Introduction to Sociology

Introduction to Sociology

Maurice C. Taylor
Laura H. Rhyne
Steven J. Rosenthal
Korsi Dogbe

Hampton University

MACMILLAN PUBLISHING COMPANY

NEW YORK

Copyright © 1987, Macmillan Publishing Company,
a division of Macmillan, Inc.

PRINTED IN THE UNITED STATES OF AMERICA

All rights reserved. No part of this book may be reproduced or
transmitted in any form or by any means, electronic or mechanical,
including photocopying, recording, or any information storage and
retrieval system, without permission in writing from the Publisher.

Macmillan Publishing Company
866 Third Avenue, New York, New York 10022

Collier Macmillan Canada, Inc.

Library of Congress Cataloging-in-Publication Data

Introduction to sociology.

   Includes index.
   1. Sociology. I. Taylor, Maurice C.
HM51.I5613   1987   301   86-12770
ISBN 0-02-419760-2

Printing: 3 4 5 6 7   Year: 7 8 9 0 1 2 3

ISBN 0-02-419760-2

to John and Rosa Taylor
M.C.T.

to Ed, Beth, Rebecca, and Megan
L.H.R.

to Mimi, Lisa, and Aaron
S.J.R.

Preface

At the heart of sociology and our experiences as social beings lies diversity. In this book we acknowledge and explore the multiracial and multiethnic character of society, and we apply the concepts of sociology to a wide array of people. These features set this book apart and represent our central concerns. Authors and publishers have recently become more sensitive to the fact that an understanding of sociology requires recognition and appreciation of diversity, and some progress has been made in the presentation of racial and ethnic experiences in sociology texts. We are convinced, however, that many more efforts are needed. We believe that the expanded coverage of diverse groups adds richness and depth to the discussion of sociological topics and thereby provides more points of identification for both students and teachers.

With this in mind, we discuss minorities' experiences throughout the book rather than only in selected chapters on race and ethnic relations or on deviance—a common approach. Chapters covering the ordinary experiences of people in society, including such topics as socialization, family, education, organizations, and gender, deal directly with racial and ethnic diversity inherent in social structures. Therefore, the family life, friendship networks, educational attainments, and occupational experiences of minorities receive attention. For example, Chapter 5, "Group Organization," includes a discussion of the impact of bureaucracy on native Americans. Likewise, Chapter 13, "Marriage and the Family," explores the strengths of Hispanic families. Also, we emphasize in our discussion of key concepts that society is much more than a community of middle-class members. Our approach is designed to enable more students to "find themselves" in the book.

Theoretical Orientation

Observations of current events in the United States, South Africa, the Middle East, and other societies might suggest that any sociological analysis involving interracial and interethnic interactions must focus on conflict and the functions of conflict in society. Nevertheless, people, regardless of their national origin, also spend a majority of their daily lives involved in routine activities such as working, playing, and visiting friends. We therefore apply both functionalist and conflict explanations of social behavior, and we also look at the contributions of social interaction theory, exchange theory, and ethnomethodology. We examine the strengths and weaknesses of the various theories in explaining social behavior in a multiracial, multiethnic society such as our own. To illustrate the power of theories and the nature of key concepts, we also employ a range of cross-cultural examples of social behavior. Thus, the expanded coverage of minorities in this book implies neither endorsement nor rejection of any particular sociological theory.

Organization of the Chapters

Each chapter contains several features to help students readily recognize major points and clearly understand the connection between topics. Objectives precede each chapter and identify five or six major points for the student to master. These objectives are followed by a general introduction that specifies the focus of the chapter. Key concepts are highlighted in boldface the first time they appear in the chapter so that students can more readily identify and learn them. In addition, these key concepts appear in an alphabetical listing at the end of each chapter. The numerous headings throughout the chapters serve as organizational guideposts that identify important topics. Chapter summaries highlight the salient topics in each chapter.

Special Features

We have planned several other features to help students and teachers. Accompanying this book is a *Student Study Guide*, written by three of the text's authors. This guide contains helpful activities, sample test questions, and suggestions for term papers. An *Instructor's Manual* has also been prepared, and it includes a list of major points for each chapter, a test bank, and suggestions for student activities. The test-bank items are unique in that students are required to read a passage and respond to questions that test not only general knowledge but also reading comprehension and abstract reasoning using sociological principles.

Two other features deserve comment. First, the language of the text is straightforward and nontechnical. We do not assume that students already know "a little" sociology, recognize sociological terms, or share the same set of experiences. Therefore, we fully explain key concepts, carefully discuss the topics, and frequently provide examples to support our points. Second, the photographs were carefully selected to highlight rather than disguise racial and ethnic diversity and to depict accurately the varied life experiences of such minorities as blacks, Hispanics, and American Indians. We hope that all students can find something of themselves in the faces portrayed in the photographs.

Acknowledgments

While there are four coauthors of this book, there are many more who helped make its final production possible. We would first like to acknowledge the contribution of Margaret N. Barnes, who wrote Chapter 11, "Aging."

The text was reviewed at various stages during its production by many professors from a variety of colleges and universities. We wish to thank the following professors for their helpful comments and suggestions: Charles W. Thomas, University of Florida; R. Kelly Hancock, Portland State University; Linda L. Green, Normandale Community College; Lynda Dickson, University of Colorado at Colorado Springs; Charlotte D. Fitzgerald, Randolph-Macon College; James Geshwender, SUNY Binghamton; Otto Sampson, Norfolk State University; Wilbur H. Watson, The Atlanta University; Herman Schwendinger, SUNY New Paltz.

We would like to extend a special word of thanks to Bill Beville for his untiring support. We also want to thank Ken MacLeod and Pat Cabeza for their efforts. It was a genuine pleasure to work with them.

There are numerous others upon whom we relied for professional assistance. Alma Orenstein provided a creative design. We wish to thank Jim Anker for his support during the early stages of the project. We want especially to acknowledge the work of Sharon Johnson, who typed the manuscripts for the text and the accompanying *Instructor's Manual* and *Student Study Guide*. We are also grateful to Melodye Mashally-DeFeo, Diane Hill, and Lessie Hollomond for their professional assistance.

Finally, we wish to express our appreciation to the administration of Hampton University. Their encouragement and support helped substantially in the preparation of this text.

M. C. T.
L. H. R.
S. J. R.
K. D.

Brief Contents

PART I Basic Concepts 1

1	**The Promise of Sociology**	3
2	**Research Methods**	19
3	**Culture**	47
4	**Socialization**	65
5	**Group Organization**	86
6	**Deviance**	107

PART II Social Inequality 133

7	**Social Stratification**	135
8	**Social Class**	156

9	Racial and Ethnic Groups	179
10	Sex and Gender	210
11	Aging	230

PART III Social Institutions 257

12	Social Institutions	259
13	Marriage and the Family	272
14	Religion in Society	300
15	Economy	329
16	Political Institutions	352
17	Education as a Social Institution	373
18	Sport as a Social Institution	392
19	Crime and the Criminal Justice System	413
20	Health Status and Medical Care	438
21	Collective Behavior, Social Movements, and Social Change	461

| Bibliography | 489 |
| Index | 507 |

Detailed Contents

PART I Basic Concepts 1

1 The Promise of Sociology 3

Objectives 3
Introduction 3
The Sociological Imagination 8
The Development of Sociology 10
Contemporary Sociological Perspectives 13
    Functionalism 13   Conflict Theory 14   Exchange Theory 14
    Symbolic Interaction 15   Ethnomethodology 16
Overview 17
Key Concepts 17
References 18

2 Research Methods 19

Objectives 19
Introduction 19
The Research Process 20
    Research Designs 22

Research Methods 25
    Survey Methods 25   Field Observations 29   Experiments 34
    Agency Data 36   Unobtrusive Measures 38
Ethics and Social Research Methods 40
    Policy, Race, and Social Research 42
Summary 44
Key Concepts 45
References 45

3 Culture   47

Objectives 47
Introduction 47
Characteristics of Culture 50
    Cultural Variability 52   Ethnocentrism 52
Factors Influencing Culture 53
    Biology 53   Environment and Extracultural Contacts 54
    Intracultural Dynamics 55   Subcultures 56
Elements of Culture 57
    Symbols 57   Values 58   Beliefs 59   Norms 59
Summary 63
Key Concepts 63
References 64

4 Socialization   65

Objectives 65
Introduction 65
Socialization Defined 66
Failures of Socialization 67
    Feral Children 67   Isolated Children 68   Hospital Studies 69
    Animal Studies 70
Learning to Behave 70
    The Controversy over Socialization 72
The Emergence of Self-Identity 74
    Looking-Glass Self 74   Generalized Other 75
    Ego Development 75
Types of Socialization 76
Agents of Socialization 78
    The Family 78   The Peer Group 79   The School 80
    The Mass Media 80
Socialization for What? 81

Summary 83
Key Concepts 84
References 84

5
Group Organization 86

Objectives 86
Introduction 86
Status and Role 87
    Status 87   Role 88
The Nature of the Group 90
    The Organized Group 92
A Classification of Groups 93
    Primary Groups 94   Secondary Groups 95   Associations 96
Bureaucratic Organization 97
    Formal and Informal Organization 97
    Public Reaction to Bureaucracy 101
    Bureaucracy in a Multicultural World 102
    Growth of Bureaucracy 103
Summary 104
Key Concepts 105
References 105

6
Deviance 107

Objectives 107
Introduction 107
Deviance Defined 108
Responses to Deviance 109
    Stigma and Social Response 109
    Deterrence and Social Response 113
Explanations of Deviance 114
    Labeling and Secondary Deviance 114   Deviance and Anomie 116
Explanations of Collective Deviance 120
    Deviant Careers 121   Deviant Subculture 122
    Mainstream Deviance 126
Functions of Deviance 128
Summary 130
Key Concepts 130
References 130

PART II Social Inequality 133

7
Social Stratification   135

Objectives   135
Introduction   135
The Nature of Stratification   136
   Contrasts in Perspectives   137
Stratification and Societal Types   138
   Caste System   139   Estate System   140   Social Class System   141
   Slave System   142
Theories of Stratification   143
   Marx   144   Weber   147   Marx and Weber Compared   149
   Race, Ethnicity, Sex, and Age   150   World-Systems Theory   153
Summary   154
Key Concepts   154
References   155

8
Social Class   156

Objectives   156
Introduction   156
   Loaded Labels   157
Subjective and Objective Approaches   158
   Subjective Approaches   158   Objective Approaches   159
The U.S. Class Structure: Two Contrasting Views   160
The Impact of Social Class   161
   Wealth and Poverty   162   Evaluation and Implications   165
   Blaming the Victim   165
Social Class as a Life-and-Death Matter   166
Social Mobility and Class Conflict   166
   Social Mobility in the United States   167
   Social Mobility and Women   168
   The Declining Significance of Race   169   Class Conflict   170
   Class Consciousness   171
Social Class in Other Countries   172
   Class Structure in Third World Societies   172
   Future Changes in Class Structure   173
Is a Classless Society Possible?   174
   The Experience of the Soviet Union   175
Summary   176

Key Concepts 177
References 177

9
Racial and Ethnic Groups 179

Objectives 179
Introduction 179
Racial, Ethnic, and Minority Groups 180
    Race 180   Ethnicity 181   Minority Groups 181
Racial and Ethnic Groups in the United States 182
    Black Americans 182   Hispanic Americans 183
    Asian Americans 183   Native Americans (American Indians) 184
    White Ethnics 184
Racism 185
    The Causes of Racism 185   Sociobiology and Racism 186
    Marxist Theory 186
Patterns of Race and Ethnic Relations 187
    Minority Group Responses 189
    Native Americans (American Indians) 190   Black Americans 192
    Asian Americans 196   Hispanic Americans 197
    European Americans—"White Ethnics" 199
Fascism and Nazism 204
Summary 207
Key Concepts 207
References 208

10
Sex and Gender 210

Objectives 210
Introduction 210
Sex and Gender 211
    Sexism and Social Inequality 212   The Workplace 212
    The Home 214
Gender and Social Institutions 216
    Socialization for Inequality: The Case of Mathematics 217
    Sexism and Racism: Similarities and Differences 220
Theoretical Explanations of Gender Inequality 221
    Biological Theories 222   Functionalist Theories 223
    Socialization Theories 224   Feminist and Marxist Theories 224
    The Controversy over Comparable Worth 226
    Women's Liberation and Minority Women 227
Summary 228
Key Concepts 228
References 229

11 Aging 230

Objectives   230
Introduction   230
Age and Aging   233
   Chronological Aging   232   Biological Aging   233
   Senility and Senile Dementia   234   Sociological Aging   235
Theories of Aging   238
   Biological Theories   238   Social Theories   238
Ageism   240
   Gerontocratic Society   240   Age Discrimination   241
Common Problems of the Aged   242
   Health   242   Income   243   Housing   244   Elder Abuse   245
The Aging Network: Informal and Formal   247
   Informal Support   247   Relevant Legislation   249
Summary   252
Key Concepts   253
References   253

PART III   Social Institutions   257

12 Social Institutions 259

Objectives   259
Introduction   259
Social Functions   261
Social Structure   262
Structural Alternatives   264
Gemeinschaft and Gesellschaft   267
   Gemeinschaft   266   Gesellschaft   267   Urbanization   267
   Specialization and Rationalization   269
Summary   270
Key Concepts   270
References   271

13 Marriage and the Family 272

Objectives   272
Introduction   272

Marriage Defined   273
Family Policy   274
Functions of Families   278
Marital Status   281
    Trends in Marital Status   282
Black Families   291
    Black Family Forms   291   Strengths of Black Families   292
    Blacks and Marital Status   294
Hispanic Families   295
    Strengths of Hispanic Families   296   Trends in Marital Status   297
Summary   298
Key Concepts   298
References   299

14
Religion in Society   300

Objectives   300
Introduction   300
The Institutionalization of Religion   302
    Beliefs   302   Practices   304   Morality   305   Collectivity   306
Perspectives on Religion   306
    A Functionalist Perspective   306   A Conflict Perspective   312
Religion as a Source of Social Change   314
    Priest and Prophet Roles   315
Religion in a Multicultural Society   317
    Religious Diversity and Political Institutions   319
    International Diversity   322
Trends in Religion   324
    Secularism and Rationalism   324   The Electronic Ministry   325
    Women in the Church   326
Summary   327
Key Concepts   327
References   329

15
Economy   329

Objectives   329
Introduction   329
Types of Productive Systems   330
    Exchange Systems   333
Theories of Economic Growth   334
    The Invisible Hand   335   The Helping Hand   336
    Dialectical Materialism   337   The Spirit of Capitalism   339
Economic Systems in the World Today   340
    The U.S. Economy and the World Economy   341

The Nature of Work   343
    Employment   343   Work Trends   346
    Unemployment and the Meaning of Work   347
Summary   349
Key Concepts   350
References   350

16
Political Institutions 352

Objectives   352
Introduction   352
Types of Government   354
    Proprietary States   354   Democratic Governments   355
    Totalitarian Governments   356
Legitimation of Authority   357
    Traditional Authority   358   Charismatic Authority   358
    Rational-Legal Authority   359
The Distribution of Power in the United States   360
    The Elitist Model   361   The Pluralist Model   362
Participation and Partisanship in the United States   366
    Political Socialization   366   Stratification   367
    Race and Ethnicity   368   Trends in Political Behavior   369
Summary   370
Key Concepts   371
References   372

17
Education as a Social Institution 373

Objectives   373
Introduction   373
Education as a Social Institution   374
    What Do Schools Teach?   375
The Social Organization of Schooling   376
The Expansion of Formal Education in Society   379
    Higher Education in the United States   380
    Blacks and Higher Education   380
Functionalist and Conflict Theories of Education   381
Education and Equality of Opportunity   385
    Busing and Affirmative Action   387
Educational Achievement   388
    Intelligence and I.Q. Tests   389
Summary   390
Key Concepts   390
References   391

18
Sport as a Social Institution 392

    Objectives 392
    Introduction 392
    Definition of Sport 393
        Sport as a Microcosm 395
    Functionalist and Conflict Views of Sport 395
        Sport and Societal Values 398   Sport and Social Class 399
    Sport and Social Mobility: The Glitter and the Reality 402
    Race, Sex and Sport 406
        Race and Sport 406   Sex and Sport 409
    Summary 410
    Key Concepts 411
    References 411

19
Crime and the Criminal Justice System 413

    Objectives 413
    Introduction 413
    Crime in American Society 414
        Types of Crime 415
    Theories of Crime 416
    Sources of Crime Data in the United States 418
        Evaluating Crime Statistics 420
    The Criminal Justice Process 423
        Law Enforcement: The Police 423
        The Judicial Process: The Courts 429
        Capital Punishment and Imprisonment 431
    Summary 435
    Key Concepts 435
    References 436

20
Health Status and Medical Care 438

    Objectives 438
    Introduction 438
    Social Forces and Mobility 439
        Age, Sex, and Disease 440   Bad Blood and Syphilis 442

Social Forces and Mortality 443
    Smoking and Health 444   Hypertension and Heart Disease 446
    Age and Cause of Death 447
Medical Care 449
    Health-care Personnel 449   Medical Diagnosis 450
    Sex and Health-care Personnel 451
    Black Health-care Personnel 453   Other Health-care Personnel 455
Income and Health Status 456
Summary 459
Key Concepts 459
References 460

21
Collective Behavior, Social Movements, and Social Change   461

Objectives 461
Introduction 461
Collective Behavior 462
    The Crowd 463   Rumors 465   Mass Behavior 467
    Cola Wars and Mass Appeal 468
Theories of Collective Behavior 470
    Contagion Theory 471   Convergence Theory 472
    Emergent Norms 473   Value-added Theory 474
Social Movements 476
    Types of Social Movements 477
    The Natural History of Social Movements 479
    Theories of Social Movements 480
Sociology and Social Change 482
    Functionalism and Social Change 483
    Conflict Theories of Social Change 484
Summary 485
Key Concepts 486
References 486

Bibliography   489

Index   505

Photo Credits

Chapter 1
p. 4	Photo by Joel Gordon
p. 5	Photo by Nagata/United Nations
p. 7	Photo by John Schultz/PAR-NYC
p. 9	Photo by Joel Gordon
p. 16	Photo by Arthur Tress/Magnum Photos, Inc.

Chapter 2
p. 26	Photo reproduced from the Archives of the Social Security Administration, Baltimore, Maryland
p. 27	Photo by Rbt. Maass/Photoreporters, Inc.
p. 31	Photo by Brent Jones
p. 36	Photo by John Schultz/PAR-NYC
p. 43	Photo by Ira Wyman/Sygma

Chapter 3
p. 48	Photo by Jacques Jangoux/Peter Arnold, Inc.
p. 48	Photo by Brent Jones
p. 49	Photo by Tom Kelly
p. 49	Photo by J.P. Laffont/Sygma
p. 55	Photo by Peter Menzel/Stock Boston
p. 56	Photo by Tannenbaum/Sygma

Chapter 4
p. 66	Photo by Tom Kelly
p. 68	Photo by Wille Vicoy from UPI/Bettmann Newsphotos
p. 71	Photo by James Nachtwey/Black Star
p. 73	Photo by Richard Kalvar/Magnum Photos Inc.
p. 74	Photo reproduced from the archives of the United States Department of Health and Human Services, Washington, D.C.
p. 77	Photo by Tom Kelly
p. 82	Photo by United Nations

Chapter 5
p. 88	Photo by David Hurn/Magnum Photos, Inc.
p. 88	Photo by Claus C. Meyer/Black Star
p. 90	Photo by Ellis Herwig/Stock Boston
p. 91	Photo by Brent Jones
p. 91	Photo by Paul Conklin
p. 91	Photo by Tom Kelly
p. 93	Photo by Tom Kelly
p. 94	Photo by Marc P. Anderson
p. 95	Photo by John Maher/EKM Nepenthe
p. 99	Photo by Marc P. Anderson
p. 100	Photo by Dave Repp/DPI

Chapter 6
p. 108	Photo by Ellis Herwig/Stock Boston
p. 110	Photo by AP/Wide World Photos
p. 111	Photo by AP/Wide World Photos
p. 112	Photo by AP/Wide World Photos
p. 115	Photo by Robert Eckert/EKM Nepenthe
p. 119	Photo by Ted Cowell/Black Star
p. 121	Photo by Robert Eckert/EKM Nepenthe
p. 123	Photo by Charles Kennard/Stock Boston
p. 128	Photo by Diego Goldberg/Sygma

Chapter 7
p. 136	Photo by David Hurn/Magnum Photos, Inc.
p. 138	Photo by AP/Wide World Photos
p. 139	Photo by AP/Wide World Photos
p. 144	Photo from the archives of German Information Center, New York
p. 144	Photo from the archives of German Information Center, New York

Chapter 8
p. 158	Photo by Martha Tabor
p. 160	Photo by Andrew Sacks/Black Star
p. 167	Photo by Hiroji Kubota/Magnum Photos, Inc.
p. 167	Photo by Costa Manos/Magnum Photos, Inc.
p. 169	Photo by Bob Adelman/Magnum Photos, Inc.
p. 169	Photo by Brent Jones
p. 171	Photo by Carl Berquist/Illustrator's Stock Photos
p. 173	Bernard Pierre Wolfe/Magnum Photos, Inc.
p. 173	Photo by Rene Burri/Magnum Photos, Inc.
p. 175	Photo by Mathew Ford/Photoreporters, Inc.

Chapter 9
p. 180	Photo by AP/Wide World Photos, Inc.
p. 187	Photo by Lionel J.M. Deleringue/Stock Boston
p. 189	Photo by Tom Kelly
p. 191	Photo by Arthur Grace/Sygma
p. 196	Photo by Dorothea Lange, Library of Congress Negative No. 210-G2-C153
p. 201	Photo from the archives of the Library of Congress, Negative No. LC-USZ62-11202

p. 206   Photo by William Campbell/Sygma
p. 206   Photo by William Campbell/Sygma

Chapter 10

p. 211   Photo by Tom Kelly
p. 211   Photo by Brent Jones
p. 212   Photo by Richard R. Collins/DPI
p. 215   Photo by Brent Jones
p. 216   Photo from ABC and Movie Still Archives
p. 218   Photo Courtesy of AT&T Bell Labs. Used by permission.
p. 223   Photo by Lois Bernstein

Chapter 11

p. 231   Photo by Brent Jones
p. 233   Photo by Paul Conklin
p. 236   Photo by Alex Webb/Magnum Photos, Inc.
p. 239   Photo by Brent Jones
p. 242   Photo by Tom Kelly
p. 248   Photo by Bruno J. Zehnder/United Nations
p. 250   Photo by Paul Conklin

Chapter 12

p. 260   Photo by Tom Kelly
p. 262   Photo by Marc P. Anderson © 1985. All rights reserved.
p. 263   Photo by Tom Kelly
p. 264   Photo from the archives of the Library of Congress, Negative No. LC 19341 MB
p. 265   Photo by Illustrator's Stock Photos
p. 266   Photo by Ira Kirschenbaum/Stock Boston
p. 268   Photo by Joel Gordon

Chapter 13

p. 273   Photo courtesy of NBC Television. Used by permission.
p. 275   Photo by Marc P. Anderson
p. 279   Photo by John Running
p. 284   Photo by Robert V. Eckert Jr./EKM Nepenthe © 1984 News Group Chicago, Inc.
p. 288   Photo by Bob Fitch/Black Star
p. 293   Photo by Brent Jones

Chapter 14

p. 301   Photo by Illustrator's Stock Photos
p. 303   Photo by Michael Thompson/EKM Nepenthe
p. 307   Photo by The Bettmann Archive, Inc.
p. 308   Photo by Dana Fineman/Sygma
p. 310   Photo by Cornell Capa/Magnum Photos, Inc.
p. 311   Photo by Tom Kelly

p. 315   Photo by Illustrator's Stock Photos
p. 315   Photo by Susan Meiselas/Magnum Photos, Inc.
p. 320   Photo by Jim Pozarik/Liaison
p. 323   Photo by Magnum Photos Inc.

Chapter 15

p. 330   Photo by Ford Motor Company from Illustrator's Stock Photos
p. 331   Photo by Jerry Frank/DPI
p. 331   Photo by Martha Tabor
p. 332   Photo by W. Marc Bernsau
p. 342   Photo from Citibank and PAR/NYC
p. 343   Photo by Martha Tabor
p. 345   Photo by Martha Tabor
p. 348   Photo by Martha Tabor

Chapter 16

p. 355   Photo from Bibliotheque Nationale, Paris-Giraudon/Art Resource
p. 356   Photo by Burt Glinn/Magnum Photos, Inc.
p. 359   Photo by AP/Wide World Photos
p. 365   Photo by Burt Glinn/Magnum Photos, Inc.

Chapter 17

p. 375   Photo by Tom Kelly
p. 376   Photo by Illustrator's Stock Photos
p. 377   Photo by Ron Stern/Illustrator's Stock Photos-PSI
p. 378   Photo by Frank Siteman/The Picture Cube
p. 379   Photo by UPI/Bettmann Newsphotos
p. 382   Photo by Robert V. Eckert, Jr./EKM Nepenthe
p. 384   Photo by Martha Stewart/The Picture Cube
p. 385   Photo by Ron Stern/Illustrator's Stock Photos-PSI
p. 387   Photo by AP/Wide World Photos

Chapter 18

p. 394   Photo by David Hurn/Magnum Photos, Inc.
p. 396   Photo by Ron Stern/Illustrator's Stock Photos
p. 397   Photo by AP/Wide World Photos
p. 398   Photo by Michael O'Brien/Archive Pictures, Inc.
p. 400   Photo by W. Marc Bernsau
p. 400   Photo by Marc P. Anderson
p. 401   Photo by United Artists Corporation from PAR/NYC
p. 404   Photo by David Hurn/Magnum Photos, Inc.
p. 407   Photo by Anestis Diakopoulos/Stock Boston
p. 407   Photo by Peter Southwick/Stock Boston
p. 409   Photo by Tom Kelly

Chapter 19

p. 418   Photo by W. Marc Bernsau
p. 419   Photo by Tom Kelly

p. 421	Photo by Tom Kelly		p. 450	Photo by Illustrator's Stock Photos
p. 422	Photo by Las Vegas News Bureau		p. 452	Photo by Paul Conklin

p. 421 Photo by Tom Kelly
p. 422 Photo by Las Vegas News Bureau
p. 422 Photo by New York Convention and Visitors Bureau
p. 426 Photo by AP/Wide World Photos
p. 428 Photo by Carl Berquist/Shenandoah from Illustrator's Stock Photos
p. 432 Photo by Tom Kelly
p. 433 Photo by Tom Kelly

Chapter 20

p. 440 Photo by Paul Conklin
p. 441 Photo by Marc P. Anderson
p. 445 Photo by W. Marc Bernsau
p. 447 Photo by Marc P. Anderson

p. 450 Photo by Illustrator's Stock Photos
p. 452 Photo by Paul Conklin

Chapter 21

p. 463 Photo by Tom Kelly
p. 464 Photo by Dan Miller/DPI
p. 465 Photo by Lauren/Matison/Gamma-Liaison
p. 467 Photo by AP/Wide World Photos
p. 469 Photo by Pepsi Cola Company. Used by permission.
p. 470 Photo by AP/Wide World Photos
p. 475 Photo by Abramson/Anderson/Hemsey/Lauren/Matison/Gamm-Liaison
p. 476 Photo by Chris Steele Perkins/Magnum Photos, Inc.
p. 485 Photo by AP/Wide World Photos

Basic Concepts

PART I

The Promise of Sociology

1

OBJECTIVES

By the end of this chapter the student should be able to:

1. Identify the major focus of sociology.

2. Comprehend what is implied in the identification of sociology as a science.

3. Understand that people in different social positions may experience the world differently.

4. Understand what is meant by the sociological imagination.

5. Trace the origins of sociology and identify some of its major figures.

6. Identify five sociological perspectives in viewing social life.

INTRODUCTION

Dance crazes appear in each generation and sweep across the country. Young people rush to learn the latest step, while their parents lament the tastelessness of the new dances and remember how good the dances were in their day. Some of the dances that have appeared in one generation and are gone by the next include the Cakewalk, the Fox Trot, the Charleston, the Lindy, the Big Apple, the Jitterbug, the Twist, the Shag, the Hully-gully, the Boogaloo, the Duck, and the Uncle Willy. Today everyone is Breaking, Popping, doing the Worm and the Bird. Dance crazes are a form of collective behavior. The communication between one person and another that spreads the dance across the country makes such behavior social in nature.

Let us look at other situations that penetrate a little deeper into our lives than such passing crazes: a working couple share household chores; a minister leads his or her congregation in worship services; a Hispanic woman keynotes a major political convention; members of an athletic team celebrate a victory; a young girl wrestles with her conscience over having an abortion; a youth gets

Sociologists focus on the social aspects of human behavior.

in trouble with the law for automobile theft; a racist group burns a cross in the yard of a black family; automobile workers go on strike; students prepare themselves for a career; a society suffers economic depression; young men and women go to war and die; young men and women fall in love and get married.

One thing that all of these situations have in common is that people, singly or in groups, are influenced by or are orienting their behavior toward other people. The quality we refer to here is the social aspect of behavior; that is, behavior that is related to group life. Humanity is not a solitary species; we are by nature social. We survive both as organisms, personalities, and peoples through our communication with others. We form groups to meet our needs and pursue our interests. This social dimension is the focus of sociology. **Sociology** is the study of social groups and their influences on human behavior.

The collective aspect of human behavior, to which sociology directs its attention, is present whether we are talking about a total society or individuals acting in accordance with standards they have learned from others. This social quality is expressed in groups. Groups surround us, ranging from the smallest, most intimate type, such as two lovers, to the largest, most inclusive group, which we call **society**. Most of our behavior occurs within the context of these relationships. Sociology concerns itself with the nature of these groups and their impact upon each other and on the individuals that comprise them.

It is sometimes difficult to identify the social element in individuals. Some of our individual behavior is not social—our physiological processes, for example. In addition, each of us has a few idiosyncracies; that is, behavior that is unique to us as individuals. An old rhyme of unknown origins said:

> I eat my peas with honey;
> I've done it all my life.
> It makes the peas taste funny,
> But it keeps them on my knife.

4 *The Promise of Sociology*

Since the habit of eating peas with honey on a knife is not shared, it is not social behavior and therefore would not be of concern for sociological study. But a great deal of our individual behavior is social behavior because it is done with an awareness of other people or groups in mind and because our previous contact with others leads us to act or think in a certain way, for example, to believe in God. These are the aspects of individual behavior in which sociologists are interested.

Had we lived in the nineteenth century, social behavior would generally have been explained to us on the basis of genetic endowment. Much of our behavior was attributed to instincts, that is, specific needs or predispositions in the human organism tied by nature to specific responses. For example, religious systems were explained on the basis of a natural fear, which was assumed to be a part of the biological or psychological equipment individuals were born with. Economic systems were explained by an acquisitive instinct humans were thought to possess; war was explained by an instinct for aggression. Similarly, certain types of personal characteristics were said to be biologically determined. Deviance was thought to be the result of "bad blood" or "bad seed," as evidenced by physical stigmata such as irregular contours of the skull, narrowness between the eyes, and the like. Poverty was seen as resulting from inferior stock. The presence of such conditions as poverty and deviance in the society was assumed to be accounted for by individual traits. These types of explanations may be called biological determinism.

Although some of these arguments persist today, we now realize that society itself is a powerful explanatory factor in understanding human behavior. *Society* refers to the organized network of social interactions within which people live their lives. These relationships comprise a reality that is greater than the sum of the individual parts, just as a watch is a reality produced by the interrelationships of its parts, not merely the sum of its parts. But these relationships create a duality: as we interact within that network of relationships, the society becomes a part of each of us. Society does not constitute some great repressive force outside ourselves with which we as individuals must continually do battle. On the contrary, society lives in each of us just as each of us lives in society. Sociologists concern themselves with the nature of this intricate web of relationships.

The discovery of predictable relationships is a part of the research involved in genetic research. The discovery of predictable relationships is also a part of sociological research.

Sociology's focus on these social relationships, however, goes far beyond interest. Sociology is also a way of acquiring knowledge and understanding of this social area of interest. Sociology attempts to study social phenomena through systematic empirical observation and logical inference. It aims at objectivity and binds itself to rules of evidence in describing and making generalizations about social life. "I heard it through the grapevine," or "Everybody knows that," or "It came to me in a vision," or "I knew a person who..." does not constitute acceptable sociological evidence. Rather, sociology attempts to gain an understanding of social life through the scientific method, which involves systematic observation, measurement, and analysis of the empirical world.

One of the basic assumptions of science is that there are regularities in the nature of things that we can discover through such study. For example, the law of gravity represents the discovery of regularity in the speed of falling objects. This discovery makes it possible for us to make predictions about how objects will act in relationship to the pull of gravity. For example, consider the number of such predictions that underlie the science of rocketry. Moon shots, space explorations, satellite launching and orbiting, the space shuttle all depend upon minute calculations made possible by generalizations growing out of the systematic observations of falling objects.

Can generalizations and predictions be made about human behavior? Many people would answer no to that question. Some of the explanations usually include, "No two people are alike," or, "It's all up to the individual." Because these ideas sometimes interfere with the ability of students to think sociologically, it is worthwhile to attempt to deal with them at the outset. It is true that no two people are exactly alike, not even identical twins. It is also true that no one is completely different from others. All of us have shared experiences with others that influence the ways we behave. This shared, or social, aspect produces regularities or patterns in behavior. For example, as Americans, we share the experiences of using the same currency, of living under the same governmental system, and of marrying only one spouse at a time. Some of us are members of ethnic or racial groups with a history of being the object of prejudice and discrimination. This means that we share with others in our group the experience of coping with that circumstance and with the special heritage of the group. We share with others our religion, our region, our community, our school, our family, our age bracket, our economic status, our profession, and our friendships. Although it is true that no two of us are exactly alike, it is also true that we are not completely dissimilar either. It is important to keep in mind that sociologists do not attempt to make generalizations or predictions about a given individual's behavior (the peas with honey problem again), but the tendencies among those who share social characteristics and experiences can be identified.

The other popular notion, "It's all up to the individual," assumes an isolated individual. The only way that statement makes sense is if the person is marooned on an island. The fact that we live among other people means that their expectations have to be considered. Keystone Kops may be funny in the movies, but as a pattern for social existence, it does not have much to recommend it. When we arrive at the point of being able to make decisions about what we shall or shall not do, the expectations of our group have already been built into our thought patterns. For example, why is the young man in the third row of your sociology class not wearing a dress today? Is it "all up to the individual"?

Sociologists are sometimes accused of being peeping toms and of invading other people's privacy.

Not really, because the individual in question has already learned from the group expectations that a dress is not appropriate for a young man; and as he has come to share that belief, it governs his behavior. Again, the sociologist is not interested in the individual in isolation but as a member of society. In that context, regularities do occur and can be discovered through the scientific method.

Students of human social behavior have some difficulties that the physical and biological scientists do not have. A chemist does not have to deal with the question of what it means to two chemical substances to be held over a Bunsen burner. The chemical reaction does not depend upon "meaning"; it happens automatically. However, humans act on the basis of the meaning that situations have for them. Such meaning is not always readily observable. Yet, if the sociologist misses this subjective aspect of the behavior, true understanding is incomplete. An early sociologist, Max Weber, used the term *verstehen* to stress the necessity to understand the meaning of social action to the actor.

Ethical problems become critical when one studies social behavior and often complicate the research process through which we gain our sociological knowledge and understanding. Chemists, botanists, and astronomers also encounter ethical problems, but these have to do mainly with either the integrity of the research process itself or with the uses made of the findings. They do not have to worry about such matters as invading the privacy of their plant and animal subjects. Seeds do not feel embarrassed if the botanist watches them germinate; a caterpillar seems unconcerned with observers of its metamorphosis; a planet goes blithely around in its orbit regardless of the telescope focused on it. But when the subjects of study are human beings, they may be injured by the research process in such ways as having their privacy invaded, their sensibilities shocked, or their dignity violated. Some of these issues are discussed in Chapter 2, "Research Methods."

Another difficulty in studying social behavior is that sociologists are a part of the thing they study. Objectivity is basic to the scientific method. A sociologist, however, has values and attitudes that have developed out of a particular social and cultural heritage, and these may intrude into the scientific process and influence the findings. For example, if sociologists were attempting to find out whether or not the Christian religion has the effect of supporting economic inequality, their study might be influenced by the fact that they were either Christians, Jews, Muslims, or atheists, as well as by their attitudes toward inequality. One of the continuing debates in sociology is whether it can be free of values. Most would agree that the sociologist cannot strip himself or herself of values. About the best that is possible is to recognize and make explicit one's own values and to keep an open and receptive mind. We recommend this attitude to beginning sociology students.

In keeping with our own advice, we wish to state at least one of the value judgments our presentation in this book expresses. Many introductory sociology textbooks appear each year. Each has its own approach and area of emphasis, and some of them are very good. One problem we have noted in most of these texts, however, is that they do not pay sufficient attention to the fact that we live in a society whose essence is diversity. We live in multiracial and multiethnic communities. Our lives are influenced by both national and international affairs. The tragedy of Bhopal, India, made us look closer at the Union Carbide plant in West Virginia and at other plants using toxic chemicals. If the focus of sociology is human interaction, we should keep before us the fact that this interaction occurs among people with a variety of racial, ethnic, and cultural heritages. Differences in these experiences are bound to influence the meanings that individuals and groups attach to social situations. We propose to keep this diversity constantly in mind, noting common experiences that transcend the differences but also recognizing that people with different racial, ethnic, and cultural heritages may experience the social world differently. We believe that this inclusive emphasis will deepen your understanding of both the richness and the complexity of multicultural society.

We invite you to join us in this exploration of the nature of social life. The only requirements are an open mind, a lively curiosity, and a genuine interest in human beings as they (we) interact with each other.

The Sociological Imagination

When an elderly friend of the authors was recently hospitalized for cancer surgery, the only available beds in the hospital at the time were in the maternity ward. Our friend's problem was immediate and personal: needing a hospital bed but feeling the inappropriateness of the maternity ward for a woman of advanced years. But this situation was also a reflection of two broad social trends: the fact that there were empty beds only in the maternity ward relates to the decided decline in the birthrate in the United States in recent years and to the increase in the elderly population. Our friend's situation marked the intersection of a personal problem with phenomena that characterize the general society.

C. Wright Mills, an American sociologist, gave the name "**sociological imagination**" to the ability to identify the interconnections between the events and situations occurring in people's personal lives and the broader trends and structures of the society. He noted the tendency for personal problems to become public issues. When individuals and their families experience a problem, they often have the tendency to regard it as their own failure and to blame their personal inadequacies. However, when the same problem repeatedly occurs in the lives of large numbers of people, the assumption can generally be made that

Both microlevels and macrolevels of social relationships are responsible for this executive's position.

broadly applicable social factors are helping to produce the situation. The problems men and women face in their personal lives, such as the painful breakup of a marriage or the loss of a job, are part of such social patterns as those involving family instability or structural shifts in the occupational structure. The logical implication of this discovery of the linkage is that the solution of the problem must be sought at the societal level, not merely at the individual level, where the hurt is felt most intensely.

The same type of interconnectedness is present as well in other behaviors and situations not specifically identified as problems. If we consider the actions of a North Carolina farmer planting a field of tobacco, we can understand them in terms of his immediate desire to sell the tobacco to make enough money to feed, clothe, and educate his family. But also impacting upon his behavior are a number of broader situations: he lives in a society where a market form of exchange operates; where the pleasures of smoking, systematically reinforced by the advertisements of tobacco companies, insure a market for his product; and where the political strength of the tobacco lobby in the nation's capital insures stability in the price of tobacco through price-support programs. His immediate situation is linked to these broader social structures and situations, and we must consider these aspects as well if we are to understand the behavior. Mills (1959) referred to these links as the intersection of the arc of biography (the individual's life) and the arc of history (social trends and structures).

Some sociologists focus on situations involving the immediate and personal interactions and experiences of individuals and small groups such as the family. This level of analysis is called **microsociology**. Other sociologists focus their attention mostly upon the broad structures and trends in the society, such as the stratification system or the urbanization of the population. This emphasis is called **macrosociology**. The specific focus of an analysis may be on either the microlevel or the macrolevel, and the sociological imagination enables one to trace the relationships between the two. When we see a young black man or woman operating successfully as an executive of a leading business, we may explain this on the basis of the individual's personal merit, achievement, and motivations as he or she has been influenced by family and peers—a microlevel emphasis. But we may also observe that the employment of blacks in business is occurring with

The Sociological Imagination 9

greater frequency than in the past. So we must understand that the explanation would also include the achievements of the civil rights movement—a macrolevel phenomenon. It is this ability to move back and forth between these two levels, sensitive to the interconnections and impacts between them, that we hope to assist the student to develop. For this approach stretches our horizons beyond the orbit of the familiar and helps us to realize how tightly the fabric of the individual's existence is interwoven with the lives of others.

The Development of Sociology

As a continuing academic discipline sociology had its origins in western Europe in the nineteenth century. It had its roots, however, in the Age of Enlightenment of the eighteenth century. The scholars of that period formed an optimistic vision of the ultimate perfectibility of mankind; humanity was viewed as capable of infinite progress. They assumed that God had created a perfectly rational universe that operated according to natural law. Comprehension of this natural law was the mission of science. Education was thought to be basic to the development of the rationality required for scientific thought.

As these ideas of science, rationality, education, and progress were applied to technological development, they produced astounding results. Invention followed invention, and by the early days of the nineteenth century the industrial revolution was in full swing. When the social philosophers of the nineteenth century looked around them, however, they did not see the social progress their predecessors had envisioned. Masses of people had migrated from the rural areas to the industrial cities. They lived in congested, vermin-infested housing; crime and disease were rampant; raw sewage flowed through the cluttered streets; children worked in the mines and sweatshops. Not a pretty picture! Where was the progress the scholars of the Age of Enlightenment had predicted?

The idea began to develop that since applying science to technology had produced progress, perhaps applying science to society might also produce progress. A Frenchman, Auguste Comte, gathered and organized various ideas along this line that were circulating and developed a new science of society, which he named "sociology." Its method was to be the positivistic, or scientific, method. Comte hoped that the findings of sociology could help in setting society on a progressive course.

Comte's counterpart in England was Herbert Spencer. He took the position that natural law would lead to progress. Spencer felt that Charles Darwin's theory of evolution could also be applied to the development of society; that is, in the struggle for existence the **survival of the fittest** would insure progress because the unfit would be eliminated. His philosophy was one of laissez-faire, and he expected that sociology would teach people not to try to tamper with natural law by implementing reforms that would permit the unfit to survive.

When sociology spread to the United States at the end of the nineteenth century, these two views of the uses of sociology developed advocates in two of the most renowned sociologists of the time: Lester Ward and William G. Sumner. Ward followed Comte. He said that humans were the only animal species that could plan their own evolutionary progress, and sociology would be a useful tool in helping that human effort. Sumner, on the other hand, adopted Spencer's laissez-faire philosophy; his famous dictum was: You cannot legislate morality, meaning that passing laws to try to change society is ineffective if they do not coincide with the prevailing sentiments in the society. His ideas were popular beyond the academic community and were thought to have been influential in the Supreme Court case of *Plessy v. Ferguson* that legitimized the "separate but equal" doctrine in race relations.

Meanwhile, the followers of Spencer, who also became intrigued with Darwin's evolutionary theory, developed a school of thought known as "social Darwinism." The questions these theorists raised concerned the evolutionary development of society: What stages did it pass through? What were the mechanisms that produced the shift from stage to stage? And what was the role of sociology in this evolutionary progress? These sociologists identified stages of development, most of which depicted a biased view in which western Europe represented the highest level. They pictured struggle between individuals, groups, and societies as the basic mechanism of change from one stage to another. Spencer's concept of the survival of the fittest was their rationale for labeling this process as progress. Some of the social Darwinians thought that sociology could be the basis for social reforms, whereas others thought that this would interfere with the natural laws that led to progress.

The social Darwinians had widespread influence in the nonacademic world. Their influence was particularly strong in the United States, where their tenets complemented the individualism that was a major part of the social philosophy of this country.

Today, however, this theory of the survival of the fittest as the path to progress is generally repudiated by most sociologists. As Hofstadter (1971:172) suggests, "Although Darwinism was not the primary source of the belligerent ideology and dogmatic racism of the late nineteenth century, it did become a new instrument in the hands of the theorists of race and struggle." Furthermore, its emphasis on laissez-faire runs counter to the prevailing idea that government has a responsibility for the quality of life of all its citizens.

The "classical period" of sociology encompasses the latter part of the nineteenth century and the early twentieth century. It includes such theorists as Emile Durkheim, Max Weber, Ferdinand Tönnies, Charles Horton Cooley and others whose ideas are discussed at various points in the chapters to follow. Although Karl Marx did not call himself a sociologist, he is generally included among the classical sociologists. This period was devoted to exploring the nature of society and social life and to laying the conceptual and analytical foundations for the new discipline of sociology. The theories developed during this time have focused the interests and set the research directions for generations of sociologists who have followed.

In the early days of sociology in the United States, the University of Chicago became the hub of activity. Although the claim to empiricism, or focus on phenomena that can be perceived through the five senses, had been made by the founders, the social Darwinians, and the classical sociologists, the sociologists at the University of Chicago made empiricism their centerpiece. Students went out in the city and studied what was actually going on. They looked at family life, delinquency, crime, mental health, the spatial development of the city, rich folks, poor folks, hobos, skid row derelicts, and race relations. Aside from the contributions to knowledge these studies made, two long-lasting results came from the efforts of sociologists at the University of Chicago. First, these areas of study became the major areas of specialization within sociology. Second, these researchers went out all over the country to found departments of sociology, most of which followed the Chicago model.

Various centers of research and teaching became well known. W. E. B. DuBois established a center for research on race relations at Atlanta University. E. Franklin Frazier followed up on such research at Howard University. The University of Minnesota became the focal point of research in rural sociology. Microlevel studies were introduced as Cooley at Michigan and G. H. Mead at Chicago began to focus on the relationship between the self and society. Sociology had branched out into many areas of interest.

American sociologists in the 1920s and 1930s began to feel very self-conscious about whether they were being scientific enough. A penchant for quantification set in: counting some phenomenon—seemed almost an end in itself. Thus, more attention was given to the method and less thought to the theoretical implications that might or might not be drawn from the studies. What resulted was a number of numerically precise studies, few of which added much to our understanding of human social life. Eventually realization of such limitations became widespread, and the attempt to blend theory and quantification now characterizes most of the research being done.

One of the countertendencies to overquantification of the trivial was the development of a major theoretical system known as functionalism. One of its principal architects, Talcott Parsons of Harvard University, pulled together many concepts developed during the classical period along with some newer ones and fitted them together into a model of a social system. The model depicts society as a unified whole made up of parts, all of which contribute to maintaining the system. This model stresses consensus and stability.

During the 1940s and 1950s this model dominated sociology. Parsons' students spread the perspective all over the academic map as they went out to various schools. But when the conflicts of the 1960s emerged in the civil rights movement, the student movement, the Vietnam protests, and the like, it became obvious that what was happening could not be explained by the consensus-stability model of the functionalist approach. A new model emerged with its roots in Marxian thought. The conflict model stressed struggle for dominance, dissension, and change.

These two models continue to compete with each other within sociology. To those less fervently committed to one perspective or the other, it seems obvious that each approach can give valuable insights into social life. In the remainder of this book we frequently contrast these approaches' interpretations of many of the topics we are considering.

This brief overview of the emergence and development of sociology shows how various sociologists have attempted to understand society. We have traced the movement from broad philosophical perspectives to more focused empirical concerns. Throughout its course, sociology has demonstrated an expanding awareness of the nature of social life from total societies to the individual in society.

Sociologists have developed theories and concepts to express generalizations about and to understand better the very social life of which they have been products. This presents some of the problems discussed earlier in the chapter. Many sociologists shared the ideologies and biases of their times and situations, which were often reflected in their work. However, they also developed a method through which the impact of such biases upon our understanding can be reduced. For example, the work sociologists have done in the study of racial and minority groups reveals a steady movement away from the kinds of biases expressed in the works of such theorists as the social Darwinians to the more analytical and objective understandings of those of today. This task is unfinished, but progress has been marked. The continuing effort to apply the scientific method to the understanding of society and ultimately to its improvement holds promise for the future.

Contemporary Sociological Perspectives

Social phenomena do not speak for themselves. The kinds of descriptions and generalizations that sociologists make about the social world depend upon the perspective from which they view it. For example, the sociological study of a factory could be made from a number of points of view. One approach might be to study the way in which the various departments of the organization cooperate to maintain the factory and to accomplish its goals. A different approach would be to look at the unequal distribution of power and privilege in the organization— for example, between labor and management; between blacks, whites, and Hispanics; or between males and females. In other words, the perspective determines what one finds interesting and significant about social life.

Five major perspectives dominate contemporary sociological study: **functionalism**, **conflict theory**, **exchange theory**, **symbolic interaction**, and **ethnomethodology**. These perspectives raise different questions about society and set different directions for sociological study and research. A brief overview of each indicates the nature of the concerns it addresses.

Functionalism

The social system is the unit of study for the functionalist. A social system may be as large as a total society or as small as a couple of roommates. It comprises a pattern of social interaction among its different parts, each of which contributes to maintaining the total system. In our hypothetical factory, for instance, the various workshops, the bookkeeping department, the research and design laboratories, the administration, and the custodial departments all contribute something to keeping the factory in operation. The social consequences each element has for the maintenance of a system and for its constituent parts are referred to as **functions**. In our factory the function of the custodial department is to provide a clean working environment for the factory operations. The function of the shop workers is to attain the production goals of the organization. If the total society is our unit of study, the family is one of its most important elements. It contributes to the maintenance and perpetuation of the society by reproducing new members, nurturing and protecting them, and teaching them how to be members of the society. These are its social functions.

When some part within the system has negative impact on the way the system operates, we speak of its consequences as a **dysfunction**. For example, if our factory has a covert policy of discrimination against Puerto Ricans in hiring for jobs and providing training, it loses much of the talent and creativity such workers could contribute if given the opportunity. This practice would be a dysfunction for the system.

The elements are organized in such a way as to achieve the goals of the system. If anything disturbs the stable relationships among these parts, the system will make adjustments to reestablish its equilibrium, or balance. If workers should strike, negotiations will occur so that production can be resumed. Functionalism assumes a basic consensus on goals and values among the parts of the system. This agreement enables the system to maintain its equilibrium, to hang together, and to meet the other needs it must fulfill to keep itself going and accomplish its goals.

The functionalist perspective leads one to ask such questions as why a given pattern exists and to look for the answer in terms of what the pattern contributes to the whole system.

Conflict Theory

The conflict perspective calls into question the emphasis functionalism places on harmony and stability. Rather than assuming shared values, it focuses on the competing interests generated by the unequal distribution of power and privilege in the social order. It examines the way in which dominance is gained and maintained. Ideologies are seen as attempts to give legitimacy, or a sense of rightness, to the claims of various interest groups in their struggle for dominance or in the defense of a dominant position. A central question for conflict theorists is, "Who benefits?" For example, in a study of our now familiar factory, conflict theorists would look at the struggle between management and labor for control over decision making or at the pattern of distribution of profits and benefits between owners and laborers. They would examine patterns whereby people in certain ethnic, racial, or gender categories either gain or are denied access to employment in high-paying jobs. They would look at the ideas that are advanced to justify the inequalities or to attack them.

Conflict theorists assume that since struggle between various interest groups grows out of inequities in the social order, the stability of social organization is problematic. Change occurs as interest groups strive to reshape the social organization to their advantage. Theorists' views differ as to whether the inequalities that produce contending interest groups are inevitable. One group, with roots in Marxist thought, assumes that inequalities in power and privilege can be eliminated with the demise of the capitalistic mode of production. Another group, deriving mostly from Weber, sees such differences as intrinsic to social organization in industrial societies. These groups have in common a belief in the centrality of interests in social organization, and they see struggle and change as the most important focus of sociological study.

Exchange Theory

The exchange perspective assumes that one of the major components in social interaction is the exchange of rewards. Exchange theorists think that it is in the nature of humans to seek rewards for themselves. Such rewards may be economic, social, or psychological; tangible or intangible. For example, a paycheck would be a reward; so would pride in oneself, acceptance by one's peers, good grades from a teacher, a pat on the back from a coach, or respect from colleagues.

Exchange theorists think that it is the desire to get rewards from others that creates social relationships. An individual tries to find profitability through a given relationship; that is, one seeks rewards that are greater than the costs in time, money, effort, self-denial, and the like. If the rewards exceed the costs, one is likely to repeat the interaction; through repetition of rewarding behavior a pattern of interaction is formed.

If the interaction proves too costly, it may be discontinued. For instance, a Hispanic machinist in our factory may be seeking rewards in terms of wages and self-respect. If he is discriminated against and insulted, these would be costs to him. He may calculate the costs to be greater than the rewards he is receiving and leave the job. If rewards are not in keeping with our costs and investments—that is, if our sense of fairness is violated—we may feel angry or frustrated. In a group project, if you do all the work and someone else gets the credit, you feel that there has not been justice in the way rewards have been distributed. When such a sense of unfairness in reward allocation is shared by many in the same situation, they may unite to challenge it; that is, they may jointly seek distributive justice. For example, our factory worker may join with others and seek action from the Justice Department to insure their rights to equal treatment.

Exchange theorists assume that **reciprocity** is vital to social interaction. That is, the exchange of rewards must be approximately equal if the relationship is to be continued. If you go out of your way to do a lot of favors for a friend, but the friend always find an excuse when you need a favor done, reciprocity is missing; and anger or hurt feelings may disturb the relationship. Evening out the rewards exchanged fosters continuation of the relationship. Exchange theorists think that examining the exchange that takes place in social interaction is the most significant task for sociologists, because they think this focus gives us the most enlightenment about the nature of society.

Symbolic Interaction

Focus on the importance of interpretation in social interaction identifies the symbolic interaction perspective. Humans communicate with each other in terms of symbols. In fact, we shape our whole universe in terms of symbols: we name things. Language is our most important set of symbols, but meaning is also communicated through other types of symbols—gestures, sounds, objects, designs, and colors, to name a few of the most obvious. A salute, a handshake, a piece of music, a flag, a skull and crossbones on a bottle of medicine, a red light, and a cross all convey meanings. The acquisition of the meanings that our social group attaches to such symbols enables us to share a common culture and to understand and respond to each other's actions and motivations.

This perspective rests on three basic premises (Blumer, 1969): (1) Human beings act toward things on the basis of the meanings things have for them. For example, a tree will have a different meaning for a botanist, a lumberman, and a poet. (2) The meaning comes from social interaction. Meaning is not a part of the inherent makeup of the thing that has meaning. It arises out of social interaction. There is nothing in the intrinsic nature of the object you are reading that requires that it be called "book" or that means it is something to be read. To nonliterate people it could be called "tunali" or something else, and it could mean a doorstop. The connection between the object and its meaning is established through social interaction. (3) Individuals go through a process of interpreting these meanings as a basis for their action. That is, in human beings usually an intervening step occurs between a stimulus and the response. That step is the interpretation of the meaning of the stimulus. So our interaction depends upon acquiring these symbolic meanings from our group and basing our actions upon our interpretation of their meanings. Symbolic interactionists find this focus fruitful in increasing our understanding of social life.

Ethnomethodology

This approach began as a critique of the overly deterministic views of the functional, conflict, and exchange perspectives. These outlooks would have us think in terms of fairly predictable patterns of social interaction determined by firmly defined interests, values, roles, or norms. Ethnomethodologists think that these approaches do not allow for what they see as one of the most interesting facets of interaction: the extent to which we make up our social reality as we go. Although many of the situations we encounter are not covered by explicit rules, we tend to act in such situations in ways that will assure ourselves that we share a common sense of order. To do this we must actively construct the meanings as we encounter the situations. A student who took a shower in the dorm with his clothes on evoked such comments from other students as "You must be crazy." "He must be drunk." "Is this a class assignment?" All of these reactions reflect an attempt to make sense of this departure from shared expectations. Thus, our interaction is creative in that we supply the meaning of it as we go along. We are continually constructing our social reality. When what is happening violates our sense of shared understandings, we try to make sense out of the situation by explaining it in categories that are familiar. For example, there is no rule that says that when two people get into an elevator, they should stand on

How do you think the young girl is trying to make sense out of this man's behavior? How is the man trying to make sense out of the woman's clothing?

opposite sides of it. Yet, if someone gets on the same side we are on, we feel uncomfortable and try to explain the behavior as "getting fresh" or "pushy." Thus, we try to make sense out of what occurs and maintain our belief in a shared view of reality. These are the aspects of human behavior that are interesting and significant to the ethnomethodologist.

Some of these approaches are more relevant when the topic is macrolevel; others emphasize microlevel analysis. It would be tedious indeed to describe how each of these perspectives would view every topic we discuss in the pages that follow; however, we offer contrasting interpretations of many of the key issues.

Overview

Chapters 1 through 6 explore the science of sociology and organization within societies. Chapter 2 focuses on the various research methods sociologists use to gather information about social behavior and should raise questions in your mind as you go through the remainder of the book about how we know what we know. The interconnections between society, culture, and the individual are examined in Chapters 3 and 4. Our emphasis there is on the shared patterns for living that societies develop and on the way in which these patterns are acquired by members of the society. Chapter 5 examines group organization. The concepts of status and role, the building blocks of social organization, are introduced and used to analyze the nature of several types of groups. In Chapter 6 on deviance we consider departures from the acceptable patterns of behavior and the social responses to this deviant behavior.

Part II, Chapters 7 through 11, focuses on inequalities that become embedded into social arrangements. Chapter 7 gives an overview of stratification. In Chapters 8 through 11 we explore inequalities in class, racial and ethnic groups, sex, and age.

Part III, Chapters 12 through 20, examines major social institutions. Family, economics, politics, religion, education, criminal justice, health, and sports are important focuses of social activity and organization in our society. In our discussion of issues in Part III, we attempt to alert you to the ways in which various racial and ethnic groups experience and participate in social institutions. We close in Chapter 21, with a discussion of collective behavior and social change.

Key Concepts

conflict theory
dysfunction
ethnomethodology
exchange theory
function
functionalism
macrosociology
verstehen

microsociology
reciprocity
social Darwinism
society
sociological imagination
sociology
symbolic interaction

References

Blumer, Herbert. (1969) *Symbolic Interactionism: Perspective and Method*. Englewood Cliffs, N.J.: Prentice-Hall, Inc.
Hofstadter, Richard. (1971) *Social Darwinism in American Thought*. Boston, Mass.: Beacon Press.
Mills, C. Wright. (1959) *The Sociological Imagination*. New York, N.Y.: Oxford University Press.
Sumner, William G. (1906) *Folkways: A Study of the Sociological Importance of Usages, Manners, Customs, Mores, and Morals*. Boston, Mass.: Ginn and Company.

Research Methods

OBJECTIVES

After reading this chapter students will be expected to be able to:

1. Understand how sociologists gain knowledge about society.

2. Identify the steps in the research process.

3. Construct a true experimental research design.

4. Distinguish between independent and dependent variables.

5. Identify the advantages and disadvantages of survey, field observations, agency data, and unobtrusive methods of social research.

6. Identify several ethical issues related to social research.

INTRODUCTION

Once upon a time, the cure for illness was the practice of bleeding patients. When a person became ill, that person would be taken to a doctor who would proceed to make an incision in a vein and let the blood run from the patient until the doctor felt that enough blood had been taken and the illness had been drained. We no longer conduct this practice because research has shown us that bloodletting is not a cure for illness. It is through medical research that cures for diseases are sought, and it is through social research that the search for causes of human behavior is pursued.

In the last chapter we discussed sociological theories. We noted that sociologists can be placed into different theoretical camps or schools. Depending on the features of society they choose to emphasize, sociologists are likely to fall into a functionalist school, a conflict school, an interactionist school, or an exchange school. These theoretical schools help to explain "social facts," or the information the sociologist has gathered about the society. The systematic gathering of social facts is called **social research**. The information collected by conducting research is called **data**. Theory guides social research and assists us in the interpretation of the data.

There are several methods for conducting social research. Each has its strong and weak points. Some methods, for example, are more appropriate for studying attitudes and beliefs, whereas other methods are more helpful in studying actual behavior. Nonetheless it is research that keeps us from guessing or merely speculating about what we know. Research then is the heart and soul of any science.

The focus of this chapter is to examine how sociologists learn what they know about societies. Social research methods are the way sociologists learn about society. In this chapter we are concerned with steps in the research process and with several research methods including surveys, field observations, experiments, agency data, and unobtrusive measures. After discussing each method we consider problems with that particular method of research. Finally, we identify a few ethical issues related to social research. A preliminary note of caution may be appropriate as you read this chapter. Remember, although we are discussing theory and research in separate chapters, in actuality theory and research are like two lovers—they go hand in hand.

The Research Process

Sociologists conduct research in an effort to collect information about society. This information helps sociologists to explain, explore, or describe characteristics of society. The process of collecting this information is very important because a haphazard collection process can lead to incomplete—and often incorrect—data. Therefore, sociologists have developed guidelines to assist them in conducting research. These guidelines serve as a model and as a checklist of items that should be included in any research process and that help to deter sloppy research (see Figure 2.1).

Researchers generally begin with an idea about society that intrigues them. For instance, an idea that is often interesting to sociologists is why a group of people behave in a certain way. For example, Harriette McAdoo, a black sociologist, was interested in factors related to stability in black families who are upwardly mobile. The idea may come as a result of something that the researcher has read or observed. After thinking about the idea, the researcher will review what others have written about the topic and thus identify what data already exist. It may be that the intriguing idea has already been explained. If the data are insufficient, however, reviewing the literature helps the researcher develop hypotheses.

A **hypothesis** is a statement about the relationship between two or more observable characteristics. The observable characteristics are called **variables** because their properties may change under certain conditions. One of McAdoo's (1978) hypotheses stated a relationship between the amount of interaction with family kin and a black family's social mobility. The two variables in McAdoo's hypothesis are kin interaction and social mobility. It is important that characteristics, or variables, be observable so that the hypothesis may be tested. To test a hypothesis means to show that the stated relationship is not false. If we developed a hypothesis about how many angels could fit on the head of a pin, our

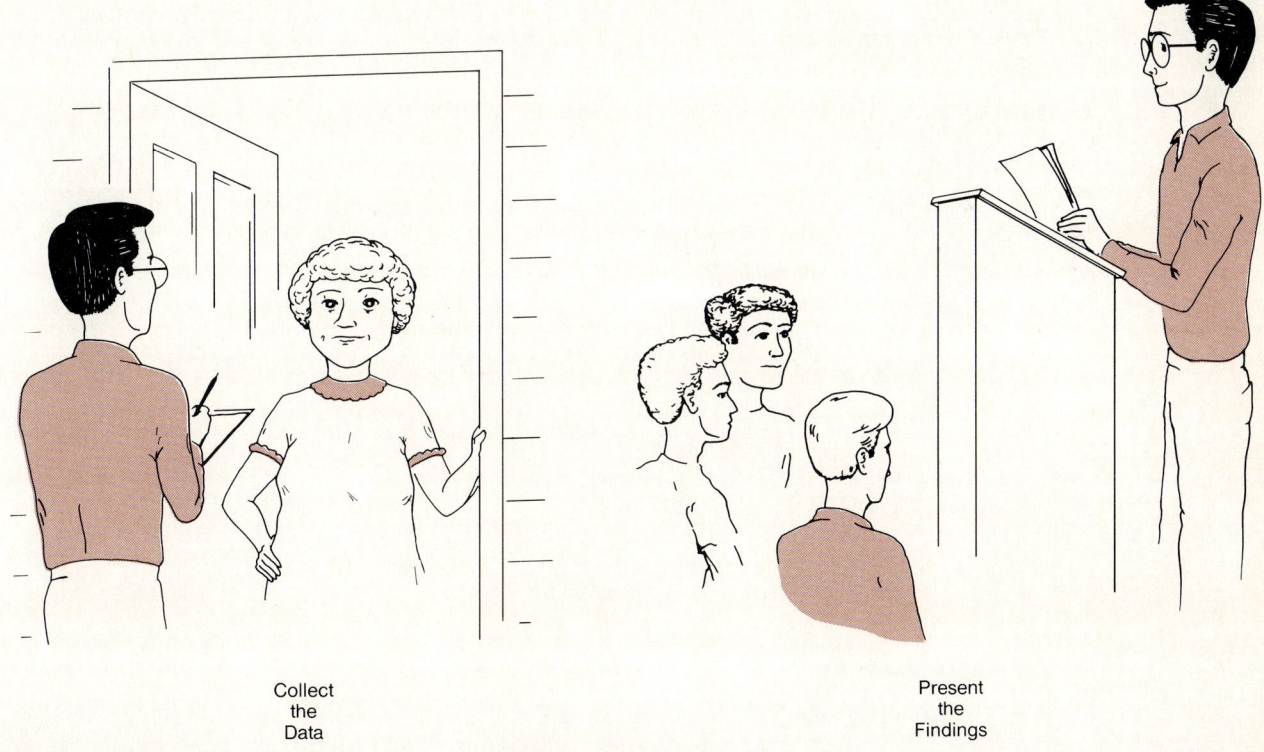

Figure 2.1

hypothesis would be useless because we cannot observe one of the variables, namely the angels.

After developing testable hypotheses, researchers construct a research design. In the research design the scientist chooses a method and selects a **sample**. A sample is a group of **subjects**—that is, the set of people who participate in a research project. The sample forms the basis for the data. Because the scientist is rarely in a position to include everyone who might provide information about the intriguing idea, it is necessary to select a sample who will be representative of all those who could provide information.

After developing the design, the researcher then actually collects the data. How the data are collected depends on the method that was decided upon in the design. Experiments, surveys, field observations, agencies, and unobtrusive measures—to be discussed further—are merely different ways of collecting data to test a hypothesis. One method is not necessarily better than another, and the method will vary according to the idea being researched. Researchers interested in studying behavior are likely to choose methods such as experiments, personal observations, unobtrusive measures, or official statistics, which will permit them to record or describe actions. On the other hand, information about attitudes or beliefs is often gathered through surveys.

The final step in the research process is to analyze the data and report the **findings**. The conclusions we reach after evaluating the data are called findings. The findings will either support or refute our hypotheses. Findings explain or describe our idea. Ideally our findings should fit neatly into some **theory**. A theory is a collection of hypotheses that explains in a more general way the relationship among related characteristics in society. A theory serves double duty in the research process. Initially a theory guides our collection of data. Upon completion and analysis of the data our theory may be reshaped and modified so as to be consistent with our findings.

In a sense the research process is never finished. When we review our data, for example, we may determine that our findings are true only under certain conditions. We may find that the relationship that existed yesterday does not exist today. One way sociologists check each others' research is to replicate a study by testing the same hypothesis using either the same or a different design.

One last point about the research process needs to be made. The purpose of the research process is to help researchers learn about social behavior; therefore, social research is only one of several ways of knowing. Not all things, however, are knowable through research. If you believe in God, your knowledge is based on faith, because the evidence that you might use to prove there is a God an atheist would use to disprove the same. Intuition and revelation are other ways of knowing. Knowledge gained through either faith, intuition, or revelation is not scientific. To say that the knowledge is not scientific is not to say that it is wrong. It is only to say that the research process, which we have outlined as the way scientists gather data, was not followed. The way that sociologists come to know about society, however, is always through the social research process.

Research Designs

Often researchers are able to manipulate variables to see how they affect the subjects. Researchers, however, do not manipulate variables haphazardly, nor do they use the "eenie, meenie, minie, mo" method. Before the researcher begins, he or she must construct a **research design**, which is a kind of blueprint of steps to be followed during the course of research.

Every imaginable variable does not have to be manipulated; in fact, often only two variables, an **independent variable** and a **dependent variable**, are needed. The independent variable is the condition that is expected to cause a change in the dependent variable. The independent variable causes the dependent variable to appear or disappear, to increase or decrease. For example, to say that prejudice causes discrimination is to say that the independent variable, the existence of prejudice, causes the dependent variable, the existence of discrimination. Therefore, research designs identify independent and dependent variables before the research actually begins, and often only the independent variable is manipulated throughout the research process.

True experimental research designs also contain **control groups**. A control group's members are like the other subjects in the research with one exception: the control group has not been exposed to the independent, or experimental, variable. Suppose you were a researcher with a social action agency and our agency has just come out with a group of three new films for reducing racial prejudice. Your job as a researcher is to test whether this package of films does what your agency claims it will. You could proceed by letting a group of subjects view these three films and then asking them about their attitudes towards different racial groups. And sure enough your subjects say they are now tolerant of different races. The design of your experiment would look like this:

$$X \quad O$$

X is the independent variable, the three films, and O is your group of subjects. Now you might be very excited about your discovery and run to report your findings. However, your boss asks you, "How do you know that the group of participants, O, were not already racially tolerant before they viewed the films?" Your boss also asks, "How do you know that they would not have said the same things if you had simply shown them a Bugs Bunny cartoon?" In other words, how do you know that the subjects are racially tolerant because they viewed this package of three films?

Back to the drawing board or, in this case, back to the research design. So you then come up with the following design:

$$O_1 \quad X \quad O_2$$

O_1 is your group of subjects before you introduce them to the independent variable, your three films. This time you ask them how they feel before letting them view the new films. This is called a **pretest**. In a pretest you find out all relevant information about your subjects before you expose them to the independent variable. In the pretest all of your subjects say they are prejudiced. This time when your participants view the films, X, you already know that they are prejudiced because you have pretested them. O_2 is the same group of subjects after viewing the films. After exposing your subjects to the films you ask them how they feel. This is called a **posttest**. In a posttest you question your subjects to find out the effects of the independent variable on their behavior. Typically a posttest asks the same questions that the pretest asked. Any changes in the response or behavior of the subjects from the pretest are then attributed to the effects of the independent variable. In your experiment you have pretested your subjects, exposed them to the films, and posttested them. After reviewing the posttest you find that again your subjects say they are more racially tolerant. Eureka! You believe that you now have indisputable proof that your agency's package of films does in fact reduce prejudice.

Again you run to report the finding of your experiment to your boss. But again your boss does not appear to be impressed and asks you a few more questions. How do you know they would not have been more racially tolerant in time anyway? How do you know they were not just giving you answers that you wanted to hear? After all, we are paying them to participate in this research. In other words, what your boss is saying is that although there was a change in your subjects after viewing the films, your research design did not permit you to control for other explanations of why there was a change in your subjects. In fact, your first two designs are called "pre-experimental designs" (Campbell and Stanley, 1963:6) because of the lack of a control group, which does not permit you to rule out other explanations of the change in your subjects. Your first design, with X and O, is called "the one-shot case study" and your second design, with O_1, X, and O_2, is called "the one-group pretest/post-test design" (Campbell and Stanley, 1963:6–7). Back to the research design.

In order to impress your boss, you must develop a research design that will permit you to control for alternative explanations of the change in attitudes of your subjects including the passage of time and the effects of your expectations on the subjects. After giving it some more thought and conducting a review of various research designs, you develop the following design to test the effects of the package of three films on the attitudes of your subjects.

Group A: O_1 X O_2
Group B: O_3 O_4
Group C: X O_5
Group D: O_6

In the above design, there are four groups. Two groups have an opportunity to view the package of films, X, and two groups have not. The two groups that have not been exposed to the films (i.e., groups B and D) are your control groups. Additionally, you decide to pretest one experimental group and one control group. One experimental group and one control group you do not pretest because you do not want the subjects to know what you expect of them.

The two groups that you pretest, groups A and B, say they are prejudiced. After exposing groups A and C to the package of films, you then ask those in all four groups how they feel about various racial groups. The two groups who were exposed to the films say they feel more tolerant of racial differences. The two groups not exposed to the films say they are still prejudiced. Cautiously, you take your findings to your boss. Your boss reviews your findings, studies your research design, and finally smiles. Your boss says the package of films does exactly what it should.

Your final research design, a Solomon four-group design (Campbell and Stanley, 1963:24), is a true experimental design. Because of your two control groups, you are able to determine exactly what effects your independent variable has on your subjects.

Our intent is not to suggest that only experiments have control groups, independent and dependent variables, and research designs. Surveys and field observation research methods also entail designs, controls, and independent and dependent variables. In fact, any research that attempts to find out the cause, or the effects of one thing on another, will contain all the elements of a true experimental design. Although our description of the use of films as an independent variable in the reduction of racial prejudice was devised to illustrate examples of pre- and true experimental designs, films actually were used in the fall of 1985 in an attempt to reduce prejudice at Tufts University. As part of their orientation, 1,200 freshmen and transfer students viewed three hours of films on prejudice and discrimination against Jews, Catholics, blacks, Hispanics, Asians, homosexuals, women, college commuters, and fraternity and sorority members (Cox, 1985:3).

Before we leave this discussion of independent variables, dependent variables, and research designs, one final point should be made. The purpose of research designs is to assist the scientist in finding the causes of attitudes or behaviors. As we have seen in the two pre-experimental designs, however, causes are not always easy to identify because factors other than the independent variable may also explain the character of the behaviors or attitudes that we are studying. Often social researchers must settle for establishing a **correlation** between the independent and dependent variables. A correlation is a regular pattern of association between variables. Establishing a correlation is not the same as identifying the cause, because some other variable that we may have overlooked could be responsible for the association between the variables we are studying. For example, although poverty is correlated with certain types of crime, to say that poverty causes crime would be incorrect, because most poor people do not commit crime and some wealthy people do.

Research Methods

Survey Methods

A **survey** is a method of research that involves asking people questions and then recording answers. The person who answers a survey is called a **respondent**. As social researchers we can also ask respondents questions about other people. When respondents answer questions about the attitudes or behavior of others, they are sometimes called *informants*. In more conventional terms, an informant is a "rat," a "squealer," or a "stoolie." Regardless of how you might feel about informants, they are important components of interviews and provide very useful data. When we use surveys, the respondents' and informants' answers to our questions form the basis for what we know.

There are two types of surveys: **interviews** and **questionnaires**. An interview is conducted by asking persons, either face to face or over the telephone, about what they know, feel, believe, or do. There are many examples of interviews. For example, in every major political campaign the candidates and the news media conduct interviews about the public's preference for candidates. Sometimes interviews are conducted about how the public feels about a certain issue, like immigration or environmental protection. George Gallup made interviews, in the form of public opinion polls, a standard way of acquiring information about how the American public feel about everything from their political to their sexual preferences. Thus, the Gallup poll asks people questions about the most admired man or woman in the world, voting preferences for presidential candidates, and the most serious social problems. Gallup made asking questions an

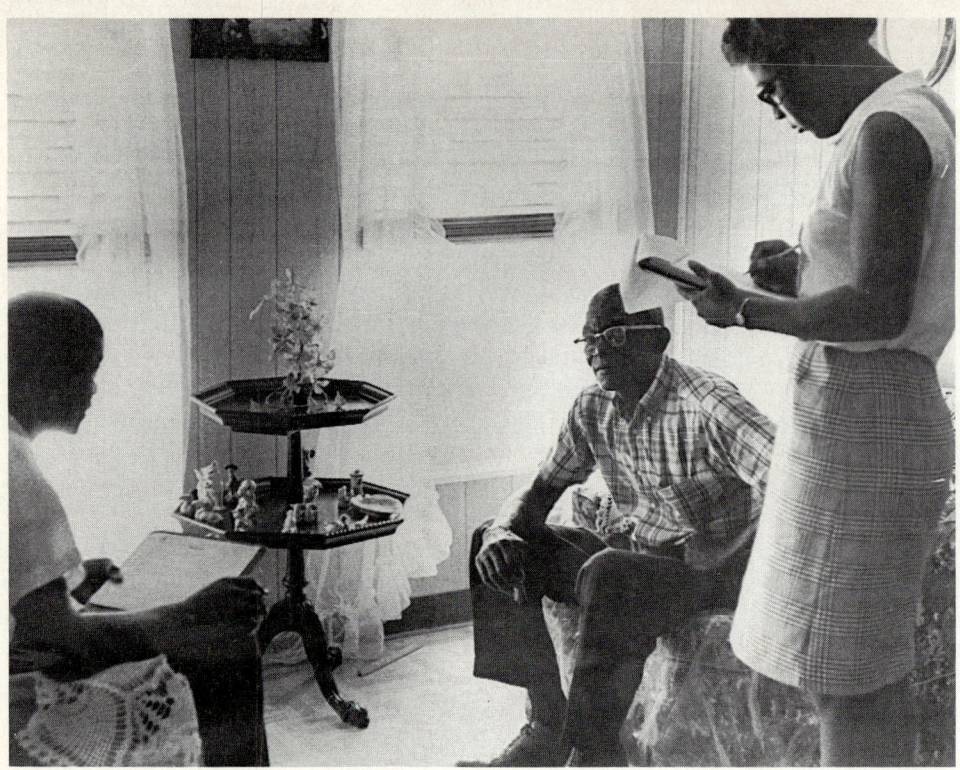

Sociologists often gather data about what people know, feel, or believe by means of an interview.

art, a science, and a business. Since then, *Time* magazine, the American Broadcasting Network (ABC), and the *Washington Post*, among others, have conducted interviews, usually by telephone, to find out information about human behavior. Sometimes interviews are conducted as voters leave voting booths, and predictions are then made as to the winner of the election. Sociologists often use interviews to acquire information about attitudes and beliefs. Specifically, interviews have been extensively used by sociologists to study crime and delinquency.

Questionnaires are a form of survey that involves respondents or informants answering a series of questions in the absence of the researcher. Survey questionnaires are perhaps the most widely used form of collecting information about human behavior. Some examples of questionnaires with which you may be familiar include the Nielsen television ratings and the United States government census. If you have ever applied for a credit card or a bank loan or made application for a job, then you have probably filled out a questionnaire.

Questionnaires used by sociologists differ from the questionnaires with which you are familiar in very subtle ways. For example, a sociologist may arrange a set of related questions throughout the questionnaire to measure aspects of the same thing (e.g., how you feel about premarital sex). When several questions are arranged on a questionnaire in such a way that the answers reflect how a person feels about the same things, the set of questions is called a **scale**. A scale is a set of related questions that attempt to reveal how strongly a person holds a given attitude.

Sociologists also relate the answers to questions on the scale with such demographic and social characteristics of their respondents as age, sex, race, religion, or political preference. In this way, we are able to tell what group of people feels strongly about any given issue.

Advantages and Disadvantages of the Survey Method. Asking people about themselves or others is an excellent way of acquiring information. A skilled researcher derives several advantages from using the survey method. Both the interview and the questionnaire have their own distinct advantages. One advantage of the interview is that the researcher has a greater degree of control over the question-and-answer setting. Because of this control the interviewer has "an opportunity to establish rapport with the respondent and to stimulate the trust and cooperation to probe sensitive areas" (Rosenthal and Rosnow, 1984:128). Thus, in an interview, a researcher may be more likely to obtain answers to sensitive questions. The researcher then may be able to derive a better quality of responses—that is, more clear and complete—from the respondent.

A second advantage of the interview method is that the interview provides the opportunity to help the respondent understand or interpret difficult questions (Rosenthal and Rosnow, 1984:128). A third advantage of the interview is a higher response rate than with the mailed questionnaire. Because the interviewer is present when the respondent is finished, the interviewer is able to collect any questionnaire that may have been used. Also, because of the interviewer's physical presence during the questioning, the respondent is likely to provide answers to more questions than would otherwise be recorded on a mailed questionnaire. In instances where the respondent is unable to read or write, the interviewer is still able to collect answers to questions. These advantages of researcher control, the opportunity to interpret difficult questions, and a higher response rate mean that the information or data derived from interviews is often a better quality data than that derived from mailed questionnaires.

There are, however, several advantages of the questionnaire that lie chiefly in its efficiency. First, the questionnaire is a relatively cheap method of collecting information. Because there are few research personnel who have to be paid, the biggest cost associated with a questionnaire is often the cost of production and mailing. Second, the questionnaire is an efficient research method because a large number of respondents may be included in the research. Having a large number of respondents is an advantage in social research because the researcher

Sophisticated survey techniques have enabled television networks to identify the winners of elections by analyzing voting patterns of a tiny fraction of the electorate.

can more accurately predict how other people who are not among the respondents might act or feel. The goal of most social research is to apply the findings of one's study of a smaller group to the largest number of people. The application of one's findings to other people who are not directly included in the research is called **generalization**.

Third, the questionnaire is efficient because it is relatively easy for the respondent to answer the questions. Most self-administered questionnaires have closed-ended, or forced-choice, answers—that is, the alternative responses are specified. In many cases all the respondent must do is check the appropriate response. In this way a respondent can answer a large number of questions in a relatively short period of time.

Finally, the biggest advantage of the questionnaire is the efficiency with which the researcher can analyze the respondents' answers. The checklist, forced-choice format of the answers means that the responses may be compared. Analysis of the answers then can easily and efficiently be conducted by use of a computer.

Frequently an advantage of the survey method of social research is that the researcher can go directly to the source, the respondents, for an explanation or insight into the attitudes or behaviors under study. Another advantage of the survey is that it is easily replicated. Researchers from different localities and even researchers from different eras can repeat the survey. In this way, a comparison of respondents' answers from different places and different times can be conducted. Thus, the survey permits sociologists to say whether their findings are true for most people most of the time or are true only for some of the people some of the time.

By now you probably are asking a few questions of your own about the usefulness of the survey. One question you may be asking is "How good are questionnaires or interviews if people do not answer truthfully?" Your question reflects a problem with the reliability of surveys. Obviously the information derived by sociologists from surveys is only as good as the answers the respondents give. In fact, there are several problems with surveys as a research method.

According to Bailey (1982), several disadvantages are common to interviews. First, interviews tend to be costly. Interview surveys often require trained interviewers who are paid, usually by the hour. In some cases the respondent or the informant is paid for participating. Finally, the trainers and the administrators must be paid. Second, interviews are time consuming because the asking and answering of questions both require a lengthy period of time, as do the interviewers' travel and arranging of the respondents' schedules. Third, when compared to the questionnaire's results the answers to the interview are more difficult to match and compare. Because interviews permit the respondents to reply in their own words, the reply of one respondent may not be comparable to those of others. Even when the respondents use similar terms, their interpretation of the terms may differ. The inability to compare responses makes it difficult to categorize the feelings or behaviors of the respondents.

The final disadvantage of interview surveys is the bias that develops from the interaction between the interviewer and the respondent being interviewed. This bias, although serious, is often very subtle. Differences between the interviewer and the interviewee in race, ethnicity, sex, social status, age, or clothing and grooming may affect the respondent's answers. For example, it is apparent that black interviewees' responses to white interviewers differ from their responses to black interviewers and that Gentile interviewees' responses to Jewish interviewers differ from their responses to Gentile interviewers (Hyman, 1954).

There are also several disadvantages of the self-administered or mailed questionnaire survey. Most of these disadvantages involve quality-control problems for the researcher. Once the questionnaire is mailed the researcher is unable to control the quality of the responses that are returned. Indeed, perhaps the most serious disadvantage of the questionnaire is the low response rate. Mailed questionnaires may receive a response rate as low as 10 percent, and a 50 percent response rate is considered adequate. Here the problem is that the researcher cannot control the number of questionnaires returned.

A second control problem facing the researcher in a questionnaire is the lack of control over those who do not respond. It could be that those who do not respond differ significantly from those who do respond. The researcher has no way of knowing whether the nonrespondents felt differently about the questions than did those who did respond or whether the nonrespondents are simply indifferent about the entire questionnaire.

A third control problem facing the researcher is the inability to control which questions will be answered. Specifically, questions that ask for information regarding sexual preferences, prejudices, political persuasion, or anything that the respondents may feel is not the researcher's business may not be answered. "Thus while 50 percent of all questionnaires may be returned, the researcher may find that only 10 percent of respondents answered a particularly sensitive question" (Bailey, 1982:158).

Finally, the researcher has no control over when the questionnaires will be returned. This lack of control over the time elapsed between the mailing and the return of the questionnaires means that the researcher may often begin analysis with an incomplete sample of respondents. These control problems affect the quality and the reliability of the research being conducted. If, for example, more people returned the questionnaires or answered more of the sensitive questions or even returned the questionnaires sooner, it is possible that the research findings would be different.

The common disadvantage of the survey method is that words are not deeds. What respondents say is not always what they do. In other words, respondents lie, have poor memories, have hidden agendas, bluff, and are not always sure of how they feel or what they would do in certain situations. Therefore, any verbal response derived from surveys must not be construed as a reflection of actual behavior. An old gambler's maxim cautions us about the disadvantages of the survey: "Never bet on anything that talks" (Nettler, 1984:70).

Field Observations

The field observation method of social research takes the previously described gambler's maxim to heart. Field observations rely primarily upon behavior rather than words as the source of data. When sociologists conduct field observations, they watch and record the behavior and interactions of the people in the society. After observing a group's behavior, researchers may ask questions of the participants. Their answers may also help to explain the observed behavior.

Such a research method was employed by sociologist Laud Humphreys while studying homosexual behavior in public restrooms (Humphreys, 1970). In order to conduct his research, entitled *Tearoom Trade: Impersonal Sex in Public Places*,"

Humphreys presented himself as a voyeur, or "watchqueen," to the men actually engaged in various sex acts in the rest rooms. By assuming the role of a watchqueen, Humphreys was useful to the other men because he served as a lookout. Most important to Humphreys, however, was the opportunity to observe the behavior and interactions of the men who come to public rest rooms to procure sexual encounters with other men. In this way, Humphreys was able to conduct his field observations without having his presence disturb the pattern of behavior under study.

Humphreys also used the survey technique to supplement his observations. After noting the license plate numbers of the cars of the men, he was able to secure the names and addresses of the participants. Humphreys than disguised himself enough to avoid recognition as the watchqueen and told the men that he was conducting a survey. Humphreys was therefore able to conduct a survey which added to his understanding of the behaviors he had observed earlier.

Humphreys's research raises a number of ethical problems with participant observation that must be addressed by researchers who choose this method of finding out. Humphreys deceived the subjects in his study by concealing his true identity as well as his true intentions. He also exposed the covert identity and the secret lives of his subjects when he attempted to collect a sample of these men to interview. Humphreys described his process thus:

> I gathered a sample of the tearoom participants by tracing the license plates of the autos they drive to the parks... Operation of one's car is a form of self-presentation that tells the observant sociologist a great deal about the operator. (Humphreys, 1970:30)

The ethical problems associated with Humphreys's research are very apparent because of the kind of secret activities he observed. As discussed later in the chapter the ethical problems of deception, concealment, exposure, and invasion of privacy face other researchers who employ the participant observation method.

Anthropologists, who often live among the society or group they are studying, make extensive use of field observations in their research. They interact with group members, observe the behavior of members of the group, and record the group's interactions and behavior. One leading anthropologist was Margaret Mead. Mead studied the small preindustrial societies of Samoa. She made field observations of child-rearing patterns, sex roles, and personality traits of members of these societies. Her field observations have provided us with a different view of other societies.

Other field observations have captured the character of intergroup relations in the United States. In *Black Like Me* (Griffin, 1961) and *Soul Sister* (Halsell, 1969), two white journalists used the field observaton techniques to record intergroup behavior between blacks and whites in Southern communities. By using skin dyes and altering their hairstyles, journalists Griffin and Halsell were able to disguise themselves as a black man and woman and observe firsthand intergroup experiences.

In unstructured ways you use field observations to collect data for personal use. Whenever you enter a new situation, a new school, or a new job, you make observations and record mental notes of how things operate there. You may even conduct a small survey by asking a few people about things and people that you have observed. The difference between your observations and those of sociolo-

Field observations have been used to capture the character of intergroup relations in small towns and on urban street corners.

gists is the more systematic and detailed character of field observations in social research.

There are several roles that the field observer may assume while conducting research. In the research of Griffin, Halsell, and Humphreys, they assumed the roles of full members of the groups they were studying. That is, each of the groups under study fully accepted the observers as members of their groups because the researchers disguised themselves as members of the group. By contrast, anthropologists, such as Margaret Mead, rarely attempt to present themselves as full members of the groups they are studying. Instead, they simply present themselves as researchers or scientists who wish to conduct a study. If they are accepted in this capacity, then they are welcomed into the group not as a full member but more as an invited guest.

Thus, field researchers need not always participate in what they are studying. Gold (1969) has identified four roles that researchers may assume while conducting field observations. A researcher may assume the roles of complete participant, participant-as-observer, observer-as-participant, and complete observer. The differences between the four roles that the researchers assume rest largely on two things: the amount of concealment necessary for the researcher to conduct the observations and the amount of the researcher's involvement in group activities. The complete participant totally conceals his identity as a researcher and is highly involved in the group's activities. An example of this type of research would include the *Tearoom Trade*.

With the role of participant-as-observer the amount of concealment is small. Group members are aware of a researcher among their midst, although they may be unaware of exactly what the researcher is studying. The researcher's involvement with the group is typically very high. The researcher literally tries to walk in the shoes of the people being studied. *Tally's Corner* (Liebow, 1967), a study of black street life in Washington, D.C., conducted by a white researcher, is an example of the participant-as-observer approach. A number of sports researchers employ the participant-as-observer technique of field observation in order to por-

	Concealment	
	High	Low
High Involvement	Complete Participant e.g.: Tearoom Trade Black Like Me	Participant-as-Observer e.g.: Coming of Age in Samoa Tally's Corner
Low Involvement	Complete Observer e.g.: A Spy	Observer-as-Participant e.g.: Sixty Minutes

Figure 2.2

tray the emotions of team members or the thrill and the possible danger involved in particular sports.

The observer-as-participant role requires no concealment from the researcher and relatively little involvement. Although group members are aware of the researcher among them, it is also clear that the researcher is there only for a story or is merely fact-finding. A good example of the observer-as-participant is a television newscaster.

Finally, the role of complete observer requires maximum concealment of the researcher's presence and absolutely no involvement by the researcher in the group's activities. In this role both the researcher's identity and the fact that the group is being observed are unknown to group members. A classic example of the complete observer is a spy, a person equipped with a microphone, field glasses, a camera, and a tape recorder to take names and record deeds.

The four roles of the field observer and examples have been summarized in Figure 2.2. Of the four roles, sociologists have made extensive use of the participant-as-observer role and, to a somewhat lesser extent, the complete participant role. As with any type of research method, there are certain ethical problems associated with the field observation method. We discuss some of these problems later in this chapter.

Researchers must give careful thought to exactly what it is they will observe in the field. Unlike in a laboratory, where the researcher can control much of the activity, in the field the researcher has to be blind to some activity while recording other behavior. In other words, the researcher must know exactly what types of behavior are important. Nachimas and Nachimas (1981:157–59) note that there are four types of behavior that may be of interest to the field observer. Those types of behavior include nonverbal behavior, spatial behavior, extralinguistic behavior, and linguistic behavior. Nonverbal behavior is any movements of the people being observed. Spatial behavior refers to the management of people and objects in the environment by those being observed. Specifically, for Nachimas and Nachimas (1981:158) recording spatial behavior would require the researcher to observe how "people move toward, move away from, maintain closeness, and maintain distance." Extralinguistic behavior includes the way the people who are being observed use their voices. For example, tone, volume, speed of speech, and the tendency to interrupt are part of extralinguistic behavior. Finally, linguistic behavior refers to actual speech. Asking questions, providing answers, telling jokes, cursing, and blessing are examples of linguistic behavior.

Awareness of the Nachimas's four types of behavior that can be observed in the field is important because the researcher needs to observe behavior in a social or cultural context. As researchers, we could be easily misled in our interpretation of behavior if we just observed what people said to one another without taking into account how they said it or what they did while they were saying it or where they were in relation to the person to whom they were speaking.

Advantages and Disadvantages of Field Observations. There are four major advantages of the field observation method over the survey method. First, field observation may provide more valid measures of human behavior, because "being there is a powerful technique for gaining insights into the nature of human affairs" (Babbie, 1983:267). A second advantage of field observations is that the researcher is able to record nonverbal behavior. Field observations permit the researcher to record spatial relationships and body movements. The old adage that "actions speak louder than words" illustrates the value of recording nonverbal behavior.

As we have seen, one of the disadvantages of surveys is that although we know what people say, we are never quite sure of what they would do in a given situation. Likewise, because experiments are often conducted in artificially controlled environments, the researcher is never really sure that the situation contrived in the laboratory would exist in real life. Thus, a third advantage of the field observation method is that the behavior being recorded happens under normal conditions.

A final advantage of the field observation method is that it usually represents a longitudinal analysis of ongoing behavior (Bailey, 1982:250). In other words, the time spent in the field is usually longer than time spent interviewing respondents or experimenting with subjects. Thus, the field researcher is able to decide whether the observed behavior is common and ordinary or whether it is a chance occurrence.

There are numerous difficulties with the field observation method. First, it is easy for a researcher to acquire "tunnel vision" by identifying so closely with the subjects being studied that objectivity in reporting and analysis is lost. The intent of research is to report the whole truth, not just the subjects' versions of the truth. Becoming too close to the people being studied can easily detract from the quality of the reporting. Incidentally, this problem of identifying too closely with people so that one's professional judgment is affected exists in other professions, too. In legal terms it is referred to as a conflict of interests. In medicine a doctor may excuse himself from a case if the patient and the doctor's relationship is such that it may affect the doctor's professional judgment.

A second and related problem with field observations is provincialism, the opposite of tunnel vision. Provincialism is the tendency to interpret behavior from one's own frame of reference. In this instance provincialism exists when "there is not enough identification with those observed, and their behavior is judged from the researcher's own point of view" (Babbie, 1983:261).

The first two problems with field observations have to do with the researcher's ability to report and analyze the data accurately. The third problem with field observations has to do with the nature of the data. Field data tend to be collected from small samples. Such data are difficult to **quantify**, and the researcher has little control over the events affecting the study. To quantify means to count, measure, rank, and statistically analyze the data. Thus, the analysis of field data is often limited to portraying impressions, feelings, and subjective interpretations rather than recording definitive patterns of behavior. These disadvantages aside, many sociologists feel that qualitative research, such as field observations, is the best way to obtain "firsthand involvement with the social world" (Filstead, 1972).

Experiments

Much of what we come to know personally we have found out through experimentation or, in more simple terms, through "trial and error." For example, the foods we like are those that through experiment we have found appetizing. In an **experiment** the researcher attempts to gain knowledge of what people will do by first doing something to them and observing how they react. In an experiment a researcher creates an environment, often similar to one that exists in the larger society, and manipulates certain variables in that environment in order to observe changes in the behavior of the subjects.

The intent of the researcher is to vary conditions to which the subjects must respond. The environment in which an experiment takes place is usually a laboratory. The laboratory for a sociological experiment is often, although not always, an artificially constructed setting, such as an artificial prison (Zimbardo, 1972) or a school setting (Milgram, 1963). The reason that experiments often rely upon artificially constructed settings is that "it is not common for real life situations to provide the kind of control that is afforded by deliberately created experiments" (Abrahamson, 1983:174).

An experiment that effectively illustrates the researcher's control of conditions in an artificially constructed setting to test subjects' responses is one conducted by Stanley Milgram (1963). Milgram was interested in whether people would obey authority to the point of killing another person even when their own lives were not threatened. To that end, Milgram devised an experiment in which he used forty men from various social classes in New Haven, Connecticut, to serve as teachers. The teachers in Milgram's experiment were seated in front of a control panel with dials, gauges, and switches; and although the teachers could not see the pupils, they could hear their answers and comments. The control panel indicated levels of electric shock ranging from a fairly mild shock of 15 volts to 315 volts. Over the voltage indicators were the labels of Extreme Intensity Shock, Severe Shock, and XXX. In order to convince the teachers of what was expected of them and what the pupils would feel, the teachers were given a mild shock. The teachers were then instructed by Milgram to ask the pupils to match up a list of word pairs and to administer electric shocks when a pupil gave the wrong answer. Indeed, not only was the teacher to administer a shock, but the voltage was to increase each time the pupil gave an incorrect response.

In response to the higher levels of shock the pupils moaned, screamed, begged the teacher to stop, complained of heart problems, and eventually became completely silent. Milgram told the teachers that silence on the pupil's part was to be treated like an incorrect response and that they should continue increasing the shocks.

Milgram found that most of the teachers, twenty-six of forty, shocked the pupils through the entire range of electrical voltage even after the pupils were silent and presumably dead. Of the remaining fourteen men, five stopped only after the pupils began kicking the wall between the teacher and themselves. The other teachers shocked the pupils through various levels of electrical voltage.

Milgram also varied the spatial distance between the pupil and teacher. The teacher was most likely to shock the pupil severely when the distance was remote or when the teacher could not see the pupil. The teacher was less likely to shock the student severely when the students were close or the teacher could see them.

Thus, the conditions—or variables—in this experiment were the researcher's authority, levels of electrical voltage, pupils' responses, and physical distance; the subjects were the teachers; the laboratory was a room in one of the buildings at Yale University; and part of the artificially contrived setting was the fake electrical control panel. Milgram brought these variables, subjects, and the laboratory setting together to learn what people would do in this, and presumably similar, situations.

As you may have guessed already, the pupils were not really shocked, although the teachers believed they were shocking them. The pupils were part of Milgram's research team and had been instructed how to act. A person who works with a researcher in an experiment but hides his identity from the subject is called a **confederate**. Confederates are most often used in experiments to create anxiety or additional pressure for a subject to respond in a given fashion. The researcher is then interested in whether the subject can withstand the confederate's pressure, requests for aid, or inducements.

Advantages and Disadvantages of Experiments. Experiments contain several advantages over other research methods. The first advantage—and clearly the most important advantage for social researchers—is the ability to determine causes. "The experiment is definitely the best method in social science for establishing causal links" (Bailey, 1982:223). Babbie (1983:205) has also contended that "the chief advantage of a controlled experiment lies in the isolation of the experimental variable and its impact over time."

A second advantage is that the experiment gives the researcher the most control over the variables that could affect the behavior of the subjects under study. The researcher is able to alter the independent variables. Thus, the researcher may elect to change the intensity of or the amount of the independent variable to which the subjects are exposed. Or the researcher may elect to change the independent variable altogether. Because of this control over the variables, the researcher can determine exactly what effects the independent variable has on a dependent variable.

A third advantage of experiments is that control groups are an integral part of the research design. Control groups permit the researcher to explore the effects of conditions other than the independent variable on behavior. Conditions other than the independent variable that may affect the subjects' behavior are: boredom, fatigue, interaction with the researcher, sensitivity to the pretest, and biased selection of subjects for the experiment. By matching subjects equally and dividing them into experimental and control groups, the researcher is able to determine the effects of these "rival hypotheses" (Campbell and Stanley, 1963:7) on the subjects in the experiment.

A final advantage of the experiment is that the research is easily reproduced by other researchers. According to Babbie (1983:205), the relatively small number of subjects as compared to the number of respondents in a survey and the corresponding low financial cost mean that "it is often possible to replicate a given experiment several times using several different groups of subjects." The replication of prior research is desirable in social research because the findings of the different researchers can be compared. When the findings of different researchers are the same or similar, we can feel more confident that the findings are accurate and apply to more than the few subjects in the study. Likewise, if the findings of researchers differ, we are more cautious about attributing causality to the independent variable.

There are two major disadvantages of the experimental method. The first is that the behavior of the subjects takes place in an unnatural setting. In other words, the effects of the independent variable on behavior may be due in part to the laboratory setting. Given the same variables in a more natural setting, the subjects might behave differently.

The second disadvantage of the experiment is the small sample size (Bailey, 1982:225). Experiments typically employ only a few subjects and often become the study of small group behavior. By contrast, sociology attempts to explain not only small group behavior but also large group behavior, such as social movements or social institutions. Therefore, the small sample size of the experiment may mean that the researcher has difficulty generalizing the findings from the experiment. The smaller the group of subjects, the less generalizable the findings.

Agency Data

Surveys, field observations, and experiments generate new data. However, a great deal of research is conducted with existing data. The existing data often take the form of official agency data. Both private and public agencies collect a variety of statistics about the people who use their services (e.g., race, sex, education, age, and income). The list of data-collecting agencies is almost infinite. A partial list of agencies that routinely collect statistics on their clients includes: hospitals, unemployment offices, welfare offices, banks, collection agencies, women's shelters, prisons, testing agencies, schools, lawyers' offices, parish churches, and credit-card-carrying institutions. All around you agencies are collecting data. How many agencies in your community can you name that routinely collect data?

The statistics collected by the Centers for Disease Control (CDC) headquartered in Atlanta, Georgia, are an excellent example of official agency data. The CDC collects data on any diseases that affect segments of the American population. Among the many different diseases currently under study and reported in the *Morbidity and Mortality Weekly Report (MMWR)* are the following: aseptic

Public agencies collect data which is often of interest to sociologists and other researchers.

meningitis, botulism, chicken pox, cholera, diphtheria, gonorrhea, leprosy, malaria, mumps, pertussis (whooping cough), plague, syphilis, tetanus, and typhoid fever. Data are also collected on accidents, heart disease, suicide, and hypertension. As new life-threatening health problems emerge, the CDC begins collecting data and conducting research into the causes and cures of the problem. A recent example of a new disease studied by the CDC is acquired immune deficiency syndrome (AIDS).

Because not everyone is likely to catch the same diseases, it is possible for researchers to determine which segment of the population is "at risk." We examine populations at risk more closely in our chapter on health. The point stressed here is that it is possible for sociologists to conduct research using the data collected by social agencies.

When sociologists use agency data we are attempting only to describe who, what, when, where, and how much.

In other words, such official agency data are **aggregate data**. Aggregate data are information about broad categories of people. When we use aggregate data, we make no attempt to identify individuals; rather our interest is in describing the behavior of people according to their membership in some category. The most common aggregate categories of agency data are: race, sex, age, income, state, region, and marital status.

Results from the analysis of agency data are therefore often referred to as descriptive statistics (e.g., the number of people in various categories). Descriptive statistics cannot determine motives behind why people behave in a certain way. The fact that agency data cannot be used to explain motives does not detract from their usefulness to researchers. Indeed, before one is able to determine why a problem exists, it is necessary first to define it. Agency data and descriptive statistics are an excellent source of data to define the scope of some problem.

Advantages and Disadvantages of Agency Data. In contrast to the number of subjects in an experiment or even the fairly large number of respondents in a survey, agency data often have the advantage of containing thousands of cases in each category. Thus, when sociologists conclude that certain behaviors vary by race or sex, they can do so confidently because of the large number of cases in agency data.

A second advantage of agency data is that they are relatively inexpensive data. Often the data published by governmental agencies are made available to everyone free of charge. For example, the *Statistical Abstracts of the United States* is published annually by the United States Department of commerce and is generally available in most libraries. Other popular annual publications of official agency data include the Federal Bureau of Investigation's *Uniform Crime Reports* of police arrests. The *Census of Population and Housing* is another example of a popular source of official data. Computer tapes of the information housed by agencies are often purchased for considerably less than the cost of conducting surveys of the same number of cases found in agency reports.

A third advantage of agency data is that longitudinal analysis and projections can be made. By comparing categories of behavior on a yearly basis, it is possible to discover long-term trends in behavior. Trend analysis is advantageous because the researcher is able to assess whether the behavior under study reflects a distinct pattern or merely an aberration. Once a pattern of behavior has been established, projections into the future can be made. Policies affecting budget preparations or crisis planning are made according to projections derived from agency data.

Most of the disadvantages associated with agency data are related to the quality of the data. There are many critics of agency data (Kitsue and Cicourel, 1963; Savitz, 1978; Nettler, 1984). Some researchers have suggested that agency data are virtually worthless. The less critical concede that it is necessary to be cautious with the interpretation of agency data. One disadvantage of agency data is that they generally underestimate the actual amount of cases. Whether the cases involve suicide (Douglas, 1967), crime (Nettler, 1984), school suspension, or wife abuse, the total amount of cases may not be reflected in the official records of the recording agency because cases are often lost with changes in personnel or coding practices.

Closely related to the underestimation of actual cases is a second disadvantage of agency data, the problem of coverage error. Coverage error is the extent to which some people are more likely to be missed in the collection of data than others. Coverage error is a recurring problem in census data. For example, as high as 20 percent of black males twenty-five to twenty-nine years of age have been missed in recent census counts. Likewise, the coverage error for other minority populations tends to be higher than for whites (Weeks, 1981:8). Thus, agency data are likely to contain coverage errors where data are collected on heterogeneous populations that include differences in age, race, sex, and income.

A third disadvantage of agency data is that it can fluctuate as a result of "reactive measures" (Nettler, 1984:42). Reactive measures are external pressures, such as political pressure or social events, that appear to cause the number of cases handled by the agency to increase or decrease. Because agency data are often used for the preparation of budgets and official reports, the number of cases may be manipulated to create the appropriate impression.

A final disadvantage of agency data is that they are often dated. Much of the agency data is published annually, but the data are a year behind the date of publication. Other data that are collected every five years may be six years old before they are finally made available to researchers. Thus, by the time a researcher has analyzed the data from a given agency, his or her conclusions may be outdated.

The disadvantages associated with agency data are readily observable when sociologists attempt to study child abuse. Several agencies including police, courts, welfare agencies, and hospitals may possess data on child abuse. Even in the same city these agencies will reveal a different number of cases of child abuse because not every case identified by one agency (e.g., a welfare agency) will be investigated by another (e.g., the police). The determination of what constitutes child abuse will also vary from the personnel in one agency to the personnel in another agency. Indeed, even personnel within the same agency will often disagree over whether a particular event should be included as child abuse. Thus, regardless of the large number of cases of child abuse cited by various social agencies, the actual number of cases is often unknown and probably larger than the number officially recorded.

Unobtrusive Measures

Sometimes, sociologists are unable to acquire information on people they wish to study by employing the survey, field observations, or agency data. When people resist being researched, do not keep records of their behavior, and are involved in illegitimate or immoral behavior, sociologists must often resort to unobtrusive measures of social behavior. Unobtrusive measures are indirect methods of identifying previous or ongoing behavior. Another term associated with unobtrusive measures is "qualitative sociology" (Schwartz and Jacobs, 1979). When sociologists employ unobtrusive measures, they often proceed as if they were detectives uncovering criminal evidence. Sociologists are likely to use four types of unobtrusive measures: physical traces, physical evidence, content analysis, and audio-visual media.

Physical traces are an indication of behavior that has occurred and can no longer be observed. Physical evidence is any item or artifact that can be collected, such as garbage. Garbology is the study of garbage to determine social behavior. In this respect, Hughes notes that the janitor and the garbage collector may be two of the most knowledgeable people in our communities. According to Hughes, "It is by the garbage that the janitor judges, and as it were gets power over the tenants who high-hat him" (Hughes, 1958:51).

A third type of unobtrusive measure is content analysis of notes, records, diaries, signs, documents, or any written account. For example, Douglas (1967) conducted a study of the meaning that suicide held for the victims by studying their suicide notes. Research on slaves has been conducted by reviewing the content of slave owners' bills of sale. Biographies of famous persons (Schwartz and Jacobs, 1979) are often written with an analysis of the letters, speeches, proclamations, or other public statements. An analysis of posted signs tells us a great deal about the problems that a community experiences.

Finally, mass media is a warehouse of unobtrusive measures. Newspapers, radio, television, records, tapes, movies, and video technology contain a great deal of information about us. Music television, MTV, now shows us the artist's interpretation of the record's lyrics. MTV, however, shows also what excites, frightens, or amuses us. It is possible therefore to develop a list of the major social concerns of a group by reviewing the content of television newscasts over a period of years. One reason why old movies or television shows amuse or bore us is because we see how differently people behaved in the past. The clothes, dances, speech patterns, and even favorite foods may be used as unobtrusive measures of behaviors. These constantly changing measures are shown through the mass media. What do you think researchers 100 years from now will say about our community when they review the content of old MTV tapes of "break-dancing," "punk rock," or Michael Jackson's "Thriller"?

Advantages and Disadvantages of Unobtrusive Measures. Unobtrusive measures are used much less frequently than other research methods. Because some unobtrusive measures may be interesting and even a little exotic, the data gathered from these measures contain a residue of incredibility. Researchers are never sure that what they have concluded from the data is correct. Therefore, unobtrusive measures suffer chiefly from the "problem of the smoking gun." There is evidence that something happened, but exactly what is not clear. As in all "who-done-its" there are many possibilities; so too with unobtrusive measures. Going back to piece together patterns of behavior from physical traces, physical evidence, content analysis, and mass media is tantamount to finding a smoking gun. For example, the content analysis of letters may suggest that a torrid love affair has taken place, but unless the letters are dated, it is difficult to say exactly when the affair occurred. Letters are misleading also since they can be written to oneself. Suffice it to say that most of the research conducted by sociologists that relies on the unobtrusive methods of research occurs when more traditional research methods are inappropriate. For example, archaeologists and anthropologists often use unobtrusive measures in their research because of an inability to survey the population of people who can answer questions about their social arrangements.

Ethics and Social Research Methods

Max Weber suggested that social research should be **value free** and that science, like justice, should be blind in both its process and its application. Value free means that the feelings of the researcher or the feelings of those being researched should not hinder the pursuit of knowledge. Value-free research, although rarely achieved, is nonetheless an ideal, a goal of researchers. In truth, values of the researcher permeate every aspect of social research, including the topics chosen, the methodologies selected, and the interpretation of research findings. The role of the values of the researcher in influencing the choice of research topics and methods and the interpretation of findings has prompted sociologist Howard Becker (1972) to ask "whose side are we on?" when we conduct studies and publish our findings.

In other words, sociologists must wrestle with several ethical concerns each time we conduct research. Ethics are a "system of moral values by which we judge behavior" (Rosenthal and Rosnow, 1984:170). There are ethical issues to be resolved concerning both the design and the politics of research. The ethics of the design refer to the moral standards that guide our research methodologies. The ethics of politics are concerned with "the substance and use of research" (Babbie, 1983:464). Regardless of the specific ethical issue, our concern is ultimately the potential harm to those who are researched because of the use of unethical research methods or the publication or application of damaging findings. Babbie (1983:452–58) notes that the ethics of process that are involved in social research include intrusion, **anonymity**, and **confidentiality**.

Perhaps the major ethical issue for sociologists is whether the intrusion into the lives of the participants is justifiable. All social research involves intrusion, and often this intrusion interrupts established customary behavior among those being researched. Even when permission to conduct the research has been granted by an authority for that group, the researcher's intrusion can stir painful memories, open old wounds, and revive repressed fears. At the very least, the research disrupts the day-to-day behavior of the participants. Although they may have initially given their consent, the intrusion and interruption may be resented by those being researched. This resentment may be seen in respondents' low return rate on questionnaires or in their refusal to answer sensitive questions in the questionnaires they do return.

The subjects in the Milgram (1963) study had certain conceptions of themselves as good citizens, as average Americans. Certainly it was Milgram's intent to get an average group of men in the study. However, participating in this research, a majority of the men altered their self-concepts as they realized that they could be executioners, given the proper authority.

Of course, unobtrusive measures such as garbology or content analysis of personal papers intentionally invade the privacy of those being researched. In fact, having to resort to unobtrusive measures to conduct research often means that the subjects of that research were either unable or unwilling to participate in this study. Researchers must determine then if their research warrants this intrusion. This ethical problem is not easily resolved because what is justifiable research rarely receives universal consensus. Typically, the sociologist is left to his own devices to determine whether the research is justifiable.

Leaving sociologists to determine for themselves what is ethical has in many instances been less than praiseworthy. For example, Warwick (1981) has cataloged a series of lies and ruses that sociologists have devised to collect data. Warwick noted that social scientists have: lied to teachers, lied to policemen, and even faked serious injury with the use of bleeding stooges on a Philadelphia subway. In an article entitled "Jokers Wild in the Lab," Rubin (1981) presented a series of "tricks" and "jokes" that social scientists have used to collect data. Rubin claimed that subjects have been tricked into believing that they were homosexuals, that they were falling in love, and that they were punishing students. Thus, for the sake of science sociologists and other social scientists have resorted to lies, deception, covert observations, and other activities that may be seen as unethical. These scientists believed that the data collected from their studies justified the questionable ethics of their research design.

Having determined that research is justifiable, the researcher shifts her or his ethical concern to the most painless way that the intrusion can be made. If there is a problem, for example with revealing the participants' identities, researchers may promise either anonymity or confidentiality. Anonymity means that the researcher cannot identify the participants by their responses. Confidentiality means that the researcher may be able to identify participants' responses but essentially promises not to do so. Anonymity and confidentiality help to reduce the pain of intrusion into the lives of those being researched by protecting their identities.

Assuring anonymity and confidentiality is often less of a problem for the researcher than the decision to reveal the researcher's true identity or the true intentions of the research. Because they rarely know the participants personally, researchers face a crisis of confidence. If participants knew the researcher's full identity and true intentions, they might choose not to cooperate. Or, if they felt coerced, the participants might choose to deceive the researcher. For example, much research is funded by the federal government. Government-sponsored research that solicits information on criminal behavior or welfare activity could be viewed suspiciously by participants.

In order to improve the confidence that the participants have in the study the researcher may elect not to make a full disclosure of either the researcher's identity or the purpose of the research. The ethical problem here is how much deception is necessary or permissible to conduct a study. Deception may improve the level of cooperation participants give to the study, but it can also threaten the cooperation that participants give in future research once their identities and the intentions of the research are publicized.

Whereas intrusion, anonymity, confidentiality, and the researcher's identity are issues related to the ethics of process, the ethics of politics are concerned with the analysis, publication, and/or application of the research findings. No data speak for themselves. Researchers must interpret and analyze data. Thus, the publication of all research reflects the interpretation of the data by the researcher. The end point of all research is the publication of the study's findings (see Figure 2.1). Yet in the case of social research the publication of findings may be very damaging to the participants. Research that has been funded, particularly government-funded research, often serves as the basis for policy and planning. For example, findings from the census influence federal allocations of monies to states and cities. Errors in the publication of census data may mean an unwarranted reduction in force (RIF) of a city's social services.

Policy, Race, and Social Research

Perhaps the consequences of ethical considerations in social research most clearly manifest themselves in studies on the subject of race. Babbie (1983:465) contends that "nowhere have social research and politics been more controversially intertwined than in the area of race relations." Joyce Ladner has called for the death of white sociology, because "historically, sociologists have portrayed Blacks as disorganized, pathological, and an aberrant group" (Ladner, 1973:xxi).

Babbie and Ladner's words draw attention to the public policy implications that research, particularly that which impacts minority groups, can have for the society. A policy (Morris, 1979) refers to the rules and regulations, or in other words the operating guidelines, that govern the delivery of human services by social organizations. Public policy then concentrates on the procedures and programs developed or controlled by the government. An example of social research that held public policy implications for blacks was that conducted by Daniel Moynihan, who as Assistant Secretary of Labor for President Lyndon Johnson wrote:

> The policy of the United States is to bring the Negro American to full and equal sharing in the responsibilities and rewards of citizenship. To this end, the programs of the Federal Government bearing on this objective shall be designed to have the effect, directly or indirectly, of enhancing the stability and resources of the Negro American family. (Moynihan, 1967:94)

Other policy-related social research includes sociologist William G. Sumner's study of folkways and mores (see Chapter 3). It was Sumner's conclusion that "stateways do not make folkways," which formed part of the Supreme Court's 1896 rationale for establishing the separate-but-equal doctrine. Findings from research conducted on the academic performance of black students in segregated schools played an important role in the reversal of the separate-but-equal doctrine in the Supreme Court's 1954 *Brown v. the Board of Education of Topeka, Kansas*.

In other social science research blacks, American Indians, Mexican Americans, and Puerto Ricans have been reported to be deficient in: mental ability, linguistic performance, logical reasoning, sorting ability, abstract problem-solving ability, and reading achievement (Barnes, 1972:66). Such characterizations of the mentality of minority group members by social researchers have led to some rather bizarre public policies. According to McCaghy (1985), between 1907 and 1937 thirty-one states enacted laws permitting the involuntary castration and sterilization of men and women who were mentally ill and mentally deficient. Prior to 1907, inmates of state institutions had been secretly sterilized for many years. Over 70,000 individuals have been sterilized as a result of being labeled mentally

Social research often has significant consequences. Research that indicates that busing accelerates white flight was used by groups that favor a return to neighborhood schools.

defective or mentally ill. A disproportionate number of those involuntarily sterilized were the poor, blacks, and members of other racial minorities. Today, the legal codes of half of the states still permit involuntary sterilization of the mentally deficient and the mentally ill (McCaghy, 1985:20). Social research continues to focus on such topics as race, I.Q., and educational achievement. Public policy is often affected by the findings of these studies. For example, in 1966 the publication of James Coleman's research on educational opportunity served as scientific evidence for those who chose to argue that school integration was not working (Babbie, 1983:455).

Perhaps the most dramatic example of a lack of ethical considerations and the implications for public policy occurred when from 1930 to 1970 the United States Public Health Service conducted an experiment on the effects of untreated syphilis on 600 black men in Macon County, Alabama. (We discuss this experiment further in Chapter 20.) As a result of this research many men died or suffered debilitating illnesses from the progression of the disease. The lives and health of their wives and loved ones were also jeopardized by this study.

In conclusion, the ethical and public policy considerations of social research can impact the lives of large numbers of research subjects and participants, as has been shown dramatically in various investigations involving minority group members. Thus, along with choosing the appropriate research design or selecting the best method for gathering data, sociologists must give some thought to the ethical and public policy implications of their research.

Summary

In this chapter we examined the methods of social research. Social research methods are a way or technique of acquiring information about groups of people. The information that is gained from research methods is called data. Sociologists employ several methods to acquire data. Chief among the methods used by sociologists are surveys, field observations, experiments, agency data, and unobtrusive measures.

Every method has certain advantages and disadvantages for the researcher. For the survey, the major advantage is that the researcher is able to ask questions directly of the respondents, whereas the major disadvantage of the survey is that respondents may say one thing and do another. The chief advantage of the field observation method is that the researcher is there to record the behavior of the people being studied. Its principal disadvantage is that a researcher may acquire tunnel vision and lose a certain objectivity in the analysis of the observations. The advantage of experiments is the ability to control the independent and dependent variables. The big disadvantage for experiments is the artificial setting in which the experiments take place. Although official agency data usually has the advantage of a large number of cases, the principal drawback is its generally poor quality. Finally, unobtrusive measures have the advantage of offering insight into behavior that otherwise would remain hidden. The major shortcoming, however, is that the researcher has no way of verifying conclusions drawn from the data.

Social research methods are not without very serious ethical considerations. The major ethical consideration for researchers is whether the inevitable intrusion into the lives of the participants is justifiable. Researchers are also faced with ethical questions of how deceptive they are with regard to their identities and the purposes of the research. The publication of research findings brings further ethical concern, particularly as the research findings hold public policy implications for various segments of the population.

Despite the disadvantages of social research methods or the very serious ethical considerations involved when conducting research, sociologists must continue to do research because the findings from social research form the basis for knowledge.

Key Concepts

aggregate data
anonymity
confederate
confidentiality
control group
coverage error
data
dependent variable
ethics
experiment
findings
generalization
hypothesis
independent variable
interview
posttest
pretest
quantify
questionnaire
research design
respondent
sample
scale
social research
subjects
survey
theory
unobtrusive measures
value free
variables

References

Abrahamson, Mark. (1983) *Social Research Methods.* Englewood Cliffs, N.J.: Prentice-Hall, Inc.

Babbie, Earl R. (1982) *Social Research for Consumers.* Belmont, Calif.: Wadsworth Publishing Co.

———. (1983) *The Practice of Social Research.* 3d ed. Belmont, Calif.: Wadsworth Publishing Co.

Bailey, Kenneth D. (1982) *Methods of Social Research.* 2d ed. New York, N.Y.: The Free Press.

Becker, Howard S. (1972) "Whose Side Are We On?" In William J. Filstead (ed.), *Qualitative Methodology.* Chicago, Ill.: Markham, pp. 15–26.

Campbell, Donald T., and Julian C. Stanley. (1963) *Experimental and Quasi-Experimental Designs for Research.* Chicago, Ill.: Rand McNally & Company.

Cox, William E. (1985) "Tufts Students Study Prejudice." *Black Issues in Higher Education, 2*(November):3.

Douglas, Jack. (1967) *The Social Meaning of Suicide.* Princeton, N.J.: Princeton University Press.

Filstead, William J. (1972) *Qualitative Methodology.* Chicago, Ill.: Markham.

Gold, Raymond L. (1969) "Roles in Sociological Field Observations." In George J. McCall and J. L. Simmons (eds.), *Issues in Participant Observation.* Reading, Mass.: Addison-Wesley Publishing Co., Inc., pp. 30–39.

Griffin, John Howard. (1961) *Black Like Me.* New York, N.Y.: Signet.

Halsell, Grace. (1969) *Soul Sister.* Greenwich, Conn.: Fawcett Publications.

Hindelang, Michael J., Travis Hirschi, and Joseph G. Weis. (1981) *Measuring Delinquency.* Beverly Hills, Calif.: Sage Publications.

Hughes, Everett C. (1958) *Men And Their Work.* New York, N.Y.: The Free Press.
Humphreys, Laud. (1970) *Tearoom Trade: Impersonal Sex in Public Places.* Chicago, Ill.: Aldine Publishing Company.
Hyman, Herbert. (1954) *Interviewing in Social Research.* Chicago, Ill.: University of Chicago Press.
Kitsue, John, and Aaron V. Cicourel. (1963) "A Note on the Uses of Official Statistics." *Social Problems, 11*(Fall): 131–39.
Ladner, Joyce A. (1973) *The Death of White Sociology.* New York, N.Y.: Random House, Inc.
Liebow, Elliot. (1967) *Tally's Corner.* Boston, Mass.: Little, Brown and Company.
McAdoo, Harriet Pipes. (1978) "Factors Related to Stability in Upwardly Mobile Black Families." *Journal of Marriage and the Family,* 40(November):761–78.
McCaghy, Charles H. (1985) *Deviant Behavior.* 2d ed. New York, N.Y.: Macmillan Publishing Co., Inc.
Mead, Margaret. (1939) "Coming of Age in Samoa." In *From the South Seas: Studies of Adolescence and Sex in Primitive Societies.* New York, N.Y.: William Morrow & Co., Inc.
Milgram, Stanley. (1963) "Behavioral Study of Obedience." *Journal of Abnormal and Social Psychology, 67*:371–78.
———. (1965) "Some Conditions of Obedience and Disobedience to Authority." *Human Relations, 18*(February):57–76.
Morris, Robert. (1979) *Social Policy of the American Welfare State.* New York, N.Y.: Harper & Row, Publishers.
Moynihan, Daniel P. (1967) "The Negro Family: The Case for National Action." In Lee Rainwater and William L. Yancey (eds.), *The Moynihan Report and the Politics of Controversy.* Cambridge, Mass.: The M.I.T. Press, pp. 44–124.
Nachimas, David, and Chava Nachimas. (1981) *Research Methods in the Social Sciences.* 2d ed. New York, N.Y.: St. Martin's Press, Inc.
Nettler, Gwynn. (1984) *Explaining Crime.* 3d ed. New York, N.Y.: McGraw-Hill Book Company.
Rosenthal, Robert, and Ralph L. Rosnow. (1984) *Essentials of Behavioral Research: Methods and Data Analysis.* New York, N.Y.: McGraw-Hill Book Company.
Rubin, Zick. (1981) "Jokers Wild in the Lab." In Theodore C. Wagenaar (ed.), *Readings for Social Research.* Belmont, Calif.: Wadsworth Publishing Co.
Savitz, Leonard D. (1978) "Official Police Statistics and Their Limitations." In Leonard D. Savitz and Normal Johnston (eds.), *Crime in Society.* New York, N.Y.: John Wiley & Sons, Inc., pp. 69–81.
Schwartz, Howard, and Jerry Jacobs. (1979) *Qualitative Sociology: A Method to the Madness.* New York, N.Y.: The Free Press.
Warwick, Donald P. (1981) "Social Scientists Ought to Stop Lying." In Theodore C. Wagenaar (ed.), *Readings for Social Research.* Belmont, Calif.: Wadsworth Publishing Co.
Weeks, John R. (1981) *Population: An Introduction to Concepts and Issues.* 2d ed. Belmont, Calif.: Wadsworth Publishing Co.
Zimbardo, Phillip. (1972) "Pathology of Imprisonment." *Society.* (April):4–8.

3

Culture

OBJECTIVES

By the end of this chapter the student should be able to:

1. Define culture and identify its major characteristics.

2. Distinguish between "ethnocentrism" and "cultural relativity" as perspectives for understanding culture and identify some of the consequences of ethnocentrism.

3. Identify factors that influence the development of culture.

4. Understand the importance of symbols for the development of culture.

5. Understand the importance of values, norms, and beliefs in shaping human interaction.

6. Understand the meaning of subcultures.

INTRODUCTION

Giant sea turtles come out at night onto the warm, sandy beaches bordering the ocean, dig a hole, and drop their eggs, usually in excess of 100, into it. Using their flippers, they refill the hole with sand and then return to the sea. Motherhood duties are over. When the baby turtles hatch, each makes its way to the ocean, swims away, finds its food, attempts to avoid its predators, reproduces, and strives daily to survive. Each baby turtle possesses a genetic code that prescribes this pattern of life.

Can you imagine what would happen to a human infant abandoned by its mother on the beach? The patterns of life through which humans go about meeting their needs are provided not by genetic programming but by culture. **Culture** refers to all those ways of thinking, acting, or feeling acquired by humans as members of human societies. Every group has such a pattern of life which provides solutions to the problems of existence. Our human infant abandoned on the beach would not be able to survive and develop as a human personality without contact with others who have themselves acquired such patterns and who will pass them on to him or her.

In the remainder of this chapter, we attempt to identify the characteristics of culture and examine some of the factors that affect it. The elements of culture that are of greatest import for defining social relationships—namely symbols, norms, values, and beliefs—are the focus of the latter part of the chapter.

Of what does culture consist? It would be impossible to catalog everything; but we can indicate some of the more important foci of cultural patterns.

Material Culture

Some of these patterns refer to **material culture,** those tangible products of social activity. Food, clothing, and shelter patterns provide ways of meeting the basic necessities. A Masai herdsman of East Africa may consume a rich mixture of milk and blood when he is hungry, whereas an American youth eats hamburgers and french fries. Each of these patterns represents a way a given group of people has developed to satisfy the dietary needs of its members.

Material culture is elaborated beyond providing the basic necessities, however. Included, too, are space rockets and spears, televisions and teddy bears, books and buildings as well as can openers and coins, bathtubs, beds, and beads. It is important to point out, however, that the patterns people practice and the ideas they have in producing, using, and giving meaning to these objects are the things that make them especially relevant as a part of culture.

The material culture has important impact on the nature of the culture in general, and of course vice versa. The cult movie *The Gods Must Be Crazy* gives us a sharp contrast between the technologically advanced culture of Johannesburg, South Africa, and the life of the Bushmen of the Kalahari Desert.

Food patterns vary widely from one society to another. Whereas Americans enjoy hamburgers and fries, members of the Libinza group in Zaire consider grubs a delicacy.

Both girls are conforming to the folkways of their cultures.

Johannesburg was portrayed as a fast-paced urban culture characterized by advanced technology, steel-and-glass skyscrapers, spaghetti-bowl highways, and sophisticated communications. The life of the Bushmen was depicted as leisurely, close knit, intimate with the environment, and having few material possessions. The movie thus suggests sociological truth: that the material culture and the meanings attached to its elements are inextricably linked.

Nonmaterial Culture

The meanings attached to material possessions are just one part of **nonmaterial culture.** It also includes knowledge, values, beliefs, laws, morals, traditions, and customs. Americans value material success not because we are born greedy, but because the culture we share defines this as a desirable goal to seek. Our art, music, dance, and ideas of beauty are a part of our culture, too. For example, most Americans think slenderness is attractive, whereas in some other societies obesity may be the ideal. There is, indeed, truth in the folk wisdom that says that beauty is in the eye of the beholder. But we should add the observation that the "eye" of the beholder has been taught through the culture to see some things as aesthetically pleasing and other things as not.

Other nonmaterial aspects of culture include patterns of family life, religion, production and exchange of goods, government, and education of the young. These patterns, which center around providing for important social needs, make up our major institutions. Also, patterns of ranking are determined by the culture. Culture defines how we are expected to treat various categories of people: patterns of discrimination against minority groups are as much a part of some cultures as patterns of respect for the elderly, loyalty to one's friends, or contempt for child abusers.

Introduction 49

Characteristics of Culture

As yet we have indicated only the general nature of culture; certain explicit characteristics may also be identified.

Learning. Culture is learned. Our physical makeup comes to us through biological transmission; that is, through the genes we inherit. Our culture, however, is socially transmitted. It is passed from parents to child, from elders to youth, from drill sergeant to army inductee, from priest to novitiate, from teacher to student, from television personality to viewer, from friend to friend, from generation to generation. This fact has important implications. It means that social contact is necessary to the acquisition of culture. If humans are not equipped by nature with cultural patterns, it is necessary for someone to teach the new members the way of life that maintains the group. Therefore, every society must make provisions for teaching new members how to be members of society.

Beneficiaries of the cultural heritage of the society, new members do not have to invent ways of solving most of the problems of living. They do not have to reinvent the wheel; ready-made solutions are available. You do not have to invent the airplane to fly home for Christmas or invent some kind of shelter from the winter cold. Culture is cumulative, and we benefit from the discoveries and inventions of those who have lived before us.

An important consequence of the fact that culture is learned is that it is subject to change if the ready-made solutions are not satisfying. Flexibility in the cultural response to individual and group needs follows from this characteristic. Consider the implications of this for our whole conception of social planning, for example. We assume that we can develop a better design for living by changing various aspects of our culture, because human nature is not fixed.

Social Transmission and Sharing. Culture is socially transmitted and socially shared. It would be very difficult to sustain social life without this shared quality. Humans depend upon one another to meet their needs. Interaction, therefore, is a fundamental process in human existence. Some degree of predictability in each other's behavior is essential to the ability of people to interact with each other. Consider a day in your life in which you could make no predictions about what anyone else would do or say: Do you wish to shower? There is no water; all of the water department personnel may be on vacation. Are you hungry? You might as well not go to the cafeteria; you don't know whether anyone will be there to cook for you. If you decide to go anyway, the person who happens to be there may decide to fry grub worms for your breakfast instead of the pancakes you were hoping for. You are taking a risk when you walk across campus to class; you don't know whether or not other students will let you pass or begin beating you with chains. Assuming that your class does meet, how will your classmates act? How do you know the other students will not saw the desks up, play drop-the-handkerchief with the flag, or pull out a knife and slash your throat? And thus through the day—providing you make it.

This digression into fantasy land illustrates how important it is for humans to be able to predict how others are going to act. A shared culture makes the necessary predictability possible.

Shared meanings enable us to communicate with and understand each other. Even a simple conversation depends upon the assumption that the meanings of the words are shared. How absurd would be the extension of our hands toward each other if we did not share the understanding of what a handshake means! How perplexing to see someone kneel before a cross unless we can understand the meaning. What would a man from Mars make of the antics of cheerleaders when he does not share our understanding of their behavior?

Shared expectations enable us to maintain a network of interaction patterns. Shared rules, moral codes, and legal codes regulate our relationships with each other and make social interaction predictable. Our activities are geared to the expectations others have of us and our expectations of them. When we deposit money in a bank checking account, our action is based on the assumption that we will be able to get it back, because we and the bank personnel share the same understanding of the rules governing such financial transactions. When we get on a city bus and pay our fares, we expect the driver to take us to the destination his route specifies. Several years ago a bus driver in New York City abandoned his bus and passengers in the middle of a busy street and took off for Mexico. The resulting chaos made the papers.

The importance of shared expectations is even more obvious when complex forms of interaction are involved, as for example, in governing a country, running a college, or operating a factory, all of which involve many people in various kinds of relationships to many other people.

To say that the expectations are shared does not mean that everyone is expected to behave in the same way. People in different positions are expected to behave appropriately for those positions. But because we share these expectations, coordination is made possible. If teachers and students share an understanding of each others' expectations, they can interact on that basis.

Dysfunctions. To this point we have focused on the adaptive quality of culture. We have emphasized the fact that it is through culture that we survive as human individuals and as societies. It provides patterns for meeting our needs and fitting ourselves into our physical and social environment. However, not all cultural patterns have this beneficial effect. Cultures may include dysfunctional patterns that are harmful to the society or to certain segments of it. Genocide, discrimination, apartheid, enslavement, and persecution; patterns of wasteful consumption; or patterns of health-threatening behavior are examples of dysfunctions because they do not enhance the ability of a society to maintain and perpetuate itself in its environment.

We have also emphasized the degree to which culture is shared. We should not assume, however, universal sharing of ideas, values, and goals. Ideas about appropriate behavior for women are now in dispute. Issues regarding abortion are hotly debated. Disagreement over budget priorities, the "guns versus butter" issue, enlivens our public debate. The patterns of distribution of wealth and power are disputed. Sumner (1906:5–6) suggested that there is a "strain toward consistency" in a culture. Where widespread lack of agreement is present, conflict may develop. The impulse to change is inherent in such situations, as the conflict theorists point out.

Cultural Variability

Out of the total array of cultural possibilities each society uses only a small segment to create its way of life. To illustrate this point we might focus on marriage and family patterns. Most Americans marry only one spouse at a time; regard the nuclear family of husband, wife, and children as the basic family grouping; trace their kinship through both the mother's and the father's lines; and leave it up to the young man and young woman to choose their own mates. Some societies may condone marriage to more than one spouse at a time; emphasize the extended family, consisting of several generations; trace lineage only through the father's line; and arrange marriages without consulting the young man and woman involved. Other societies may "mix and match" these patterns or select other alternatives. Out of the almost infinite range of potential patterns every society develops a valid way of life for its members. The rich diversity of cultures tells us that there are many ways of being human.

However, cultural variability may create problems. When people with different cultures come in contact with each other, misunderstandings may arise. The following story illustrates this point.

An American tourist stood by a quiet village road in Ghana, West Africa, and thumbed up in the usual American way to ask the driver of an oncoming vehicle for a lift. The driver, a Ghanaian, stopped the vehicle, got out of it, held the American tourist by the collar of his shirt, and forced him to explain why he (the American) was insulting his mother. The American tourist had the "culture shock" of his life, trying to explain to the Ghanaian driver the American meaning of the gesture that he had made. He was further shocked because he had been told, prior to his travel to West Africa, about the renowned Ghanaian hospitality, which makes the Africans there go out of their way to show kindness and hospitality to visitors and strangers. In addition, the whole incident was complicated by the fact that the American tourist was black; therefore, the Ghanaian driver found it extremely hard, initially, to understand why another black person could confuse local symbols so badly. But after everyone involved listened to each side of the story, they both understood the danger that could result from such a clash of cultures. Whereas the symbol made by the American truly means "please drop me off at your next stop," in Ghana, among the Ga people, it is an insult that roughly means "your mama."

Ethnocentrism

Difficulties in relating to those whose culture is different from one's own follow from the tendency a group has to develop ethnocentric attitudes. **Ethnocentrism** refers to the tendency to judge other cultures as inferior to one's own. The patterns of life of other cultures are viewed as absurd, weird, funny, barbaric, stupid, uncivilized, or just plain wrong. One's own culture is the standard against which other cultures are judged and found to be inferior.

Another aspect of ethnocentrism is the tendency to interpret traits of other cultures in terms of the categories of meaning of one's own. Let us illustrate what we mean by looking at essentially the same behavior in our culture and in a different culture. Americans regard the abandonment of an unwanted baby to die, as for example by stuffing it in a trash can, as an act of murder. Perhaps our tendency would be to interpret the behavior of the Arapesh in New Guinea in abandoning an unwanted child in the bush in the same light, that is, in terms of the same category of meaning. However, to the Arapesh a baby does not become a person until it goes through the birth ceremony, so the meaning of the act in the context of the culture in which it occurs is very different. By interpreting such behavior in terms of what it means in our culture is to be ethnocentric. The opposite idea is to try to understand a given behavioral pattern in the context of the culture in which it occurs, a stance known as **cultural relativism.** We recommend this attitude to sociology students as one that increases one's understanding of society and culture.

Ethnocentrism hampers our ability as individuals, as a people, and as a government to relate to other peoples of the world. Superior attitudes are a hindrance to amicable international relations and understanding.

Ethnocentrism has another face as well. It promotes social solidarity, or unity, among members of a society who share a culture. Commitment to the standards, values, beliefs, and customs of one's culture develops as people are brought up to learn their own language, love and understand their own standards and values, eat their own staple dishes, and clothe themselves according to the geographic and climatic conditions that affect their culture. They internalize these life patterns and develop a loyalty to them and to those who share them. Although unity and commitment to cultural values and beliefs can give strength to a society, they can also create a nationalistic urge to assert forcibly the society's superiority over others. War and aggression are often the consequences.

McLuhan (1967) has suggested that the world is becoming a "global village," where the development of a global culture is foreseen. In our supersonic age, people can travel to any part of the world faster than ever before. Trade, commerce, sports, and recreation establish international contacts. People can sit at home and see whatever is going on in other parts of the world via satellite communication. The import of these developments for the reduction of ethnocentrism is promising.

Factors Influencing Culture

Although no one factor can explain why cultures develop as they do, some factors exert a strong influence on cultural themes and emphases. In some cases they set the bounds within which the patterns will fall. We discuss several of these factors in the following subsections.

Biology

In recent years sociobiology has been introduced as an explanatory concept for culture. The basic idea in this theory is that humans are motivated, as are other animals, by the biological necessity to preserve the species and that our cultural arrangements express this innate urge. Patterns of family, property, government, warfare, and social relationships all are reducible to the genetically determined need to give preference and concern to those most like ourselves. For example, racial and ethnic patterns of discrimination are seen as attempts to preserve the genetic links between our biological past and future. We have altruistic feeling toward those who are genetically close to us, whereas we have hostile feelings toward those who are biologically distant from us. We incorporate these feelings into our institutional structures, where they become elements of culture.

The thrust of this theory is to lead us away from the conception of culture as learned, or socially acquired, and shared, adaptive, and variable. Sociobiology generally runs counter to major sociological understanding. Furthermore, it has the potential of returning us to old conceptions of biological superiority and inferiority that in the past attempted to justify patterns of prejudice and discrimination.

Although we may reject genetic factors as the major determinants of culture, we must recognize that if a society is to exist, its cultural patterns must provide for the biological needs of its members. A culture must define ways of getting the nutrition and protection that the members depend on for their survival as biological organisms. For example, the human body's need for food sets an imperative upon culture. Every culture must have patterns to provide these things. But the kind of food people eat, the time, place, and manner of its consumption, and the organization of tasks required to get it from its original state to the site of consumption may vary widely from one culture to another.

Other biological urges and needs similarly must be dealt with by the culture. Provisions must be made for elimination of body wastes, for sexual activity and reproduction, for sleep and rest. But these needs are modified and channeled in various ways by culture. For example, in some cultures people sleep on mats; in others, people sleep on beds or in hammocks.

Humans are born in a helpless state and must be cared for. They go through the maturation cycle and die. All cultures must pay attention to the differing needs and capabilities of infants, children, and adults. Aging and death are facts of life that a culture must take into account. The age divisions a given culture recognizes may differ from those another acknowledges, and the treatment deemed appropriate for people at different stages of the life cycle may vary. For example, in our society, elderly people are often treated as a social problem. In African societies they are respectfully regarded as the source of knowledge, wisdom, and authority. Some early Eskimo groups abandoned their old when they could no longer care for themselves.

Biological realities set requirements and impose limits on what cultures can be and include. They also explain why some basic similarities may be found in very different cultures.

Environment and Extracultural Contacts

The geographical setting and climatic conditions in which a society exists influence the nature of a culture. People must adapt to their physical setting: they use materials at hand; they cope with the soil, the sea, the heat, the terrain, the desert, or the ice. As a case in point, people who live in hot, humid countries tend to construct shelters that allow for free circulation of air, whereas people in cold climates usually try to build airtight structures. Culture allows great flexibility in ways of adapting to the physical setting. The ingenuity of humans produces many varied responses to the environment and keeps reducing the limits of the impossible. But the limits do exist; the environment does set boundaries upon what can or cannot be done.

The social environment within which a society exists also influences how a

Climatic and geographical factors have an influence on the way cultures develop.

culture will develop. A society that is relatively isolated from contact with other cultures lacks the infusion of new ideas and practices that may be found in cultures that have close contact with other cultures. This will have an impact upon the way it develops. Contact among cultures promotes the diffusion, or spread, of cultural traits. Where the contact between cultures is amicable and where power relations are not an element in the situation, a given society will selectively take on cultural traits of another and adapt them for its own purposes. Where domination or conquest is a part of the contact, the culture of the stronger society may be imposed upon the weaker. The process by which one group takes on the cultural patterns of another is called **acculturation.** It has the potential for being a two-way street, but symmetry in the exchange of culture rarely occurs.

Intracultural Dynamics

Some factors within a given culture have been pinpointed by various students of culture and society as having primary influence on what the remainder of the culture will be. The level of technological development is one such factor. A culture centering around industrial production can be expected to differ greatly from one based on agriculture. The division of labor, the patterns of ranking, family organization, governance, goals, and patterns of relationship all seem to reflect such differences in the level of technology in the society. Without making presuppositions about technology as *determining* culture, we can recognize that

Factors Influencing Culture

the kind of technology a society utilizes will at least influence much of the rest of the culture.

Another factor within a given culture that has been identified as especially significant in shaping the rest of the culture is its structure of dominance. Some groups in a society have the position and power to impose their cultural preferences on others in the society. An illustration of this may be seen in the Anglicizing of culture in the United States and the assumptions that non-Anglo groups will adopt these dominant patterns. For example, the racial and ethnic diversity in America is reflected in the many languages and dialects of its people. Yet the process of public education and acculturation places great pressure on members of these groups to adopt English as their primary if not their only language.

Of course, central to any explanation of a given culture is its own cultural heritage. This is the unique core that gives continuity and character to a culture. It predisposes a society toward selection of options from the range of possibilities afforded by inventions, discoveries, and cultural contacts.

Subcultures

Where there is diversity in the makeup of a given society, it is likely that subcultures will develop. A **subculture** is a pattern of life in which much of the general culture is shared but in which some unique patterns may be found. Although this definition allows us to include such small units as families or clubs, the term usually is reserved to characterize patterns that develop among different racial, ethnic, or religious groups or within distinctive milieux. We may speak of racial or ethnic subcultures of such groups as blacks, Mexican-Americans, and Japanese-Americans; or of religious subcultures of such groups as Jews or the Amish;

Many subcultures exist in the United States.

or distinctive life-styles such as the carnival culture or the homosexual culture. Distinctive language usages, religious practices, food preferences, music, celebrations, styles of dress, historic identification, and pride of heritage may represent departures from the broader society. For example, most Mexican-Americans share with each other a knowledge of Spanish, a commitment to the Catholic religion, food preferences derived from their Mexican heritage, a historic identification with Mexico, and pride in being Mexican-Americans. They may share with the broader society patterns of governance, rules of driving, types of money, love of country, and aspirations for their children. Coping strategies for dealing with the broader society are a part of the subcultures of groups that have faced prejudice and discrimination from the broader society.

Some of the differences among both cultures and subcultures can be very subtle. Edward Hall (1959) suggests, for example, that the "silent language" of the use of space is very different between people in the United States and people in Latin America.

> In Latin America the interaction distance is much less than it is in the United States. Indeed, people cannot talk comfortably with one another unless they are very close to the distance that evokes either sexual or hostile feelings in the North American. The result is that when they move close, we withdraw and back away. As a consequence, they think we are distant or cold. . . . We, on the other hand, are constantly accusing them of breathing down our necks, crowding us, and spraying our faces. (Hall, 1959:164)

We could expect that such differences might carry over into subcultures in the United States.

Mark Zborowski (1952) studied differences in responses to pain between Jewish, Italian, and "Old American" stock. He found that Jews and Italians display very emotional reactions to pain. The Jewish response seems to indicate concern about threat to future health. The Italian response calls for immediate relief of the pain. Zborowski found that "Old American" patients tend to report on their pain. They attempt to assume the detached role and describe the situation as objectively as possible to assist diagnosis. Emotional reaction to pain is expressed mainly while one is alone. Thus, we see that subcultures vary not only in such obvious characteristics as food preferences and celebrations, but also in ways not always consciously recognized.

Elements of Culture

Culture comprises inumerable elements. Some of these, however, are of more significance in shaping social relationships than others. Symbolic systems, norms, values, and beliefs are of particular interest to sociologists because they define the goals people seek and regulate the relationships they create in pursuing these goals.

Symbols

A **symbol** is a composite of two things: a meaning and a physical structure, for example, a sound, an object, an act, a color, or a design. "The physical form or structure is the vehicle by means of which the meaning is transmitted" (White, 1973:3–4). The meaning is arbitrarily assigned by the society; it is not intrinsic to the thing itself. Let us go back to our American tourist again. The meaning "your mama," which he conveyed to the Ghanaian automobile driver by thumbing up to him, was a behavior that had nothing at all to do with thumbs, per se. Therefore, by itself, thumbing up as a form of behavior would not have carried with it the meaning "your mama" in Ghana had not Ghanaians made the behavior acquire such a meaning. In the same manner, thumbing up in the United States to mean "please give me a lift" has nothing to do with thumbs, per se. It is a symbol, the meaning of which is culturally defined.

Humans organize their world symbolically: they name things. Language is the basic set of symbols through which meaning is communicated. To acquire language is to learn to share the meanings that enable us to interact with one another. The story of Helen Keller highlights the dramatic breakthrough that occurred when she as a child who was deaf and blind suddenly realized that things could be represented by symbols. Communication of meaning is essential to interaction; language makes this possible. Language enables us to accumulate and store knowledge. Thus, it frees us from the limitations of what we can learn and experience in the immediate situation. For example, Pavlov's dogs learned to salivate at the sound of a bell, but they had no way to explain this to other dogs or to elaborate its meaning to more complex behaviors. They were tied to the immediate situation. Language enables us to learn about things in the past or to speculate about the future. It allows us to experience in our imagination things that have happened in other places or envision things that never were. It permits us to think about abstract qualities like love or peace or equality and to conceptualize our experiences. Culture is transmitted through communicative interaction, and language is basic to this process.

However, as indicated above, meaning may be conveyed through other physical forms or structures. We use color to symbolize a range of qualities: red for danger, black for mourning, purple for royalty, and white for purity. Objects such as a wedding ring, a cross, a star of David, and a flag convey meaning. Gestures such as "high five," a salute, a handshake, "the finger," a wink, and a clinched fist communicate meanings to those who share the symbols. Sounds such as a national anthem, an alma mater, or a wolf whistle are symbols. We use space, time, and numbers in symbolic ways. Becoming members of a society means in one sense to acquire the knowledge of the symbols through which meanings are communicated. Thus, symbols are a major part of any culture.

Values

Values are an important element of culture because they specify the types of goals we seek. Every culture teaches its members ideas about what is desirable and worthwhile. These are the cultural values, and they define the goals we are expected to strive for. For example, in American society we value material success. Many of the goals we are taught to pursue are related to this value: getting an education, finding a job, or learning a trade. Our personal motivations tend to be geared to culturally specified goals. When we say, "My goal is to get a job, make money, and get married," what we are saying is that we have learned to strive for those things that our culture has defined as valuable.

Although some values seem to be overarching for the whole society, we cannot always assume unanimity or consistency in cultural values. In the first place, our values sometimes include contradictory qualities: health and indulgence; security and adventure; or a common problem facing college students, education and partying. Myrdal (1944) defined one of the major dilemmas of Americans as being the contradiction between the value we place on democracy and the value we attach to white racial superiority. Secondly, values may vary relative to different positions in the social structure. For example, the managers of a factory may value freedom from government intervention, whereas workers in the same factory may value security through government regulation of wages and hours and bargaining rights. But whether values are universally or partially shared, they shape the goals the members of a society deem worth pursuing.

Beliefs

The cognitive element in culture consists of what we think to be true. **Beliefs** are important in shaping our behavior because we act on the basis of what we believe to be true, regardless of what the objective truth might be. We have beliefs about the nature of the physical world. For example, creationists believe that human beings were created by God; evolutionists, however, assert that human beings evolved from earlier forms of life. What one group regards as knowledge another considers to be ignorance or superstition.

Our collective beliefs about the social world help to shape our relationships to each other. If we believe men are superior to women, our differential treatment of men and women will reflect that. Belief in racial stereotypes has provided a basis for hideous patterns of persecution. Belief that all humans are created equal has led to expanding patterns of inclusion.

Our beliefs about the supernatural or the cosmic order give direction to our behavior. A culture that has a conception of a sacred way or one that envisions an omnipotent God will bear the imprint of those beliefs in myriad activities and relationships: in our religion and in our moral codes, for instance.

Beliefs sometimes become linked into systems of ideas that embody fundamental truths about the nature of the world or the cosmos as its exists and as we should relate to it. Such belief systems constitute ideologies. Ideologies tend to generate strong emotions. They are defended fervently and opposed with equal ardor. Revolutions, crusades, and mass movements may be set in motion by true believers. Early Protestantism, democracy, fascism, communism, and white supremacy are examples of ideologies that have had far-reaching impact on the nature of society.

Norms

It is doubtful that any human society could exist without some kind or degree of normative order. **Norms** are the culturally determined expectations about how people should behave in specific situations. They provide guidelines for the way we live our lives. As people develop a sense of obligation to follow them, they become a sort of blueprint for human behavior.

Sociologists are particularly interested in norms because they regulate human interaction. The norms of our society tell us that we should marry only one spouse at a time, that we should nurture our children, that we should not burp in someone's face, that we should not commit incest, that we should bathe

Elements of Culture 59

regularly, that we should go to school, and that we should not steal. The fact that most of us feel obligated to follow such expectations gives predictability to what we expect others to do and how we are expected to treat them. These mutual understandings enable us to maintain a network of interaction.

Norms that specify what we should or should not do are sometimes called **ideal norms.** These may be distinguished from **statistical norms,** which describe what people actually do. For example, while premarital chastity has been the ideal norm, research shows that premarital sexual experience is becoming the most typical pattern of behavior. In this case the statistical norm and the ideal norm are not in sync. When this happens, the ideal norm often shifts in the direction of what actually occurs. The norms at one time indicated that women should not smoke and that men should not wear wristwatches (they were thought to be sissy). But as more women began to smoke and more men began to wear wristwatches, the expectations shifted to accommodate actual behavior. However, it is generally the case that there will be fairly close correspondence between the "should be" and the "is," because it is our feeling of obligation to follow the normative expectations that give order to society.

However, in a diverse culture, normative patterns tend to vary. Commitment to certain norms will be strong among some groups and weak among others. So the patterns of nonconformity are present alongside patterns of conformity. We find patterns of people resisting the draft, fighting for civil rights, following gay life-styles, dressing and behaving in punk rock ways, or participating in drug cultures. The point is that there are patterns of nonconformity amidst the more general normative expectations. Reactions to these nonconformist ways may range from overt hostility to legal action to laissez-faire.

Explanations as to how norms emerge differ among sociologists with different perspectives. Exchange theorists tell us that patterns take on permanence as we repeat those behaviors that are rewarding to us and abandon those that are not. For example, people get more positive responses from others when they bathe frequently; therefore, they tend to repeat this behavior until it becomes a pattern. Functional theorists think that norms emerge through the common experience of the members of a society as over time they work out solutions for meeting their needs. Conflict theorists suggest that many norms will reflect the interests of the dominant group in a society because they are in a position to influence the direction the society takes. As a case in point, norms concerning property rights reflect the interests of those who own property.

Norms may be expressed in a positive or a negative way. Norms that tell us what we should do are **prescribed:** we should respect our parents, go to church, vote on election day, and use deodorant. Norms that indicate what we should not do are **proscribed.** We should not commit murder, abuse our spouses, betray a friend, spit on the sidewalk, embezzle from a business, or eat human flesh. Whether positively or negatively stated, however, norms regulate our relationships with each other in the manifold spheres of experience: the family, the school, the playground, the amusement center, the military service, the government, the athletic arena, and the doctor's office as well as the dance floor, the elevator, the sidewalk, and the parked car in lovers' lane.

Folkways and Mores.   There are several types of norms that indicate important distinctions to sociologists: **folkways, mores,** and **laws.** The first sociologist to bring folkways and mores to the attention of the scientific world was William Graham Sumner. Sumner taught that folkways develop in every society out of custom. As customary rules of conduct, therefore, folkways are interpreted as a people's way of introducing patterns of etiquette into society or of specifying appropriate modes of behavior that people should exhibit in particular situations for social acceptability. For instance, in most West African societies, it is not polite behavior to give somebody something with the left hand. Therefore, most West Africans are horrified to see Westernized churchgoers giving their Sunday offering to God with the left hand. But since folkways are only polite or customary ways of behaving, the society's overall survival or welfare does not necessarily depend on them. In our society it is a matter of custom that we should not slurp soup or wear sneakers with a tuxedo and that we should brush our teeth, mow our lawns, and eat with silverware. One who goes contrary to a folkway is not regarded as immoral or bad. In most cases he or she is simply regarded as an uncouth person.

Mores, however, are standards of behavior that members of society regard very highly and respect a great deal. They carry connotations of good and evil, moral and immoral, or right and wrong. People who sexually abuse children are not regarded as just uncouth; they are considered immoral. Societies view the infraction of mores more seriously than folkways because mores are very important for the society's welfare. Violations of the mores impair or threaten the ability of the group to preserve the interactive network through which it maintains itself. We may illustrate this point by referring to the Ten Commandments, which express a central moral code of the Judeo-Christian tradition. Viewed in terms of their sociological significance, six of the commandments instruct us in ways of preserving group harmony: thou shalt not kill, steal, covet, bear false witness, or commit adultery, and thou shalt honor thy father and thy mother. It is easy to imagine a whole society of noisy soup slurpers who adhere to these commandments and are able to cooperate with one another for broader social needs. It is more difficult to envision such interaction when indiscriminant killing is rampant.

Enforcement of the Norms. Clusters of norms define our ways of meeting our needs as a society: how we produce our food, govern ourselves, entertain ourselves, maintain our unity, and educate our children. Because the norms are such an important feature of our communal existence, every society develops ways of insuring compliance. The most efficient way is through teaching the norms to each new generation so that people will wish to do what they are supposed to do. This process is the focus of the following chapter. The family, the school, the church, the peer group, and the mass media contribute to children's acquisition of norms. From all these sources children adopt norms that become part of their own ways of thinking. When norms have become internalized, the sense of obligation to conform begins to come from within. Conformity is fostered by feelings such as pride, self-esteem, guilt, or shame.

However, enforcement of the norms comes from sources external to the individual as well; that is, from society. **Sanctions** are rewards or punishments used by society to bring about conformity to the norms. Each individual is a part of the public opinion to which other individuals respond. Every time one snubs a show-off, expresses horror at a murder, frowns at a drunk, disapproves of someone's sloppy manners, praises an act of kindness, casts a vote, or admires a virtuous person, he or she is a part of that public opinion that is attempting to exercise control over the behavior of others. Granted, some people are in positions in which their opinions count more than others, such as employers or judges; but we are all society.

Society uses a wide range of sanctions for insuring compliance. These are by no means all or even mainly punitive and restrictive. The desire for approval and acceptance is strongly motivating in the lives of us all. The need to belong is a powerful psychic force. Some of the rewards that society holds out address these needs. The type of satisfaction that a small child gains when his parents praise his demonstration that he has learned to tie his shoes stays with us always. The desire for the approval of others, especially the high regard of those people who are most meaningful in our lives, is a positive goal toward which we strive.

Those techniques that are often felt to be more restrictive as we experience them are the negative measures through which society exercises control. We sometimes feel them to be a "Thou shalt not" response to our "I want to." Through the punishment of the offender society reasserts the norms. Doubtlessly a long list could be compiled of the informal ways in which disapproval may be expressed: frowns, laughs, sneers, snickers, reprimands, raised eyebrows, a shake of the head, averted glances, or verbal criticism. If the violation of the norm is not serious—that is, if the behavior merely violates a folkway—these techniques suffice to express public disapproval. If the mores are violated, however, harsher techniques may be employed: public ridicule, bad publicity in the press, ostracism from the group, physical harm, or even taking the life of the offender. Religious sanctions are often attached to mores to give them added support. Legal sanctions, too, reinforce them. For example, murder not only violates public opinion, but it is also considered a sin and a crime. Together these supports strengthen the norm.

Laws. Laws are social rules that have been formally encoded. They have been enacted, usually by a legislative or regulatory body; thus they are "official." Laws regulate our conduct and give predictability to our interactions. Violations of the law—that is, the criminal law—constitute crimes. Functionalists regard the law and its enforcement by an official body as the way the people in a society protect their common life through the agency of the state, which represents them. Criminal cases are listed on the docket as "the state v. John Doe" or "the people v. Jane Doe." This indicates that in violating the law the offender has attacked not only the actual victim but the communal bonds as well. Conflict theorists often see law as the way in which one powerful group imposes it rules upon the rest of the society, using the state as its agency to do so.

There are, of course, interconnections between the folkways and mores on the one hand and law on the other. For example, mores that form the basis of prohibition against betraying one's country may also be the foundation of a law against treason. Sumner maintained that we cannot legislate morality. Unless the laws are in keeping with the mores of the society, they will not be obeyed. The widespread disregard of the Nineteenth Amendment, which prohibited the sale of alcoholic beverages, is a well-known case in point. However, there is also evidence that legislation may create folkways and mores. For example, civil rights legislation changed the expected patterns of interaction between races in this country. Social Security legislation changed our norms about how people in need are to be treated. Although Sumner may have been on the right track, he probably overstated his case. Laws may lead as well as follow the folkways and mores.

Summary

In this chapter we have regarded culture as behavior that one acquires as a member of human society. It is through culture that human societies meet their needs. One of the major characteristics of culture is that it is learned, which gives its practitioners great flexibility in making adaptations to the physical and social environments. Culture is also shared, creating the common understandings that make interaction possible.

Some of the factors that influence culture are biological characteristics of humans, the physical and social environment, the level of technological development, and the structure of dominance within the society. The special heritage of each society provides the core around which selections from the range of cultural possibilities are made.

Subcultures develop among various racial, ethnic, and religious groups. Subcultures combine some features of the broader society with patterns that are unique to a particular segment of the population. Subcultures add much richness and diversity to a culture but can also be a source of strain in relationships with the broader society.

People tend to become committed to their own culture and usually will develop ethnocentric feelings, that is, feelings that their culture is the best. Such feelings promote group solidarity but play havoc with relationships outside the group.

The major elements of culture that interest sociologists are the symbolic systems that make the communication of meaning possible; the beliefs of the culture, which provide the cognitive framework in terms of which we interact; the values, which define the things we think to be worth striving for; and the norms, which provide the guidelines for behavior and regulate our interaction. Folkways are norms that specify polite or customary ways of behaving. Usually they are not stringently enforced. Mores are norms relating to the welfare of the society and accordingly receive much stronger sanctions. Laws are codified rules of conduct that are officially enforced. Usually they do not stray too far from the folkways and mores; but there are numerous cases to the contrary: stateways are not always folkways.

Key Terms

acculturation
beliefs
cultural relativism
culture
ethnocentrism
folkways

> ideal norms
> laws
> material culture
> mores
> nonmaterial culture
> norms
> prescribed norms
> proscribed norms
> sanctions
> statistical norms
> subculture
> symbols
> values

References

Hall, Edward T. (1959) *The Silent Language.* Greenwich, Conn.: Fawcett Publications, Inc.

McLuhan, M. H. and Q. Fiore. (1967) *The Medium is the Message.* New York, N.Y.: Random House, Inc.

Myrdal, Gunnar. (1944) *An American Dilemma.* New York, N.Y.: Harper and Brothers.

Sumner, William G. (1906) *Folkways.* Boston, Mass.: Ginn and Company.

White, L. A. (1973) *The Concept of Culture.* Minneapolis, Minn.: Burgess Publishing Company.

Zborowski, Mark. (1952) "Cultural Components in Responses to Pain." *The Journal of Social Issues,* 8(4):16–30.

4

Socialization

OBJECTIVES

Upon completion of this chapter students will be expected to:

1. Define and identify four types of socialization.
2. Discuss the impact of the failure of socialization on human development.
3. Compare and contrast theories of how self-identity develops.
4. Discuss opposing viewpoints on oversocialization.
5. Describe the characteristics of total institutions.
6. Understand how members of various groups often experience a different pattern of socialization.

INTRODUCTION

In Chapter 3 we saw how culture contributes to the form of collective life. Culture outlines for its members everything necessary to insure the survival of group members. Matters of taste for particular foods, preferences for sexual gratification, and appropriate forms of shelter are only a few examples of social behavior that is culturally determined. The question for us in this chapter is why? Why is culture the primary method of survival for humans? Why can we not rely on our biological instincts? Why must we survive in groups?

The answer to all of these questions is **socialization.** Studies that examine the failure of socialization demonstrate very clearly that to be human is to be social. Being social is not an automatic process. We learn to be social when we develop attitudes and behaviors that are similar to those of other members of our society. Thus, through socialization we literally learn to become human. The focus of this chapter is the socialization process. In many ways it is perhaps the single most important concept in the study of sociology because any specific attitude (e.g., love, hate, prejudice) or behavior (e.g., crime, deviance, conformity) presupposes socialization. In this chapter we define socialization, review

Through socialization we learn attitudes and behaviors appropriate for members of our society. Here a child learns the meaning of love.

studies on the failure of socialization, tell how socialization is learned, examine agents of socialization, and review theories of how self-identity develops. The idea to keep in mind as you read this chapter is that human behavior is diverse and complex. Just look around at the diversity among your classmates. Yet, all of this diverse and complex behavior had to be learned from others. Socialization is this learning process.

Socialization Defined

Socialization is the process by which we acquire the attitudes and behaviors that are appropriate for the members of our society. Although the attitudes and behaviors that we learn in our society distinguish us from members of other societies, the socialization process operates in the same manner in all societies. The purpose of socialization is to insure that our attitudes and behavior will be acceptable to a majority of the members of our respective societies. Although there is evidence that some socialization occurs among animals (Harlow, 1971), to the degree that humans rely most heavily on socialization for survival, the socialization process also distinguishes us from other animals. Put another way, socialization is the process that makes us act like human beings.

In order for socialization to be successful in transforming us from an organism capable of seemingly endless behavioral adaptations to a person who is easily recognized as a member of a given society, socialization must impart to the members certain specific information. Thus, socialization may be seen as the learning process whereby members of the society acquire personalities; learn the social rules that govern their behavior in the situations and social positions in which they find themselves; and transmit the storehouse of knowledge, skills and techniques of the culture.

Socialization is a continuous process. Whereas it is easy to understand the importance of socialization in the transformation of the child into an adult, the role of socialization may not be as readily apparent in the lives of adults. Adults, however, must be constantly socialized as they move in and out of new groups—adults change jobs, marital statuses, states of residence and even citizenship. Each of these changes requires socialization in order for the persons to behave appropriately in their new situation. As a student in college you had to be socialized to the proper attitudes and behavior expected of you as a college student. Each stage of the life cycle requires additional socialization. As we examine in the chapter on aging, people are socialized to the appropriate attitudes and behaviors expected of the elderly. Socialization then is a lifelong process. It is continuous from the womb to the tomb.

Failures of Socialization

One way for us to explore the importance of socialization in the development of humans is to examine instances where socialization has failed. The failure of socialization may be seen in studies of feral children, children raised in relative isolation, hospital studies, and animal studies. As we examine each of these failures, you should keep in mind that each example represents another possibility of what we all could become. An adaptation of an old expression seems appropriate here: "There but for the grace of socialization go we."

Feral Children

Feral means wild, untamed, or undomesticated. **Feral children** are children who have purportedly been raised by animals. Although it is doubtful that most children would be able to survive without the constant care and supervision of an adult, there have been a few substantiated reports of children who have survived in the wilderness and/or have been cared for by animals. One such case involved the wild boy of Aveyron. Apparently separated from humans when he was very young, the boy had managed to survive in the woods until he reached puberty. Found in France around 1800, the boy could not speak. He would, however, behave like an animal. He liked to swing from trees, go around naked, and be outdoors to experience the elements. He disliked prepared foods and preferred potatoes, which he pulled from a fire with his bare hands. Efforts to teach him to speak failed. Even after living with other humans for about twenty-five years, the wild boy of Aveyron never learned to speak or interact with other people in a socially acceptable fashion.

Brown (1972) discussed another case of feral children. Named Kamala and Amala, the two girls were found in India in a wolf's den, where they had apparently survived as "cubs" among the wolf's offspring. The older girl, Kamala, was eight, and the younger, Amala, was about one and a half years old. Both girls behaved like wolves. For example, they moved about on their hands and knees, ate raw meat, and sniffed their food. Their teeth were like canines. They avoided interacting with other children and liked to prowl around at night.

The wild boy of Aveyron, Kamala, and Amala demonstrate how the lack of interaction with others resulted in these children behaving in a nonhuman fashion. The failure of socialization in these feral children permitted them to assume the attitudes and behaviors appropriate for their environment but not for life among humans. Admittedly these two cases are extreme. There are other examples of children who were raised among humans but not with them. These are children who were raised in relative isolation.

Isolated Children

Perhaps the most celebrated cases of children raised in relative isolation are Anna and Isabelle. Davis (1948) noted that Anna had been kept isolated in an upstairs bedroom for almost six years before she was found by authorities. So complete was her neglect that when she was found she could not walk, talk or feed herself. She suffered from malnutrition. When she was found, she showed no emotion or acknowledgment of people in her surroundings. After being in the care of authorities for a period of time, Anna did manage to feed herself with a spoon and speak in rough phrases. Anna died four and a half years after her discovery. She never really recovered from the failure of socialization brought

Children who are raised in isolation often manifest problems in their physical, psychological, and social development.

about by the early years of relative isolation. When she died, Anna had managed to develop only to the stage of a two-year-old.

Isabelle, like Anna, was an illegitimate child. Isabelle's mother was a deaf mute, and their communication consisted only of gestures. When she was discovered in 1938, Isabelle was more than six years old. She could not speak. She made only gutteral noises and reacted to strangers, particularly men, with fear. So great was her fear that she behaved like an enraged animal when strangers approached. Later, after being in the care of the authorities for some time, Isabelle became more accustomed to people, and a therapist began teaching her to speak. The first test for her level of maturity revealed that Isabelle's score was the equivalent of an infant's. By the age of nine, after about three years of custody, she had made rapid progress and was able to enter school. Isabelle went on to overcome the effects of extreme isolation and eventually behaved appropriately for her age. Her case, like Anna's, demonstrates again the effects of failed socialization on a child's ability to behave in a fashion even remotely resembling human behavior.

The final case of a child raised in relative isolation that we will consider is Genie. Genie was discovered in 1970 (Pines, 1981). At the time California authorities found her she had been isolated in a room for almost thirteen years. Genie had been neglected and could not speak. Even by the time she was eighteen years old Genie was at the level of a child of three or four. The lack of socialization, particularly in the early years of development, left Genie at best severely retarded in terms of appropriate social behavior. Anna, Isabelle, and Genie's cases have the element of neglect common to all of them. This element of neglect compounds the lack of socialization. Some studies suggest that among institutionalized populations where children receive relatively good physical care, the failure of socialization may still be evident.

Hospital Studies

Studies that compare children raised by parents to children raised in institutions (Spitz, 1964, Goldfarb, 1945) demonstrate that socialization is more than just physical care. Spitz (1964) compared children raised in an orphanage to children raised by their mothers in a women's prison nursery. Spitz found that within a two-year time period the children who were raised in the orphanage were physically and emotionally retarded. Many of the children died of a variety of ailments. The common element in these deaths was **marasmus.** Marasmus is a withering away or wasting away because of a lack of social interaction. Spitz found that less than 25 percent of the children in the orphanage between the ages of two and four could walk unassisted. In contrast to the problems of the children raised in the orphanage, the children raised by their mothers suffered little of the retardation experienced by their institutionalized counterparts. This happened despite the fact that the children in the orphanage received relatively good physical care.

Research by Goldfarb (1945) which compared children who were raised in an orphanage from birth until they were three years old to foster children offers additional support for Spitz's observations. In Goldfarb's study the children who were raised in an orphanage suffered from a variety of problems. In comparison to the foster children the orphans were more immature, possessed lower IQ scores, and were more indifferent to other people. Even after the orphans were placed in foster care, many of the problems of development persisted. Spitz's and

Goldfarb's research indicates that even minimum failure of socialization can have profound physical and psychological implications for human growth and development.

Animal Studies

For ethical reasons it is difficult to conduct controlled experiments on children raised in isolation. All of the cases of feral, neglected, and institutionalized children that we have discussed were simply recorded by researchers. Animal studies have traditionally been used to provide insight into human behavior. Harlow (1971) conducted a series of controlled experiments with rhesus monkeys who were isolated from their mothers and from other monkeys. Harlow found that the isolated monkeys developed severe emotional problems. The isolated monkeys behaved in an autistic fashion and often gathered themselves into a corner and rocked back and forth. Harlow raised some of the isolated monkeys with surrogate mothers. The surrogate mothers were of two types. The first was simply a wire-mesh form with a milk bottle attached for feeding. The other surrogate mother consisted of a wire-mesh form covered by terry cloth. Harlow wanted to see which of the surrogate mothers the isolated monkey would prefer. Of course if the monkey was hungry it would go to the wire mesh mother to feed. It spent most of its time, however, attached to the terry-cloth mother. When Harlow frightened the monkeys with a mechanical monster, he found that the monkeys who had previously spent time with the terry-cloth mothers ran to her, and their fear gradually abated. When those monkeys who were isolated even from terry-cloth mothers were frightened, they tried to escape from the mechanical monster by running down an alley, gathering themselves into a corner, and resorting to autistic rocking, apparently still terrified by the monster.

Each of the cases of failed socialization that we have considered dramatizes the importance of socialization in the development of humans. And though some caution must be exercised in extrapolating the findings of animal studies to humans, Harlow's research is consistent with the findings of cases of human isolation. To be human, and according to Harlow, to be a well-adjusted rhesus monkey, is to be social. Being social requires that we have opportunities to practice being human through constant socialization and social interaction.

Learning to Behave

If socialization is the key to becoming human, then learning is the key to the socialization process. In other words, we must learn to be human. Socialization is learned both directly and indirectly. We acquire socialization directly in either of two ways, through instruction and through the application of sanctions. When we learn to behave in a human fashion through instruction, we serve as an apprentice. A master shows us how it is done. Formal education is an obvious example of instruction. The most important lessons, however, are not necessarily taught in school. Recall the times you were shown how to do something correctly. Perhaps it was in the kitchen, the backyard, or the playground or at your grandparent's feet. We learn to take care of ourselves by being taught how to cook, wash, iron, sew, and shop. We have many teachers in our lives, and each of them has had a part in instructing us on the proper ways of behaving.

Many of the lessons we learn are joyous; others are painful. We remember the lessons because of the consequences of doing what we did. When we did something very well, we were rewarded with money, a smile, a hug, a handshake, and sometimes a cookie. But when we did something bad, we were punished with a frown, a spanking, embarrassment, or a cross word. As discussed in Chapter 3, the rewards for behaving properly and the punishments for misbehaving are called sanctions. We acquire socialization, in part, as a direct result of the consequences of our behavior. Of course, not all behavior is rewarded or punished. Indeed most behavior is simply not acknowledged at all. We have only done what was expected of us.

Direct socialization experiences are perhaps the most dramatic but not the most common. As we get older, we rely on more indirect socialization to help us behave properly. Socialization is acquired indirectly through imitation and observation. Much of what we do is the result of our imitating what we have seen others do. We did not ask them to instruct us, nor did they offer to show us. We often imitate dress, manners, preferences, style, walk, and speech. We see a gesture that we like and imitate it. We see a pose and copy it for ourselves. Children are great imposters. They mimic adults and other children. This imitation of others, however, helps us to behave properly. Imitation provides us with a range of models for our behavior.

Finally we learn to behave properly merely by observing others. Observation is an indirect method of acquiring socialization. When we observe others we may

Imitation provides us with a range of models for our behavior.

not copy their behavior. We may simply watch how they do what they do. Indeed, we may not even aspire to behave as they do. By observing them, however, we have learned additional behavior. We may be able to teach others how to behave, even when we have not been called upon to exhibit the appropriate behavior. For instance, coaches and critics are examples of persons who observe appropriate behavior and tell others what is inappropriate in their behavior, yet they may not be able to behave appropriately themselves. They know what they do largely by observing the appropriate behaviors of others. We learn to behave in a human fashion largely through the indirect methods of imitation and observation.

We do not learn to behave just to receive praise or merely for the sake of imitating a model. The point of learning to behave is that we do so because we believe it is right and proper. The goal of socialization is to induce us to internalize the social justifications for behaving acceptably. When we wait at a red light although no one will see us or we do not beat up someone who angers us although we are sure that the person is defenseless, we have internalized the social justifications for rules of traffic safety and prohibitions against personal violence. This then is the aim of socialization—to induce us to behave in socially acceptable ways because we believe it to be wrong to do otherwise.

Learning to behave is not a purely haphazard process. During the socialization process we learn the social rules of our society. Some of those rules are formal in the sense that they are written and enforced as laws. Prohibitions against violent personal crimes, such as rape or murder, are examples of formal rules. Other social rules are informal. Informal rules have to do with matters of preference, such as style, taste, and manners. Every society has formal and informal rules that govern the behavior of its members. These social rules are called norms. An important aspect of learning to behave is internalizing norms.

The Controversy over Socialization

Some sociologists have objected to what they feel is an "oversocialized conception of man" (Wrong, 1961). According to Wrong, too much emphasis has been placed by sociologists on the internalization of norms as the mechanism by which we become socialized. "The view that man is invariably pushed by internalized norms or pulled by the lure of self-validation by others ignores—to speak archaically for the moment—both the highest and the lowest, both beast and angel, in his nature" (Wrong, 1961:191).

For Wrong the assumption that the internalization of norms is the essence of socialization does not allow for a sufficient range of motives underlying conformity. Such a view minimizes the degree to which conformity is frequently the result of coercion rather than conviction. According to Wrong, humans are more than merely status seekers whose sole motivation is the approval and acceptance of others. We are also prompted to behave in a given fashion by material interests, sexual drives, and the quest for power. Ultimately, this means that we may be "social but not entirely socialized" (Wrong, 1961:191).

Other sociologists (Wilson, 1974; Turk, 1965) have suggested that the idea that we may be oversocialized is much ado about nothing. For Wilson (1974) the increased number of people in big government, big industry, big unions, big military, and big classes leads to a suppression of individuality. Today we find ourselves entwined with the lives of so many others that we are unable to behave purely on the basis of self-interest. For example, a strike in one plant affects employment, sales, purchases, and prices in many other areas. Thus, today we are socialized, coordinated, manipulated, and otherwise induced to conform "because a complex and interdependent system requires it." Thus, people are restricted in their conduct by others' conceptions of what is right and wrong. Wilson argues that conformity is both necessary and desirable. Accordingly he writes:

> Social relationships are necessary. The evidence suggests that outside of that system of human relationships we call a group, we find only sub-human behavior. Removed from social intercourse, the individual never becomes a person; worse, he can suffer traumatic collapse of what personality he has (Wilson, 1974:119).

Similarly, in "An Inquiry into the Undersocialized Conception of Man" (1965), Turk argues that the application of internalized norms to others may be the principal source of order in the society. In other words, socialization serves not only as a way of making each of us internalize behavioral expectations, but it also assists us in controlling the behavior of others. According to Turk (1965:521), "In internalizing culture, that individual not only acquires a personal morality but he also becomes a component of the collective conscience". Thus, Turk felt that any theory of socialization should take into account both the feelings of guilt that appear when we misbehave and the "passionate reaction" that we feel when others misbehave.

The controversy over socialization is further heightened when we consider that members of a community may share similar but not necessarily identical socialization experiences. In societies like America, where there is a variety of economic, racial, ethnic, and regional communities, the content of socialization often varies. This means some people will internalize a different set of norms and perceive their position in the community differently than others in the society. The public manifestation of these differential socialization experiences may be easily seen in the diversity and deviance associated with human behavior.

In societies where there are different economic, racial, and ethnic communities the content of socialization often varies.

The Emergence of Self-Identity

Sociologists view the self-identity as a product of socialization. The self gradually emerges as a result of the interaction with others. The two prominent theories of the emergence of self-identity in sociology are the theories of Charles Horton Cooley and George Herbert Mead. In addition to examining these theories we will borrow theories from other disciplines in order to compare and contrast their approaches to the development of self-identity.

Looking-Glass Self

Charles Horton Cooley (1964) is credited with the "looking-glass self" theory. Cooley contended that the personalities of people evolve as a result of social interaction and the encountering of social experiences, social forces, and events by individuals.

Infants do not have a self-concept or self-awareness. As they go through the process of maturation, they involve themselves with others through social interaction. As this social interaction intensifies, children begin to listen more carefully to the comments of other people involved in this interaction and begin to let such comments affect the way they view themselves in the larger society. They begin to imagine a self-concept that they think others have of them and start to feel and act accordingly. If this imagined self-concept is positive, they will immediately develop positive attitudes and demonstrate positive behaviors towards

The "looking-glass self" theory claims that other people show us who we are.

the others. Conversely, if the imagined self-concept is negative, they will develop negative attitudes and behavior patterns.

The "looking-glass self" teaches that other people in society are, in fact, our image makers. We all walk, talk, and work in society every day with a picture at the back of our minds, representing what we think other people think or make of us. There are three elements in this "looking-glass self" process. First, we imagine the way in which others view our behavior. Second, we imagine how such behavior is judged by others. Third, depending on how the behavior is judged—as positive or negative—we feel good and proud about ourselves or bad and ashamed of ourselves. Ultimately, we imagine an overall personality for ourselves.

Generalized Other

George Herbert Mead (1934) is the second important sociologist who helped in the understanding of how the "self," or personality, develops in society. Mead explained that before children develop a concept of the self, they go through three stages: the preparatory, the play, and the game stages. Children imitate the behaviors of others a great deal during the preparatory stage. As they grow out of the preparatory stage, they begin to put themselves in the shoes of others or play the roles of others in their social group, community, or society. Children may sometimes play the family and assign each other the different roles that people play in the family, such as the roles of father, mother, son, daughter, or even a baby. At this stage children may also play the roles of a teacher or a friend. Mead termed this playing the roles of "the significant other." During the game stage, children begin to internalize roles of the larger society. By doing this children perceive the larger community as what Mead calls "the generalized other." In this way they expand their role playing to include not only significant others but also many different people in the larger society itself. Thus, children are able to place themselves within the context of the larger society.

According to Mead, the self has two major parts: **"I"** and **"me."** The "I" never really gets socialized. It is that part of the self that remains at the stage of impulsivity and independent creativity. But the part of the self that is called the "me" is socialized. It is the part of the self that has internalized the appropriate, community-sanctioned attitudes and roles in the child's society. A maturing personality is one that begins to consider the disapproval of others when considering gratifying the "I." As an adult the rewards for gratifying the "me" are usually more important than those that come from satisfying the "I." In conclusion, the social self for Mead means the internalization of a structure of attitudes by which we are able to judge our own behavior. In this way the self and society become inextricably linked.

Ego Development

Sigmund Freud (1958) introduced the psychoanalytic viewpoint of personality development. This viewpoint is also known as the conflict theory of growth. Freud believed, as Cooley and Mead did, that the self is a social product. But unlike Cooley and Mead, he taught that the self consists of three components that are always fighting with one another. These components of the self he called the id, ego, and superego. The id is the seat of all antisocial acts. It is unruly, pleasure seeking, and impulsive. It dominates the life of everybody from birth to death and manifests itself through the unconscious.

Whereas the id remains unconscious and is full of energy, the ego is conscious and is the seat of rational behavior. It is the aspect of the self that is in constant debate with the id. Freudians believe that as children grow up and interact with others, they begin to acquire the component of the self that is called the ego. The acquisition of this component of the self indicates that the child has acquired its own objective position within the environment and in relationship to other humans and nonhumans. And as children mature, their ego increasingly acts as a judge of their actions. This way, the ego controls the impulsive, unconscious, and antisocial acts of the id to bring those acts in line with what society teaches.

The part of the self that represents the tenets of society is the superego. Children acquire this aspect of the self by interacting, first and foremost, with the primary groups in society, such as family members and the peer group. Through the acquisition of the superego, children learn to identify with their parents. Thus, the superego becomes the conscience of the growing child. It becomes the seat of appropriate, socially approved behavior, as the child grows up to internalize the norms, rules, and values of society. It is the superego that helps the growing child to select from a list of behavior patterns the most appropriate, desirable, and acceptable ones for his particular society and culture.

Types of Socialization

As we have seen, socialization is not a simple matter. It is a complex process which does not stop with infancy or childhood but goes on until the person dies. Sociologists say that socialization is a lifelong process, encompassing the entire life cycle of a person. In some societies, as may be found in preindustrial Europe and some Third World countries today, there are only three recognizable stages of the life cycle, namely, infancy and childhood, adulthood, and old age. But in industrial, postindustrial, and space-age societies, such as the United States, six stages of the life cycle are discernible, namely, infancy, childhood, adolescence, youth, adulthood, and old age. As people go through these stages of the life cycle, they acquire different images of the self and commit themselves to the imbibing of society's values and norms with different degrees of fervor. For at these different stages of the life cycle, society's expectations of the individual differ from one stage to the next; different roles are played and different statuses attained. These changes between stages of the life cycle call for adjustments in the socialization process. In all, sociologists identify four types of socialization, including primary, anticipatory, reverse, and resocialization. The four types tend to occur in all societies, no matter how many stages of the life cycle a society may recognize.

Primary socialization occurs during the infancy and childhood period. Language and preoperational skills are acquired at this stage. Also, at this stage children are expected to internalize the norms and values of their culture, learn the appropriate sex-role behaviors, and develop the appropriate emotional relationships expected of members of that society.

Anticipatory socialization occurs as we learn to play future roles.

Anticipatory socialization occurs as children learn to play future roles appropriately. Learning to play "mother" or "father" is an anticipatory socialization technique to instill in children appropriate future roles they may play as parents in their society. Schooling, or formal education, is fundamentally a process of anticipatory socialization. The career programs and training projects of the school are all built to prepare the student to play future roles in accordance with the standards of society.

Traditionally, socialization is something that is transmitted to the younger generation from the older generation. **Reverse socialization** turns this process around. Often the younger generation transmits norms and values to the older generation. Reverse socialization usually takes place when social change is very rapid and some members of the adult world are unable to catch up with new behaviors. For example, children of immigrants who are born in the new domicile of their parents may know more about the cultural cues of their newfound home than their immigrant parents. In these cases the younger generation becomes the interpreters of the new norms and values to the older generation.

Resocialization is usually a process whereby adults must learn new standards, values, and behavior. This process takes place in varying degrees when people are converted to another religion or when they make another society and culture their home. Resocialization occurs in **total institutions.** The characteristics of a total institution have been outlined by Goffman (1961). In his work on asylums, Goffman describes the experiences of mental patients and other inmates who are institutionalized. In total institutions authorities have a great deal of control over the activities of those in their charge. The residents are isolated from some previous life-style, and they spend much of their time in the institutions in the company of others much like themselves. The people are alike in that they are institutionalized for the same reasons. They are not necessarily identical, however, because they come to the institution from a variety of backgrounds. Once institutionalized, residents find that their identities are systematically destroyed. This ritual shedding of identity is referred to by Goffman as **mortification ceremonies.** The purpose of mortification ceremonies is to create new identities among the residents that are more compatible with the goals of the institutions. Examples of mortification ceremonies include strip searches, tonsure, and issuing of institutional clothing.

Total institutions are also characterized by regimentation. Regimentation means that day-to-day activities proceed according to a prescribed time period. The residents conform their daily rituals to preordained time periods set by authorities. Finally, once institutionalized, residents are not free to leave. Usually the residents are institutionalized for a predetermined amount of time, although in some institutions, such as mental hospitals, the residents' stays may be indeterminate.

Examples of total institutions include prisons, the military, particularly the boot-camp experience, and prison camps. Additionally, cloistered societies including convents and monasteries qualify as total institutions. Some institutions, although not completely closed, have many of the features of total institutions. For example, schools, particularly boarding schools and colleges, hospitals, and some jobs that require training periods, such as in sports camps and police academies, possess many of the features of a total institution. Total institutions are particularly important in the continued socialization of adults. In many ways total institutions become a way of resocializing their residents.

Agents of Socialization

Most of the examples we have seen in the acquisition of socialization have been informal. These examples do not mean that socialization is simply a chance occurrence. Such a key process in the development of society's members cannot be left to chance. The people and institutions of the society that have primary responsibility for socializing its members are called **agents of socialization.** These agents of socialization consist mainly of the family, the peer group, the school, the mass media, and total institutions.

The Family

Charles Horton Cooley called the family a **primary group.** Primary groups are characterized by intimate face-to-face association and cooperation, and as such they are critically important in the formation of the social nature and ideals of the individual. As a primary group, the family is characterized by closeness, warmth, love, empathy, trust, and interdependence, and it is the major social institution that is largely responsible for the socialization of the child. It is in the family that the child first develops the skills of intergroup life. He or she learns the language and other communication skills through the family and acquires an understanding for the likes and dislikes of his or her community and culture.

Also, as a primary group, the family serves as the first reference group of the child. What this means is that the family is the first social institution in society to provide the child with the best role model in society. The attitudes, mores, norms, and values of the family become those of the child, and equipped with such the child begins to interpret and understand the world outside.

For a child to develop a socially acceptable personality, he or she must receive support from the family to meet his or her basic needs, such as food, shelter, and love. In short, human contact is very important for personality development. Anything short of that may create problems in the development of a personality for the child. For instance, Harlow's (1971) research revealed that monkeys raised in isolation behaved schizophrenically toward one another. The feral children we read about earlier in this chapter failed to develop emotional ties to family members. All these research findings point to the fact that if children are deprived of love, care, and human contact, there is a great likelihood that they will not become interested in themselves, others, or their community and that they may be unable to learn some of the socially desirable skills or proper behavior.

The Peer Group

The peer group is also a primary group and as a socialization agent is very important in influencing the development of personality and self of the child. As a primary group, the peer group is usually small and close knit. Children in the group are, therefore, afforded the opportunity to develop intimate, face-to-face, and trusting relationships, built mostly on egalitarian values. The child freely participates in such a social milieu on an equal basis and feels almost obliged to internalize the group's values and standards.

A child's peer group is made up of different groups of children, some consisting of neighbors' children, some composed of a neighborhood gang, others being a group of schoolmates, and still others congregating as playground friends. Peer groups usually stay apart from the adult world and govern themselves according to a system of rules and regulations they build for themselves, or in accordance with the logic of a language they create for themselves.

In a study on child socialization, McCandless (1969) notes that the peer group is second only to the parents in socializing the child, and as children grow older, (e.g., about junior high school), the peer group assumes increasing importance in the socialization process. The author suggests further that the peer group provides the child an opportunity to rehearse and act out adult roles before reaching adulthood by acting out courtship, cooperative, competitive, aggressive, and dependent behaviors and rehearsing appropriate sex roles for themselves (McCandless, 1969:808).

Additional research on juvenile delinquency (e.g., Cohen, 1955; Moore, 1978; Elliot and Ageton, 1980) suggests that the peer group may be more important in the overall socialization process of the lower-class child than the middle-class child and of lower-class boys than of lower-class girls. These peer groups tend to consist of same-sex children.

The School

The school is a third socializing agent in society, even though it is less personal than both the family and the neighborhood peer society. But it is in the school that the child comes into contact with teachers, administrators of the school, and children from other homes and backgrounds. The school serves as a socializing agent in several ways. First, because youth spend so many formative years there, schools are able to transmit important societal values such as patriotism and respect for authority. Second, the school helps to crystallize normative expectations for youth by presenting models of appropriate behavior in the form of teachers, coaches, administrators, guidance and career counselors, and visiting guests. Third, schools also assist in the development of a self-identity and a personality by providing a set of significant and generalized others with whom youth can interact on a regular basis. Finally, the schools also help to resocialize adult members of the community through such activities as continuing education and parent-teacher associations (PTA).

In the United States, where racism, discrimination, and poverty still affect many people, the school's role as a socialization agent has become even more significant over time. Research indicates that a majority of teachers and school administrators consider themselves middle-class Americans. School practices such as tracking and the neighborhood school concept tend to place children of the same socioeconomic, racial, and ethnic backgrounds into the same academic program or keep them in the same schools. Teachers and administrators with middle-class values who work in schools situated in low-income neighborhoods socialize the children in these schools with middle-class values. In some schools children from minority families have experienced problems with the socialization process. For example, some minority children in integrated schools "have a functional peer group in the school setting" (McCandless, 1969:811). As minority children move into bigger junior and senior high schools, they may be increasingly excluded from "social and extracurricular aspects of social life. The socialization record becomes worse as the child moves from first to twelfth grade" (1969:811).

The Mass Media

The mass media consist of newspapers, radio, movies, television, books, magazines, videotapes, and disks. Although sociologists find it difficult to measure the extent to which the mass media influence the socialization process in society, many assert that their influence is very significant. In the United States it has been said that television has the most influence among all the media. Estimates are that at least 95 percent of American homes have a television set. Changing values and norms are quickly picked up by youth and are faddishly followed or permanently internalized. The powerful, affluent group uses television to reinforce traditional values in American society. For instance, television continues to portray the woman as a housewife who is constantly concerned with cleanliness, and she remains a sex object in many of television's commercials and advertisements. Miller Lite beer commercials combine humor and good times to transmit normative behavior and values that extol the virtue of alcohol. Members of minority groups are often assigned subordinate roles on American television programs.

The development of cable and satellite systems has increased the potential of the mass media to socialize both children and adults. For example, Music Television (MTV) on cable television programs a variety of music videos. The lyrics, the music, and the images combine to transmit powerful messages to a largely teenage and young adult audience. Often the messages include references to death, Satan, violence, and horror. Videos that include Satan and sacrifice or other symbols of devil worship have been seen on MTV. Late-night, religious, and health-oriented cable channels focus their attention on an older cohort. The values of good health, good sex, and good behavior are broadcast twenty-four hours a day on the adult channels. Thus, the broadcasting of normative behavior and values via the mass media extends the socialization process beyond family, friends, and the school.

In summary, the family, peer groups, schools, and the mass media are important agents of socialization. They are not, however, the only agents of socialization. Every group to which we belong and every institution in our society contributes to the socialization process. The professional organizations, the voluntary associations, and the churches to which we belong assist in socializing us. Normative expectations and societal values are also transmitted on the job, in the courts, and in the military. The point here is that from the moment of birth socialization is an ongoing process, and although a few groups and institutions are most important in teaching us to behave, every group and institution in the society makes a contribution to our socialization.

Before we leave this section on agents of socialization, one final note needs to be added. Often the agents of socialization do not transmit the same set of norms and values. Schools, particularly colleges and universities, sometimes erode norms and values learned at home. Media images offer a cornucopia of conflicting norms and values. Specifically, the family is likely to impart rather strong prohibitions against violence and casual sexual behavior. Television ratings, however, traditionally have been tied to the frequency and the explicitness of episodes of sex and violence. Thus, although agents of socialization induce us to internalize norms and values of the community, the specific behavioral expectations transmitted by them often conflict with one another.

Socialization for What?

Socialization in America has traditionally meant learning mainstream American values, such as thrift, frugality, deferred gratification, rugged individualism, independence, and upward mobility. There is, however, a seamy side of socialization. Mainstream norms and values have often been reserved for select groups, whereas other groups have been socialized to absorb divergent norms and values. Lewis (1965) observed that some children of the poor are socialized to absorb a culture of poverty. Because poverty contributes to the advantages enjoyed by the well-to-do (Gans, 1971), some socialization encourages the poor to perform distasteful economic and social functions. Coles (1967; 1971) has carefully outlined the divergent norms and values transmitted to the children of poor black, Mexican American, and Puerto Rican migrants and of sharecroppers and mountaineers by their parents and teachers. According to Coles (1971:511), "The migrant child

Some researchers argue that children of the poor are socialized to absorb divergent norms and values.

learns right off that he has no particular possessions of his own, no place that is his to use for rest and sleep, no objects that are his to look at and touch and move about and come to recognize as familiar." A black child from Atlanta remembered the message he received from his mother when he spoke during the 1960s of racial integration in the schools. "Mamma started praying out loud, and quoting the Bible to me about getting into heaven by being poor, and if I tried to go to school with whites and rise up, I'll probably lose my soul" (Coles, 1967:108).

In stark contrast, evidence (Veblen, 1973; Domhoff, 1971) suggests that the wealthy are socialized to internalize a different set of norms and values. Domhoff notes that "members of the upper class not only have more, they have different" (1971:91). Upper-class individuals are able to recognize one another by school ties, accent, understated dress and behavior, common assumptions and values, standards of behavior, and a sense of noblesse oblige (Domhoff, 1971). These characteristics are transmitted to the children at home and in private schools. The same characteristics are later reinforced in adults in private clubs and formal organizations such as the Junior League and informal groups such as Bohemian Grove. Veblen's (1973) research offers corroboration that the socialization of the wealthy is different from other groups in the society. According to Veblen, the leisure class is characterized by conspicuous leisure, conspicuous consumption, pecuniary standards of living, and pecuniary canons of taste and dress as an expression of a pecuniary culture. Thus, the poor and the rich are likely to internalize different norms and values. Likewise, learning to behave will mean radically different things for the two groups, although their members are raised ostensibly in the same culture.

The institutions that assist in socializing various groups in the society also transmit different messages. The Bureau of Indian Affairs (BIA) is a case in point. The BIA, begun in 1834, was set up to manage the affairs of Indians and to assist in their assimilation into the larger American culture. A century and a half later the BIA has been criticized as one of the major factors in the continued plight of American Indians. For example, Collier (1980) feels the BIA's paternalism keeps the Indian dependent and in a state of "perpetual juvenilization." According to Collier, "Thus, the BIA's overseership of human devastation begins by teaching bright-eyed youngsters the first formative lessons in what it is to be an Indian" (Collier, 1980:412).

The BIA's boarding schools for the youth of Indian reservations are riddled with accounts of physical abuse and the initiation of a failure orientation. The Indian students' education often teaches them that they are powerless and inferior. As one author notes,

> Having spent his youth being managed and manhandled, the Indian is accustomed to the notion that his business must be taken care of for him. He is thus ideally equipped to stand by and watch the BIA collect mortgages on his future (Collier, 1980:413).

Similar evidence of the transmission of other-than-mainstream norms and values in public schools is offered by Rosenthal and Jacobson (1968). Their research, described in *Pygmalion in the Classroom,* illustrates how teachers socialize poor, largely Mexican American youth for failure. Thus, although we look to the socialization process and to the agents of socialization to inculcate within the members of society a common set of normative expectations, the extent to which we share common norms and values will depend on the other groups to which we belong.

Summary

The focus of this chapter was socialization. We defined socialization as the process whereby we acquire the attitudes and behaviors that are appropriate for our society. It is socialization that allows us to act like humans. Without socialization we would have problems developing. These developmental problems are seen most clearly in the cases where socialization has failed. Cases of feral, isolated, and institutionalized children illustrate that without socialization we would have difficulty in walking, talking, and feeling like a human being. Animal studies on rhesus monkeys also support the importance of socialization.

We are socialized both directly and indirectly. We are socialized directly through instruction and the application of rewards and punishments. Indirectly we are socialized through imitation and observation. Socialization is so important in developing conforming members of the society that it is not left to chance. Those persons and institutions that have the responsibility of socializing members of the society are called agents of socialization. The agents of socialization include the family, peer groups, schools, and the mass media.

There are four types of socialization. The types of socialization include primary, anticipatory, reverse, and resocialization. These four types of socialization demonstrate the lifelong experiences of socialization. We are constantly being socialized and resocialized. Socialization does not end after childhood. We are socialized from the womb to the tomb.

Self-identity is a product of the socialization process. According to Cooley, the self emerges as a result of peering into the looking glass of others. Mead says that we develop a social self as we learn to call up in ourselves the expectations of a generalized other. Freud's theory also illustrates the importance of others in influencing our self-identity. Finally, we noted that socialization in America is not a homogeneous experience. Different subcultural groups may experience different lessons in their socialization.

Key Concepts

agents of socialization	mortification ceremonies
anticipatory socialization	peer group
ego	primary group
feral children	primary socialization
"I"	resocialization
id	reverse socialization
looking-glass self	self
marasmus	socialization
"me"	superego
total institution	

References

Brown, Roger. (1972) "Feral and Isolated Man." In V. P. Clark et al. (eds.), *Language.* New York, N.Y.: St. Martin's Press, Inc.
Cohen, Albert. (1955) *Delinquent Boys.* New York, N.Y.: The Free Press.
Coles, Robert. (1967) *Children of Crisis.* New York, N.Y.: Dell Publishing Company, Inc.
———. (1971) *Migrants, Sharecroppers, Mountaineers.* New York, N.Y.: Little, Brown and Company.
Collier, Peter. (1980) "Better Red Than Dead." In Glen Gaviglio and David E. Raye (eds.), *Society As It Is.* New York, N.Y.: Macmillan Publishing Co., Inc.
Cooley, Charles H. [1902] (1964) *Human Nature and the Social Order.* New York, N.Y.: Schocken Books, Inc.
Davis, Kingsley. (1947) "Final Note on a Case of Extreme Isolation." *The American Journal of Sociology, 3*(March):432–37.
———. (1948) *Human Society.* New York, N.Y.: Macmillan Publishing Co., Inc.
Domhoff, G. William. (1971) *The Higher Circles.* New York, N.Y.: Vintage Books/Random House, Inc.
Elliot, Delbert S., and Suzanne S. Ageton. (1980) "Reconciling Race and Class Differences in Self Reported and Official Estimates of Delinquency." *American Sociological Review 45*(February):95–110.

Freud, Sigmund. (1958) *Civilization and Its Discontents.* New York, N.Y.: Doubleday/Anchor.

Gans, Herbert J. (1971) "The Uses of Poverty: The Poor Pay All." *Social Policy, 2*(July/August):20–24.

Goffman, Erving. (1961) *Asylums: Essays on the Social Situation of Mental Patients and Other Inmates.* New York, N.Y.: Doubleday and Company, Inc.

Goldfarb, William. (1945) "Psychological Privation in Infancy and Subsequent Adjustment." *American Journal of Orthopsychiatry, 15*(April):247–55.

Harlow, Harry F. (1971) *Learning to Love.* New York, N.Y.: Ballantine.

Lewis, Oscar. (1965) *LaVida.* New York, N.Y.: Random House, Inc., 48–54.

McCandless, B. R. (1969) "Childhood Socialization." *Handbook of Socialization Theory and Research.* In D. A. Goslin (ed.), Chicago, Ill.: Rand McNally & Company.

Mead, George H. (1934) *Mind, Self and Society.* Chicago, Ill.: University of Chicago Press.

Moore, Joan W. (1978) *Homeboys.* Philadelphia, Pa.: Temple University Press.

Pines, Mayor. (1981) "The Civilizing of Genie." *Psychology Today, 15*(September):28–34.

Rosenthal, Robert, and Lenore Jacobson. (1968) *Pygmalion in the Classroom.* New York, N.Y.: Holt, Rinehart and Winston.

Spitz, Rene. (1964) "Hospitalism." In Rose Coser (ed.), *The Family: Its Structure and Functions.* New York, N.Y.: St. Martin's Press, Inc. 1964.

Turk, Herman. (1965) "An Inquiry into the Undersocialized Conception of Man." *Social Forces, 43*(May):518–521.

Veblen, Thorstein. [1899] (1973) *The Theory of the Leisure Class.* Boston, Mass.: Houghton Mifflin Company.

Wilson, Everett K. (1974) "Conformity Revisited." In George Ritzer (ed.), *Issues, Debates, and Controversies: An Introduction to Sociology.* Boston, Mass.: Allyn & Bacon, Inc.

Wrong, Dennis H. (1961) "The Oversocialized Conception of Man in Modern Sociology." *American Sociological Review, 26*(April):183–93.

5

Group Organization

OBJECTIVES

By the end of this chapter the student should be able to:

1. Understand the nature of status and role and see them as the basic components of social organizations.

2. Distinguish between social aggregates, categories, and groups.

3. Identify the characteristics of groups.

4. Differentiate primary and secondary groups.

5. Understand the nature of the formal and the informal structure of bureaucracy and some of its social consequences.

INTRODUCTION

Interaction is the basic process of social life. Interaction means that actors orient their behavior toward one another; that is, the action of one takes the other into account. Accidentally bumping into someone in the hall is not interaction; but when one person then says, "Why don't you look where you're going?" and the other apologizes, interaction occurs, because what each does takes the other into account.

Interaction is not usually random bumping into each other, however. Most interaction is patterned; that is, it is organized into relationships that are somewhat stable and predictable. In this chapter we examine some of the elements and forms of social organization.

Status and Role

The basic components of social organization are **status** and **role.** Often referred to as the building blocks of social organization, they are the units in the network of relationships that define societies and groups. Status and role are closely related to each other. Status is the positional element; role refers to the behavioral expectations associated with the position.

Status

A status is a position in a social system. It may be a unit in the general social structure: black, white, male, female, the young, the old, the rich, the poor, labor, management, or the military. It may also be a position in a particular group. For example, statuses in a family are father, mother, and child. Statuses in an army are general, major, captain, sergeant, and private. Statuses are, for the most part, built into the system; that is, they are attributes of the social organization itself. Usually, the status precedes the individual as a part of the organizational network, and it remains when the individual moves on. For example, the pitcher is a position on a baseball team that was a part of the organization of the group before Fernando Valenzuela became a pitcher. The status, or position, will continue to be a part of the team long after Valenzuela's arm has given out. So in this respect, a status is independent of the individual who occupies it.

A given individual will occupy at least one status in each group of which he or she is a part as well as various statuses in the general society. A man may be a father to his family, a welder in a factory, a member of his union, the captain of his bowling team, a precinct worker in the Democratic party, a communicant in the Catholic Church, and a citizen of the United States.

Statuses are filled according to two fundamental principles: ascription and achievement. **Ascribed status** refers to a status that is filled on the basis of individual characteristics that are present at birth or that develop through maturation; that is, characteristics over which the individual has no control. Sex, race, age, and ethnic and kinship statuses are ascribed statuses. One may be a daughter, a female, a child, and a native American without any effort on her part. That she occupies these statuses is beyond her control.

Achieved statuses are those that are filled through some purposeful activity on the part of the individual: doctor, teacher, coal miner, student, athlete, office holder, prom queen, political activist, or dancer. Achieved status does not necessarily imply successful achievement on the part of the individual but that the status is filled as a result of what the individual does. For example, occupational statuses in our society are not assigned automatically merely through being born and staying alive. Achieved statuses are up for grabs, and many of them are filled through some degree of competitive effort, win, lose, or draw.

It is obvious that there is an interplay between ascribed and achieved statuses. Being born female or a member of a minority group or a member of a poor family has considerable influence over which achieved statuses one may fill. The predominance of white males in high-level occupational positions demonstrates the impact of ascribed status on achieved status. Efforts to eliminate the effects of irrelevant ascribed statuses in filling achieved statuses have been the focus of

This child occupies the following ascribed statuses: daughter, female, child, Native American. Achieved statuses are those we must strive to fill.

the civil rights movement and the women's movement in recent years. The candidacy of the Reverend Jesse Jackson for the Democratic presidential nomination in 1984 may be seen as an effort to break through these barriers to achieved status.

Every society uses both principles in filling its positions: some statuses are ascribed; some are achieved. However, when we compare contemporary societies with the societies of the past, it is obvious that there has been a shift in the relative emphasis between the two patterns. In more traditional societies, age, sex, and kinship statuses were relatively more important than they are today. One reason for this is that the occupational statuses were relatively undifferentiated except by sex, and the kinship group was the most important organizational unit for a broad range of social activities. "Who is your family?" was a more salient question for identification than "What do you do?" In modern societies the kinship unit has been separated from occupation and other social activities. Occupations have become specialized, individualistic, and competitive. Therefore, achieved statuses are of relatively greater importance than they were in the past.

In a highly urbanized society much interaction takes place between individuals on the basis of their occupational statuses rather than their personal acquaintances. Symbols of status become very important in identifying each other: the uniforms of the policeman, the fireman, the doctor, the airline pilot, the nun, the waitress, the gasoline station attendant, the nurse, the grocery clerk, and the postman give clarity to status identity in situations in which it is important to have confidence that the person is who he or she claims to be. Other symbols such as office furnishings, wedding rings, briefcases, hard hats, and various insignia also help to identify status.

Role

Role refers to the behavioral expectations that are normatively attached to a given status. Expectations as to how one should act, think, or feel in a given status are defined by the society and are learned by individuals through the socialization process. For example, a father is expected to love, nurture, guide, and support his children. The expectations attached to a doctor's role are that he or she will diagnose and treat the patient according to accepted medical practice, observe professional standards of conduct toward the patient, and maintain confidentiality. Note that the expectations involve interaction with other roles.

Sometimes the role performance departs from the role expectations. For example, a father might abuse his children; a doctor may spread the word about Mr. Hermann's weak heart. Individuals performing the same role may carry it out differently. They may have different interpretations of it or different personalities, motivations, and experiences to bring to it. In addition, as the ethnomethodologists point out, some of the role behavior is not spelled out and is subject to improvising by the individual. You may be taking classes with five different instructors. The expectations are the same for all of them, and they must keep these expectations in mind or expect to lose their jobs. However, you may find that one professor is a clown, one uses the class for moralizing, one puts the class to sleep, one is permissive, and one is a strict disciplinarian. No two of them perform the role in exactly the same way. Role performance, then, combines role expectations generated by the group with individuality in carrying out the expectations.

At times individuals who perform several roles find themselves in a position in which the behavior expected in one role is incompatible with that expected in another role. This situation is called **role conflict.** For example, a union man's loyalty to his striking union may be in conflict with his need to provide for his family. A female student with children may find that her role as student and her role as mother are often in conflict with each other. Her big exam in organic chemistry is scheduled at the same time her son is appearing as Sneezy in his school's production of "Snow White and the Seven Dwarfs." She is expected to appear for both occasions. The expectations of one role run counter to the expectations of the other. Given the relative emphasis on achieved roles in our society, traditional family roles are frequently an element in role conflict, though role conflict is by no means confined to such situations.

Various patterns of adjusting to role conflict may be noted. In some cases the conflict may go unresolved and become a continuing irritant or source of frustration. Sometimes one performs an intricate juggling act in an effort to meet as many expectations of both roles as possible. At times, priorities are established as a guideline for resolving the conflict. For example, in the award-winning movie *Chariots of Fire* one of the major characters was caught in a role conflict because his role as an Olympic runner required him to compete on Sunday, whereas his role as a minister carried the expectation that he would not contend on his Lord's day. He resolved the conflict by assigning a higher priority to his role as a minister than to his role as an Olympic runner.

Roles do not exist in a vacuum. They are reciprocally linked to other roles. This is why they are basic components of social organization. It is difficult to describe the expectations of a role without identifying its links to other roles. For example, how does one describe a teacher's role without referring to the student's role, or the parent's role without tying it to the child's role? The expected behaviors generally specify how one is to act toward those in related roles: doctor–patient, lawyer–client, employer–employee, or husband–wife. Exchange of rights and obligations takes place between roles. Role performance is a matter of social interaction. As one acts out his or her role, the interactive process is involved, because the role performance links the actor's role to other roles.

However, exchange between roles is not always equal. Sometimes power is a strong element in the role relationship: master–slave, employer–employee, male–female, teacher–student, or jailer–prisoner. This fact raises important questions as to the degree to which such role expectations are basically defined by

Role definitions are often determined by those in dominant positions.

those in whose interest the power operates. Conflict theorists point out that those with power see to it that expectations of their roles and related roles serve to maintain their own dominance. For example, in the history of the continuing relationships between blacks and whites in this country, the role expectations were defined by the dominant group and imposed upon the subordinate group rather than through some original consensus between them. Using other terms, Marx applied this idea to the role relationships between capitalist owners and laborers in the factories. Dahrendorf applied it to modern bureaucratic structures in terms of those roles having authority and those that do not (Dahrendorf, 1959). These situations have in common the fact that the role definitions and relationships are defined by those in positions of power and maintained by rules created by those in power. Such issues serve to remind us that both conflict and consensus are involved in role definitions and relationships.

A given status may have several role relationships attached to it. Such ties clustered around a given status are a **role set** (Merton, 1968). For example, a social worker has role relationships with clients, colleagues, administrators, and secretarial staff. Sometimes the expectations involved in the various relationships contrast with each other. The dilemma resulting from incompatibility in the expectations of members of the role set is called **role strain.** For example, social workers may experience role strain because their clients expect them to give personal commitment to meeting their particular needs, whereas the administrators expect them to conform strictly to eligibility rules in providing services. Tension is generated because members of their role set are expecting different behaviors from the social workers. In spite of the conflict and strain individuals experience in performing their roles, the relationships that link one role with other roles are the materials out of which group life is made and maintained. The network of linked roles is an important element in social organization.

The Nature of the Group

Although the group is a central unit of sociological analysis, its meaning has often been imprecise. For example, we may speak of a number of people waiting on the corner for a bus as a group. We may think of "the elderly" as a group. Or we may refer to a hospital staff as a group. These examples reflect important sociological differences. The first refers to a number of people who happen to be at the same place at the same time. It carries no implication of any similarity between them and no assumption about interaction among them. We may refer to such a gathering as a **social aggregate.** Other examples of social aggregates are people at a rock concert, passengers on an airplane, shoppers at a mall, and drivers on a freeway. People in such situations may or may not be doing the same thing; the distinctive feature is that they are physically together.

Social aggregates are interesting to sociologists for three main reasons. First, they may indicate a social trend; for example, mall shopping or crowded freeways. Secondly, they are subject to crowd reactions when some stimulus is introduced; for example, panic in a burning theater or frenzy at a rock concert. Thirdly, being together may lead to interaction; for example, motorists who stop for a wreck on a highway may work together to rescue the victims and redirect traffic.

The second of our original examples, "the elderly," refers to a number of people who have a characteristic in common: they are old. As such, they constitute a **social category;** that is, they share at least one sociologically relevant characteristic that permits them to be classified together. Other examples might

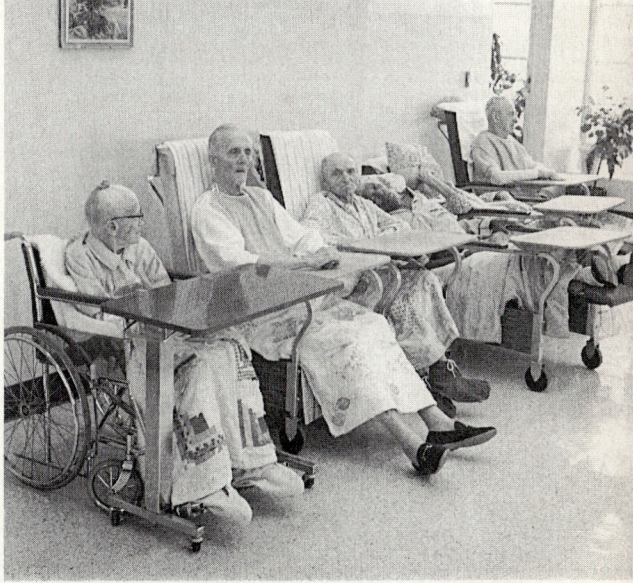
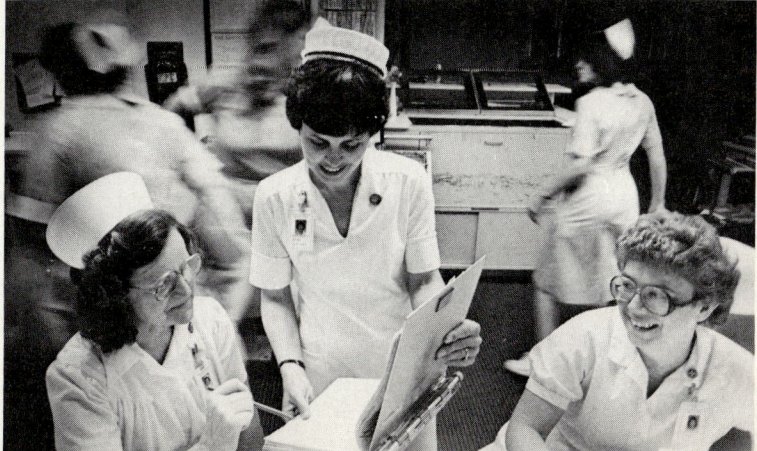

"Group" has been applied to all these situations. However, many sociologists use "aggregate" to refer to such situations as waiting for a bus, elderly people as a "category," and situations that include social interaction and internal structure as "organized groups."

be people of Puerto Rican descent, students with a 3.5 or higher grade point average, urban dwellers, criminals, fat people, sailors, break-dancers, and people with an income under $10,000. There is no implication of interaction or physical proximity among the people in the category.

Social categories are important to sociological analysis because people who have the same social characteristic may share attitudes and interests relevant to that characteristic. For example, farmers may share certain attitudes because they belong to the same occupational category. Factory workers tend to have similar economic and political interests. We express this same idea when we generalize that Hispanics tend to vote Democratic in this country or that military officers tend to support high defense budgets. A second reason why social categories are important is that they frequently form the basis upon which organized groups are created. For example, factory workers, a category, may form a labor union, an organized group, to further the interests they share as laborers. Jews are a category; the Anti-Defamation League is an organized group that expresses the interests of Jews.

The third and most important usage of the term group is the **organized group.** A hospital staff would illustrate this meaning. The organized group refers to recurrent interaction among members, patterned on the basis of norms and roles and maintained by some kind of social control. Examples of organized groups are a family, a club, a government agency, a corporation, a union, a college, a sports team, a ship's crew, a professional organization, and a friendship clique. The smallest group is made up of two individuals; for example, sweethearts, a married couple, or roommates. The largest group to which we belong is the society. Such groups form the context in which most of our social experience is gained and expressed; therefore, they are of primary importance to sociologists. The remainder of this chapter focuses on the organized group, particularly upon its internal structure.

The Organized Group

Although a married couple, a football team, a labor union, and the United States Senate have many obvious differences, they also have some important similarities. All of them have a means of establishing a boundary that separates members from nonmembers. All involve an interaction network of statuses and roles. The behavior of members is regulated by group norms, which are enforced by sanctions. These are the elements of group organization.

Boundaries. In the sense described above, your class is an organized group. Its boundaries are officially defined through registration. This does not imply that new members cannot be added. Rather, it means that it is possible to distinguish those who are members from those who are not. Boundaries may be drawn in many ways. They may be defined by official rules or law; by paying dues or fees; by blood relationship; by a uniform, an insignia, or a particular handshake; or by physical or spatial criteria. Some groups, such as high school cliques, are maintained by subtle boundaries of mutual acceptance or feelings of identification.

Statuses and Roles. Groups differentiate among their members as to who is expected to do what. Statuses and roles may be formally recognized through official designations, such as the officers and members of a club, the organizational chart of a college or corporation, or the job descriptions of a government agency. They may be rooted in long-standing custom; for example, family roles or age-graded units such as those found in Masai society. On the other hand, roles may be very informal. A friendship group, for example, may distinguish the leader, the clown, the confidante. The relationships between and among the roles give the group its organizational framework. A patriarchal family and an egalitarian family may be composed of the same roles. The relationships among those roles give each group its character.

Norms and Sanctions. Expectations that group members will behave in a certain way are a part of every group organization. The norms may be official (e.g., an eight-hour workday), or they may be unofficial (e.g., the obligation of loyalty and support to other group members). The norms do not necessarily coincide with the norms of the broader society; some groups may require their members to flout convention or the law, such as an organized crime syndicate or Murder, Inc. Norms serve to pattern the interaction of the group. They are enforced by sanctions the group has at its disposal, among which acceptance or rejection as continuing members of the group are basic. For example, the threat of excommunication from a church organization, dismissal from a job, dishonorable discharge from military service, or ostracism from a social group exerts social control over the behavior of group members. The desire to be accepted as a member in good standing is a potent force in maintaining conformity to the group norms. Many other penalties (fines, denunciations, jail sentences, loss of position, disapproval and the like) and rewards (such as raises, praises, awards, and approval) are used by groups to regulate the behavior of members. In addition, as the group norms become internalized by members, one's feelings of guilt or pride act as mechanisms of social control over his or her behavior.

A Classification of Groups

Although all groups have these organizational constants, the quality of the relationships within groups varies widely. Variations in expectations in role relation-

The "we-feeling" is strong in a primary group.

ships are socially patterned. Attempts to classify groups have focused on the distinction between those embodying relationships that are intimate and personal, that is, expressive, on the one hand and those that are impersonal, or instrumental, on the other.

Primary Groups

As discussed in Chapter 4, the concept of the primary group was developed by Charles H. Cooley. By primary group, he meant small groups characterized by "intimate face-to-face association and cooperation" (Cooley, 1962:23). He further emphasized the extent to which a "we-feeling" develops through the "fusion of individualities into a common whole" (Cooley, 1962:23). Examples of groups embodying mostly primary relationships are families, friendship groups, neighborhood groups, and small villages. The small size and physical closeness of the primary group intensify the interaction, permitting personal ties to develop.

In a primary group members share a broad range of unspecified activities and obligations. For example, in the old rural community the same men may hunt and fish together, go to church together, hang around the stove at the country store together, help each other out at harvest time, visit each others' family on Sunday afternoon, attend school activities together, hang over each others' fences to chat, share family picnics at the river, and so on through many other such activities. Furthermore, they would feel that if something unexpected arose, such as a fire, a death, or a lost child, they could count on each other for support and cooperation.

Where the bonds are deep and personal, the relationship is durable. Its lasting quality is supported by the caring that develops out of the shared experiences. The maintenance of the primary group relationship is for members a goal in itself, which transcends any particular activity or situation. Immediate gain for a given individual is not the sole purpose of the relationship. Rather, the value of the relationship itself is its own justification.

The fusion of individualities in the primary group refers to the fact that anything that affects one affects all. When the father of a family loses his job, the

The degree of relaxation we feel at a music recital depends upon whether it is our child or someone else's.

situation carries not only economic but also emotional import for the whole family. Parents who sit placidly through the program of a music recital get sweaty palms and raw nerves when their child performs. Their identification magnifies each wrong note and intensifies their pride in a successful presentation. Primary group members have as one of their goals the welfare of other members of the group (Davis, 1949).

Secondary Groups

The quality of secondary relationships contrasts with that of the primary relationship. It is impersonal; that is, the emotional identification is minimal. This does not mean that it is hostile; rather that it is neutral. We do not hate our postman; we just do not invest any emotional content in the relationship. Secondary relationships are formed in order to achieve particular goals of the participants. The utilitarian nature of the relationship suggests that the only reason for the contact is that it furthers the interests of the parties to it. For example, if you wish to buy a new car, you must establish some kind of relationship with a car salesman. The relationship, however, is very specific. It is to accomplish a particular purpose on your part and on the salesman's part, and its obligations do not extend beyond that purpose. You do not have to know or care about the salesman's arthritic Aunt Thelma or his dog, Rover. You do not have to invite him to your home for dinner or date his sister. The relationship is limited to the specific transaction for which the contact was made.

Secondary groups, then, are groups in which secondary relationships are

The relationship between salesperson and customer is a secondary relationship. It will not last beyond the specific transaction.

predominant. They are large, impersonal groups that involve their members in specific and limited contact. Examples are large corporations, universities, labor unions, professional organizations, and governmental agencies. Within secondary groups some primary relationships may develop, such as close friendships among coworkers in an office or factory, but these are not the overall relationships that typify such large-scale organizations. In such groups impersonal relationships predominate and express the definitive quality of the group.

Many secondary relationships involve a contract, either written or understood. A contract involves mutual, specified, and carefully circumscribed, impersonal obligations. Furthermore it embodies the idea that when the obligations have been met, the relationship ends. The contact you establish with a taxi driver, for example, ceases to exist when you have reached your destination and he or she has received the fee. A contract expresses the essential spirit of the secondary relationship.

Another characteristic of the secondary relationship is the interchangeability of the parties to it. In the checkout counter at the grocery store, it does not matter who checks one's groceries; the point is to get it done. If one person can do the job as well as another, then the relationship easily shifts from one to another. If register number three is busy, go to number four. A great many of the role relationships in large urban centers involve this interchangeability of personnel. This is one source of the feeling that we often do not see each other as human personalities but merely as means to the ends we seek to accomplish.

Associations

Large-scale secondary groups that are deliberately created to accomplish a specific purpose are called **associations.** The United States has been referred to as an associational society because the rational pursuit of goals through formal alignment with others who wish to accomplish similar ends is a dominant motif in our culture. In the names of large-scale organizations words like association, council, society, company, union, alliance, corporation, federation, organization, agency, and coalition express the idea of joining together to pursue an interest or goal. Examples are the American Sociological Association, the National Puerto Rican Coalition, the Farmers Alliance, the National Council on Alcoholism, the Society for the Prevention of Cruelty to Animals, the Greyhound Corporation, the National Wildlife Federation, and the Coca-Cola Company. However, it is not the name itself but the organizational qualities of the group that make it an association.

Voluntary Association. Associations may be classified into two broad categories: **voluntary associations** and **bureaucracies.** These types are not mutually exclusive and may interpenetrate each other. The voluntary association includes such groups as interest groups, professional organizations, philanthropic societies, civic groups, and groups espousing causes. The distinguishing characteristic of the voluntary association is that the occupational career of most of the members is not pursued within the organization. However, many such organizations may employ a professional staff, which is likely to be organized bureaucratically. Examples of the voluntary association are the American Cancer Society, the Parent–Teacher's Association, the Sierra Club, the American Red Cross, the Democratic party, and the League of Women Voters.

Bureaucracy. The second type of association is the bureaucracy, and even more than the voluntary association it is a hallmark of modern societies, both East and West, and increasingly of Third World societies. A bureaucracy has the characteristics of associations: it is a large-scale organization of secondary relationships deliberately created to achieve a particular goal(s). In addition it has a specialized division of labor; it is coordinated through a hierarchy of authority; it operates through a set of abstract rules; and it is the focus of the career of workers within it (Weber, 1946).

This type of social organization emerged as a pervasive form alongside the development of capitalistic economics and nontraditional governments. In several important ways it marked a departure from older forms of social organization. Its organization separated the office from the person; that is, the authority structure and its division of labor created an impersonal system of statuses and roles defined in such a way that the obligations and rights were vested in the office, not in the person. In addition, it circumscribed the boundaries of the organization, separating it from the household and personal life of its members. It also freed its personnel from the personal fealty that characterized feudal forms. The deliberate aim of its organization was to maximize efficiency, and each of its major features can be related to this goal.

The expansion of bureaucracies is obvious when we consider the growth of corporations and the proliferation of governmental agencies, as well as the organization of schools, hospitals, churches, unions, political parties, sports, entertainment, and recreation along bureaucratic lines. Weber (1946) thought that these impersonal, rationally designed structures were a major source of alienation in modern society. He referred to bureaucracy as an iron cage. Organizational efficiency has been achieved at the expense of the personal, emotional, traditional, and expressive values that have been a source of belongingness. Those values are still viable, but the areas of social life reserved to them have been steadily shrinking as bureaucracy has expanded.

Bureaucratic Organization

Because bureaucracy occupies such a prominent position in modern social life, it is important to understand its characteristics and its impact. Its internal structure will be our next consideration.

Formal and Informal Organization

Like other social groups, the college you attend is organized in terms of statuses and roles, norms, criteria of admission, and social controls. Some of these elements of organization are specified in the official guidelines and procedures of the college. For example, the duties and responsibilities of president, registrar, dean, instructor, student, department chairperson, and other positions are spelled out. The criteria for admission as a student or employment as an instructor, secretary, or dietician serve to limit the membership and thus help to define the boundaries of the organization. Directives identify the expectations regarding the level of performance and conduct (e.g., a student must maintain a 2.0 GPA, an instructor must submit a grade for each student). Guidelines for registering, paying fees, getting a meal ticket, or earning tenure or promotion are worked out by the appropriate officers of the college and have official sanction. Rewards and penalties are defined: promotions for faculty based on experience and/or performance; passing or failing grades for students; dismissal of secretaries for "Teh pooor typits." All of these things are a part of the formal organization of the college.

However, other patterns develop within the organization that are not officially designated. Among students word gets around about courses and instructors: "Professor Featherhead is an easy grader," "Professor Moralez is tough but fair," "Professor Dullard is boring and pedantic," "Introduction to Sociology is a neat course," "Basket Weaving 101 is a breeze." These informal evaluations become criteria of course selection. You may note that certain faculty members have lunch together every day, and chances are they will vote together on departmental affairs. An official may use his or her position to build a power base for furthering a personal career. Such patterns are not a part of the official design of the college; they arise spontaneously through the interaction of people within the organization. They constitute the informal organization of the college.

Other bureaucratic structures—businesses, unions, government agencies, and hospitals—have a similar kind of dual organization: the official, or formal, organization and the nonofficial, or informal, organization. Actually, the formal and the informal organization are two aspects of the same structure. They develop because the people who are members of the bureaucracy interact as human personalities, not as robots, and because the entire range of interactions cannot be programmed in advance. We shall look at the characteristics of both informal organization and formal organization in more detail.

Formal Organization. The official, deliberately designed plan is the **formal organization.** It follows in general the elements Weber (1946) identified as the characteristics of bureaucracy, or as he saw it, the characteristics that would be present in a completely rational organization.

Specialization of Task. The work of a bureaucracy is divided among various positions. Job descriptions define the responsibilities. Mastery of increasingly complex and technical knowledge requires such specialization of task and personnel. The assumption built into the structure is that efficiency is increased, because expertise develops through the division of labor.

Hierarchy of Authority. When the work is divided into small units, the need for coordination becomes critical. The coordinating, or authority, structure of a bureaucracy may be represented geometrically by a pyramid shape. This form distributes decision making through different levels of the organization; it allows for coordination of activities and decisions; and it provides a channel for two-way communication through the organization. It also builds marked inequalities into the system.

Impersonality. The official expectation is that the affairs of the bureaucracy will be handled without the intrusion of personal or emotional relationships. Hiring, firing, promoting, and evaluating, as well as carrying out everyday activities and procedures, are designed to be handled in an impersonal way. For

Police departments generally operate according to bureaucratic principles.

example, a surgeon usually does not operate on members of her family; a professor is expected to grade on the basis of how well the student performs, not on how well he likes the student. A social worker is not expected to become personally involved with a client. Personal relationships are generally regarded as less efficient than impersonal relationships.

Merit Criteria. One of the specific applications of the impersonality principle is that performance standards are used as a basis for hiring, firing, promoting, appointing, contracting, and the like. Efficiency criteria are built into the official expectations. Job qualifications rest on training and experience.

Abstract Rules. A system of official procedures provides uniformity and predictability within the organization. For example, rules that define the requirements for graduation apply across the board. You either meet them or you do not. Your case is not regarded as unique. The pertinent question is, "Have you met the requirements specified by the rules?"

Written Records. A filing system guarantees continuity of operations by freeing the business of the organization from dependency upon the memory or longevity of any particular member. If the registrar of your college elopes to South America with an accordian player from Toledo, have no fear: your records will be in the file cabinet or computer awaiting the new registrar.

Bureaucratic Organization

These graduates had to meet the formal requirements of their educational bureaucracy in order to get diplomas.

These official, "on-paper" characteristics can be identified in every bureaucratic organization. They are calculated to accomplish efficiently the goals for which the organization was formed. Yet, when we see bureaucracies in operation, we become aware that they do not always adhere to this pattern. Some of the discrepancy comes from the **informal organization.**

Informal Organization. Alongside these official patterns in the bureaucracy, other patterns spontaneously develop. They are not a part of the formally designated organization, but the network of personal relationships and informal practices may have significant impact upon the operation.

The characteristics of the informal structure are not easily enumerated. Some tendencies, however, may be identified. Personal relationships frequently develop among workers who are brought together in the course of their jobs; for example, among members of an army platoon, secretaries in an office, workers in a shop, or faculty members within a department. Such relationships may have positive effects for the organization (e.g., high morale, cooperation) or negative ones (e.g., time wasted through chitchat or horseplay). The relationships may also involve personal antipathy, which may make cooperation difficult. Preferential treatment may be shown to personal friends. Informal patterns involving giving and seeking advice, helping out colleagues under pressure, and orienting newcomers will usually be present. Activities that protect one's turf or consolidate one's position in the organization are a part of every bureaucracy and have the potential for serious impact on the structure. For example, the demand for loyalty from those one supervises may override considerations of proficiency when evaluations are made. The old saying "He who makes waves finds himself in rough water" applies here. Contacts with proven facilitators are also a part of the informal network. Patterns that identify whose door to knock on for help, whose office to bypass, or what type of approach is useful in certain situations develop through the process of working with others in the organization.

Members tend to develop spontaneous norms that pattern expectations. For example, informal expectations concerning how much work should be done in a day may evolve among group members (Homans, 1950). The degree of participation in expected, though nonofficial, activities of the workers may distinguish "one of the gang" from the social isolate. "Old boy" networks that are hard for newcomers or outsiders to break into or even deal with form within the organization, influencing the flow of work, decision making, and many other aspects of the work situation. Informal practices for accomplishing the formal tasks may depart from the official procedures or may fill in around aspects of the tasks not specified in the directives. Sexual harassment is often built into the informal structure.

The formal and informal structures of bureaucracy mutually influence each other. The interaction required by the formal structure produces the informal structure as well. The informal structure will feed back into the formal structure as the network of relationships and informal practices enhances, undermines, or otherwise alters the official design of the bureaucracy.

Public Reaction to Bureaucracy

Although efficiency is the criterion of bureaucratic formal organization, bureaucracy evokes much criticism from its personnel and from the general public who have to deal with it or who must bear its impact. Reaction to bureaucracy may be directed at the formal or the informal structure. Cronyism is a complaint against failure of the organization to maintain impersonality and performance criteria in its operations. Playing favorites violates the official norms and justifies the criticism of unfairness. Goal displacement refers to the extent to which bureaucratic personnel direct their efforts toward maintaining the structure itself and their place within it to the detriment of the goals that provide the rationale for the existence of the organization. These kinds of criticisms are a reaction to the operation of the informal structure.

Other criticisms hit at the heart of the formal structure. For example, bureaucracy is regarded as cold and impersonal. Clients who deal directly with government agencies often feel that the agency does not care about them as persons. Abstract rules do not make adjustments to the unique circumstances of each case about which decisions are to be made. This makes the bureaucracy appear to be heartless.

The rigidity of procedures in a bureaucracy evokes the criticism that it stifles creativity. The necessity to conform to the official rules, backed up by official sanctions, is generally perceived as producing ritualistic adherence to established procedures rather than encouraging initiative and imagination. Such rules are also the source of the complaint against bureaucratic red tape. The requirement of submitting multiple copies of a given form or seeking a decision through seemingly endless layers of the chain of command may facilitate coordination within the organization; but from the vantage point of the outsider attempting to relate to the organization, its procedures appear hopelessly ensnarled in pointless rules.

The Peter Principle (1970) suggests that personnel in a bureaucracy tend to be promoted until they reach their highest level of inefficiency. That is, if they do their jobs well in a given position, they are given more and perhaps different responsibilities until they reach the point at which they are operating at a level that is beyond their ability. This situation presumably places many incompetents in high-level positions in the bureaucracy. Whether or not this "principle" is a serious attempt at analyzing the structure of bureaucracies, the visions it stimulates are intriguing.

A final major criticism of bureaucracy is the inequality embedded in it. Its hierarchy of authority concentrates power in the hands of a few people and gives them effective control over the resources of the entire organization. Those in the lower echelons become entrapped in a permanent state of powerlessness. This state is perpetuated by the rules of the organization.

Bureaucracy in a Multicultural World

In traditional cultures and subcultures, where familistic ties are the major focus of social organization, bureaucratic structure enters as an alien form. Its appearance alters the patterns of social organization in seemingly irreversible ways. For example, bureaucratic organization was the administrative instrument of colonialism, and it became a symbol of economic and political exploitation. Even in colonial societies where the indigenous system of chiefs was maintained, the administrative expectations of impersonality, inflexible rules, and performance criteria often ran counter to the expectations of the people regarding the behavior of their chiefs (Beattie, 1960). As colonies moved toward independence, these bureaucratic principles were incorporated into the new administrative structures, in large measure supplanting precolonial patterns of governance. However, lack of deep-rooted cultural commitment to such principles has been a source of instability in political institutions in the new nations. At the same time, external economic bureaucracies have been a continuing presence in such societies. Colonial societies, then, have usually experienced bureaucracy as a means of political and economic dominance that has undermined much of their cultural tradition. Despite such continuing difficulties, however, bureaucracy now provides their bridge to the rest of the modern world.

In the United States bureaucracy has had varying impact for different groups. For the native American population, the impact of bureaucracy has resembled the colonial experience in many respects. "The bureaucracy" was the Bureau of Indian Affairs. Its administration was often viewed in a confrontational context. Its policies vacillated between extremes of exploitation and concern but were for many long years constant in their lack of understanding of Indian culture.

Other groups have had different experiences as they have encountered bureaucracy. In earlier days, when rural areas and small towns were the focus of American life, the support most people received to supplement the household was a matter of help from relatives and neighbors (Warren, 1978). For example, fire protection depended upon a "bucket brigade" of neighbors or a volunteer fire department. Care of the elderly was a family responsibility. Today specialized agencies provide such supports. Hospitals, fire departments, recreational programs, welfare agencies, transportation systems, and commercial establishments are bureaucratically organized to provide services that once friends and family offered.

One of the consequences of this shift has been the depersonalization of the services. Although we have lost much of the personal touch in the provision of services, there are some important compensations. For example, for black Americans in the old rural South, one source of personal support for nonlandowning farmers was the paternalistic system. A landowner usually looked out for his "hands" (the term itself is instructive), often providing such things as food, hand-me-down clothing, and medicine. Although usually very limited, such services were important supplements to the meager incomes of black sharecroppers and wage laborers. The exchange was a costly one for blacks; the reciprocal value was deference and accommodation to an inferior status. This was a personal relationship subject to revocation by the landowner if the tacitly understood terms of the agreement were violated. Any challenge a black worker made to the existing racial norms could only result in withdrawal of the patronage. Because options were so severely limited outside this system, a man had to weigh seriously any action that would separate him and his family from it.

Bureaucratic organization, which has come to characterize the new urban, industrialized South, provided a challenge to the paternalistic system. Its impact has been strong in several areas. First, in depersonalizing the work situation, activity in pursuit of civil right objectives became more viable. Where work depended more on performance and less on personal fealty, men and women could protest racial norms with less jeopardy to their financial security. Secondly, when workers entered bureaucratic work structures, they came within the scope of impersonal wage and hour laws and union activity. Some economic protection has been provided through these measures. Thirdly, many of the services provided through paternalistic arrangements are now provided through bureaucratic organizations on the basis of entitlement programs. Eligibility rules for such programs as care for the elderly, child protection, welfare, and unemployment compensation are universalistic and do not require particularistic subservient response.

It would be unrealistic to assume that the depersonalization built into such programs has rid them of prejudice against blacks and other minorities. Programs are administered by individuals, whose actions often reflect the varied attitudes of the broader society. However, according to the organizational principles of bureaucracy, race and ethnic origin are irrelevant criteria. The thrust of these features is to diminish their effects. Measures such as the Civil Rights Act of 1964 and various affirmative action programs have goaded bureaucracies to adhere to impersonal performance-based principles. Minorities have gained better access to these structures as a result.

However, some of the abstract rules have differential impact on minorities. Wage policies based on seniority favor employees who have been in the organization for the longest period of time. Minorities, particularly blacks and Puerto Ricans, have entered the bureaucracies more recently on the whole. In times of retrenchment the consequences of the employment norm "Last hired, first fired" are that minorities, in general, bear the brunt of unemployment.

Growth of Bureaucracy

Bureaucracy has extended itself into manifold areas of life. Political, economic, educational, health, recreational, human service, criminal justice, and religious organizations have increasingly taken on bureaucratic form. The whole concept of social planning has been expressed through bureaucracy. The tendency to meet a human need through the creation of a specialized structure is one of the hallmarks of Western culture. Hardly any aspect of our public life has escaped its impact. The enlargement of its scope is a trend that continues uninterrupted.

The increasing centralization of power has been a further characteristic of the relationship between bureaucracy and the rest of the society. The model of bureaucracy we have developed depicts it as an independent unit of social organization. For example, your college exists as a bureaucracy in itself. This helps us to understand the internal structure of bureaucracy; but when we look at the relationship of bureaucracy to the total society, it is important to note the pyramiding effect that has occurred. One obvious trend in bureaucratic organizations in the United States is the extent to which they transcend local community boundaries. Local organizations have strong ties to state, regional, and national organizations. For example, fast-food restaurants are linked to parent companies far removed from the locale in which they fry (or flame broil) their hamburgers. Similar patterns exist in factories, businesses, and financial and commercial enterprises. Government operations also have such ties. For example, local welfare agencies are closely linked with state and federal human service agencies. This arrangement of "vertical linkages" orients the local institutions and their employees to institutions, that is, higher levels of the bureaucracy, outside the community (Warren, 1978). It also removes much of the decision making that affects the community from the locality itself. For example, decisions to close a factory in a given community may be made in board rooms half a continent away. Emphasis on hierarchies outside the community has diminished local autonomy and has accelerated the trend toward political and economic centralization of power in the country.

In spite of sporadic governmental initiatives to return control of various programs to the states and localities, this trend is unlikely to reverse itself in any broad-scaled fashion. Economic bureaucracies have evolved from family enterprises to national and international structures. Bureaucracies are extending into ever-expanding areas of life, and they are continuing to grow in size, scope, and power. If, as Weber suggested, they are the source of alienation in modern society, the pressures they generate can be expected to increase in our individual and communal lives.

Summary

Status and role, not the individual, are the building blocks of social organization. Individuals are connected to the social organization as they occupy statuses, play the roles attached to them, and interact with others playing related roles. Stability in social relationships comes from the patterning of role expectations.

Expressing the next level of social organization is the group. Groups differ from social aggregates and social categories in that they are organized. They involve interaction networks which are given stability through role relationships, through norms and sanctions which provide social control, and through ways of defining their own boundaries and distinguishing between those who belong and those who do not.

One of the most meaningful classifications of groups is that which distinguishes primary and secondary groups. A small, face-to-face group that is characterized by mainly personal relationships is a primary group. The primary group is especially important in guiding the socialization process, supporting feelings of belongingness, and meeting the desire for response. In a secondary group, impersonal, functionally specific relationships are dominant. The instrumental quality and the interchangeability of personnel often lead us to think of such groups as dehumanizing and manipulative.

Large secondary groups deliberately created for a specific purpose are called associations. Both the voluntary association, which does not employ its membership, and the bureaucracy, which does, are important forms of social organization in modern industrial societies. Bureaucracies have a dual structure. The formal structure is the officially designed part of the organization, whereas the informal structure arises spontaneously in the process of interaction.

Many criticisms have been directed at bureaucratic coldness, red tape, inequality, and rigidity as well as its lapses from impersonality and performance standards. Not all groups have experienced bureaucracy in the same way; but as it has challenged familism and tradition, its seal has been firmly stamped on the social life of the modern world.

Key Concepts

achieved status
ascribed status
association
bureaucracy
formal organization
informal organization
organized group
role

role conflict
role set
role strain
secondary group
social aggregate
social category
status
voluntary association

References

Beattie, John. (1960) *Bunyoro: An African Kingdom.* New York, N.Y.: Holt, Rinehart and Winston.
Cooley, Charles H. [1909] (1962) *Social Organization.* New York, N.Y.: Schocken Books, Inc.
Dahrendorf, Ralf. (1959) *Class and Class Conflict in Industrial Society.* Stanford Calif.: Stanford University Press.
Davis, Kingsley. (1949) *Human Society.* New York, N.Y.: Macmillan Publishing Co., Inc.
Homans, George. (1950) *The Human Group.* New York, N.Y.: Harcourt Brace Jovanovich, Inc.
Marx, Karl, and Friedrich Engels. [1848] (1955) *The Communist Manifesto.* New York, N.Y.: Appleton-Century-Crofts.

Merton, Robert. (1968) *Social Theory and Social Structure.* 2d ed. New York, N.Y.: The Free Press.
Parsons, Talcott. (1957) *Toward a General Theory of Action.* Cambridge, Mass.: Harvard University Press.
Peter, Lawrence J., and Raymond Hull. (1970) *The Peter Principle.* New York, N.Y.: Bantam Books.
Warren, Roland L. (1978) *The Community in America.* 3d ed. Chicago, Ill.: Rand McNally & Company.
Weber, Max. (1946) *From Max Weber: Essays in Sociology.* Translated by H. H. Gerth and C. Wright Mills. New York, N.Y.: Oxford University Press, Inc.

6

Deviance

OBJECTIVES

Upon completion of this chapter the student should be able to:

1. Define deviance.
2. Explain the distinction between deviance and crime.
3. Identify several social responses that are used to control deviants.
4. Compare and contrast explanations of why deviance occurs.
5. List the contributions that deviance and deviants make to society.

INTRODUCTION

Thus far we have concentrated on expected patterns of behavior. The chapters on culture, socialization, and groups have explored normative expectations for people as they occupy a variety of social positions. We have concentrated on what makes people accepted in their respective groups. But what happens when people do not conform to norms and rules of the group? Why do people break rules? And what are the social responses to these nonconformists?

The focus of this chapter is behavior that departs from normative expectations. Our concern is with the behavior that is disapproved of by large numbers of people. We examine the ways groups attempt to control **deviance.** Specifically, we discuss: the relationship of crime to deviance; stigma and deterrences as forms of social response; explanations of deviance; deviant careers; and deviant subcultures. Finally, we identify the functions of deviance.

Deviance Defined

The mention of deviance often stirs up ideas of people regarded as nuts, sluts, slick, and sick. Others (Bavak-Glantz and Huff, 1981) refer to deviants as "the mad, the bad, and the different." In fact, even before we have a clear definition of deviant behavior, we are often presented with a picture of the deviant as the boogeyman. The boogeyman is a vaguely sketched chimera (Sykes, 1978) who is capable of unspeakable abnormal acts of violence and/or perversion. According to Sykes (1978:30), the search for the deviant or criminal has largely been a search for a monster. Yet, this character of the deviant as boogeyman is misleading. Because no society can exist without deviant behavior, we are left to conclude along with Durkheim that deviance is normal. Research seems to bear this out, because law-abiding citizens often secretly break the law (Wallerstein and Wyle, 1947; Becker, 1973:20).

A **deviant** is a person who violates expected rules of conduct. The expected conduct may be formally written in a code book, as in the case of a law book or a code of ethics for doctors and lawyers. Often, however, the expected conduct may be generally shared by members of a community but not officially encoded. For example, certain table manners prohibit noise while eating, including burping, flatulence, lip smacking, slurping, and humming—behaviors that are generally disapproved. People who break these informal rules of expected behavior are nonetheless regarded as deviant, labeled as such, and treated accordingly. Yet, no formal set of written rules exists governing table noise. Likewise, there are no formal rules of expected behavior governing obesity, left-handedness, or being crippled. However, persons who overeat, who grab with their left hand, or who are lame are seen as rule breakers and treated as deviant. Thus, deviance is any behavior that departs from expected norms.

A deviant is a person who violates expected rules of conduct.

Although deviance is any activity that departs from expected rules of conduct, it is not necessarily behavior that is disapproved. Genius is deviance. However, the Educational Testing Service (ETS) was established in part to identify genius. Schools and colleges may then reward the tested geniuses with scholarships. Ultimately, whether the deviant act is disapproved or rewarded depends upon the social context and social consequences of the act. For example, an abortion is either a sin or a right, depending on whether the judge is the Moral Majority or the Supreme Court. However, most deviance studied in sociology is behavior that departs from the expected rules of conduct and is disapproved of by a large group of people.

Deviance that departs from expected rules of conduct that have been formally encoded into law is called **crime.** Crime includes acts of commission, which occur when people behave in ways that laws prohibit. Larceny, civil disobedience, computer sabotage, and conspiracy are acts that are prohibited by law. Crime may also include acts of omission, which occur when people fail to behave in ways that the laws require. For example, you may be arrested and held criminally responsible if you behave recklessly or negligently and your actions lead to the harm of others.

Crime is most often thought of in terms of street crimes committed by poor black and other minority males who commit often violent acts against strangers. However, this conception of crime is largely a stereotypical image that fits the idea of the deviant as the boogeyman.

It is clear however, that crime as well as other forms of deviance occurs in all social groups regardless of race or social class. The thing that all crime has in common—regardless of type, its perpetrator, or its victim—is that crime violates the expected rules of conduct for a large number of people. Crime occurs when the violation of expected rules of conduct leads to an official response such as fines, sentencing, and imprisonment from law enforcement agents.

Responses to Deviance

People who violate expected rules of conduct are not automatically viewed and treated as deviant. The response to deviance depends upon many factors, including the actor's public identity (Garfinkel, 1956), the setting in which the deviance occurs (Drus, 1975), the audience judging the act (Becker, 1973), and the time that has elapsed between commission of the deviant act and discovery of it. Thus, in many ways deviance is negotiated (Wiseman, 1970; Trice and Roman, 1970). For example, plea bargaining in criminal court is an illustration of negotiated deviance. The negotiation of deviance suggests that accused persons engage in formal (e.g., plea bargaining) or informal arbitration (e.g., kangaroo courts) with agents of social control to minimize the effects of labels designed to stigmatize them as deviant or deter them from future deviance.

Stigma and Social Response

Labels assigned to deviants have the effect not only of identifying that their behavior (e.g., child molesting, prostitution, drinking) is unacceptable but of sig-

Vanessa Williams, winner of the 1983 Miss America pageant, is shown here with outgoing Miss America, Debra Moffett.

nifying to others that this person's moral character is undesirable. This is particularly important because very few persons spend the majority of their time engaged in deviant pursuits. Even those who make a career of deviant activity, such as thieves, hookers, homosexuals, junkies, and radicals, spend most of their time in pursuit of rather normal activity, including eating, playing, and conversing with others. However, the assignment of a deviant label to what they do has the effect of being generalized to what they are. This generalization of deviant behavior or the "dramatization of evil" (Tannenbaum, 1938) to a person's entire moral character is called **stigma.**

The term *stigma* was originated by the Greeks to refer to bodily signs designed to reveal something unusual and bad about the moral status of a person (Goffman, 1963). According to Goffman, "The signs were cut or burnt into the body and advertised that the bearer was a slave, a criminal, or a traitor—a blemished person, ritually polluted, to be avoided, especially in public places" (1963:1). Nathaniel Hawthorne's classic novel about adultery in Puritan New England, *The Scarlet Letter,* shows how techniques of stigmatizing individuals evolved from branding to burnishing. Today other forms of public stigmatization exist to advertise that the bearer is an undesirable character.

For example, prison garments and numbers stigmatize the wearer as evil. This becomes even more evident when you remember that there is nothing in the prison garment or number that differentiates the cold-blooded murderer or the rapist from the tax evader. Wearing prison garments not only dramatizes evil and thereby stigmatizes the wearer, but it also equalizes evil by hiding differences in the degree of deviance. Generally the stigmatization process equalizes evil

Later, she negotiated her penalty for past deviance at a press conference by resigning rather than face being stripped of her title by pageant officials.

among many deviants. Adulterers, homosexuals, racists, leftists, and prostitutes are stigmatized not according to the number of times they performed their undesirable acts but by the consensus of others. Therefore the degree of involvement is often unimportant in terms of how others respond to the stigmatized individual once he or she has been identified as deviant.

Sociologists (Goffman, 1963; Birenbaum, 1970; Pfuhl, 1980) have identified four types of stigma: physical stigma, character stigma, tribal stigma, and courtesy stigma. Physical stigma exists when a person possesses some physical trait that many persons view as undesirable. Examples of physical stigma include albinos, obese persons, pregnant women, and the physically handicapped.

Character stigma exists when a person is viewed as possessing an undesirable personality trait. For example, people have a character stigma when they are referred to as spineless, as sneaky, or as a snake. Goffman (1963) described character stigma as blemishes of individual character perceived as weak will, domineering or unnatural passions, treacherous and rigid beliefs, and dishonesty. Often character stigma is inferred from the records of past deviant behavior. For example in the 1972 McGovern–Nixon presidential campaign (in which Senator Thomas Eagleton was initially selected as McGovern's running mate) and the 1983 Harold Washington–Bernard Epton Chicago mayoral campaign, records that identified candidates as having had psychiatric consultation proved to be damaging to Senator Eagleton's and millionaire candidate Epton's efforts to convince the voters that they were competent enough to hold office.

Tribal stigma exists when a person belongs to an undesirable collective such as a group, a race, a caste, or a religious order. In many cases tribal stigma are ascribed statuses such as race, sex, age, or national origin, and persons become

Responses to Deviance

The character stigma which is attached to those who had psychiatric consultation may have cost Bernard Epton, 1983 Chicago mayoral candidate, some public support.

stigmatized although they have not actually done anything deviant. Tribal stigmas often elicit responses directed at the entire group of stigmatized persons. For example, Auschwitz and other German concentration camps, internment camps in America during World War II, the Crusades of the Holy Roman Empire, and apartheid policies of South Africa are all examples of group responses to tribal stigma.

Courtesy stigma exists when otherwise normal persons are perceived as undesirable because they "share a web of affiliations" (Goffman, 1963; Birenbaum, 1970) with other persons who possess a physical stigma, character stigma, or tribal stigma. Examples of courtesy stigma include parents of stigmatized children, children of stigmatized parents, and friends and lovers of stigmatized individuals.

According to Birenbaum (1970), there are three types of courtesy stigmas. First, there are the friends and relatives of publicly identified radicals, homosexuals, criminals, or mental patients. Second, there are the parents of handicapped children or children of divorced or handicapped parents. Third, there are the friends and lovers of members of pariah groups in society, such as the "nigger lover," who become branded as not fully competent. Sometimes people may share a courtesy stigma by their affiliation with each other. Interracial couples are an example of people who share courtesy stigmas.

Chances are very high that you probably have experienced one or more of these four types of stigmas. It is difficult to live in a modern, complex, economically diverse society like ours and not offend somebody who in turn will attempt to stigmatize you among a body of your peers. Names such as "teacher's pet," "brownnoser," or "apple-polisher" are common attempts to stigmatize the overly ambitious student.

Regardless of the type of stigma or the seriousness of label, the purpose of stigmatizing deviants is to justify efforts to punish or treat them for their deviance. In short, stigmatization often precedes the efforts of social control agents to deter the deviant and others from future deviance.

Deterrence and Social Response

Deterrence means that the effects of social response on the deviant will be to convince the stigmatized to return to conformity and adhere to normative expectations. Social control agents, whether formal such as police and the courts, or informal, such as relatives and friends, intend to make the price that the stigmatized will pay so severe that the deviance will not be worth committing again. This is called specific deterrence (Nettler, 1978). Specific deterrence suggests that the pain of incarceration, expulsion, avoidance, isolation, and ridicule will be enough to prevent the deviant from repeating the same or similar acts of deviance.

Earlier forms of punishment were designed to make a public spectacle of the offender. Authorities were less concerned about the specific deterrent qualities of their punishments than they were about the general deterrent qualities of the punishment. General deterrence suggests that stigmatizing and punishing one deviant will have the effect of deterring many other would-be deviants. According to Walker.

> In early times, savagery and violence were considered ideal deterrents and were regularly meted out; death was commonplace and delivered by an overwhelming number of ingenious methods. For minor offense, degradation was popular, the thinking of the ancients and indeed the not-so-ancients was that if a villain was to be made to look a fool, the public ought to witness his downfall and misery. Punishment and deterrence were thus combined. It became fashionable to concoct complicated and sadistic penalties. (Walker, 1973:16–17)

Forms of early punishments meant to deter the general populace included a litany of horrors, notably crucifixion, live burials, the wheel, the pillory, drowning, dragging, branding, stretch-neck, mutilations, stocks, quartering, Halifax Gibbet, hanging, brank and gag, dunking stools, whippings, finger pillories, and body presses as well as having the offenders thrown off cliffs, pushed from towers, or burned at the stake. Although these punishments often resulted in the death of the deviant, they were not reserved only for violent offenses. In fact, the sentences were widely inconsistent. For example, citizens of Sparta could be whipped if they became too fat, and in Rome bachelors were fined and ridiculed if they were not married by a certain age (Walker, 1973:25).

Modern ideas behind deterrence were developed by Cesare Becarria (1764), and eighteenth-century reformers who were attempting to reform early forms of punishment and the legal code in Italy and England. Beccaria published an anonymous appeal to authorities to cease brutal torture, sadistic punishment, and capital punishment, which he felt had little deterrent value. Instead, in his essay *Crime and Punishment*, he wrote that "public murder should not be used to prevent private murder, that life imprisonment was a better deterrent than death" (Walker, 1973:86).

Today, both specific and general deterrence are contained in the medical treatment, prison incarceration, and capital punishment of criminals. Specific deterrence can be seen in work-release educational and treatment programs. Treatment is often more severe than punishment for the criminally insane, who often endure a "tyranny of treatment" (Nettler, 1978:46). Thornberry and Jacoby's (1979:1) review of residents at Farview State Hospital in Pennsylvania led the authors to conclude that the criminally insane suffer from the double stigma of being both mad and bad, and this has led many states to create maximum-security mental hospitals for their treatment. Often those found incompetent to stand trial for a criminal offense are sentenced to mental hospitals, where they end up doing life sentences or remaining incarcerated for a longer period of time than if they were simply found guilty and sentenced only for their offense. Thornberry and Jacoby (1979:3) note that at the Farview Hospital for the Criminally Insane, of the 1,229 patients discharged from 1945 to 1960, the average length of stay was six years and four months and the most common discharge disposition was death.

Incarceration has a twofold purpose: (1) preventing criminals from committing their deviant acts again by physically restraining them, and (2) serving as the most visible form of punishment and, therefore, being useful as general deterrence. The most common justification for capital punishment, or the death penalty, is general deterrence. However, killing people both prevents them from repeating their deviance and prevents them from returning to conformity. Thus, the focus of capital punishment is to deter or prevent the general populace from committing the same or similar act for which another was put to death.

Today in the states that have the death penalty there is a great controversy over the effectiveness of the death penalty as a deterrent. Many people see the death penalty as an act of revenge by the state. Specifically, the death penalty is viewed as a tool of racial oppression. In recent years, although the number of whites outnumber the number of black, brown, and red convicts who have been officially put to death, more minorities await execution on death row than whites.

Explanations of Deviance

Much deviant behavior remains unobserved. Think a moment about all of the deviant behavior with which you have gotten away. Perhaps you have gotten away with shoplifting, cheating, embezzlement, larceny, or lying. And although you may not have gotten away with murder, approximately one-fourth of all murderers do get away. Because you were not caught, you are still accepted as a good person. Further, there may be many reasons to explain why you committed these rather serious acts of deviance. However, because you were not caught committing these primary acts of deviance, your reasons are important only to you, given that no explanation and, more importantly, no official defense of your behavior are necessary.

Labeling and Secondary Deviance

Some sociologists (Lemert, 1951; Shur, 1971; Becker, 1973) contend that the most instructive form of deviance is that which has been observed and elicits some public response from a social audience. These sociologists argue that deviance that has been publicly acknowledged or punished leads to **secondary deviance.** According to Lemert:

> When a person begins to employ his deviant behavior or a role based upon it as a means of defense, attack, or adjustment to the overt and covert problems created by the consequent societal reaction to him, his deviation is secondary. (Lemert, 1951:76)

Thus, secondary deviance is viewed by sociologists as the violation of expected rules of conduct which occurs because the social audience's response to a person's initial or primary deviance has created an environment where increased deviance is likely. For example, a person's arrest and incarceration for primary deviance increase the likelihood of avoidance by law-abiding citizens and acceptance by others who have been arrested and incarcerated for the same or similar deviance. This approach to the study of deviance is called **labeling.**

The labeling approach encompasses three distinct ideas (Gibbs, 1981:35). First, some sociologists contend that labeling one as deviant leads to a self-fulfilling prophecy (Gove, 1975; Orcutt, 1983). Contrary to the old adage "sticks and stones may break my bones, but names will never hurt me," labeling theory contends that names do in fact hurt. Furthermore, labeling theorists hold that persons "labeled as deviant by powerful agents of social control and treated as outcasts by conventional society may actually come to see themselves as the thing they have been labeled" (Orcutt, 1983:20). In other words when people, particularly powerful people, say something or label something, often they create conditions that bring about its existence.

The second idea encompassed in labeling theory is that deviance is more the product of societal reaction to traits of the accused and the accuser than solely the behavior of the accused. This idea of labeling notes that whether a given act comes to be identified as deviant depends upon such traits as (1) the social identity of the individuals, including race, sex, income, and education;

Labeling theorists believe that persons labeled as deviant and treated as outcasts may come to view themselves as the thing they have been labeled.

(2) the social identity of the reactors; (3) the specific rules that were alleged to have been broken; and (4) the circumstances surrounding the act, including time, setting, and outcome (Gibbs, 1981:35–38). The societal reaction proposition of deviance points out that two people accused of the same act may not necessarily be treated the same way because of their racial, sexual, or economic differences.

The third idea encompassed in labeling theory is that of the secret deviant. This idea suggests an act is deviant if and only if it is so labeled (Becker, 1973; Gibbs, 1981). For example Becker (1973) and Pfuhl (1980) have noted that the "secret deviant" is one who is not publicly labeled as deviant but nonetheless has privately violated normative expectations. The unmarried woman who has had an abortion, the shoplifter, and the incestuous father are examples of secret deviants. Notice that it is not necessary for absolutely no one to know of their hidden behavior in order to be a secret deviant. Rather, it is important that those who do know of private and hidden normative violations choose not to make a public issue of the behavior. The incestuous father's deviance is known to the daughter or son and even perhaps by the mother. However, he is a secret deviant and can remain an acceptable member of the community as long as the victim or his spouse chooses not to reveal him as a true deviant.

Deviance and Anomie

Sociological explanations of deviance typically attribute violations of expected behavior to adjustments people make to their social environment. We saw earlier that labeling theorists claim that people are likely to become increasingly deviant as they make adjustments to stigmas initiated by a variety of social responses. **Anomie** explanations of deviance contend that people become deviant in response to structural problems in society. These structural social problems, such as divorce, economic misfortune, or economic success, affect a large number of people. For example, the dual problems of unemployment and inflation mean that many people, not just an individual, have had to make difficult adjustments to living with less money. For example, the suicide rate increased following the decade of the 1950s, when both unemployment and inflation were lower than in subsequent decades. In his classic study of suicides, Durkheim (1951) noted that suicides may be a collective response to collective problems.

Interestingly, anomie theories of deviance began as an explanation of suicide. Emile Durkheim, a French sociologist, believed that the norms, values, and traditions in any society helped people feel a sense of belonging. When social problems caused the norms, values, and traditions to change, people had to adjust. One way people adjusted to change was to commit suicide. Suicide was not the only adjustment to change, but Durkheim chose to study rates of suicide to illustrate that deviance is often a collective, rather than an individual, response to social problems in the organization of society. According to Durkheim, suicides should not be studied only as separate, unrelated occurrences. He felt that the study of suicides in a given society should focus on the total number. "It appears that this total is not simply a sum of independent units, a collective total, but is itself a new fact sui generis, with its own unity, individuality and consequently its own nature—a nature furthermore dominantly social." (Durkheim, 1951:46)

Thus, Durkheim's research sought to establish suicide as a collective response to structural problems, such as social change, in the organization of society. Durkheim identified four types of suicide, including anomic, altruistic, egoistic, and fatalistic. First, suicides are more likely to occur in situations of excessive individualism. He studied marital status, religion, and political crises. Rates were higher among single people than among married people. Protestants had a lower rate than Catholics. Durkheim called this type of suicide *egoistic.* He concluded that the tighter the group integration, the lower the rates of suicide. The opposite situation is one in which there is excessive commitment to the group. *Altruistic suicide*, this second type, involves a willingness to sacrifice one's life for the group or for failure to live up to the group's ideals. The kami-kazi pilots of World War II, who made suicidal attacks on American warships for the glory of the Japanese emperor, would be an example. Although he did not offer research to support the type, the third type, *fatalistic suicide* results from extreme rigidity of regulation and control. Such a condition could be found in prisons or concentration camps. Anomie was a state of deregulation when traditional rules that govern a person's life have lost their authority (Durkheim, 1951:253). Anomic suicide occurred when people took their lives because the norms governing their lives suddenly changed. For example, people who have experienced divorce, bankruptcy or who have won a $5 million lottery have also experienced a sudden change in norms. Thus, anomic suicide represented a collective adjustment many people made to social problems brought about by dramatic social changes. Although Durkheim's research was conducted across Europe in 1897, many of his findings of higher rates of suicide among the divorced, Protestants, single people, and men still hold true today (Maris, 1969; Taylor, 1982).

In 1938 Robert Merton expanded Durkheim's concept of anomie. Merton's primary aim was "discovering how some social structures exert a definite pressure upon certain persons in the society to engage in nonconformist rather than conformist conduct" (Merton 1938:672). Merton saw anomie as the condition existing in society when people realize that traditional means of acquiring success do not always work and feel it necessary to make adjustments that are not normally right. For example, you may believe that by attending college you will get a good job. That is, you feel a good education will lead to a good, high-paying job. However, education does not guarantee economic success. Think about the cars that your professors drive. How many of them do you envy? Table 6.2 shows average salaries of college professors. Although you may feel that the $30,000 or more paid to full professors is a good salary, remember that on the average full professors have been teaching over twelve years and are at the height of their career. Likewise, hard work does not automatically guarantee economic success. Economic success depends a great deal upon the type of work you are doing. In fact, the more physical the work, the less you are likely to achieve economic success, even though physical labor is hard work.

Table 6.1** **Adjustments to Anomie

Methods	Emphasis on goals	Emphasis on means
Conformity	+	+
Innovation	+	−
Ritualism	−	+
Retreatism	−	−
Rebellion	•	•

Note: (+) = accept (−) = reject (•) = replace

FACT-FILE

Average Faculty Salaries by Rank and Type of Institution, 1984-85

	SALARY				1-YEAR CHANGE			
Academic rank	Public	Independent private	Church-related	All	Public	Independent private	Church-related	All
Category I: Doctoral institutions								
Professor	$42,560	$49,880	$44,710	$44,100	+ 6.6%	+ 6.1%	+ 7.1%	+ 6.5%
Associate professor	31,370	34,130	33,270	31,910	+ 6.4%	+ 5.5%	+ 6.6%	+ 6.3%
Assistant professor	26,100	27,840	27,200	26,480	+ 6.9%	+ 6.1%	+ 7.0%	+ 6.7%
Instructor	19,330	21,760	22,110	19,790	+ 6.4%	+ 4.2%	+ 5.4%	+ 6.0%
Lecturer	22,880	23,560	24,360	23,030	+ 7.1%	+ 5.8%	+10.9%	+ 6.9%
All ranks	33,860	39,020	34,640	34,830	+ 6.6%	+ 6.0%	+ 6.9%	+ 6.5%
Category IIA: Comprehensive institutions†								
Professor	37,090	37,980	37,110	37,190	+ 8.0%	+ 6.2%	+ 5.7%	+ 7.6%
Associate professor	29,620	29,730	29,190	29,590	+ 7.3%	+ 5.9%	+ 5.3%	+ 6.9%
Assistant professor	24,420	23,890	24,130	24,320	+ 7.1%	+ 5.9%	+ 5.2%	+ 6.7%
Instructor	19,640	17,810	19,170	19,370	+ 7.0%	+ 5.2%	+ 6.1%	+ 6.7%
Lecturer	19,900	22,380	23,170	20,360	+ 6.8%	+ 5.6%	+11.4%	+ 6.8%
All ranks	29,930	29,200	29,170	29,770	+ 7.5%	+ 6.0%	+ 5.5%	+ 7.2%
Category IIB: Baccalaureate institutions								
Professor	33,850	36,500	29,510	32,830	+ 7.9%	+ 5.7%	+ 5.4%	+ 6.2%
Associate professor	28,160	27,670	24,130	26,230	+ 7.6%	+ 6.0%	+ 5.4%	+ 6.2%
Assistant professor	23,540	22,530	20,350	21,850	+ 7.3%	+ 5.8%	+ 5.5%	+ 6.1%
Instructor	19,000	18,330	16,940	17,840	+ 7.0%	+ 5.8%	+ 6.1%	+ 6.4%
Lecturer	21,080	22,230	16,430	20,690	+ 8.4%	+ 7.5%	+ 6.4%	+ 8.2%
All ranks	26,880	27,790	23,360	25,600	+ 7.6%	+ 5.8%	+ 5.5%	+ 6.2%
Category IIC: Specialized institutions								
Professor	40,860	37,840	25,850	35,920	+ 5.5%	+ 6.1%	+ 6.0%	+ 5.8%
Associate professor	31,670	29,620	22,890	29,410	+ 6.8%	+ 6.7%	+ 5.2%	+ 6.6%
Assistant professor	27,570	25,240	19,480	25,240	+ 7.5%	+ 6.2%	+ 6.0%	+ 6.7%
Instructor	21,720	19,940	16,030	19,890	+ 6.1%	+ 5.5%	+ 4.6%	+ 5.7%
Lecturer	23,250	22,680	‡	23,030	+12.2%	+ 8.0%	*	+11.2%
All ranks	32,520	28,450	22,470	28,860	+ 6.4%	+ 6.3%	+ 5.8%	+ 6.3%
Category III: 2-year institutions with academic ranks								
Professor	33,230	24,680	21,290	32,880	+ 6.1%	+ 3.7%	+ 4.1%	+ 6.1%
Associate professor	28,200	22,970	18,300	27,950	+ 5.8%	+ 4.9%	+ 6.4%	+ 5.8%
Assistant professor	23,630	19,320	17,630	23,370	+ 5.9%	+ 6.8%	+ 3.1%	+ 5.9%
Instructor	19,630	15,560	15,210	19,340	+ 5.5%	+ 4.7%	+ 2.8%	+ 5.4%
Lecturer	18,070	11,370	*	17,740	+ 7.3%	+ 9.1%	*	+ 7.4%
All ranks	26,460	20,370	17,440	26,120	+ 5.9%	+ 5.1%	+ 3.9%	+ 5.9%
Category IV: 2-year institutions without ranks								
No rank	24,830	16,240	18,010	24,550	+ 5.8%	+ 6.2%	+ 6.1%	+ 5.8%
All categories combined except IV:								
Professor	39,640	44,130	33,510	39,870	+ 7.0%	+ 6.1%	+ 5.9%	+ 6.7%
Associate professor	30,210	30,930	26,810	29,910	+ 6.8%	+ 5.8%	+ 5.6%	+ 6.4%
Assistant professor	25,020	25,040	22,080	24,610	+ 6.9%	+ 6.0%	+ 5.7%	+ 6.6%
Instructor	19,530	18,990	17,500	19,150	+ 6.5%	+ 5.1%	+ 6.0%	+ 6.2%
Lecturer	21,830	23,100	21,780	22,020	+ 7.2%	+ 6.0%	+10.2%	+ 7.1%
All ranks	31,240	32,950	26,250	30,960	+ 6.9%	+ 6.0%	+ 5.8%	+ 6.6%

† Institutions that award degrees beyond the bachelor's degree but do not qualify for Category I.
‡ Too few individuals to warrant publication of data.
* No data reported.
Note: Salary figures are based on reports of 2,059 institutions. Percentage changes are based on reports of 1,736 institutions that provided comparable data for both 1983-84 and 1984-85.

SOURCE: AMERICAN ASSOCIATION OF UNIVERSITY PROFESSORS

Table 6.2 From The Chronicle of Higher Education 30 *(5), April 3, 1985.*

Merton called this problem of emphasis on culturally induced success goals divorced of a coordinated institutional emphasis *anomie*. Merton identified five possible adjustments to anomie, according to whether people emphasized the success goal or the institutional, traditional means of success. The five methods of adjusting to anomie are listed in Table 6.1. When faced with anomie, most people continue to conform by accepting success goals and traditional means of achieving these goals. However, some people attempt to achieve success by deviant or illegitimate means. These people accept the cultural goals but "eliminate" or reject cultural means. Crime, including white-collar types, is an example of innovation because it represents a creative way of acquiring goals that most people use traditional means to achieve.

When faced with anomie, many people give up trying to achieve success and simply go through the motions of holding on to their jobs. This method of adapting to anomie is called ritualism. Examples of ritual behavior include many bureaucratic positions in government and much assembly-line work. However, students and teachers often engage in ritual behavior when they go about their respective tasks, bored and disinterested with each other. Retreatist behaviors such as suicide, drug addiction, alcoholism, and mental illness are a means of withdrawing from both the success goals and the institutional means like work or education of acquiring those goals.

Finally, rebellion is an adjustment to anomie that seeks to replace established goals and means with new goals and means. The focus in rebellion is to introduce a "new social order." Although rebellion, the complete overthrow of an old order and the introduction of a completely new order, is rare outside of political coup d'etat and violent revolutions, there are many examples of dramatic reforms that have led to the introduction of new social order. For example, the

Cesar Chavez, president of the United Farm Workers of America, organized boycotts and strikes to press for reforms. His efforts may be explained as a response to anomie.

civil rights movement was precipitated by Rosa Parks's refusal to relinquish her seat to a white rider in Montgomery, Alabama's segregated bus system. The ensuing boycott led by Dr. Martin Luther King, Jr., began a decade of reforms which ushered in changes in the social order for blacks. Likewise, "Ladies' Day in the House" referred to a passage of the 1964 Civil Rights Act that forbade discrimination based on race, creed, national origin, or sex. Sex was included in the act initially to sabotage the passage of the bill, which was intended to improve the status of racial minorities. However, the bill passed with the last-minute addition of the word "sex," and since then women have used the bill more successfully than racial minorities to prosecute cases of discrimination.

These five methods of adaptation to anomie may be described as conformist, aberrant, and nonconformist behavior. When faced with anomie, most people continue to conform to the cultural success goals and adhere to traditional means of working towards those goals. However, most deviance is **aberrant behavior.** "Aberrant conduct, therefore, may be viewed as a symptom of dissociation between culturally defined aspirations and socially structured means" (Merton, 1938). Aberrant behavior is characterized as a private, hidden discontent with the social arrangement. Deviants who resort to aberrant conduct seek only a personal adjustment to anomie. Their justifications for deviance apply to their specific condition (Merton, 1938; McCahgy, 1976).

By contrast, nonconformist behavior seeks to make public the discontent with social goals and routine means. The nonconformist often forms groups to press for advantages that will benefit persons besides themselves. Nonconformists claim that values such as justice, freedom, equality, and liberty justify their protest for systematic changes in existing social arrangements, goals, and norms.

Explanations of Collective Deviance

Some deviance, such as child molesting, incest, and some forms of homosexuality (Humphreys, 1970), is highly secret and very personal. People who commit these acts are not likely to join with others to engage in further deviance. However, much deviance is shared. The justifications, techniques, and operations are shared with others to carry out further deviance. For example, the gay liberation movement has done much to present the justification for homosexuality to other gays as well as heterosexuals. Additionally, gay activism has helped to protect gay operations, including bars, nightclubs, and residences, from legal and social embarrassment.

Another example of collective deviance is delinquent gangs. Gangs help youth justify their deviant activities. Techniques of shoplifting, robbing, and using drugs are taught and learned in the context of gang deviance. The operations of the gang may require a group effort. One member may provide a lookout while another provides a diversion and still another burglarizes, robs, or otherwise steals from the victim. Collective deviance such as homosexuality and gang delinquency often lead to development of deviant careers, subcultures of deviance, and cultural conflict.

Finally, a much-overlooked form of collective deviance is corporate deviance. Typical activities associated with corporate deviance include bribery, illegal political contributions, tax evasion, and antitrust violations. Each of the criminal categories may involve other forms of deviance such as conspiracy, fraud, perjury, and obstruction of justice. Although much deviance is seen as shadowy behavior committed on back streets and in backwoods, corporate deviance is main street and mainstream behavior.

Deviant Careers

A career is an occupation, a profession, or a job. The term *career* denotes activity that a person works at on a daily or regular basis. Dentist, dancer, and demolition expert are a few examples of popular careers. What career are you preparing for? What career do you currently possess? Additionally, a career is shared with others. that is, the process of becoming a professional in any career is similar for everyone who aspires to that career. Some sociologists (Goffman, 1961; Becker, 1973; Rains, 1982) have employed the term *careers* to explain and draw attention to certain patterns of deviant behavior. The activities of prostitutes, burglars, strippers, fences, card hustlers, bank robbers, and marijuana users have been described in sociological studies as **deviant careers** (Rains, 1982).

Three important elements lead to the development of deviant careers. These elements represent the shared or collective experiences of persons engaged in deviant careers. First, "one of the most crucial steps in the process of building a stable pattern of deviant behavior is likely to be the experience of being caught and publicly labeled as a deviant" (Becker, 1973:31). Being publicly identified as sick, slick, mad, or bad means that the social response of others often blocks efforts by the deviant to return to conformity. For example, those officially and publicly identified as whores, gays, or thieves may find that the opportunity to hold certain jobs, specifically government or defense occupations, is closed to them. Conformist friends, relatives, and acquaintances may begin to avoid them for fear of acquiring a courtesy stigma. In this way, opportunities for returning to conformity are limited, and the probability of association with other deviants like themselves for companionship and employment is increased. Edward Sagarin has identified several voluntary associations among social deviants. According to Sagarin:

> During the past twenty years, a new hope of formal association has begun to flourish in the United States; it is the organization of the special deviant. The

Being publicly identified as sick or mad may hinder later efforts by the deviant to return to conformity.

members of such a voluntary association may consist of alcoholics, gamblers, narcotic addicts or ex-convicts among others. (Sagarin, 1967:8)

Thus, the public identification of one as a deviant may limit associations with conformists and increase association with other deviants.

Second, deviants often experience the effect of the "ban" (Matza, 1969) on their deviance. The ban is the moral restriction against an activity. It is the ban that makes one feel guilty even in instances where no one else knows of the activity. In an effort to hide both the guilt and the banned activity a person often becomes involved in other deviance. The logic of the ban creates the strong possibility that the subject will become even more deviant in order to deviate (Matza, 1969:148).

For example, a man who is an adulterer may wish to sleep with another woman. However, in order to accomplish this, he may have to lie to his wife and to his employer in order to make available the time to rendezvous. And if this rendezvous is on company time and at company expense, then the man is also guilty of misappropriation of funds. So too, alcoholics and drug addicts may find that in order to carry out their deviant desires they need to commit acts of additional deviance that even they find distasteful. In other words, people who take up activities that are disapproved of by others will for reasons of either practical or moral self-protection find themselves more deeply involved with deviance than they might have first bargained for (Rains, 1982).

Third, deviance tends to become a **"master status"** (Hughes, 1945). A master status is one that dominates our social interaction with others. It is predominant in its influence on others' perception of and interaction with us. Ascribed statuses such as sex, age, and race tend to be master statuses. Because deviant tends to be a master status, others tend to pay less attention to the many minor or auxiliary statuses occupied by the deviant. For example, an elementary school teacher who is a male, a member of the Big Brothers organization, a pilot, a Boy Scout troop leader may still be unwelcomed because it is known that he is gay. In fact, once it is publicly known that he is gay, this male may have a difficult time continuing as an elementary school teacher, a Big Brother, and a Boy Scout leader. According to Becker (1973), possession of deviant master status may have a generalized symbolic value such that people automatically assume that its bearer possesses other undesirable traits allegedly associated with it.

Thus, public identifications, banning, and master statuses are shared experiences of many deviants. These shared experiences often lead to deviant careers. That is, persons may often find themselves engaged in regular patterns of deviant activity because the public label, the effects of the ban, and the dominance of the deviant status make it difficult for them to do otherwise.

Deviant Subculture

The old adage "birds of a feather flock together" is the core idea behind subcultural explanations of deviance. "Deviant subculture refers to the shared ways of thinking, feeling, and acting, that members of a deviant group have developed for engaging in deviant behavior, organizing relations among themselves, and defending themselves against social punishment" (Rubington, 1982:69).

There are two essential ideas that account for the formation of deviant subcultures. The first is that confirmed deviants recruit otherwise conforming or

"Birds of a feather . . ." is the core idea in subcultural explanations of deviance.

"drifting" (Matza, 1964) persons into a network of deviant activities and teach them techniques and accompanying rationalizations, and neutralizations, for committing deviance. These subcultural theories of deviance began in the 1930s with the Chicago School's explanation of juvenile delinquency (Rubington, 1982:53).

The second important idea in the formulation of deviant subcultures is that persons experiencing similar problems with conformity, such as anomie, lack of opportunity, or failure in school, come together to create subcultural standards and protect themselves against conformist moral entrepreneurs. This formulation includes differential opportunity theory and cultural conflict theories. The difference between these subcultural explanations of deviance is a matter of emphasis. The first explanation emphasizes the recruitment or teaching process that turns otherwise conforming people into deviants. The second explanation emphasizes the discontent with the conformists that encourages some people to come together and try to resolve this discontent through deviance. Despite these differences all subcultures tend to have in common characteristics that differentiate them from the conformists. These characteristics include language, symbols or signs, dress, values, and behavior.

Recruiting Subcultures. Subcultures that recruit deviants are based on the idea that deviance, including crime, is learned (Sutherland, 1939). Researchers (Burgess, 1925; Shaw and McKay, 1942) at the University of Chicago became interested in explaining the higher rates of deviance that existed in certain sections of Chicago. They noticed that in the areas immediately surrounding the downtown rates of deviance, including mental illness, delinquency, drug abuse, and crime, were higher than in any other section of the city. When Shaw and McKay (1942) reviewed past rates of deviance, they found that even though the times changed and the racial and ethnic composition changed, rates of deviance

Explanations of Collective Deviance 123

remained high in these areas. The researchers concluded that a subculture of deviant values, beliefs, and attitudes was culturally transmitted from one generation to the next.

It was left for Edwin Sutherland (1939) to make the first claim that deviance is learned. According to Sutherland:

> Criminal behavior is learned. Negatively, this means that criminal behavior is not inherited, as such; also, the person who is not already trained in crime does not invent criminal behavior, just as a person does not make mechanical inventions—he has been trained in mechanics. (Sutherland and Cressey, 1978:80)

Thus, persons are recruited and taught how to behave in a deviant fashion. Sutherland goes on to say that the teaching and learning involve not only techniques of committing deviance but also rationalizations that justify committing deviant acts. Sutherland's theory is called differential association theory.

The notion that people learn rationalizations to justify deviance intrigued some researchers (Sykes and Matza, 1957; Matza, 1964). These researchers began to explore **techniques of neutralization** that permit youth to rationalize their behavior and "drift" into deviance. The techniques of neutralization include denial of responsibility, denial of injury, denial of the victim, condemnation of the condemners, and appeal to higher loyalties. Denial of responsibility occurs when the delinquent claims someone else should be held accountable. The reply "It's not my job, man," is a denial of responsibility. Denial of injury occurs when the delinquent acknowledges responsibility but claims no one was hurt. Vandalism and consensual sexual deviance are often rationalized away through denial of injury. Denial of the victim occurs when youths claim that those persons injured deserved the harm because they are unacceptable. Injuries to so-called fags, bums, niggers, drunks, junkies, wops, chinks, and dikes are often denied. Condemnation of the condemners occurs when youth claim that their delinquency is no worse than the deviance of their advisors. "Listen to the pot calling the kettle black" is a phrase that illustrates the idea that the accuser (the pot) is just as wrong as the accused (the kettle). The appeal to higher loyalties occurs when youths claim that their deviance is justified because a power greater than themselves, and greater than the conforming norms, required them to behave in a delinquent manner. Any behavior that violates expectations but is done in the name of God, loyalty, justice, or honor is an appeal to higher loyalties.

Delinquent youth are able to recruit and teach these techniques of neutralization to youth who are wandering or drifting between adherence to conformist expectations and acceptance of deviant desires. The delinquent subculture is important because it provides "the situation of company" (Matza, 1964:51–59) in which delinquency occurs.

Thus, the various subcultural theories of deviance that emphasize the recruitment and training process by which one becomes deviant have in common the idea that deviance is learned in the company of others. According to Matza:

> The major contribution of sociology to the understanding of deviance has consisted of two fundamental insights. First, persistent deviance is not a solitary enterprise; rather, it best flourishes when it receives group support. Second, deviance typically is not an individual or group innovation; rather it has a history in a particular locale. (Matza, 1964:63)

Some subcultural theories of deviance concern themselves primarily with the problems certain segments of the society—typically lower-class, poor, and minority males—have with conforming to white middle-class standards. The major emphasis in these theories is not the recruitment and training process but the common problems that deviants share which lead them to reject conformist standards or place them in opposition to the larger culture. These theories can be called opposition subcultures views.

Opposition Subcultures. Theories of deviance based upon the idea of opposition generally contend that there is a core set of values and norms within a subculture that differs from the larger culture, rejects some major component of the larger culture, or directly conflicts with the larger culture. For example, the idea that cultural conflict could explain deviance was developed by Thorsten Sellin (1938). Sellin developed his theory during a time when immigration from Europe to America was very high. He noticed that as these various racial and ethnic groups began to coexist, they often came into conflict when the conduct norms of one group were incompatible or clashed with the conduct norms of another group. According to Sellin, cultural conflict led to deviance when norms of one group migrated into another group's territory and were subsequently punished as improper. Norms resulted in conflict when they were border norms, extended norms, or transposed norms. An example of a border norm would be deviance that occurs when groups and cultures have geographic proximity, such as the United States and Mexico, and the norms conflict along the border. The controversy over illegal Mexican aliens in California and in Texas reflects the idea of border norms and cultural conflict.

Extended norms exist when one group dominates, occupies, or imposes their norms on another. Apartheid in South Africa, the American Revolution, and the American occupation of Japan after World War II are examples of extended norms. A current example of an extension of norms can be seen in Russia's influence over life in Poland. For example, one of the leaders, Zbigniew Bujak, of the underground trade union movement Solidarity, claims that the Polish leader Wojciech Jaruzelski, has admitted that he is subordinate to Moscow (*Newsweek,* September 2, 1985:33). Solidarity has emerged not only as a force for change in Poland but also as a symbol of resistance by the Polish people to the extension conduct norms from Russia over their lives. An example of migrating norms includes unassimilated immigrants who violate expectations because they are following the conduct norms of their parent culture instead of the host culture. "When in Rome, do as the Romans do," is a phrase that reflects the warning that you may be guilty of a deviant act if you do not learn the ways of the culture to which you are migrating.

Walter Miller (1958) has argued that the lower-class culture is a breeding ground for collective deviance, in particular gang delinquency. Miller believes:

> In the case of "gang" delinquency the cultural system which exerts the most direct influence in behavior is that of the lower-class community itself. (Miller, 1958:6)

Specifically, it is the focal concerns of the lower-class culture that generate a milieu conducive to gang delinquency. Miller contends that concerns in the lower-class culture over trouble, toughness, smartness, excitement, fate, and autonomy create an environment that is conducive to delinquency. Miller concentrates much of his explanation on the influence lower-class definitions of masculinity have on collective deviance. Miller feels that because a significant number of lower-class males are raised in female-headed households, these males become obsessed with proving their masculinity. It is this subcultural attempt largely by lower-class males who demonstrate their masculinity through violence, sex, honky-tonk activities, and use of alcohol that leads to collective patterns of deviance and the formation of delinquent gangs.

Another popular explanation of collective deviance is differential opportunity theory (Cloward and Ohlin, 1960). This theory identifies three different types of deviant subcultures, including the criminal subculture, the conflict subculture, and the retreatist subculture.

The criminal subculture occurs when lower-class youth are exposed to models of success who have acquired their wealth illegitimately. Numbers runners, pushers, pimps, bootleggers, and prostitutes are likely to have visible cash on hand and make impressive ostentatious displays of success. Additionally, they may form relationships—casual, working, or friendly—with local youth whereby an "age-grading of criminal learning and performance can occur" (Cloward and Ohlin, 1960).

The conflict subculture develops in areas where "transiency and instability become the overriding features of social life" (Cloward and Ohlin, 1960). In such areas violence becomes the means of acquiring success. Successful people in a conflict subculture are those who possess a reputation. A reputation, or "rep," is the distinguishing mark of success in the conflict subculture.

The retreatist subculture arises from failure to achieve legitimate or illegitimate success because of internal values or social barriers (Cloward and Ohlin, 1960). Thus, the retreatist subculture emerges when people not only fail to become doctors and lawyers but also when the same people fail to become successful criminals or fail to acquire a rep. Therefore, the retreatist subculture is filled with "double failures." Members of retreatist subcultures pursue kicks and drugs. Cloward and Ohlin (1960) contend "that retreatist behavior emerges among some lower-class adolescents because they have failed to find a place for themselves in criminal or conflict subcultures."

Other research (Hirschi, 1969) on delinquency has identified the loosening of social controls as a breeding ground for deviance. Control theory holds that when one's stake in conformity or bonds to conformity are weakened, one becomes free to commit deviant acts. Essentially, control theory suggests that rarely does the gang recruit good boys and turn them bad, but rather a boy takes up with delinquent peers and commits delinquent acts because he has lost his stake in conformity. Specifically, the stakes in conformity are attachment to school and parents and the commitment, involvement, and belief in correctional norms. When these stakes are weak, then social controls are loose, and youth are freer to become involved in deviant activities (Hirschi, 1969).

Mainstream Deviance

The deviance that is committed by individuals acting on behalf of corporations poses several problems that differentiate it from other forms of collective deviance. For example, gang delinquency and drug subcultures are comprised of individuals whose actions are disapproved of by a majority of people. Once identified as having committed a deviant act, an individual faces a social response that is often swift and resolute in punishing representatives of these deviant subcultures. Additionally, the activities of most forms of collective deviance are legally prohibited by the criminal code. Thus, the activities of those who participate in collective forms of deviance such as burglary, assault, possession of narcotics, and peddling kiddie pornography are prohibited by the criminal law.

By contrast, mainstream deviance exists in a kind of legal limbo. According to Clinard (1979:xxii), there are three problems in the criminal prosecution of corporate deviance. First, because of the division of tasks within a corporation, it is not easy to determine the criminal liability of any one person. Second, corporate deviance is more complex than other forms of conventional deviance. Third, the effects of the deviance are so diffuse that it is not easy to identify who was harmed. Where there are no complaining victims, there is likely to be little concern in identifying criminals. Additionally, although there is likely to be little disagreement over the legal penalties given to conventional deviants, there are often differences of opinion of how white-haired, white-collar deviants should be punished. In a study of 582 of the largest publicly owned corporations in the United States, Clinard (1979) examined enforcement actions initiated or imposed by twenty-four federal agencies during 1975 and 1976. This study revealed that the penalties imposed on top corporate management were quite lenient. Few members of corporate management were ever incarcerated when they were convicted of some offense. Most mainstream deviants were placed on probation or given suspended sentences and had a fine levied against them. According to Clinard (1979:xxii), "The average prison sentence for all those convicted, whether or not they went to prison and regardless of the offense averaged 2.8 days".

These problems are clearly evident in the recent case involving E. F. Hutton. In May 1985, E. F. Hutton pleaded guilty to 2,000 separate charges of mail and wire fraud. These charges stemmed from a check-kiting scheme which officers at E. F. Hutton devised to obtain interest on money that had not been deposited. According to *Time* magazine (July 16, 1985:54), executives at E. F. Hutton issued overdraft checks which amounted to no-interest loans at a time when rates were 20 percent. Beginning in July 1980, the company obtained as much as $250 million a day on freebie loans on which it could earn interest. Estimates suggest that the amount of money defrauded from banks ranged from a low of $8 million to as much as $30 million.

The Justice Department fined E. F. Hutton $2 million and decided not to prosecute any officers of the corporation because "it would be legally fruitless" (*Newsweek,* July 22, 1985:45). *Newsweek* magazine reported that representative William Hughes, chairman of the House Judiciary subcommittee investigating Hutton, accused the firm of "attempting to frustrate the investigation by releasing documents in spits and dribble" (July 22, 1985:45). A later investigation of the check-kiting scheme authorized by top officials at Hutton singled out fifteen employees who were involved. The 183-page report highlighted a peculiar management structure in which no one admitted being the immediate boss of the cash manager at Hutton. Although none of the fifteen officials suffered criminal penalties, Hutton announced plans to discipline fourteen with firings and/or fines.

Mainstream deviance is often initiated by big business to obtain financial gain or advantage over corporate competitors. The effects of the activities may be diffuse, but they are no less serious. The deviance of corporate officials can lead to unsafe automobiles, toxic drugs, flammable clothing, carcinogenic additives, tainted meats, and unsafe work environments. Likewise, the economic costs to the society of mainstream deviance from such activities as price fixing and unscrupulous sales and repairs in the automobile industry far exceed the costs to society from other forms of deviance. Finally, mainstream deviance, like gang activities or deviant subcultures, is collective deviance. Conspiracy, the act of meeting together to devise methods of conducting illegal behavior, is a common component of mainstream deviance.

Functions of Deviance

Not all deviance is punished, nor are all deviants mistreated. Some people have become rather famous and very wealthy because they did not conform to social expectations. Notable because of his deviance, Muhammad Ali changed the sport of boxing in several ways. Muhammad Ali had a boxing style that did not conform to the expectations of heavyweight boxers. He fought with his hands down. He fought backing away from attacks. He made the jab an offensive weapon. He fought on the ropes with a rope-a-dope. He expended unnecessary energy with his Ali-shuffle. Yet, each of these deviant performances served to make him in the eyes of many the greatest boxing champion of all time and served as a model for future boxing champions, like Sugar Ray Leonard and Larry Holmes.

Neither did Muhammad Ali conform to the expectations for boxers outside the ring. For example, Ali made predictions about the fate of his opponents. He bragged on himself, and he refused military induction. Yet this deviant behavior made him ultimately a popular, well-known, and well-liked personality. Other boxers, most notably Joe Frazier, became wealthy also by representing, although unsuccessfully, those who would have had Ali conform. In fact, in recent years "bad boys" like Ilie Nastase, Jimmy Connors, and John McEnroe have done much to popularize the sport of tennis and at the same time enhance their personal wealth.

Thus, deviance also serves important functions for the individual deviant. It may be easier to be deviant than to attempt to conform. Some people who receive unemployment, welfare, and medicaid benefits may find this assistance threatened if they attempt to work. Students may find it easier to accept labels like slow learner, educationally mentally retarded (EMR), and dumb jock than to strive for academic excellence.

John McEnroe's popularity may be due in part to his deviant antics on the tennis court.

Individuals may use deviance to solicit attention and services that might not ordinarily be forthcoming. For a long time many researchers have identified attempted suicide as a "cry for help." So by attempting suicide, people—mostly women and teenagers—can solicit attention and love from their families and friends. In other instances, fathers have deserted their families or committed a variety of criminal offenses to solicit services from welfare agencies, employers, hospitals, and correctional facilities for which they ordinarily would not have been eligible. Deviant behavior often qualifies individuals for the services of self-help groups like Alcoholics Anonymous (AA), drug detoxification programs, and homosexual service groups.

Finally, deviant behavior can help to identify the values and beliefs of the deviant. The social response to individuals' deviance may intensify their belief in the rightness of their deviant behavior, or the social response may convince them of the error of their ways. In any event, their deviance and the ensuing social response helped to clarify and solidify their beliefs.

Additionally, deviance serves certain important functions (Durkheim, 1950; Coser, 1967; Erikson, 1966; Dentler and Erikson, 1959) for the society. One function that deviance serves is to increase the sensitivity of others to the norm that is being violated. Kai Erikson (1966) has called this process the boundary maintenance function of deviance. In this way, decisions can be made to intensify support for the norm or alter that norm. The late senator Joseph McCarthy became a political force and built a career on identifying or threatening to identify the deviance (e.g., membership in the communist party) in others. During the 1970s the American Indian Movement's (AIM's) tactic of reclaiming ancestral lands served to bring the issue of treaties to the courts, where boundary maintenance and the articulation and clarification of the meaning of the treaties could occur.

Deviance also functions as a method of ventilating collective grievances and publicizing social injustice. Social movements such as the civil rights movement, the labor movement, or the women's liberation movement have all included some form of civil disobedience and flagrant violation of the law. These actions permit members of the movement to voice their objections to social arrangements. The injustice in the social arrangements is dramatized by public defiance of the laws that protect these arrangements. For example, the marches and the subsequent arrest of those who marched on the South African embassy served to publicize the injustice of apartheid in South Africa. The occurrence of such actions indicates that the society is open for change. In the instances of civil disobedience, fads, and fashions, deviance also points the way to changes that eventually become accepted as normal (Durkheim, 1980; Coser, 1967). Desegregation, shorter dresses, longer hair, and bilingual signs have all become accepted as appropriate because of behaviors that were initially perceived as deviant. Deviance contributes to group solidarity as people band together to identify, punish, or treat the deviant (Durkheim, 1950). The emergence of self-help groups like the Guardian Angels in New York is the result of norm-abiding citizens getting together to identify and catch deviants. In some instances, groups also induce and encourage deviant behavior and protect the deviants from expulsion from the group (Dentler and Erikson, 1959).

Thus, given the nature of American society, if we lived in a state where there were no deviants, we would be forced to import them from nearby states so that we could hold elections, take up collections, have a need for ministers and Sunday sermons, maintain a police force, hire social workers, listen to counselors, and, yes, write chapters on deviant behavior in introductory sociology texts. To a large extent, deviant behavior is a normal, inevitable, integral, necessary factor in all healthy societies (Durkheim, 1950).

Summary

When people do not conform to group expectations, they are regarded as deviants. Although not all nonconformist behavior is unwelcomed, most discussions of deviance center upon behavior that departs from the expected rules of conduct and is disapproved of by a large group of people. Crime is deviance which violates the laws of the community. Not all deviance is crime. Crime requires an act which is undefensible and violates a written law. A common social response to deviance is to stigmatize nonconformists. In addition to being stigmatized, deviants are often punished. The intent of punishment is to deter the deviants and others from violating the rules of the group. Explanations of deviance focus on either the social response to primary deviance or upon strains in the social structure which create deviance. Some deviance results in long-term careers and subcultural adaptations. Finally, deviance serves certain functions. Deviance can be viewed as contributing to boundary maintenance, pointing the way to change, indicating that the society is open, and contributing to group solidarity.

Key Concepts

aberrant behavior	**deviant careers**
anomie	**labeling**
crime	**master status**
deterrence	**secondary deviance**
deviance	**stigma**
deviant	**techniques of neutralization**

References

Bavak-Glantz, Israel, and C. Ronald Huff (eds.). (1981) *The Mad, the Bad and the Different: Essays in Honor of Simon Dinitz.* Lexington, Mass.: Lexington Books (D. C. Heath and Co.).

Becker, Howard S. (1973) *Outsiders: Studies in the Sociology of Deviance.* New York, N.Y.: The Free Press.

Bequai, August. (1978) *Computer Crime.* Lexington, Mass.: D. C. Heath & Company.

Birenbaum, Arnold. (1970) "On Managing a Courtesy Stigma." *Journal of Health and Social Behavior, 11*(September):196–206.

Black, Donald. (1970) "Production of Crime Rates." *American Sociological Review, 35*(August):733–48.

Burgess, Ernest W. (1925) "The Growth of the City: An Introduction of a Research Project." In Robert E. Park, Ernest W. Burgess, and R. D. McKenzie (eds.), *The City.* Chicago, Ill.: University of Chicago Press, 47–62.

Clinard, Marshall B., Peter C. Yeager, Jeanne Brissette, David Petrashek, and Elizabeth Harries. (1979) "Illegal Corporate Behavior." U.S. Department of Justice, Law Enforcement Assistance Administration. Washington, D.C.: U.S. Government Printing Office.

Cloward, Richard A., and Lloyd E. Ohlin. (1960) *Delinquency and Opportunity: A Theory of Delinquent Gangs.* New York, N.Y.: The Free Press.

Coser, Lewis A. (1967) *Continuities in the Study of Social Conflict.* New York, N.Y.: The Free Press.

Dentler, Robert A., and Kai T. Erikson. (1959) "The Functions of Deviance in Groups." *Social Problems, 7*(Fall): 98–107.

Durkheim, Emile. [1895] (1950) *Rules of the Sociological Method.* 8th ed. New York, N.Y.: The Free Press.

———. **[1897]** (1951) *Suicide: A Study in Sociology.* New York, N.Y.: The Free Press. Translated by John A. Spaulding and George Simpson.

Elderhertz, Herbert. (1970) "The Native Impact and Prosecution of White Collar Crime." U.S. Department of Justice, Law Enforcement Assistance Administration. Washington, D.C.: U.S. Government Printing Office.

Erikson, Kai T. (1966) *Wayward Puritans.* New York, N.Y.: John Wiley & Sons, Inc.

Garfinkel, Harold. (1956) "Successful Degradation Ceremonies." *American Journal of Sociology, 61*(March):420–24.

Gibbs, Jack P. (1981) *Norms, Deviance and Social Control: Conceptual Matters.* New York, N.Y.: American Elsevier Publishing Co., Inc.

Goffman, Erving. (1961) *Asylums; Essays on the Situation of Mental Patients and Other Inmates.* New York, N.Y.: Doubleday/Anchor Books.

———. (1963) *Stigma Notes on the Management of Spoiled Identity.* Englewood Cliffs, N.J.: Prentice-Hall, Inc.

Gove, Walter R. (ed.). (1975) *The Labeling of Deviance: Evaluating a Perspective.* New York, N.Y.: John Wiley & Sons, Inc.

Hirschi, Travis. (1969) *Causes of Delinquency.* Berkeley, Calif.: University of California Press.

Hughes, Everett C. (1945) "Dilemmas and Contradictions of Status." *American Journal of Sociology, 50*(March):353–59.

Humphreys, Laud. (1970) *Tearoom Trade: Impersonal Sex in Public Places.* Chicago, Ill.: Aldine Publishing Company.

Lemert, Edwin M. (1951) *Social Pathology: A Systematic Approach to the Theory of Sociopathic Behavior.* New York, N.Y.: McGraw-Hill Book Company.

Maris, Ronald. (1969) *Social Forces in Urban Suicide.* Homewood, Ill.: Dorsey Press.

Matza, David. (1964) *Delinquency and Drift.* New York, N.Y.: John Wiley & Sons, Inc.

———. (1969) *Becoming Deviant.* Englewood Cliffs, N.J.: Prentice-Hall, Inc.

McCahgy, Charles. (1976) *Deviant Behavior: Crime, Conflict, and Interest Groups.* New York: Macmillan Publishing Co., Inc.

Merton, Robert. (1938) "Social Structure and Anomie." *American Sociological Review 3*(October):672–82.

Miller, Walter B. (1958) "Lower Class Culture as a Generating Milieu of Gang Delinquency." *Journal of Social Issues, 14*(Fall):5–19.

Nettler, Gwynn. (1978) *Explaining Crime.* 2d ed. New York, N.Y.: McGraw-Hill Book Company.

Newsweek. (1985) "Up From the Underground." (September 2):33.

———. (1985) "The Nightmare at Hutton." (July 22):45.

Orcutt, James D. (1983) *Analyzing Deviance.* Homewood, Ill.: The Dorsey Press.
Pfuhl, Erdwin H. (1980) *The Deviance Process.* New York, N.Y.: D. Van Nostrand Company.
Rains, Prue. (1982) "Deviant Careers." In M. Michael Rosenberg, Robert A. Stebbins, and Allan Turowetz (eds.), *The Sociology of Deviance.* New York, N.Y.: St. Martin's Press, Inc., 21–41.
Rubington, Earl. (1982) "Deviant Subcultures." In M. Michael Rosenberg, Robert A. Stebbins, and Allan Turowetz (eds.), *The Sociology of Deviance.* New York, N.Y.: St. Martin's Press, Inc., 42–70.
Sagarin, Edward. (1967) "Voluntary Associates Among Social Deviants." *Criminologica,* 5(May):8–22.
Savitz, Leonard D. (1978) "Official Police Statistics and Their Limitations." In Leonard D. Savitz and Norman Johnson (eds.), *Crime in Society.* New York, N.Y.: John Wiley & Sons, Inc.
Sellin, Thorsten. (1938) *Culture Conflict and Crime.* New York, N.Y.: Social Science Research Council Bulletin 41.
Shaw, Clifford R., and Henry D. McKay. (1942) *Juvenile Delinquency in Urban Areas.* Chicago, Ill.: University of Chicago Press.
Shur, Edwin M. (1971) *Labeling Deviant Behavior.* New York: Harper & Row, Publishers.
Sutherland, Edwin H. (1939) *Principles of Criminology.* 3d ed. Philadelphia, Penn.: Lippincott.
Sutherland, Edwin H, and Donald R. Cressey. (1978) *Criminology* (tenth edition). Philadelphia, Penn: Lippincott.
Sykes, Gresham M. (1957) "Techniques of Neutralization: A Theory of Delinquency." *American Sociological Review, 22*(December):644–70.
———. (1978) *Criminology.* New York, N.Y.: Harcourt Brace Jovanovich, Inc.
Tannenbaum, Frank. (1938) *Crime and the Community.* Boston, Mass.: Ginn and Company.
Taylor, Maurice C. (1982) "Black Male-Female Suicide: A Case Study of Occupation and Rates of Suicide by Race and Sex." *Western Journal of Black Studies, 6*(Fall):124–29.
Thornberry, Terrence P., and Joseph E. Jacoby. (1979) *The Criminally Insane: A Community Follow-up of Mentally Ill Offenders.* Chicago, Ill.: University of Chicago Press.
Time. (1985) "Placing the Blame at E. F. Hutton." (September 16):54.
Trice, Harrison M., and Paul M. Roman. (1970) "Delabeling, Relabeling and Alcoholics Anonymous." *Social Problems, 17*(Spring):4.
Walker, Peter N. (1973) *Punishment: An Illustrative History.* New York, N.Y.: Arco Publishing Co.
Wallerstein, James S., and Clement J. Wyle. (1947) "Our Law-Abiding Law-Breakers." *Probation, 25*(March/April):107–12.
Wiseman, Jacqueline P. (1970) *Stations of the Lost: Treatment of Skid Row Alcoholics.* San Diego, Calif.: University of California Press.

PART II

Social Inequality

7

Social Stratification

OBJECTIVES

By the end of this chapter the student should be able to:

1. Define what is meant by stratification and identify its major dimensions.

2. Contrast the functional and conflict perspectives on stratification.

3. Characterize several types of stratification systems.

4. Understand and contrast two classic theories of stratification: Marx's theory of class and Weber's theory of class, status, and party.

5. Identify inequalities that create differential access to ranking systems.

6. Understand the basic implications of world system theory for stratification.

INTRODUCTION

A student in a southern university once announced to her sociology class that there were no social classes in her hometown, a small manufacturing town in eastern North Carolina. "How often do you date the boys who work in the mill?" a skeptical classmate asked. She replied, "Oh, my mother wouldn't let me date anybody who works at the mill." The idea of equality runs as a vigorous theme in the minds of most Americans even in the face of the most blatant evidence of inequality. In this and the chapters to follow we are concerned with various manifestations of inequality. In the present chapter we focus on the general nature and types of stratification. Sociologists have advanced many theories to explain why stratification exists. We shall look at several attempts, examining in particular the assumptions about consensus or conflict each makes.

The Nature of Stratification

Everywhere we look, we recognize differences among people: some are male; others are female. Some are young; some are old. Some are athletes; others are musicians. Some drive Jaguars; others drive Ford pickup trucks. Some make A's; others make C's. Some are Hispanic; others are Japanese. Sorting people according to socially recognized characteristics occurs in all societies. This is what we mean by social differentiation. Not all the differences between people have social relevance. For example, generally we do not differentiate people with oily earwax from those with crumbly earwax or those with inward or outward navels. But all societies recognize and consider significant some differences between people.

Not all of the distinctions we draw are judgmental. For example, backstroke swimmers are different from breaststroke swimmers, but we do not rank one group as superior to the other. For many other distinctions, however, we make evaluations, establishing a ranking of the differences that leads to important advantages or disadvantages. For example, one such evaluation concerns physical appearance. How would you evaluate being good-looking or being ugly? What are the advantages or disadvantages of being one or the other? We make similar evaluations concerning many other qualities. We value youth over old age; having a job over being unemployed; living in a nice house over living in a tenement; having an education over being illiterate. Through the judgments and evaluations we make about social differences, we create inequalities. Because, as the symbolic interactionists point out, we act on the basis of our perception of things, the judgments have consequences for the ranked individuals and groups. The point is that inequalities are not just opinions but are manifested in the way people live their lives.

Some inequalities become predictable elements of social organizations and are perpetuated from generation to generation. When inequalities become embedded in the institutional arrangements of the society, they create social

When ranked differences become embedded in our social structure, social stratification has set in.

stratification. Not all inequalities become institutionalized. For example, homely parents may have good-looking kids; intellectual geniuses may have average or even dumb kids. But rich parents are going to have rich kids, and the advantages are going to accrue to them. Parents of Puerto Rican descent are going to have Puerto Rican kids, and whatever inequalities they have experienced will very likely be experienced by their children.

Stratification implies that the unequal access people have to scarce and valued things the society has to offer gets built into the structure of society. Most sociologists, following Weber, recognize that wealth, prestige, and power are the most consequential dimensions of social stratification. Differentials along each of these dimensions create a ranking along each axis that persists as a stable pattern in the social order.

Contrasts in Perspectives

Functional and conflict theories were introduced in Chapter 1. Perhaps at no point is the contrast between functional and conflict theories more sharply drawn than in their perspectives on social stratification. The functional perspective, which was developed by Talcott Parsons and by Kingsley Davis and Wilbert Moore, has as its primary thrust the relationship between stratification and the division of labor. Ideas that identify a functional perspective are the following: (1) There is a societal need to see that the most important roles that make up the division of labor are competently filled and performed. (2) There is basic consensus regarding the contributions of different roles to the maintenance of the society. (3) A ranking is established among these roles in terms of rewards. High rewards are attached to functionally important positions that are difficult to fill. Relatively unimportant positions or important positions that are easy to fill have lesser rewards attached to them. (4) Basic agreement on the essential fairness of rewards gives stability and coherence to the social system. This perspective sees stratification as contributing in a positive way to the adaptive capacity of a society by motivating qualified individuals to prepare for and perform important tasks of the society.

Conflict theory today centers around four major ideas: (1) It assumes that individuals and groups in different positions in the social structure develop different interests. (2) As these groups struggle with each other for the advancement of their interests, some groups succeed in establishing dominance over less successful groups. (3) Ideas become weapons in the struggle for power and are used by the ruling group to legitimate the system that supports their privileged position. (4) Because subordinate groups continue to pursue their interests and seek changes in the distributive system that deprives them, instability is inherent in social organization; therefore, change rather than stability is the major theme in society. Conflict theorists regard stratification as having a negative impact on the society because it benefits the few at the expense of the many.

Because functional theorists have focused their attention on explaining the ranking of occupational roles implicit in a complex division of labor, they have paid little attention to identifying who fills the roles. For example, they have not analyzed the differential access to the hierarchy of roles based on race, ethnicity, sex, age, or other social characteristics. For conflict theorists on the other hand, such differences in access are at the heart of social stratification as members of the dominant group, which they usually identify as white, middle-class males,

The high salaries that athletes and entertainers make raise questions about whether the most important jobs receive the highest salaries.

reserve the positions of privilege for themselves and use their power to keep subordinate group members in less valued positions.

Stratification and Societal Types

Patterns of stratification are variable in many ways. Two types of variation seem particularly significant. One of these is the degree of difference in access to economic goods, prestige, and power the system permits. Systems also differ in the amount of vertical mobility that is afforded to individuals in the society; that is, the opportunity they have to move up or down the ranking scale. The first of these refers to the gaps between levels; the second refers to the rigidity of the levels.

Variation in the degree of inequality in a society seems to be related to the technological level of the society. Lenski (1966) has identified a pattern in distributive systems in which the degree of inequality in power and privilege is directly associated with the amount of surplus goods the society produces. A society must meet the basic needs of its members. When, through technological development, its productive capacity exceeds the maintenance needs of the group, the struggle to control the excess creates a stratified system. The greater the surplus produced, the greater the gap between those who gain control of it and those who do not.

Lenski began with hunting and gathering societies, where surplus is small and the sharing ethic strong. He found little evidence of entrenched inequality in such societies. As the technology of food production improves from digging stick to hoe to plow and as other developments such as irrigation, fertilization, and domestication of animals increase productivity, conflict over control of the surplus becomes more extreme, and the discrepancy between the haves and the have-nots increases. Lenski suggested that the agrarian society produced the greatest extremes in wealth. Although the industrial society produces even greater surpluses, Lenski says that certain factors mitigate against increasingly extreme inequalities. The spread of literacy, the existence of an egalitarian ethic, and the dependence of those in control upon the knowledge, skill, and goodwill of their subordinates have interrupted the trend toward increasing disparities in power and material wealth. However, inequities are still deeply embedded in the fabric of industrial societies. These are the focus of our ensuing chapters on social inequality.

Stratification systems, then, have existed throughout much of human history. Some of the best-known systems embodying inequalities of power and privilege are caste, estate, class, and slave systems. These systems vary in many ways, of which the degree of mobility each permits is one of the most important.

Caste System

The prototype of a caste system, the most rigid form of stratification, is the traditional caste system of India. Many changes within India and in India's relationship to the modern world have somewhat blurred the features of the system, but elements of the pattern that persisted through 3,000 years survive into the present. Other caste societies are identified in the degree to which they approach the old model.

The Indian caste system is one of the most rigid systems of stratification.

Caste constitutes a closed prestige system where access to valued material resources has also generally followed caste lines. The ranking is sustained by a number of features. Caste membership is hereditary. It is an ascribed status in that the child at birth assumes the rank of his or her parents and remains in that stratum throughout the life span. Movement upward or downward within the caste may occur. For example, a merchant may become richer or poorer—but movement across the caste line is prohibited.

Most stratification systems tend toward **endogamy** in the choice of marriage partners; that is, the expectation that one will choose a partner from within one's social group. The caste system makes it mandatory to marry within one's own caste. This pattern has the effect of unifying family and caste identification because caste lines are inclusive of family units.

A caste is further unified by its identification with a given occupation. The decision with which many college students wrestle, What kind of work shall I do? is irrelevant in the caste system. One enters the occupation associated with his family's caste. A son born into a family of the leather-working caste becomes a leather worker. This characteristic minimizes intercaste competition and eliminates a possible source of challenge to the system.

Intricate rules govern the behavior of caste members. One is obligated to conform to norms regulating the relationships between members of different castes. Examples include restrictions on who may cook the food one eats, whom one may eat with, associate with, touch, or, in some cases, let one's shadow fall upon. Ritual purification is required when one has been contaminated by violations of social distance rules by less-clean caste members.

Sanctions for these observances are imposed by the community and the caste itself. The ultimate sanction, however, is the Hindu religion. Through its doctrine of transmigration of the soul the caste system is justified and strengthened. This belief holds that one's soul goes through a series of reincarnations until it blends with the Infinite. Caste rankings form a ladder for the soul's journey. If one lives a good life in his or her present embodiment by carefully observing the caste rules, in the next reincarnation the soul will be born into a higher caste. One is therefore promoted or demoted in the next life according to how faithfully one conforms to the caste rules in this life. In this way religious doctrine is used to legitimate the caste system.

Estate System

A line of thought in early feudal times in western Europe identified three types within the human community: "Those who prayed, those who fought, and those who worked" (Bloch, 1964:291). These ranked orders emerged as the elements in the estate system of the later feudal period. It is a pattern of stratification that has its counterpart in many other times and places.

"Those who prayed" were, of course, the clergy. The power of the church was enhanced by its vast landholdings and its feudal ties to secular powers. The clergy recruited its membership from the other orders. The source of recruitment was usually reflected in the rankings within the ecclesiastical hierarchy; leadership within the church tended to come from the higher levels of the laity (Adams, 1969:89). The priesthood embodied a hierarchy within its own ranks ranging from the rich and powerful bishops and archbishops down to the lowly country priests, whose life-style closely resembled that of the peasants among whom they lived and worked. Some mobility through the ranks was possible, but it was limited.

"Those who fought" referred to the knights. Theoretically the land belonged to the king. Knighthood was bestowed as a result of one's personal fealty and service in warfare to the king or to a great lord. Usually control over land was bestowed along with the title. Gradually as the right to the title and to the lands became hereditary, the nobility was established as a legally recognized and privileged group. The noble status was transmitted to one's posterity and came to imply a knightly lineage. Administrative control over the feudal estates gave to the nobles political, legal, and economic jurisdiction over the land and the people who occupied it.

A hierarchy of wealth, power, and prestige among the nobility was supported by law and custom (Bloch, 1964:322). The greatest lords received lands directly from the kings or territorial princes. They granted lands and titles to lesser nobles, who became their vassals. The vassals in turn could become lords as they granted lands and titles to lesser noblemen. The lowest nobles were those who had no other knights as vassals. Despite these gradations, the nobility were united in their values, in their life-style, in their commitment to warlike pursuits, and in their belief in their superiority over those of common origins. The overriding significance of lineage in establishing superior status was supported by the pattern of endogamy in the selection of marriage partners.

The common people were "those who worked"—the producers. They were not a homogeneous group, however. Some were tied to the land; some were free to move. Some were peasants; some were artisans, craftsmen, and merchants. Some were well-to-do; some were poor. Indeed, as manufacturing and commerce grew among the people, the bourgeoisie, the rising capitalists, emerged as a very wealthy class. The bond between the commoners was their shared exclusion from the power and prestige of the nobility and their subjection to its political and administrative dominance.

The estate system was a hierarchical ranking system sanctioned in law and custom. It was protected by religious ideas such as the divine right of kings and the God-given nature of the social order. Essentially closed, it was, however, somewhat less rigid than the caste system. The occupational linkages were looser. The rules governing contacts between members of different strata were less stringently enforced. Some economic mobility within each stratum was possible. A modest crossing of lines was possible as lords occasionally rewarded faithful servitors with grants of lands or titles.

Social Class System

In comparison with caste and estate systems, a social class system is relatively more open. This is the system that typifies modern industrial societies. Class strata are primarily economic groups rather than prestige groups. Efforts to characterize their nature and number have engaged social scientists for a long time. Classification attempts run into problems such as just which criteria identify classes and where the cut-off points between one class and another occur.

That such problems exist reflects to some extent a degree of flexibility in the class system itself. As Bottomore has (1966:12) suggested, classes are not constituted on the basis of any legal rules. Class membership does not confer or deny "special civil or political rights." Religious sanctions for class differences (for example, the idea that "God maketh the righteous to prosper") have been advanced, but these supports have not been formally codified, and contrary ideas (such as the equality of souls before God and the brotherhood of man) have mitigating effects. Sanctions are for the most part, then, custom and public opinion.

Endogamy is widely practiced, though this is not required by law. One is permitted to marry outside one's class, though many factors insure that this does not happen often. Patterns of association make it likely that one will choose a marriage partner from one's own class. For example, to which social class (e.g., lower, middle) do the members of the opposite sex you associate with belong? We tend to marry those who are similar to ourselves in social background. The fact that in most class societies a young man and a young woman choose their own mates rather than having their parents make the arrangements gives the illusion that the choice is more open than in fact it is. Still, interclass marriages do occur, especially between members of adjacent classes.

A social class system theoretically minimizes the importance of hereditary privilege. Mobility in the system is held to be possible for everyone. Obviously the reality departs substantially from this principle. A child assumes the class position of his or her family, and this is one of the strongest factors in determining the class level that can be achieved. Factors such as race, ethnicity, sex, and age strongly influence access to wealth and privilege. They also have impact upon the degree of mobility that occurs. However, for some in the society mobility does occur. Modern industrial societies throughout most of their history have had expanding economies, which have opened up opportunities for many. In a class system, one is less likely to remain in the stratum one is born into than in a caste or estate system.

Reports of a conversation between Ernest Hemingway and F. Scott Fitzgerald have it that Fitzgerald observed, "The rich are different," to which Hemingway replied, "Yes, they have money." This anecdote suggests another feature of class systems. Someone in a particular class is not presumed to be a different order of person from someone in another. And no ceremony or official recognition is required to confirm one's status if one moves into a different class (Bottomore, 1966:12).

Slave System

Slave systems may exist within any of the other types of stratified societies. The essential feature of slavery is that one person owns the body and labor of another. Slavery may or may not be an inherited status. In the United States during most of the seventeenth century, children of slaves were presumed to be free. This practice, proving uneconomical to slaveowners, was discontinued, and the slave status assumed a hereditary character.

Force is the chief support for the slave system. Major original sources of slaves have been through military subjugation and through capture and kidnapping. In societies where the slave status is inherited, children of slaves make up the bulk of the slave population. Legal sanctions are usually applied to preserve the slave system. Slave codes define the rights of and the restrictions upon slaves and slave owners. Some basic protections were secured for slaves in Mediterranean regions through the Justinian Codes. Transported to Latin America, these codes influenced the legal rights of slaves in Brazil (Tannenbaum, 1963). But

English legal systems prior to the American experience had developed no tradition of legal protection for slaves (Elkins, 1963). The result was a system in which the human personality of the slave was denied. Slave codes mostly defined restrictions on slaves. Such basic rights as freedom to travel, to make contracts, to be educated, or to assemble were prohibited. One of the few restrictions on the slave owner was on killing a slave. Because the testimony of slaves against a master was not recognized, even this basic right had no legal protection.

Often support for slavery has been sought in religion. Much salving of Christian conscience was achieved through the injunctions to passivity toward temporal inequalities to be found in New Testament scriptures. And one of the arguments used to justify slavery and the slave trade was to rescue the heathens and to Christianize them.

Slavery in this country was reinforced by the ideology of racism. This was a part of the dehumanization of black slaves that allowed slave owners to talk about equality and freedom at the same time they defended their slave system. If blacks were thought to be subhuman, then they were not included in the purview of the "self-evident truth" that all men are created equal. The economic utility of this doctrine is also a "self-evident truth."

Marriage patterns in slave systems were endogamous, though they were not always regularized through ceremony. In Brazil the Church insisted upon formal recognition of the marriage of slaves. In the United States, however, such recognition was denied. Marital commitments of slave men and women to each other existed without legal sanction and under the constant threat of separation by one of the partners being sold or by coercion of the female partner by the slave master.

For the most part, the slave system permits little mobility. In this country, some slaves were freed by their masters before Emancipation, particularly in the Upper South, where the economic feasibility of slavery was becoming questionable. In Brazil some slaves, mostly artisans, were permitted to buy their freedom by working for pay a certain number of days each month. Even so, mobility was severely restricted in both situations.

Slave systems have been in existence since ancient times. And according to the Anti-Slavery Society of Britain, slavery continues to flourish in many parts of the world.

Theories of Stratification

In our review of Lenski's thesis the emphasis was on the amount of inequality between strata in a society. The discussion of types of stratification systems focused on the degree of mobility between strata. A more basic question is why stratification exists at all. Our discussion of caste, estate, class, and slavery included some consideration of the kinds of justifications that are used to support the inequalities. However, explanations such as the result of divine purpose or the working out of some metaphysical principle are a part of the system they purport to explain. Sociologists attempt to transcend specific systems and make empirical generalizations that have wide applicability. Is stratification a necessary and inevitable component of all societies that develop any degree of complexity

Marx and Weber were the two major pioneers in the study of social stratification.

in the division of labor? Is it possible for a modern society to eliminate inequality? Does consensus or conflict underlie the distributive system in a society? Many sociologists have attempted to answer such questions. The most far-reaching influence has come from theories developed by Marx and Weber.

Marx

Marx focused on the economic, or class, dimension of stratification. He considered other types of inequality to be derivatives of class differences. His insights have stimulated generations of social scientists to investigate the nature and consequences of class, and even those who have disagreed with him have had to come to grips with the power of his argument. Many conflict theorists of the present trace their ideas directly to him.

Marx was particularly interested in the emergence of capitalism in the Western world and, as he saw it, in its inevitable decline. He developed an analytical model that placed the capitalistic system in the context of historical development. The starting point of his analysis is the fact that humans create what they require to survive, that is, their subsistence. In producing the material conditions of their survival, individuals must form relationships with other people; that is, they create a social order. At any given period of history a society will use a particular means of producing its subsistence and develop a characteristic set of social relationships associated with the means used.

In early periods of history the basic means of production were communally owned. The whole group shared in what was produced. Patterns of land usage, however, led some people to claim the land as their own. At this point, according to Marx's analysis, social classes made their appearance. When some people claimed the basic means of producing the group's subsistence as their private property, other people were left without access to what they needed to survive. Their only recourse was to work for those who owned the land, in short, to sell their labor. This new development brought a change in social relationships. Now there were two very different groups of people: one group owned the land; the other group worked the land. Here are the origins of social class. To Marx a social **class** is a group of people similarly related to the means of production. In the situation we have described, one class owned the means of production, whereas the other class did not.

If we push the fast-forward button of history, we find ourselves in the medieval period of western Europe. The pattern of social classes was well entrenched. The feudal lords controlled the land; the peasants worked it. Through their control of the land, the feudal lords could control the conditions under which the peasants gained access to it. One of those conditions was that the lords claimed the right to appropriate much of what the peasants produced for their own use.

According to Marx, the value of an object is equal to the amount of labor required to produce it. The peasants created value with their labor only to have it appropriated by the lords of the manor. Their interest as a class would be served by drastically changing the system that exploited their labor. On the other hand, it was in the interest of the nobility to defend a system that gave them such advantages. Class struggle is inherent in opposing class interests.

Within the feudal structure new classes began to emerge as former peasants left the land to become craftsmen and wage workers in the cities. With the growth of manufacturing, the basis of production began to shift from land to factories. The feudal system, too narrow in its social relationships to contain the dynamic forces of the new means of production, was overthrown.

With the emergence of the new system, which was based on manufacturing and commerce, a new set of polarized class relationships developed. The **bourgeoisie**, the capitalist class, owned the factories and businesses. The **proletariat** were those who had to sell their labor to have access to subsistence. The owning class's pattern of appropriation of surplus value created by the labor of the working class repeated itself in this new context of production.

Workers in industry produced value beyond that required to produce their own labor. This surplus was appropriated by the capitalist owners. Marx said that this exploitation is expressed as the "iron law of wages." As long as workers bargain individually with owners, they will receive only subsistence wages. To pay less means that the labor is not produced. To pay more is to reduce the amount of profits the capitalist owner derives from his enterprise.

Marx believed that unemployment was a necessary condition of capitalist production. A large pool of unemployed workers—the industrial reserve army—made it possible for capitalist owners to pay workers a mere subsistence wage, that is, just enough to produce their own labor, maintain their families, and reproduce workers for the system. As workers competed with each other for jobs, owners could always find a substitute from the unemployed ranks for any worker who insisted on higher wages. Marx said that the only remedy for this situation is for workers to band together and jointly demand higher wages. Out of this union activity political awareness and true class consciousness would develop among the workers.

Because the capitalist system of appropriation (the relations of production) is too narrow to contain the burgeoning productivity of the laborers (the forces of production), Marx predicted that class struggle between the capitalist class and the working class would eventually lead to the overthrow of capitalism and the emergence of the communist system. In the new system the workers themselves would jointly own the means of production and would share in what was produced. Because there would no longer be private ownership of the means of production, there would be no classes. In Marx's vision of the communist society, domination and class struggle disappear with the abolition of private property. The formula for the new conditions of life would be: From each according to his ability; to each according to his need.

Revolutionary class struggle between those who own the means of production and those who must sell their labor to gain access to subsistence drives history from one period to another. Except in the final classless stage, as each new economic system emerges, the new ruling class puts its stamp upon the whole society, creating a set of institutions and ideologies to support its own interests. Marx distinguished the economic foundations of the society, the **infrastructure**, from the rest of the social structure, the **superstructure**, which consists of other institutions and the dominant ideas of the society. The infrastructure comprises two elements. One facet of the economic base is the forces of production: land, tools, factories, raw materials, technology, worker skills, scientific knowledge, work organization, and everything else that contributes to productivity. The other aspect is the social relationships of production, which essentially refers to social classes with their differential access to whatever is produced.

The superstructure is built upon these economic foundations and changes as the economic base changes. The institutional structure is altered to fit the needs of the dominant class. Law, education, government, family, and religion are shaped by the economic forces and relationships. For example, Marx thought that government existed solely to further the interests of the ruling class. His original insight on this point came from a newspaper story about a poor man who was caught gathering firewood from the forest of a wealthy landowner. He was put in jail for poaching. Marx concluded that the law protects the rights of the property owner and neglects the needs of the poor man. He predicted that when private property is abolished and the class structure dismantled, there will no longer be any need for government.

The prevailing ideology of the society is also a part of the superstructure. In Marxian thought, ideas are tools of dominance or the struggle for dominance, and they grow out of the material conditions of life. This is to say that the ideas one holds result from one's position in the economic organization of the society. When one group is in a dominant position, the ideas it develops to support its interests will be the dominant ideology, taking on the form of universality for the whole society. When the bourgeoisie were on the rise, they developed a set of ideas to support their class interests—individualism, free enterprise, equality, and democracy being prominent among them. When they became the ruling class, these ideas became the dominant ideology of the society.

The point is that the nature of the society, its institutions, and its major ideas all rest on the economic foundations and serve to stabilize the system and preserve the privileged position of the owning class. The ruling class encourages society-wide commitment to these institutions and ideas. When the exploited workers give allegiance to the ideas and institutions that support the interests of their exploiters, they experience, in Marx's terms, false consciousness. That is, their values and beliefs are not supportive of their own class interests and do not contribute to their self-actualization. An example of false consciousness would be the commitment of wage workers to the free-enterprise system.

But Marx thought that each system based on private ownership of productive property, being flawed, contained the seeds of its own destruction. An exploited class will eventually become aware of what its true interests are and will develop a set of ideas around which it can unify as a political force. It develops a true class consciousness, a necessary step in its coalescing into a revolutionary force to pursue its interests and eventually to overthrow the system that exploits its members.

Weber

In a classic essay Weber (1946) made the case for expanding the study of stratification to cover three dimensions of social ranking: class, status, and party. Although Weber recognized that these three ranking systems often coincide and certainly influence each other, he insisted that they refer to distributions of different things. **Class** refers to economic differences; status stratification refers to the distribution of prestige; party concerns the inequality of power.

Class. According to Weber, a class is a group of people who share similar life chances in the marketplace. "Life chances" refers to the economic capability for securing "a supply of goods, external living conditions, and personal life experiences" (Weber, 1946). In other words, included are the chances to have food, clothing, housing, education, health, travel, and all of those other things that contribute to sustaining the quality of life. A class, then, represents people whose economic power to acquire those things is similar and whose source of economic power is similar. The similarity rests on like opportunities for impersonal exchange of what one has for what one needs or wants in a commodity or labor market situation. This would exclude slavery or serfdom, because in such situations one is not free to exchange in the market.

What are the bases that determine one's life chances in the marketplace? Weber agreed with Marx that the ownership or nonownership of property constitutes basic categories in differentiating classes. Those who own factories have better access to economic power than the workers in the plant. Further differentiation rests on the type and amount of property that is owned. A large-scale Texas rancher is in a more favorable market position than a family that owns a small subsistence farm. And both of them have a different economic base from a large shareholder of a telecommunications firm.

The kinds and levels of knowledge, skills, and services people have to offer can create differences in life chances and, therefore, differences in classes. A surgeon may own nothing but a toothbrush and a scalpel, but he or she can exchange the skill (market it) for what is needed to make life comfortable. A professional athlete, an artist, and a welder all can exchange their skills for what they want and need. A hairdresser, a tax accountant, or a maid can provide services that other people desire and for which they are willing to pay. Individuals who have no property and who are unskilled and can offer no valued service have very poor life chances in the marketplace. They have little to exchange for what they need.

Weber thought that individuals will compete in the market for their individual advantage. But he did not think that competitive struggle as a unified class is inevitable. He did not think of classes as constituting necessarily self-conscious groups, or "communities," as he puts it. Whether a nonprivileged class attacks the economic system depends on the situation, including such factors as how many people are in the same position and how directly they can connect the source of their problems with the structure of the economy and identify a concrete target for their protest.

Status. President Franklin Roosevelt once brought down the wrath of the Daughters of the American Revolution upon his head when he opened an address to their convention with the words, "My fellow immigrants." The claim to special honor and respect by those whose ancestors fought for American independence was diminished by words which seemed to lump all Americans together as newcomers to these shores. The DAR illustrates the kind of grouping Weber had in mind when he spoke of status groups.

As classes represent economic stratification, so status groups represent stratification based on prestige, or as Weber calls it, social honor. Status ranking is usually expressed through differences in life-style. Variations in the consumption of such items as education, travel, housing, furnishings, clothing, entertainment, and use of leisure and the arts establish a hierarchy of prestige. Members of a particular status group share a style of life not only in the sense that it is similar to that of other members, but also in the sense that they have intimate access to each other. They associate with each other; they marry each other. Katharine Hepburn said to Spencer Tracy, "Guess who's coming to dinner" in an award-winning movie by that name. Although the movie answer was a surprise (namely, their daughter's black fiancé), in reality it is usually someone from one's own status group who comes to dinner.

The style of life that people maintain is, of course, closely related to the economic advantages or disadvantages they possess. One cannot support a high-status life-style without adequate financial resources. Weber recognized that economic power is one important source of prestige. But the economic dimension is analytically separable, and it is not the only source of social honor. Old money carries more social respect than new money, further evidence that sheer economic power is not the sole component of status ranking. The nouveaux riches have always been a slightly suspect group.

Social subordination of one group by another is often based on ethnic or racial categories. Sometimes these rankings become rigidly fixed, and a caste system develops. Type of occupation is a further source of prestige. In the old French hierarchy, for example, a real gentleman would not engage in trade. The merchant, no matter how successful, lacked refinement by the very nature of his work. The social distinction between blue-collar jobs and white-collar jobs reflects prestige ranking. Descendants of historically significant ancestors or royalty may claim special honor. The grounds upon which certain groups set themselves apart and claim social honor may be one of any number of characteristics.

Parties. When Weber spoke of the social action of parties, he was speaking of power rankings. Through means ranging from violence to "dirty tricks" to television speeches and kissing babies, groups struggle to gain the power to make communal decisions supporting their interests. As some groups, parties, or factions gain dominance over others through this struggle, a power ranking comes into being. Weber defined power as "the chance of a man or of a number of men to realize their own will in a communal action even against the resistance of others who are participating in the action" (1946:180). The organized pursuit of power eventuates in elections won or lost or in some countries perhaps a coup d'etat or a revolution, which is a very emphatic way of expressing power relationships. The interests political parties represent may be class interests, status interests, or other kinds of interests, or as Weber points out, frequently a combination of these. Because most modern-day political parties are the umbrella type, with each covering a range of interests, factions frequently develop within them, each striving for preeminence. In the United States in recent times the conservative wing of the Republican party has usually had more power than the moderate wing. In the Democratic party, the liberal wing has had more power than the moderate wing.

But Weber did not intend to limit the meaning of parties to political parties as we generally understand them. Any group that coalesces to pursue its interest in opposition to other groups constitutes a party in Weber's sense. Labor unions, women's organizations, gay rights groups, advocacy groups for racial and ethnic minorities, manufacturers' associations, environmental groups, and antinuclear groups all contend for power to have their goals carried out. We usually refer to such groups as interest groups.

In addition to groups that contend with each other in affairs involving public policy or governmental action, factions may develop in many other kinds of social organizations and compete with each other for power. Religious organizations, social clubs, businesses, universities, professional groups, and unions have their own brand of politics resulting in power rankings that fall as neatly into Weber's idea of party stratification as political parties do. Weber left only brief comments on party stratification, but many social scientists have been stimulated by these fragments to pursue the topic of power relationships.

Marx and Weber Compared

Weber and Marx are both regarded as conflict sociologists. However, the answers their theories provide for some of the issues raised earlier are in some cases very different.

Weber's conception of stratification is broader than Marx's. Weber thinks that class, status, and power, although certainly interrelated, are analytically separable. They may or may not coincide. For example, a black businessman may be in the same economic category, or class, as a white businessman; but their status categories, reflecting racial and ethnic criteria, may be different. To Weber these three dimensions may be regarded separately. To Marx the primary element of stratification is the economic, or class, dimension, as determined by the relationship to the means of production. Status or power differences are derived from the economic dimension; they would reflect the class differences.

Although both Marx and Weber used *class* to refer to the economic hierarchy, they defined it a bit differently. To Marx the criterion of class was clear-cut: the relationship to the means of production. Owners constituted one class and nonowners another, though Marx did recognize the existence of some subsidiary classes. Weber's criterion of class was one's life chances in the market place. People who have similar wealth, property, or skills to insert into the open market to obtain what they require or desire constitute a class. To Weber, classes are not dichotomous but are ranged along a continuum.

Marx and Weber also differed in their assessment of the inevitability of the development of class consciousness. Marx thought that the development of true class consciousness among workers was an inescapable step in the revolutionary process. Workers in industrial society are drawn together in one place and also develop mental contact with one another. They become aware of their exploitation at the hands of the capitalist class, and eventually they develop the realization that only through class action can they combat it. Such class consciousness provides the basis for unified revolutionary action.

Weber would say "maybe yes, maybe no." People in the same economic group may be in different status groups, and this difference could prevent the development of class consciousness. For example, certain categories of white-collar workers and blue-collar workers may be in similar economic positions, that is, they may have similar chances in the marketplace to obtain what they need and want to live on. But white-collar workers and blue-collar workers are in different status categories, and this may well prevent them from uniting in the pursuit of economic interests. The history of conflict between black and white workers is another example of people of similar class but different status groups finding it difficult to develop class solidarity. Other factors such as the social and political context may also prevent the development of class consciousness, although Weber realized that sometimes class consciousness does develop.

As conflict theorists, Marx and Weber agreed that people would pursue their differing interests either collectively or individually. Is this conflict of interests a necessary and inevitable part of society? What are the prospects of an egalitarian, conflict-free society? Again, Marx and Weber gave differing answers. Marx said that conflict in the capitalist society is the result of the private appropriation of the means of production by the capitalist class. He thought that if this capitalistic mode of appropriation is abolished through revolutionary action of the workers, such conflicts would cease. If everyone owns the means of production and shares in what is produced, then the inequalities that characterize a capitalistic society would no longer exist. To eliminate class is to eliminate the major root of antagonism in the society. In the communistic society equality would prevail and conflict would be eliminated.

Weber thought that differing interests are an integral part of modern, complex society and that these varied interests would be pursued and form a potential basis of conflict in socialist societies, just as they do in capitalistic societies. Furthermore, bureaucratic organization with its authority differentials is endemic to modern industrial society. The power to coordinate activities is built into bureaucratic structure. Weber says that a workers' revolution would not eliminate bureaucracy. Indeed, with the emphasis on planned productivity, bureaucracy in socialist society would likely increase rather than decrease. This means that power differentials will persist and can be converted to other types of privilege. So he foresaw no prospects of eliminating conflict and inequality in modern society.

Race, Ethnicity, Sex, and Age

What are the implications of these theories for the differences we can observe in today's society between racial, sexual, ethnic, and age categories? Although neither Marx nor Weber systematically addressed these issues, some relationships can be deduced from their theories.

These theories posit a ranking of privilege and power. Access to the hierarchies of class, status, and power that make up a stratification system is not randomly distributed among members of a society. Racial and ethnic group membership, sex, and age are factors that strongly influence one's placement in the rankings of wealth, prestige, and power. The interplay between the hierarchies has impact upon access.

Marx's emphasis was on the division of labor, that is, the division between owners and workers. How are race and ethnicity related to this division? One among many sociologists who have addressed this issue is Oliver C. Cox, a black sociologist (1948). According to Marx, each class develops an ideology to support its economic interests. Applying this theme to the analysis of race relations, Cox sees racial prejudice as the rationalization used to justify and facilitate the systematic economic exploitation of blacks and poor whites in our capitalistic system.

Racial antagonism, Cox says, had its rise only in modern times, emerging as a concomitant of the development of modern capitalism (1948:322). One of the conditions for the existence of capitalism is the proletarianization of the masses of workers. Labor must be converted into a commodity that can be bought and sold according to the laws of the market—meaning paying the lowest price possible for it and getting as much productivity out of it as possible. The ideology of racism had the effect of justifying the assignment of blacks to those tasks that were arduous, dirty, and monotonous, but necessary to capitalistic production. It also used the assumed degradation of blacks to justify paying lower wages for their labor. Another important effect was to prevent the coalescing of black and white workers into an active, organized, united force to combat their mutual exploiters. Cox suggested that race hatred was deliberately introjected into group relationships by the dominant group. The ideology of racism sets white worker against black worker and binds the white worker to the exploiting capitalist with bonds forged of race loyalty.

Similar arguments have been made regarding the economic exploitation of other ethnic groups. The need for cheap labor has been a continuing factor in the degrading treatment of ethnic minorities. For example, the need for low-paid farm labor in the California produce business has been an important consideration in the treatment of Hispanic workers there. "The lower the wages, the higher the profits" is a traditional interpretation of capitalistic enterprise, according to Marxist analysis, and the degradation of racial and ethnic minorities may be seen as a deliberate attempt to keep wages low. According to this view, racism is a ploy of the capitalist class to advance their own interests and thwart the interests of workers.

Marx's theme of the capitalist exploitation of labor has also been applied to sexual differences. Women provide needed labor at wages that average only about 60 percent of men's wages. Industry and business bring them in when labor is in high demand and shut them out when the demand is low. In addition, women's labor in the household is not paid labor and is not even considered as part of the gross national product. Housework is unpaid, unrecognized, and undervalued.

A Marxist interpretation of the treatment of the aged in our society would depict the elderly as the discards of our economic system. Their productive juices having been sucked dry, they are cast out of the labor force and devalued by the society.

For Weber race and ethnic groups would constitute status groups. With the claims of white Anglo-Saxons to high prestige, blacks, Hispanics, Asians, and other racial and ethnic groups would occupy lower positions in the status hierarchy. Status positions have an impact on the economic and power dimensions, as these three systems of ranking, although analytically distinguishable, are interrelated.

Weber points out that status groups are relatively more emphasized during long periods of economic stability, whereas classes become more important in the overall structure of a society in times when technological innovation produces dynamic shifts in the production and distribution of material goods. The estate system, a status system, developed out of the Middle Ages in western Europe when little innovation occurred in the basic ways goods were produced and distributed. This system yielded to more fluid class arrangements when rapid technological development and capitalistic economic organization occurred.

According to Weber's generalization, we would expect that our society gives more emphasis to class than to status. It is true that in the United States the ideal is that status groupings will not interfere with the open market process upon which, according to Weber, classes are based. This is what we speak of as equal opportunity to compete. It is also true that even though some progress has been made in this direction, status groupings still exert considerable influence over access to economic positions. The privilege claimed by white, Anglo-Saxon status groups has prevented blacks, Hispanics, Puerto Ricans, and others from having open access to the market. Furthermore, as Weber suggests, the formation of class consciousness and class action may be inhibited by virtue of the fact that people in the same class may be in different status groups. We see evidence of this in the difficulties black and white workers in the United States experienced in forming unions. The Reverend Jesse Jackson's concept of the Rainbow Coalition may be seen as an illustration of social action calculated to transcend status differences between groups in order to focus on economic, or class, similarities between them. That the coalition did not quite succeed in doing this attests to the continuing strength of status stratification.

However, we have also seen a major increase in the black middle class. The development of a class of young black urban professionals with a sophisticated life-style is an expression of the dynamic interplay of these three dimensions. We may interpret this partly in terms of the power blacks have been able to exert in furthering their economic interests and status position. So in this instance we can see the intertwining of class, status, and power as they mutually influence each other.

Weber's theory has little to say about sexual differentiation because he regarded the family as a unit in the hierarchies. That is, a family shared a class position or a status position, and he made no distinction between males and females in the family. However, one may look at the women's movement as an example of a power grouping. As a faction, women have united to pursue their interests. The same may be said for the aged. They demonstrate unequivocally the way in which an interest group or faction may use its power to improve its class position.

Issues relating to inequality between racial and ethnic groups, between sex and age groups, and between social classes are the focus of the four chapters to follow. These issues represent groups with unequal access to the rankings of power and privilege in the society. These rankings of class, status, and power may be regarded as ladders. The inequities in terms of who has access to which rungs of the ladder are our focus in this section of the book.

World-Systems Theory

Weber and Marx mainly focused on the differentiation within nations. More recently students of stratification have begun to look at the international ramifications of stratification as they are expressed in patterns of dominance between rich nations and poor nations.

One of the more influential efforts along this line is Wallerstein's world-system theory (1974). World-systems are "defined by the fact that their self-containment as an economic material entity is based on an extensive division of labor and that they contain within them a multiplicity of cultures" (Wallerstein, 1974:348). Wallerstein has contended that from its beginning capitalism has involved one world economic system, though related to a multiplicity of political systems and cultures. For example, the trading patterns that Dutch merchants established in the Sixteenth Century already manifested the inclusion of many nations within the economic system. This capitalistic economy has continued to take the form of a world-system, though there is no corresponding political system transcending states and cultures.

The division of labor cited in the definition of world-systems is not merely functional, or occupational, but also geographical. Areas of the world-system are divided into three categories. The core states are those in which capitalism originated and/or developed strongly. Included would be the advantaged nations of Western Europe, Great Britain, the United States, and Japan. In these states the tasks involve high levels of skills and greater capitalization (Wallerstein, 1974:350). The peripheral areas are those that provide raw labor power for capitalistic development. Generally they include the former colonial states of Africa, Asia, and Latin America and other Third World countries. The third group is made up of semiperiphery nations, which act as a kind of buffer between core and periphery areas. Included are such nations as Portugal, Mexico, Brazil, and other countries that have shown some industrial growth. Some of these are former periphery nations.

Wallerstein contended that the core nations established dominance over the peripheral areas as early as the sixteenth century and have continued to draw more from them than they contribute to them. The colonization of the peripheral areas was essentially an arrangement for economic exploitation. Colonization was an important process in formalizing and maintaining the capitalistic world-system.

A stratified relationship has been established between these three groups. Wallerstein saw the strong national states of the core areas as opposed to the weaker political forces in peripheral areas as "guarantors" of the world economy. However, he also noted the counterassertiveness of the peripheral areas as they reject the forces that oppress them. He states, "Exploitation and the refusal to accept exploitation as either inevitable or just constitute the continuing antimony of the modern era, joined together in dialectic which has far from reached its climax in the twentieth century" (Wallerstein, 1974:357).

Summary

Stratification refers to the institutionalized inequalities built into the social system. The most important dimensions of stratification are class, status, and power. Types of stratification vary along many axes, two of the most important of which are (1) the amount of inequality between levels of the ranking system and (2) the degree of flexibility, or mobility, the system permits. Lenski links the amount of inequality to the amount of surplus the system produces, though mitigating factors reduce this association in industrial societies. Caste, estate, class, and slavery—some of the best-known types of stratification systems—differ in the degree of mobility they allow.

Sociologists have attempted to explain the existence and nature of stratification. Functional and conflict theorists differ mainly in terms of their assessments of the consequences of stratification for the society, functionalists seeing it as principally adaptive for the society, and conflict theorists seeing it as detrimental to the society.

Marx and Weber developed theories of stratification that continue to orient students of stratification. Marx posited the economic factor as the determinant of other differences among members of a society. Weber maintained that class, status, and power form separable dimensions of stratification, though they may be interrelated.

Wallerstein's world-system theory extends stratification to the global dimension, with the core capitalistic societies dominating and drawing from the peripheral areas. He also sees counterassertiveness among peripheral societies.

This chapter has attempted to provide theoretical and historical background for the further consideration of inequalities of class, race, ethnicity, sex, and age, which follows.

Key Concepts

bourgeoisie
caste
class (Marx)
class (Weber)
class consciousness
core nations
division of labor
endogamy
false consciousness
forces of production
inequality
infrastructure
labor theory of value
periphery nations
power
proletariat
relations of production
semiperiphery nations
specialization
status
stratification
superstructure
world-system

References

Adams, Jeremy du Quesnay. (1969) *Patterns of Medieval Society.* Englewood Cliffs, N.J.: Prentice-Hall, Inc.

Bloch, Marc. (1964) *Feudal Society.* Chicago, Ill.: University of Chicago Press.

Bottomore, T. B. (1966) *Classes in Modern Society.* New York, N.Y.: Vintage Books/Random House, Inc.

Cox, Oliver C. (1948) *Caste, Class, and Race: A Study in Social Dynamics.* Garden City, N.Y. Doubleday and Company.

Dahrendorf, Ralf. (1959) *Class and Class Conflict in Industrial Society.* Stanford, Calif.: Stanford University Press.

Davis, Kingsley, and Wilbert Moore. (1945) "Some Principles of Stratification." *American Sociological Review, 10*:(April) 242–49.

Elkins, Stanley. (1963) *Slavery: A Problem in American Institutional and Intellectual Life.* New York, N.Y.: Grosset & Dunlap, Inc.

Lenski, Gerhart. (1966) *Power and Privilege.* New York, N.Y.: McGraw-Hill Book Company.

Tannenbaum, Frank. (1963) *Slave and Citizen: The Negro in the Americas.* New York, N.Y.: Vintage Books/Random House, Inc.

Wallerstein, Immanuel. (1974) *The Modern World-System.* New York, N.Y.: Academic Press, Inc.

Weber, Max. (1946) *From Max Weber: Essays in Sociology,* Translated by H. H. Gerth and C. Wright Mills. New York, N.Y.: Oxford University Press.

8

Social Class

OBJECTIVES

A student who learns the material in this chapter should be able to:

1. Recognize and be sensitive to unscientific and imprecise use of social class labels.

2. Compare and evaluate the strengths and weaknesses of the subjective, reputational, and objective approaches to the study of social class.

3. Describe the functionalist and conflict views of the U.S. class structure and analyze four important differences between them.

4. Discuss how social class is closely related to economic status and describe the unequal distribution of wealth and income in the United States.

5. Define social mobility, class conflict, and class consciousness and discuss how they are measured and studied.

6. Compare the U.S. class structure with that of other countries.

INTRODUCTION

The concept of social class is one of the most important concepts in sociology. Whether they are studying social, economic, or political inequality in society or how members of different groups in society display different life-styles or patterns of behavior, sociologists are likely to use the concept of social class in order to understand and explain what they are studying.

In this chapter we note that it is easy to apply social class labels in unclear or biased ways that may reinforce negative stereotypes about members of particular social classes. To overcome these problems, sociologists have developed at least three different approaches—known as the subjective, reputational, and objective approaches—to defining and measuring social classes. Also, functionalist and conflict sociologists have set forth rather different analyses of the class system in the United States and other countries.

As a result of the class system, there are great economic inequalities in the United States. Great concentration of wealth and very high incomes are at the top, but widespread poverty is at the bottom of the United States class structure. As we discuss later, there are several different kinds of theories that try to explain the persistence of poverty. Some theories tend to "blame the victim," whereas others "blame the system."

Members of a social class sometimes are able to move into a different social class. At other times they may become involved in conflict or struggle against other classes. These two social processes are known as **social mobility** and **class conflict,** and we shall examine what sociological research has discovered about them.

Toward the end of this chapter we compare social class in the United States with social classes in other types of societies. We conclude by taking up the question of whether it is possible to create a classless society. We try to answer the question by reviewing the experiences of Soviet communism.

Loaded Labels

"Middle class," "lower class," and "upper class" are labels most of us often use to refer to particular groups in our society. We also use such labels as "working class," "underclass," or "ruling class" to describe certain groups or to argue a political point. If you were challenged to come up with precise definitions for these labels, you would probably find it very difficult. If you ask a class of sociology students to define "social class" and to indicate who belongs to which class in our society, you are likely to start a never-ending argument.

This is also true among sociologists, for sociologists do not agree among themselves on how to define, describe, or measure social classes. Nor are these disagreements merely over minor details. They are often disagreements about the most important and fundamental issues relating to the subject of social class. Almost all sociologists do agree, however, that *social class* is one of the most important concepts in sociology and that the concept can help us understand a great deal about human behavior and social structure.

Back in the 1940s pollster Elmo Roper did a survey for *Fortune* magazine in which he asked Americans whether they belonged to the upper, middle, or lower class. Roper reported that 79 percent of those asked said that they were middle class and, therefore, that the United States was an overwhelmingly middle-class society. This view was soon challenged by Richard Centers (1949), a social psychologist, who did a nationwide survey in which he added the category "working class." He reported that about 50 percent of those asked now said that they were working class, whereas only 43 percent answered "middle class."

These surveys show us that answers people give in choosing a social class depend a lot on the choices. Most people clearly did not want to describe themselves as lower or upper class. They therefore answered "middle class." When Centers included a fourth choice, "working class," people's responses were radically different. The majority now answered "working class" instead of "middle class."

Also, most people avoid labeling themselves "lower class." Many people associate the "lower class" with poverty, laziness, slums, crime, and racial and ethnic minority groups. Most people do not label themselves as upper class. They feel they are not that rich or high up in society, and they do not wish to sound like snobs. The term "upper-middle class" is more acceptable, because it implies that, even if you are pretty well off, you are all right because you are still part of the middle class. Similarly, the term "working class" is acceptable to more people, because it suggests a class of people who work for a living and contribute to society.

More recently, the National Opinion Research Center (NORC) has annually asked a representative sample of Americans whether they are lower, working, middle, or upper class. The results have been quite stable from year to year. During the mid-1970s the following small range of variations was obtained:

Lower class:	4 to 6 percent
Working class:	45 to 48 percent
Middle class:	44 to 49 percent
Upper class:	2 to 3 percent

Subjective and Objective Approaches

Subjective Approaches

Asking people to choose which class they belong to is known in sociology as the subjective approach to measuring and defining social class. This approach has advantages and disadvantages. The main advantage is that it reveals what people think about their social class position (Kerbo, 1983). The main disadvantage, however, is that subjective opinions are by nature often inaccurate, less than honest, or unscientific. The subjective approach may only tell us what people have been socially conditioned to believe about their position in society. It may only reveal how people respond to various "loaded labels."

Although many people associate middle class with whites and lower class with racial minorities, people of different racial groups are often in the same class.

This is particularly true when some people compare different racial and ethnic groups in the United States. Some people tend to equate middle class with whites and lower class with blacks, Puerto Ricans, Mexican Americans, and other racial and ethnic minorities. This kind of racial stereotyping gets in the way of developing an accurate and scientific way to define, describe, and measure social class in American society.

Closely related to the subjective approach to the study of social class is what sociologists call the reputational approach. In the subjective approach people are asked to indicate their own social class. The reputational method asks people to indicate the social class of other people in their community. Researchers interview various residents of a community and try to put together a picture of how the members of that community define and describe social classes. The best-known and most influential example of this approach was the study of Newburyport, Massachusetts, a town of some 17,000 people, by Warner and Lunt (1941).

This method has proven to be well suited to small communities in which many people know one another. It has provided insight into how community residents see the social classes that make up their town. This approach has also been used in cities (Hunter, 1953), but it would be virtually impossible in entire societies, because respondents would have no personal contact with most of the population they were being asked to describe (Gilbert and Kahl, 1982).

Objective Approaches

Both the subjective and the reputational approaches are based on gathering people's subjective views and opinions about social class. The alternative to these methods is known as the objective approach. The sociologist who employs this method selects one or more objective criteria such as income, occupation, education, place of residence, or ownership of property and then divides the population into classes based on these criteria. An early example of a study using this approach was Hollingshead's study of New Haven, Connecticut (1949). Hollingshead used the criteria of place of residence, occupation, and educational level to divide the city's population into five social classes.

The Marxist approach is also an example of the objective approach to the study of social classes. Karl Marx defined a social class as a group of people who share a common relationship to the means of production. The means of production are the farms, factories, offices, and the like. The capitalists, therefore, are a class because they are owners of the means of production. Workers are a class of nonowners. The ownership of property enables the capitalists to be employers—to hire workers. The nonownership of property compels the workers to sell their labor power to the capitalist for a wage or salary.

Although Marx regarded capitalists and workers as the two main classes in modern capitalist societies, he also identified middle-class elements who occupy a position in between the capitalists and workers. An example of this approach is the model offered by Wright and Perrone (1977). Wright and Perrone identify a capitalist class, a working class, a class of managers, and a class of small capitalists ("petty bourgeoisie"). Wright and others (1982) further refined this approach by emphasizing control or lack of control over economic and political decision making and over the work of others.

Karl Marx asserted that modern capitalist society is mainly divided between the capitalist class and the working class.

The objective approach also has certain advantages and disadvantages. The advantages are that it can provide clear-cut measurements of social classes based on fairly easily obtainable official statistics, and it can avoid the sometimes vague and biased opinions that come from subjective studies. The main disadvantages are that the researcher may select arbitrary criteria for defining social classes. Hence, the objective method may be biased by the personal choices of the sociological researcher.

The U.S. Class Structure: Two Contrasting Views

There are two main views of the class structure of the United States found in the studies that have employed either subjective or objective methodologies. The term **class structure** refers to the classes that make up a society and the relationships of those classes to each other. The traditional, or mainstream, view of the U.S. class structure divides the society into an upper class, a middle class, and a lower class. Sometimes, each of these classes is further subdivided into an upper and lower class.

Other sociologists present a contrasting view of the U.S. class structure. At the top is a small but powerful capitalist class, including no more than 1 percent of the U.S. population. Below them is a middle class of managerial and professional people, comprising some 15 to 20 percent of the population. The rest of the population—over 80 percent—are part of the working class. As Sherman and Wood (1979) point out, this radical, or Marxist, view presents a sharply differing picture of U.S. society.

There are four differences between these two views of the U.S. class structure. These differences hold several important implications.

1. Which is the largest class in U.S. society? According to the mainstream view, the middle class is the largest class. It includes skilled blue-collar workers, white-collar workers, professionals, managers, and their families. These groups comprise more than two-thirds of the U.S. population. The upper class is estimated to comprise 1 to 3 percent of the population and consists of the wealthiest property-owning families. The lower class includes those who remain, between one-fourth and one-third of the population, consisting of unskilled workers, the unemployed, and welfare recipients—the poorest groups in society.

   According to the Marxist view, the working class is the largest class. It includes all those who must sell their "labor power" to earn a living and are therefore employees of the property-owning capitalist class. It therefore includes both blue- and white-collar workers, and many who are labeled professionals but are salaried employees. It also includes the unemployed, welfare recipients, and nearly all of the poorest groups in society. All these groups comprise between 80 and 85 percent of the U.S. population. The capitalist class comprises about 1 percent of the population, and the middle class consists of those 15 or 20 percent who are in between the working class and the capitalist class. This includes small-business people, managers and executives, doctors, lawyers, engineers, college professors, and similar professionals, and others who have higher incomes and greater independence than workers usually do.
2. Which class is most influential and powerful? The mainstream view tends to see U.S. society as dominated by the cultural values of the middle-class majority. The Marxist view holds that the capitalist class controls the government and all other important institutions in society.
3. Which class is at the bottom of society? The mainstream view holds that the lower class is at the bottom of society, because it is made up of those people who have the least economic resources and political power. The Marxist view holds that the working class is the lowest class in society, and under capitalism part of the working class is kept unemployed, poor, and dependent. Virtually all working-class people experience periods of poverty or unemployment from time to time. This does not move them out of the working class; it is part of the fate of the working class under the capitalist system.
4. What changes in the class structure are recommended or predicted? The mainstream view sees the expansion of the middle class as a continuing and desirable trend in society. The Marxist view sees a sharpening of struggle by the working class against the capitalist class until the working class overthrows the capitalist class and creates a socialist or communist society in which class differences are eventually eliminated.

The Impact of Social Class

There is probably no area of social life that is not deeply affected by the impact of social class. We will focus our attention on the impact that social class has on the lives of people in our society. Specifically, we will concentrate on social factors and theories associated with wealth and poverty.

Wealth and Poverty

Economic status is closely related to social class. Both income and wealth are highly unequally distributed in the United States. Those who are in the upper class or the capitalist class receive the highest incomes and own most of the wealth. Government statistics indicate that the top 20 percent of U.S. families receive nearly half of all income (wages, salaries, etc.) annually and own over three-fourths of all wealth (stocks, bonds, real estate, trusts, etc.). The bottom 20 percent, in contrast, receive only about 5 percent of annual income and own only 0.2 percent of all wealth. There has been little change in this pattern throughout the entire twentieth century.

Not only the amount but also the sources of income and wealth differ between upper and lower groups in society. The very rich obtain 80 to 90 percent of their incomes from property ownership (business profits, stock dividends, capital gains, etc.), whereas all others receive almost 90 percent of their incomes from wages and salaries. This pattern is consistent with the Marxist assertion that capitalist property owners receive high incomes, whereas workers who do not own property receive low incomes as sellers of their labor power. This inequality, or course, was a major reason why Marx condemned private ownership of the economy.

The tax structure in the U.S. helps to maintain and promote economic inequality between social classes. Although some people believe that the tax system works to reduce economic inequality by taxing richer people more heavily and transferring more money to poor people, careful studies have shown that this is not the case. High-income families also avoid payment of billions of dollars of taxes annually by not reporting certain kinds of income. Some critics have labeled the tax system a "welfare system for the rich." The popular stereotyped idea that the tax system takes money from white, middle-class taxpayers and gives it to lower-class minorities serves to scapegoat poor minorities and deflect attention away from the tax advantages enjoyed by the rich.

The program of tax cuts enacted under the Reagan administration in the early 1980s substantially favored the rich; the wealthiest of U.S. families received an extra $36 billion in income, whereas the poorest 20 percent lost $1.2 billion. Corporations also receive tax breaks amounting to over $40 billion, most of which went to the very largest corporations (Lekachman, 1982).

Politicians often hold out the promise of tax reforms that might benefit poor and middle-income taxpayers, but powerful lobbyists for the very wealthy have thus far been highly successful in shaping tax reform along lines that mainly benefit the upper class.

Because poverty coexists alongside great wealth in the United States, it is an emotional issue. It is difficult to separate the question of why poverty exists from the question of who or what is to blame for poverty. Social scientists have distinguished between **absolute** and **relative poverty.** Absolute poverty is defined as being too poor to have the most basic necessities, such as food, clothing, and shelter. The U.S. government uses this kind of definition to measure the extent of poverty in our society. Relative poverty is defined as being too poor to afford the things that most people in society have. It is not defined in terms of a specific standard, but by means of a comparison with better-off groups in society.

During the early 1960s, when the U.S. government declared a "war on poverty," the government drew the absolute poverty line at $3,000 a year for a family of four persons. Adjusting that figure for inflation and other factors, the government increased the poverty line to around $10,000 a year by the middle of the 1980s. According to this official absolute measure of poverty, there were about 33 million Americans who were poor in the mid-1960s. As "entitlement" programs (welfare, food stamps, etc.) grew during the late 1960s and early 1970s, the number of poor people declined somewhat. As these entitlement programs were reduced in the early 1980s, the numbers of poor people again rose to about the same level that existed in the 1960s.

When relative poverty is measured over time, we find also that it has not decreased in recent decades. Data on income distribution referred to earlier show that the poorest 20 percent of the U.S. population consistently have received only about 5 percent of annual income throughout the twentieth century.

Who Are the Poor? Poverty is much more widespread among some groups in the U.S. population than others. Although the majority of those in poverty are white, the poverty rate for blacks is roughly three times as high as the rate for whites. The National Urban League report on the Status of Black America (1984) found that 35 percent of black Americans were below the official poverty line, compared with 12 percent of whites. Some 50 percent of Native Americans and 26 percent of Hispanics were living below the poverty line during the mid-1980s. Within the Hispanic population, poverty rates were greater among Puerto Ricans, Mexicans, Mexican Americans, and recent immigrants from Central and South America and lower among Cubans and Spanish Americans.

Feminization of Poverty. This phrase became popular during the early 1980s as poverty among women drew increasing attention. More than one-third of all families headed by women are below the poverty level, compared with only about 7 percent of two-parent families. This higher poverty rate among female-headed families is directly attributable to two factors. First, women workers are concentrated in lower-paying jobs and receive only about 60 percent of the wages and salaries men receive. Second, many female heads of families depend upon welfare programs, whose payment levels are below the poverty line.

Poverty rates are particularly high for black women. They face the "double jeopardy" of both race and sex discrimination. Statistics indicate that a majority of female-headed black families live in poverty.

Poverty is also concentrated among the elderly in the United States. Between one-fourth and one-half of all elderly citizens live in poverty, according to different analysts. Approximately 60 percent of all persons over the age of sixty-five are women. Therefore, poverty is particularly widespread among elderly women. Elderly blacks are also more likely than elderly whites to be living in poverty. Elderly black and other minority women who face the combined effects of ageism, racism, and sexism are victims of what some writers call "multiple jeopardy."

Not only the elderly but also the young are more likely to live in poverty. Children under the age of eighteen make up some 40 percent of all those living in poverty. Finally, disabled or handicapped people are more likely to be living in poverty. Overall, then, poverty is most highly concentrated among racial and ethnic minorities, women, older and younger persons, and the disabled.

Causes of Poverty. National surveys have shown that many Americans tend to blame poor people themselves for poverty. Feagin (1975) found that about one-half of his respondents cited alleged lack of thrift, lack of effort, lack of ability, loose morals, and drunkenness as important reasons for poverty. Other researchers have found that more-affluent white Americans are relatively more likely to attribute poverty to individualistic failings of the poor, whereas those closer in status to the poor themselves put the blame elsewhere.

Cultural Explanations. Social scientists also subscribe to different explanations of the causes of poverty. Those who tend to blame the poor themselves for poverty put forward cultural or biological explanations, whereas those who blame society or "the system" put forward structural explanations of poverty. The main cultural explanations are the "culture of poverty" and the "social disorganization" views. These theories note that poverty may have arisen from structural causes, but they focus on how poverty is perpetuated by the cultural values or the social disorganization of poor people themselves. According to the culture of poverty theory, poor people develop a set of cultural values that emphasize immediate gratification of living for today, a fatalistic belief that things cannot be changed, and a general lack of self-discipline or desire to work or improve oneself. This produces a life-style that perpetuates poverty. Children reared in this culture "learn" to follow this lifestyle and remain poor, rejecting any opportunities to better themselves.

Closely related to the culture of poverty theory is the social disorganization theory. The most influential and best-known version of the social disorganization theory is associated with Daniel P. Moynihan, a social scientist and a U.S. Senator. Moynihan's writings have focused on poverty among blacks, which he attributes primarily to female-headed, single-parent families. In Moynihan's view, this type of family is common among blacks because black culture does not value stable, intact two-parent families, dominated by the father. Black men who are unable to assume the role of successful family providers turn to crime and other antisocial behavior, thereby causing welfare dependency and a "tangle of pathology" in the black community.

Another version of this kind of explanation of poverty was put forward by Banfield in his book *The Unheavenly City* (1970). Banfield asserted that poverty and other urban problems are caused by the "lower class." The "lower class," in his view, consists of those people who are "radically present-oriented" and lack the capability to imagine or plan for any future.

Biological Explanations. Similar to these cultural explanations of poverty are the biological explanations. Two somewhat different kinds of biological explanations can be distinguished. First, there is the view that certain individuals or groups are genetically inferior in inherited ability or intelligence and therefore are biologically doomed to living only at the lowest level of society. In the United States various writers have used I.Q. test results to "explain" poverty among racial minorities (e.g., Jensen, Shockley) and lower social classes (e.g., Herrnstein) in biological terms.

Since the mid-1970s a second kind of biological explanation of poverty has been put forward by social scientists associated with what is called "sociobiology." As described in Chapter 3, sociobiologists believe that there is an underlying "biological basis" for all human social behavior. They assert that there are universal genetically programmed traits of human nature that have evolved according to Darwinian principles of "natural selection." That is, those traits that have survival value are retained; individuals who have those traits have a competitive edge. It is the social Darwinian "survival of the fittest," notion. Thus, if selfish competition is "human nature," it is more or less inevitable that there will be impoverished losers in society.

Structural Explanations. Structural explanations locate the causes of poverty not in any inborn or learned deficiencies of poor people but in the structure of the larger society and its institutions. Gans (1971), for example, suggests that affluent and powerful groups in society benefit in numerous ways from the existence of poor people. Poor people provide cheap labor; their existence creates many jobs for welfare workers, government bureaucrats, police officers, and others. Some economists argue that high unemployment and low wages are "built into" the U.S. economy, thereby structurally creating a large group of poor people.

Other analysts argue that race, sex, and age discrimination are built into the U.S. economic and social system, thus causing widespread poverty among racial minorities, women, and the elderly. Radical and Marxist writers go further, arguing that poverty is an inevitable part of capitalism. Capitalists increase their profits by lowering the standard of living of minority and women workers and neglecting the needs of the elderly and the disabled.

Evaluation and Implications

Biological explanations of poverty generally correspond to conservative political ideologies. Conservatives usually attribute economic and social inequalities to individual differences in ability and effort. Consequently, conservatives regard such inequalities as "natural" and deserved. They oppose efforts by government or others to interfere with these inequalities. Cultural explanations of poverty are generally associated with liberal political ideologies. Liberals usually reject biological explanations of poverty, but liberals share with conservatives the belief that poor people themselves exhibit deficiencies that cause their own poverty. The difference between conservatives and liberals is that the liberals view these deficiencies as learned or acquired and, hence, potentially changeable. If the poor are biologically inferior, as conservatives allege, nothing can be done about it. However, if the poor are culturally inferior, as liberals allege, government programs to modify the culture and behavior of the poor can be established. This is what was often attempted under the so-called War on Poverty during the early 1960s.

Structural explanations of poverty do not regard biological or cultural inferiority as causes of poverty. Because the structural explanations focus on economic and political institutions, they are associated with more radical ideologies that call for major changes in society's institutions. Structural explanations tend to blame poverty on the great concentration of wealth and power in the hands of upper-class groups.

Blaming the Victim

Those who subscribe to structural explanations regard biological and cultural explanations of poverty as examples of what William Ryan (1977) called "**blaming the victim.**" Victim-blaming occurs when the persons or groups who suffer most from a social problem are blamed for causing that problem. Blaming the victim, according to Ryan, is a way of "scapegoating" the poor, that is, blaming them for something caused by others in society.

Ryan argued that all racial, ethnic, and social class groups have an equal capacity to learn and contribute to society. Poor people are concerned about the future and often struggle to achieve a better life for themselves and their children. The rich are just as likely as the poor to seek "immediate gratification" on many occasions. Blaming the victim, Ryan argued, is an ideology that justifies and perpetuates poverty and inequality in American society and undermines attempts to promote social change. Because the rate of incidence of poverty is greater among racial and ethnic minorities, blaming the victim can be seen as a racist ideology.

On the other hand, those who subscribe to biological and cultural explanations of poverty criticize the structural explanations in equally sharp ways. They argue that people must take responsibility for their own position in society and stop blaming somebody or something else for their own failures and shortcomings. They assert that there is nothing fundamentally wrong with the system. The opportunity to get ahead is there for anyone who wishes to take advantage of it, including racial and ethnic minorities.

Social Class as a Life-and-Death Matter

When the trans-Atlantic luxury liner the Titanic rammed an iceberg and sank in 1912, more than 1,500 of the 2,200 passengers on board died. Women and children were saved first in the too-few lifeboats. The official casualty lists indicated that only 3 percent of the first-class female passengers died. Sixteen percent of the second-class female passengers died, and 45 percent of the third-class female passengers drowned. Social class apparently had a significant impact in this famous disaster on what Max Weber called life chances.

Social Mobility and Class Conflict

Social mobility and **class conflict** reflect two different perspectives on "getting ahead" in American society. The first concept, social mobility, refers to the American ideal of individually achieving a higher class position in society. The second concept, class conflict, refers to the attempt to achieve collective or group upward social mobility, that is to raise the position in society of an entire class of people by means of collective class struggle. Sociologists study both social mobility and class conflict. Functionalist sociologists regard individual social mobility as the "American way" to get ahead and see class conflict as harmful and destructive to society. Conflict sociologists may regard class conflict as better for the working class because it can benefit larger groups of people and create more equality in society.

Although social mobility generally refers to changes in class position, it has most frequently been measured in terms of changes in occupational status or prestige. For example, a person who moves from an assembly line to a white-collar clerical job has achieved upward social mobility by achieving higher occupational status. Such movement upward or downward is called **vertical mobility.** Movement from one occupation to another on the same level is called **horizontal mobility.**

Most large-scale studies of social mobility by sociologists have focused on white males. Most commonly, these studies have compared the occupational status of fathers and sons, thereby measuring what sociologists call **intergenerational mobility** among white males. More recent studies have sought to overcome these limitations by including women and all racial and ethnic groups.

What are the main questions about social mobility that sociologists attempt to answer? First, sociologists want to estimate how much upward (vertical) mobility exists in American society. Second, they want to compare social mobility today with the past. Are opportunities to get ahead greater or smaller than in the past? Third, sociologists want to compare social mobility in the United States with social mobility in other countries. Is there greater opportunity to get ahead in the United States than in other countries? Finally, with the inclusion of women and minority groups in social mobility studies, how does social mobility compare among different groups in American society? Sociologists are pretty much in agreement on the answers to these questions, but, as we shall see, they disagree in their interpretations of some of the answers.

Social Mobility in the United States

Social mobility is not as widespread in the U.S. as the "rags-to-riches" ideology suggests, but considerable upward mobility does exist. Lipset and Bendix (1964) found that most business leaders have always come from upper-class backgrounds. Blau and Duncan (1967) and Hauser and Featherman (1977) found considerable upward social mobility in the U.S. but also considerable inheritance of parents' occupation from one generation to the next. They also found that great

Despite the existence of social mobility in American society, these children are very likely to occupy the same class positions as their parents.

upward leaps are rare; most upward mobility consists of small steps up the occupational scale.

Sociologists have also found that the extent of social mobility in the United States has not changed a great deal during the past 200 years. Opportunities have neither greatly increased nor decreased. Comparative mobility studies have found much similarity in social mobility rates among industrialized societies throughout the world. The U.S. does not provide significantly more opportunities for upward mobility than do European countries or Japan, for example (Lipset and Bendix, 1964; Blau and Duncan, 1967).

The amount of social mobility in the United States depends to a great extent on one's definition of what constitutes social mobility. Most social mobility during the twentieth century has consisted of movement out of farm or factory jobs into clerical and similar white-collar jobs. Whether this is movement upward from the working class into the middle class depends upon one's definition of middle class. If all white-collar workers are classified as belonging to the middle class, then clearly there has been a great deal of upward social mobility into the middle class in the United States. On the other hand, most clerical jobs do not provide higher earnings than blue-collar jobs. If the growth of white-collar employment is seen as merely a change in the composition of the working class, then very little upward social mobility has taken place in the U.S. Workers generally remain workers; capitalists remain capitalists; and the middle class has grown only modestly.

Social Mobility and Women

Throughout American history opportunities for social mobility for women and racial and ethnic minorities have been limited. Female and minority workers were overwhelmingly concentrated in lower-status occupations. Since the 1960s there has been increased social mobility for women and minority groups. Although there is general agreement that there have been improved opportunities for female and minority workers to enter higher-status occupations, there is substantial disagreement over how much change has actually occurred. Although some sociologists assert that race and sex are no longer barriers to occupational advancement, others argue that gains have been limited and that race and sex discrimination still significantly reduce social mobility for females and minorities.

The distinction between ascribed and achieved status is helpful in analyzing the occupational status and social mobility of females and minorities. Societies in which ascribed status predominates have relatively little social mobility. Societies in which achieved status predominates have relatively high rates of social mobility.

In recent decades women have entered previously male-dominated occupations in increasing numbers. In the mid-1980s, for example, women made up about one-third of the entering classes in medical and law schools in the United States. Nevertheless, we should not exaggerate the amount of social mobility that women have experienced in recent years. Women still are only about 15 percent of the doctors and lawyers in the United States and only about 6 percent of the engineers. Although women are 81 percent of all clerical workers, they are only 28 percent of the managers and administrators of those workers. The concentration of women in certain occupations has not changed a great deal over the past two decades. Women are still 92 percent of all nurses, dieticians, and therapists,

81 percent of all librarians, and 71 percent of all public school teachers. These still predominantly female occupations are sometimes referred to as "pink-collar" jobs. The earnings of women who work full-time year-round remain only about 60 percent of the earnings of similarly employed males. Moreover, as noted earlier in this chapter in the discussion of poverty, the percentage of poor people who are female has actually increased in recent years. Thus, although some women have experienced upward mobility, others have evidently experienced either no social mobility or even downward social mobility (U.S. Dept. of Labor, 1983). The ascribed status of being female thus continues to limit social mobility for over one-half of the U.S. population.

The Declining Significance of Race?

According to black sociologist William J. Wilson (1978), black Americans have experienced "dramatic upward social mobility since the 1950s." There has been a "remarkable shift in the black occupational structure." For example, the percentage of black males employed in "middle-class occupations" increased from 16.4 percent to 35.3 percent between 1950 and 1970, reflecting "increased white-collar job opportunities for more talented and educated blacks" (1978:129). Although "talented and educated blacks are now entering positions of prestige and influence at a rate comparable to or, in some situations, exceeding that of whites with equivalent qualifications, the black underclass is in a hopeless state of economic stagnation, falling further and further behind the rest of society" (1978:2).

Wilson interpreted this growth of inequality or stratification within the black population as evidence that "class has become more important than race in determining black access to privilege and power" (1978:2). In other words, achieved status has become more important than ascribed status for blacks.

Those who disagree with Wilson have made several important criticisms of his analysis. First, they have objected to his definition of the term *middle class*.

While some Blacks have achieved upward social mobility, others face a hard struggle for survival.

Wilson includes in the middle class all those persons who come under the U.S. Census Bureau categories "clerical, sales" and "craftsmen, foremen," as well as owners, managers, and professional and technical workers. More than 70 percent of the middle class as defined by Wilson consists of these white-collar and blue-collar workers. If these groups were redefined as part of the working class, then the middle class would shrink to only 10 percent of the black population, and much of the upward social mobility claimed by Wilson would disappear.

Second, critics have disagreed with Wilson's claim that racial discrimination against blacks has significantly declined in the economic sphere. Critics point out that unemployment rates among blacks have consistently remained more than twice as high as among whites during the 1970s and 1980s. Third, critics have pointed to a pattern of "learning without earning" among blacks. Although blacks have reached levels of educational achievement nearly equal to whites, they have not been able to translate educational gains into economic equality with whites. Thus, qualified blacks are not experiencing equal treatment with whites in the economic sphere.

Finally, critics have pointed out that the economic achievements of a minority of blacks have often been cited as proof that racism is not a barrier to the advancement of poorer blacks. Critics charge that this is a way of using those blacks who have "made it" to keep down those who have not (Brewer, 1982).

The extent of social mobility among other racial and ethnic minorities can be compared with that of blacks. Some Hispanic groups, for example, have fared somewhat better than blacks, but others have probably fared worse. A relatively large part of the Cuban American population hold professional, technical, managerial, and administrative jobs, whereas Mexican Americans and Puerto Ricans, like blacks, are heavily concentrated in low-paying blue-collar, service, and clerical jobs.

Class Conflict

Class conflict occurs when members of different or opposing social classes do battle against each other to achieve economic, political, or other objectives. The most common example of class conflict is a strike, in which the interests of workers and capitalists are arrayed against each other.

Although many social scientists view class conflict as a rare occurrence in U.S. history, labor historians have pointed out that the U.S. has perhaps had the most violent class conflict of any Western industrial nation (Taft and Ross, 1969). Class conflict may be viewed negatively as a divisive and disruptive force that prevents stability and national unity, or it may be viewed positively as a collective method through which oppressed groups fight to improve their position in society.

An example of collective achievement of group social mobility is the success of labor unions during the late 1930s and early 1940s. During this period the major mass production industries (auto, steel, electrical, etc.) were successfully unionized, as more than ten million workers joined the CIO and AFL. Much of this was accomplished through militant strike action, often accompanied by considerable violence. Class conflict thus improved the economic status of millions of working-class families. A second more recent example is the civil rights movement and the ghetto revolts of the 1960s. These mass movements produced changes that improved the status of large numbers of people of many racial and ethnic groups.

A strike is the most common form of what Karl Marx called class struggle or class conflict between workers and owners.

Class Consciousness

Karl Marx predicted that working-class people would develop a collective awareness that they belonged to a class oppressed by the capitalists. This class consciousness would sharpen to the point that workers would see the need to rise up and overthrow the capitalist system and establish a worker-run communist society. Sociologists have conducted many studies aimed at measuring the extent of class consciousness among workers. They have generally reported that class consciousness is relatively low among U.S. workers and have focused their analysis on identifying the factors responsible for this low class consciousness.

The factors most often cited include: (1) widespread upward social mobility, which enables individuals to move from one class to another and thus lessens identification with a particular class; (2) the ideologies of opportunity and individualism, which are opposed to collective struggle; (3) racial and ethnic rivalries, which undermine working-class solidarity; (4) the promotion of patriotism, which unites people of all classes and thus reduces awareness of class differences; (5) popular culture, which offers various status symbols, heroes, and so forth that all people can identify with, regardless of social class; and (6) the success of the labor movement in obtaining government assistance in improving the position of workers in U.S. society.

Critics of this analysis have countered with the following arguments. First, sociologists who are eager to show that workers have very low class consciousness sometimes employ methods of measuring class consciousness that significantly underestimate working-class consciousness. Second, the ideologies such as patriotism, racism, and individualism that divide workers and undermine the development of class consciousness are often deliberately promoted by the capitalist upper class to control the working class. Third, critics have suggested that class consciousness is particularly high among members of the upper class, who are very aware of common class interests and act together in a well-organized

Social Mobility and Class Conflict 171

and well-coordinated manner (Domhoff, 1967, 1970, 1974; Useem, 1978, 1983). A small, powerful upper class would be expected to have greater class consciousness than a large, relatively powerless working class.

Social Class in Other Countries

Industrial societies in other parts of the world have class structures much like that in the United States. Great Britain, France, West Germany, Japan, or Australia are different, however, in some important ways from the U.S. For example, they do not have as much extreme poverty as the U.S. They do, however, have small, wealthy upper classes, large working classes, and middle classes comparable to those in the United States. Because of these similarities, many people can easily make the mistake of assuming that "all societies" are pretty much alike, that "human nature" is the same everywhere, and that the way things are is the way they always have been and always will be. By examining other societies we can see that there are different kinds of class structures.

First, let us examine the class structure of two Third World countries, one in Latin America and one in the Middle East, and contrast these to the class structure of the United States. Then let us look at two different ways of predicting how the class structure will change in the future. Will there be a steady, gradual expansion of the middle class, or will there be a growing division or polarization between the upper class and the working class, leading to possible revolutions?

Class Structure in Third World Societies

In most Third World countries there is a small, wealthy upper class, a middle class that is considerably smaller than the middle class in industrial societies, and a very large working class. The working class usually includes large masses of both rural and urban poor people. In Mexico, a country with a population of over eighty million, there is a very wealthy upper class that holds the most political power. The middle class is somewhat larger than in most Third World countries but still smaller than in fully industrialized societies. The working class includes many urban industrial workers as well as even greater numbers of rural farmers, who either own very little land or no land at all. Unemployment is extremely widespread among both urban and rural workers and is a major reason why many Mexican workers enter the United States legally or illegally to seek work. Although expanded industrial development and oil revenues have led to some expansion of the middle class, at least one-third of the people are classified as living in poverty. Although there has been much migration to large cities, more than one-third of the Mexican population remains rural and dependent upon agriculture.

Egypt, which is an African country with a population approaching fifty million, has greater poverty than Mexico. There is a small, wealthy upper class and a small middle class, but the majority of people who live both in the cities and in the rural villages are poor and working class. Half of the population consists of rural farmers, and more than half of the people of Egypt cannot read and write. Although parts of Egyptian cities consist of wealthy and affluent neighborhoods,

In many developing countries there are stark contrasts between the upper and lower classes.

the cities are dominated by overcrowded, dusty, poor areas. There are some Third World countries in which class differences and inequalities are not as great as those in Mexico or Egypt, but in general Third World countries present a more extreme version of the class inequalities of industrially developed countries.

Future Changes in Class Structure

Two contrasting views of future changes in class structure have been put forward by sociologists. One view holds that the middle class will continue to expand, whereas the upper and lower classes will shrink. According to this view, the solution for minority groups that are concentrated in the lower ranks of society is the gradual movement of their members out of the lower class and into the expanding middle class. William J. Wilson, whose analysis of stratification among blacks was discussed earlier in this chapter, argues that considerable expansion of the black middle class has already taken place and that further change must focus on finding ways to help the black "underclass."

Another view holds that, under capitalism, society will become increasingly polarized between a small, wealthy, capitalist elite and a large working class. The overwhelming majority of working-class people will never be able to rise into the middle or the capitalist classes. The only way workers can improve their lot is to unite, overthrow the capitalist rulers, and create a classless, egalitarian, communist society. This view holds that workers from racial and ethnic minority groups suffer the greatest oppression under capitalism and have the greatest need to overcome racial divisions, unite the working class, and overthrow capitalism.

Is a Classless Society Possible?

Many sociologists, particularly functionalists, argue that it is impossible to maintain a classless society. They assert that society needs unequal classes in order to get the most essential functions accomplished. Many sociologists also point to the experience of the Soviet Union and other societies that have undergone communist revolutions as evidence that attempts to create classless societies are probably doomed to failure. Some conflict sociologists reject the functionalist arguments but acknowledge that the Soviet Union today clearly has a class structure. The experience of the Soviet Union, however, can be interpreted in different ways.

Karl Marx argued that a classless society could only be established after a workers' revolution overthrew capitalism and abolished private ownership of the means of production. Private ownership of the economy necessarily divided society into an owning class and a nonowning working class. If the economy was collectively operated for the good of all, if people were taught to work for the good society and not for personal gain, and if rewards were more or less equally distributed, a classless egalitarian society could be built.

Many critics have dismissed the goal of a classless society as utopian, that is, as a dream impossible to achieve. The most common arguments put forward by Marx's critics are (1) that a classless society is contrary to human nature, because competitiveness and selfishness will always cause some human beings to desire and struggle to have more than others; and (2) that such a society requires centralized political leadership, and that the leaders will always become a privileged and powerful elite standing over the rest of society; and (3) that attempts to create a classless society in the Soviet Union and other countries have turned out to be disastrous failures.

Defenders of the goal of a classless society have responded to these criticisms as follows: (1) There is no such thing as a fixed "human nature." Human nature is a social product; in different cultures people can be taught to be either competitive and selfish or cooperative and unselfish. Most individuals and groups display both "communist" and "capitalist" behaviors and values. (2) In a worker-run communist society, leaders would come from the working class, receive no special privileges, and get paid no more than the average income of other workers. (3) Attempts to build a classless society have not been total failures or total successes. People can learn from both the mistakes and the accomplishments.

The Experience of the Soviet Union

In 1917, during World War I, Russian workers, peasants, and soldiers, under the leadership of the Bolshevik (communist) party, carried out a revolution and set about building a classless, communist society. Today the Soviet Union has a class system that has come more to resemble the class system of Western capitalist societies. Although economic inequality is probably not as great in the Soviet Union as in the United States, there are great differences in economic status between bosses, managers, and administrators at the top and workers and farmers at the bottom. Political power is largely concentrated in political leaders who are career bureaucrats, administrators, officials, and managers. Profit is the goal of economic enterprises, and many writers have described the Soviet system as a kind of "state capitalism." Thus, Soviet society does not come close to being a classless society.

How and why did this come about? Needless to say, a great many people have offered all kinds of answers and drawn all kinds of lessons from the Soviet experience. Sociologists who still believe in the possibility and desirability of a classless society have generally emphasized the following points: First, the Soviet Union did achieve some notable successes. They transformed an economically backward country into an advanced industrial society in a relatively short period of time. They brought education, health care, and modern culture to virtually all the citizens of the Soviet Union. They made significant progress in improving the status of ethnic minorities and women. They played a vital role in defeating worldwide fascism and Nazism during World War II.

The Soviet Union and China have not created classless communist societies.

Second, the Soviets were forced to act under great pressure from anticommunist nations who wanted to destroy the communist system. Soviet leaders had no previous models of a classless society to follow. Consequently, they made many serious mistakes. They copied or borrowed many capitalist methods of doing things and reintroduced more and more inequalities into Soviet society. Eventually these policies produced a new class structure. Privileged classes took over political control. Although the new Soviet elite pretended to be following communist policies, in reality it moved to consolidate its own capitalistic position in society. Thus, sociologists who subscribe to the notion of a classless society assert that future revolutionary movements could learn from these mistakes, avoid repeating them, and perhaps succeed in creating a classless society.

Summary

Social class is one of the most important concepts in sociology, but sociologists disagree among themselves about how to define and measure social classes in society. The three principal methods of studying social classes are the subjective, the reputational, and the objective methods. The subjective and reputational methods may be biased by the views of the people surveyed, whereas the objective method may be biased by the criteria chosen by the sociological researcher; but each method has its strengths as well.

Social class is closely related to economic status. Great wealth is concentrated in the upper class, but there is extreme poverty at the bottom of the class structure. Poverty is disproportionately found among racial minorities, women, the elderly, children, and the disabled. Cultural and biological explanations of poverty locate the causes of poverty in the characteristics of the poor themselves. Structural explanations of poverty locate the causes of poverty in the characteristics of the society. The former blame the victim; the latter blame the system.

Social mobility refers to changes in the position of individuals or groups within the class structure of society. Although there has been considerable upward social mobility in the United States, most of it has been in small steps. Discrimination has limited opportunities for social mobility for women and racial and ethnic minorities, who continue to be overconcentrated in lower-paying occupations.

Class conflict has been widespread and often violent in U.S. history and has sometimes enabled the working class and minority groups to improve their position in society. Class consciousness refers to awareness of and identification with one's social class. Sociological research has often found class consciousness to be relatively low among U.S. workers and relatively high within the upper class. The class structure of other industrialized nations is not very different from that of the United States, but the class structure of Third World countries is significantly different. The middle class in Third World countries is much smaller, and the working class is larger, much poorer, and still more heavily involved in rural agriculture.

The experience of the Soviet Union has not settled the question of whether it is possible to create and maintain a classless society. Today the USSR has a definite class structure, but perhaps people who seek to create a classless society can learn from the Soviet experience and be more successful in the future.

Key Concepts

absolute poverty
blaming the victim
capitalist class
class conflict
class consciousness
class structure
classless society
horizontal mobility
intergenerational mobility
lower class
middle class
relative poverty
social class
social mobility
upper class
vertical mobility
working class

References

Baltzell, E. Digby. (1964) *The Protestant Establishment: Aristocracy and Caste in America.* New York, N.Y.: Random House, Inc.

Banfield, Edward C. (1970) *The Unheavenly City.* Boston, Mass.: Little, Brown and Company.

Blau, Peter M., and Otis Dudley Duncan. (1967) *The American Occupational Structure.* New York, N.Y.: John Wiley & Sons, Inc.

Brewer, Rose M. (1982) "Neglected Issues in *The Declining Significance of Race:* A Comment." *The Black Sociologist,* 9(Winter):69–72.

Centers, Richard. (1949) *The Psychology of Social Classes.* Princeton, N.J.: Princeton University Press.

Domhoff, G. William. (1967) *Who Rules America?.* Englewood Cliffs, N.J.: Prentice-Hall, Inc.

———. (1970) *The Higher Circles.* New York, N.Y.: Vintage Books/Random House, Inc.

———. (1974) *The Bohemian Grove and Other Retreats.* New York, N.Y.: Harper & Row, Publishers.

Feagin, Joe R. (1975) *Subordinating the Poor: Welfare and American Beliefs.* Englewood Cliffs, N.J.: Prentice-Hall, Inc.

Gans, Herbert J. (1971) "The Uses of Poverty: The Poor Pay All." *Social Policy,* 2:21–23.

Gilbert, Dennis, and Joseph Kahl. (1982) *The American Class Structure.* Homewood, Ill.: Dorsey Press.

Hauser, Robert M., and Featherman, David L. (1977) *The Process of Stratification.* New York, N.Y.: Academic Press, Inc.

Hodge, Robert W., and Donald J. Treiman. (1968) "Class Identification in the United States." *American Journal of Sociology,* 73:535–547.

Hollingshead, August B. (1949) *Elmtown's Youth.* New York, N.Y.: John Wiley & Sons, Inc.

Hunter, Floyd. (1953) *Community Power Structure.* Chapel Hill, N.C.: University of North Carolina Press.

Kerbo, Harold R. (1983) *Social Stratification and Inequality.* New York, N.Y.: McGraw-Hill Book Company.
Lekachman, Robert. (1982) *Greed Is Not Enough: Reaganomics.* New York, N.Y.: Pantheon Books, Inc.
Lipset, Seymour Martin, and Reinhart Bendix. (1964) *Social Mobility in Industrial Society.* Berkeley, Calif.: University of California Press.
Lord, Walter. (1955) *A Night to Remember.* New York, N.Y.: Henry Holt.
Marx, Karl, and Friedrich Engels. (1959) *Basic Writings on Politics and Philosophy.* Edited by Lewis Feuer. Garden City, N.Y.: Anchor Books/Doubleday & Company, Inc.
Moynihan, Daniel Patrick. (1967) "The Negro Family: The Case for National Action." In Lee Rainwater and William L. Yancey (eds.), *The Moynihan Report and the Politics of Controversy.* Cambridge, Mass.: The M.I.T Press.
National Opinion Research Center. (1970–1979) *General Social Survey.* Chicago, Ill.: University of Chicago Press.
National Urban League. (1984) *The Status of Black America.*
Ryan, William. (1977) *Blaming the Victim.* Rev. ed. New York, N.Y.: Vintage Books/Random House, Inc.
Sherman, Howard, Jr., and James L. Wood. (1979) *Sociology: Traditional and Radical Perspectives.* New York, N.Y.: Harper & Row, Publishers.
Taft, Philip, and Philip Ross. (1969) "American Labor Violence: Its Causes, Character, and Outcome." In Hugh David Graham and Ted Robert Gurr (eds.), *The History of Violence in America.* New York, N.Y.: Praeger Publishers, Inc.
U.S. Department of Labor, Bureau of Labor Statistics. (1983) *Employment and Earnings.* Washington, D.C.: U.S. Government Printing Office.
Useem, Michael. (1978) "Inner Group of the American Capitalist Class." *Social Problems,* 25(February):225–40.
———. (1983) *The Inner Circle: Large Corporations and the Rise of Business Political Activity in the U.S. and U.K.* New York, N.Y.: Oxford University Press.
Warner, W. Lloyd, and Paul S. Lunt. (1941) *The Social Life of a Modern Community.* New Haven, Conn.: Yale University Press.
Willie, Charles V. (1979) *Caste and Class Controversy.* New York, N.Y.: General Hall Inc.
Wilson, Edward O. (1975) *Sociobiology: The New Synthesis.* Cambridge, Mass.: Harvard University Press.
Wilson, William J. (1978) *The Declining Significance of Race.* Chicago, Ill.: University of Chicago Press.
Wright, Erik Olin, and Luca Perrone. (1977) "Marxist Class Categories and Income Inequality." *American Sociological Review,* 42(February): 32–55.
Wright, Erik Olin, Cynthia Costello, David Hachen, and Joey Sprague. (1982) "The American Class Structure." *American Journal of Sociology.* 88:176–209.

Racial and Ethnic Groups

OBJECTIVES

The student who completes this chapter should be able to:

1. Define race, ethnicity, and minority group.
2. Know the principal demographic characteristics of the Native American, Black American, Latin American, Asian American, and European American groups that make up the American population.
3. Define racism and explain different theories of the causes of racism.
4. Identify six dominant group policies toward minority groups and four minority group responses to dominant groups.
5. Give important historical examples of majority group policies toward various minority groups and examples of minority group responses.
6. Explain fascism and Nazism as the most extreme forms of racism and apply these concepts to analysis of the Ku Klux Klan and South Africa.

INTRODUCTION

> The problem of the twentieth century is the problem of the color line.
>
> W. E. B. Du Bois

Early in the twentieth century, W. E. B. Du Bois identified racism as the central problem of humanity in this century. Du Bois's words may remain equally true in the twenty-first century, for humanity has made only limited progress in eradicating racism from various societies throughout the world. Although a chapter in a textbook is not likely to contribute much to the elimination of racism, or what Du Bois called "the color line," perhaps the concepts, theories, and information in this chapter will leave you better equipped to make such a contribution.

We begin by examining the concepts of race, racial group, ethnic group, and minority group. Next, some rather detailed information about the size, economic status, and geographic location of racial and ethnic groups in the

W. E. B. DuBois earned a Ph.D. in Sociology from Harvard University in 1893. For nearly seven decades he was both a brilliant sociological interpreter of the problems of racism and a leader of the struggle for equal rights for people of all races.

United States is presented. A definition of racism is then offered, followed by an examination of different theories that seek to explain the cause or origins of racism.

We discuss the fact that dominant groups can adopt many different policies toward minority groups and that minority groups can respond to oppression in several different ways. We examine both the past and present experiences of minority groups in the U.S. in some detail in order to identify some patterns in these dominant group policies and minority group responses.

Focusing on an important topic that is usually not covered in sociology texts, we examine fascism and Nazism as the most extreme and dangerous forms of racism. We analyze the Ku Klux Klan as an example of a fascist organization, and we look at South Africa as an example of a fascist society.

Racial, Ethnic, and Minority Groups

Race

Most sociologists, along with most other scientists, recognize that race as a biological concept is virtually meaningless. All humans are biologically and genetically far more similar to each other than different. Differences in skin color and other physical characteristics are the result of adaptations human groups have made to the different environments in which they live. Nonetheless the most common definition of **racial group** is one whose members are more or less physically identifiable and distinguishable from other people in society.

Although humans differ in some physical characteristics that they inherit from their parents, there is no evidence that different groups inherit different psychological characteristics, temperaments, or levels of intelligence or general ability. Race, therefore, has almost no significance for the sociologist, who is concerned with explaining human behavior and the structure of societies.

Race as a social concept, however, has acquired an enormous and often deadly significance in human societies during the past 300 years. When large numbers of people come to believe that there are unequal racial groups and treat one another on this basis, they are socially defining people as "belonging" to different races and constructing a systematic ideology or set of beliefs. Thus, although race as a biological concept is not a sociologically significant concept, race as a social concept is highly significant.

Ethnicity

The difference between race and ethnicity is the difference between physical and cultural characteristics. An ethnic group is one whose members are not physically different but rather culturally identifiable and distinguishable from other people in society. These cultural differences may include language, religion, nationality, cuisine, or historical heritage. Whereas black Americans and native Americans can be regarded as racial groups, Jewish Americans and Italian Americans can be regarded as ethnic groups. Thus, in the United States the distinction between race and ethnicity means in practice that white groups are regarded as ethnic groups, whereas people-of-color groups are regarded as racial groups. Neither racial nor ethnic groups have any inborn psychological or behavioral traits that distinguish them from other people: there are no innately "lazy," "industrious," "warlike," or "inscrutable" racial or ethnic groups.

Minority Groups

Sociologists have a very specific meaning for this important concept. Louis Wirth (1945) first defined a minority group as "a group of people who, because of their physical or cultural characteristics, are singled out from the others in the society in which they live for differential and unequal treatment and who therefore regard themselves as objects of collective discrimination." Since then, sociologists have generally agreed that this definition implies the following five characteristics of minority groups:

1. Members of a minority group suffer disadvantages or discrimination at the hands of dominant groups. Whereas the minority group suffers exploitation, prejudice, discrimination, segregation, and claims of inferiority, the dominant group reaps economic, political, and social advantages.
2. Socially visible group characteristics are used to define membership in a minority group. All people who share a particular skin color, language, religion, culture, or nationality are lumped together. No matter how arbitrary the characteristic chosen, the dominant groups elevate it to great social importance.
3. Members of a minority group tend to have or develop a strong sense of "group consciousness" or "group identification." Their awareness of group persecution strengthens feelings of group loyalty and solidarity.
4. People usually are not able to choose whether to become members of a minority group. They are born into it; it is an ascribed status.

5. Members of a minority group generally marry within the group. This is partly caused by necessity, because members of dominant groups are strongly discouraged from marrying minority group members. It is partly caused by choice, as group consciousness leads minority group members to select marriage partners from within the group.

Not included in these five characteristics of a minority group is any reference to size, even though the term *minority* implies that the group is outnumbered by a *majority*. Consequently, a minority group may actually be a numerical majority in a particular society. Blacks in South Africa are about 75 percent of the population, but their subordinate position in that society makes them a minority group in the sociological sense of the term. Similarly, women in the United States and other countries are a numerical majority, but most people would agree that they fit the first four of the five previously described characteristics of a minority group.

Racial and Ethnic Groups in the United States

The United States is one of the most multiracial and multiethnic societies in the world. Historically, slavery, conquest, and immigration have brought people of all racial and ethnic groups from all over the world to what is now the United States. Today, changing immigration patterns continue to increase the racial and ethnic diversity of American society.

The United States is made up of many groups of Black Americans, Latin Americans (or Hispanics), Asian Americans, native Americans (American Indians), and European Americans ("white ethnics.")

In the first part of this chapter we defined such concepts as race, ethnicity, and minority group. In this section we identify the specific racial and ethnic groups in U.S. society and survey their major demographic features. **Demography** refers to the study of population patterns, so we investigate in this section the size, areas of geographic concentration, and current population trends for racial and ethnic groups in our society. Statistics presented are taken from the latest (1980) census taken by the U.S. government, unless otherwise indicated.

Black Americans

Just over twenty-six million black Americans were counted in the 1980 census, making blacks 12 percent of the total U.S. population. Substantial concern was raised about the possible failure to count many urban blacks, resulting in an undercount as high as several million. Since this issue has not been resolved, we may estimate that there are twenty-six to thirty million blacks in the United States, comprising 12 to 14 percent of the U.S. population. Over fourteen million blacks, some 53 percent, live in the South, but southern blacks, like blacks in all other regions of the country, are overwhelmingly urbanized. Over one-third of all blacks—more than nine million—live in just five states: New York (2.4 million), California (1.8 million), Texas (1.7 million), Illinois (1.7 million), and Georgia (1.5 million). Since the 1970 census there has been no further overall pattern of black migration out of or into the South.

Within the black population are hundreds of thousands of black immigrants from the Caribbean Islands. The 1980 census included some 253,000 people who identified their ancestry as Jamaican, some 171,000 as Dominican, and 91,000 as Haitian. Adding to this smaller populations from the many other Caribbean Islands, there are at least half a million blacks from the "islands" in the United States, of whom between 70 and 90 percent live in the Northeast.

Hispanic Americans

The 1980 census counted 14.6 million Hispanics in the United States, but Hispanics, like blacks, were probably undercounted. There are anywhere from one to several million undocumented workers (so-called illegal aliens) in the United States, the majority of whom are from Latin American countries, so that the actual Hispanic population could number close to twenty million. In any event, those Hispanics counted increased 61 percent between 1970 and 1980, increasing from 4.5 to 6.4 percent of the U.S. population. Some analysts predict that Hispanics will outnumber blacks in the United States by the end of the century.

The Hispanic population in the U.S. consists of Mexican Americans, Puerto Ricans, Cuban Americans, and smaller numbers of immigrants from many nations of Central and South America. European Americans of Spanish ancestry are also usually counted as Hispanics. Mexican Americans number almost nine million and thus make up the single largest Hispanic group. Puerto Ricans on the U.S. mainland number just over two million. There are also about 3.3 million people on the island of Puerto Rico. Cuban Americans number just over 800,000. All other Hispanics total just over three million. They include between 100,000 and 200,000 people from war-torn El Salvador, a roughly equal number from such South American countries as Colombia and Ecuador, as well as smaller numbers from other countries in Central and South America.

Over two-thirds of all Hispanic people in the United States live in just four states: California (4.5 million), Texas (3 million), New York (1.7 million), and Florida (.9 million). Different Hispanic groups, however, are concentrated in different parts of the United States. Mexican Americans are mainly concentrated in the five states of the Southwest (i.e., California, Texas, Arizona, New Mexico, and Colorado). Some 7.2 million Mexican Americans—83 percent of all Mexican Americans—live in these five states. The largest group of Mexican Americans outside the Southwest is in Illinois.

About one million out of two million mainland Puerto Ricans live in the state of New York. New Jersey (242,000) and Illinois (132,000) have the next largest numbers of Puerto Ricans. While the population of Puerto Rico has grown to 3.3 million, the mainland population of Puerto Ricans increased from 1.4 million in 1970 to 2 million in 1980.

Nearly 60 percent of all Cuban Americans reside in Florida. In addition to the nearly half million Cuban Americans in Florida, there are about 80,000 each in New York and New Jersey.

Asian Americans

The U.S. census uses the category of "Asian and Pacific Islander" in counting this population group in the U.S. It found over 3.5 million people in this category in the 1980 census. This included 812,000 Chinese Americans; 782,000 Filipino Americans; 716,000 Japanese Americans; 387,000 Asian Indians; 357,000 Koreans; 245,000 Vietnamese; and about 200,000 other Asian Americans.

In addition, there has been a substantial immigration of Asians from other countries of Indochina (Cambodia and Laos) and from Middle Eastern countries (particularly Iran and Israel) during the 1970s and 1980s. It is estimated that 626,000 Indo-Chinese refugees had come to the United States by 1982 (1984 *Statistical Abstract*:94). There were approximately 200,000 Iranian and 200,000 Israeli immigrants in the United States in the early 1980s as well.

Some 40 percent of all Asian Americans—nearly 1.5 million—live in the state of California. According to the 1980 census, about 40 percent of the Chinese, Filipinos, Japanese, Korean, and Vietnamese in the United States reside in California. The second largest concentrations of Chinese and Korean Americans are found in New York. The second largest groups of Filipino and Japanese Americans live in Hawaii. The largest groups of Asian Indians live in New York and California. The second largest group of Vietnamese is found in Texas.

Native Americans (American Indians)

The number of native Americans (American Indians) identified in the 1980 census was nearly 1.5 million, an increase of nearly half a million since the 1970 census. California (228,000), Oklahoma (171,000), Arizona (154,000), and New Mexico (107,000) have the largest populations of native Americans. About one-half of American Indians live in urban areas, whereas the other half live on reservations. The concentration of native Americans in Western states reflects the extermination and forcible removal of those Indians living east of the Mississippi River from the sixteenth century to the end of the nineteenth century. The largest group of native Americans remaining east of the Mississippi is in North Carolina (mainly Cherokee), whose ancestors escaped removal by fleeing into the mountains during the first half of the nineteenth century.

White Ethnics

About 80 percent of the U.S. population today is white. The 1980 census counted about 181 million whites and provided a partial breakdown of the ethnicity (nationality or ancestry) of the white population.

Historically, the major division among whites has been between Protestant immigrants from Northern and Western Europe who came to the United States before about 1890 and largely Catholic and Jewish immigrants from Southern and Eastern Europe who entered the United States after 1890. Of those Americans for whom the census identified a single ancestry, about fifty million were of northern and western European origin, whereas about twenty-five million were of southern and eastern European origin. The pattern is about the same for Americans who report "multiple ancestry," that is, ancestors from more than one ethnic group. Over 110 million Americans were reported by the census to have some English, German, or French ancestry, and about 60 million Americans were reported to have some Irish, Italian, or Polish ancestry.

Racism

Racism may be defined as systematic practices and ideological beliefs that victimize any racial or ethnic minority groups. Although this sounds simple and self-evident, there are a number of important issues involved in selecting a definition of racism.

First, the definition of racism needs to recognize both the practices and the ideas of racism. The practices are acts of discrimination carried out against racial or ethnic minorities. The ideas include prejudiced beliefs as well as any other ideas that justify or encourage unfair treatment of minorities. Racism is thus not the same thing as either discrimination or prejudice; it includes both discriminatory actions and prejudiced beliefs (Schaefer, 1979:53).

Second, the definition of racism refers to actions and ideas that are harmful to any racial or ethnic group. The targets of that racism may be socially defined in terms of physical, cultural, religious, or nationality differences. Third, the alleged inferiority of a group may therefore be attributed to inborn genetic traits or to acquired cultual and psychological traits. This definition also includes what is often called "institutionalized racism" (Carmichael and Hamilton, 1967); that is, laws, customs, and practices that reflect and produce racial and/or ethnic inequalities, regardless of whether there is a conscious racist intent among all the individuals involved.

The Causes of Racism

There are many explanations of the causes of racism, but most of the explanations are superficial and unscientific. For example, if you ask people where racism comes from, they are likely to tell you that people learn it from their parents or friends. If you then ask where their parents and friends learned it, you have pushed this "explanation" about as far as it can go.

The two major theoretical orientations in sociology are the functionalist approach and the conflict approach. There are theories of racism associated with each of these approaches.

Functionalist Approach. The main theories of racism associated with functionalism are the assimilationist and pluralist theories. Functionalists assume that shared cultural values enable a social system to function harmoniously. If there are problems in racial and ethnic relations, these occur either because the dominant group does not abide by society's values of offering equal opportunity for all or because minority groups do not embrace the society's values. For the assimilationists, the solution requires that minority groups with deviant values embrace the dominant values of the society and that the dominant group "practice what it preaches." For the pluralists, the solution requires that the society as a whole become more tolerant of cultural differences. Minority groups can thus embrace key societal values, but they can be allowed to retain important cultural values of their own.

Either way, the value conflicts between the society and minority groups can be resolved. Both the assimilationists and the pluralists see no fundamental conflict of interests between different groups in society. No one has a powerful vested interest in racism. Everyone would benefit from progress toward racial and ethnic harmony.

Conflict Theory. This approach focuses on competition among unequal groups in society. Conflict theorists assume that a dominant group is trying to protect economic, political, and social advantages that it enjoys at the expense of racial and ethnic minorities. Racism is thus seen as being caused not by differences in cultural values but by differences in interests. The ideology and the practice of racism enable the dominant group to perpetuate its privileged position.

Two additional theories take the conflict theory of racism further, but in totally opposite directions. The first is the theory of sociobiology, and the second is the theory of Marxism.

Sociobiology and Racism

Sociobiologists believe that a universal human nature has evolved, so that all humans are genetically predisposed to be competitive, aggressive, and racist. Van den Berghe (1978) argues that humans naturally identify with those genetically most like themselves and oppose those genetically most different from themselves. The alleged reason for this is that when we protect others genetically similar to ourselves, we are in effect partially protecting ourselves. Racial conflict is thus seen as a natural and biologically advantageous form of behavior. Van den Berghe's conclusion is that societies that practice racism have an advantage over those that do not. To the sociobiologists, racism is genetically rooted in human nature. It cannot be eliminated from human society.

Marxist Theory

To Marxist sociologists, in contrast, the root of racism lies in capitalism, and the way to eliminate racism is through working-class revolution. Marxists argue that capitalist ruling classes seek to maximize their profits and power. Racism is the capitalists' method of "divide and rule" that enables them to maximize profits and power. Specifically, racism serves the following five functions for the capitalists:

1. Racism creates a large pool of cheap labor. Minority workers are forced to work for less, creating higher profits for capitalists. The lower wages of black and Hispanic workers are examples.
2. Racism is used to divide the working class along racial and ethnic lines, thus placing groups of workers in competition with each other. Workers who are divided within their own class cannot unite to wage a class struggle effectively against the capitalists.
3. Racism thereby lowers the standard of living of all sections of the working class. Capitalists are able to use the lower wages of minority workers and the disunity between groups of workers to drive down the wages of all workers. On this point the Marxist analysis differs from virtually all other theories. The Marxists hold that only the capitalist class actually benefits from racism. All workers, including white workers, are harmed economically by racism.
4. Racism is used to scapegoat racial and ethnic minorities. That is, the capitalists blame minorities for problems caused by the capitalist system. For example, crime and poverty are blamed on poor blacks.

Racism encourages the scapegoating of minority groups.

5. Racism is used to justify and mobilize support for imperialistic military actions against other countries. For example, racist stereotypes were used to build popular support for World War II, the Korean War, and the Vietnam War.

Marxists thus believe that workers have a strong interest in overcoming racism so that they can overthrow the capitalist system. Once workers have created a socialist or communist society, they can struggle to eliminate racism from society completely.

Patterns of Race and Ethnic Relations

Multiracial and multiethnic societies may exhibit different patterns of relations among the many racial and ethnic groups they contain. Relations between dominant and minority racial and ethnic groups may be relatively harmonious and equitable, or they may involve much conflict and oppression. Simpson and Yinger (1972) have identified six possible patterns of dominant group–minority group relations in society and have arranged them into a typology.

Assimilation occurs when members of a minority group are absorbed into a dominant group. Forced assimilation compels a racial or ethnic minority to give up its own culture, religion, language, and the like and take on those of the dominant group. Voluntary assimilation occurs when members of a minority group choose to do this. Structural assimilation takes place when minority group members achieve the same economic, political, and social status in society as the dominant group. Cultural assimilation without structural assimilation strips a group of its culture without changing its disadvantaged status. Assimilation of a small portion of a minority group into the dominant society is often called "tokenism;" it is not full-scale structural assimilation. On the other hand, some writers argue that cultural assimilation must take place in order then to achieve structural assimilation. That is, a minority group must take on the culture and values of the dominant group in order to succeed in society.

Pluralism is a pattern of race or ethnic relations in which minority groups are permitted to retain their cultural identity while nevertheless being incorporated into the larger society of the dominant group. Concessions to pluralism may involve a tolerance of different religions, languages, and customs. These forms of tolerance may be embodied in laws establishing more than one official language in a society, guaranteeing equality of religion, or celebrating various ethnic holidays. Pluralism, in comparison with assimilation, implies a greater tolerance of cultural differences, but it does not necessarily imply economic, political, or social equality for minority groups. A pluralist pattern of race or ethnic relations may exist in a society where there is considerable racial and ethnic inequality. On the other hand, a pluralist pattern may be established or maintained among racial and ethnic groups who enjoy equal status with each other. For example, pluralism and inequality coexist in the United States and Canada, whereas pluralism and equality coexist in Switzerland among the Germanic, French, Italian, and Romansch groups.

Legal protection of racial and ethnic minorities may be the prevailing pattern of race and ethnic relations in society. Such protection may or may not be sincere or effective, for the dominant group may not support the laws and may refuse to enforce them.

Population transfer is forced relocation of a minority group by a dominant group from one place to another within a society. It may involve removing a group from valued land or removing them from contact or proximity with the dominant group to a more isolated and remote location. This policy was, of course, widely used in North America against native Americans.

Continued subjugation takes place when a dominating group maintains a policy of exploitation and oppression of minority groups. Although a dominant group may sometimes acknowledge that it is following a policy of continued subjugation, a dominant group is more likely to claim or pretend that it is working to end subjugation of minorities, whether or not this is the case.

Extermination, or **genocide,** is the actual destruction of part or all of a racial or ethnic group by a dominant group. This is, of course, the most extreme policy that can be adopted. Genocide, as defined by the United Nations Convention, refers not only to the total annihilation of a group, but also to partial destruction and to "indirect" extermination brought about by imposing upon a group conditions that destroy the lives of many of its members. The Nazi extermination of six out of nine million European Jews during World War II is the most terrible modern example of genocide. The United Nations has adopted a "convention" against genocide.

The continuation of dominance and of racial and ethnic inequality may occur under any of the six policies defined above. A greater likelihood of progress toward racial and ethnic equality may be associated with assimilation, pluralism, and legal protection, but racial and ethnic exploitation may take place even under these policies.

Minority Group Responses

In the previous section we only considered the various policies that may be adopted by a dominant group. At least as important is a consideration of what racial and ethnic minorities who are the target of those policies may do. What is the range of minority group responses to domination?

The sociology of minority groups has too often omitted analysis of minority group responses to domination. This is because it has often been assumed that race and ethnic relations would be shaped exclusively by the policies of the dominant group and that the minority group would be only the passive object of dominant group actions. This perspective also assumed that change or improvement in race and ethnic relations would come from the actions of the dominant group and only when and how the dominant group chose to make such changes.

The history of race and ethnic relations during recent decades in the United States has revealed the inadequacy of this perspective. At the same time, it has enabled us to identify more clearly the different responses to domination that may be chosen by minority group members. The responses discussed range from acceptance of inequality to revolutionary struggle against it.

Accommodation refers to the process of "living with" patterns of racism in society. Accommodation is rarely advocated as desirable in itself; it is more often

Many people prefer to live in integrated neighborhoods.

suggested as a necessary temporary means of survival until circumstances improve and a more aggressive approach can be taken. Accommodation usually involves a major role for minority group leaders who seek to accommodate or adjust the conflicts between the dominant and the minority group. Such leaders are sometimes perceived as having "sold out" to the dominant group.

Reform includes several different strategies for improving the position of minority groups within the existing system. The emphasis may be on legal change accomplished through legislation or though the courts. Or the emphasis may be on the integration of jobs, neighborhoods, and schools accomplished by mass protest and demonstration.

Separatism, or nationalism, involves an emphasis on self-help and self-organization. The emphasis may be on the relatively conservative promotion of minority-owned businesses, or it may be on the more radical promotion of militant nationalist struggle against the dominant group. Separatism, or nationalism, sometimes includes a strong aspect of accommodationism, such as when black separatists and white segregationists collude to maintain racial inequality. On the other hand, separatism or nationalism sometimes includes a strong aspect of reform, such as when separatist or nationalist efforts are mainly directed toward producing reform in society.

Rebellion and revolution refer to sometimes violent collective efforts to challenge or overthrow the existing system. Rebellion is usually an unplanned, spontaneous uprising of large masses of people, whereas revolution is a planned, long-term struggle aimed at the overthrow of the dominant group and the government. Revolutionary ideologies usually blame the capitalist system for racism and call for uniting workers of all racial and ethnic backgrounds in a common struggle against racism and capitalism and for socialism or communism.

Native Americans (American Indians)

The population of native Americans in North America at the onset of the European invasion in the sixteenth century may have been as high as several million. Over the next three centuries scores of Indian tribes were wiped out by warfare, disease, deprivation of food sources, and forced relocation. By 1890 the U.S. census counted no more than 200,000 native Americans. When Theodore Roosevelt announced that he agreed that "the only good Indian is a dead Indian," he was endorsing what had been U.S. policy toward the great majority of native Americans. Whereas extermination or genocide was the principal policy toward native Americans, forced relocation and forced assimilation were imposed upon the survivors. Virtually all Indians east of the Mississippi were forcibly relocated in the West. Many tribes were relocated several times. Each time valuable agricultural or mineral resources were discovered where native Americans lived, treaties and promises were broken, and the Indians were uprooted again.

The reservations which at last became permanent areas of settlement for Indians generally consisted of the most barren and undesirable land, thus condemning the Indian population to extreme poverty. Comparisons can be made between the U.S. policy of creating Indian reservations and the contemporary white South African policy of forcibly relocating millions of blacks onto so-called Bantustans.

Forced assimilation of native Americans was also attempted, particularly during the late nineteenth and early twentieth centuries. For example, the U.S.

Native Americans organized to demand reforms during the 1960s and 1970s.

government sought to impose the capitalistic concept of individual private ownership of land upon Indian tribes that had historically regarded the land as a collectively shared gift of God and nature. Similarly, the U.S. government sent young Indian children away to boarding schools. The children were forbidden to speak their native language or practice native religious customs. The goal was forced assimilation into the dominant culture.

Native Americans responded to these policies in various ways, but rebellion and assertion of Indian nationalism have probably been the main responses. Though they were up against the greater numbers and more powerful weapons of the Europeans, native Americans fought to preserve their way of life. Their survival today is no doubt due to the struggle they waged.

Native Americans have also pursued nationalist or separatist goals. They have sought restoration of tribal lands and rights, promoted traditional culture, and encouraged some forms of separation from the dominant society.

Over the years accommodation has also been a response of some native Americans. The U.S. government set up the Bureau of Indian Affairs (BIA) to control the lives of native Americans. The BIA distributed government aid, provided patronage jobs, policed reservations, and appointed native leaders who would work with the BIA. The more militant American Indian Movement (AIM) that grew up during the late 1960s and early 1970s came into conflict with those Indian leaders who were identified with the BIA.

Whether the focus of future Indian struggle will be the separate reservation communities is difficult to predict. Approximately half of all native Americans

Patterns of Race and Ethnic Relations

now live in urban areas under social and economic conditions roughly similar to those of black and Hispanic minority groups.

Conflict theories of racism easily fit the experiences of native Americans. There was clearly a conflict of interest between native Americans and those Europeans who wanted to get rich by exploiting the land and resources occupied by the Indians. Whites justified their own greed and brutality by promoting a racist ideology that degraded native Americans and exalted white behavior as "manifest destiny."

Black Americans

Blacks have experienced the full range of dominant-group policies from genocide, forced relocation, and continued subjugation to assimilation, cultural pluralism, and legal protection. Blacks have also responded in various ways from accommodation and reform to rebellion, separation, and revolution.

Slavery and Abolitionism. Slavery was a brutal system of exploitation, and blacks fought back against slavery in a variety of ways. About one-fourth of all southern white families were slave owners. A small percentage of wealthy families owned large numbers of slaves; many other southern white families were extremely poor. Lerone Bennett (1976) has argued that wealthy whites developed the system of slavery and racism to divide, control, and exploit both blacks and poor whites.

The Civil War led to the abolition of slavery, but it was not originally begun for that purpose. The conflict between two economic systems, one based on slave labor and one based on wage labor, had intensified during the nineteenth century. Northern business interests were not necessarily opposed to slavery; rather, they opposed its further expansion. President Abraham Lincoln's position was similar. After the southern states seceded from the Union, Lincoln announced that his aim was to preserve the Union, whether that required freeing all of the slaves, some of the slaves, or none of the slaves.

Two years of military stalemate convinced President Lincoln that abolishing slavery in the Confederate states and opening up the armed forces of the Union to blacks were necessary in order to win the war. These moves turned the tide of the war. Some 200,000 blacks served in the Union army, blacks made up over one-fourth of the Union navy, and hundreds of thousands of other blacks fought as guerrillas behind Confederate lines or worked as civilians for the Union forces.

Reconstruction and Betrayal. After the Civil War ended, the defeated southern rulers tried to reimpose virtual slavery upon blacks again (the "Black Codes"). The federal government stepped in and put the South under military rule. State conventions of blacks and poor whites were elected to write new constitutions guaranteeing democratic rights. Then these states could be readmitted to the Union. Black-white coalitions thus built new Reconstruction governments in southern states, threatening to destroy the power of the former slaveowners forever. At this point, former slaveowners and Confederate officers organized the Ku Klux Klan as a violent racist secret society aimed at destroying any unity of blacks and whites and terrorizing blacks and whites who worked with blacks into submission.

Following the disputed presidential election of 1876, northern and southern white leaders reached an agreement (the Compromise of 1877) ratifying a betrayal of blacks. Northern white leaders agreed that they would not interfere on behalf of blacks in the South, and southern leaders agreed to open up the South to investment by northern capitalists. The South thus became a region of racism, segregation, poverty and low wages, not simply because southern white leaders fought to make it that way, but more importantly, because the U.S. national leadership wanted the South that way. For example, in 1896, when the U.S. Supreme Court, in the famous *Plessy v. Ferguson* decision upheld the "separate-but-equal" doctrine by announcing that the courts could not make "inferior" blacks equal to "superior" whites, only one of the justices was a southerner.

By this time the great majority of blacks had been reduced to the status of indebted sharecroppers, again working to enrich white landowners. Laws deprived blacks of any political voice and required all-around racial segregation. The still-small number of blacks who lived outside the South faced widespread racial barriers as well. Lynchings were commonplace, and law enforcement authorities not only did nothing to prevent them or punish the killers; on many occasions they participated.

The black leadership that emerged at the end of the nineteenth century pursued a strategy of accommodation. Booker T. Washington urged blacks to provide loyal industrial and agricultural labor for whites and accept their current political and social status.

Soon, however, other black leaders came forward to challenge Washington's philosophy and urge blacks to fight for equality and full rights of citizenship. W. E. B. Du Bois, who received a Ph.D. in sociology from Harvard University, became the most prominent black advocate of active struggle against all forms of racism.

During the first half of the twentieth century, dominant whites maintained a policy of continued subjugation to racism and segregationism for blacks. Blacks mounted legal struggles through organizations like the NAACP (National Association for the Advancement of Colored People), supported nationalist movements like that led by Marcus Garvey during the 1920s, and joined unions and the Democratic party in great numbers during the 1930s. Smaller numbers of blacks joined the Communist party and other radical groups during the 1930s and 1940s.

Meanwhile, a fundamental transformation of the position of blacks in U.S. society was rapidly taking place. Between World War I and the 1960s millions of blacks were moving from rural to urban areas and from the South to other regions of the country. Blacks became concentrated in the nation's largest cities and employed in the lower ranks of the nation's basic industries.

The Civil Rights Movement and Black Rebellion. Between 1954 and 1963 a mass movement of blacks and whites brought about the elimination of virtually all of the segregationist laws that had been erected against blacks. Under the leadership primarily of Martin Luther King, Jr., millions marched, picketed, lobbied, and sat in to integrate schools and public accommodations and to win the right to vote for blacks. Although some blacks and whites were killed by the Ku Klux Klan and thousands were beaten and arrested by racist mobs or local law enforcement personnel, they won the intervention of federal authority in the South and the passage of new civil rights and voting rights laws during the early 1960s.

The victories of the civil rights movement did not eliminate racism or improve the position of all blacks in American society. Most urban blacks still faced segregation in ghettoes, unemployment rates more than twice as high as whites, police brutality and harassment, high prices for inferior merchandise in ghetto stores, and a median family income less than 60 percent that of white families. From 1964 until the beginning of the 1970s these conditions produced hundreds of massive black rebellions in American cities.

While politicians played upon white racial fears by labeling these revolts "race riots" and blamed them on "outside agitators," many sociologists refuted these views. The term *race riot* implies that the uprisings were antiwhite and senselessly violent and destructive. In reality, the rebellions were mainly directed against police, government, and businesses. There were very few instances in which white civilians were attacked just for being white.

The rebellions were not the work of outside agitators. They were not planned by any leaders. The revolts were spontaneous outbreaks usually triggered by police shootings or beatings of ghetto residents. There was widespread participation in the rebellions by ghetto residents, including young and old, employed and unemployed, recent arrival and long-term resident.

The main activity of participants in the rebellions was looting—property crime. The police, national guardsmen, and army units brought into the ghetto, however, engaged in widespread and often deadly violence against ghetto residents. Investigations documented many instances of unnecesary killings by law enforcement personnel, as well as smashing and looting of black-owned businesses. In fact, the methods used to suppress the rebellions usually generated greater popular anger than the conditions that caused the rebellions in the first place.

Blacks in the U.S. Today. Black gains have been threatened during the 1970s and 1980s. Five important examples have been the following: (1) the revival of arguments about inherited differences in I.Q.; (2) the revival of the Ku Klux Klan; (3) opposition to affirmative action and concern about "reverse discrimination"; (4) the rise of antibusing movements; and (5) federal government budget cuts and "Reaganomics."

Professors Arthur Jensen, William Shockley, and Richard Herrnstein have revived the argument that blacks inherit less intelligence than whites. Scientists have shown that I.Q. tests are culturally biased and do not measure intelligence, that major studies of the influence of heredity were fraudulent, and that I.Q. tests have had a long history of being used to justify racially discriminatory practices.

The Ku Klux Klan has received publicity from the mass media and police protection far out of proportion to its size. Its members have killed antiracists in Greensboro, North Carolina, and been acquitted of all criminal charges.

Efforts to achieve black equality with whites in employment and education through affirmative action have been attacked as "reverse discrimination." Federal agencies and the U.S. Supreme Court have ruled against affirmative action programs that involve numerical "quotas" for hiring, promoting, or admitting minorities. Critics of affirmative action have argued that quotas give unfair preference to less-qualified minorities and discriminate against qualified white males who are not guilty of having discriminated against minorities.

Defenders of affirmative action have replied that minorities are not any less qualified, and that privileged white males have often imposed arbitrary and invalid definitions and measures of what being "qualified" means. They have also pointed out that racial minorities continue to be greatly underrepresented in higher paying jobs and higher status educational programs and that white males continue to disproportionately dominate such privileged positions. Thus, there can be no such thing as "reverse discrimination" until and unless racial minorities actually begin to occupy more than their share of valued positions in society. As long as black unemployment rates are more than twice as high as whites', as long as blacks are only 6 percent of all medical students and only 1 percent of all corporate and banking executives, there can be no such thing as reverse discrimination.

The cry of "reverse discrimination" can be seen as a dangerous form of scapegoating that encourages whites to blame their inability to obtain the employment or educational opportunities they seek on blacks, whose opportunities are actually more limited than those of whites. Such scapegoating is similar to the way Hitler sought to blame the Jews for all problems in Germany in the 1930s. The Ku Klux Klan makes agitation about "reverse discrimination" one of its central themes.

Court-ordered busing programs have been in effect in a number of cities since the early 1970s to create racially balanced schools in communities whose housing patterns were racially segregated. Opposition to busing has arisen from a mixture of racist and nonracist motives and has probably accelerated so-called white flight from urban public school systems and from the urban areas themselves.

During more than three decades since the U.S. Supreme Court outlawed segregated schools in the 1954 *Brown* decision, many forms of white opposition to integration have persisted. Many black and white children attend highly segregated schools, and many children of all races attend inferior schools that are failing educationally. Antibusing agitation often arouses racist anger against blacks and distracts attention away from solving educational problems.

Budget cuts imposed under the Reagan administration in the early 1980s disproportionately affected poor blacks. Cutbacks in social services, food stamps, educational assistance, and the like substantially increased the numbers of blacks living below the poverty line during the early 1980s. Defenders of "Reaganomics" argued that such cutbacks did not damage the social "safety net," which protects the "truly needy," and that the cutbacks would encourage people not to depend upon government but on their own efforts. Critics of "Reaganomics" argued that the Reagan administration was favoring the rich at the expense of the poor and that such favoritism had a highly racist impact upon blacks and other racial minorities.

Despite the changes and progress of recent decades, the overall status of black Americans in the mid-1980s was not better than it was a quarter century earlier, during the early stages of the civil rights movement. Black median family income in 1984 was down to 57 percent of white median family income, after having climbed to 63 percent in the early 1970s. It was thus back to about the same level as that of the 1950s. Black unemployment rates continued to be more than twice as high as those of whites. Although blacks had closed much of the educational gap with whites, they, like females, continued to experience "learning without earning." Closing the educational gap has not generally been translated into closing the income gap.

Economic deprivation has taken an increasing toll on black families. In the mid-1980s 40 percent of black families were single-parent families, and a majority of black children were growing up in such single-parent families. Black female heads of families, as victims of both racism and sexism, had the highest poverty rate of any family category. Meanwhile, blacks continued to make up 50 percent of the growing prison and death-row populations in the United States. The struggle for a decent life for blacks in American society is clearly far from over.

Asian Americans

Immigrants from China were the first large group of Asians to come to the United States. They were brought to the West Coast of the United States to work in mines and on railroads during the middle part of the nineteenth century. They soon became victims of intense discrimination, segregation, and mob violence. Laws were passed forbidding further Chinese immigration, barring Chinese from many jobs and neighborhoods, and prohibiting interracial marriage.

When Japanese immigrants arrived in the United States during the late 1800s and early 1900s, they therefore faced already well established patterns of anti-Asian racism. Excluded like the Chinese from many occupations, many Japanese immigrants entered farming. During hard economic times, Chinese and Japanese Americans were attacked for competing with white workers for jobs. Politicians aroused and manipulated public opinion and collective violence against Asian Americans.

There was thus a long history of anti-Asian racism on the West Coast prior to the Japanese attack on Pearl Harbor, Hawaii, in 1941. In early 1942 the U.S. government uprooted 110,000 people of Japanese background, 70,000 of whom were American citizens, from their West Coast homes and interned them in hastily built concentration camps, which were euphemistically called "relocation centers." The justification set forth by U.S. politicians and military leaders was that there was a real military danger of sabotage, spying, and other acts of disloyalty by Americans of Japanese ancestry.

In reality, no evidence was ever found of disloyal activity among Japanese Americans. When Japanese Americans were allowed in 1943 to enlist in the U.S. armed forces 33,000 served. The all–Japanese-American 442d Regimental Combat Team was one of the most highly decorated units in the war. Moreover, tens of

Over 110,000 Japanese-Americans were forcibly taken from their homes and resettled in prison camps during World War II.

thousands of German and Italian aliens residing in the United States were not interned, even though the United States was also at war with their countries. Nor were the 157,000 Hawaiin residents of Japanese extraction interned, even though Hawaii, not California, had been attacked by Japan.

Earl Warren, attorney general of the state of California and later chief justice of the U.S. Supreme Court, explained the internment of Japanese Americans in the following terms:

> We believe that when we are dealing with the Caucasian race we have methods that will test the loyalty of them, and we believe that we can, in dealing with the Germans and the Italians, arrive at some fairly sound conclusions because of our knowledge of the way we live ... But when we deal with the Japanese we are in an entirely different field and we cannot form any opinion that we believe to be sound. (Carlson and Colborn, 1972: 242–43)

The stereotype of the "inscrutable Oriental" was thus put forward to try to justify one of the most lawless actions ever taken by the U.S. government. Japanese Americans lost millions of dollars worth of property and possessions and spent a year or more in crude, uncomfortable camps.

Anti-Japanese racism carried over into the propaganda and methods used by the U.S. government in waging war against Japan. The ultimate result of this racism was the dropping of atomic bombs on the Japanese cities of Hiroshima and Nagasaki in August 1945 at the end of the war. Although U.S. leaders justified this use of nuclear weapons and the destruction of two Japanese cities in terms of saving as many as one million American lives by shortening the war and avoiding the necessity of a U.S. invasion of Japan, subsequent scholarship has cast doubt on these justifications. The Japanese were already beaten and were seeking a means of surrendering before the bombs were dropped. It has been argued by critics that the United States dropped the bombs to demonstrate American power to the Soviet Union. The use of nuclear weapons by the United States can thus be viewed more as the first act of the Cold War with Russia than the last act of World War II (Alperowitz, 1965).

Racism experienced by other groups of Asian Americans has also been tied in with U.S. wars against their countries of origin. Filipino, Korean, and Vietnamese Americans all come from countries against which the United States has waged highly destructive wars. The United States fought to install or preserve pro-American governments in the Philippines from 1898 to 1913, in Korea from 1950 to 1954, and in Vietnam from 1950 until 1975.

The status of many Japanese and Chinese Americans has improved considerably since the World War II years. Japanese and Chinese Americans have among the highest percentages of college graduates of any ethnic groups in the United States. But, whereas there is little poverty among Japanese Americans, about one-fourth of the Chinese American population is poor and under educated. Poverty rates are relatively low among Korean and Filipino Americans, but as many as one-fourth to one-third of Vietnamese Americans live below the poverty level (1983 Census).

Hispanic Americans

Puerto Ricans. Both the 2 million Puerto Ricans on the U.S. mainland and the nearly 3.3 million on the island of Puerto Rico suffer the disadvantages of minority group status. Mainland Puerto Ricans have a lower median family income ($10,734) and a higher percentage of people living in poverty (40 percent) than black Americans. Island Puerto Ricans as a whole have an even lower standard of living.

Puerto Rico was taken over by the United States as a result of the U.S. defeat of Spain in the Spanish-American War of 1898. During most of the first half of the twentieth century, U.S. business interests made Puerto Rico into a "one-crop" sugar economy. Since World War II there has been a great increase in U.S. industrial investment on the island, taking advantage of low wages and low taxes. Puerto Rico's formal status today remains that of a "free associated state," but many Puerto Ricans critically describe it as an oppressed colony of the United States. Different political parties among Puerto Ricans favor full statehood, independence and/or socialism, or preservation of its current status.

Puerto Ricans on the U.S. mainland are concentrated in low-wage jobs and segregated, ghetto-type housing. They experience discrimination in education because of language and cultural differences. In New York and other metropolitan areas they are sometimes pitted against blacks in competition for access to government programs and benefits. Puerto Ricans have worked to improve their position in society through diverse movements ranging from such traditional channels as the Democratic party to the militant Young Lords organization formed in the 1960s.

Mexican Americans. The position of Mexican Americans in the Southwest historically resembles that of blacks in the South. Mexican Americans have been exploited as cheap immigrant labor since the mid-nineteenth century. They have been treated as an inferior race by the white ranchers, farmers, mine owners, and industrialists who have employed them. Whereas the movement of blacks was controlled and regulated first by slavery and then by segregation laws, the movement of Mexican Americans has been controlled and regulated by immigration policies. When Mexican labor was needed, millions of workers were admitted either legally or illegally in the U.S. When Mexicans were no longer needed, millions were deported from the United States and doors were closed.

Mexican workers were heavily concentrated in agriculture and mining in the decades before World War II, but today they are much more concentrated in urban industries. Median family income for Mexican Americans, according to the 1980 census, was $14,765, about $2,000 higher than the median for blacks but nearly $7,000 lower than that for whites. Over 20 percent of Mexican Americans were living in poverty—not quite as high as blacks but three times as high as whites. These figures, of course, exclude illegal Mexican immigrants, whose economic conditions are generally much worse.

Mexican Americans have experienced Anglo violence, racial stereotyping, police brutality, and inferior educational opportunities—minority group disadvantages similar to those experienced by blacks. They have responded in various ways, through traditional party politics, militant nationalist organizations, and union and communist movements. In the 1980s Mexican Americans felt particularly threatened by proposed legislation to tighten controls over undocumented workers, so-called illegal aliens.

Most of the people who have entered the United States illegally in search of work are from Mexico, although sizable numbers have also come from other Latin American and Caribbean countries. "Illegal aliens" have been accused of taking jobs away from American citizens and legal immigrants and of using schools and social services paid for by American taxpayers. These claims are highly misleading. Unemployment among U.S. workers has not been caused by illegal aliens, but by problems in the U.S. economy itself. The hundreds of thousands of U.S. auto and steel workers who lost their jobs during the 1970s and early 1980s, for example, did not lose them to illegal aliens.

Undocumented workers are recruited mostly for jobs for which citizens are rarely hired. This is because the employers of such workers are seeking higher profits by paying undocumented persons lower wages and forcing them to accept inferior working conditions. Employers know that illegal aliens usually must accept these conditions because they face immediate deportation if they complain or protest. Illegal aliens are therefore the victims of widespread exploitation, rather than the cause of it. Blaming them for various problems can be seen as a form of scapegoating.

Legislation that would make it a crime for an employer knowingly to hire an illegal alien has been strongly opposed by Mexican Americans, because they fear it would lead employers to suspect all Mexican Americans of being illegals. This would cause widespread discrimination and harassment against all Mexican Americans, as well as against other Hispanics who might "look" illegal.

Cuban Americans. Most of the Cubans who came to the United States during the first decade after the 1959 Cuban Revolution were middle- and upper-class people who opposed the social, economic, and political changes taking place in Cuba. They not only had the advantages that come with business and professional backgrounds; they also had the political advantages of being welcomed and assisted by U.S. leaders, who tried unsuccessfully to use Cuban exiles to overthrow the Cuban government headed by Fidel Castro. Consequently, many of these earlier Cuban immigrants have done well in the United States and enjoy middle- or even upper-class status. More recent arrivals, however, have included mostly working-class Cubans, including former inmates of Cuban jails and mental institutions. Many of these more recent immigrants, particularly the so-called Marielistas, who arrived during the big "boat lift" of 1981, have faced unemployment, poverty, and resentment in the United States.

Thus, although Cuban Americans as a whole have a higher standard of living than other larger Hispanic groups such as Puerto Ricans and Mexican Americans, there is considerable class differentiation in the Cuban American community today. More than a quarter of a century has now passed since the Castro revolution. Most Cuban Americans now no longer see themselves as temporary exiles, and they have become increasingly aware of racial and ethnic inequalities in the United States (Portes, 1984). There has also been conflict between Cuban Americans and blacks in South Florida. Many blacks feel that Cubans have been favored over them for jobs. Feelings ran especially high after a black youth was shot and killed in a video arcade in the Overtown section of Miami by a Cuban American police officer in 1982.

European Americans—"White Ethnics"

Since the upsurge of black struggle during the 1960s, concern with "white ethnics" has frequently been misused to arouse anti-black feelings among whites and to distract attention away from efforts to improve the position of blacks. Too often it has been argued that white ethnics faced the same problems racial minorities now face and that white ethnics overcame those problems through hard work without special government programs to give them an unfair advantage. This view must be refuted before we can learn anything truly useful from the experiences of white ethnics in the United States.

White ethnics faced far more racism during the late nineteenth and early twentieth centuries than most people realize today, but they did not encounter the same problems faced by black, native American, Asian, or Hispanic people. Moreover, white ethnics often responded to racism by fighting back in many of the same ways racial minorities have fought back in more recent decades.

The dominant whites in the United States have mainly been upper-class people whose ancestors came to North America from England, Germany, France, and other countries of Northern and Western Europe. The term *white ethnics* refers to Americans whose ancestry derives from Southern and Eastern European countries. The two groups of whites are also often distinguishable in terms of religion: the dominant whites have usually been Protestants; white ethnics have more often been Catholics, Eastern Orthodox, or Jewish.

The first white ethnics who came to the U.S. in large numbers were Irish Catholics fleeing famine and political oppression in Ireland. In the 1840s and 1850s, as they arrived in cities like Boston, New York, and Philadelphia, the Irish were subjected to extreme racist attacks. Their Catholic institutions were attacked by mobs and they were allowed only the worst jobs, stereotyped as drunken, violent criminals, and forced to live in impoverished slums. Irish Catholics fought back against their oppressors by organizing many of the first major unions and strikes during the 1870s and 1880s. The Molly Maguires in Pennsylvania and the Knights of Labor, one of the first national labor organizations, were mainly formed by Irish Americans.

Between the 1880s and World War I, Irish Americans were joined by tens of millions of other white ethnic immigrants. From Italy, Poland, Russia, Hungary, Greece, and other countries of Southern and Eastern Europe, workers poured into the rapidly growing urban industrial centers of the Northeast and Midwest. Soon, from one-third to two-thirds of the population of New York, Boston, Philadelphia, Pittsburgh, Cleveland, Buffalo, Chicago, and Detroit consisted of white ethnics.

White ethnics got the jobs at the bottom of U.S. industry, working for poverty wages under dangerous and unhealthy conditions. They lived in overcrowded slums and had little formal education. They suffered high rates of unemployment, especially during the economic depressions that occurred every five to ten years. Meanwhile, their labor created the fortunes of the Rockefellers, Carnegies, and Vanderbilts.

Soon white ethnic workers fought back against this exploitation. Their economic struggle focused around the fight to form labor unions. Much of their political struggle involved supporting the Democratic party as well as socialist and communist political parties.

Upper-class whites sought to control this increasingly organized and militant class of white ethnic workers through a combination of violent repression and racism. From the 1890s down through the 1930s the United States had what some historians consider to be the most violent labor struggles of any country in the world (Taft and Ross, 1969). The upper class and the government regarded strikes and labor unions as illegal and un-American. Workers faced strikebreaking local police forces, private police forces, private detective agencies (labor spies), the

Southern and Eastern European immigrants struggled against Nativism during the early decades of the Twentieth Century.

national guard, ad hoc vigilante groups, and even the U.S. army. Hundreds of workers were killed in labor battles with these groups.

Racism was a major weapon used by upper-class whites in this prolonged struggle. They promoted a racist ideology that is best known to historians as **nativism.** The doctrine of nativism held that "native born" Americans (not Indians, but the earliest Anglo-Saxon immigrants) were superior to foreign-born recent immigrants from southern and eastern Europe. The "new" immigrants were supposedly biologically and culturally inferior and were threatening to destroy the American way of life. They allegedly created slums, poverty, drunkenness, and crime and brought with them alien ideas about labor unions and socialism. Their language and religious differences made them impossible to assimilate into American culture.

This nativist movement grew stronger and stronger during the first two decades of the twentieth century. It had far-reaching goals, which included the following: (1) immigration laws, with quotas limiting entrance into the United States of persons from "inferior" races and nationalities; (2) deportation from the United States of "undesirable" and "subversive" persons; (3) laws prohibiting interracial marriage, i.e., antimiscegenation laws; (4) laws mandating sterilization of "feebleminded" and other "inferior" persons, so that they would not "breed more of their kind;" (5) laws and policies to prevent or eliminate labor unions and socialist or communist political parties; (6) promotion of eugenics, the supposedly scientific effort to breed a so-called master race, by encouraging breeding among "superior" races and discouraging breeding among "inferior" races; and (7) encouraging a revival of vigilante organizations such as the Ku Klux Klan to terrorize groups opposed to or victimized by nativism.

By the 1920s all of the above goals of the nativist movement had been achieved in the United States. In the early 1920s the U.S. Congress, following recommendations of the Dillingham Commission, adopted new immigration laws that explicitly discriminated against future immigrants from southern and eastern Europe, Africa, and Asia. The door was left open to import cheap labor from Central and South America, to offset a possible labor shortage that might be caused by cutting off immigration from other continents. From 1919 to 1920 the Justice Department conducted the infamous Palmer Raids, illegally seizing thousands of immigrant workers in coordinated raids, holding them arbitrarily, and deporting hundreds from the United States without any due process. Most of those singled out for deportation had been labor union leaders and political activists.

By the end of the 1920s most states in the United States had adopted both laws prohibiting interracial marriage and laws permitting forced sterilization of those designated as the feebleminded, the criminally insane, paupers, and prostitutes. Earlier, during and just after World War I, the U.S. government imprisoned leaders of the Socialist party, the Industrial Workers of the World, and other radical political organizations. Congress had passed legislation making it illegal to speak out against World War I and the draft. Socialists who denounced the war as a capitalist and imperialist war and urged the working class not to support it were arrested and imprisoned.

During the 1920s the United States became a world leader in the promotion of eugenics. National organizations grew up, international conferences were held, books and journals were published, and eugenics became a standard part of the college and medical school curriculum in the United States. By the 1930s the eugenics movement was the common cause that found support in the United States, Great Britain, fascist Italy, and Nazi Germany (Chase, 1977).

The nativist movement was so successful in the United States because it had the support of top political, business, and educational leaders. An example of the support of political leaders was President Calvin Coolidge, who signed the Immigration Restriction Act into law in 1924. Coolidge had in 1921 as vice-president written an article for *Good Housekeeping* magazine titled "Whose Country Is This?" in which he answered this question by asserting:

> There are racial considerations too grave to be brushed aside for any sentimental reasons. Biological laws tell us that certain divergent people will not mix or blend. The Nordics propagate themselves successfully. With other races, the outcome shows deterioration on both sides. Quality of mind and body suggests that observance of ethnic laws is as great a necessity to a nation as immigration law. (Carlson and Colborn, 1972:343)

Support for nativism also came from the highest levels of American business. Rockefeller and Carnegie and the foundations they established provided the funding for eugenics research, publications, and conferences. The corporate owners whose fortunes were made from white ethnic labor were also the so-called philanthropists who funded the movement that attacked white ethnic workers and justified their exploitation.

Finally, nativism had the support of educational leaders. The top professors and university presidents from such institutions as Harvard, Princeton, and Stanford contributed to the nativist movements by providing "scientific proof" of the racial inferiority of white ethnics and other minority groups. The major contribution to nativism from university scholars was the I.Q. test. Test results were used during the 1910s and 1920s as "proof" of the innate inferiority of white ethnics, blacks, Hispanics, native Americans, and Asian Americans, and therefore as justification for all of the racist programs instituted by the nativist movement.

The most influential scientists associated with early I.Q. testing all contributed directly to the cause of nativism. Lewis Terman of Stanford introduced the Stanford-Binet I.Q. test and argued that the test proved that black, Mexican, and white ethnic children had lower intelligence and therefore should receive only education that would prepare them for menial occupations. Henry Goddard of Princeton was hired by the U.S. Public Health Service to administer I.Q. tests to white ethnic immigrants arriving at Ellis Island in New York harbor. Goddard reported in 1916 that he had found some 80 percent of the Catholic and Jewish immigrants from Russia, Poland, Hungary, and other eastern European countries to be "feebleminded," and that his testing had led to a vast increase in the deportation of such feebleminded aliens. Robert Yerkes of Harvard headed a team of scientists chosen by the U.S. government in 1917 to administer I.Q. tests to the millions of Americans drafted into the armed forces during World War I. Yerkes and his associates testified before Congress in the early 1920s in favor of immigration quotas, asserting that his testing program had shown that white ethnic immigrants were nearly as inferior as the non-European minority groups found in the United States (Kamin, 1974; Chase, 1977; Carlson and Colburn, 1972).

This pattern of racism kept white ethnics in a severely oppressed position in U.S. society until the 1930s. During the decade of the Great Depression white ethnic workers led the fight for unionization in basic industries, achieving a level of class solidarity that overcame racial and ethnic divisions. Sit-down strikes, mass marches and demonstrations, and violent confrontations were commonplace. The Communist party played a prominent part in many of these actions.

After World War II, blacks and Hispanics began to replace white ethnics on the lower levels of American industry and also in the inner-city ghettoes and neighborhoods. Many white ethnics became middle-class suburbanites, but many others have remained within the working class. The gap between white ethnics and other whites has closed considerably, but not completely. The sharp racism that was previously directed against white ethnics is now primarily directed against black and Hispanic groups.

Comparisons between the experiences of white ethnics and racial minorities yield important insights into the nature of racism in American society. First, for nearly half a century white ethnics experienced racist victimization that was in many ways similar to that experienced by racial minorities. Moreover, the same people were responsible for racism against both groups. For example, the same I.Q. tests that have been used to attack blacks and Hispanics were used for decades to "prove" the inferiority of white ethnics.

Second, white ethnics turned to many of the same militant and radical methods of fighting back that racial minorities have adopted since the 1960s. Third, because racial minority groups have experienced more brutal and longer-lasting racism than white ethnics have experienced, one should expect the struggle of racial minorities to be even harder than was that of white ethnics. If white ethnics and racial minorities acquire a better understanding of both the similarities and the differences in their experiences, relations among them will no doubt improve considerably.

Fascism and Nazism

The most extreme and deadly form of racism in modern societies is fascism or Nazism. These two terms mean basically the same thing. Fascism refers to the repressive system established in Italy under Mussolini in 1922, and Nazism refers to the system set up under Hitler in Germany in 1933. Both regimes were destroyed in World War II. Fascism may be defined as a violently racist, nationalistic regime under which people have few rights and the government's rule by force faces few limits. Although there have been many kinds of repressive governments throughout human history, fascism as such is a twentieth-century phenomenon that evolved after World War I.

Although fascism arose in Italy and Nazism in Germany, they have not been limited to those two countries. Fascist movements have appeared essentially in every country in the world, and during World War II fascist rule was extended to a majority of the world's nations.

Fascists subscribe to the most crudely racist ideologies and attack racial minorities for whatever problems exist in society. The target may be Jews in Germany, blacks in the United States, Koreans in Japan, or Asians and West Indians in Great Britain. Fascists promote the most extreme and fanatical nationalism or patriotism. Fascists also promote the most extreme and violent anticommunism.

There is a logical connection between the racism, nationalism, and anticommunism of fascist movements and governments. Twentieth-century capitalist societies have been profoundly threatened by communist-led working-class movements. This threat has been greatest during the crises created by world wars or worldwide economic depressions. Communist parties have attempted to create international and interracial working class unity against the capitalist system. Fascist movements have tried to do just the opposite. They have attacked communist governments, and they have promoted divisions within the working class by building nationalism and racism. Communism and fascism are sometimes mistakenly portrayed as being essentially the same, because they are both violent; however, they are actually violently opposed to each other. Fascism seeks the preservation of capitalism at all costs; communism seeks the overthrow of capitalism.

Fascist movements have existed in the United States during much of the twentieth century. The nativist movement analyzed earlier in this chapter displayed many of the characteristics of a fascist movement. It is thus no accident that many nativist leaders enjoyed friendly relations with Nazi Germany and fascist Italy. Similarly, the Ku Klux Klan can better be understood as not only a violently racist organization but as a fascist organization as well.

The Ku Klux Klan that was revived in 1915 was different in several important ways from the Klan that was organized after the Civil War to destroy Reconstruction. The twentieth-century Klan's racism was not only directed against blacks but also against Jews, Catholics, other white ethnics, and other racial minorities. It also was no longer just a southern rural organization. When the Klan's membership grew to several million during the early 1920s, it was strong in all regions of the country, and it was concentrated more in urban than in rural areas.

In addition to this broadened racism, the Klan also emphasized patriotism, anti-unionism, and anticommunism. During World War I the Klan attacked Americans who were opposed to U.S. involvement in the war, attacked workers' strikes, and condemned socialists and communists. During the 1930s the Klan formed an alliance with Nazi and fascist groups in the United States. During the 1950s and 1960s the Klan denounced integration as a "communist plot," thus combining its racism and anticommunism. Even more recently, in 1979 the Klan joined with Nazis to murder five members of the Communist Workers Party in Greensboro, North Carolina. Other violently racist Nazi-type groups have been active in the United States during the 1980s.

An example of a fascist government in the world today is South Africa. In South Africa all political power is in the hands of the 13 percent of the population that is white. Blacks, who make up about 75 percent of the population, have no rights whatsoever, and the remaining "coloured" (mixed-race) and Asian populations have very limited rights. Under the system of apartheid (which means "separate development") blacks are not even regarded as citizens in the land that was taken from them by Dutch and English colonial invaders during the late nineteenth century. Eighty-seven percent of the land—including all good farmland, mineral wealth, and urban areas—is reserved for the whites. The remaining 13 percent—the most barren land—is divided into reservations called Bantustans.

Blacks are allowed in the white areas only to provide cheap labor for the whites. Blacks do all of the heavy and dangerous labor in the gold mines, industries, and farms, as well as in the homes of the whites. Black workers typically earn about one-sixteenth of the wages paid to whites. Laws prohibit a black worker from being in any position of authority or supervision over a white. Blacks who work in the white areas must return to their segregated townships at the end of their shifts. These townships (like Soweto, with a population of some 1.5 million) are the world's largest and most oppressive black ghettoes. Black domestic workers must by law live in a separate detached dwelling and not under the same roof as the white family they serve.

Black workers are unable to have other members of their families live with them. Most black workers must live in single-sex barracks and can only see their spouses or children once a year. Black children, workers without jobs, or elderly blacks are forced to live on the Bantustans, often hundreds of miles away. All blacks must carry passports that indicate where they are allowed to be. Each year hundreds of thousands of blacks are arrested for violations of the passport laws.

This system of apartheid enables employers in South Africa to exploit black workers as the cheapest, most tightly controlled labor in the world. The exploitation is so severe that between one-third and one-half of all black children in South Africa die of malnutrition and disease before their fifth birthday. Meanwhile, white South Africans enjoy one of the highest standards of living in the world.

Because of the high profits that can be made from cheap black labor, multinational corporations and banks have invested heavily in South Africa. Some 400 U.S. corporations, including most of the largest corporations, have factories, assembly lines, and offices in South Africa worth several billion dollars. U.S. banks also have several billion dollars invested in South Africa. The United States has

The system of *apartheid* in South Africa, in which Blacks have few political rights, is an example of a fascist political system.

for years been South Africa's largest trading partner as well. Although U.S. businesspeople claim that their presence in South Africa helps blacks to break down the system of apartheid, the evidence suggests just the opposite.

Whereas South Africa is more or less a democracy for whites, it is essentially a fascist dictatorship for blacks. Those whites who oppose the system also have their rights taken away. It is against the law in South Africa to advocate racial equality and integration. Laws such as the Suppression of Terrorism and Suppression of Communism acts enable the government to crack down on any protest or dissent.

Despite this enormous repression, there has been widespread protest and rebellion in South Africa. Nonviolent resistance was widespread in the late 1950s, but resistance became violent when black rebellion developed in the 1970s, with workers and students engaged in massive strikes and uprisings. These actions continued for several months; the government killed several hundred blacks in the process of suppressing the uprisings. In the mid-1980s, protest and rebellion became even more widespread, and anti-apartheid activity became a mass movement in the United States as well. It appeared that South Africa might become engulfed in all-out revolutionary civil war.

Comparing South Africa with the United States yields insights into patterns of racism in both countries. Racism, inequality, and oppression are obviously far more severe in South Africa than in the United States, and the racial composition of the populations is very different. Also, the South African government fully supports racism, whereas the U.S. government's position is more mixed. Still, there are also some significant similarities. Economic exploitation severely threatens black family life in the U.S. as well as in South Africa. Racial minorities in the U.S. live largely in segregated housing. Native Americans were forcibly relocated on Bantustans called reservations when whites took their land. Mexicans are exploited as cheap migrant labor and deported back to their homeland, as South African blacks are. Finally, many of the same businesses that make high profits from racism in South Africa also exploit minority labor in the United States.

Summary

Racial groups are physically distinguishable, whereas ethnic groups are culturally distinguishable. Minority groups are self-conscious, socially defined groups that suffer disadvantages at the hands of dominant groups in society. Racism consists of practices and ideas that victimize racial and/or ethnic minority groups.

There are different sociological theories of the causes of racism. Functionalist theories emphasize cultural assimilation or pluralism, whereas conflict theories emphasize competition between groups with different interests.

There are a great number of racial and ethnic minorities in American society. Most are socially and geographically segregated and suffer economic disadvantages. Dominant groups may pursue different policies toward minority groups, and minority groups may respond to the dominant group in different ways. The history of minority groups shows that they have been victims of many oppressive dominant-group policies and that they have responded in several different ways to that oppression. Fascism and Nazism are the most extreme forms of racism. The Ku Klux Klan and South Africa are examples of fascism.

Key Concepts

accommodation	demography
apartheid	ethnicity
assimilation	eugenics
continued subjugation	fascism

> genocide
> minority group
> nativism
> Nazism
> pluralism
> separatism
> population transfer
> race
> racism
> reverse discrimination
> scapegoating

References

Alperovitz, Gar. (1965) *Atomic Diplomacy: Hiroshima and Potsdam.* New York, N.Y.: Simon & Schuster, Inc.

Bennett, Lerone, Jr. (1970) "The Road Not Taken." *Ebony,* August 71–77.

Block, N. J., and Gerald Dworkin. (1976) *The I.Q. Controversy.* New York, N.Y.: Pantheon Books, Inc.

Boyer, Richard O., and Herbert M. Morais. (1970) *Labor's Untold Story.* 3rd ed. New York, N.Y.: United Electrical Workers of America (UE).

Carlson, Lewis H., and George A. Colborn (eds.). (1972) *In Their Place: White America Defines her Minorities, 1850–1950.* New York, N.Y.: John Wiley & Sons, Inc.

Carmichael, Stokely, and Charles V. Hamilton. (1967) *Black Power: The Politics of Liberation in America.* New York: Random House, Inc.

Carsten, F. L. (1971) *The Rise of Fascism.* Berkeley: University of California Press.

Chalmers, David M. (1965) *Hooded Americanism.* Garden City, N.Y.: Doubleday & Company, Inc.

Chase, Allan. (1977) *The Legacy of Malthus: The Social Costs of the New Scientific Racism.* New York, N.Y.: Alfred A. Knopf, Inc.

Cherny, Robert. (1977) "Economic Theories of Racism." In *Problems in Political Economy.* 2d ed. David M. Gordon (ed.), Lexington, Mass.: D. C. Heath & Co., 170–82.

Cox, Oliver. (1970) *Caste, Class, and Race.* New York, N.Y.: Monthly Review Press.

Feagin, Joe R. (1984) *Racial and Ethnic Relations.* 2d ed. Englewood Cliffs, N.J.: Prentice-Hall, Inc.

Fitzpatrick, Joseph P. (1971) *Puerto Rican Americans.* Englewood Cliffs, N.J.: Prentice-Hall, Inc.

Foster, William Z. (1954) *The Negro People in American History.* New York, N.Y.: International Publishers.

Geschwender, James. (1978) *Racial Stratification in America.* Dubuque, Ia.: William C. Brown Company, Publishers.

Higham, John. (1975) *Strangers in the Land, Patterns of American Nativism, 1860–1925.* New York, N.Y.: Atheneum Publishers.

Jones, Faustine Childress. (1977) *The Changing Mood in America, Eroding Commitment?* Washington, D.C.: Howard University Press.

Kamin, Leon. (1974) *The Science and Politics of I.Q.* New York, N.Y.: Halstead Press.

Moore, Joan W. (1976) *Mexican Americans.* 2d ed. Englewood Cliffs, N.J.: Prentice-Hall, Inc.

Perlo, Victor. (1975) *Economics of Racism.* New York, N.Y.: International Publishers.

Pinkney, Alphonso. (1975) *Black Americans.* 2d ed. Englewood Cliffs, N.J.: Prentice-Hall, Inc.

Portes, Alejandro. (1984) "The Rise of Ethnicity," *American Sociological Review,* Vol 49, (June) 383–397.

Reich, Michael. (1981) *Racial Inequality.* Princeton, N.J.: Princeton University Press.

Schaefer, Richard T. (1979) *Racial and Ethnic Groups* Boston: Little, Brown, and Company.

Sherman, Howard J., and James L. Wood. (1979) *Sociology: Traditional and Radical Perspectives.* New York, N.Y.: Harper & Row, Publishers.

Simpson, George E., and J. Milton Yinger. (1972) *Racial and Cultural Minorities.* 4th ed. New York, N.Y.: Harper & Row, Publishers.

Szymanski, Albert. (1976) "Racial Discrimination and White Gain." *American Sociological Review, 41*(June):403–14.

Taft, Philip, and Philip Ross. (1969) "American Labor Violence: Its Causes, Character and Outcome." In Hugh David Graham and Ted Robert Gurr (eds.). *The History of Violence in America.* New York: Praeger Publishers, Inc.

U.S. Dept. of Commerce, Bureau of the Census. (1983) *General Social and Economic Characteristics, United States Summary, Vol. I, 1980 Census of Population.* Washington, D.C.: U.S. Government Printing Office.

Van den Berghe, Pierre. (1978) *Man in Society: A Biosocial View.* New York, N.Y.: American Elsevier Publishing Co., Inc.

Wax, Murray L. (1971) *Indian Americans.* Englewood Cliffs, N.J.: Prentice-Hall, Inc.

Wilson, Edward O. (1975) *Sociobiology.* Cambridge, Mass.: Harvard University Press.

Wilson, William Julius. (1978) *The Declining Significance of Race.* Chicago, Ill.: University of Chicago Press.

Wirth, Louis. (1945) "The Problem of Minority Groups." In Ralph Linton (ed.), *The Science of Man in the World Crisis.* New York, N.Y.: Columbia University Press.

Woodward, C. Vann. (1955) *The Strange Career of Jim Crow.* New York, N.Y.: Oxford University Press.

10

Sex and Gender

OBJECTIVES

Students who complete this chapter should be able to:

1. Distinguish between sex and gender and define sex, gender roles, and sexism.

2. Describe the main forms of gender inequality women experience both in the workplace and in the home.

3. Describe how other social institutions contribute to gender inequality in society and how some of these institutions are changing.

4. Discuss the similarities and differences between sexism and racism.

5. Understand and explain the four major theories of gender inequality.

6. Understand the controversy over "comparable worth."

7. Understand and discuss whether minority women need women's liberation.

INTRODUCTION

In the presidential election year of 1984 one major U.S. political party nominated a woman as its vice-presidential candidate, and the other had appointed the first woman to the U.S. Supreme Court. Women made up 50 percent of the delegates at both parties' nominating conventions. As of 1984 women made up approximately one-third of the entering students in U.S. medical and law schools. At the Los Angeles Olympics thousands of women athletes displayed their skill and competitiveness to hundreds of millions of television viewers throughout the world.

Nevertheless, in the mid-1980s, women were 60 percent of all Americans living in poverty; women working full time year round earned only 59 percent of what their male counterparts made; and women workers who had attended college still earned less than male workers who had not even finished high school. Rape, wife battering, sexual abuse, and sexual harassment inflicted

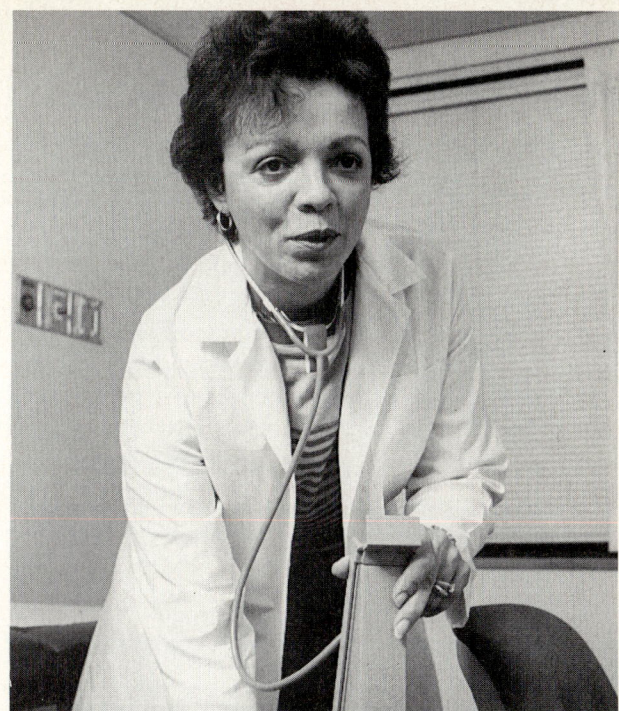

Women achieve success in many fields in American society.

physical violence and emotional trauma on great numbers of women. Women continued to work for low pay in traditionally sex-segregated occupations in the labor force and to do most of the housework and child care in the home for no pay.

It thus seems that some women have come a long way, although many other women have made very little progress during recent decades. Although the struggle against sexism and for equal rights for women has produced important changes in U.S. society, great numbers of women still suffer from many forms of oppression. This chapter reviews and analyzes the changes in the status of women in society, both in the workplace and in the home. It examines similarities and differences between sexism and racism. It compares the major theories that seek to explain social inequalities between women and men. It concludes with discussions of the issue of comparable worth and of the relevance of women's liberation for minority women.

Sex and Gender

Throughout history many people have believed that men and women naturally occupy different positions in society and exhibit different behaviors. Sociologists today recognize that most of what people often see as natural, or biologically determined, positions or behaviors are actually learned and thus socially determined. Sociologists therefore emphasize the distinction between **sex** and **gender.** Sex refers to biological differences between males and females that are genetically determined and expressed in genital differences. Gender refers to characteristics and behaviors that are viewed as masculine or feminine in a particular culture.

Sex and Gender 211

Sex is a fixed and almost unchangeable biological characteristic, but what is associated with the masculine or feminine gender varies considerably from one culture to another and from one time period to another within the same culture. A recognition and appreciation of the distinction between sex and gender is thus fundamental to an awareness that existing **gender roles** are not sacred and unchangeable. Gender roles—that is, the generally expected behaviors or positions of males and females in society—are not biologically fixed, but rather are cultural creations of humanity.

Sociologists also recognize that differences between masculine and feminine genders may be greatly reduced, so that individual male and female members of society may display highly similar traits. Such people are **androgynous.** An androgynous society is one whose culture makes relatively minor distinctions between masculine and feminine gender roles.

Sexism and Social Inequality

Sexism refers both to ideas that justify unequal rights and opportunities and to practices that deny those rights and opportunities to females. Sexism has become the most widely used term for ideas and practices that have also been called "male chauvinism" or "male supremacy." Sexism perpetuates patterns of gender stratification and inequality in society that oppress women in all areas of American society. People who treat sexism as a joking matter may not realize the great harm it inflicts on women.

The Workplace

Although growing numbers of women have entered previously male-dominated occupations and professions, the majority of women workers still work in relatively low-paying clerical or service jobs.

The entry of increasing numbers of women into the paid labor force is sometimes mistakenly equated with the "liberation" of women. Many women view their employment outside the home as a step forward, and many others view it simply as a necessity. In either case, women in the labor force encounter inequalities in many forms.

During the 1950s only one-third of all adult women in the United States were in the labor force. In the mid-1980s well over 50 percent of all women were in the labor force. During this same time period the percentage of men in the labor force declined 10 percent, from 87 to 77 percent. Women are now some 43 percent of all workers and may approach half of the labor force by the year 2000. In dramatic contrast to the traditional notion of women staying home with children, two-thirds of all women with school-age children are in the labor force today.

The entry of vast numbers of female workers into the labor force does not mean, however, that women have entered the same occupations as men or that women earn wages and salaries comparable to those of men. U.S. Department of Labor statistics for 1982 showed that 54 percent of all women workers were clerical or service workers, compared with only 16 percent of all male workers. On the other hand, men dominated the managerial and administrative category, 15 percent male compared to 7 percent female, and the skilled craft category, 20 percent to only 2 percent. Higher-paying occupations are clearly dominated by men, and lower-paying occupations are dominated by women.

Women not only experience occupational segregation: they also earn lower wages and salaries than men. The median earnings of women are about 60 percent of those of men and have actually fallen slightly during the past three decades. This pay gap is experienced by women with all levels of education and in all occupational categories. For example, women with four years of high school who worked full time year round in 1981 received median earnings 60 percent those of their male counterparts. Women with four or more years of college received median earnings that were 63 percent of their male counterparts' median earnings.

When we consider the impact of race and ethnicity as well as gender, we find that the earnings gap between minority women and minority men is much smaller than the earnings gap between white women and white men. This is essentially because racism depresses the median earnings of black and Hispanic men. Black and Hispanic women have median annual earnings that are about three-fourths of the median annual earnings of black and Hispanic men, whereas white women have median annual earnings that are less than three-fifths of the median annual earnings of white men.

A detailed study by Almquist (1984) suggests that gender and race are both influential in determining the occupations and earnings of minority women. Black and Hispanic women have median annual earnings that are about 90 percent of the median annual earnings of white women. Black women have historically had a higher rate of participation in the labor force than white women, but this difference has become very small in recent years. In 1983, 54 percent of black women and 52 percent of white women were in the labor force. The labor force participation rate for Hispanic women was 48 percent in 1983.

Black and Hispanic women are more heavily concentrated in factory and service occupations than are white women. About 38 percent of black and Hispanic women were classified as "operatives" or service workers in 1983, in contrast to just 24 percent of white women. Although these differences are significant, occupational differences between all males and all females are even greater.

The concentration of women in lower-paying and "female" occupations has further harmful consequences. Women workers are often dependent on male supervisors, confined to jobs with few opportunities for advancement and promotion, and subject to **sex-role spillover** (Gutek and Morash, 1982). Sex-role spillover occurs when women workers are expected to perform traditional female roles in the job. Women workers, for example, are often expected to serve coffee to their male bosses, run personal errands, and do other "housework" at their workplace. In addition, women secretaries, waitresses, and other workers are expected to dress in a sexually attractive or even provocative manner as part of their occupational duties. Regardless of their attire, women workers are often subjected to sexual harassment in many forms, ranging from verbal abuse to physical assault.

Research on sexual harassment suggests that a large percentage of women workers experience some kind of sexual harassment and that minority and lower-status workers experience the most frequent and most severe kinds of sexual harassment. In recent years the federal government and private employers have established policies to deal with sexual harassment, but punishment of harassers has remained relatively rare (Martin, 1984).

If women encounter so much sexist victimization in the workplace, why do women work outside the home, and why have they been doing so in such rapidly increasing numbers? There appear to be two answers to these questions.

First, economic necessity has clearly drawn increasing numbers of women into the paid labor force. The U.S. Department of Labor estimated in 1982 that some 45 percent of all women workers were single, widowed, divorced, or separated from their husbands. Women living with their husbands worked mainly to augment husbands' earnings that were not adequate to maintain the family. Wives contributed about 25 percent of all family earnings among whites and 33 percent of all family earnings among blacks.

Working not only is an economic necessity for the families of most working women. It is also regarded by increasing numbers of people as necessary for the economic and social independence of women themselves. Few believe that women can achieve equality with men if women are financially dependent upon men.

The second answer to why women work outside the home emphasizes not the desires of women themselves but the demand for cheap female labor on the part of business, industry, and government. Valerie Oppenheimer (1970) has argued that the demand for clerical workers, teachers, nurses, service workers, and the like could only be met by drawing into the labor force large numbers of women who previously were not expected to work outside the home. Thus, the changing needs of the economy, as well as the needs of women themselves, have brought about the tremendous growth in women's participation in the labor force.

The Home

Patterns of sexism in the workplace are similar to patterns of sexism in the home for many women. The division of labor with regard to housework and child care usually requires women to assume most of the burden for the performance of this vast amount of unpaid but necessary labor. Surveys first undertaken during the late 1970s and early 1980s continue to report that women are responsible for about 80 percent of the housework and child care in American families. This holds true, whether the woman works outside the home or not. Although most men say they are willing to "help out" around the house and in fact do so, they still expect women to do most of the work, whether the women work outside the

Although women and men both do housework, women still do much more housework than men.

home or not. Women who do not work outside the home spend an average of over fifty hours a week on housework and child care, whereas employed women spend about half as much time on domestic tasks.

Even more serious than the unequal division of domestic labor is the spouse abuse that affects many women each year. National statistics indicate that 95 percent of all violent instances of spouse abuse consists of assaults by men on women (U.S. Department of Justice, 1983:21). Although men are more likely than women to be victimized by violent crime at the hands of a stranger, women are more likely than men to be victimized by violent crime at the hands of a relative or acquaintance.

Gender inequality in the home is often so extreme, according to Jesse Bernard, that there are really two marriages in some marital unions—"his" and "hers" (Bernard, 1972). "His" marriage is frequently much better than "hers." Statistics indicate that marriage is highly beneficial to men: Married men live longer, are physically and mentally healthier, and are more economically successful. Married women, in contrast to married men, show far greater rates of physical and mental illness. On the other hand, unmarried women generally show better physical and mental health than unmarried men. Bernard's explanation for this pattern is that married women suffer what she calls "status denigration" as "housewives"—that is, relegation to low status, no pay, dependency, and hard labor.

Bernard has also concluded that married women who work outside the home have "overwhelmingly" better physical and mental health than housewives, despite the demands placed on them by their dual roles of worker and homemaker.

Sex and Gender **215**

Gender and Social Institutions

Women encounter gender inequality not only in the workplace and in the home but also in other major social institutions in American society, including political institutions, criminal justice institutions, educational institutions, religious institutions, and the mass media.

Women make up only about 4 percent of national political leaders and 12 percent of state political leaders in the United States. Although large numbers of women participate in various forms of political activity, elite positions of power remain overwhelmingly in the hands of men. Men also dominate top corporate and banking positions, which carry a great deal of national political influence. Studies of national political elites indicate that men continue to control the inner circles of political power in the United States (Domhoff, 1983).

Although polls have consistently shown majority support for the Equal Rights Amendment (ERA) to the U.S. Constitution, the ERA has been defeated. The legal rights of women have also been challenged in such areas as abortion rights and equal participation in sports. In the criminal justice system women are working for better treatment of victims of spouse abuse and rape and more protection from men who abuse and rape women. This requires reforms in traditional practices of law enforcement and judicial agencies.

In educational institutions women are 71 percent of all elementary and secondary school teachers but only 35 percent of all college and university teachers and only 5 to 10 percent of the principals, administrators, superintendents, and presidents. Similarly, women make up only 14 percent of all religious workers, and the hierarchies of all major religious denominations are almost completely male dominated. In the mass media most positions of authority are occupied by males, whereas females serve more frequently in subordinate or even decorative roles. In sports, despite impressive gains for female athletes, big-time professional and collegiate sports are still overwhelmingly dominated by male owners, male coaches and managers, and male athletes.

The gender inequality in these institutions parallels the gender inequality found in American society as a whole. Nevertheless, these institutions do more than just reflect larger patterns of gender inequality. They also contribute to the perpetuation and reinforcement of gender inequality by systematically socializing

Children's television programs have contributed to socialization of boys and girls into traditional masculine and feminine gender roles.

females and males into at least partial acceptance of male dominance and female subordination.

The earliest gender-role socialization occurs primarily in the family. Researchers have found that differential treatment of males and females by parents begins with newborn children. Parents use different voice tones in speaking to their female and male infants and use different adjectives to describe them. As early as the age of six months, many parents offer sex-stereotyped toys to babies (Weitzman, 1984:159–61). On the other hand, much other research has failed to document consistent differences in socialization during early childhood. Such differences are well documented, however, in research focusing on socialization by other social institutions during later years of childhood and adolescence.

Studies of children's books during the 1970s showed that males dominated and females were nearly invisible. Male characters were involved in adventures and activities that built self-confidence and independence, whereas those female characters who did appear were portrayed as passive, dependent, and confined to traditional domestic and supporting roles (Weitzman, 1984:164).

Children's television programs, according to researchers, also contain more male than female characters, and the male characters are more dominant, aggressive, active, and successful. Moreover, many children's programs that are widely viewed date from the 1950s and 1960s and present extremely stereotypical treatment of males and females to their young audiences.

When children enter grade school, they are exposed to books that encourage gender-role stereotyping and teachers who often favor boys over girls in subtle ways. Studies of elementary school readers have found that male characters greatly outnumber female characters. Moreover, the male characters display such traits as bravery, heroism, initiative, independence, and perseverance, whereas female characters are passive, docile, and dependent. Males engage in adventure and exploration, but females are portrayed doing domestic chores and often crying. Although school systems and publishers have taken steps to remove sexism from school books in recent years, such patterns are still frequently found in many classrooms.

Teachers often encourage similar inequalities in their treatment of boys and girls. Some researchers have found that teachers pay more attention to boys and praise their creative efforts more. They often assume that boys' success in school is a result of talent, whereas girls' success comes from hard work. Boys may receive more encouragement in such areas as math and science, whereas girls are discouraged from excelling in these areas.

School policies also frequently promote gender stereotyping and inequality. For example, many school systems have traditionally tracked or channeled girls into such areas as home economics, typing, secretarial skills, English, or social studies, while they have directed boys toward skilled crafts, science, engineering, and the like. Until recently, school systems also strongly reinforced gender inequality through their athletic programs: boys became athletic heroes, while girls became decorative cheerleaders.

Socialization for Inequality: The Case of Mathematics

Although some researchers have claimed that there are genetic differences in mathematics abilities between males and females, there are a great number of

Girls who excel in mathematics are able to enter many high status professional and scientific fields.

studies that describe how the socialization process in educational institutions produces unequal achievement in mathematics for boys and girls. Because math skills are necessary for entry into virtually all of the most prestigious occupations—medicine, science, engineering, and business—unequal achievement in mathematics plays an important role in maintaining gender inequality in society. One researcher (Sells, 1972) found that only 8 percent of all women entering college had sufficient math prerequisites to enter those majors that lead to math-based occupations, whereas 57 percent of all males entering college had these prerequisites. The same author repeated the study in 1977 with similar findings. She also found that only 20 percent of black males and 10 percent of black females had these math prerequisites.

How are women filtered out of mathematics? In the early grades girls do at least as well—often better—in mathematics than boys, and girls and boys report liking math equally well. Also, in the elementary years, girls and boys believe that they are equally good at math. By high school, however, most boys and girls believe that boys are better at math than girls. Girls' performance in math declines sharply with the beginning of adolescence. Girls who excel at math are subject to severe stereotyping. A large percentage of teachers believe that boys do better at math than girls, and such expectations contribute to a self-fulfilling prophecy. Math teachers focus more attention on boys than girls. All of these influences combined undermine the self-confidence, motivation, and achievement of females in mathematics, and mathematics-based occupations continue to be overwhelmingly male-dominated (Weitzman, 1984:210–15).

Further evidence that unequal math achievement is the result of socialization influences comes from experimental programs that have made special efforts to encourage math achievement among girls. These programs (Weitzman, 1984:214–15) have obtained striking results when circumstances have been created to promote math excellence among girls.

Religion. The socialization process for many people is strongly influenced by their religious training. Not only are boys and girls directly exposed to the influence of religious institutions, but the values transmitted by parents to their children are also often strongly influenced by parents' religious beliefs and affiliations. Most major religious denominations in the United States and throughout the world have traditionally emphasized very different roles for women and men. Women have been taught that their most important roles are those of mother and wife and that they must serve and obey men, including husband, clergy, and the deity.

In recent years the role and position of women has been discussed and debated a great deal in most religious denominations. Some denominations have modified their practices and doctrines to encourage more equal roles for women and men. Other more conservative religious denominations, however, have strongly held to traditional teachings and have opposed not only changes within their own denominations but also changes in the larger society. Major religious groupings, for example, were highly active on both sides of the struggle over the Equal Rights Amendment.

Mass Media. Gender-role stereotyping in the mass media has been widely recognized and criticized in recent years. Television, newspapers, and magazines have consistently portrayed a world dominated by men in which women are subservient sex objects. Researchers disagree as to how much such stereotyping in the mass media actually influences attitudes and behaviors, but many sociologists regard it as extremely harmful.

Television programming and advertising portray men in positions of dominance and authority and women in subordinate, domestic, protected, and decorative roles. Although occasional television commercials challenge traditional stereotypes, most continue to try to sell products by selling gender stereotypes.

Other media, such as motion pictures, newspapers and magazines, follow a similar pattern. There are noteworthy exceptions in all areas, but the overall thrust of the content and influence of these institutions still reinforces gender-role inequality.

Sport. Until the 1970s sport was an overwhelmingly male domain. Women participated in those individual sports that emphasized grace and beauty, such as swimming, diving, and gymnastics, but were virtually excluded from aggressive team sports such as basketball, football, baseball, or soccer. Colleges with multimillion-dollar budgets for male athletic programs spent only a few thousand dollars on women's sports. Youth sports programs were exclusively run for boys; no girls were allowed on Little League baseball teams or other youth sports teams.

The changes since the early 1970s, however, have been significant. Legislation popularly known as Title IX mandated equal opportunities for females in sports and required that programs receiving federal funding had to provide roughly equal sports programs for females and males. Consequently, female participation in sports has grown rapidly, so that nearly as many girls as boys are involved in Little League, high school, and college sports. The quality of athletic performance by females has improved dramatically as well, as clearly evidenced by the success of U.S. women during the 1984 Olympic games in such sports as basketball, volleyball, gymnastics, and track and field.

Over one million girls in the United States play soccer—a team sport requiring aggressiveness, competitiveness, and physical skills.

These changes have challenged traditional gender stereotypes in fundamental ways. The image of females as fragile, passive, and docile is shattered by the aggressive, talented play of outstanding female basketball or soccer teams. Although males still observe female cheerleaders, they now also see thousands of female athletes whose accomplishments they respect.

Nevertheless, despite important changes, much gender inequality remains in sport. Professional, big-money sports are still overwhelmingly male. Media coverage mainly emphasizes male athletes. Less money and resources are still provided in many areas of female sports. Despite these inequalities, however, sport no longer socializes males and females into highly unequal gender roles as it clearly did in the past. It is doubtful if females who have now discovered the excitement and fun of competitive sports will ever again settle only for the sidelines.

Sexism and Racism: Similarities and Differences

There are a great many similarities between sexism and racism in society and a few important differences. An examination of these similarities and differences may be helpful to our understanding of both sexism and racism.

A first similarity is that women are a minority group in most of the same ways that racial and ethnic groups are minority groups. Women are a recognizable, socially visible group; they experience economic, political, and social inequality at the hands of a dominant group; they are born into an ascribed minority status; and they increasingly display a group consciousness of minority status.

These are four of the five characteristics of minority group status usually cited by sociologists (See the discussion on racism in Chapter 9). The fifth characteristic of minority group status, segregation or social distance from the dominant group, does not for the most part apply to women. Women, of course, marry and interact intimately with men. On the other hand, there are important areas of male activity, such as private clubs, recreational and business organizations, from which women have been largely excluded.

Several other important similarities between sexism and racism exist. The ideological justifications for sexism and racism are similar. Sexist and racist ideologies allege inferiority of the victim and their suitability for subordinate roles in society. Such ideologies are frequently put forward as scientific truths by influential "scholars."

The economic consequences of sexism and racism are highly similar. For example, median family income for blacks compared to whites and median income of full-time female workers compared to male workers are both about 60 percent, and this ratio has remained fairly constant for decades. Racial minorities and women make up a disproportionate percentage of the poor and of those on welfare. Both groups are victims of a great deal of occupational segregation that concentrates them in low-paying jobs.

Both racial minorities and women are victims of widespread violence at the hands of members of the dominant group. Racial minorities have experienced violence from the Ku Klux Klan, from white mobs, and from law enforcement personnel. Women have been violently attacked by abusers and rapists, both strangers and close acquaintances. Lynchings have been a weapon of terror to keep racial minorities "in their place"; rape and spouse abuse have been forms of violence used to keep women "in their place." An important difference, however, is that violence against racial minorities has often been organized by large groups, whereas most violence against women has been carried out by individuals.

Finally, both racial minorities and women are frequently blamed, or scapegoated, for the problems that victimize them. Whereas racial minorities have been blamed for much of the violent crime and property crime in society, women have been blamed for the sexual and other assaults against them. Racial minorities and women have been blamed for the poverty and deprivation they suffer, and racial minorities and women as parents have been blamed for the misdeeds of children in our society. Criminal justice agencies have failed to protect both racial minorities and women from many forms of criminal victimization.

The differences between sexism and racism are probably not as significant as the similarities. First, there is greater segregation and social distance between racial groups than between women and men. It is arguable that this leads to greater hostility and violence toward racial minorities than toward women, but it should be noted that the worst violence against women comes from the men closest to them. Secondly, women are numerically much larger than any racial and ethnic minorities in the United States. But, just as women are a numerical majority in the United States, blacks are a numerical majority in South Africa. Still, the greater numbers of women in U.S. society probably give women some relative advantages in gaining access to political, economic, and educational opportunities. For example, women greatly outnumber blacks in graduate and professional schools, in university faculties, and in many prestigious occupations, even though women remain substantially underrepresented in all these areas.

Third, women are more widely dispersed throughout the entire class structure of society than are racial minorities. Because women marry men of all social classes, there are of course large numbers of upper-class and middle-class women. Although most of these women have much less power than their male counterparts, they nevertheless enjoy many of the same privileges of their higher-class position. Although women of all classes may be oppressed by sexism in some ways, women in the higher classes certainly experience many compensating advantages that make them more accepting of the status quo in society. An example of this can be seen in comparing female and black voting behavior. During the early 1980s there was much attention paid to the "gender gap." That is, women gave less support to President Ronald Reagan than did men. This gap never began to approach the "racial gap" between white and black support for Reagan. Whereas as many as two-thirds of whites expressed support for Reagan, no more than 10 to 15 percent of blacks did so. This suggests that the politics of race are more dangerously divisive than the politics of gender. Overall, then, there are many important similarities in the nature and consequences of sexism and racism, and several important differences as well.

Theoretical Explanations of Gender Inequality

There are four major kinds of theories that attempt to explain systematic inequality in society. They are (1) biological theories, (2) functionalist theories, (3) socialization theories, and (4) feminist and Marxist theories.

Biological Theories

Some biological explanations of gender inequality express the idea that "anatomy is destiny," that is, anatomical differences between males and females determine the social positions or destiny of men and women in society. There are several different versions of biological theories that emphasize different arguments. One version emphasizes the childbearing function of females and asserts that women are naturally suited to having and raising children, whereas men are naturally suited for the "breadwinning" and protective functions. This argument is usually supported by noting males are naturally larger and stronger than females and therefore naturally suited for more aggressive and competitive roles.

Another version emphasizes alleged hormonal differences between women and men that supposedly make women by nature more emotional, irrational, and dependent and men more rational, aggressive, and independent. Men should therefore assume leadership positions in society, and women should perform expressive and supporting roles.

A more recent version of biological theory is sociobiology. Sociobiologists have argued that male dominance and female subordination have evolved through the process of natural selection. Natural selection has produced males who are genetically programmed to be highly aggressive, competitive, violent, warlike, and territorial. Men compete against each other to pass on these genetic traits to offspring by impregnating women. Women, in contrast, by natural selection are genetically programmed to attract and capture the loyalty of one man who will protect them and their offspring. Sociobiologists therefore claim that there is a genetic basis for what is commonly referred to as the "double standard" of sexual behavior. They also claim that general male dominance in society is equally biologically determined.

The biological explanations of gender inequality rest on evidence from animal studies, but there is little evidence drawn from studies of humans. Although it is obviously true that there are certain inborn biological differences between males and females, scientific research has not shown that these differences *cause* social inequalities in human societies. Women in American society today spend an average of less than three years of their adult lives in pregnancy or nursing babies. That leaves them with an average of nearly sixty years to do other things such as working outside the home or participating in government. Childrearing can be done more or less equally well by females and males, if they wish to do so.

Although men are on the average larger and stronger than women, many women are larger and stronger than many men. More importantly, very few tasks or jobs in society depend on size and strength. Women have proven that they are quite capable of performing physically demanding jobs such as construction work, law enforcement, and competitive sport. If women are not naturally suited to play professional football, neither, after all, are men. The career of the average male professional football player lasts only four to five years, and men must lift weights fifteen to twenty hours a week to build up the muscles to play big-time college football as well as professional football.

Nor does scientific evidence support the claim that hormonal differences produce different temperaments for men and women. Differences in temperament that do exist have been shown to be primarily due to differences in socialization or conditioning. Women have as much potential as men to be rational, aggressive, and independent, and are therefore potentially as capable as men of filling leadership or other positions in society that require such traits. Likewise, men have the capacity to be emotional, passive, dependent, nurturing and caring.

Scientists have not discovered any genes that influence people to behave competitively or cooperatively, aggressively or passively, violently or peacefully. Not only are these behaviors culturally learned, but even what these terms mean is greatly influenced by culture. Human behavior changes and varies too quickly and too frequently to be explained by genetic factors. Critics of sociobiology have argued that sociobiologists offer ideological justifications for existing social inequalities rather than scientific explanations of those inequalities.

Functionalist Theories

Functionalist sociologists have approached the explanation of gender inequality from the perspective of how it contributes to the maintenance of the society as a whole and the maintenance of the family as a social institution. Functionalists assert that within social groups there are both **instrumental** and **expressive functions** that must be performed. Instrumental functions are those involved in organizing and leading the group to accomplish tasks and achieve goals. Expressive functions are those involved in making people feel happy, encouraged, motivated, and able to get along with other group members.

According to Parsons and Bales (1953), the family as a social group functions best when there is a division of labor in which the man performs the instrumental function and the woman performs the expressive function. Women, because they bear and nurse children, are best suited for homemaking, while men are best suited for breadwinning. The socialization process teaches women and men the content of these two roles and also teaches them to conform to these roles. This division of labor is also in the best interests of the society as a whole because it insures that the home and children will be properly looked after (by women) whereas the necessary work in factories and offices will be performed by men.

Defenders of the functionalist approach assert that they are not insisting that women ought to fill expressive functions and men ought to fill instrumental functions. They are only explaining how this particular division of labor has served certain societal functions. On the other hand, critics argue that functionalists have attempted to persuade people to accept a certain division of labor as functionally necessary to the survival of the family and the society. Critics have also emphasized the disadvantages of this particular division of labor. First, the instrumental role is more highly regarded and more highly rewarded in our society. The man thus enjoys much higher economic and social status, whereas the woman is made subordinate and dependent. Second, the unequal positions of the man and women introduce much conflict and disruption into the family and the society. This contributes not to the maintenance but to the breakdown of social institutions.

Third, it is possible for both instrumental and expressive functions to be jointly shared by both men and women. This is in fact what has been increasingly taking place in American society and in many other societies throughout the world. As increasing numbers of women have entered the paid labor force, they have taken on a growing share of instrumental functions. To the extent that the division of labor in the home has been changed, men have taken on a growing share of expressive functions. These changes have reduced gender inequality in both the workplace and in the home. As a result, males and females do not have to be socialized to conform to such distinct masculine and feminine social roles.

Socialization Theories

Socialization clearly has a lot to do with gender inequality in society. We have already in this chapter analyzed how major social institutions in our society contribute to gender-role differentiation and gender inequality by the ways they socialize males and females. In contrast, then, to the biological and functionalist theories, there is considerable scientific research supporting the idea that differences in socialization of males and females are related to gender inequality in society.

Before you leap to the conclusion that the question of what causes gender inequality has been answered, however, there is a further question that must be confronted: Why are males and females socialized for gender inequality? Socialization theories describe the process through which people are taught gender roles and encouraged to accept gender inequalities, and, therefore, they are extremely valuable in increasing our awareness of how gender inequalities are perpetuated in society. Socialization theories, however, do not explain why all this takes place.

Feminist and Marxist Theories

Feminist theories locate the cause of gender inequality in the patriarchal structure of society and its institutions. That is, gender inequality stems from male dominance of the family, the economy, the government, and other important institutions in society. Marxist theories locate the cause of gender inequality in the capitalistic structure of society. That is, gender inequality is a basic feature of capitalism and benefits the capitalist class in various ways.

Feminist and Marxist theories are often combined into a single framework that analyzes both patriarchy, that is, male dominance, and capitalism, that is, capitalist dominance in society. Some writers, however, place greater emphasis on the analysis of patriarchy, whereas others place greater emphasis on the analysis of capitalism.

Feminists tend to argue that the oppression of women is the most fundamental type of oppression in society, and therefore that the struggle for the liberation of women is the central task in creating a better social order. Marxists tend to argue that class oppression, that is, the exploitation of the working class by the capitalist class, is the most fundamental type of oppression. Most women belong to the working class and, because of sexism, are oppressed more than male workers. A minority of women belong to the capitalist class, and although they may be oppressed to some extent by sexism, they have more in common with male capitalists than with female workers. For Marxists, then, the central task in creating a better social order, is to unite all workers to overthrow capitalism. Feminists often criticize the Marxist view for giving insufficient attention to the oppression of women. Marxists criticize the feminist view for downplaying class exploitation and class differences among women.

Marxist and feminist theorists have attempted to combine these theories by analyzing the way that women's oppression is linked to the structure of capitalism. They have argued that sexism, like racism, serves the interests of capitalism in important ways and divides and harms the working class. Specifically, these theories assert that:

1. Sexism creates an increasing pool of cheap labor for capitalism, as more and more women are drawn into the paid labor force.
2. Sexism provides and justifies a vast pool of free labor in the form of the housework and childbearing that are done mainly by women. This unpaid labor is essential to the functioning of capitalism. Capitalism has separated "home" and "work" and downgraded the status of housework.
3. Sexism divides male and female workers from each other and prevents their solidarity as a class against the capitalist class.
4. Sexism makes women the scapegoats for many of the problems of capitalist society. Women are often blamed for problems that occur within the home and for much of the physical and sexual abuse they suffer. Blaming women for these problems and encouraging men to vent their anger against women keeps blame and anger from being directed against the capitalist system.
5. The sexual exploitation of women, ranging from advertising to pornography and prostitution, produces profits for capitalism and greater social control over both men and women by capitalist society.

The Marxist and feminist theories do not assert that capitalism "invented" the oppression of women. The oppression of women existed in feudal and ancient societies as well, but capitalism has perpetuated it in both old and new forms.

The Controversy over Comparable Worth

The concept of **comparable worth** evolved during the early 1980s as a means of achieving "equal pay for equal work" for female workers. As we have seen earlier in this chapter, there is a great deal of occupational segregation by sex in the U.S. economy, and occupations in which there are the greatest concentrations of women generally pay lower wages or salaries. Moreover, this includes many occupations, such as nursing and teaching, which offer low pay despite having relatively high educational and training requirements.

Advocates of equal pay for women have argued that it is not sufficient to require equal pay for women and men who do the same jobs, because women and men so often have different jobs. There must also be a requirement of equal pay for jobs of "comparable worth." That is, where women and men do different jobs, if women do work that involves as much education and training, responsibility, and complexity as work performed by men in other jobs, then the pay of such women should be comparable to that received by men.

Blatant examples of undervaluing the worth of occupations performed by women can be found in the *Dictionary of Occupational Titles* published by the U.S. Department of Labor. This federal government manual rates the level of complexity of some 30,000 jobs in the United States. One of the lowest ratings is for "foster parent," who:

> rears children in own home as members of family. Organizes and schedules activities, such as recreation, rest periods, and sleeping time. Insures that child has nutritious diet. Instructs children in good personal and health habits. Bathes, dresses, and undresses young children. Washes and irons clothing. Accompanies children on outings and walks. Disciplines children when required . . . may work under supervision of welfare agency. May prepare periodic reports concerning progress and behavior of children.

As Coser and associates (1983:251) have pointed out, this occupation is rated just above "coin-machine collector" (who "collects coins from parking meters or telephone pay stations") and just below "driver helper," who "loads and unloads trucks." Thus, work done by women is grossly undervalued when compared to work done by men.

Biological theories of gender inequality justify the undervaluing of work done by women by alleging that women are naturally subordinate to men and biologically destined to fulfill inferior roles. Men are to be more highly rewarded for dominance and leadership, and women are simply not comparable to men.

Functionalist theories could be used to support either side of the controversy over comparable worth. Functionalists might argue that the functions performed by women workers are just as socially necessary as those performed by men and thus should be comparably rewarded. On the other hand, some functionalists have argued that certain functions are more important than others and require greater talent and training, and thus are more highly rewarded (Davis and Moore, 1945).

Socialization theories call into question the occupational segregation and lower pay of women workers by focusing attention on how the cultural values of our society socialize us to undervalue the work performed by women. The essential contributions performed by women both in the paid labor force and in the home are undervalued because we are socialized to degrade the value of women in our society. As a result, women tend to be overqualified and underpaid in the work they do. This cultural bias can be changed if we recalculate the value of women's contributions and provide equal pay for jobs of comparable worth.

Marxist and feminist theories also support the demand for equal pay for jobs of comparable worth and point out that this issue exposes how the capitalist system rests upon the profitable exploitation of cheap female labor. Marxists point out that the opponents of equal pay for jobs of comparable worth defend the right of capitalist employers to underpay women. Marxist and feminist theories assert that the struggle for full economic equality for women must lead to a struggle to replace the capitalist system itself with an egalitarian socialist or communist society.

Women's Liberation and Minority Women

Do black women and other minority women in the United States need women's liberation? There has been considerable argument over the answer to this question. There are at least six reasons that have been set forth by those who argue that minority women do not need women's liberation. First, it is argued that minority women are already liberated. They have had to be strong and work outside the home to support their families in a hostile society. Second, minority women, especially black women, allegedly do not need to be liberated because they are already the dominant sex. The matriarchal tradition in black families has produced a pattern of female dominance. Third, minority women should not seek liberation because African tradition (or Latin tradition or Asian tradition) sanctifies male dominance and female subservience. Women's liberation is thus contrary to minority cultural traditions. Fourth, racism is the principal problem facing minorities, and women's liberation is a distraction that cannot be afforded. Fifth, women's liberation is essentially a plot to divide minority women and men against each other and disrupt the unity necessary for minority progress. Sixth, and finally, the women's liberation movement is a white middle- and upper-class movement that is not relevant to the needs of most minority women.

Some of these arguments have partial validity, whereas others are mere rationalizations, and still others contradict each other. A strong case can be made for the view that racism is a greater threat to minorities than sexism and that unity of minority women and men is essential. Also, there is some validity to criticisms of racism in many organizations that comprise the women's liberation movement. On the other hand, the other arguments are highly dubious. Minority women are not already liberated. Being liberated does not mean having to be strong in the face of oppression and concentration in the worst jobs. Black and other families are not matriarchal. Although many minority families are single-parent families, this is not an indication of the power and dominance of females. It is more a reflection of severe economic deprivation, high unemployment rates, and the difficulty of forming and maintaining stable two-parent families under such stressful conditions.

Invoking minority cultural tradition to justify male dominance is the same excuse used by white male chauvinists to support gender inequality. Finally, much evidence indicates that sexism is a severe problem for minority women and for minority communities as a whole.

A few examples illustrate this point. First, a careful analysis by Almquist and Wehrle-Einhorn, "The Doubly Disadvantaged: Minority Women in the Labor Force" (1978), shows that gender seems to be as important as ethnicity in accounting for occupational discrimination against minority women workers. Second, minority women are victims of high rates of violent abuse and rape, primarily at the hands of minority men. In conclusion, even if it is acknowledged that racism is a more severe problem than sexism, women's liberation is necessary and relevant to minority women.

Summary

Sociologists distinguish between sex as a biological characteristic and gender as a social characteristic. Gender refers to roles that are deemed masculine or feminine. Unlike sex, gender roles are changeable and vary considerably in different societies and different times. Sexism refers to ideas and practices that deny equal rights and opportunities to females.

Although there have been significant changes in the status of females in American society, many women continue to suffer from major inequalities both in the workplace and in the home. These include lower pay, occupational segregation, and sexual harassment in the workplace and an unequal division of labor, dependency, and violent abuse in the home.

Social institutions such as education, religion, the mass media, government, and sport contribute to the perpetuation of gender inequality in American society. Some of these institutions, such as sport and education, have begun to provide greater equality of opportunity to females.

There are important similarities between sexism and racism, and also a few significant differences. There are four kinds of theories that attempt to explain the causes of gender inequality. These are biological, functionalist, socialization, and feminist and Marxist theories. These theories have different implications, as we can see when we attempt to apply them to a concrete issue such as the controversy over "comparable worth." Although it has been argued that minority women do not need women's liberation, evidence suggests that minority women are victims of many forms of sexism and would benefit from gender equality at least as much as white women.

Key Concepts

androgyny	gender roles
comparable worth	instrumental functions
expressive functions	sex
gender	sexism
sex-role spillover	

References

Almquist, Elizabeth M. (1984) "Race and Ethnicity in the Lives of Minority Women." In Jo Freeman (ed.), *Women: A Feminist Perspective.* 3d ed. Palo Alto, Calif.: Mayfield Publishing Company.

Almquist, Elizabeth M., and Juanita L. Wehrle-Einhorn. (1978) "The Doubly Disadvantaged: Minority Women in the Labor Force." In Ann H. Stromberg and Shirley Harkness (eds.), *Women Working.*

Bernard, Jessie. (1972) *The Future of Marriage.* New York, N.Y.: Bantam Books, Inc.

Coser, Lewis A., Buford Rhea, Patricia A. Steffan, and Steven L. Nock. (1983) *Introduction to Sociology.* New York: Harcourt Brace Jovanovich, Inc.

Davis, Kingsley, and Wilbert E. Moore, 1945 "Some Principles of Stratification" *American Sociological Review.* 10(April)242–49.

Domhoff, G. William. (1983) *Who Rules America Now? A View for the Eighties.* Englewood Cliffs, N.J.: Prentice-Hall, Inc.

Gutek, Barbara, and Bruce Morash. (1982) "Sex Ratios, Sex Role Spillover, and Sexual Harassment of Women at Work." *Journal of Social Issues, 38*:55–74.

Jaggar, Alison M., and Paula S. Rothenberg. (1984) *Feminist Frameworks: Alternative Theoretical Accounts of the Relations Between Women and Men.* New York, N.Y.: McGraw-Hill Book Company.

Joseph, Gloria I., and Jill Lewis. (1981) *Common Differences: Conflicts in Black and White Feminist Perspectives.* New York, N.Y.: Anchor Books/Doubleday & Company, Inc.

Martin, Susan Ehrlich. (1984) "Sexual Harassment." In Jo Freeman (ed.), *Women: A Feminist Perspective,* 3rd ed. Palo Alto, Calif.: Mayfield Publishing Company, 54–69.

Oppenheimer, Valerie Kincade. (1970) *The Female Labor Force in the United States.* Berkeley, Calif.: University of California Press.

Parsons, Talcott, and Robert F. Bales. (1953) *Family, Socialization, and Interaction Process.* Glencoe, Ill.: Free Press.

Sells, Lucy. (1978) "Mathematics—A Critical Filter." *Science Teacher,* (February)28–29.

Sokoloff, Natalie J. (1981) *Between Money and Love.* New York, N.Y.: Praeger Publishers, Inc.

U.S. Bureau of the Census. (1982) *Statistical Abstract of the United States, 1982–1983.* Washington, D.C.: U.S. Government Printing Office.

U.S. Department of Justice, Bureau of Justice Statistics. (1983) *Report to the Nation on Crime and Justice.* Washington, D.C.: U.S. Government Printing Office.

U.S. Department of Labor. (1977) *Dictionary of Occupational Titles.* Washington, D.C.: U.S. Government Printing Office.

U.S. Department of Labor, Bureau of Labor Statistics. (1983) *Employment and Earnings 30.* Washington, D.C.: U.S. Government Printing Office.

Weitzman, Lenore J. (1984) "Sex-role Socialization: A Focus on Women." In Jo Freeman (ed.), *Women: A Feminist Perspective.* 3d ed. Palo Alto, Calif.: Mayfield Publishing Company.

11

Aging

OBJECTIVES

Upon completion of this chapter the student should be able to:

1. Recognize various socially defined connotations of aging.

2. Understand the processes associated with aging.

3. Identify specific impacts of the rapid growth of the aged population in the United States.

4. Recognize aging-related problems and issues.

5. Identify societal efforts to address aging-related problems and issues through legislation, policies, and programs.

INTRODUCTION

> When I Was Young?—Ah, woeful When!
> Ah, for the change 'twixt Now and When!
>
> —from "Youth and Age"
> by SAMUEL TAYLOR COLERIDGE

[1]Growing older is a universal phenomenon, escapable only by death. To experience growing older, an individual has merely to live. The inevitability and universality of the phenomenon often narrow the attention individuals give to the actual process of growing older. When, perchance, we do reflect on how much we have aged, we are astounded by how much change occurred with the passage of time.

As we age, multiple changes (as in appearance and life-style) are expected. Yet, inattentiveness to personal aging processes may, unfortunately,

---

[1]This chapter was written and contributed by Margaret N. Barnes, Director of Gerontology at Hampton University; co-founder and first president of the Association of Gerontology and Human Development in Historically Black Colleges and Universities, Inc.

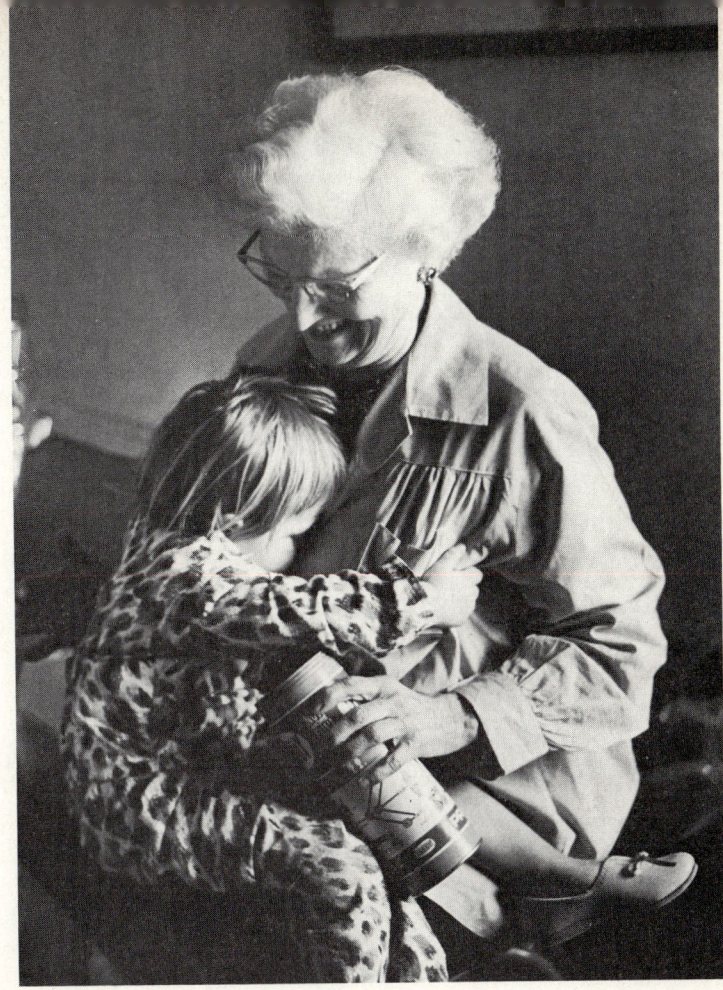

Aging includes biological, psychological, and social processes that occur throughout our lives.

also result in inadequate retirement plans and marked declines in health status in later years. At the macro level, inattentiveness to aging can result in inadequate housing, medical care, labor force policies, and other programs and services to accommodate a society's aged population.

When individuals and society do attempt to manage their own aging and the aging of others, they need assistance in addressing the issues and problems they encounter. Education, research, information, special programs, and services are important elements in preparing for and adapting to aging changes. **Gerontology** is the study of aging processes, issues, and problems. Gerontology strives to help us understand our own aging and the aging of others.

Aging, as a concept, includes biological, psychological, and sociological processes that occur throughout life. Therefore, issues and problems paramount to aging may be found in all aspects of our society. Sociologists, economists, architects, biologists, politicians, psychologists, nutritionists, physicians, fashion designers, social workers, and the like all have a vested interest in gerontology as their roles are impacted by the growing number of people who are living longer.

In this chapter we discuss gerontology, with emphasis on aging in America. As the number of older Americans increases, our society becomes more concerned about the processes of aging and the role of the aged. Limited income, poor health, inadequate housing, and age discrimination are described as problems faced by many older persons. Yet, we note that minority group members have special aging characteristics and need special consideration in the development of appropriate responses to aging issues.

One way our society responds to its increasing aged population is through the development of more services and programs targeting older persons, thus creating an aging service network. Allied professions join in the discussion of gerontological issues, provision of aging services, and advocacy for aged persons. Likewise, older persons themselves make contributions to society as they cope with their own aging and the aging of others.

As we discuss aging and the various ways the aged may be described, we realize that there are no two persons who age exactly the same. Stereotypes and myths suggest that all aged are the same, but even personal experiences with and recollections of older relatives and friends tell us they are not homogeneous.

Although it is not clear why humans age, it is certain that they do. As they age, change occurs within and around them. This chapter is an overview of aging—its incidence, processes, problems, and treatment in America.

Age and Aging

When we ask, "How old are you?" we generally expect a response that declares a measure of the time (e.g., years, months, weeks) a person has lived. However, the response we receive may vary, depending on the respondent's interpretation of the question and/or willingness to respond. Age may be and is expressed in a variety of ways.

Chronological Aging

From birth, chronological, biological, psychological, and sociological clocks tick to mark sequels of our aging processes. At any point in our lives these clocks may be used to describe our age. **Chronological age** is perhaps the most common method of expressing age. By using calendar benchmarks such as years or weeks we are able to communicate a dimension of aging—the passage of time. A famous comedian did little to support the usefulness of chronological measures of age when he coined the response "I'm thirty-nine" for any inquiry about age after the thirty-ninth birthday. Chronological age is accurately expressed if it descrbes all the calendar time between birth and the point in time that the measurement is taken. Birth certificates, records in family Bibles, and baptism certificates are commonly accepted as valid indicators of age.

The most common chronological age used to classify the "aged" is sixty-five; however, not all spheres of our society subscribe to the "sixty-five years of age and older" demarcation for identifying the aged (Atchley, 1983:11–12). Programs and services designed for older Americans utilize varied eligibility ages to qualify their target populations. The eligibility age for aging services is as low as fifty-five for some services.

How long people are expected to live should be a major consideration when utilizing chronological age to classify the aged. **Life expectancy** is the average length of life, based on the population's current mortality rate, or the probability

Although people may share the same chronological age, the aging process for each may be quite different. Successful aging is characterized by a transfer of social roles and a continuing of social interaction.

of surviving to a particular chronological age. Utilizing death rates, life expectancy is computed annually for birth cohorts. A **birth cohort** is a group of persons born during a given year. Thus, a life expectancy of 70.8 years for 1970 means that persons born during 1970 are projected to live an average of 70.8 years.

Life expectancy varies between different birth cohorts and among the same birth cohorts. Sex and race are specifically identified as contributors to differential life expectancies (Giles, 1983:53). National Center for Health Statistics (1980) data indicate that the 1980 life expectancy is 77.8 years for white females; 70.2 years for white males; 73.6 years for nonwhite females; and 65.0 years for nonwhite males. Differential life expectancies have enormous implications for individuals and our society, including who will become eligible for aged services and for how long.

The life expectancy of the general population in the United States has increased from an average of about 47 years for those born in 1900 to an average 73.7 years for those born in 1980 and 79.8 years for those born in 2050. Listed in Table 11.1 are life expectancies in the United States from 1900 to 2050. Fluctuations in the longevity projections, including projections for sex and race, are often attributed to such factors as medical advances, political climates, and social environments.

Biological Aging

Age may also be described in terms of biological or physical changes that affect the human body. Although aging does entail incremental processes (i.e., the growing, strengthening, and building up of the body), much more attention in gerontology is given to the decremental factors of aging. Physical decrements are biological events that result in a lessening or complete demise in the body's ability to function. Thus, biological aging is often referred to as "the body's gradual loss of the ability to renew itself" (Atchley, 1980:6).

Physical changes in aging affect the appearance and functioning of the body.

Table 11.1 *Life Expectancies at Birth and Age 65 by Sex and Calendar Year*

Calendar year	Male		Female	
	At birth	At age 65	At birth	At age 65
1900	46.56	11.35	49.07	12.01
1910	50.20	11.38	53.67	12.10
1920	54.59	11.81	56.33	12.34
1930	58.01	11.38	61.36	12.91
1940	60.89	11.92	65.34	13.42
1950	65.33	12.81	70.90	15.07
1960	66.58	12.91	73.19	15.89
1970	67.05	13.14	74.80	17.12
1980	69.85	14.02	77.53	18.35
1990	72.29	15.11	79.85	19.92
2000	73.42	15.71	81.05	20.81
2010	73.93	16.08	81.62	21.27
2020	74.42	16.45	82.18	21.73
2030	74.90	16.81	82.74	22.18
2040	75.37	17.18	83.29	22.64
2050	75.84	17.55	83.84	23.11

Source: Social Security Administration, Office of the Actuary, September 1982.

If we want to present a picturesque description of aging, we might include visible characteristics commonly associated with old chronological age, such as gray hairs, wrinkled skin, and crooked posture. A functional description might include reduced strength, cardiovascular diseases, and slowed movement. Although these descriptions may have their merits, individuals do not physically age at the same rate; thus, the descriptions do not apply to all individuals at any given chronological age.

Although they evolve at different rates within different individuals, there are certain aging processes that occur within all human bodies. Postmaturational aging, or **senescence,** refers to processes occurring within the bodies of all humans that contribute to their functional decline and eventual death. The functioning of the kidneys, blood vessels, immune system, and muscular system are among the many body components affected by senescence. It is usually middle age when these aging-related changes are most noticed. Because the various changes involve gradual processes, their cumulative effects are often erroneously perceived as sudden. However, evidences of senescence such as menopause and hardening of the arteries are not overnight occurrences; they merely culminate and become noticed suddenly.

Senility and Senile Dementia

Another commonly used descriptor for the aged is senile. **Senility** is a term generally used by laymen to explain a wide range of aged behaviors that suggest mental incapacities. At the first sign of confused behavior, including forgetfulness, short attention span, paranoia, and incoherent speech, the older person is labeled senile. A younger person who occasionally forgets escapes such as a label. Boredom and legitimate suspicions are seldom attributed to the aged to explain their behavior. Actually, sensory losses that alter how well we hear and what we see may account for some inability to follow conversations and feelings of loneliness or of being left out. However, senility should not be confused with senescence, as many of the symptoms associated with senility are not normal processes of aging and are often treatable.

Symptoms commonly associated with senility may be caused by brain diseases or disorders. Specific diseases that affect mental faculties include Alzheimer's disease, Pick's disease, Huntington's disease, multiple sclerosis, and multiinfarct dementia. (For more information, see Omen, 1977; Jarvik, 1980; Weeks, 1984). It is estimated that more than 10 percent of the aged experience cognitive impairments. In fact, **senile dementia,** the gradual onset of impaired orientation, memory, judgment, and intellectual functioning in the absence of major neurological deficit (Fox et al., 1975:557), is a primary psychiatric disorder among the aged.

Many of the brain diseases and disorders found frequently among the aged are mistakenly perceived as "old-age diseases" and elicit surprise when younger persons are stricken. For example, Alzheimer's, a type of senile dementia characterized by disorientation, a decline in intellectual functioning, and personality changes, accounts for about one-half of the dementia or chronic organic brain syndrome found in the later stage of life. Although Alzheimer's is diagnosed most frequently in the elderly, younger people also suffer from the disease and are afflicted with presenile dementia. Many brain diseases, like Alzheimer's reflect gradual and progressive deterioration of brain cells that usually culminates in late life.

The causes, some of which are reversible, of mental confusion demonstrated by older persons are many. Unfortunately, the catch-all diagnosis of senility hinders the proper diagnosis and treatment for many older persons. In some cases, treatment is not even sought, as caregivers attribute the symptoms to old age and conclude that such symptoms are to be expected and are not treatable. Yet, many of the symptoms are misdiagnosed and/or are treatable. Careful examinations will help to identify treatable symptomatic dementia (Jarvik, 1980:180–87) induced by drugs, intracranial lesions, malnutrition, depression, stress, and paranoid disorders.

Sociological Aging

Socially defined positions are commonly used to describe individuals as they age. What people do and are expected to do, in relation to the society as a whole, is linked to numerous other variables, including age, socioeconomic status, ethnicity, race, health, and education. Among the elderly these variables affect marital status, living arrangements, familial support patterns, income, and other social participation patterns (Jackson, 1980: 117–59). Norms and statutes help to regulate participation in our society and guide individuals through usual, normative social development. Statutes or laws legalize norms—standards for behavior—and legally prescribe what must be done, when it can be done, and/or how it must be done.

Age grading is used to categorize, through status and roles, a society's populace. In its simplest form an age-grading system might distinguish individuals as either children or adults. A plural system of age grading is evident in the United States. For example, although statutes recognize eighteen as the legal adult age and allow entry into the political system with voting privileges, family network and economic system may not view individuals as adults until they are employed and self-supporting. Similarly, grandparenthood and exit from the work force are correlated with passage into later maturity and old age. Individuals who have reached old age but can work and continue to do so effectively may not be viewed as old by their colleagues or co-workers. Within the family, however, the same individuals, as grandparents or great-grandparents, may be labeled "old." Social meaning is attached to chronological age, just as statuses and roles provide sociological age definitions.

Life-course stages play a vital role in defining roles and behaviors for people in our society. Major life events that individuals are expected to experience are categorized in life-course stages such as adolescence, young adulthood, adulthood, middle age, later maturity, and old age. The life-course stages describe the ideal positions and experiences expected of and by individuals as they participate in society and grow older. These stages are expressively normative patterns that can be used to determine how an individual is progressing socially with respect to the social developments of birth cohorts and to societal expectations.

As individuals grow older, they experience changes in their behavior and the behavior of others toward them. In the earlier life-course stages, schools, occupations, affiliations, families, and friends provide individuals an abundance of social roles and opportunities for social interactions. The later life-course stage provides fewer opportunities for social interaction. Fewer role options are found in old age, as biological, economic and sociocultural factors systematically place limitations on the life space of individuals. Though it is increasingly more common to hear of aged individuals marrying, beginning new careers, and returning to school, most older persons exit major roles by ascription, "act their age," and experience old age in widowhood and retirement.

Roles provide individuals with social identity and contribute to self-concept and self-esteem. Unfortunately, older persons experience—often beyond their control—accumulative losses that influence their behavior and access to societal roles. Declining health, retirement, reduced income, and death of family members and friends often force individuals to exit from socially sanctioned and personally satisfying roles. Because such role exits are more common in later life than are role transitions, the social identity of the aged diminishes. Thus, the societal role of aged individuals is frequently questioned by them and others. It affects what the individuals expect and what others expect of them. The loss of major roles

Unsuccessful aging is characterized by a loss of social roles, loneliness, and social isolation.

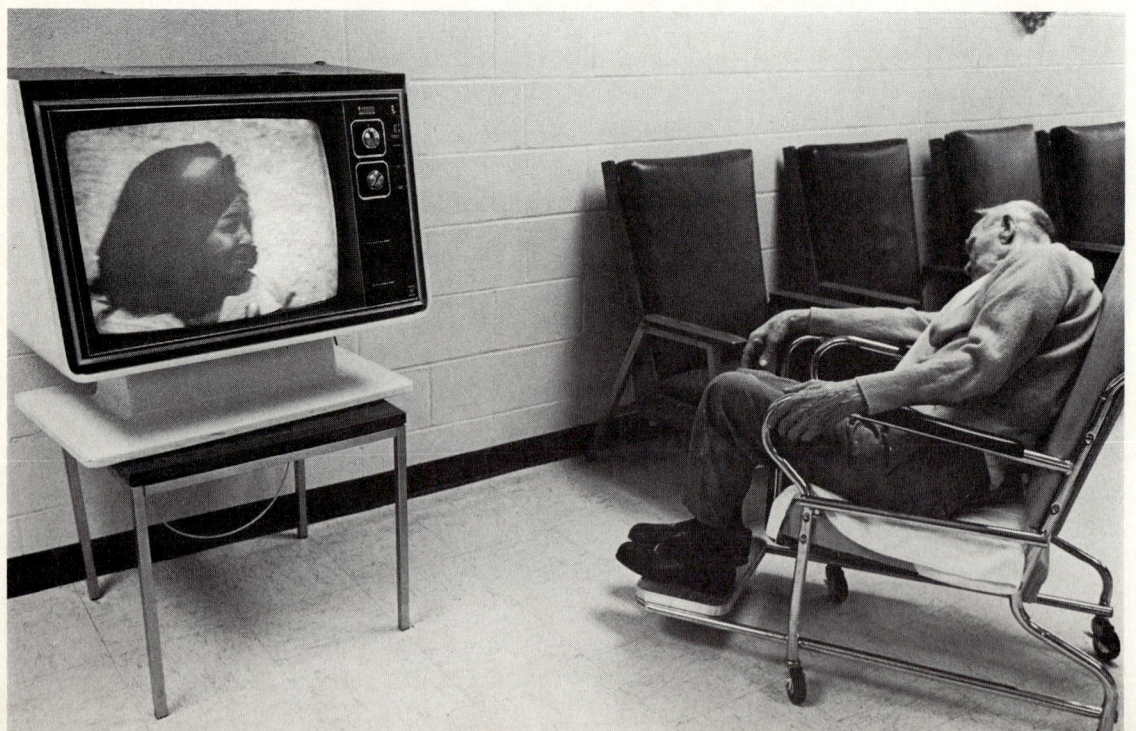

has already been linked to increased vulnerability, suicides, and shortened life spans among the aged.

Chronic illnesses and physical limitations restrict and reduce the activity of the older person. In addition, sensory acuity, lessened through the aging process, is affected; consequently, smelling, touching, seeing, hearing, and tasting become less reliable and enjoyable. Suffering from what has been called environmental impairment, or the inability to receive complete information from the environment, older persons may find themselves excluded from important social interactions such as conversations, dinner parties, and group projects. Poor health and other physical losses may even result in the movement of aged persons from their usual social habitats to institutions where they can receive the supervision and care required by their ailments.

Most older persons, due to poor health, forced retirements, and/or voluntary resignations are unemployed. Although retirement has been viewed as a part of the "golden era," with time not committed to an occupation, it usually marked decreased income for the retirees also. Less and inadequate income will affect the retirees' ability to participate in certain activities and to access services and commodities. In addition, retirement marks the end of a major social role and the social interactions and status that accompanied that role. Likewise, the accumulated deaths of family members and friends subtract social roles and relations, helping to disintegrate the individual's social network.

Special programs and groups have evolved to help aged individuals cope with the social losses associated with aging. When they are able, aged individuals fill the social gaps themselves. Volunteer work, special transportation, support groups, new friends, surrogate families, public assistance, senior centers, and hobbies are a few of the avenues used by the aged to compensate for other losses. Hearing aids, glasses, walkers, and other equipment also enhance effective participation in society. Yet, most of the losses associated with old age are irreversible and are not compensated or replaced. Individuals who have passed through the earlier life stages find themselves at a dead end, without another socially prescribed stage, save death, that they can enter. Thus, the position and role of the aged are greatly influenced by the resources and opportunities available to them in the society.

In conclusion, because the large number of persons living to late maturity and old age is a fairly recent trend, there are few aging role models. Consequently, norms and roles for the aged are neither empirically nor clearly defined. Observations of the aged reveal that they may assume a variety of social roles. Retirement and the death of family members and friends have varied consequences. Health status and incomes also vary. Discrimination and historical factors add other dimensions to social role and status among the aged. What we observe may range from a retired couple cruising the Mediterranean to a poverty-stricken widow living in housing without indoor plumbing.

Although some aged are experiencing relatively healthy living, others are suffering from chronic illnesses that limit their social involvement and may result in institutionalization. The rate and circumstances of aging vary. So, as we visualize the decrepit recluse among the aged, we also see the active and engaged aged in our society. In either case, the aged individuals are only a part of the equation that determines sociological descriptions of their old age. Societal factors (e.g. expectations, retirement laws, and discrimination) complete the equation and influence how individuals age in our society.

Theories of Aging

There are numerous theories of how and why aging occurs. None of these theories can be universally applied, as they do not account for all the biological and sociological consequences of aging nor consider special characteristics of certain aged populations. There are no generally accepted theories of aging. Among the existing biological theories are wear-and-tear, programmed time clock, error, and immune system. Social theories of aging include modernization, activity, and disengagement.

Biological Theories

The **wear-and-tear theory** of biological aging views bodily functions much like the functioning of a machine. Machine parts eventually wear out because of constant use and cause the machine to operate improperly or not to operate at all. Similarly, body organs in constant use are said to wear out and cause bodily dysfunctions and/or death. Unlike the machine, however, the human body can repair itself, and constant use does strengthen rather than weaken some bodily functions.

The **programmed theory** of aging holds that aging is genetically preprogrammed and that cellular reproduction is limited to a fixed number of times. Thus, death is not only inevitable; if left to natural causes, its timing may even be predetermined or inherited. The most identifiable support for this theory is similarities in senescence rates among humans with similar heredity. Conversely, the ability of some cells to continue to reproduce and live refutes the theory's general applicability.

Another genetic theory is the **error theory**, which explains the aging of body cells as caused by errors in the synthesis of protein. Genetic codes on DNA prescribe the normal protein synthesis. When errors occur, the cells are not compatible with the code, cannot function properly, and eventually die. Cumulative cellular losses result in a decline in bodily functions and eventually death.

The **immunological theories** refer to the ability of the body's immune system to recognize and combat substances in the body that cause harm or damage with antibodies. If the immune system fails to destroy harmful substances in the body or produces antibodies that instead destroy normal, good cells, harmful cells are allowed to live within and damage the body (Shock, 1974; Finch and Hayglick, 1977; Rockstein and Sussman, 1979).

Social Theories

The **modernization theory** resolves that declines in the social status among the aged are due to modernization. In his description of the modernization theory, Cowgill (1974:123–46) pinpointed four basic processes that reduce the status of older persons. These four processes—urbanization, economic developments, advances in health technology, and formal education—are common in developed and modern societies.

The theory explains first that medical advances increase longevity for more people and force the young and old to compete for limited positions in the society. Second, new occupations introduced by economic technology pay higher salaries to the qualified younger worker and make many of the skills possessed by older persons obsolete. Third, more formal and technical education provided younger people makes the older persons less informed about the modern society. Finally, urbanization that increases the migration of younger people further polarizes the young and old by leaving aged persons in older, usually deteriorated neighborhoods. In each of these processes, the older person is believed to emerge with lower status on the basis of income, employment, residence, and useful information.

The **modernization theory** assumes that older persons had high social status prior to modernization. However, the status of the aged may not, in fact, have been high, and not all older persons are negatively affected by modernization. Not all industrialized, modern societies note a decline in social status for their aged. In addition, the theory relates only to a specific period of a society and does not deal with the effects of social change on the aged after that period. Consequently, the modernization theory is a good demonstration of how social change may alter the social staus of older persons but is limited in its applicability in explaining the social role and status of the aged.

The **activity theory** purports that older persons who maintain a high level of activity are better able to cope than are inactive ones. When an activity or role, such as an occupation or a spouse, is lost, the older person is said to substitute new roles or more activity. Theoretically, older persons are able and/or want to be involved. Watson (1982:12) points out that failing health, individual adjustment differences, and multiple hazards of aging and the aged lend little support to this theory.

The **disengagement theory** is always included in discussions of the aged as social beings. In an attempt to explain how and why older persons leave social roles, the disengagement theory proposes that individuals necessarily and inevitably withdraw from social roles and experience increased introversion (Cumming et al., 1960:23–25; Cumming and Henry, 1961). In a sense, older persons respond to a societal responsibility to move aside, experience their old age while awaiting death, and make room for younger members of the society.

Activity theory claims that older persons who maintain a high level of activity are better able to cope in later years.

Disengagement is neither a universal nor inevitable response to aging among the aged. Not all older persons mutually disengage from society. In addition, many aged do not have the luxury of the myriad of social roles, assumed by the theory, from which to withdraw. In his analysis of the theory Rey (1982:192–93) commented on the theory's applicability to minority aged, stating that

> The disengagement theory provides a conceptual filter that can block out the day-to-day, as well as the historical, life experiences of older people; and as such, it eliminates minority seniors from those who choose to pretend that all is rosy with the elderly to the very end.

Whether older persons voluntarily withdraw from social roles that they held when they were younger or whether older people are pushed out of these roles by younger members of society, social roles are, nonetheless, among a variety of losses experienced by many of the aged. Most older persons manage to cope with the losses they experience. Some must overcome numerous barriers, such as too little income, discriminatory policies, and unavailable services, to meet the standards for successful aging set by most theorists. Successful aging, as a concept, places positive values on certain adjustments made by older persons to cope with aging (Atchley, 1980:239). Valid theories of aging must consider individual differences in histories, experiences, values, and preferences when defining successful aging. Without such considerations, theories of aging will continue to be proven invalid by exceptions.

Ageism

Monolithic inscriptions provide evidence that as early as 3000 B.C. the role and social status of the elderly were being identified and recorded (Freeman, 1979:20). However, neither historical data nor present-day investigations have produced a single model of the elderly's role and social status that is universally demonstrated. The social role and status of the aged vary from one society to another. A **gerontocratic** society places elderly in higher positions and provides them greater respect and honor than any other type of society.

Gerontocratic Society

In a Kenyan village, the Gikuyu provided their elderly with rubric respect and obedience (Cox, 1977:2–10). Their societal structure and ethos dictated that younger tribe members afford respectful behavior to all elders, simply because of their age. The elders were permitted to judge the behavior of other villagers and comprised the village's decision-making core. Elderly women substituted for their earlier childbearing obligations to the society new obligations to assist young girls in meeting these expectations. Young boys who wanted to marry or touch the breasts of young girls first consulted their male elders. In explaining the status of villagers' male elders, one elder said:

> By age sixty he has cooled down. He can reflect on all his actions. When he does a wrong it is intentional and therefore very serious. He must stand by his actions as a rational man and may be called to judge the actions of others. The wise man

at this stage admits to the impossibilities of life; he stops swearing at life and gives way. He has much experience and a wide range of opportunities to express his intelligence to others. He is senior elder and people listen to him for he knows all there is to know (Cox, 1977:3).

Gerontocratic societies, dominated and controlled by elders, result from laws and religious dogma that revere older members of their populaces. Age and wisdom usually secure these elders governing powers and property rights not attainable by the young. Junior elders, those in their early forties, of the Akikuyu village strove for the additional years and wisdom gained from experiences that would categorize them as senior elders, so they would be eligible for the maximum social status in the village. Note that the reverence of age found in gerontocracies may even follow older persons to the grave, as religious commandments sometimes require descendants to be duteous after the older person's death.

Numerous theories attempt to explain declines in social roles and status among older people. Declines in the number of gerontocracies are reportedly due to epidemics, starvation, wars, and youthful upheavals that virtually annihilate elderly populaces and/or their influences (Freeman, 1979). On another hand, supporters of the modernization theory, discussed earlier in this chapter, might offer urbanization, economic technology, and more formal, technical education for younger people as reasons for declines in social roles and status among older persons.

Age Discrimination

What is true, though, is that negative myths and stereotypes do little to raise the social status of older Americans. These myths and stereotypes buttress much of the **ageism** in our society against older persons. Ageism is a form of discrimination based solely on age.

Ageism against older persons is demonstrated in institutional and attitudinal manners (Weeks, 1984:307). Institutional ageism includes discriminatory hiring practices, retirement policies, insurance enrollment criteria, and lending requirements. It involves inherent discriminatory practices, built into the rules and regulations governing an establishment's or program's normal operations. Attitudinal ageism refers to the personal prejudices of individuals, based solely on age. Individual ageism may be displayed in a variety of ways, including writings (books, newspapers, etc.), medical treatment considered reasonable, and daily interactions with older persons.

As ageism works to diminish the status given the older person in our society today, other factors create double and triple jeopardy for minority elderly. Double jeopardy applies to those persons who are not only aged but are also a member of a minority group. Their double jeopardy—race and age—make aging in America twice as difficult for this group. Triple jeopardy adds a third handicap, sex, and means that discrimination against women will add an additional burden for aged women who are members of minority groups. Multiple jeopardy is a term that allows special consideration for other attributes or characteristics (e.g., physical handicaps) that give rise to discriminatory practices.

Much effort is being made to eradicate many of the stereotypes and myths that distort views of aging and older persons. Children's books, television commercials, and television programs are being monitored to flag ageism; laws making age discrimination illegal are being passed; and education is being used as an instrument to dispel erroneous myths. Older persons may be productive; they can learn; and they continue to experience sexual sensations.

Common Problems of the Aged

Health, income, and housing are common problems among the aged. More recently elder abuse has been recognized as a national issue. Fear of crime, loneliness, transportation, and ageism may be easily added to the list of problems encountered by older Americans. Various programs, discussed later in the chapter, address some of the aged's needs and aging-related problems in our society. Yet, older persons still find themselves burdened with numerous problems particularly prevalent in their age group.

Health

Illnesses may be classified in two categories: acute illnesses and chronic illnesses. Acute illnesses are generally short-term and have rapid onset. Chronic illnesses develop gradually and are long-term or permanent conditions. Both acute and chronic illnesses afflict humans of all ages and can be disabling and/or cause death. Chronic illnesses are prevalent among the aged. It is estimated that 80 percent of all aged have one or more chronic conditions (Woodruff and Birren, 1983:85).

Declining health, retirement, reduced income, and substandard housing are common problems among the elderly.

Table 11.2 *Prevalence Rate of Top Chronic Conditions in U.S. Population 17 Years and Older, 1981*

	Rate per 1,000 Persons AGE		
Condition	17–44	45–64	65 plus
Arthritis	47.4	246.5	264.7
Hypertension	54.2	243.7	378.6
Hearing impairments	43.8	142.9	283.8
Heart conditions	37.9	122.7	277.0
Chronic sinusitus	158.4	177.5	183.6
Visual impairments	27.4	55.2	136.6
Orthopedic impairments	90.5	117.5	128.2
Arteriosclerosis	0.5	21.3	97.0
Diabetes	8.6	56.9	83.4
Varicose veins	19.0	50.1	83.2
Hemorrhoids	43.7	66.6	65.9
Frequent constipation	9.2	22.4	59.2
Disease of urinary system	25.8	31.7	56.1
Hay fever	100.2	77.5	51.9
Corns and callosities	14.0	35.8	51.9
Hernia of abdominal cavity	8.9	33.1	49.1

Source: National Center for Health Statistics, Division of Health Interview Statistics, unpublished; Adapted from U.S. Senate Special Committee on Aging, *Aging America: Trends and Projections.* (PL3377–584) Washington, D.C.: GPO, 1983, p. 58.

In 1981 arthritis, hypertension, hearing impairments, and heart conditions were the most common chronic conditions affecting older Americans. Table 11.2 shows the prevalence rate (per 1,000 persons) of leading chronic conditions among the U.S. adult population aged seventeen and older. Note that the conditions are increasingly more prevalent with age for each of the conditions, except hay fever. Consequently, as more people live longer, we can expect chronic illnesses to become even more dominant among health-care needs.

Although chronic illnesses are common among the aged, they do not deter most older persons from living independently. A relatively small number of the aged are severely disabled by their chronic illnesses. Only about 5 percent of the aged population, at any one time, may be found in nursing homes.

Chronic illnesses, however, may account for more frequent physician visits, more hospital stays, and greater health-care expenditures experienced by older Americans. A U.S. Senate Special Committee on Aging Report (1983:52–76) indicated that persons over age sixty-five use hospitals an average of 2.8 times per year, whereas those forty-five to fifty-four years of age average 4.7 visits per year. The sixty-five-and-older group accounts for 33 percent of the country's total health-care expenditures. Health and the consequences of poor health are major issues in aging. However, it is important to note that life experiences, environment, and heredity play major roles in the determination of health status in later years; thus, health considerations should include conditions and processes that cover the life span.

Income

Wages and earnings generally account for most income received by U.S. residents. Older Americans who are retired and experience a reduction in income and those who work but receive lower pay are more economically disadvantaged than younger workers. Older women and minority groups are notably most disadvantaged. The U.S. Senate Special Committee on Aging report summarizes: "Elderly white men had a poverty rate of 8.3 percent in 1982, but elderly white women were twice as likely as their male counterparts to be in poverty (17.5 percent), elderly black men four times as likely, and black women five times as likely (42.4 percent)." One of seven (14.5 percent) of America's elderly lived in poverty in 1982.

Income sources for older Americans may be direct and/or indirect. Direct income has transferable value and includes social security, other job-related pensions, cash public assistance, interest, and gifts. Indirect income is not transferable, being earmarked for the recipient only, and includes public assistance and informal support provided individuals. Noncash public assistance benefits include rent subsidies, food stamps, and health-care insurances. Although poverty-level computations do not consider noncash public assistance that improves economic conditions, it is important to note that in 1981, 49 percent of the aged poor received no public assistance.

In Table 11.3 the percentages of older persons receiving income from earnings, social security, public pensions, private pensions, and public assistance in 1978 are shown. After age sixty-five, people increasingly rely on all other income sources except earnings because of retirement. A larger percentage of couples than single persons begin to receive social security, but single persons continue to be the dominant receivers of public assistance among the aged.

Today, social security remains the primary source of income for the aged, especially the black aged. In 1981 social security represented 47 percent of the income for black heads of households sixty-five years of age and older and 37 percent for all elderly heads of households. Similarly, it represented 46 percent of the income for all aged persons living alone and 62 percent for black aged persons living alone (U.S. Senate Special Committee on Aging, 1983:33).

Housing

Although many older persons own their own homes, most live in a house whether they own or rent. Unfortunately, most of these homes are older dwellings with structural and environmental problems. As discussed earlier, modernization has resulted in increased mobility and income for younger persons who move to newer housing and away from old neighborhoods. Older persons, 50 percent of whom have lived in their present homes since before 1959, are left to live in the

Table 11.3 *Percentage of Older Households Having Income from Selected Sources by Age and Household Type, 1978*

	Ages 62–64		Ages 65 and Older	
Source	Couples	Single Persons	Couples	Single Persons
Earnings	77	50	41	15
Social security	46	58	91	89
Public pension	13	9	16	12
Private pension	19	13	31	14
Public assistance	2	10	5	14

Source: Social Security Administration. "The Income and Resources of the Elderly in 1978." *Social Security Bulletin* 44:12, 1981.

older neighborhoods. In urban areas especially, such movements have created older neighborhoods void of usual community resources (e.g., corner store); filled with dilapidated, boarded, abandoned, or unkept buildings; and plagued by crime.

In addition, the older homes are usually structurally inadequate. The homes may be too large, in need of repairs, and/or not navigable by the older residents. A home once the residence of spouses and children may have excess living space for an older couple, widow, or widower whose children have left. Insufficient dollar resources often hinder older persons in making needed repairs or renovations to accommodate their physical handicaps. Often ramps, widened doorways for wheelchairs and hand-support fixtures in the bath are needed, if older persons are to continue functioning in their homes.

Retirement communities and other senior housing facilities have met the housing needs of many older persons for whom these options are available and affordable. Designed specifically for the aged, they usually meet the structural and environmental needs of their older residents. Services and special security provisions such as meals, social activities, medical care, in-home services, and checks on residents who live alone are also becoming more common in alternate housing arrangements for the elderly.

Elder Abuse

Abuse of individuals within American families is not a new phenomenon. A national study of violence in the family (Straus et al., 1980) suggested that the family, next to the military in times of war, is the most violent single institution in American society. The impact of abuse against children and spouses (particularly battered wives) has been recognized both politically and socially since the 1960s and 1970s, respectively. Only recently has **elder abuse** begun to receive national attention.

As a result of a year-long investigation of elder abuse, a report (April, 1981) by the House Select Committee on Aging stated:

> Elderly abuse is far from an isolated and localized problem involving a few frail elderly and their pathological offspring. The problem is a full-scale national problem that exists with a frequency that few have dared to imagine ... the problem is increasing from year to year.

In addition to almost daily media accounts of elder abuse in the United States, several studies (Lau and Kosberg, 1979; Block and Sinnott, 1979; O'Malley et al., 1979; Douglass, et al., 1980) of professionals, service agencies, caregivers, and actual client records provide evidence of chronic and repetitive elderly abuse.

Although there are other perpetrators of abuse, most elder abusers are related to their victims and may be suffering from stress. Typically, the elderly victim is viewed as the source of the stress. In generationally inverse situations, where the older generation or parent is dependent on the younger generation or child(ren), there is a reversal of a complex set of rights, responsibilities, and obligations (Steinmetz, 1978: 54–55). Both generations change patterns and expectations of themselves and others.

The responsibility of caring for the older person may be an additional burden for the individual who must perform other roles such as parent, spouse, and employee. The combined demands of these roles contribute to the probability of neglecting the elderly and may lead to abusive behavior towards them. In their study of caregivers, Steinmetz and Amsden (1983: 179–91) found that responsibility for doing tasks for the elderly, stress resulting from the older person's dependence on the caregiver, and feelings of a sense of burden increased the likelihood of abusive and disruptive family interactions. It is estimated that about 10 percent of those elderly who are dependent on others are at risk of abuse.

However, recent data have indicated a "web of interdependency" (Astrein et al., 1984:11) between the elderly victims and the abusive relatives or caregivers. For example, the elderly individual may be dependent on the abuser for assistance with daily living activities, whereas the abuser may be dependent on the elder for emotional and/or financial support. Although most reported cases of elder abuse are found in the lower socioeconomic strata, a significant number are found in the middle and upper classes. Alcoholism, addiction to other drugs, marital problems and/or financial difficulties are also characteristic of abusers.

The profile of the elderly most vulnerable to abuse includes females; older elderly (above age seventy); dependency on the abuser, usually because of physical and/or mental disabilities; and residency with the abuser. Although about 4 percent of older Americans are actual victims of moderate to severe abuse, only one of every six cases (about half the report rate for child abuse) is reported. Most cases of elder abuse are reported by service providers, relatives and friends. A study of actual abuse reports at a clinic in Cleveland conducted by Lau and Kosberg (1979: 10–15) found that only 5 percent of the abused elderly reported the abuses. Twenty-three percent of the elder abuse cases were reported by hospital staff; 21 percent by nursing agencies; 21 percent by relatives; and 10 percent, by friends.

Several factors contribute to the small percentage of elder abuse cases reported. First, there is a reluctance among abused elderly to report abuse. Intimidations, threats, and other fears prevent the abused elderly from seeking help. Most often, the abused elderly fear retaliation from the abuser, are doubtful that a remedy is possible, or do not want to prosecute the abuser, who may be a family member. If the abuser is a primary caregiver, additional fears are generated when undesired institutional care or no care at all are seen as alternatives.

Second, the common isolation of vulnerable elderly is a deterrent to the reporting of elder abuse by others. The abusers, who usually have the most contact with the abused elderly, will seldom report their maltreatment of the older person. Limited mobility and social interactions minimize opportunities for others (e.g., service providers, friends, and relatives) to observe the treatment and conditions of isolated elderly. Yet, trends point out the important role for service providers, friends, and relatives in the actual reporting of elder abuse.

Third, varying definitions of abuse hinder the classification and documentation of elder abuse. Many reports of elder abuse are unsubstantiated, as the reporters are uncertain about what classifies abuse. Other observations of elder abuse are not reported because potential reporters are not familiar with detection and reporting procedures. Further, various categories of neglect—particularly the failure to provide proper care and abuse and maltreatment that causes injury or harm—have been used to document elder abuse cases. The absence of consistency in the classifications used in recording cases makes the compilation of available data difficult.

Physical abuse, psychological abuse, and material abuse are frequently used to categorize elder abuse. Block and Sinott (1979) have further delineated abuse to the physical body and have added medical abuse to their classifications:

1. Physical Abuse: maltreatment that causes malnutrition and injuries such as bruises, welts, sprains, dislocations, abrasions, or lacerations.
2. Psychological Abuse: maltreatment characterized by verbal assaults, threats, fear, or isolation.
3. Material Abuse: maltreatment that involves the theft or misuse of money or property.
4. Medical Abuse: maltreatment evidenced by the withholding of medications or aids (e.g., glasses, false teeth, and hearing aids).

The majority of the states mandate the reporting, usually by certain professionals and public employees, of elder abuse. The laws are not uniform but recognize the need systematically to identify and stop abuses against the elderly. Additional laws exist to help insure the proper care and protection of the elderly. Ironically, some of these laws are themselves viewed as abusive and as violating the rights of the elderly (Krauskopf and Burnett, 1985:219–55).

When involuntary commitments, guardianships, and other court-ordered remedies are applied to the elderly, legal and ethical arguments evolve around the methods used to determine the need for such remedies and the older person's role in the determination. Paramount in these arguments are the rights of the older persons to maintain as much autonomy as they desire over their affairs and person. It is not always clear when the courts are infringing upon rather than insuring the rights of the individual. Family members and other caregivers are frequently confronted with the same dilemma. When, if ever, should adults not be able to choose the type and condition of the environments in which they live (or die)? Do some laws inflict societal values disparately upon aged adults and other adults? Are some laws legal means to abuse elderly and their material possessions? These are but a few of the questions posed by vulnerable elderly and their advocates as our society attempts to protect its elderly members.

The Aging Network: Informal and Formal

Formal and informal services from both public and private sources are available to older Americans. Although they do not meet all the needs of all aged persons, they constitute a wide variety of services. Collectively, they form a network for aging and are the source of much information and many services and special programs for the aged.

Informal Support

Most elderly prefer to live independent lives; however, crises, impairments, and other frailties often require elderly individuals to seek assistance and help from others. In such cases, the personal autonomy of the elderly individual is enhanced by the availability of viable options. In old age, as throughout life, a primary source of such options is the informal support network, family members, friends, and neighbors. For the elderly, the high prevalence of death among elderly friends and spouses usually spawns increased elderly reliance on other family members, especially their children, and the community.

The myth of abandonment has been refuted by numerous studies (Shanas, 1979; Bild and Havighurst, 1976). Children and other family members do not, en masse, abandon elderly parents and kin. Family members provide the elderly in need of assistance a range of services from help with activities of daily living to social interaction and financial support. When they need assistance, most elderly prefer help from adult children rather than any other kin or nonfamily support system (Cicerelli, 1979: 3–4).

However, familial support and expectations vary among individuals and groups. The extended family and filial piety are frequently referred to when discussing the kin network of minority groups. These kin networks are especially important among first-generation elderly (Woodruff and Birren, 1983:60–61). For example, within the traditional Japanese family, children are expected to care for elderly parents. Similarly, the extended family among Mexican Americans and blacks is chronicled as a primary source of support for its elderly members. Most recently, increased assimilation of ethnic and minority groups is being investigated for its impact on the traditional values and customs in minority subcultures and their family structures.

Unfortunately, not much attention has been given to current population trends regarding the age group of the children from whom support is expected. At the turn of the century about 4 percent of the elderly in the United States were "old-old," or over the age of eighty-five. In 1980, 10 percent of the elderly, or 2.2 million Americans, were over the age of eighty-five. It is estimated that by the year 2000 there will be 5.1 million Americans in the old-old category. Consequently, the children of the old-old, from whom the elderly prefer assistance, will

The degree of care and respect for the elderly is affected by race, class, and culture.

themselves be elderly, between the ages of sixty-five and eighty-five years, or "young-old."

Other social institutions and groups comprise the aged individual's informal network. Organizations such as social clubs, fraternal groups, and churches lend support and assistance to the elderly, especially members, in their communities. Associations developed through membership may provide social interactions, services, and assistance to the aged. Other elderly benefit from special projects and activities that target them. However, most elderly belong to no more than one such organization, excluding the church (Riley and Foner, 1968:483–510). Church membership and participation are generally continued. Thus, the church is viewed as a primary institution in accessing and aiding the aged. Nonetheless, as discussed earlier in this chapter, poor health, limited mobility, and other barriers also hinder the ability of the aged to participate in church and other activities. Without these important societal links and associations, the aged individuals may be deprived of another potential source of support.

Although informal support systems are vital sources of support for the elderly, the ability of these systems to provide such support should be neither overstated nor assumed. Evidenced by the demand for public assistance and services, there are gaps between what the elderly need and the ability and/or the willingness of informal support systems to meet those needs. Laws, programs, and services do exist to help fill these gaps.

Relevant Legislation

The federal government enacts legislation and appropriates funds to support aged persons in their efforts to live and participate in the American society. In Table 11.4 some of the major legislation that impacts the lives of older Americans is identified. Over the years amendments to these acts have added new dimensions or foci but have not altered the primary impact of the acts. For example, survivors' benefits (1939), disability insurance (1956), and medicare (1965) were merely new features of the Social Security Act. Amendments in 1956, 1959, and 1964 to the Housing Act of 1937 authorized, respectively, mortgage-insurance financing of housing for the aged; low-cost loans for those with moderate and above-average incomes, and expanded low-rent public housing for the aged; and specific provisions for relocation assistance and an extension of the mortgage-in-

Table 11.4 *Major U.S. Legislation that Affects Older Americans*

Year Passed	Title of Act	Primary Impact
1935	Social Security Act	Provided for minimal retirement income for many older persons
1937	Housing Act	Provided low-rent public housing for the aged and poor
1965	Older Americans Act	Established a national network of agencies to service the aged and made provisions for federal support of aging services
1967	Age Discrimination in Employment Act	Set the minimum age for mandatory retirement
1975	Age Discrimination Act	Outlawed age discrimination in all federally-funded programs

surance program for rural elderly (Woodruff and Birren, 1983:399–400). Although a 1978 amendment to the **Age Discrimination in Employment Act** raised the minimum age for mandatory retirement from sixty-five to seventy, the amendment did not alter the act's role in controlling mandatory retirement policies.

Social security and medicare are perhaps the most commonly known federal programs that provide assistance to older Americans. The Social Security Act was enacted in 1935 and, as noted in the previous section, is a primary source of income for older persons. As social security eligibility is based on age at retirement, amount of time in the work force, and income while working, it is inherently discriminatory against women, blacks, and other minority groups. The eligibility of these potential social security recipients is most often hindered by patterns of interrupted careers resulting from pregnancies, "last-hired–first-fired" policies, and other discriminatory employment practices. Shorter life spans (except for white females), lower salaries, employment (such as housekeeping) not covered by the Social Security Act, and poor health resulting in early retirement are also among the characteristics that reduce or deter social security benefits.

The medicare program was introduced by Congress in 1965 as a health insurance program for older Americans. It includes both hospital and medical benefits. Its policies require recipients to pay a premium and set sixty-five as its eligibility age. Unable to pay the premium, some poor elderly do not benefit from all its provisions; others, with shorter life expectancies, do not anticipate receiving any of its benefits.

Other formal programs and services available to older persons include nutrition, transportation, employment (paid and volunteer), outreach, and education. Senior centers in community settings usually serve as the prime source for many of these services, including information and referral, recreation, friendly visiting, and telephone reassurance. These formal services are in addition to the similar services provided informally by family members, friends and neighbors.

Many other services are available to aged persons. Some of the services are age specific; other services are not age specific. **Age-specific services** are those that utilize age criteria and target one specific age group for servicing. Most of the services discussed thus far in this section have been age specific. However,

Age-specific services such as adopt-a-pet programs help aged individuals to cope with the social losses associated with aging.

it is important to note that there are many other programs and services that are not age specific and/or include the aged in their target populations.

Numerous funding sources, programs and services, professional organizations, educational institutions, advocacy groups, caregivers, and elderly themselves form the formal and informal links of the aging network. Including family members and other informal caregivers, the aging network encompasses the national, state, and local levels and functions to address problems and issues salient to aging processes, the aged, and an aging society. Collectively, they provide many resources and much direction, information, and support for the development of adequate services and policies in aging.

Older Americans Act. In the aging network one of the most important pieces of federal aging legislation is the **Older Americans Act** (OAA). First enacted in 1965, it has undergone numerous revisions but continues to provide much of the funding for aging programs and services. In addition to serving as an avenue for congressional appropriations for aging programs, the OAA establishes and guides the operations of the Administration on Aging (AoA). To illustrate the impact of the OAA on the network, a schematic view of the AoA and its resulting links is provided in Table 11.5.

AoA is a unit of the Office of Human Development Services (HDS). The chief AoA officer, the Commissioner on Aging, is directly responsible to the Secretary of HDS. Regional offices are established as administrative arms of AoA. Each state operates a state unit (usually a department or office) on aging. To help develop, coordinate, and implement aging programs and services at the local level, local units on aging (commonly known as area agencies on aging) exist. The total number and size of these local units vary from state to state.

Primarily, AoA oversees its regional offices and provides funding for state and local agencies on aging (including U.S. territories). Yet, its ensuing network

***Table 11.5** Aging Network Links Resulting from Older Americans Act*

National Level
National aging agencies
Other federal agencies
Administration on Aging (AoA)

Regional Level
Regional Administration on Aging Offices

State Level
State units on aging
Other state departments and units
State legislatures
State association on aging
State advisory boards
State colleges and universities

Local Level
Area Agencies on Aging
Local advisory boards
Family members and other informal service providers
Other local agencies
Old Americans Act-funded programs and services
Local governments

incorporates other agencies, organizations, institutions, and individuals at each of its levels. This sharing and coordinating of information is vital to the network and part of AoA's mandate. Further expanding its network, AoA also provides financial support for research and demonstrations that target specific aged populations, issues, and problems.

Some professional areas have established organizations that address issues more related to their specific aging activities. Examples of these organizations are the National Association for Nursing Homes, the National Association for State Units on Aging, the National Association for Area Agencies on Aging, and the Association for Gerontology in Higher Education. Other organizations target aged members and have large elderly constituents. The Gray Panthers, National Retired Teachers Association/American Association of Retired Persons, and the National Council for Senior Citizens are among the largest organizations for older persons.

Generally, the poor, women, blacks and other minority groups are not represented by these organizations (Atchley, 1983:101). In recognition of the limited participation of minorities in such organizations, organizations targeting minority members and aging interests have emerged. The National Caucus and Center on the Black Aged primarily focuses on black aging; the National Association for Spanish Speaking Elderly, on Hispanic aging; the National Indian Council on Aging, on native American aging; and the National Pacific/Asian Resource Center on Aging, on Asian American aging. In 1981 the Association for Gerontology and Human Development in Historically Black Colleges and Universities incorporated to provide its members a forum in which they could address issues relevant to their aging activities. Similar groups are forming to fill the gaps in other areas left by organizations in addressing the needs of the poor, female, and minority aged. Wider participation of minorities in the aging service delivery system (as providers and recipients) and in the system as a whole is a current issue in the aging network.

Summary

Although individuals and society contribute to the consequences of growing older, aging is universal and inevitable. As researchers attempt to understand aging—how and why it occurs—they postulate various theories that contribute to what we know about aging; yet, none of the theories is generally applicable. However, a group of processes, referred to as senescence, is found to occur at varying rates in all humans.

In the United States the aged population has increased dramatically and is expected to exhibit more growth through the next century. The prevalence of aged persons in our society forces attention. Consequently, problem areas related to the aged such as health care, income, abuse, and housing are major societal issues for this century and the next.

Perceptions of aging are influenced by myths and stereotypes. How our society deals with the problems and issues of aging will depend on the availability of accurate data and information about aging and the aged. Such data and information have already promulgated many laws, policies, and programs to address the aged. Yet, with gerontology, the study of aging and aging processes, our society can expect programs to be altered and added, new laws enacted, and new policies implemented.

Key Concepts

activity theory
Age Discrimination in Employment Act
age grading
age-specific services
ageism
aging
birth cohort
chronological age
disengagement theory
elder abuse
error theory
gerontocratic society
gerontology
immunological theories
life expectancy
modernization theory
Older Americans Act
programmed theory
senescence
senile dementia
senility
wear-and-tear theory

References

Astrein, Bruce, Adria Steinberg, and Joann Duhl. (1984) *Working with Abused Elders: Assessment, Advocacy and Intervention.* Massachusetts: University Center on Aging, University of Massachusetts Medical Center.

Atchley, Robert C. (1980) *The Social Forces in Later Life.* New York, N.Y.: Wadsworth Publishing Co., Inc.

———. (1983) *Aging: Continuity and Change.* New York, N.Y.: Wadsworth Publishing Co., Inc.

Bild, Bernice R., and Robert J. Havighurst. (1976) "Family and Social Support." *The Gerontologist, 16*(February):63–69.

Block, Marilyn R., and Jan D. Sinnot (eds.). (1979) *The Battered Elderly Syndrome: An Exploratory Study.* College Park, Md.: Center on Aging, University of Maryland.

Bostwinick, Jack. (1981) *We Are Aging.* New York, N.Y.: Springer Publishing Co., Inc.

Butler, Robert N. (1975) *Why Survive? Being Old in America.* New York, N.Y.: Harper & Row, Publishers.

Cicirelli, Victor G. (1981) *Helping Elderly Parents.* Boston, Mass.: Auburn House Publishing Company.

Coleridge, Samuel Taylor. (1983) "Youth and Age." In Virginia S. Reiser (ed.), *Best Loved Poems in Large Print.* Boston, Mass.: G. K. Hall and Company, 232–33.

Cowgill, Donald O. (1974) "Aging and Modernization: A Revision of the Theory." In Jaber Gubrium (ed.), *Late Life Communities and Environmental Policies.* Illinois: Charles C. Thomas.

Cox, Frances M., and Ndung'u Mberia. (1977) *Aging in Changing Society: A Kenyan Experience.* Washington, D.C.: International Education on Aging.

Cumming, Elaine, Lois R. Dean, Davis S. Newell, and Isabel McCaffrey. (1960) "Disengagement: A Tentative Theory of Aging." *Sociometry, 23*(March)23–25.

Cumming, Elaine, and William E. Henry. (1961) *Growing Old: The Process of Disengagement.* New York, N.Y.: Basic Books, Inc., Publishers.

Douglass, Richard L., Tom Hickey, and Catherine Noel. (1980) *A Study of Maltreatment of the Elderly and Other Vulnerable Adults.* Ann Arbor, Mich.: Institute of Gerontology, University of Michigan.

Finch, Caleb E., and Leonard Hayglick (eds). (1977) *Handbook of the Biology of Aging.* New York, N.Y.: Van Nostrand Reinhold Company.

Fox, Jacob H., Jordan L. Topal, and Michael T. Huckman. (1975) "Dementia in the Elderly—Search for Treatable Illnesses." *Journal of Gerontology, 30* (September):557–64.

Freeman, Joseph T. (1979) *Aging: Its History and Literature.* New York, N.Y.: Human Science Press.

Giles, Helen Foster. (1983) "Differential Life Expectancy Among White and Nonwhite Americans: Some Explanations During Youth and Middle Age." In Ron C. Manuel (ed.), *Minority Aging.* Westport, Conn.: Greenwood Press, Inc.

Jackson, Jacquelyne J. (1980) *Minorities and Aging.* New York, N.Y.: Wadsworth Publishing Company, Inc.

Jacobson, Solomon G. (1982) "Equity in the Use of Public Benefits by Minority Elderly." In Ron C. Manuel (ed.), *Minority Aging.* Westport, Conn.: Greenwood Press, Inc., 161–70.

Jarvik, Lissy F. (1980) "Diagnosis of Dementia in the Elderly: A 1980 Perspective." In Carl Eisdorfer (ed.), *Annual Review of Gerontology and Geriatrics.* New York, N.Y.: Springer Publishing Company, Inc.

Krauskopf, Joan M., and Mary Elise Burnett. (1985) "The Elderly Person: When Protection Becomes Abuse." In Harold Cox (ed.), *Aging.* Guilford, Conn.: Dushkin Publishing Group, Inc.

Lau, Elizabeth E., and Jordan I. Kosberg. (1979) "Abuse of the Elderly by Informal Care Providers." *Aging, 299*(September/October):10–15.

Manuel, Ron C., and John Reid. (1983) "A Comparative Demographic Profile of the Minority and Nonminority Aged." In Ron C. Manuel (ed.), *Minority Aging.* Westport, Conn.: Greenwood Press, Inc.

O'Malley, Helen, Howard Segars, Ruben Perez, Victoria Mitchella, and George Knuepfel. (1979) *Elder Abuse in Massachusetts: A Survey of Professionals and Paraprofessionals.* Boston, Mass.: Legal Research and Services for the Elderly.

National Center for Health Statistics. (1982) *Health, United States: 1982.* (PHS 83–1232) Washington, D.C.: U.S. Government Printing Office.

Omen, Gilbert S. (1974) "Behavior Genetics." In James Birren and K. Schaie (eds.), *Handbook of the Psychology of Aging.* New York, N.Y.: Van Nostrand Reinhold Company.

Rey, Antonio B. (1982) "Activity and Disengagement: Theoretical Orientations in Social Gerontology and Minority Aging." In Ron C. Manuel (ed.), *Minority Aging.* Westport, Conn.: Greenwood Press.

Riley, Matilda White, and Anne Foner. (1968) *Aging and Society. Volume One: An Inventory of Research Findings.* New York, N.Y.: Russell Sage Foundation.

Rockstein, Morris, and Marvin Sussman. (1979) *Biology of Aging.* New York, N.Y.: Wadsworth Publishing Co. Inc.

Shanas, Ethel. (1961) *Family Relationships of Older People.* Chicago, Ill.: Health Information Foundation.

Shock, Nathan W. (1974) "Biological Theories of Aging." In Morris Rockstein (ed.), *Theoretical Aspects of Aging.* New York, N.Y.: Academic Press, Inc.

Slaughter, Oliver, and Mignon O. Batey. (1982) "Service Delivery and the Black Aged: Identifying Barriers to Utilization of Mental Health Services." In Ron C. Manuel (ed.), *Minority Aging.* Westport, Conn.: Greenwood Press, Inc.

Social Security Administration. (1981) "The Income and Resources of the Elderly in 1978." *Social Security Bulletin, 44:*3–11.

Steinmetz, Suzanne K. (1978) "The Politics of Aging, Battered Parents." *Society* 15 (July/August):54–55.

———. (1983) "Dependent Elders, Family Stress." In Timothy H. Brubaker (ed.), *Family Relationships in Later Life.* Beverly Hills, Calif.: Sage Publications, Inc.

Straus, Murray A., Richard J. Gelles, and Suzanne K. Steinmetz. (1980) *Behind Closed Doors: Violences in the American Family.* New York, N.Y.: Anchor Books/Doubleday & Company, Inc.

U.S. Senate Special Committee on Aging. (1983) *Aging America: Trends and Projections.* (PL 3377–584) Washington, D.C.: U.S. Government Printing Office.

Watson, Wilbur. (1982) *Aging and Social Behavior.* Beverly Hills, Calif.: Wadsworth Publishing Company, Inc.

Weeks, John R. (1984) *Aging: Concepts and Social Issues.* Beverly Hills, Calif.: Wadsworth Publishing Company, Inc.

Woodruff, Diana S., and James E. Birren. (1983) *Aging: Scientific Perspective and Social Issues.* Monterey, Calif.: Brooks/Coles Publishing Company.

PART III
Social Institutions

12
Social Institutions

OBJECTIVES

Upon completion of this short chapter, the student should be able to:

1. Understand social institutions.

2. Identify social function and social structure as they apply to social institutions.

3. Contrast functional and conflict perspectives on the nature of social institutions.

4. Discuss issues related to change in social institutions and the possibility of more equitable structures.

5. Contrast gemeinschaft and gesellschaft societies.

6. Identify factors in the gesellschaft society that have converged to produce the impersonal, specialized, and bureaucratized structures of modern social institutions.

INTRODUCTION

Social institutions may be defined as sets of norms and activities clustered around the fulfillment of particular needs or interests of a society. For example, one of the needs a collectivity has is to renew itself by reproducing new members and socializing them into the culture of the group. Numerous norms focus on the way a given society goes about doing this: norms regulating courtship and marriage, norms defining who is a member of one's kinship group, norms defining role obligations between marriage partners, norms specifying the expectations concerning how the children are to be nurtured and taught. Of course, these norms all cluster around the family. The family is one of the most important social institutions.

A great many such clusters of norms may be found in most societies. Some of the most easily identified are those related to governance; to the production, exchange, and consumption of goods and services, that is, the economy; to education; and to religion. These have long been major institutions in our society. Our society is dynamic, however, and new clusters of norms continually

Sports has become one of our major institutions. The bureaucratic organization of sports is a far cry from the sandlot games of earlier years.

form around specific kinds of activities. To illustrate this we may think of the growth in the past fifty years in sports activities such as professional football and basketball, the development of youth sports programs, the sudden popularity of gymnastics, and the emergence of televised sport. Sport has become one of our important social institutions. Similar observations may be made about health-related activities. Health care has emerged as one of our major social institutions as a whole complex of norms related to health delivery systems and medical research has developed. Norms have changed with medical developments such as transplant surgery and artificial hearts, like the Jarvik 7 and Penn State ones. Although the village constabulary has been in existence for some time, the development of a network of norms centering on the criminal justice system—the police, the courts, the prisons—has been fairly recent. This system, too, has become an important social institution in our society.

In this section of the book the following eight social institutions are the subject of our analysis: family, economy, education, politics, religion, criminal justice, sport, and health. This list by no means exhausts the total number of social institutions; however, it does include those that seem most relevant for our contemporary society. Obviously, these institutions do not exist in hermetically sealed compartments; they impinge upon one another at many points. The close interplay of government and the economy is a case in point. The problematic relationship between religion, education, and politics is another, with issues such as prayer in the schools at stake. We indicate many of these interconnections as we proceed.

The present chapter introduces some general characteristics of social institutions, particularly their functions, their structures, and the conflicts that become embedded in them. We also attempt to provide a general social context for the changes in the kinds of relationships and activities that modern social institutions embody.

The Criminal Justice System of today has very slight resemblance to the village constabulary of old.

Social Functions

Those social arrangements that have consequences for the maintenance and perpetuation of the society or for its major components are called social functions. For example, in our analysis of socialization, we indicated that one of its functions is to perpetuate the culture the group shares by passing it on to each new generation. The emphasis in the concept of social function is the impact on the society; that is, on the network of social relationships, not specifically on the individual in the society. For instance, when we speak of the social function of religion, we are not referring to the fact that the individual believer may find strength and comfort through faith. Rather, the reference is to such concerns as what the consequences of religion are for maintaining solidarity in the society or for reinforcing the norms that maintain the network of social relationships.

As with many other issues raised in this book, two very different perspectives, each with its own insights, can be brought to bear on the nature of social institutions and the functions they perform. In general, functionalist sociologists assume that social institutions provide the framework through which a society meets its needs. The family provides nurture for new members, and education passes on the accumulated knowledge and skills to new generations. The government defines collective goals and insures that divisiveness and disorder will be held to a minimum. Functionalists assume a widespread agreement on the values embodied in the institutions. Where problems occur, functionalists assume that the society will make readjustments so that balance can be restored.

Conflict theorists, on the other hand, assume that social institutions are defined and organized in such a way as to serve the interests of the dominant group in a society. In this view the differing interests of the dominant group and the subordinate group are irreconcilable. The dominant group exerts its power to maintain the kinds of institutions that work to its advantage. For example, an economic elite dominates governmental policy in order to further the interests of business. A white middle-class society creates a criminal justice system that systematically selects blacks and Hispanics to people its prisons. In this view of institutions, conflict of interests rather than shared values characterizes the social arrangements.

Merton (1958), a functionalist sociologist, distinguished between social functions that are explicit, intended, and publicly recognized on the one hand and those that are unintended and largely unrecognized on the other. The former are called **manifest functions.** The manifest function of our health-care system is to provide medical services to the people. All the other social institutions have such intended or manifest functions. The unintended consequences Merton called **latent functions.** For example, although the manifest function of a college or university may be to educate the young adult, one of its latent functions is to serve as a matrimonial agency for young men and women of marriageable age. It places people of similar background in contact with one another and through its social activities facilitates mate selection. So the same institution has both manifest and latent social functions.

Not even functionalists think that all of the consequences of social institutions are beneficial to the society. Those arrangements that have negative effects on the society or components of the society, Merton called dysfunctions. To illustrate: the Dutch Reformed Church in South Africa carries a strong Calvinist thrust with an implication that its adherents are God's elect people, predestined to carry out His will here on earth. The white Afrikaners use this religious doctrine to justify their domination of the black population of the country. The religion, then, is dysfunctional because it serves to create tension and oppression in the society. These concepts, manifest and latent function and dysfunction, are used in the analysis of some of the institutional arrangements in the following chapters.

Social Structure

The social functions of institutions are carried out through **social structures.** By this we mean that there are some relatively stable and predictable patterns of organization relating to the particular activity that forms the core of the institution. The functions of the family, for example, are carried out through the organized social relationships that make up the family. Consider, too, the organized procedures, requirements, role relationships, and activities through which your college attempts to perform its educational function.

The elements of social organization that have been discussed in earlier passages of the book are the principles that define such structures. The norms of the society give predictability to the patterns of activity that are the focus of social institutions. For example, one of the norms in our society is that the individual is expected to marry only one spouse at the time. This normative expectation is very important in giving a predictable form to the family. A social norm that specifies that one will pay for the goods and services one receives in the open market gives structure to our economic institutions.

The norms that define role relationships are particularly important in defining the structures of social institutions. Roles are interwoven with each other to provide a network of predictable relationships. It is necessary to determine who has what kinds of rights and obligations relative to whom in order to carry out the activities for which the social institution is responsible. For example, the role relationships between church hierarchy, the ministers, the church officials, and the laity provide stable patterns of interaction in religious institutions, enabling the religious institution to perform its functions. The roles of laborer, employer, distributor, retailer, and consumer all mesh to provide a network through which our economic institution can produce and exchange goods and services.

Interrelationships between groups are also prominent features of the social structure of institutions. For example, the predictable competition between various interest groups in pursuit of power gives structure to the political process in our society. The predictably lower quality of health care available to minority groups is a part of the structure of our health-care institution. Tolerance of the commitment of ethnic groups to their traditional churches attests to the pluralistic character of our religious institutions.

Members of the society are socialized in such a way that they internalize the normative expectations of the social institutions. They are socialized to fill the roles that make up the network of institutional relationships. Some of this role preparation is a part of general socialization: learning to be a mother, a citizen, a patient, a consumer. Other roles require specialized training, however, and provision for such socialization is a part of the institutional arrangements: training for nurses, teachers, police officers, or professional athletes.

Our discussion of social institutions, as we have attempted to show, builds on the concepts and principles of social organization that have been discussed earlier in the text. They are the elements that provide structure to social institutions: norms, roles, groups, and socialization. Through these structures the functions that social institutions perform are carried out.

The religious functions are performed through a structure of interrelated roles.

Structural Alternatives

At an earlier time in history the assumption was made that the structure of institutions was unalterable. In some instances, it was assumed that the social order was decreed by God and therefore was not subject to change through human tampering. The patriarchal (father-dominated) family, the "divine right" of kings to rule, the economic order as a network of fixed statuses:—such ideas about social institutional structures pervaded the society.

One of the hallmarks of the modern age is the challenge to the inevitability of such structures. What we now realize is that a given social function can be carried out by very different structures; that is, we recognize the viability of **structural alternatives.** For example, functions of the family may be carried out by the traditional family consisting of father, mother, and children with the father the undisputed head. But these functions may be carried out equally effectively by families with multiple spouses, mother-dominated families, families where authority is shared, single-parent families, or by families consisting of a great variety of household occupants. One of the biggest breakthroughs in the modern era came with the realization that structures could be deliberately created that would carry out the governing functions more effectively than the traditional monarchies. Thus, constitutional government came into being. Alternative structures are a characteristic of the modern age.

The major governing processes in this country are expressed in the Constitution.

In addition to the idea that within a given institution the functions can be carried out by a variety of structures, modern history has demonstrated that a given function may be assigned to different institutions. For example, education was at one time assigned to the family: one learned one's adult roles in the household. This function now is assigned to the educational institution. Care of the sick was at one time a family function. Now much of this function has been shifted to health-care facilities.

The import of what we are saying here is that it is possible to carry out the collective functions through a variety of structures. Structures are subject to change and are often adaptable through deliberate design. In the light of some of the issues raised in the preceding chapters on inequality, these conclusions are particularly salient. The idea that existing institutional structures carry out their collective functions in ways that often benefit some groups more than others is a major source of conflict in modern institutions. What alternative structures might be more equitable? Can we create economic structures that diminish extreme class inequality or eliminate it altogether? Can we create a criminal justice system that punishes the well-to-do felon as well as the poor felon? Can we provide education and health-care services that benefit minority populations on a par with dominant-group members? These are issues that will continue to engage our attention not only as sociology students but also as responsible members of our society.

Gemeinschaft and Gesellschaft

In earlier times if one's house caught on fire, neighbors rushed in to help. The bucket brigade passed pails of water from a well or stream to the house to quench the fire, while friends removed belongings from the burning building. Fire pro-

The modernization of fire protection has been a bonus for urban residents in spite of its impersonality.

tection was handled on the basis of personal acquaintances coming to each other's aid. Contrasting with this method of meeting a recurrent need, today professional units of fire-fighters converge upon the scene; and using their specialized personnel and equipment, they attempt to put out the fire and rescue the people trapped by it. Such fire-fighters do not know personally the people whose house or family members they are attempting to save. The activity is carried out on an impersonal basis. Parallels to this contrast may be found in myriad social activities.

The shift from a friends-and-neighbors approach to meeting collective needs to an orientation characterized by impersonal, specialized organizations responding to such needs is an important development in the nature of social institutions. It roughly parallels the shift from preindustrial society to industrial society. The terminology most frequently used by sociologists to describe the contrast in social relationships embodied in the shift was developed by Ferdinand Tönnies, a German sociologist. Tönnies used the terms **gemeinschaft** and **gesellschaft** to describe contrasting types of societies as well as the different modes of mentality and behavior that characterize them.

Gemeinschaft

Tönnies postulated that out of the desire of men and women to associate with one another comes a unity of human wills. The foundations of such unity, as Tönnies saw them, were kinship, physical proximity, or neighborhood, and intellectual proximity, or shared culture. These constitute the basis of gemeinschaft relationships. Functioning in a homogeneous group, where there is little diversification of interests, and values, the gemeinschaft embraces the intimate, private, and exclusive elements of living together. The ties are emotional, intense, and durable. Contacts, which usually involve face-to-face relationships, are diffused over a wide area of interests and activities, strengthening the bonds of association by their number. Living in a gemeinschaft is an end in itself rather than a means toward some extrinsic end. Relationships are formed not for the

Many of the functions that were at one time performed by the family are now carried out by specialized institutions.

profit to be derived from them but for the value of the contact itself. Specific ends are subsidiary to the maintenance of the relationship. Understanding forms the basis for mutual aid, love, and trust, which are manifestations of the gemeinschaft attitude. The sentiments of the gemeinschaft are bound up in its folkways, mores, and religion, which serve as controlling agents in the society.

Members of the true gemeinschaft feel no need of economic regulation because a private economy is unknown to them. Land is communally owned and cared for. Although the division of labor is rudimentary, such specialized goods and services as are available are personally exchanged and shared. The kinship and neighborhood groups constitute the major institutional focus, and most of the collective needs of the society are addressed by these units.

Tönnies neglected to identify any friction and hostility that were undoubtedly present in gemeinschaft societies; but Tönnies was developing a typical model, or ideal type, to characterize a particular historical manifestation of social relationships.

Gesellschaft

Tönnies's contrasting type, the gesellschaft, is the totality of individuals who enter a relationship according to their own individual wills or motivations for an achievement of their own purposes. The aim of the relationship is to profit each individual who enters it; each strives for his or her own advantage.

The factors giving impetus to forming relationships are mutual, rational pursuit of self-interest. These rational ties connect people at a single point of contact; that is, the areas involved in the relationship to the checkout clerk in a grocery store are specifically limited to the exchange of your money for the merchandise. When the association accomplishes the purpose for which it was formed, the bonds are dissolved. It may be said, then, that the bonds are utilitarian, segmental, temporary, and shallow.

Tradition loses its grip on members of the gesellschaft as the chief medium of social control. Mores lose their rigid nature. New approaches to old problems are found. Civil law dominates the legal system. To Tönnies the law of contract is the typical expression of the gesellschaft relationship. When you contract to buy a car, for example, the relationship between you and the car dealership is limited to the terms specified in the contract. When those specified obligations have been fulfilled, the relationship is dissolved.

The gesellschaft is based upon an elaborate economic system involving rules of exchange that have as their principal components the use of money and credit and the creation of contracts. The individual contributes commodities or services as a means of securing a share of desired goods and services. Exchange takes place within an institutional framework formalized in the state.

Urbanization

What we are describing here is our contemporary industrial society. Our modern institutional structures reflect the historical shift from gemeinschaft to gesellschaft. The differentiation of the economic system from the family system was one of the most profound changes in this shift. From personal, communal sharing and exchange of goods and services, the impersonal market came into being. In the system of exchange that emerged with the modern era, self-interest became

In the Gesellschaft, the rational pursuit of self-interest is the factor that stimulates people to form social relationships.

a visible component of the market relationship. Competition replaced communality. The division of labor became complex as individuals sought advantages by offering different goods and services. The impact on the institutional structure was the emergence of specialized agencies to address the collective needs.

One of the consequences of the industrial society has been the **urbanization** of the population. Urbanization means that an increasing proportion of a society's people live in large cities and their surrounding metropolitan areas. Although agricultural production also took on the commercialized quality of the gesellschaft, the major impetus was toward the cities. Urbanization was the result of the push-pull effect. As agriculture became increasingly mechanized, less farm labor was required, and people were thus pushed toward cities for employment. Periodic setbacks in farm prices also pushed people off the farms. The pulls of the city were the opportunities for employment in its industries and businesses, higher wages, the appeal of the bright lights, and perhaps escape from devalued statuses. The city offered alternatives and opportunities that people responded to in masses. In this country at the time of the first census in 1790, 5.1 percent of the population was urban. The halfway mark occurred in 1920 when over half of the population was classified as urban. Today, approximately 74 percent is urban. Although much of this growth came from migration from the farms, a great deal of it came from immigration. Typically, immigrants who came during the peak period of immigration, 1890 to 1920, settled in the cities of the Northeast and Midwest.

The city is not to be equated with gesellschaft. In a real sense, from its earliest times our society in both its rural and urban settings has constituted a gesellschaft because of its economic organization geared to the impersonal exchange of goods and services. However, the emergence of the gesellschaft was paralleled by the development of cities as the industrial system concentrated population in urban areas.

The city is a Janus-faced entity: its virtues are often the flip side of its vices. For example, the city offers anonymity to its members. One may not even know one's next-door neighbors. This permits a certain degree of privacy and freedom to the urban dweller. However, it can also result in loneliness and isolation. Individuality is enhanced in the urban setting. One is relatively freed from the grip of the group and seeks recognition on merit rather than on ascribed characteristics. Alternatives are many, and freer exercise of choice is permitted. Relationships tend to be fleeting and reciprocally utilitarian and as such pose few restrictions on one's total being. Individuality is enhanced.

However, because many relationships tend to be merely utilitarian, someone else would serve the purpose as well. Someone else who can do as well or better can easily be substituted in situations where impersonal standards, geared instrumentally to the achievement of specified goals, are applied. One becomes interchangeable with others. If you are buying stamps, for example, it really does not matter whether Mr. X., Mrs. Y., or Ms. Z. or a stamp machine sells you the stamps. All you are interested in is the transaction. The relationship itself being immaterial, one person does as well as another, providing that an adequate level of competency is present. One's value to others, then, tends to be instrumental, not intrinsic; segmental and not total. This is one of the sources of alienation in modern society. One of the consequences for social institutions of such impersonality is to render the friends-and-neighbors approach to collective needs obsolete.

Another characteristic of city life is its heterogeneous character. The complex division of labor promotes different interests among members of society. Cultural backgrounds are varied among city dwellers; and life-styles, mores, and religion reflect the diversity. One of the results of this has been increasing tolerance for differences. But the opposite has also been true: the city has been the arena for bigotry and conflict between people with diverse interests, values, and ancestry. An institutional response to this situation has been the growth of formal structures of social control, for example, our criminal justice system and a growth of regulatory governmental agencies.

Specialization and Rationalization

One of the characteristics of the industrial society is the shift from a **traditional orientation** to social activity to a **rational** one. Weber (1968) suggested that in the preindustrial society one orients one's behavior to tradition. "How has it always been done?" serves as the guide to how one acts in the pursuit of goals in any given situation. This type of orientation toward work, authority, family relationships, and the like gives a stable quality to social institutions.

However, as Weber suggested, a shift occurred toward the type of orientation that characterizes modern society: movement toward a rational orientation to action. By rational Weber meant that one chooses a course of action or behavior on the basis of weighing the alternatives and deliberately choosing the most effective means to achieve a given goal. This orientation applies not only to interpersonal relationships and technology but especially to social institutions and gives a dynamic quality to the whole society. The rationalization of business means systematic attempts to calculate and implement effective productivity, profits, and career development. The rationalization of government means the deliberate creation of designs for performing state functions.

The rationalization of other types of services resulted in the development of specialized agencies to carry out functions that had earlier been carried out by friends and family. This **specialization** is evident in many ways. The production of consumer goods such as food and clothing; health care; education; protection of property; care of the elderly, the indigent, and the handicapped; and recreation and entertainment has become the focus of specialized agencies. Provision of such specialized services is made through two channels: either through commercialized activity or through governmental action (Warren, 1978). Both these types of providers depart from the personal relationships that had characterized preindustrial institutions. Both types have culminated in an ever-expanding bureaucratic organization of institutions, which embodies in an intense fashion the specialization and rationalization of activity that we have described.

The convergence of these factors that characterize the gesellschaft, or industrial society, has resulted, then, in the shift of many social functions to impersonal, specialized, bureaucratic, deliberately designed social institutions. This profound change provides the social context in which our contemporary institutional structures may be examined.

Summary

The purpose of this chapter has been to provide an orientation to social institutions. Social institutions are clusters of norms focused around the pursuit of some interest or fulfillment of some need in the society. Social institutions have structures that perform functions. Whereas functional sociologists see social institutions as providing a stable framework through which collective needs are addressed, conflict theorists see them as structures that benefit the dominant groups in the society and often work to the detriment of other groups.

The fixed nature of social institutions has been challenged in the modern age. We no longer regard them as set in concrete. We now confront the issues of designing social institutions that provide more equitable consequences for members of society.

Social institutions have shown the impact of the profound historic shift from the gemeinschaft to the gesellschaft type of society. Factors such as separation of work and family; urbanization; competition, self-interest, and impersonal social relationships; and rational orientations to action have resulted in a shift of many social functions from the old family-and-friends structures to specialized, bureaucratic commercial and governmental structures.

Key Concepts

gemeinschaft
gesellschaft
latent function
manifest function
rational
rational orientation
social institutions
social structure
structural alternatives
traditional orientation
urbanization

References

Merton, Robert K. (1958) *Social Theory and Social Structure.* New York, N.Y.: The Free Press.
Tönnies, Ferdinand. *Community and Society* (Gemeinschaft und Gesellschaft). Translated and edited by Charles P. Loomis. East Lansing, Michigan: Michigan State University Press, 1957.
Warren, Roland L. (1978) *The Community in America.* 3d ed. Chicago, Ill.: Rand McNally College Publishing Company.
Weber, Max. (1968) *Economy and Society.* Totowa, N.J.: Bedminster.

13

Marriage and the Family

OBJECTIVES

Upon completion of the chapter the student should be able to:

1. Identify several definitions of the family and note the implications of these definitions for social policy.

2. Identify the functions and strengths of family life.

3. Understand the impact of changing economic conditions and changes in the status of women on the family.

4. Discuss trends and differences in the experiences of people according to their marital status.

5. Discuss differences in family life by race and ethnicity.

INTRODUCTION

Our first experiences with social interaction occur in the context of the family. Thus, the family is a primary agent of socialization. In recent years, however, the institution of the family has experienced significant changes. Patterns of marriage have changed, and more people are choosing either to remain single longer or seek divorce sooner. These new marriage patterns mean that we may encounter a variety of family forms, including increased numbers of single-parent families, childless couples, and families blended together by remarriage. These changes in marriage patterns and family forms require a reexamination of marriage and the family. To that end, this chapter reviews the concept of marital status; examines alternative definitions of family; reviews social policy implications for such definitions; describes cross-cultural comparisons of families; reviews trends among divorced, widowed, and single persons; and identifies racial and ethnic variations in marital status.

Marriage Defined

Marriage is a public and legal statement whereby a man and a woman agree to share certain social and sexual privileges and adhere to contractual obligations. The privileges associated with marriage are largely tied to sexual intimacy. Once married, an adult may engage in sexual activity without fear of legal intervention or social stigma, as long as the sexual activity is confined to one's spouse. Although there are some state laws that regulate certain kinds of sexual activity permitted among consenting adults, these laws are rarely applied to married couples.

Having children who are regarded as legitimate and being accepted as part of a community are privileges derived from socially approved sexual intimacy. The obligations associated with marriage are by and large financial. The contractual and legal responsibilities for which married couples are held accountable insure that the married couple, and not others in the community, pay for the privileges associated with their marriage. For example, although raising a family free of social stigma is a privilege of marriage, the legal contract between the couple assures that the welfare of the children will be paid for by one or both of the spouses. Additionally, the legal contract between the married couple inhibits one or the other of the spouses from seeking sexual privileges elsewhere. The major factor of that legal contract inhibiting spouses from casually discarding one another and seeking sexual privileges elsewhere is financial loss.

Bill Cosby's TV family, the Huxtables, represent for many an ideal family. Today, family life varies widely from this ideal.

Admittedly, our definition raises a number of issues about marriage. One issue that may be raised is whether homosexuals can get married. As it is defined here marriage takes place only among heterosexuals. Although some homosexuals have had weddings, such unions have yet to be recognized legally as marriage (Duvall and Miller, 1985:6).

Another issue highlighted by this definition of marriage is the idea that sexual activity is permitted only if a couple is married. Obviously, much of sexual activity is premarital or even extramarital. Sociologists are not naive. Sexual activity that is free from social stigma and legal reprisal, however, is guaranteed only when a couple is married. Many religious denominations regard any sexual activity outside of marriage as a sin. And many state laws regard fornication, such as premarital sex, as a crime.

A final issue that this definition of marriage raises is that it ignores religious principles that are associated with marriage. It is common for marriages to receive public acknowledgement through church weddings. Religious dogma often suggests that marriages are made in heaven and that matrimony is an institution where God joins a man and a woman together to raise a family. Although our definition of marriage does not preclude religious interpretations of the significance of matrimony, our definition does suggest that the most apparent consequences of marriage are social and legal. Regardless of a person's religious affiliation, believers and nonbelievers are subject to the same conditions of the marriage contract.

Some states recognize **common law marriages.** A common law marriage occurs when a couple have, without prior legal sanction, lived together long enough for the state to acknowledge any contractual obligations of marriage they may have incurred during the tenure of their relationship. Usually the issue of a common law relationship only surfaces in court when the couple cannot decide between themselves the terms of their separation. Although common law relationships are not the norm, they are not infrequent. Because both a legal marriage as well as a legal divorce can be expensive, poor people may sometimes opt for a common law relationship.

Perhaps the most celebrated common law relationship surfaced when actor Lee Marvin was sued for financial support by his long-time companion, Michelle Triola. In the case of *Marvin v. Marvin,* Ms. Triola sued the actor for a kind of alimony on the grounds that their relationship was enduring enough to warrant financial support for her. The name that was given to this financial support in recognition of the common law relationship in this and other cases is palimony. **Alimony** is a financial allowance given to a spouse, usually the woman, after legal separation or divorce. Because no legal marriage ever existed in a common law relationship, palimony is the popular label given to the financial allowance given to one's "pal" upon termination of a court-acknowledged common law marriage.

Family Policy

Although marriage and family are often considered in the same context, it is clear that a marriage does not necessarily result in children. Conversely, many people

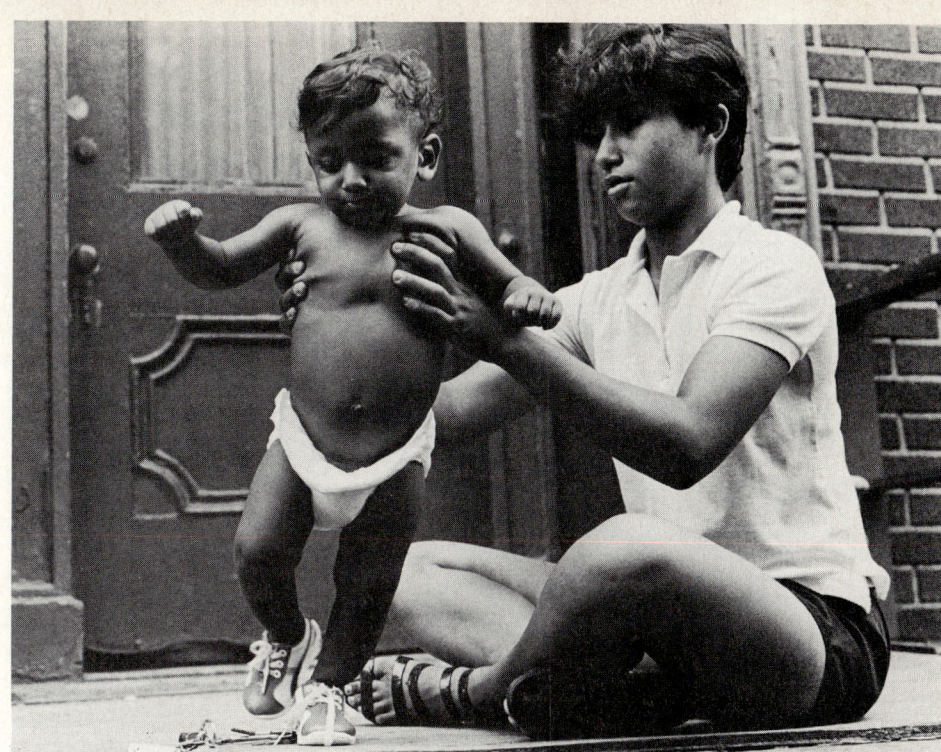

Any definition of family raises numerous social policy issues.

have children without the sanction of marriage. Can either of these two situations be regarded as a family? Or, must a family include a legally married couple and their children? The answers to these questions require more than a casual reflection, because any definition of family raises numerous social policy issues. For example, your definition of family affects how you feel about such policy matters as governmental support for family planning, abortion, and in vitro births. Likewise, other governmental policies are likely to receive your support or criticism depending upon whether you feel these policies enhance or weaken the family as you define it.

Views toward the family have influenced a variety of trends in recent years. For example, several governmental policies, such as Aid to Families with Dependent Children (AFDC), marriage taxes, no-fault divorces, life insurance benefits, and mortgage payments, have all been subject to criticism because of the perceived impact of these policies on family life. The political debate over the Equal Rights Amendment (ERA) has often centered upon its perceived impact on the family. Additionally, the police response to domestic disturbances has been reevaluated. The common response in the past for police intervening in family disturbances was to attempt to quiet the persons involved and to avoid arresting the hostile family members. Now the police are somewhat more likely to arrest perpetrators of family violence, who are usually men, and remove them from the home.

The controversy over the definition of family was highlighted in 1980 when former president Jimmy Carter called a national conference to discuss issues related to the American family. The conference has come to be known as the White House Conference on Families. The goal of the conference was to develop a set of recommendations that the government could use to guide its policies for strengthening the family. The White House Conference on Families succeeded less in presenting recommendations and more in providing several definitions of family.

According to Melville (1983:13–14), essentially four perspectives on family emerged from the conference. First, the Coalition for the White House Conference on Families argued against stereotypical definitions of the family. The coalition claimed that a wide diversity of family types ought to be recognized as legitimate families. Second, the gay task force offered their definitions of family "as any two or more persons who love and take responsibility for each other" (Melville, 1983:13). Third, the gay task force also suggested that children and the adults who care for them ought to be recognized as a family. Fourth, the conservatives, or the "pro-family" lobby, felt that the concept of family meant more than one's personal preference of life-style. The conservatives favored a more traditional definition of family that included a legally married man and woman and their offspring.

These definitions of family occur because of conflict between a social ideal and the immediate realities in which people live. The socially ideal type of family that was favored by the "pro-family" lobby at the White House Conference is called a traditional nuclear family by sociologists. A **nuclear family** is a married couple and their children. Although ideally it may be desirable to define a family as a married man and woman and their offspring, many people find themselves in situations that vary dramatically from this social ideal. Economic conditions, racial and ethnic orientations, for example, may shape experiences quite different from those in the traditional nuclear family.

For example, one's concept of family life varies by class and race. Poor people, and particularly poor blacks, are likely to experience family life that differs from the traditional nuclear family because a large percentage of these families are likely to include single parents. In Table 13.1 the percentages of single-parent families by race, sex, and ethnicity are presented. Additionally, some families are likely to include extended family members. "For example, Chinese or Japanese families living in the United States are two to three times as likely to be vertically extended (having aged parents living with them) as are those of Irish and German descent" (Duvall and Miller, 1985:7). An **extended family** is a nuclear family plus relatives of any one of the nuclear family members, including aunts, uncles, cousins, nephews, grandparents, and grandchildren.

Other individuals who are likely to view themselves as members of a family include those who find themselves for various reasons in foster care, adopted, or deserted by their parents or legal guardians but cared for by someone else, as well as others who may rely upon someone or some group to provide emotional

Table 13.1 Percent of Single Parent Family by Race and Sex, 1982

	Race						
Family Type	U.S. (%)	Asian (%)	Black (%)	Indian (%)	Mexican (%)	Puerto Rican (%)	White (%)
Total families	100.0	100.0	100.0	100.0	100.0	100.0	100.0
Female householder	15.4	10.8	40.6	22.7	17.7	44.7	15.4
with children	9.6	5.9	28.4	16.0	12.8	37.0	9.6
Male householder	3.3	4.8	4.3	5.5	4.1	4.5	3.3
with children	1.1	1.2	1.5	2.9	1.0	2.3	1.1

Source: U.S. Bureau of the Census, *Statistical Abstracts of the United States, 1984*, 37–40.

and physical needs. People in these situations often define themselves and their caregivers as family units because the relationship among the group members may be as intimate and as nourishing as that of the nuclear family. Persons who consider themselves a part of some family, although they may not be part of the traditional family, are quick to point out that many of the traditional, nuclear families are characterized by incest, abuse, neglect, and violence. Therefore, there is nothing in conforming to the socially ideal nuclear family form that assures that its members will be any better off than members of other types of families.

These issues illustrate that definitions of family are not value free. Sociologists, demographers, and census administrators have devised terms that are primarily intended to reflect the composition of the family and thereby avoid stigmatizing families that may not conform to traditional values. For example, children develop within their **family of orientation,** which includes their siblings and their parents. When children are old enough to marry, they are expected to begin their **family of procreation,** which includes their spouse and their offspring. It is through the overlap of families of orientation and families of procreation that in-laws emerge. Mother-, father-, brother-, and sister-in-laws are the parents and siblings from a spouse's family of orientation.

The Bureau of the Census defines a family as a "householder and one or more other persons living in the same household who are related to the householder by birth, marriage, or adoption" (Bureau of the Census, 1980:B–2). The Census Bureau has two criteria that it uses to identify families. First, a family must have a householder. A householder is any adult in whose name a house, apartment, or room is rented or owned. Second, a family must contain other people who live with and are legally related to the householder. In Table 13.2 data on family type by race and ethnicity are presented. According to Table 13.2, the most common type of family regardless of race or ethnicity is a married couple. Of all the racial and ethnic groups in Table 13.2, Asians have the highest percentage (84.4) of families where the married couples live in the same household. Half (50.8 percent) of all Puerto Rican families are married couples. The Census Bureau figures in Table 13.2 include both families with and without children.

Table 13.2 *Family Type by Race for the United States, 1982*

Family Type	U.S. (%)	Asian[a] (%)	Black (%)	Indian[b] (%)	Mexican (%)	Puerto Rican (%)	White (%)
Total families with	100.0	100.0	100.0	100.0	100.0	100.0	100.0
children	50.8	62.0	61.1	66.1	71.4	75.1	50.8
Married couple	81.3	84.4	55.1	71.8	78.2	50.8	81.3
with children	40.1	54.9	31.2	47.2	57.6	36.0	40.1
Female householder	15.4	10.8	40.6	22.7	17.7	44.7	15.4
with children	9.6	5.9	28.4	16.0	12.8	37.0	9.6
Male householder	3.3	4.8	4.3	5.5	4.1	4.5	3.3
with children	1.1	1.2	1.5	2.9	1.0	2.3	1.1

Source: U.S. Bureau of the Census, *Statistical Abstract of the United States, 1984*, 37–40.
[a]Asian includes Pacific Islander
[b]Indian includes Eskimo and Aleut

Functions of Families

The decade of the sixties witnessed an increasing number of women who criticized the wife and mother roles. Some women charged that the family benefitted men and children at the expense of women. As an increasing number of women have begun to seek work and careers outside of the home, they have called for greater equality in the sharing of family duties. Despite some vocal and articulate criticisms of family life, another set of facts is equally significant. These facts suggest that despite the problems and criticisms, most people continue to marry and raise families. About 90 percent of all Americans will marry at some point in their lives. It appears that Americans are not deterred by divorce either. Although there are approximately 1.2 million divorces each year in America, four out of five divorced people eventually remarry (Furstenberg and Spanier, 1984:37; Melville, 1983:21). Of the forty-five million married-couple households in 1980, nine million, or one in five, of those households involved a remarriage. One in four marriages among blacks and one in six marriages among Hispanics involved a remarriage (Furstenberg and Spanier, 1984:39). Thus, marriage and the family, although radically altered in their modern forms, endure as a viable social institution because they continue to meet certain functions that people find important. Researchers have identified several functions and strengths of marriage and family life (Jackson et al., 1981; Melville, 1983; Duvall and Miller, 1985; Hill, 1971). Five of these functions are as follows.

First, marriage continues to provide the only socially acceptable place for sexual intimacy. In American society sexual intimacy within marriage is characterized by monogamy. **Monogamy** refers to marriage and sexual intimacy between one man and one woman. Some societies, however, permit polygamy. **Polygamy** refers to marriage and sexual intimacy among several spouses. *Bigamy*, a form of polygamy that is illegal in America (though practiced within some religious communities), is marriage and sexual intimacy among a person of one sex and two of his or her spouses of the opposite sex. Of the societies that permit polygamy, most allow a wealthy male to have several wives. This form of marriage is called *polygyny*. A few societies, usually where there is a severe shortage of males, permit women to have more than one husband. This practice is referred to as *polyandry*.

When married couples in America require a change in partners, they must first become divorced. In their search for intimacy an increasing number of persons have been divorced more than once. This exchange of spouses through divorce in order to acquire intimacy through remarriage is called **conjugal succession** (Furstenberg and Spanier, 1984:47). Conjugal succession in America has also been described as *serial monogamy*. The importance of this idea is that although sexual intimacy may involve a number of mates over the period of one's life, in order for the intimacy to be socially acceptable the mating must be to one spouse at a time and in succession, or in a series.

A second function of marriage and the family is to legitimize the bearing and rearing of children. Legitimacy is tied to the contractual obligations, responsibilities, and privileges associated with marriage. Matters of birthright and inheritance rely upon the designation of children as legitimate heirs to family property. Likewise, issues relating to parental responsibility for the care and protection of children presuppose the legitimacy of offspring. In short, marriage is the social prerequisite for raising a family. Although the census data indicate an increase in the number of unwed mothers over the past two decades, marriage is still regarded as the optimum context in which to raise a family. Some researchers have found that premarital births are likely to decrease a woman's chances of getting married. Teachman and Polonko (1984:249), for example, note that young unwed girls are often encouraged not to get married soon after a premarital birth. On the other hand, women who have already delayed marriage beyond the normative childbearing years may be reluctant to get married for the sake of appearances. Likewise, a young child further deteriorates the prospects of marriage for older women because the relative number of older men available for marriage is reduced. Despite trends to the contrary, marriage is still the only context in which children are regarded as legitimate.

A third function of marriage and family life is socialization of children and adults. The function of socialization serves the larger society because children first learn the rules of proper social conduct within the family. Duvall and Miller (1985) suggest that the family acts as the transmitter of cultural heritage. According to the authors, "Within the family individual members first learn the rules, rights, obligations, and responsibilities characteristic of human societies" (Duvall and Miller, 1985:9). This process of parents teaching their offspring the values of the larger society reinforces those same values in the parents. Thus, the family may be considered the primary source of socialization for any society.

A fourth function of marriage and family life is the development of group identity. Developing group identity involves recognizing the symbols that mark one as a member of the group and acquiring the values and beliefs common to group members. Thus, depending on the parents, children may develop strong group identities for their social class, their religion, their race, or their family name.

Developing group identity through the family may be clearly seen in the family life of native Americans. According to Miller and Moore (1979), because the word *Indian* means very little to Indians, the first thing to ask upon meeting an Indian is What tribe are you? A tribe is "not belonging to a country, or a

The development of group identity is an important feature of Native American family life.

sorority, or a church. It's all of that and more, a difficult concept to grasp" (Miller and Moore, 1979:448). From 1972 to 1975, Miller and her associates at the Native American Research Group studied 120 native American families living in the San Francisco Bay area of California. Part of the focus of the research was to identify ways that native Americans who lived in or near the city of Oakland, California, maintained their tribal identities. There are over 100 tribal groups in the Bay area. Miller concentrated on identity development and identity maintenance among the Sioux, the Navajo, the California tribes, and twenty-one other tribes.

Miller found three factors used by native American families to maintain their tribal identity in the face of pressures to modernize in the city. The three factors were tribal language; the extent of home teaching of tribal ways, values, and norms; and each mother's stated preference for her child's marriage partner. After measuring the strength of these factors in each of the four groups of native Americans, Miller and Moore (1979:470) found that "Navajo mothers ranked highest on all Indian-identity indicators, the mothers of the California tribes the lowest, and the Sioux and others somewhere in the middle. In Table 13.3 data regarding the native American respondents' views toward these three factors are presented.

Finally, marriage and family life function as a shock absorber and support system for family members. In outlining family strengths in normal families Olson (1983:18) has suggested that "Unfortunately, most of the problems individuals have either begin or end up in the family." Thus, families absorb the frustrations and the failures that both adults and children face on a day-to-day basis. Ordinary shocks, frustrations, and failures for adults include accidents, job dissatisfaction, financial problems, illness, and environmental stressors such as noise, pollution, overcrowding, and weather-related mishaps. Extraordinary shocks experienced by adults that the family may be required to absorb include job loss, drug addiction, criminal victimization, spouse abuse, and death of family members.

Likewise children experience ordinary, day-to-day, shocks, frustration, and failures. These include parental constraints, peer pressures, sibling rivalries, failed relationships, pubescent changes, and school-related problems such as required attendance, teacher personalities, and failed tests. Extraordinary shocks that may be experienced by children include drug addiction, criminal victimization, sexual abuse, divorce of parents, and death of family members.

In summary, the statuses that people hold in the larger society often present situations and circumstances that subject them to harsh criticism, close scrutiny, and impersonal interaction. Most individuals first turn to their family for help in restoring self-esteem and finding resources to resolve the problems associated

Table 13.3
Respondents' View of Three Indicators of Indian Identity, by Tribe (Percentage)

	Know Language	Teach Indian Ways	Prefer Indian Marriage for Child
Sioux	47%	73%	42%
Navajo	93%	77%	81%
California	0%	47%	70%
Other	45%	54%	72%
TOTAL	46%	63%	67%

Source: Miller, Dorothy L. and Charlotte Dickinson Moore "The Native American Family: The Urban Way." in *Families Today: A Research Sampler on Families and Children* (Vol. 1) pps. 470. National Institute on Mental Health Science Monographs. Printed 1979 by U.S. Department of Health, Education, and Welfare. Rockville: MD

with holding these statuses. Needy persons are first likely to turn to members of their nuclear family. As the shocks and failures become more extraordinary and the nuclear family lacks the resources to resolve these problems, individuals may turn to extended family members.

Marital Status

Sociologists usually refer to four types of **marital statuses,** including married, single (i.e., never married), divorced, and widowed. Although persons may be separated from their spouse or living with a lover, these are not ordinarily recognized as separate and distinct marital statuses. A person who is separated is still legally married, and a person who is "living in" is presumably still single.

The important idea expressed by marital status is that being married has been the accepted position in society for adults. In other words, adults are expected to marry, and most adults—about 90 percent—conform to this expectation at some point in their lives. Other adult statuses tend to be viewed as deviations from the married norm. Traditionally, being single, divorced, and widowed have been seen as less desirable conditions than being married.

Although some of the traditional attitudes that support the sanctity of marriage have been weakening over the past decades, largely because more people are choosing to remain single or seek divorce, we will see that many of the issues related to marital status are tied to assumptions about the importance of traditional expectations of marriage for adults.

In Table 13.4 data are presented regarding the marital status of Americans from 1970 to 1982. Over the past decade there has been a decline in the percentage married, an increase in the percentage of those remaining single, a slight decline in the percentage widowed, and over twice the percentage of those divorced. As shown also in Table 13.4, the largest percentage of adults eighteen years and older continues to prefer marriage. Despite the decline from 1970, in 1982 slightly more than two-thirds of all adults were married, a fifth were single, and less than one-tenth were widowed or divorced.

Marital status varies somewhat by sex. Males are more likely to be either married or single than females, and females are more likely to be widowed or divorced than men. The differences in marital status by sex may be attributed largely to higher rates of remarriage and mortality among males. Males remain single longer than females, but when they marry, they do so to younger women.

Table 13.4 Marital Status of the Population, 1970–82

Marital Status	1970 (%)	1980 (%)	1982 (%)
Married	71.7	65.5	64.5
Single	16.2	20.3	20.9
Widowed	8.9	8.0	7.7
Divorced	3.2	6.2	7.0

Source: *U.S. Bureau of the Census, Statistical Abstract of the United States, 1984,* 104th ed., 44.

When men and women get divorced, the woman is likely to remain unmarried longer (in part because she is older and the number of eligible males older than she has diminished); and her ex-spouse is likely to remarry a younger, and often single (i.e., never-married), woman.

This arrangement seems somewhat unfair to women. After being married to a woman for the best years, or at least the youngest years, of her life, a man can divorce her and have a relatively easy time remarrying a younger woman. For those female students who are now crying "foul play!" a small consolation may be that men are generally expected to pay the costs for this foul in terms of higher court fees, alimony, and child support. Findings from the 1980 census however, showed that only about 1 in 7 women who divorced were awarded alimony and only about ⅓ of those who were awarded alimony received it. Also, only about half of the women who are awarded child support actually receive it. Under no-fault divorce laws these trends have actually worsened.

Trends in Marital Status

In the past, ideas about the desirability and sanctity of marriage meant that adults had in effect only two marital statuses from which to choose. The choices were the state of marriage or a state of "ness"—loneliness if you were single, sadness if you were widowed, and unhappiness if you were divorced. So engrained was the idea that adults should be married that there was a time when "in many New England towns, bachelors had to pay extra taxes on the theory that sin and iniquity ordinarily are the companions and consequences of the solitary life" (Melville, 1983:150). Recent trends suggest that more people are making conscious decisions about their marital status. Although being widowed is still a matter of chance rather than choice, men and women are delaying marriage and opting in increasing numbers to leave marriages that are unsatisfying. In the upcoming sections of the chapter we review trends and developments in the life-styles of those who are single, married, widowed, and divorced.

Single. Since 1965 there has been a gradual but steady increase in the percentage of those electing to remain single. The percentage of the population, 14.9 percent, that was eighteen years and older and single in 1965 rose to 20.9 percent by 1982. The percent of single males is slightly higher than the percent of single females. In 1965, 10.3 percent of all males and 7.9 percent of all females were single. By 1982 almost a fifth (19.1 percent) of the males and 15.3 percent of the females were single. The percentage of single males is only higher than the percentage of single females when totals are considered. Otherwise, the ratio of single males to single females varies depending upon age and region of the country. An article from *Money* magazine underscores this point. Table 13.5 is a reprint from the *Money* article entitled "Figuring the Odds in the Marriage" and illustrates the changes in the ratio of single males and females by age and city of residence.

Reasons to Remain Single. Notions about singles as swingers, spinsters, or spastic personalities are beginning to erode. Despite the popularity of magazines such as *Playboy, Penthouse, Playgirl, Hustler,* and *Screw,* much evidence indicates that a majority of singles are not swingers. Ironically, research funded by the Playboy Foundation found that the median number of sexual partners

Table 13-5 The Marriage Market. Eligible men for every 100 single women.
Source: *Money*, 13 (December) 1984, pp. 34–35.

AGE	Anaheim	Atlanta	Baltimore	Boston	Buffalo	Chicago	Cincinnati	Cleveland	Columbus	Dallas	Denver	Detroit	Fort Lauderdale	Houston	Indianapolis	Kansas City	Los Angeles	Miami	Milwaukee	Minneapolis-St. Paul	Nassau-Suffolk counties, N.Y.	Newark	New Orleans	New York City	Philadelphia	Phoenix	Pittsburgh	Portland, Ore.	Riverside, Calif.	Sacramento	San Antonio	San Diego	San Francisco	San Jose	Seattle	St. Louis	Tampa-St. Petersburg	Washington, D.C.	AGE
20-24	135	131	133	123	117	129	122	128	122	128	137	119	135	149	116	119	135	117	120	121	113	119	141	125	125	128	117	126	130	118	123	179	136	142	131	119	127	130	20-24
25-29	93	91	84	81	70	85	77	86	72	87	95	78	97	111	73	80	97	78	78	78	66	77	97	90	78	84	70	86	83	75	70	110	104	100	90	73	82	97	25-29
30-34	75	74	70	62	54	68	61	68	55	72	79	63	82	90	60	66	82	68	62	62	49	59	83	75	60	69	54	71	68	62	56	83	91	81	74	58	70	82	30-34
35-39	57	54	55	47	43	52	48	51	42	54	59	50	64	68	48	51	65	56	50	46	37	44	64	57	48	54	41	55	53	49	44	62	73	63	57	45	57	62	35-39
40-44	46	41	48	42	40	44	42	44	37	43	46	43	50	53	40	44	54	47	47	39	34	39	53	47	43	45	36	44	46	43	38	49	58	51	46	39	49	48	40-44
45-49	39	33	42	40	38	42	37	39	33	37	40	40	40	45	38	39	46	40	45	37	33	37	46	42	39	39	35	39	42	40	37	44	47	42	42	36	42	42	45-49
50-54	34	28	38	38	37	38	33	36	30	33	36	36	35	37	36	34	42	36	41	35	31	36	41	36	35	35	33	38	40	40	35	39	41	36	40	33	38	38	50-54
55-59	29	24	34	36	34	34	32	34	29	29	33	33	31	35	32	30	37	33	37	34	31	34	37	33	32	31	32	36	38	39	33	35	36	31	38	31	36	33	55-59

within a year for single men under twenty-five was two. For single men between the ages of twenty-five and thirty-four the median number of sexual partners was four. For comparable age groups of single women the median number of sexual partners in a year was two and three respectively (Melville, 1983:173). Although these data do not support a pattern of celibacy among singles, they also do not illustrate a swinging life-style of casual sex. Likewise, in his research on "men who don't fit the mold" Darling (1981) observed that bachelors are not basically different types of people, rather it is the timing, definition, and perception of events in the lives of bachelors that differed from those men who married early. The research on singles illustrates that although singles may not be radically different from married persons, there are reasons why some people remain single.

The reasons why males remain single are not necessarily identical to the reasons that females remain single. For example, some women may choose to remain single because they do not wish to change their names—a social expectation though no longer a legal requirement. Other women may avoid marriage because they do not wish to have children. Some women are simply enjoying the freedom of the single life-style, an option that men have always had but which is fairly recent for women. On the other hand, some men are remaining single because they feel that marriage is an economic disadvantage because their salary will not permit them to support a wife and family financially. The dedication to career and professional success may consume the time that some men might ordinarily spend in the marriage market.

Although some reasons for remaining single vary by sex, Melville (1983:157) has noted two factors that in recent years have contributed to the increase in the number of singles. The two factors include a change in values and an increase in the opportunities that support a singles life-style. Changes in values about morality, family size, the roles of women, marriage, and the purpose of dating have made remaining single a respected if not respectable marital status. Increased educational and occupational opportunities for women mean that a large number of women can afford to be single. Single women can now afford apartments, homes, cars, and travel. The increased opportunities of single women also encourage men to remain single because males do not always have to assume the financial obligations of dating. As values about sexual morality have

Changes in values and opportunities have combined to make being single a more appealing lifestyle for many women.

changed and the improved methods of birth control have decreased the likelihood of pregnancy, couples have increasingly been able to enjoy sexual intimacy without fear of reprisal or unwanted pregnancy. Thus, changes in both values and opportunities have combined to make being single a more appealing life-style for many men and women.

Married. Over the past decade the percentage of those who are married has steadily declined. In 1970 about 72 percent of Americans eighteen years and older were married. By 1982 less than two-thirds of all adults were married. The downward trend in marriage may be explained in part by examining changes in the reasons people marry. The reasons people marry change according to economic conditions and the status of women in the society. It is possible to examine the status of women in three general periods of time—the agricultural revolution, the industrial revolution, and the technological revolution—and observe their impact on why people marry.

During the agricultural revolution land was the most pronounced feature of social and economic life. Social prestige and economic wealth were determined by the amount of land one possessed. In many parts of the world marriages were arranged in order to secure or increase families' ownership of land. Additionally, women provided labor in the form of another "hand." As such, along with her other household duties, she often became a farmhand or a ranch hand helping men clear the land, tame animals, or serve in other capacities when the situation demanded it.

The status of women during the agricultural revolution was a property status. Thus, the value of women during this time period was tied to the amount of real property they could fetch for the groom or the groom's family. This motivation for marriage, which could be called marriage for property, has existed throughout much of recorded history. Examples of this motivation to marry range from the marriages of English nobility to secure kingdoms to the marriages of poor peasants to acquire a **dowry.** A dowry is money, goods, or property that a woman brings to her husband when they marry. Even today, in places characterized by poverty (places in India, for example) or places characterized by land-based economy (e.g., some developing nations) a woman's family is expected to provide a dowry to the groom at marriage.

During the industrial revolution, manufacturing became the most pronounced feature of economic life. Wealth, power, and prestige were related to the production and the sale of consumer products. And although some marriages during this time helped to cement corporate mergers and family fortunes, the status of women had changed to conform with the economic conditions. The industrial revolution created a social order in which a man earned a salary and supported his wife and children. Once again, however, women were called upon to provide labor for which there was little monetary compensation such as house cleaning, child-rearing, meal preparation, and bill paying. Amidst the set of social arrangements during the industrial revolution women became dependent on their husbands for their social and economic standing.

The industrial revolution idealized the dependency and helplessness of women. Further, a man now married not for the property that his wife could offer but for the prestige that her beauty would bring to him in the eyes of others. By her beauty and her praise a woman added to a man's self-esteem. Thus, a woman's beauty became her dowry. The industrial revolution lifted women out of their property status and placed them on a pedestal to display their beauty and helplessness. The motivation for men to marry became capturing the woman on the highest pedestal. Ideas about love and romance supported the pedestal status of women during this period because these ideas added emotional fervor to the

Source: © 1984, New Group Chicago, Inc.

pursuit of beauty and helplessness. Not so coincidentally, love and romance served also to eliminate women from the competition for jobs in industry because men could marry the competition and keep it at home.

Today, the technological revolution has once again changed economic conditions and the status of women. Technology is the application of science to social processes. Harnessing the principles of science requires skilled professionals such as scientists, engineers, and systems analysts. In the technological revolution knowledge and information are more valuable than one's sex or physical strength. The labor that women provide during this period of technology and information is closer in kind to that provided by men than in other periods of time. Further, the dependency of women on men that men enjoyed during earlier periods of time simply has become too expensive. A man's salary has become too meager to support a family, and women have been encouraged or often forced to seek employment outside of the home. The status of women has changed from property and pedestal to that of a person in order to better meet the needs of the new technocracy. Therefore, those women fortunate enough to acquire the necessary technological skills are able to work alongside men in the labor force and earn comparable salaries.

This is not to suggest that today there is no sexism. Although prejudice and discrimination against women still exist, enough women are able to support themselves so that the dependency on men for their financial and social standing has been eroded. More women are able to achieve success in the high-paying fields of entertainment, medicine, law, mass media, and aeronautics. Thus, during this period of the technological revolution, the economic conditions of the labor force have changed enough to make room for the contributions of women and have reduced the necessity for women to marry while they are still young and presumably beautiful. Men and women now marry primarily for affection and companionship. A man may still seek to marry a woman because she is beautiful or because he hopes to improve his economic position by adding her property to his; however, women are increasingly able to reject relationships of this kind.

Changes in economic conditions and the status of women also affect residence patterns of the newly married and the society's rules for family descent. During the agricultural revolution, newly married couples were often absorbed into either the husband's parents' family or the wife's parents' family. That is, young newly married couples during this era usually established either **patrilocal** or **matrilocal** residences. Patrilocal means that the married couple lives with the husband's family. Matrilocal means that the married couple lives with the wife's family. Many societies continue to support the newly married by absorbing them into patrilocal and matrilocal residence patterns. Beginning with the industrial revolution and particularly in the technological revolution, the residence patterns of the newly married have become increasingly **neolocal.** Neolocal means that the newly married establish a new residence separate from both the husband's and wife's family.

Social norms governing family history, inheritance, and blood lines are determined by the rules of descent. As the status of women and economic conditions have changed through the agricultural, industrial, and technological revolutions, the rules of descent have also changed. In those societies where women possessed a property status, descent was likely to be **patrilineal.** Patrilineal means that a family's descent is traced through husband or father. In some societies where women held a somewhat higher status, a family's descent often was **matrilineal** and traced through the wife or mother. As the status of women changed through the industrial and technological revolutions and women began to have a greater voice in social and family matters, the rules of descent became increasingly **bilateral.** Bilateral means that a family's descent is traced equally through both spouses or parents.

Tracing that status and the economic conditions through the agricultural, industrial, and technological revolutions is not to say that all societies have progressed in such a linear fashion. Vestiges of each revolution may be found in many different societies. Marriage trends will, however, continue to reflect the dominant features of economic conditions and the status of women in a society. Specifically, marriage trends, the reasons for marrying, residence patterns, and the rules of descent will be linked to changes in these areas.

Divorced. Earlier in this chapter we defined marriage as a public and legal contract between a man and a woman. **Divorce** is the legal dissolution of the marriage contract. Other than divorce however, a marriage may be legally dissolved by annulment and separation. An annulment "is the legal erasure of a marriage for reasons of force, fraud, bigamy, insanity, falsified age at marriage, or any gross misrepresentation by either party that voids the contract" (Duvall and Miller, 1985:334). A legal separation is usually a precondition for divorce. It is a specified amount of time whereby the couple are required by law to live apart from one another. During the time they are separated the couple may not marry anyone else and must provide for the care of children born while they were married. Of course, not all separations are legal. Many separations are private agreements between spouses.

Marriages may also end because one of the spouses deserted another. The line between separation and desertion is not always clear, because a couple can agree that the marriage should end yet not agree on exactly when to end it. In such a case the desertion occurs because one spouse decided when to end the marriage without consulting the other. In most instances, however, the desertion is not expected. Contrary to the stereotype of the lower-class male who deserts his family, evidence suggests that the typical male who deserts his family is forty-four to fifty-one years old and college educated (Duvall and Miller, 1985:335). He is likely to be a salesman or an executive. The number of women deserting their families has increased over the past decade. Like her male counterpart, the woman who deserts her family is likely to be well educated. She is likely, however, to be slightly younger, deserting her family at about age thirty-five.

Through the twentieth century divorce rates have been increasing, though not continuously. For example divorce rates declined for a time after World War II and remained fairly stable during the baby-boom years. Since about 1970, the divorce rate per 1,000 increased dramatically to its present level. Weed (1980) contends that about half of all marriages occurring today will end in divorce.

Despite this rather alarming forecast by Weed, Americans are not deterred from marrying because of the prospects of divorce. Although there are approximately 1.2 million divorces each year in America, four out of five divorced persons eventually remarry (Furstenberg and Spanier, 1984:37; Melville, 1983:21). About half of all divorced persons remarry within three years of their final divorce decree (Spanier and Thompson, 1984:12). Of the forty-five million married-couple households in 1980, nine million, or one in five of those households, involved a remarriage. This figure varies somewhat by race and ethnicity. For example, one

As societal values have lessened the stigma of divorce, an increasing number of families are comprised of single parents and their children.

in four marriages among blacks and one in six marriages among Hispanics involve a remarriage.

The differences in rates of remarriage by race suggest that divorce rates depend upon one's social group. Divorce rates are higher for blacks than for whites. According to Spanier and Thompson (1984:13), the divorce rate is inversely related to education. With the exception of women with graduate degrees, the higher the education level, the lower the divorce rate. Women with graduate degrees have a disproportionately high rate of divorce. Most divorces occur fairly early in a marriage, somewhere between two and five years after the marriage. The long-term projection for trends in the divorce rate is at best a leveling off of the rates. As long as the status of women and economic conditions continue to erode the dependency of women on men and the values of the society continue to lessen the stigma associated with divorce, we can expect the rates to remain high. Indeed, "considering separation, divorce, remarriage, and redivorce, it can be projected that a majority of all marriages among young adults today will not remain intact" (Spanier and Thompson, 1984:13).

Reasons for Divorce. The sociological explanations of why people get divorced are not the same thing as the legal grounds for divorce. Grounds for divorce are the legal conditions under which a marriage may be terminated. The grounds for divorce may vary from state to state. Some states, like Nevada, have traditionally had very liberal grounds for divorce. The most common legal grounds for divorce include cruelty, desertion, nonsupport, adultery, habitual drunkenness, drug addiction, impotence, conviction of a crime, and insanity (Duvall and Miller, 1985:340). The more grounds for divorce that a state acknowledges, the easier it is to secure a divorce. Generally those states with liberal divorce laws have higher rates of divorce than those states that acknowledge only a few grounds for divorce. The introduction of "no-fault divorce" proceedings in some states has been generally accompanied by higher rates of divorce. A no-fault divorce is one in which the spouses are permitted to legally terminate a marriage without demonstrating that one of the partners has violated the conditions of the marriage. Ordinarily, contested divorces are costly because of lawyers' fees, child support, alimony, and property settlements. When the spouses are able to agree before the divorce proceedings on these matters, no-fault divorces are relatively cheap.

The sociological reasons for divorce are linked not so much to the legal grounds but to the societal changes that make divorce possible and acceptable. First, divorce is possible because the status of women has changed and women are not as dependent upon men for their livelihood. This change in status includes increased education and salaries. Indeed, some of the high rates of divorce among blacks can be explained by the relative parity in education and income among black men and women. Staples (1981:173) noted that "unlike the white family, which was a patriarchy and was sustained by the economic dependence of the female, the black dyad has been characterized by more equalitarian roles and economic parity in North America." To the extent that educational levels and salaries of men and women in the larger society converge as they have already done in the black community, the rates of divorce will reflect that convergence.

Second, divorce has increased because values and norms of the society have lifted much of the stigma associated with being divorced. These changing values and norms can be seen in the more liberal divorce laws, ministers' attitudes towards parishioners who are divorced, and the acceptance of marriage counseling as an occupation. In some Roman Catholic churches, which have traditionally rejected divorce, there are church-sponsored support groups for their divorced members. The change in values that lessens the stigma of divorce and the social opportunities that support an independent life-style have created a situation such that people will continue to seek marriage yet will view divorce as an acceptable and even an attractive option when their spouses disappoint them.

In addition to the above reasons there are several other factors that contribute to a high divorce rate. As men and women marry primarily for happiness, love, companionship, or other affective reasons, we can expect divorce rates to remain high. According to Kennedy (1986:76), "If either wife or husband has a change of heart, grows bored with or comes actively to dislike the other then the sole reason for being married will be lost." Even remaining married for the sake of the children has lost some appeal today because many of the child-care and child-rearing functions have been subsumed by other social agencies, including schools, courts, and social welfare agencies. Finally, the erosion of religious values that support marriage also contributes to higher divorce rates.

Widowed. The percent of the adult population that is widowed has remained fairly stable, at about 8 percent, since 1950. In 1965 the rate for widowed persons rose to 9 percent and by 1982 had declined to slightly less than 8 percent. When we compare widows, women whose husbands are deceased, to widowers, men whose wives are deceased, we see that the percentage of widows is higher than the percentage of widowers. In fact, since 1975 the percentage of widows has remained about six times as high as the percentage of widowers. Much of the difference in the ratio of widows to widowers can be explained by longer life expectancies of women. Women may live as many as ten years longer than their husbands; and although life expectancies have increased for men over the past several decades, women are also enjoying increased longevity. Therefore, the gap in life expectancy between males and females has not closed. Future projections of trends among the widowed suggest little change in the differences between widows and widowers, because there is little reason to believe that the causes of death for elderly males and females will change dramatically in the next decade. Middle-aged and elderly men experience higher rates of death from natural causes such as heart disease, cancer, and stroke than middle-aged and elderly women. Perhaps more significantly, however, are the differences in deaths due to violence between the two at this age. For example, middle-aged and elderly men are roughly five times more likely to die from homicide and suicide than women of the same age. Further, these men are more than twice as likely to die from accidents as women of the same age. As long as men continue to suffer higher rates of deaths from unnatural causes, medical advancements that extend the natural life will have little effect on unnatural causes of death, and middle-aged and elderly women will continue to outlive their husbands.

Experiencing Widowhood. The experience of widowhood is not the same as the experience of divorce. According to Spanier and Thompson (1984:14), divorce is a response to an unsuccessful marriage relationship. It is characterized by the realization that one has made a poor choice of mates, a lack of personal commitment to the relationship, and disenchantment with one's spouse. And, although divorce may be painful for both spouses, the pain of living together is apparently greater. In comparison to the widowed, divorcees have the advantage of preparing themselves for the termination of an unsuccessful relationship.

By contrast, those who are widowed are more likely to have been involved in a relationship that was satisfying. At the very least, they had not decided to terminate the relationship and may not have had time to prepare themselves for a life of being alone. Suffering a loss is characteristic of widowhood. This suffering and loss are likely to be heightened by the accompanying funeral. One measure of this sense of suffering and loss can be seen in the rates of suicide and mental illness. Rates of suicide are higher among the widowed than among the married. This is particularly true for widowers. Apparently, widows do better without their husbands than widowers do without their wives. Melville (1983:163) noted that in a study of one Florida retirement community the death of a spouse hit elderly males harder than elderly females. Widows in this community were more inclined to carry on housekeeping chores, kin relationships, and community activities. By contrast, widowers tended to become isolated. It is this isolation that is seen as a major factor in the suicides of widowers. Thus, the experience of widowhood is more than merely being alone. Although singles and the divorced are alone, the widowed, particularly widowers, are likely to experience loneliness and isolation.

Black Families

In 1965 the assistant secretary for the Office of Policy Planning and Research of the United States Department of Labor, now senator (Democrat, New York), Daniel P. Moynihan released a report entitled "The Negro Family—The Case for National Action." In this report, Moynihan claimed that "the family structure of lower class Negroes is highly unstable, and in many urban centers is approaching complete breakdown" (Moynihan, 1967:51). Moynihan further noted that these black families including large numbers of broken families, suffered from a "tangle of pathology" characterized by high rates of illegitimacy and a matriarchal authority structure. It was these features of the black family, particularly its matriarchal authority structure, that impeded progress for lower-class blacks and resulted in economic dependency and high rates of crime and delinquency. A **matriarchy** is a family where important decisions are made by a female head of household. In this context Moynihan was suggesting that lower-class black women are the heads of their families because they control the family's finances and decide the most important family matters. In many instances these black women headed their families because a large percentage of lower-class black fathers were absent from the home.

In contrast to the matriarchal structure of the black family Moynihan (1965) suggested that white families possessed patriarchal or egalitarian authority structures. A **patriarchy** is a family where important decisions are made by a male head of household. In **egalitarian** families important decision making is shared by both male and female heads of household. Moynihan noted that the differences between blacks and whites in the rates of crime, delinquency, educational level, and poverty could be attributed to the difference in their family structure. Since that report many researchers have objected to Moynihan's findings. For example, Hill (1971) and McAdoo (1982) have outlined the strengths and stress-absorbing systems of black families. The following section of the chapter reviews a statistical profile and identifies the strengths of the black family.

Black Family Forms

A majority of all black families include married couples (see Table 13.2). Although not all black families contain children, a majority of black families with children are headed by married couples. Regardless of family form, black families have more and younger children than families of other racial and ethnic groups. This is particularly true of female-headed black families. As a result of higher fertility rates among single black women, a majority of black children are raised in single-parent families. According to Glick (1981:110), in 1980, 45.8 percent of all black children lived with a single parent, 42.2 percent lived with both parents, 10.7 percent lived with other relatives, and 1.3 percent lived with nonrelatives. Of those who lived with single parents, 96 percent lived with the mother only. According to the *Statistical Abstracts* (1984:54) the average black female head of household is thirty-eight years old, and 70 percent have children under eighteen living at home. About a third are single (i.e., never married), a fourth are separated, and about a fifth are either widowed or divorced.

The data in Table 13.2 illustrate that there is no prototypical model of the black family. In contrast to the matriarchal family structure identified in Moynihan's (1967) report, these statistics reflect the basic black family forms, including married but childless black couples, married black couples with children, and black women with children. In addition to these three forms of black families a significant number of black families may be characterized as **"kin-assisted families"** (McAdoo, 1982). Kin-assisted families involve extended family members, often grandparents, in the care and rearing of children (McAdoo, 1982:483). Thus, many black children are raised by grandparents or other relatives. This "kin assistance" is often given to single mothers, but it is not infrequently extended when both parents are still together. Others have noted the diversity in the forms of black families (e.g., Willie, 1981; Glick, 1981).

Other racial and ethnic group family forms are not quite as diverse. For example, 84 percent of Asian families consist of married couples. Of the racial and ethnic groups described in Table 13.2 Asian families also have the lowest percentage of female-headed families. In fact, with the exception of black and Puerto Rican families, at least 71 percent of all other racial and ethnic groups' families consist of married couples (*Statistical Abstracts*, 1984). Children in these families are likely to be raised by both parents.

Strengths of Black Families

We have identified the strengths and functions of marriage and family life in an earlier section of this chapter. Some researchers have argued that the "continuing significance of race" has meant that the black family has had to provide additional strengths and functions for its members (Willie, 1981:27). In addition to the five strengths and functions of families that we identified earlier, Robert Hill, director of the research department of the National Urban League, has identified five strengths that are characteristic of black families. According to Hill (1971:3), family strengths are "those traits which facilitate the ability of the family to meet the needs of its members and the demands made upon it by systems outside the family unit." The five strengths of black families include the following: strong kinship bonds, strong work orientation, adaptability of family roles, strong achievement orientation, and strong religious orientation.

Strong kinship bonds are evidenced by the finding that black families are more likely to take in other relatives than white families. Specifically, black families are likely to absorb related minors and elderly individuals. "When we examine census data for families with no children of their own under 18 at home, we find that black families are much more likely than white families to take in other young related members" (Hill, 1971:5). Strong kinship bonds are further evidenced by an informal adoption network among black families. Hill (1971:7) has estimated that more than 160,000 out-of-wedlock black babies were absorbed in 1969 by existing black families. Finally, the absorption of subfamilies (i.e., families who lack their own housing), or "doubling up," is a declining but significant feature of black families.

A strong work orientation is a feature of both two-parent and single-parent black families. Traditionally, more wives in married-couple black families have worked than the wives in married-couple white families. Even with the contributions of the wife's earnings, the median income of black families remains lower than the median income of white families, whose income is more often a reflec-

Adaptability of family roles is one of the strengths of black families.

tion of the husband's income. Likewise, a majority—three-fifths—of the black women heading their own families work. Despite the work ethic of black female heads of household, half of these families have incomes below the official poverty level.

Adaptability of family roles is reflected in the adjustments to adversity that members of black families have had to make in order to preserve family life. For example, since more black mothers work than white mothers, black husbands and children have had to do more of the domestic and traditionally feminine chores. Thus, traditional sex roles and household distinctions of women's work and men's work were not as severely engrained in the black family. Less stigma was associated with black men who could wash clothes, cook, sew, and clean the house. Likewise, seeing black women come home from work in the uniforms of their occupations has been a longstanding feature of the black community. When it was necessary because of death or disaster, black family members shifted roles easily to keep the family going. Hill (1971:21) has suggested that even the higher percentage of single-parent families in the black community can be seen as evidence of the adaptability of black parents to maintain their families in the absence of a spouse.

High achievement orientation can be seen in educational aspirations of lower-class black youth. Hindelang (1970) and Cosby (1971) have suggested that low-income blacks have higher educational and occupational aspirations than their low-income white counterparts. Further, evidence from college and university records indicate that a larger proportion of black students are from families who require financial assistance in order for their children to attend school. Although blacks continue to face economic hardships and racial restrictions, their families manage to instill in them a strong dose of the American dream of becoming a successful person.

Religious orientation has been a traditional bulwark for the black family. Much of the history of the advancement of black people can be traced in the sermons of black ministers. Black ministers such as Father Divine, Adam Clayton Powell, Leon Sullivan, and Reverend Ike have encouraged blacks to seek financial independence. Other black ministers, including Wallace D. Muhammad, Benjamin Hooks, and Martin Luther King, Jr., have used the force of their religion to instill a sense of social and civil rights in their largely black congregations. Most recently, the most successful black candidate to run for president of the United States was a minister, the Reverend Jesse Jackson.

Blacks and Marital Status

Since 1960 young adult blacks have been postponing marriage longer than their white counterparts (Glick, 1981:115). Thus, what we see when we examine trends in the marital status of blacks over the past two decades is an increase in the percentage single, a decline in the percentage married, a decline in the percentage widowed, but an increase in the percentage divorced. For example, in 1970 one-fifth of the black population eighteen years old and over was single. By 1982 almost a third (32 percent) of blacks in this age category remained single. This trend becomes even more evident when we examine black singles by sex. Almost a quarter (24.3 percent) of black males were single in 1970, but by 1982 the figure had risen to 35 percent. The corresponding figures for black women were 17.4 percent and 29.6 percent, respectively.

One reason for this trend in postponing marriage is the "marriage squeeze" faced by black women. During the prime marrying ages for men, twenty to twenty-six, black women face a shortage in the number of eligible mates. According to Glick (1981:115), "by 1970, the number of Black men 20 to 26 years of age was only 82 percent of the number of women 18 to 24." The marriage squeeze for black women is further exascerbated by higher educational levels among black women and interracial marriage. Although formal and informal rules of endogamy, which restrict the selection of marriage partners to members of one's own group, kept the percentage of interracial married couples at less than 2 percent of the total married couples in 1982, black males were more than twice as likely as black females to select mates from another racial or ethnic group.

As the percent of blacks remaining single has increased, the percent of blacks who are married has decreased. Some of the decline in the percent of black married couples is also because of an increase in the percent of divorced blacks. In 1970 about two-thirds (64 percent) of blacks were married. By 1982 the proportion married had declined to one-half. Getting married and remaining married are closely tied to the economic position of black males and females. For example, Glick (1981:117) notes that as the income level of black men increases, the likelihood that they will have intact first marriages increases. The relationship between economic success and marital stability is strongest at the lowest end of the financial continuum. That is, "marital permanence for men depends less on being well-to-do than it does on not being poor" (1981:117).

On the other hand, economically successful black women are less likely to have intact marriages. Staples (1981) has noted that the relative freedom to work that black females have traditionally experienced in the labor market has made them less dependent on black men for economic security. Further, college-educated black women outnumber college-educated black men two to one. Marital stability that rests between the twin pillars of patriarchy and economic dependency of a woman on a man is simply not possible for the majority of black women.

Finally, death and divorce appear to be changing places as reasons why blacks who were once married are now without a spouse. As the percentage of divorced blacks more than doubled from 1970 (4.4 percent) to 1982 (9 percent), the percentage of widowed blacks declined from 11 percent in 1970 to 9.2 percent in 1982. Part of the explanation for this shift in death and divorce rates is the longer life span for blacks. When death rates were higher for both black males and females because of poor health care, a troubled marriage may have been prematurely terminated by the death of a spouse. Improved health care and longer life spans for blacks increase the opportunities for divorce. Likewise, the continued erosion of the dependency of females makes divorce less of a threat to their economic and emotional security.

Hispanic Families

Although the term Hispanic is used to lump Americans with Spanish surnames into a single category for data collection and research purposes, all Hispanic persons do not share a common identity. Persons with Hispanic ancestry may include a variety of groups, including Mexican, Puerto Rican, Cuban, Dominican, Colombian, Spanish, Ecuadoran, and Salvadoran. Of these groups the two with the largest populations in America are persons whose ancestry is either Mexican or Puerto Rican.

The differences among the Hispanic populations can be readily observed by examining the types of families. The data in Table 13.6 deal with the family types for Mexican, Puerto Rican, and "other" Hispanics. Also, as seen in Table 13.6, the type of family varies depending upon the type of ancestry. A larger percentage of Mexicans and Puerto Rican families have children than other Hispanics. The similarities in family types between Mexicans and Puerto Ricans end here. For example, whereas better than three-fourths (78.2 percent) of families of Mexican ancestry are married couples, only half (50.8 percent) of the families with Puerto Rican ancestry are married couples. More children in Mexican families are likely to be raised by a married couple, whereas Puerto Rican children are as likely to be raised by a single female parent as they are a married couple. In fact, as shown in Table 13.6, with the exception of the higher percentage of children, families of Mexican ancestry are more likely to conform to the family types of "other" Hispanics than are families of Puerto Rican ancestry.

Puerto Rican families resemble black families in the diversity of their family types. That is, Puerto Rican families are likely to consist of childless married couples (14.8 percent), married couples with children (36 percent), or single

Table 13.6 *Family Types Among the Spanish-Origin Population; 1982*

Family Type	Total (%)	Mexican (%)	Puerto Rican (%)	Other (%)
All families	100.0	100.0	100.0	100.0
with children	68.7	71.4	75.1	58.8
Married Couples	73.0	78.2	50.8	73.7
with children	50.7	57.6	36.0	43.0
Female householder	22.7	17.7	44.7	21.8
with children	16.7	12.8	37.0	14.2
Male householder	3.3	4.3	4.1	4.5
with children	1.3	1.0	2.3	1.7

Source: U.S. Bureau of the Census. *Statistical Abstract of the United States, 1984,* 104th ed., 41.

females with children (37 percent). One feature of Puerto Rican families that differs from whites, blacks, and other Hispanic families is that Puerto Rican fathers are about twice as likely to raise their children by themselves than are the fathers of other groups. According to statistics derived from the U.S. Bureau of the Census for 1982, the percentage of single male householders with children under eighteen years of age at home is 2.3 for Puerto Ricans, 1.1 for whites, 1.5 for blacks, and 1.3 for other Hispanics.

Hispanic families tend to contain more family members than white or black families. The family members include both children and other relatives. Compared to white or black families, Hispanic families are less likely to have no children under age eighteen and more likely to have two or more children under eighteen years of age. According to other research (Duvall and Miller, 1985:364–65), about 30 percent of Hispanic families consist of five or more persons. Hispanic couples with more than two children tend to reside in nonmetropolitan areas, whereas Hispanic females with children tend to live in metropolitan areas.

Strengths of Hispanic Families

As we have seen earlier, all families have functions and strengths. Because the history of Hispanics in America is different from whites, blacks, native Americans, or Asians, their family strengths will reflect their history. In addition to the functions and strengths of families, which were noted earlier, Hispanic families have three other important strengths that have helped them survive in America. Those strengths include bilingual orientation, la familia, and uniform religious orientation.

The bilingual orientation of Hispanic family members serves several purposes. It helps family members retain their cultural identity. For example, in areas with large Hispanic populations such as Miami, New York, California, and parts of the Southwest, newspapers, radio stations, television stations, public transportation terminals, and restaurants have information communicated in Spanish. This bilingual orientation has also assisted other family members who were less fluent in English to interact with the larger Anglo society by using other bilingual family members as interpreters. The shock of assimilation and involvement in the larger society is therefore buffered by the bilingual orientation of the Hispanic family. The language also becomes a way of maintaining a private conversation within a crowd of people. Because Hispanic persons may have a variety of racial and ethnic colors and ancestry, the bilingual orientation becomes a way of identifying that person as a member of the Hispanic community.

La familia refers to the kin assistance network among Hispanic families. According to Jaime Sena-Rivera (1979:91), la familia refers to the sense of obligation to help each other in times of economic trouble or illness with small loans, household services, or child care. Intermarriage is common among some Hispanic populations. La familia helps to include in-laws who may not be Hispanic in origin into the family network. This ability of la familia to integrate non-Hispanic in-laws is an important strength. Intermarriage can confuse bloodlines, ancestry, and inheritance. La familia helps assure that racially mixed couples and their children continue to belong to the community. La familia also becomes a way of transmitting important values in Hispanic families through generations far removed from their culture of origin. One of the values important in many Hispanic communities that is transmitted by la familia is respect for the elderly. Elderly Hispanics often play a more important role in family matters than the elderly in other families.

The uniform religious orientation of Hispanic families is Catholicism. This is not to say that all Hispanic families are Catholic. It is to say, however, that the Catholic church has traditionally been very influential in both the private and public lives of the people of Mexico and other Latin American countries. For example, in his research on Mexican American families Rivera (1979:123) found that Catholicism is taken for granted in their lives. This uniform religious orientation serves as a strength of Hispanic families because the Catholic church typically has been conservative in its orientation towards family life. For example, the Catholic church has frowned upon divorce, abortion, and premarital sex. The Catholic church has generally supported a patriarchal family structure. All of the conservative traditions support a traditional family. Religious doctrines are presented to generations of Hispanics without being diluted with conflicting religious orientations. Specifically, within the uniform religious orientation of Catholicism generations of Hispanics are raised to believe that the family is sacred.

Trends in Marital Status

The effects of the strengths of Hispanic families can be seen in the trends of their marital status. Over the past decade the marital statuses of Hispanic persons have not conformed to the general pattern of increased numbers of singles and a decreased number of married persons. For example, the percentage of single Hispanics has declined since 1975 and the percentage of married persons has increased. In fact, the percentage of single Hispanic females dropped from 27.1 percent in 1975 to less than 20 percent (19.5) in 1982. Nearly two-thirds (65.9 percent) of Hispanic families were married in 1982 as compared to less than two-thirds (60.3 percent) in 1975. However, the strengths of Hispanic families have not completely insulated them from the patterns in marital trends of the larger society. While the percent of Hispanic singles has declined and the percent of married persons has increased, the percent of divorced persons doubled from 1970 to 1982 for both Hispanic males and females. Divorced Hispanic females follow the pattern of the larger society in that there are more divorced females than there are divorced Hispanic males.

Summary

The focus of this chapter was issues related to marriage and the family. Marriage was defined as a public and legal contract between a man and a woman. Such a definition raises issues about whether homosexuals can be married; whether sexual activity outside of marriage is legal; and whether religious definitions of marriage are sufficient. The definition of family was shown to be controversial. Depending upon one's social circumstances or political beliefs, family may be variously defined. Four marital statuses were identified: single, married, divorced, and widowed. Of these four marital statuses, marriage has been traditionally accepted as the norm for adults. Recent changes in economic conditions and in the status of women have meant that other statuses, specifically being single and being divorced, are now more acceptable.

Trends in marital statuses were reviewed. As societies changed from agriculture, to industry, to technology as the basis for economic production, trends in marital status shifted. In a technological society there is greater opportunity for a person to remain single or support herself or himself in the event of divorce or death of a spouse. The strengths and functions of families including black and Hispanic families were identified. Issues related to marital status among blacks and Hispanics were discussed. It was shown that portraying all Hispanic families as if they represented one type family is an error. Puerto Rican families, for example, demonstrate a greater variety of family types than do Mexican families.

In conclusion, we have observed that the family has experienced many changes. These include changes in the reasons couples marry, controversies over definitions of family, and changes in the roles of women. Although these changes have led many to postpone marriage, most people will continue to marry and raise a family. This is so because despite social and economic changes, marriage and familylife continue to provide the primary source of affection and emotional support for a majority of individuals.

Key Concepts

alimony	matrilineal
bilateral	matrilocal
common law marriage	monogamy
conjugal succession	multilineal
divorce	neolocal
dowry	nuclear family
extended family	patriarchy
family	patrilineal
kin-assisted families	patrilocal
marital status	polygamy
marriage	single
matriarchy	widowed

References

Cosby, Arthur. (1971) "Black-White Differences in Aspirations Among Deep South High School Students." *Journal of Negro Education,* (Winter); 17–21.

Darling, Jon. (1981) "Late Marrying Bachelors." In Peter J. Stein (ed.), *Single Life.* New York, N.Y.: St. Martin's Press, Inc.

Davis, Frank G. (1981) "Economics and Mobility: A Theoretical Rationale for Urban Black Family Well-Being." pps 127–138 in Harriet P. McAdoo (ed.), *Black Families,* Beverly Hills, Calif.: Sage Publications.

Duvall, Evelyn M., and Brent C. Miller. (1983) *Marriage and Family Development.* New York, N.Y.: Harper & Row, Publishers.

Furstenberg, Frank F., Jr., and Graham B. Spanier. (1984) *Recycling the Family: Remarriage After Divorce.* Beverly Hills, Calif.: Sage Publications.

Glick, Paul. (1981) "A Demographic Picture of Black Families" pp. 106–126 in Harriette P. McAdoo (ed.), *Black Families*, Beverly Hills, CA, Sage Publications.

Hill, Robert B. (1971) *The Strengths of Black Families.* New York, N.Y.: Emerson Hall Pub., Inc.

Hindelang, Michael J. (1970) "Educational and Occupational Aspirations Among Working Class Negro, Mexican-American and White Elementary School Children," *Journal of Negro Education, 39*(Fall):351–53.

Jackson, James S., Wayne R. McCullough, and Gerald Gurin. (1981) "Group Identity Development Within Black Families." pp 252–263 in Harriette P. McAdoo *Black Families.* Beverly Hills, Calif.: Sage Publications.

Kennedy, Robert E., Jr. (1986) *Life Choices: Applying Sociology.* New York, N.Y.: Holt, Rinehart and Winston.

McAdoo, Harriette P. (1982) "Stress Absorbing Systems in Black Families." *Family Relations* 31(October) 479–488.

Melville, Keith. (1983) *Marriage and Family Today.* New York, N.Y.: Random House, Inc.

Miller, Dorothy L., and Charlotte Dickinson Moore. "The Native American Family: The Urban Way." pps 441–484 in *Families Today: A Research Sampler on Families and Children* (vol. 1) National Institute of Mental Health Science Monographs. U.S. Department of Health, Education and Welfare. Rockville, MD. 1979.

Moynihan, Daniel. (1965) *The Negro Family: The Case for National Action.* Washington, D.C.: Office of Policy Planning and Research, U.S. Department of Labor.

Olson, David H. (1983) *Families—What Makes Them Work.* Beverly Hills, Calif.: Sage Publications.

Sena-Rivera, Jaime. (1979) "Extended Kinship in the U.S.: Competing Models and the Case of La Familia Chicana." *Journal of Marriage and the Family, 41*(February):121–129.

Spanier, Graham B., and Linda Thompson. (1984) *Parting: The Aftermath of Separation and Divorce.* Beverly Hills, Calif.: Sage Publications.

Staples, Robert. (1981) *The World of Black Singles*. Westport, CT.: Greenwood Press, Inc.

Teachman, Jay D., and Karen A. Polonko. (1984) "The Timing of Marriage." *Social Forces, 63*(September):245.

U.S. Bureau of Census. (1980) *Current Population Reports,* Series P–60, No. 125. Washington, D.C.: U.S. Government Printing Office.

U.S. Bureau of Census. (1984) *Statistical Abstracts of the United States.* Washington, D.C.: U.S. Government Printing Office.

Weed, J. A. (1980) *National Estimates of Marriage Dissolution and Survivorship: United States.* Vital and Health Statistics: Series 3, Analytic Statistics, No. 19. Washington, D.C.: U.S. Government Printing Office.

Willie, Charles V. (1981) *A New Look at Black Families.* Bayside, N.Y.: General Hall, Inc.

14

Religion in Society

OBJECTIVES

At the end of this chapter the student should be able to:

1. Identify the realm of the sacred.
2. Understand the process of institutionalization of religious beliefs, practices, and collectivities.
3. Distinguish functional and conflict perspectives on the role of religion in society.
4. Identify ways in which religion may promote or inhibit social change.
5. Understand some of the issues relating to religious diversity in the United States.
6. Identify several trends in religion in this country.

INTRODUCTION

What is the difference between the water in the bathtub at your house and the water in the baptismal pool in a Baptist church? If we see, feel, or taste the water in each or have it chemically analyzed, our answer would probably be, "There is no difference." Yet when we immerse ourselves in the former, we lather up and wash our bodies; when we are immersed in the latter, the soul, rather than the body, is cleansed. We feel there is a difference. Whatever its basis, our understanding tells us that it is there. Similar understandings are present in the circumstances described in the following illustrations:

> In a Mexican community, two Zinacantecan specialists in the rain-making ceremony make a pilgrimage to the summit of Junior Great Mountain. Facing east, they offer candles and incense to the gods who inhabit the mountain and pray to them to release the rain which they control (Vogt, 1970:98).
>
> A group of holy men of the Cheyenne Indians gather in the Medicine Arrow Lodge and carefully open the fox-skin bundle in which four Medicine Arrows are kept. They

are performing the renewal ceremony for the arrows, which were a gift to the Cheyenne people from their culture hero, Sweet Medicine, who is said to have brought them many of their traditional ways of life (Hoebel, 1960:7–8).

In a church in the southern part of the United States, a man and a woman, surrounded by their friends and relatives, kneel before a golden cross set upon an altar and ask for divine blessings upon their marriage.

A mountain, four arrows, a golden cross:—what do these things have in common? In all of these situations the particular item or object arouses in a group of people a feeling of awe and reverence. Junior Great Mountain is not just another tall hill. In this mountain the rain gods live; this sets Junior Great Mountain apart as a special object of awe and reverence for the Zinacantecans. The four Medicine Arrows are not arrows one would use to kill game for the evening meal. The Cheyenne keep these particular arrows wrapped in a special bundle which only the medicine men can handle because they are thought to be so powerful. And the symbol of the cross evokes for our American Christian couple and their relatives a feeling of reverence because it represents the death and sacrifice of Jesus. Doubtlessly a garden rake would arouse no such feelings in the young couple and their friends; Christians do not feel reverence for garden tools.

These examples point to the answer to our initial question concerning the difference between water in the bathtub and water in the baptismal pool. What we are describing is the quality of sacredness. The emotions that are the identifying mark of it may be attached by a given group of people to any tangible or intangible item: person, plant, animal, inanimate object, design, sound, idea, time, place. The awe and reverence accorded these things by a group of people sets them apart from ordinary, everyday things, thereby creating the realm of the **sacred** (Durkheim, 1961:52).

Concern with the sacred is the essence of religion. Ultimate meanings are rooted in it; the group's experience is expressed through it. Questions of explaining it, expressing it, and relating to it are the central concerns of any

The feelings of awe and reverence make this water sacred and different from bathtub water.

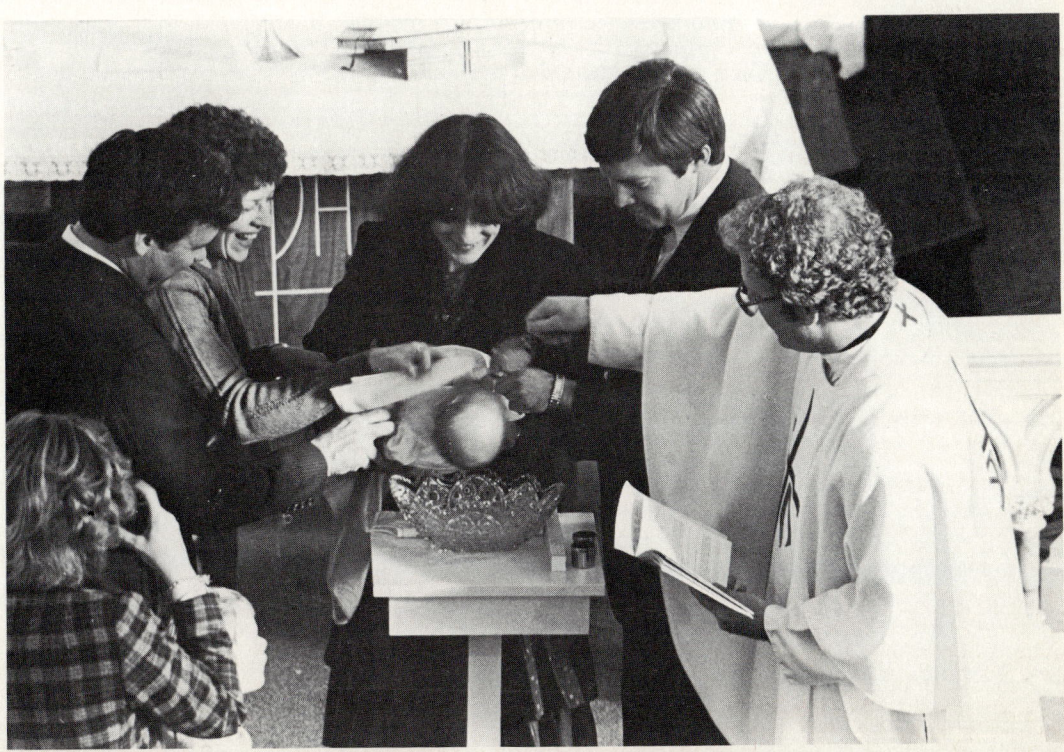

particular religion. There is no known human society that does not have some form of religion. Throughout history it has been a constant, usually dominant, motif in the cultural equipment and social activity of human groups.

With this preliminary identification of the realm of the sacred, we turn to the process through which collectivities, beliefs, and practices relating to this realm become institutionalized. We attempt to identify cohesive and disruptive impacts of religion as well as its potential for stability and change in the society. We close with a discussion of religious issues and trends in a society, our own, which is characterized by religious diversity.

The Institutionalization of Religion

Though manifested in a rich variety of patterns from one group to another, four aspects are present in any institutionalized religion: beliefs, practices, morality, and collectivity. These elements may be relatively vague and unfocused at the inception of a given religion. Oftentimes, a high degree of spontaneity and emotionalism characterizes the early stages of development. There is a tendency, however, for the elements to become more regularized; that is, the patterns become stable and predictable. This is what is meant by the **institutionalization** of religion. We consider each of these elements in turn.

Beliefs

Ideas about the realm of the sacred are a part of every religion. Not all religions involve belief in a supernatural being or beings; some may focus on a sacred principle or way of living, as in Buddhism. The institutionalization of beliefs occurs as a process of development of a logically coherent system of ideas. Elaborated and formalized ideas constitute the theology of the religion. For example, the Apostles' Creed, which communicants often repeat in Christian worship services, represents a distillation of Christian theology:

> I believe in God the Father Almighty, maker of Heaven and Earth, And in Jesus Christ his only Son, our Lord; who was conceived by the Holy Spirit, born of the Virgin Mary; suffered under Pontius Pilate, was crucified, dead, and buried; the third day he rose from the dead; he ascended into heaven, and sitteth at the right hand of God, the Father Almighty; from thence he shall come to judge the quick and the dead. I believe in the Holy Spirit, the holy catholic Church, the communion of saints, the forgiveness of sins, the resurrection of the body; and the life everlasting.

Here the Christian beliefs in God, the divinity of Jesus, the Virgin birth, the resurrection, and eternal life are given succinct expression. The Apostle's Creed is a theological statement.

Social groups have held varied beliefs concerning the nature of the supernatural entities they recognize. The conceptions have profound import for the rest of the culture. Students of religion have attempted to categorize broadly some of the differences in belief systems. One set of categories distinguishes personal and impersonal deities. **Deism** is the name given to the conception of a god who created the world and everything in it according to a set of logical and immutable principles, then retired and let it operate according to these divine laws. An

"Lord!, help me pass this test. Next time, I'll study for it."

analogy might be the clockmaker who fashions an intricate clock, winds up his creation, and sits back to watch it run. This impersonal view of God, the creator of a mechanistic universe that operates according to his established principles of cause and effect, has been prominent in Western thought since the Age of the Enlightenment, beginning in the seventeenth Century. Positing natural law in the universe, it was a potent stimulus to the development of modern science. The assumed task of the scientist was to discover God's unchanging laws, for example, the movement of the planets and the principle of gravity.

Theism is the conception of a God (or gods) who not only created the world but continues to take a personal interest in its operation. This conception depicts the supernatural entity (or entities) as perpetually intervening in nature and in the everyday affairs of men and women. Greek mythology furnishes myriad examples of this. For example, during the Trojan War, the gods and goddesses lined up on opposite sides. At one climactic point of the war, Athena, the goddess of war and wisdom, protected her favorite, the Greek hero, Achilles, by sending a puff of wind to turn aside Hector's spear; while Apollo, the sun god, caught up his favorite, Hector, the Trojan prince, in a cloud of dust to avoid Achilles' spear.

We do not have to go to ancient religions, however, to find examples. A student who prays to God to let him pass a test for which he has not studied demonstrates belief in a theistic deity—one who will intervene personally on one's behalf. The implications of this view for scientific development are obvious. Science is based on predictability rooted in regularities of cause and effect in nature. Theistic beliefs assume that God will contravene these causal sequences on behalf of a supplicant. For example, the Biblical story tells of God commanding the sun to stand still as a result of Joshua's plea on behalf of the Israelites. The same orientation is illustrated in the case of a young lady planning a garden wedding who believes that if she prays hard enough for fair weather, God will be moved to send sunshine, whatever the prevailing weather patterns might indicate. The predictability that is the core of science is not assumed to be present under theistic conceptions; the tensions between science and religion are partially an effect of this conception.

Categories of belief based on the number of deities are **monotheism,** belief in one god, and **polytheism,** several gods. Judaism is a monotheistic religion,

The Institutionalization of Religion 303

from which both Christianity and Islam are derived. Most Christians would say that they believe in one God, which is monotheism, but many invoke the Holy Trinity: Father, Son, and Holy Spirit. The mythologies of various peoples are replete with examples of polytheism. For example, the Bahima, the cattle-raising segment of the Baziba groups in Uganda, worship Wamara and his four sons, to whom he distributed various spheres of reality: Kagoro, mythical hero; Mugasha, god of water; Kazoba, god of sun and moon; and Ryangombe, god of cattle (Grimal, 1973:523). Among the ancient Greeks, although Zeus was the king of the gods, other gods and goddesses controlled various aspects of existence: Ares was the god of war; Aphrodite, the goddess of love; Demeter, goddess of the harvest; Hades, god of the underworld; Poseidon, god of the sea, and so on through an extensive array of gods and functions. Among polytheistic religions, the gods rule those aspects of existence that are most salient for the society. The ancient Greeks' preoccupation with warfare is demonstrated by the fact that both a god and a goddess of warfare inhabit their pantheon of deities. Similarly, the god of cattle projects the occupational emphasis of the Bahima. In monotheism, the single god is usually depicted as an all-powerful entity covering all realms of reality.

Supernatural entities are usually endowed with human-type characteristics; that is, man creates his gods in his own image. The tendency of a group to incorporate this idea into its conception of the deity or deities is called **anthropomorphism.** The gods may be conceived in human physical form and exhibit the same emotions and motivations that humans do. Gods and spirits reward, punish, pity, feel sad, weep, play tricks, take vengeance, walk, talk, love, sulk, lust, feel anger, jealousy, and compassion. This aspect of religious belief is a powerful force for social control, because discretion would dictate that one not offend an entity with human-type passions and supernatural ways of expressing them.

Embodying this anthropomorphic principle in an intensive way, though with less emphasis on physical form, **animism** has been an important form of religion in some preliterate societies. This is the belief that immanent spirits pervade all nature. Trees, mountains, rivers, animals, the sky, the fields, the wind, the rain are imbued with supernatural forces that must be continually placated. It is obvious that technological development, which depends upon the impersonal, rational manipulation of nature, would be seriously impeded by this belief. The interpretation one might put upon this depends upon how well one likes automobiles and air-conditioned classrooms—or smog and high electric bills. But we may say with certainty that the development of modern technology depended upon man's emergence from what Weber referred to as the "enchanted forest."

Practices

Every religion involves some type of activities or practices. These may include such behaviors or activities as prayer, chanting, exhortation or preaching, singing, playing instruments, dancing, reciting codes, sacrifices, retreats, vigils, pilgrimages, scarification, flagellation, fasting, feasting, or the use of trance-inducing drugs, paintings, masks, or icons. These behaviors may involve group participation or may be privately performed following the group definitions of what is appropriate.

In the early stages of the development of a religion the activities associated with it are often characterized by a high degree of spontaneity; one may act in ways that express the emotional content of the experience. There is a tendency, however, for the behaviors to become stylized, or patterned, among group members. Worship assumes a stable form. Rituals represent the institutionalization of the religion. There is acceptance of the idea that "this is the way it should be done." One may find an illustration of this point by looking in the hymnals found in Christian churches. There one may find the order of worship for regular services, for special seasons or events in the church calendar, for communion, baptism, confirmation, marriage, and funerals. The words to be spoken by the minister and by the other participants may be specified, the prayers written out, and the musical responses identified. Times to stand, to sit, to kneel are designated. In the traditional Hopi Indian culture, the ritual of the Rain Dance was so meticulously prescribed that the slightest variation in the performance was thought to be sufficient cause for the deity controlling the rain to refuse to release it. Although the cultural settings of these two examples are very different, both represent a high degree of institutionalization of religious practices.

Morality

Durkheim suggested that the **collective conscience,** that is, the shared values and beliefs of a group, are given religious sanctions in order to reinforce them. That is to say that the norms and beliefs that are most important to sustaining the group are proclaimed as sacred edicts and are enshrined as holy writ. Once this has occurred, they take on a reality and a continuity of their own. They become the moral code of the religion, providing guidance for believers in their social relationships. They are the mores of the society. For example, the Ten Commandments of the Old Testament prescribe and proscribe behaviors that result in smooth social interaction. Such actions as adultery, murder, theft, and bearing false witness are behaviors that disrupt the patterns of cooperation and trust that are important to group life. This code of morality is tied securely to maintaining solidarity among believers. Other established religions have also developed ethical guidelines. These are expressed in the most cherished religious writings, as in the Judeo-Christian Bible, the Koran of Islam, the Laws of Manu of Hinduism, or the Tripitaka of Buddhism. Similar ethical themes may be found in such sacred writings. For example, some variation of the Golden Rule is to be found in almost every major religion.

Moral codes sometimes go beyond the behaviors that deal with group unity. The Puritan codes of the Massachusetts Bay Colony were so rigid that they exceeded their usefulness in producing harmony. Even though religious sanctions give stability to moral codes, they do change over time. Behavior that is regarded as immoral at one point may not be so regarded at a different period. For example, at the beginning of this century women who smoked were regarded as immoral. Abortion was unequivocally immoral. Today both of these practices have widespread acceptance.

One of the results of the student movement of the 1960s was that many of our moral directives were stood on their heads and new ethical themes were introduced. For example, there was a loosening of concern with strict personal moral standards and a new emphasis on the moral imperatives of social responsibility. Martin Luther King, Jr., expressed this shift in his image of the beggar on the Jericho road. The Good Samaritan followed his personal ethical code in offering aid. Without denigrating this act of love, King suggested that a higher ethic would be to create a society in which there were no beggars on the Jericho road. Many religious bodies have moved in the direction of social activism as a part of their moral responsibility.

Morality is one of the major elements of institutional religion. The major ethical systems that have been developed in the world have been rooted in and encapsulated in religious codes.

Collectivity

One of the intrinsic qualities of religion is that it is social in nature. Although one may worship in private, one generally incorporates the beliefs and practices of a group into one's religious behavior. Having a religion all by oneself is a contradiction in terms. A number of people who share a similar belief and engage in religious practices together tend to identify with each other; they form a self-conscious collectivity. Sometimes, particularly in preliterate societies, the religious collectivity is coterminous with the society. Members of the society participate in the religion of the whole group, and the organization of the religious group may be indistinguishable from that of the society, though generally the specialist in dealing with the sacred will be a recognized role. In multigroup societies, such as ours, many religious collectivities may exist, and the separation of political and religious organization usually occurs, though they may interpenetrate.

As people associate with one another in religious activity, they develop a pattern of roles and predictable relationships. In other words, religious groups become organized. The structure may be relatively simple; for example, the leader, who is a specialist in dealing with the supernatural, may be the only role that is differentiated from the other members of the group. But organizational roles tend to become specialized and formalized. For example, in an emerging contemporary religious group, Miss Kumquat may volunteer to play the piano once or twice at worship services. Soon, she is expected to play for services. Eventually she may be designated "the church pianist" or perhaps "director of music." Once the position is built into the organization, it exists independently of the specific person who fills it. If Miss Kumquat moves to Peoria, she does not take the position away; someone else then becomes "director of music." Other positions follow a similar pattern, and the structure becomes more stable and predictable; the deacons, the usher board, the youth director, the director of religious education, the church secretary, and so on become formal roles that have specified requirements and continuity. Institutionalization has occurred.

Perspectives on Religion

A Functionalist Perspective

The fact that a collectivity shares a system of beliefs and practices relative to sacred things has profound import for the society. Functional analysis is concerned with those consequences; that is, with the social functions it performs.

Durkheim was one of the first sociologists to make a detailed study of the social functions of religion.

What we refer to here is not what religion does for individual believers, but what it does in terms of the maintenance of the group itself. It is this social aspect of religion that caught Durkheim's attention; and any analysis of the social functions of religion must begin with him.

Durkheim (1961) said that religion both expresses the solidarity of a society and at the same time serves to maintain and strengthen that solidarity. In its elementary forms, he says, religion probably was a means of celebrating the unity of the group. We continue to find this characteristic in it. The quality of sacredness becomes attached to objects or ideas that symbolize the collective experience. Thus, in Durkheim's thought, religion is the projection of a society's reverence for its own communality, and every society has something of this quality in it.

But Durkheim also insists that religion contributes to maintaining the solidarity of the group. Humans link the sacred realm with the "collective conscience." That is, they attribute the source of morality and ultimate group values to supernatural entities or sacred principles. And of what does morality consist? For the most part, it is social norms that have important consequences for maintaining the solidarity of the group. For example, six of the Ten Commandments express how people should relate to one another; in effect, how to avoid social conflict. Religious codes typically encourage believers to subordinate individual goals to group cohesion. Injunctions against stealing illustrate the point; stealing may be a direct way to further one's goals, but the group's ability to cooperate to meet its collective needs may be impaired by the activity. Every major religion includes some form of the Golden Rule: "Do unto others as you would have them do unto you." The implications of this dictum for social harmony are obvious,

Perspectives on Religion

as are such admonitions as "Love thy neighbor as thyself." This sanctification of the rules that facilitate social interaction is one of the major ways in which religion contributes to group cohesion. An old hymn goes:

> Blest be the tie that binds
> Our hearts in Christian love.
> The fellowship of kindred minds
> Is like to that above.

This "fellowship of kindred minds" is a powerful cohesive force. Those who share the same beliefs and ultimate values draw together in a moral community. "We think alike" is one of the strongest elements in building group identification. In the face of external challenge to those beliefs and values, such unity may be strengthened through an intensified awareness among believers of sameness and difference. For example, many of the pietistic sects that faced religious persecution in Europe during the sixteenth and seventeenth centuries flourished as a result of their fervid defense of the faith.

The group exercises social control over its members through its sacred rules and the religious sanctions attached to them. When one sins, he or she feels guilty; so the control becomes internalized. Some of the sanctions are imposed by religious law or by the decree of religious functionaries. The Spanish Inquisition, whose duty it was to seek out and punish heresy, was administered through a tribunal of the Roman Catholic church. Excommunication of offenders is the prerogative of the Pope in Catholic tradition. Excommunication and denouncement from the pulpit were techniques used by the Puritans. Black Baptist churches sometimes used public denouncement of offenders. Under Islamic law, the thief's hand is cut off, and the married adulterer is stoned. But even stronger sanction is that attributed to the supernatural realm itself. Religious beliefs that include concepts of heaven and hell or some other depiction of life after death usually tie them to earthly behavior. In most religions the individual is able to influence his or her destiny in eternity by following the sacred rules in this life. Early Calvinist beliefs in predestination were a notable exception.

Unmarried pregnant girls were once publicly punished or humiliated in church congregations.

Either fear of a vengeful god or love for a beneficent one that intervenes in ongoing human activity is also a powerful stimulus for conforming conduct. Many religions incorporate the notion of **moral determinism,** the idea that the events of one's life are determined by the morality of one's behavior. The connecting link is the intervention of a deity that is angry and punishing or pleased and rewarding, as the case may be. In many societies illness or misfortune is explained as the punishing action of some offended supernatural being. Therefore, to cure an illness, one must consult the specialist in dealing with the supernatural; that is, the shaman or **priest.** In Biblical stories Sodom and Gomorrah were destroyed because the inhabitants were evil. The flood wiped out the earth's inhabitants because they were bad; Noah and his family were saved because he was good. When we hear someone who has good fortune say, "I must have been living right," we are hearing an example of moral determinism in our own culture: right living is thought to bring good fortune. Social control is integral to this notion. In order to avoid misfortune one must attempt to placate the supernatural powers that reward or punish one according to whether one's behavior follows the divinely decreed rules. Such rules are usually the mores of the society.

Ritual plays an important part in revivifying for members of the collectivity their "fellowship of kindred minds." It evokes the heritage of shared beliefs and sacred rules and renews commitment to them. The symbols embodied in ritual are charged with meanings rooted in the group's cultural history. Ritual confirms these meanings and rejuvenates them so that they retain freshness and continuity within the group. But Durkheim says that the particular external forms of ritual are not as important as the reaffirmation of communal ties that underlie them:

> To become conscious of itself, the group does not need to perform certain acts in preference to all others. The necessary thing is that it partakes of the same thought and the same action; the visible forms in which this communion takes place matter but little. Of course, these external forms do not come by chance; they have their reasons; but these reasons do not touch the essential part of the cult . . . before all, rites are means by which the social group reaffirms itself periodically (Durkheim, 1961:432).

For example, the symbols of the Star of David, the Ark of the Covenant, and the Menorah used in Jewish rituals have meaning in the context of the cultural heritage and social experience of Jews. But it is not these particular sacred items themselves or their particular use in religious ceremony that have maintained unity among Jewish people. Participating together periodically in rituals that evoke through these symbols the common life and heritage that they share perpetuates the group and keeps it vibrant and alive.

Another of the social functions of religion is to provide legitimacy for the social world. According to Peter Berger (1969), every human society constructs its own world of reality. Its language, its knowledge, its norms, its social institutions are all ways of imposing order upon the otherwise chaotic experiences of individuals. The distinction people in our society make between green and blue, either of which may have light and dark shades, is reality to us. Another society may think of the light shades of what we would call blue and green as one color and the dark shades as another color. That is their reality. We order reality in the social world as well as in the physical world. In our society one does not marry a first cousin on either the mother's or the father's side. That is our social reality. In another society the cousins on one side or the other are exactly the group from which one selects a mate. That is their reality.

It is the joint experience of worshipping together that keeps the Jewish religion fresh and vibrant.

The socially constructed world of reality rests on shaky grounds. The social world, especially, is subject to challenge: Why should I not kill a person who insults me? Why must I respect my parents? Why should I not sleep with my father (or mother)? Why should I be faithful to my spouse? Why should I kneel before the king? Why should I not take wood from someone else's land if I am cold or take food from a supermarket if I am hungry? The normative world requires some kind of legitimacy if it is to maintain its order and stability in the face of doubts and questions that challenge the way things are.

One of the stongest legitimizers for social reality is religion. Religion has the capacity for placing man's everyday experiences in the context of cosmic order. This provides legitimation, which helps to sustain the reality (Berger, 1969:35). For example, why do some of us close up our businesses on Sunday and sit around most of the day in our best clothes? Because our religion tells us that God said, "Remember the Sabbath day and keep it holy," and Christians interpret this to mean Sunday. This ties our socially constructed reality (i.e., we close our businesses on Sunday) to the cosmic order (God's commandment) and is a much stronger legitimation for our practice than "that's just the way we do it." The belief that God commands us to honor our parents gives legitimation to our norm of parental respect. "God says so" gives religious support to this aspect of social reality. Religious validation of marriage also gives support to the family institution: "Whom God hath joined together" gives marriage divine sanction. We cite examples here to demonstrate the point; but in societies in which secularization has not seriously challenged cosmic decree, the social order in its totality may be legitimized through religion: the world is as it is by divine plan. Sometimes secular legitimations take on religious overtones precisely because they perform the same function, e.g., "democracy" or "communism" may provide an overarching support for social reality. That such legitimation gives stability to social institutions is obvious. But one of the crucial effects of imbuing human institutions with sacred significance is that it renders them impervious to change. The assumption about our social institutions that "What we have made we can change" provides a ground upon which improvement may be attempted. But the assumption that God has made our social order means that we tinker with it at our own peril.

Religious endorsement of social arrangements may legitimize severe inequalities in social structure. For example, the traditional caste system of India, which we discussed earlier, manifested inequalities so profound that the very shadow of a member of the "untouchables" was thought to be contaminating to upper caste members upon whom it might fall. Rigidly stratified, endogamous, hereditary, and occupationally linked, the castes were legitimized through the Hindu religion. One was thought to have been born into a certain caste because of what one was and did in a previous existence. The notion of reincarnation is

Religion legitimizes marriage norms giving them some degree of stability. Legitimation of social norms is one of the functions of religions.

tied to the principle of karma, which promises that if one lives a good life (which means obeys the caste rules), he or she will be advanced in the next reincarnation to a higher position in the social structure. This means, then, that one deserves the caste position or the outcaste status into which he or she is born. Therefore, it behooves one to comply with all the rules governing one's position so that in the next life one may be "promoted" to a higher caste. The Brahmins are the highest caste because they deserve to be; they have worked themselves up the caste ladder. When they die, their souls will not be reincarnated but will join the Infinite. To challenge this system is to risk "demotion" in the next life. The social order thus is given immutability by religious legitimation.

To turn to our own society, we may note that religion has been used to legitimate racial and economic inequality. The legitimation it gives to traditional women's roles becomes apparent every time we go to a wedding in which the bride promises to "obey" her husband and the minister reads scriptural passages enjoining her to stay at home and be a helpmate to her husband. Religion, then, not only reconciles us to the uncontrollable events that confront us—illness, natural disasters, and death—but also to the social institutions that shape our lives. It provides, in Berger's imagery, a "sacred canopy" for the reality we jointly have constructed.

A Conflict Perspective

Conflict theorists disagree with some of the assumptions that functionalists make about religion in society and reinterpret others. We must look to Marx as having formulated the position.

Strongly attracted to the humanitarian ethic of Christianity, Marx was intensely concerned with religion in his early years. However, he grew increasingly hostile toward it as he came to see its emphasis as transcendent and God-centered. The impact of such a focus was, he thought, passiveness toward the world. Religious exaltation was "a hot-water bottle for some individual souls," he said in his doctoral dissertation. But Marx, passionately interested in the real world of human activity, decided that religion, in emphasizing the Absolute as opposed to man immersed in that real world, was alienating to man.

His subsequent discussions of religion place it in the context of his general theories of alienation and false consciousness. His basic premise is that man makes religion; religion does not make man. That is, religion is a social product. Man creates religion because he "has not found his feet in the universe." He has not developed a sense of his true reality as a human being. Religion, not man himself, becomes the source of logic, morality, motivation, and the basis for consolation and justification. The more of himself he invests in supernatural beings, the less he has left for his own actualization. For example, in attributing the source of morality to God, he robs himself of the realization of his own moral capacity. Furthermore, these religious systems confront him, as his political and economic creations also confront him, as objective forces that limit and coerce him. They are, therefore, alienating in that they set one part of man against another part of himself.

At the same time, religion is an expression of human suffering:

Religion is the sigh of the oppressed creature, the sentiment of a heartless world, and the soul of soulless conditions. It is the opium of the people (Marx, 1967:250–51).

Marx said that it brings to men an illusory happiness; but his major concern is the consequences such preoccupation with illusion has for maintaining conditions that are so painful that man must resort to illusions in order to endure them. By focusing on the illusory world, man's attention is deflected from the need to create the conditions of his true happiness in the real world. In this sense, religion is "false consciousness;" for it does not contribute to true self-awareness and identity, these being the products of material rather than spiritual conditions. Marx believed that by focusing attention on life beyond the grave, religion distracts the working class in particular from the task of bringing about the radical economic change that will reduce oppression. He held that because religion in this way discourages radical change, it serves the interest of the ruling class; by eliminating it man can get on with the business of changing the economic and political structures that cause him pain in this world.

Furthermore, Marx saw the content of the Christian ethic as inimical to the interests of the oppressed class. Its social principles, he says, preach "self-contempt, abasement, submission, humility" when the working class needs "its courage, its self-esteem, its pride and its sense of independence more than its bread." In effect it encourages cringing, when revolutionary action is required (Marx, 1959:268–69).

Later Conflict Studies. Some American writers of the conflict perspective have identified specific situations in which religion has been used to support the interests of the ruling class. Their interpretations echo Marx's analysis. For example, one interpretation is that in the early days of this country, slave owners deliberately sought to Christianize the slaves because they thought religion would keep them docile. It was, in effect, a tool for maintaining dominance. The otherworldly emphasis in Christianity would lessen their resistance to servitude in this world; and the ethic of meekness and love, a requisite for attaining that salvation, would reconcile them to their subservient position.

In this mode we may note the appeal to the Bible for justification of existing social arrangements. For example, the Biblical story of God's cursing Ham and sentencing his descendants forever to be hewers of wood and drawers of water was used by many white supremacists as a legitimation for discrimination against blacks. During the days when the Reverend Martin Luther King, Jr., was invoking Christian precepts to challenge continuing racism and segregation in the South, many white Bible Belt church men and women fell back on their conception of the universe as an expression of God's immutable purposes: If God had meant for sparrows and robins to mingle with one another, He would have made them all the same. Translation: God condones segregation; if He had meant for blacks and whites to mingle with each other, He would have made them all the same color.

Liston Pope's (1942) classic study, *Millhands and Preachers,* illustrates clearly the tendency of religion to support class interests and resist social change. Set in Gastonia, North Carolina, in 1928, this study explores the interrelationships of religious and economic institutions as they came into focus during one of the earliest attempts to unionize the textile mills of the South. The churches of Gastonia tended to draw from different segments of the population, with established denominations drawing mostly from the middle and upper economic levels, whereas churches of a more expressive, informal type appealed to the mill workers. The textile companies had subsidized the mill churches, maintaining that religion makes not only good workers but also good citizens.

When labor organizers entered one of the large mills to attempt to establish a union, the whole community became embroiled, and the churches were in the thick of it. Pope had expected to find that the established churches supported the textile companies. Would the workers' churches support the union? On the contrary, Pope found that the mill churches vehemently opposed the union and took an active part in condemning the "Communist outside agitators" for destroying the community. Religion in Gastonia stood steadfast in its resistance to this threat to existing class relationships.[1]

Similar questions concerning the relationship between religion and social action prompted the research of Gary Marx (1967) in the 1960s. It has often been cited to support the contention of the conflict school that religion sustains unjust social arrangements. From a national survey of black adults, Marx found an inverse relationship between religiosity and militancy: the higher the degree of religiosity among respondents, the lower the level of militancy. It should be noted that the majority of militants in the study were religious. However, religious fundamentalism, belief in the literal interpretation of the Bible, was strongly associated with nonmilitancy. The fatalistic outlook that confronts a social problem with the idea of putting everything in "God's hands" seemingly absolves humans of the necessity to take action to correct it. If God's will is being done, then man need not—in fact, should not—get involved. This fatalistic point of view helps to explain the type of association Gary Marx found.

A further point of disagreement between functionalist and conflict sociologists is the extent to which a religion unifies its adherents. One need only refer to the chronicle of schisms, heresies, factional disputes, and dogmatic spinoffs that have characterized Christianity since its early days (and as recently as yesterday's newspaper accounts of Protestant-Catholic conflict in Northern Ireland) to identify a strong divisive tendency within it. "Blest be the tie that binds," says the old hymn; but the susceptibility of those ties to rupture is amply demonstrated by the history of denominational differentiation and conflict that continues to the present.

Religion as a Source of Social Change

Both the functionalist and conflict perspectives view religion as essentially a stabilizing force in the society.[2] But evidence abounds that religion can also be a basis for change. For example, the black church was the strategic arena from which the civil rights movement of the 1960s was launched. The black church, the only meeting place not under white domination in the South, was the site of

---

[1] In a restudy of religion in Gastonia some twenty-five years after Pope's study, researchers found that with the increasing complexity of the social structure and the greater differentiation of churches that reflected it, the willingness of some churches to challenge existing relationships increased. This was true particularly regarding integration (Earle et al., 1976).

[2] Conflict theorists do not deny that religion can produce change. However, they do not see religion-induced change as altering the basic structures of class relationships.

protest meetings and strategy sessions. Black leadership skills were honed in the church. The roster of black church men who led the movement included not only such distinguished and familiar names as the reverends Martin Luther King, Jr., Ralph Abernathy, Andrew Young, and Jesse Jackson, but also numerous unsung local ministers who were active in their communities throughout the region, challenging segregation customs, raising funds for civil rights organizations, leading registration drives for black voters, and mobilizing their parishioners for action. The role of the church as an effective source of change in this instance cannot be denied.

Max Weber was a sociologist who identified the dynamic potential for change that religion represented. We now look at one of his discussions that expressed this recognition.

Priest and Prophet Roles

Weber (1964) developed concepts embodying the stability and change roles of religious functionaries: priest and prophet. These are ideal, or pure, types; in actuality, they may be combined in the experience of any religious figure. The

The priest is a member of an established church. The prophet challenges the existing order.

priestly role is mainly to perpetuate and strengthen sacred tradition. The priest is a functionary of an organized religious body and directs the power of his office toward reinforcing the interests of that collectivity. His authority derives from his institutional position. Usually this commits him to preserving the doctrinal heritage of the group, though Weber says this is not universal, and to reinforcing its association with a particular normative order. Most of the ministerial figures that appear in the pulpits of American churches on Sunday mornings represent this role. They interpret the scriptures according to traditional precepts, attempting to bring comfort and provide spiritual and moral guidance to their congregations. The pattern is one of accommodation to or with the existing order. Stability and continuity are maintained through this clerical emphasis.

The role of the **prophet,** on the other hand, is to challenge the existing order. The prophet, either by his personal example or through his commitment to a set of ethical principles, attempts to create a new order to replace a defective existing order, which may be depicted as evil or as lacking in vitality and direction. Many, though not all, prophets have been lawgivers. For example, Moses in Hebraic law and Mohammed in the law of Islam set forth divinely sanctioned ethical codes to regulate the relationships of individual with individual and individual with God. But more central to the role of the prophet is his or her calling the people to a higher conception of spiritual and ethical life. The prophet proclaims a religious doctrine or divine commandment. The truth he or she reveals attempts to integrate social and cosmic views into a meaningful whole to which individual conduct must be oriented.

Charisma is an important factor in establishing the authenticity of the prophet. The acceptance of a prophet by the laity is generally based upon the powers imputed to him that distinguish him from ordinary men and women. He may become the object of a cult. Most of the founders of the major religions were such charismatic figures: Jesus, Mohammed, and the Buddha. Charisma works to galvanize the fervor of the people to follow the prophet.

In recent years an example of this type of religious leader is Ayotollah Khomeini. His leadership of the Iranian revolution, which unseated the Shah of Iran, was based only partially in political revolutionary fervor. His main motivation seems to have been a rekindling of the fires of Islam; he advocated return to the Islamic principles of earlier times. Conceiving of him as demonstrating particular gifts of the spirit that set him apart from ordinary people, his followers dedicated themselves to achieving the goals he enunciated.

Dr. Martin Luther King, Jr., was also a prophet and a charismatic figure. He directed his prophetic voice toward social reform. Employing the precepts of traditional doctrine, he called the nation to a higher application of its basic ideals. So profoundly did he embody in his exhortations this challenge to the existing order to revivify the ideals of brotherhood and equality explicit in its religious and political codes that the nation was stirred to action. The charismatic impact of his ministry was so forceful that one public figure, obviously lacking in identification and sympathy with King's objectives, was moved to remind the country of a doctrinal priority, "It's 'God is King', not 'King is God' ".

As indicated earlier, Weber developed these concepts as ideal types; but in actuality the roles of prophet and priest may be combined as dual functions of any religious leader. A clergyman may minister to his congregation in traditional doctrinal terms but may also attempt to stir them to social action. However, most ministers tend to see the priestly role as more appropriate for themselves than the prophetic role (Earle et al., 1976:155). A "priestly" view is well demonstrated by the minister of a prestigious Southern church who publicly stated while controversy swirled around his community during the 1960s, "My concern is religion; I don't have anything to do with desegregation." Laymen, as well, seem more comfortable with the priestly role for the minister (Earle et al., 1976:155). This is hardly surprising given that the mission of the prophet is to make people uncomfortable. It is through this prophetic role, however, that the potential for social change is galvanized and expressed in the church.

Religion in a Multicultural Society

Religion has been a major element in the diversity of cultural heritages that has characterized the United States. For example, E. Franklin Frazier (1963) described the way the church has served to unify blacks at three different periods of rapid change. Under slavery the "invisible church," centered around the slave preacher, brought blacks together in worship and common activity, provided a stabilizing moral code, and kept hope alive.

After Emancipation the church helped to define the black community, often giving it its name and boundaries as well as its network of social relationships. The activity of building the church established patterns of economic and social cooperation and mutual support. Seeing land ownership as one means of stabilizing the family, the church encouraged its members to acquire farm land. Church support for education compensated in some measure for the neglect black schools suffered. Skills gained in governing the church gave political experience to men and women shut out of the broader political life of the society. The church served as a refuge from the hostile white world and as a focus for black communal life.

Frazier notes that when blacks migrated to the cities, the church began to reflect the diversity that was developing in the black community itself. Storefront churches gave continuity to those who yearned for the intimacy of worship in the small rural churches they had come from, whereas the large churches turned their attention toward a broad range of concerns, both sacred and secular, that confronted blacks in the urban environment.

The creative use of the black church as a focus of communal life has demonstrated resilience and ingenuity in the face of oppression. It was not surprising that the civil rights movement was launched from the black church; for it was in the church that much of the unity and strength of the black community was forged.

The ethnic church was a focal point around which immigrant groups from Europe established communities in the new world. Intolerance was often directed toward Catholics and Jews as a part of the broader prejudice expressed toward immigrant groups upon their arrival on these shores. Discrimination in employment, education, and housing as well as personal harassment characterized much of the experience of non-Protestant groups. But religion has been one of the cultural elements most resistant to change in the assimilation that has occurred among such groups. Milton Gordon has suggested that the United States has had a triple melting pot. Whatever blending of ethnic groups there may have been has occurred mostly within, not across, the three major religious groups: Protestant, Catholic, and Jewish (Gordon, 1964:205). So religion has not only exemplified cultural diversity; it has also served to maintain it, though the impact of American culture has been noticeable on these identifications.

A recent study of 1,000 Hispanic Catholics in the New York archdiocese indicated that Hispanics strongly adhere to the fundamental tenets of the Catholic faith, despite the fact that 36 percent said they did not attend mass and an additional 24 percent said they went only occasionally (Fitzpatrick, 1983:185). There are 835,000 Hispanics in the New York archdiocese, about 65 percent of whom are Puerto Ricans. Results of this study indicate that being a part of a Catholic community that celebrates the faith through such activities as processions, fiestas, and important commemorative events is more important in religious identification than attending mass. The study showed that traditional religious practices are still widely carried out among churchgoers and nongoers alike: "Candles, incense, shrines in the home, the rosary, wearing medals, blessings, prayer at meals, sprinkling holy water, especially on the newborn child, reading the Bible (Fitzpatrick, 1983:186)." (See Table 14.1)

The impact of American culture on Hispanic religion, however, is also clearly indicated in the study. The higher the educational level attained, the lower the identification with the church appeared to be. Perhaps more significant, as bilingualism increases, religious practices decrease. The Spanish language and the preservation of the faith seem interrelated. These findings bring into focus the issues of cultural assimilation and cultural pluralism.

A countertendency has also been noted. Because tolerance for religious diversity has been at least an official value in this society, doctrinal extremes have been muted. Herberg noted the homogenizing of religion among the three major religions, all of them emphasizing those values shared by most Americans: humanitarianism, tolerance, individualism, equality, and democracy (Herberg, 1955). Bellah (1970), borrowing a phrase from Rousseau, spoke of our "**civil religion,**" which embodies a nonspecific, nondoctrinal conception of God, who

Table 14.1. *Survey of 1,000 Hispanic Catholics*

	First generation (%)	Came to the U.S. before 8 years old (%)	Second generation (%)
Wear medals, crucifixes, scapulars or rosaries	42.6	36.1	38.9
Practice self-imposed penance	22.0	22.2	15.8
Say the rosary	30.1	19.4	21.1
Read the Bible	56.1	61.1	48.4
Give thanks before meals	50.8	50.0	30.5
Burn incense	20.0	22.2	14.7
Keep candles in the house under a religious image	23.1	22.2	16.8
Bless house or property	47.2	33.3	34.7
Keep images of saints or an altar at home	36.9	27.8	32.6
Make pilgrimages or visit shrines	12.3	8.3	5.3
Sprinkle holy water	27.3	30.6	18.9

Source: Archdiocese of New York

represents the transcendent moral standards to which the nation should and, in Bellah's opinion, does aspire.

Religious Diversity and Political Institutions

The relationship between religious and political institutions is a crucial one for any society. There are many variations in the patterns that define the nature of the connection. In some societies religions and political institutions are tightly intertwined, as for example in Iran today.

Diversity in the United States. Such a situation contrasts strikingly with that found in the United States. The doctrine of the separation of church and state is built into the First Amendment to the Constitution and it might be viewed as one of the main supports for the edifice of multiculturalism:

> Congress shall make no law respecting an establishment of religion, or prohibiting the free exercise thereof; or abridging the freedom of speech, or of the press; or the right of the people peaceably to assemble, and to petition the Government for a redress of grievances.

Although this amendment enjoins Congress, it has been interpreted by the courts to apply to the states and their creations as well. As it relates to religion, the first amendment stresses two themes. First, it prohibits the government from establishing or supporting any religion or giving one faith preference over any other. There is to be no officially supported religion. The second part prohibits the government from interfering in religious worship. Together these two aspects of the First Amendment establish the doctrine of separation of church and state. It is intended to maximize religious freedom.

Although the formal doctrine of the separation of church and state has been taken seriously in the structuring of our institutions, in reality the interrelationship of church and state has been much in evidence. Religious symbols pervade our public ceremonies and are incorporated into much of our political activity. Our currency states, "In God we Trust." The Great Seal of the United States claims (in Latin), "God has favored our undertaking." The pledge of allegiance to the flag proclaims, "one nation, under God." Various oaths of office are sworn on the Bible and end, "So help me God." Our armed services provide a chaplaincy. Prayers open many official gatherings, such as the meetings of Congress. Bellah calls attention to the references to God in the inaugural addresses and major speeches of the presidents (Bellah, 1970:168–72). They stress a higher judgment upon our action beyond ourselves and remind us of our obligation to discern and carry out God's will. The use of essentially religious themes and symbols that give transcendent meaning to the major events of our national history is a part of our "civil religion." It lacks embodiment in any specific church or religious body but seems to be securely established in the shared orientations of most Americans. The civil religion has sometimes been invoked for corrupt and selfish ends; but Bellah argues that this ultimate dimension has also underlain the nobler aspirations and accomplishments of the nation. As an example of this, some sense of the ultimate rightness of it helped to produce the Voting Rights Act of

1965. Selma marchers and other civil rights activists invoked this theme. When he went before Congress to ask for its passage, President Johnson concluded his message with these words:

> God will not favor everything that we do. It is rather our duty to divine his will. I cannot help but believe that He truly understands and that He really favors the undertaking that we begin here tonight (quoted in Bellah, 1970:181).

Such references do not refer to the God of any particular religion but to some ultimate entity to whom most people can relate. They serve as a demonstration that the separation of church and state is not as complete as we sometimes assume.

The boundaries of this doctrine have been repeatedly tested, both in the courts and in public discourse. One of the most provocative issues has been the extent to which the church or religious functionaries should participate in political life. Assumed to be nonprofit organizations, churches are exempt from property taxes. Religious contributions are also tax deductible. The presupposition underlying these exemptions is that churches will be pursuing only religious objectives. But distinguishing religious from nonreligious objectives is very difficult. For example, some churches, both black and white, were active in the campaign to end segregation; and church men and women contributed much of the leadership for the movement. The overriding concern with desegregation obscured the issue of "mixing religion and politics" in this situation, and little controversy focused on this question at the time. It was to be resurrected in the presidential campaign of 1980 and again in 1984, however, in an attempt by some religious figures to identify a precedent for injecting religious activism into the election.

The Moral Majority, an organization of mostly fundamentalist men and women, was founded by the Reverend Jerry Falwell, a television evangelist. Advocating a return to a more disciplined and puritanical standard, they entered the political

The Reverend Jerry Falwell, founder of the Moral Majority, delivers a Sunday sermon heard by millions over 500 radio and 392 TV stations.

arena on behalf of candidates who were committed to the same ethic; that is, candidates who supported prayer in the schools and who opposed abortion, gay rights, women's rights, and, in general, permissiveness in American society. They also took a strong stand on economic and military preparedness issues.

The Moral Majority mobilized a group of people who had had little prior involvement in the political process, predominantly lower-middle-class white Protestants. Leaders of the movement asserted their right to be involved and defended the organization as a forum through which they could express themselves effectively. They compared their involvement with some churches' earlier advocacy for civil rights, claiming that opposition to the Moral Majority was based on the conservatism of their program rather than on any real concern with the issue of separation of church and state.

Opponents claimed that the involvement of the Moral Majority in politics did violate the principle embodied in the First Amendment. The "hit list" in particular was held to be objectionable and dangerous. Some opponents did not see some of the issues of concern, such as economic and military matters, as having religious relevance. The Moral Majority's stand on other issues, such as abortion, gay rights, and prayer in the schools they interpreted as an attempt by the Moral Majority to force its religious beliefs upon the rest of the society. As such, it was seen as a threat to religious pluralism and religious freedom.

The Moral Majority is one of several groups that constitute what the press calls the "religious right." Lobbying on behalf of such matters as an amendment against abortion and for prayer in the schools forms a major part of the political agenda of these groups. Whether the "religious right" is viewed as an expression of religious freedom or an attack upon it seems to rest not so much on the First Amendment (to which both sides appeal) as upon one's ideological commitment. So far, the issue has been debated in the media, where the verdict is not definitive, rather than in the courts. It probably will remain a focus of controversy for some time to come.

Another facet of the relationship between religion and politics to be explored in public debate is whether or not the First Amendment guarantee of freedom of religion takes precedence when the religious practices run contrary to law. For example, do Indian groups whose religion calls for the use of peyote in producing trances have the right under the First Amendment to use hallucinogenic drugs prohibited by law? Do snake-handling cults of the rural South have the right to thrust poisonous snakes upon children? Do family members whose religion forbids consulting a doctor have the right to deny medical attention to someone who is dangerously ill? In 1983 Bob Jones University, a fundamentalist religious college in South Carolina, was denied tax exemptions because its policy prohibiting interracial dating violates the Civil Rights Act of 1964. The university claimed that the policy was based on religious belief and that the action of the Supreme Court violated their freedom of religion. Generally when such cases have arisen, the courts have ruled in favor of the secular laws rather than the religious practices.

A third type of situation that creates controversy over First Amendment rights involves the introduction of religion into secular areas of concern. One issue of this type is particularly emotional: whether prayer in the schools is permissable. Mandatory prayer in the public school has been ruled by the courts to be a violation of the First Amendment. By interpretation, this ruling applies to any teacher-directed period in which the children may or may not pray, as they see fit. The issue is debated in terms of "prayer in the schools," though this is not technically the difference in the positions. Private prayer is not prohibited; the ban covers only prayer instigated or arranged for by school personnel.

A ruling by the Supreme Court in 1985 in a case involving the state of Alabama established the principle that even periods of silence, if they were designed by teachers or other school personnel to encourage students to pray, ran counter to the First Amendment and therefore could not be instituted in the classroom. The "moment of silence" had been widely used as a way around the prohibition on school-organized prayers.

Those who oppose "prayer in the schools" in this sense cite the guarantee in the First Amendment that government will not establish any religion. Adherents of this position say that the rights of children of non-Christian faiths, or of no faith, would be violated by formally arranged prayer in the schools because most public school teachers and students are Christian. Even when prayer is not made mandatory, children of other faiths are frequently the victims of peer rejection if they do not participate. Opponents claim that religious freedom for all faiths is enhanced by keeping religious observances out of schools. The policy avoids what de Tocqueville called the "tyranny of the majority." That is, the Christian majority does not violate the rights of non-Christians or non-believers.

Proponents of prayer in the schools cite the other aspect of the First Amendment: that government shall not interfere with the right of people to worship as their conscience dictates. They see prayer in the school as a part of such freedom: children should be allowed to pray as a part of their freedom of worship, though those who do not wish to do so should have the right to abstain. Some proponents also point out that because the majority of the children are Christian, democracy is thwarted by a ban on prayer in the schools; that is, the desires of the minority prevail over those of the majority. They also refer to the increasing violence in and declining effectiveness of public schools since the Supreme Court ruled out prayer: they assert that prayer would counteract the slide into permissiveness and would strengthen discipline so that the schools could accomplish their educational mission more effectively.

The concerns we have discussed are merely examples of the kinds of issues that can arise from the diversity of religious groups in a nation where that very diversity is assured by the Constitution. The guarantees of the First Amendment are buttressed by the equal protection clause of the Fourteenth Amendment to provide legal underpinnings for religious freedom. But, as we have seen, legal interpretations as well as public perceptions may vary widely as to just what that means.

International Diversity

When we look at religious diversity on an international level, it becomes at once apparent that it is a powerful source of conflict. Religious and political interests become identified so that the resulting hostility is both a religious mission to protect or extend the faith and a struggle for dominance of the political apparatus that would make that possible. The struggle of Protestants and Catholics in Northern Ireland is a political and a religious struggle. On the Indian subcontinent, the clash of Moslem and Hindu represents both. The beleaguered Middle East illustrates this political and religious strife as Moslems, Jews, and Christians war with one another.

Even within countries where one religion is overwhelmingly dominant, factions develop. For example, various Islamic sects struggle with one another in Middle Eastern countries. Even in Latin American countries where the Catholic Church claims 80 to 90 percent of the population, internal factions have developed. The emergence of "liberation theology," although not confined to the Catholic Church, has produced dissident factions within that body.

The traditional Christian social doctrine of the church has focused on a vision of humanity that allows it to embrace all persons without assuming any particular political stance. Liberation theologists label this approach as naive and ineffective. They assert that the mission of the church should be to align itself with the poor and oppressed people of the world and to engage actively in their fight to liberate themselves from their oppressors. Such a stance requires political commitment and activism in pursuit of the goals of liberation. Some clerics have advocated violence and revolution as acceptable strategies to achieve these goals.

The economic well-being and human dignity of the people who live in poverty is the major goal of this liberation theology. Because class struggle is a major aspect of oppression, opting for the oppressed class as against the oppressing class is to face the issue in a confrontational manner. This has meant in many situations an alignment of the liberation church with socialist movements in Third World countries. This affiliation has been a major source of opposition from within the traditional church, because the atheism of socialist doctrines is antithetical to religious interests. Additional opposition comes from the doctrine that the church should serve people from all walks of life and not commit itself to one segment in conflict with another. Liberation theologists submit that neutrality is not possible in today's world.

The economic well-being and human dignity of those who live in poverty is the major goal of liberation theology.

Liberation theology has been particularly prominent in Latin America, where the opposition within the Catholic clergy has become acute. African societies have also been attracted to this religious innovation.

Trends in Religion

Secularism and Rationalism

The most obvious long-term trend relating to religion is the dual advancement of secularism and rationalism. Religious accounts of the origin of the physical world have yielded ground to scientific explanations of origins; and ideas of cause-and-effect relationships in the natural world have challenged the notions of moral determinism and a capriciously intervening God. Nevertheless, there is still much controversy over creationism and evolutionism.

Traditional religious legitimations for the social world are also being replaced by rational supports. Freud (1957) posed a question as to whether the restraints on conduct that are necessary for human beings to work together to meet their needs could be maintained without religious legitimations. Noting the extent to which secularism and rationalism have weakened religion, he asked what happens to the curbs, particularly upon our sexual and aggressive tendencies, when the religious legitimation is too weak to support them? Freud welcomed our liberation from unnecessary restraints but voiced alarm that we may be freed from our necessary restraints as well. The solution he proposed to avert social chaos is to teach people rational explanations. Reason would make us less resistant to the necessary restrictions and less likely to cast them aside if religion declines. And Freud thought that unnecessary restraints should be discarded. Perhaps in the greater permissiveness of our contemporary society we may see Freud's point reflected.

We have seen religion move from being the central focus of community life to occupying a compartmentalized role in the society. It no longer dominates our concepts of health, wealth, family, warfare, and governance. It occupies its assigned slot, as these other institutions occupy theirs.

For some people in the society the belief in God remains a relevant component of their system of ideas, but they do not affiliate themselves with a church. This, too, is an impact of secularism. The belief that religion is a personal matter that does not depend upon attending church or participating in group religious activities reflects the reduced role of the church in public life. Some express actual hostility to organized religion, although maintaining their private forms of worship. There has tended to be an increase in the numbers of such people in our society.

Secularism has been accompanied by a humanistic approach to social life. The emphasis on secular humanism is expressed in social action that enhances individual life and dignity. The focus is humanity, not God. The criteria for desirable action and social policy are the impact they have on individual well-being. There has been little effort to institutionalize secular humanism. However, as it is given voice in books, magazines and other media, and especially in social programs, it is clear that it is a strong motif in contemporary American culture.

Fundamentalist Christian groups have launched broadside attacks on this outlook. To label a particular political or social stance as representing a secular humanist approach is deemed by some to be a resounding denunciation.

Churches have not been passive in the face of secular trends in the society. One response has been the growth of ecumenical efforts aimed at reestablishing the unity of Christianity. Although little action has been taken in that direction, continuing discussion has resulted in declarations of linkages across denominational lines among some major denominations in the United States. This development may be seen as an effort to mobilize the strength of the church to counteract the effects of increasing secularization of culture.

The Electronic Ministry

From the early days of television, local stations have presented Sunday morning worship services. At first ongoing community worship services were passed along to home audiences. In the 1970s, however, the number of evangelists addressing a nationwide television constituency began to increase. In the time since then the leading evangelists have attracted a large audience. According to Gallup polls, 50 percent of Protestants surveyed in 1980 said they had watched in the past year. Estimates of the size of the national audience for the electronic church have ranged from 130 million per week to 7 to 10 million, peaking to 23 million occasionally (Heinz, 1983:138).

The fund-raising strategies of television evangelists have been spectacularly successful. It is estimated that one billion dollars in contributions are received annually by television evangelists (Heinz, 1983:138). They have used these funds for building schools, churches, hospitals, and colleges, and in some cases for promoting political agendas.

Television evangelists have been one of the important factors in the mobilization of the New Christian Right. Combining evangelical and political concerns, this movement has sought to influence government in its social policy. It has developed a program of social policies that expressed the conservative political agenda and has encouraged its adherents, many of them swayed through television evangelism, to defeat those candidates for office who do not support the approved program: anti-abortion, anti-homosexuality, anti–women's liberation, anti-pornography, and anti-permissiveness. The three most important organizations in the New Christian Right have been widely supported by television evangelists. The Christian Voice has received support and television access from Pat Robertson's "700 Club." The Moral Majority is guided by Jerry Falwell. The Roundtable, too, has received exposure from the electronic ministry. These three organizations constitute the core of the New Christian Right. The role of the television evangelist has been supportive and stimulating in the mobilization of this movement but has not been definitive. About half of the leading TV evangelists, such as Oral Roberts, Jimmy Swaggert, and Rex Humbard, have refused to introduce political issues into their ministries and have remained independent of the New Christian Right movement.

The television ministry will probably continue to attract a wide audience of viewers, whether or not the political emphasis is expressed. The impact of the electronic church upon community-based worship is a question that has not been adequately explored. Do people go to church and then watch James Robinson or Jim Bakker for additional worship; or do they watch such evangelists as a substitute for attending church? The answer could have profound impact for the role of the traditional church in the contemporary community.

Women in the Church

Although women have for many years been dutiful participants in religious organizations, they have occupied auxiliary positions, for the most part. Church power has rested in the hands of men, and nowhere more emphatically than in the pulpit itself. Recently, women have successfully challenged the ordination laws and customs in many of the larger denominations. Increasing numbers of women are entering seminaries; and church bodies are faced with the need to place them in church positions.

In spite of this so-called opening up of the ministry to women, the patterns that emerge reflect old norms and conventional attitudes. Many women members are assigned to small rural charges, where conservative resistance to female ministers is predictably strong and pay is low. Many others are assigned to be assistant ministers to senior pastors, performing for the most part a "fetch-and-file" role with vestments. Appointments to senior positions in large churches are rare.

Strong opposition to the ordination of women has come especially from two large denominations, the Southern Baptist church and the Catholic church. Internal conflict over the issue has fragmented both bodies, but power has remained in the hands of the resisters. Factional disputes over this issue create newspaper headlines whenever the Baptists meet in national conference. Disputes within the Catholic church usually take the form of individual challenges to the church hierarchy.

Women's issues have also become matters for debate and conflict in church organizations. Abortion is condemned by the Catholic church and by many Protestant organizations as well. Within church bodies many women are adopting a prochoice stance, which sets them in opposition to prevailing religious doctrine and decree. Social control strategies such as excommunication have been used by various church groups to attempt to discourage and punish unacceptable views on abortion.

Controversy over women's liberation has developed in some church bodies. Biblical injunctions to women to be subservient helpmates to their husbands are seriously regarded by many church groups. For example, some ministers will not perform marriage ceremonies without such instructions to the bride. Equity in husband-wife relations is regarded as a violation of such directives. This issue, too, has set many women at odds with the power structure of their church bodies.

Doctrinal changes that emphasize equality have generally been rejected. For example, the thrust of some women's rights advocates to project androgynous images of God—that is, images that combine masculine and feminine characteristics—are regarded as outrageous by many church bodies and their members. Combined images of God, the Mother, as well as God, the Father, are apparently too much for most church groups to encompass (Giele, 1978:339). In summary, although there has been some movement toward equity for women in church organization and policy, the traditional attitudes are very persistent, and power relationships are slow to change.

Summary

In this chapter we have identified the sacred as something that is set apart and regarded with awe and reverence by a group of people. Beliefs, practices, and collectivities relating to the sacred usually go through a process of institutionalization, that is, they become stable and predictable.

Sociologists differ in their interpretations of the relationship between religion and the rest of the society. Functionalists emphasize its contribution to the integration of society through shared values and the social control it exerts. It is also a major legitimizer of social reality. Conflict theorists, on the other hand, focus on its potential for divisiveness, on its ratification of injustices, and on its diversion of attention from the oppression of this life through its emphasis on the afterlife.

Religion has potential for both social stability and social change, as illustrated by the contrasting roles of priest and prophet. Weber's tracing of the role of the prophet suggests a dynamic potential in religion.

Religion has been one of the important dimensions of cultural diversity in the United States. Although religious tolerance has been a major theme, religion has often been the source of persecution and discrimination. Nevertheless, diverse ethnic and racial groups have found in their religion a focus of solidarity and support.

Protection of religious diversity is offered by the doctrine of separation of church and state embodied in the First Amendment. At the same time, the bitterness stirred by such issues as prayer in the schools, tax exemptions for churches, and participation of religious figures in politics indicates that the boundaries between church and state have not been firmly defined.

Increasing secularism has been a longtime trend in our society. Changing legitimations for social realities seem to be a consequence of this development. Other trends include an ecumenical impulse, an expanded role for women, and a growth in the electronic ministry.

Key Concepts

animism
anthropomorphism
civil religion
collective conscience
deism
ecumenical impulse
institutionalization

monotheism
moral determinism
polytheism
priest
prophet
sacred
theism

References

Bellah, Robert N. (1970) *Beyond Belief: Essays on Religion in a Post-Traditional World.* New York, N.Y.: Harper & Row, Publishers.

Berger, Peter. (1969) *The Sacred Canopy: Elements of a Sociological Theory of Religion.* Garden City, N.Y.: Anchor Books/Doubleday & Company, Inc.

Durkheim, Emile [1915]. (1961) *The Elementary Forms of the Religious Life.* New York, N.Y.: Collier Books.

Earle, John R., Dean Knudsen, and Donald W. Shriver, Jr. (1976) *Spindles and Spires.* Atlanta, Ga.: John Knox Press.

Fitzpatrick, Joseph P. (1983) "Hispanics in New York: An Archdiocesan Survey." *America,* (March 12):185–88.

Frazier, E. Franklin. (1963) *The Negro Church in America.* New York, N.Y. Shocken Books, Inc.

Freud, Sigmund. (1957) *The Future of an Illusion.* Garden City, N.Y.: Anchor Books/Doubleday & Company, Inc.

Giele, Janet. (1978) *Women and the Future.* New York, N.Y.: The Free Press.

Gordon, Milton. (1964) *Assimilation in American Life.* New York, N.Y.: Oxford University Press, Inc.

Grimal, Pierre. (1973) *Larousse World Mythology.* New York, N.Y.: The Hamlyn Publishing Group, Ltd.

Heinz, Donald. "The Struggle to Define America" in Liebman, Robert E., and Robert Wuthnow (1983.) New York, N.Y.: Aldine Publishing Co.

Herberg, Will. (1955) *Protestant, Catholic, Jew.* Garden City, N.Y.: Doubleday & Company, Inc.

Hoebel, E. Adamson. (1960) *The Cheyennes: Indians of the Great Plains.* New York: Henry Holt and Company.

Liebman, Robert C., and Robert Wuthman. *The New Christian Right,* 1983. New York, N.Y.: Aldine Publishing Co.

Marx, Gary. (1967) *Protest and Prejudice.* New York, N.Y.: Harper & Row, Publishers.

Marx, Karl. (1959) *Communism of the Paper Rheinischer Beobacter.* Reproduced in Feuer, Louis (ed.), *Basic Writings on Politics and Philosophy: Karl Marx and Friedrich Engels.* Garden City, N.Y.: Anchor Books/Doubleday & Company, Inc.

———. (1967) *Critique of Hegel's Philosophy of Right.* Reproduced in Easton and Guddat (eds.), *Writings of the Young Marx on Philosophy and Society.* Garden City, N.Y.: Anchor Books/Doubleday & Company, Inc.

Morgan, Edmund S. (1958) *The Puritan Dilemma: The Story of John Winthrop.* Boston, Mass.: Little, Brown and Company.

Pope, Liston. (1942) *Millhands and Preachers: A Study of Gastonia.* New Haven, Conn.: Yale University Press.

Vogt, Evon Z. (1970) *The Zinacantacos of Mexico: A Modern Way of Life.* New York, N.Y.: Holt, Rinehart and Winston.

Weber, Max [1922]. (1964) *The Sociology of Religion.* Boston, Mass.: Beacon Press.

15

Economy

OBJECTIVES

Following this discussion of the sociology of economic institutions the student should be able to:

1. Understand the social functions of economic institutions.

2. Compare and contrast theories of economic development.

3. Compare the main kinds of economic systems.

4. Analyze the role of multinational corporations in the international economy.

5. Understand the nature and meaning of work in our society.

INTRODUCTION

The production and distribution of goods and services within a society are essential to its existence. **Goods** are those products that are needed, such as food, clothing, and shelter, or that are desired, such as televisions, cars, watches, and washing machines. **Services** are those activities that are performed in order to benefit someone, such as government service, medical and health care, teaching, car maintenance, and entertainment.

If each of us could provide for ourselves all the goods and services we require, there would be no need for economic systems. However, we do not have that capacity. We meet our needs through a division of labor. This refers to the fact that the tasks of maintaining the requirements of the society are broken up in such a way that people are performing various aspects of the activities: some individuals grow food, some build shelters, some provide medical services for the sick, some offer spiritual guidance.

The division of labor is fundamental to a society's ability to survive. It is through this productive process that needs are met and the "extras" are provided. This is accomplished through the exchange relationships that are established as those who produce a product or provide a service exchange what

A division of labor involves us in relationships with others thereby creating a social network.

they have to offer with those who produce what they need. The performance of these tasks constitutes our work. That our work involves us in relationships with others creates a social network that helps to bind a society together.

In this chapter we consider production and exchange relationships. Such relationships are embedded in various kinds of economic systems, of which several are examined. Economic theories abound; we consider several that have particularly significant sociological relevance. We close with a look at worker relations and job satisfaction.

Types of Productive Systems

Every historic period is characterized by a specific method of producing the goods the society needs. For example, in early times production took the form of hunting game and gathering roots, berries, and nuts. Later, the discovery that people could grow their own food made horticulture and, later, agriculture the basic way of producing what the society required. Manufacturing then developed as the way in which most of our goods were produced. This continues into the present, although today the provision of services has assumed increasing importance.

Colin Clark (1940) developed a set of labels that we continue to use to identify these types of productive activity: the **primary sector,** the **secondary sector,** and the **tertiary sector.** Each type of productivity tends to create a characteristic set of social relationships.

The primary sector includes agriculture, herding, fishing, forestry and extractive activities such as mining. The emphasis in this type of productive system is on using what nature provides and adapting it to human use. In societies where such activities are most common, the division of labor is relatively simple. Most of the members are engaged in the same occupation, with only a minimal surplus produced to support specialists in nonessential activities. The human relationships in such societies are intimate and personal. They are enriched by the shared values and norms that characterize the way of life they follow.

The primary sector involves working with natural resources.

The secondary sector involves the production of finished goods from raw materials.

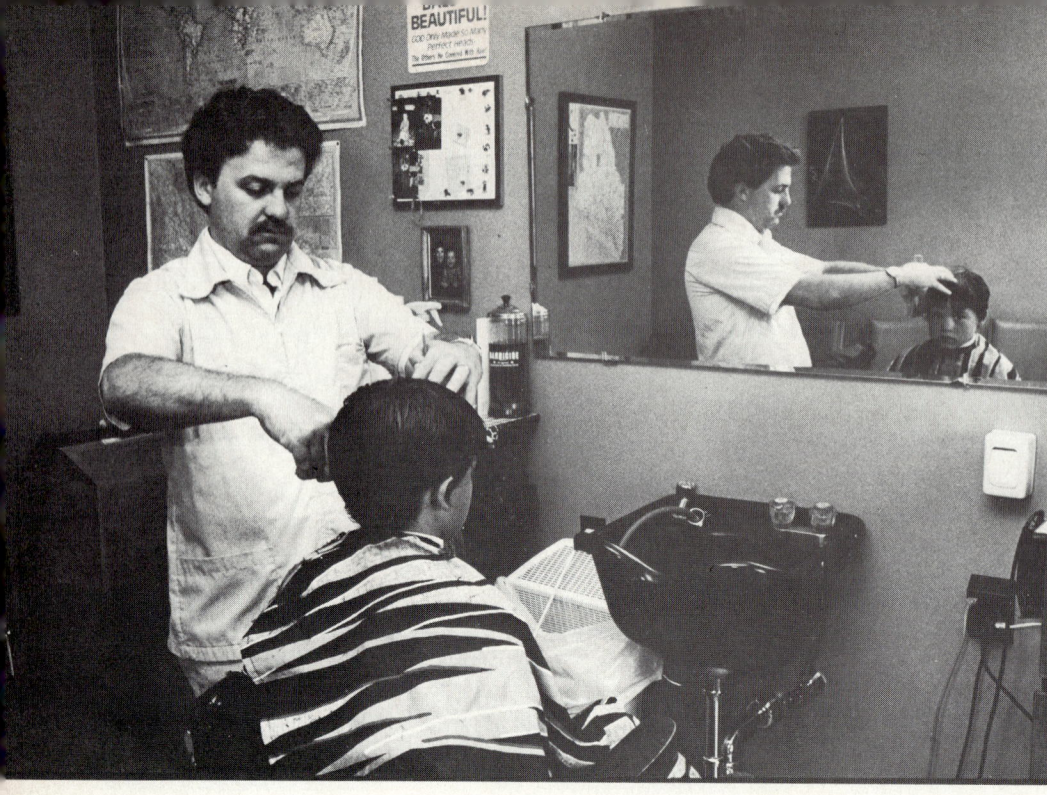

The tertiary sector involves the provision of services.

    The secondary sector is concerned with producing finished goods out of raw materials. Manufacturing involves the use of machines and an increasingly complex division of labor. The use of nonhuman, non-animal sources of power to run the machines, the improvement of transportation and communication facilities, the continuing rationalization of activity to improve the efficiency of production all contributed to the industrial revolution. The specialized division of labor of this mode of production fragmented the shared way of life that had characterized preindustrial society. Furthermore, workers now confronted machines rather than one another. Industrialism was for many an alienating system of production. This system, however, raised the standard of living for most members of industrial societies to unprecedented heights as a result of the tremendous increase in productive capacity the system permitted.

    The tertiary sector focuses on the provision of services. Daniel Bell (1973) has referred to the emergence of service provision as a major focus of productivity as creating the postindustrial society. Although we still depend upon the secondary sector, that is, on manufacturing, to produce the goods that we need, more and more our division of labor is being skewed toward the provision of services. The most obvious increase is in the area of government services at local, state, and national levels. The planning and delivery of services to the poor, the needy, the sick, the elderly, and dependent children as well as the various regulatory agencies increase the number of care providers. This is only one area where the provision of services has grown. When we look at the growth in health care, education, legal representation, entertainment and the like, it is obvious that the service area represents a major shift in our division of labor. An important implication of this shift is that it places people in relationship to other people again in contrast to the individual—machine relationship characterizing the secondary sector.

Exchange Systems

In the primary sector exchange relations were at first personal. Hunting and gathering societies depended upon a sharing ethic. Such societies were small and often were composed of kinship groups. Their relationships were such that what one could produce, all could share. The division of labor was minimal because most people were engaged in the same productive activities.

As more advanced productive capacities within the primary sector increased the division of labor, exchange relations became more complex. More people became specialists in various areas of producing goods and services. A system of **bartering** developed within and between societies. Bartering is a method of trade whereby one object or service is exchanged for another. However, bartering is awkward (Levy, 1967:15), because it depends on a "double coincidence of wants" (Lipsey et al., 1984:650). In effect this means that for bartering to work, you must have exactly what I want in the amount that I desire, and vice versa. Another problem inherent in bartering is that there is no way to assign a standard value to objects or services being traded.

These problems grew acute as exchange relationships became more impersonal. Traders sought some medium of exchange that could be standardized in value and could avoid the problem of mutual desires. **Money** evolved as a result of these problems. Money is any medium of exchange which buyers and sellers agree has some relatively fixed value.

When you think of money, you probably think of dollar bills and coins. These are fairly recent developments in the evolution of money. The earlier forms of money consisted of bags of grain. As early as 2000 B.C., barley was used in Egypt and Babylonia "to fix the prices of goods, rents, and wages" (Levy, 1967:16). Other popular forms of money have included animals such as cows or oxen, land, produce, and labor. Because these items were often perishable, the use of coins or various metals was more convenient and predictable. What makes cows or coins or any other medium of exchange useful as money, however, is not the intrinsic value of the medium, but the general confidence that people have in its value. It is this confidence that makes it valuable as money, though regulation by official agencies gives support to these understandings. In its simple forms or in the sophisticated concepts of banking and credit of today's financial world, money facilitates the distribution of goods and services in a society.

Another important development in the trend toward impersonality of exchange was the concept of the **marketplace.** When you think of a marketplace, you might recall one of the famous downtown markets with which you are familiar, such as the Lexington Market in Baltimore, the Fulton Fish Market in New York City, or the Farmer's Market in Philadelphia. Or you may think of malls, shopping centers, stock markets, and flea markets. What all these markets have in common is that they are places where a variety of individuals and businesses gather in order to buy, sell, or exchange their goods and services. They represent a departure from the ancient open-air markets where trading partners haggled over their exchanges, but they serve the same purpose.

The impersonality of today's market means that the exchanges occur in the context of secondary group relationships. The parties to the exchange are usually strangers with neutral attitudes toward one another. The provision of services, although facilitating person-to-person relations, involves relationships shaped by bureaucratic rules of exchange, as, for example, in government agencies. As we have seen, bureaucracies dominate our contemporary forms of social organization.

The complexity in the division of labor no doubt contributed to the trend toward impersonality in the marketplace. Specialization enables one to have an advantage in exchange relationships. Offering a product or service that is not readily available elsewhere increases one's chance of favorable trading. Although mutual interdependence of individuals in a society with a complex division of labor draws members of the society together in a cooperative network, individuals can gain competitive advantage from the specialized goods or services they offer for exchange.

Our exchange relationships have undergone a transition over time from personal transactions involving particularistic relations in the period when the primary sector prevailed. Today's impersonal, universalistic exchange in the open market, using a standardized, impersonal medium of exchange in the buying and selling of goods and services, represents a profound change in our exchange systems. When production and exchange become as complex and impersonal as in today's world, some official regulation of the process seems inevitable. Ideas about the role of political institutions in regulating economic activities have varied, sometimes violently. How best to manage the production and exchange of goods and services becomes the subject of intense disagreement. Such ideas are debated in theoretical conception and are manifested in various economic systems. Our discussion now turns to an examination of these concerns.

Theories of Economic Growth

There are generally two opposing theoretical camps of economic development. The conflicting ideas at the heart of each of these theoretical camps is a debate over whether economic growth should be above all efficient or whether economic growth should be shared equitably by all sectors of the economy. Although economic theorists come to be known by many names such as conservative, liberal, classical, or supply siders, the central debate among them is an argument over efficient economic development or equitable economic development. The debate is more than an academic exercise, because such a debate over efficiency or equality involves governmental policy. The efficiency argument that has come to be known as the classical school of economics was outlined by Adam Smith in his text the *Wealth of Nations*. This text was published in 1776, the year of the American Revolution. The equality argument, sometimes known as the liberal position on economic development, is closely identified with John Maynard Keynes and his text *The General Theory of Employment, Interest, and Money*. Keynes's text followed Smith's work by some 160 years; it was published in 1936, while America was still suffering from the Great Depression.

In addition to these two opposing theoretical ideas on the nature of economic development, there are two other theorists whose ideas on capitalism have had a profound effect on how we view economic behavior. These two theorists are political philosopher Karl Marx and sociologist Max Weber. Marx's works, the *Communist Manifesto* and *Das Kapital*, outlined the inevitable conflict between the workers and those who employed them. Weber's work entitled *The*

Protestant Ethic and the Spirit of Capitalism examined the influence of religious doctrine in supporting capitalist enterprises. Together the works of Smith, Keynes, Marx, and Weber have had profound influence on economic thought. A word of caution here is necessary. Remember as we review these theories that their authors lived at different times. In their times they were faced with different economic and social problems. Although it is interesting to view these authors as captains of their respective theoretical camps, careful reading of their works reveals two things: (1) in many instances the authors are addressing separate questions of economic—specifically, capitalist—activity; and (2) the theoretical differences among the authors are not always as clear as they are sometimes purported to be.

The Invisible Hand

When Adam Smith wrote the *Wealth of Nations*, England was a "nation of shopkeepers." That is to say that England's economy at the time of publication of the text consisted primarily of the goods and services of independent small businesses. There was little in the way of huge manufacturing concerns and each small business was regulated by the self-interests of the proprietor. In the *Wealth of Nations*, Smith wrestled with the question of how economic order is achieved. Given the unregulated self-interests of a shopkeeper economy, how is economic order, in terms of stable prices, sufficient quality, and fair wages, obtained?

In developing this question, Smith noted that businessmen were driven by their self-interest to make a profit. If businessmen were motivated only by profit, however, they would manufacture only items that would bring the most money, charge the highest prices, and pay the workers the barest of wages. Yet, Smith noted that a fairly wide variety of goods were being produced and that the prices being charged for those goods were reasonable and did not vary too greatly among similar products. In short, Smith pointed out that despite the unregulated activities of English businesses a certain economic order emerged that met the needs of the larger society, kept prices in line, and assured that workers were paid a fair salary.

Smith concluded that the answer to how economic order is obtained is "the **invisible hand**" of the free market. The invisible hand is the laws of a free market that not only regulate prices and assure appropriate incomes for workers but also insure that goods are produced in sufficient quantity to meet the needs of society. According to Smith, two important laws of the free market that produced economic order are the law of competition and the law of supply and demand. Smith noted that if a manufacturer in a line of business, for example a pin factory, charged too much for his pins and paid his workers inappropriate wages, a competitor pin manufacturer would step in, charge lower prices for pins to the consumer, and pay higher wages to his workers. In this fashion the pin manufacturer who charged too much and paid too little would be forced to alter his methods or to go out of business.

Likewise, if there are two products, for example pins and needles, and one product (pins) is in short supply whereas the other product (needles) is in abundant supply, manufacturers will charge higher prices for pins than they will needles. When others see the opportunity to make more money in pins than in needles, they will begin to manufacture more pins. The manufacturing of more pins, while producing less or the same amount of needles, will increase the supply of pins to meet the demands of the society and gradually reduce the overall price of the pins. Thus, a potentially very sticky situation of too few pins and too many needles is gradually brought into balance by the laws of competition and supply and demand. Smith argued that if government wanted to best help the economy it would leave it alone and permit the invisible hand to regulate the market. Proponents of Smith's theory were quick to adopt this sentiment into a doctrine that came to be known as **laissez faire.** Laissez faire means let it be. The doctrine of laissez faire became both the rationale and a slogan for anyone who was opposed to government intervention in the economy as well as government attempts to reform social ills and redistribute the wealth of the nation in a more equitable fashion.

In actuality, Smith was not as concerned about government intervention as he was concerned about **monopolies.** A monopoly is "a market structure in which the output of an industry is controlled by a single seller or a group of sellers making joint decisions" (Lipsey et al., 1984:976). Smith wrote: "People of the same trade seldom meet together, but the conversation ends in a conspiracy against the public, or in some diversion to raise prices" (Smith, 1965). It is the development of monopolies, multinational organizations, trade fairs, and mergers that changed the face of capitalism from a nation of shopkeepers to a world of **oligopolies.** Oligopolies occur when a small number of businesses dominate an entire industry. It was these and other developments such as the Great Depression that led John Maynard Keynes to develop an opposing view of the market.

The Helping Hand

When Keynes wrote *The General Theory of Employment, Interest and Money,* both England and America were facing severe economic crises. In America the Great Depression had brought economic activity to a virtual standstill. In England, preparations for World War II were under way, and the problem of financing the war stymied the English economy. The question for Keynes was how to stimulate a sluggish economy, when "the bottom had fallen out of private investment" (Heilbroner, 1972:267). Whereas Smith concerned himself with factors that maintain economic order, Keynes focused on factors necessary to revive an economy on the verge of collapse.

The key features of Keynes's theory are savings and investment. According to Keynes, investments are the key to economic prosperity. The source of all investment capital is savings. Individual consumers save money from their wages. When their savings are placed in a bank, the bank is then able to lend money to businesses for expansion. Likewise, businesses save money for their profits in order to finance expansion, exploration of new markets, and experimentation with new products. Therefore, investments bring about more jobs because there is more work. Workers save more and coincidentally are able to purchase more. The new ventures for businesses result in greater profits and in turn more savings for future investments.

Just as savings and investments are the keys to economic prosperity when the economy is strong, they are also twin nooses that could strangle a weak economy. In hard economic times, such as they were in America during the Great Depression and in England during the World War II era, there was little in the way of investments taking place because people were either living off their savings or they had lost their savings as the sectors of the economy in which those savings were invested collapsed. Thus, the failure of banks, stocks, and businesses meant several things for the economy. Failure above all meant a loss of savings both for consumers and corporations. Failure also meant a loss of jobs as well as a loss of profits. Smith noted that supply swells to meet demand. Keynes countered several decades later that there are few demands if there is no work. When the entire economy is on the verge of economic collapse, the invisible hand of the free market is not enough to revive economic activity. Rather than an invisible hand the economy needs a "helping hand" (Heilbroner, 1972:268).

The helping hand that could revive the economy was the government. Specifically, the government could put people to work and thereby create a demand for more goods and services. By reducing unemployment, the government could begin the flow of money again by creating income that in turn became savings, profits, and investments. This is precisely what President Roosevelt did with the public works projects of the New Deal era. Thus, the rationale for government spending was born during a time when capitalist economies teetered dangerously on the verge of collapse. That rationale was nurtured and encouraged in Keynes's theory. Keynes felt that government intervention—that is, government spending—should be used to stimulate an economy in which savings, investments, and business activity had fallen dangerously low. The government intervention would thereby serve as a helping hand for the resurgence of a strong economy.

Just as Smith's *Wealth of Nations* formed much of the intellectual justification for a doctrine of laissez faire, Keynes's *General Theory* formed much of the rationale for government spending and government intervention into the economy. Keynes's theory provided proponents of government intervention with intellectual ammunition in their war with their laissez faire opponents. Actually, Keynes felt that government intervention should be used only to the degree that was necessary to stimulate the economy. Smith's theory serves as the core argument in supply-side economics, or Reaganomics. The idea expressed by all those who cite Smith, although sometimes too emphatically, is that the economy will work more efficiently when the marketplace is unfettered by government intervention, including spending, price controls, and regulations, and the invisible hand of a free market is left to achieve economic order.

By contrast, Keynes is cited by those who wish government to intervene in the marketplace to encourage business investments or to redistribute incomes more equitably. As such, special-interest groups and professional lobbyists have endorsed the idea of the government as a helping hand to advance their specific causes. Today, special-interest groups and lobbyists include "not only the standard villains of the policy processing—big business, big labor, the farm lobby, and others of their ilk—but also the far more numerous factions, from environmentalists and anti-abortionists to Gray Panther grandmothers" (Navarro, 1984:39). Keynes's theory serves as the core argument in liberals' position, or those who argue for equity in the distribution of wealth. The idea expressed by those who cite Keynes, again sometimes too emphatically, is that the government has a role in regulating the economy and assuring that distribution of the wealth of the nation is equitable and beneficial to all members of the society.

Dialectical Materialism

Both Smith and Keynes were proponents of capitalism. Despite the problems of prices, quantity, income, and depressions, both Smith and Keynes felt that capitalism offered the best hope for the prosperity of all. In contrast to these two advocates of capitalism, Karl Marx felt that capitalism was only a stage in the progression of economic history. Marx is perhaps the most influential critic of the capitalist economy. Marx and his often neglected English collaborator, Friedrich Engels, based their perception of capitalism largely on observations of England's fledgling manufacturing industry during the early nineteenth century. The conditions of the workers at that time were severe. It was nothing for a workweek to be as long as eighty or more hours. And for the length of such a workweek, a laborer could expect subsistence wages—often not even enough to support a family. Children worked in the factories and were not protected by laws or moral outrage. Marx, who was German, was not interested in merely describing the social misery of the workers or simply attacking the capitalist economy. Marx sought to identify the pressures within capitalism that would lead ultimately and inevitably to its demise. In short, Marx was interested in the laws of change. He contended that capitalism, as formidable as it might appear, was only a link in the chain of history.

Marx's theory is called **dialectical materialism.** The theory is introduced in the *Communist Manifesto* published in 1848 and further developed in what Heilbroner (1972:156) calls the "Doomsday Book of Capitalism," *Das Kapital* (Capital). Dialectical materialism suggests that change occurs because of internal conflicts or contradictions in the way a society is organized. The change from one economic system to another is caused by the conflict between the forces of production and the relations of production. The forces of production are the technology and machinery that produce at a certain level of efficiency and productivity. The relations of production are the social relations between the class of owners and the class of workers in society. The capitalists, or bourgeosie, were the owners of factories and the means of production. The workers were the proletariat, who sold their labor in exchange for wages.

Marx believed that capitalism brought about increased production of material goods, because capitalist business owners were competing with each other to find more efficient and cheaper ways to exploit workers' labor. Although the workers' collective labor produced everything, the capitalist owners reaped the profits. The capitalist system was thus based on the exploitation of workers by the capitalist owners.

Struggle between these two classes was the main social conflict in modern capitalist society, according to Marx. He believed that this class struggle would intensify for several reasons. First, the rate of capitalist profits would tend to fall, causing the capitalists to exploit the workers even more ruthlessly. Second, the workers would become increasingly more conscious of their oppression and increasingly organized to fight against their capitalist rulers. Eventually, workers would overthrow the capitalist economic system and the capitalists' government in a violent revolution and create a classless communist social order.

Marx's theory of dialectical materialism and of the role that a capitalist economy plays in that theory is very complex. *Das Kapital* alone includes four volumes that took forty-three years of editing and publishing largely by Engels and over twenty-four hundred pages before it was completed. The theory is developed in other writings of Marx including the *Communist Manifesto*. The value of Marx's works lies in his ability to identify the internal and inherent conflicts within a capitalist economy. The greatest threat to the capitalist way of life is not so much the external and competing ideologies of communism or socialism. The greatest forces leading to the collapse of capitalism lie with capitalism itself. Heilbroner (1972:159) noted that the prediction of the demise of capitalism cannot be taken lightly.

> In Russia and Eastern Europe capitalism has disappeared; in Scandinavia and Britain it has been partially abandoned; in Germany and Italy it drifted into fascism and emerged from its bath of fire in less than perfect health. And while wars, brute political power, exigencies of fate, and the determined efforts of revolutionaries have all contributed their share the grim truth is that these changes occurred largely for the very reason Marx foresaw: capitalism broke down. (Heilbroner, 1972:159–60)

The Spirit of Capitalism

Another of the contributions of Marx was his examination of the relationship of ideas and ideology to the economic order. Specifically, Marx noted that religion was one of the ideas that supported capitalism and thereby supported the bourgeoisie in their conflict with the proletariat. German sociologist Max Weber thoroughly researched the relationship between religion and capitalism in a series of three articles published from 1904 to 1906, which have been collected and published as *The Protestant Ethic and the Spirit of Capitalism.*

The spirit of capitalism, as Weber saw it largely through the writings of Benjamin Franklin, is characterized by the quest of making money purely for the sake of making money. According to Weber (1958:53), the *summum bonum* of the spirit of capitalism is the earning of more and more money, combined with the strict avoidance of all spontaneous enjoyment of life. This ethic of capitalism is foreign to all peoples not under capitalistic influence.

The question that Weber asked was, How did the capitalist spirit, specifically the unabashed pursuit of profits by the bourgeoisie and the dedication with which the workers applied themselves to their tasks, emerge? This was an important question because the most influential religion of that time, Catholicism, held that making money was at best a necessary evil. Weber (1958:75) noted that even in fourteenth- and fifteenth-century Florence, Italy, the money and capital market of all the great political powers, the capitalistic attitude towards money was considered ethically unjustifiable, or at best to be tolerated. Ideally, excess profits should be given either to the church or distributed to the poor. The Catholic church particularly frowned upon the practice of usury, or moneylending to make a profit. And, as we have seen, lending money in order to make money is now one of the most important functions of money. According to Parsons (1958:le), the question for Weber was, Why did a rational capitalist spirit triumph "over the conventional attitude which had regarded the appetitus divitiarum infintus—the unlimited lust for gain—as anti-social and immoral"?

Weber found the answer to why the spirit of capitalism emerged in religion. The spirit of capitalism, however, was not consistent with just any religion. As we have seen, the Catholic church frowned upon many of the common capitalist practices. Rather, the spirit of capitalism is a product of the Protestant Reformation. The Protestant Reformation changed the idea that the way to God and to salvation was through monastic isolation. According to Weber (1958:80), the new idea offered by the Reformation was that "the fulfillment of duty in worldly affairs is the highest form which the moral activity of the individual could assume." It was this idea that gave everyday worldly activity a religious significance. Weber went on to refer to the spirit of capitalism, particularly as it developed in America, as a "calling." A calling is a moral duty to behave in a certain way. Although it was the commercial center of the world, fourteenth- and fifteenth-century Florence, Italy could only ethically tolerate the pursuit of profits.

> But in the backwoods small bourgeois circumstances of Pennsylvania in the eighteenth century, where business threatened for the simple lack of money to fall back into barter, where there was hardly a sign of large enterprise, where only the earliest beginnings of banking were to be found, the same thing was considered the essence of moral conduct, even commanded in the name of duty. (Weber, 1958:75)

Thus, Weber felt that the American economy as reflected in the spirit of capitalism was given the blessings of the Protestant ethic. Capitalism thrives in America in part because religious doctrines support it. It is no longer necessary to be poor in order to be blessed. In fact, an important idea in America is that being blessed is the result of hard work. And blessings along with the grace of God may also include dollars and cents. Television evangelists often preach this ethic in their Sunday sermons.

Economic Systems in the World Today

Capitalism and communism are often considered to be the two main kinds of economic systems in the world today, but most economists and sociologists believe that there are no truly capitalist or communist systems actually in existence. If capitalism is defined as a economic system in which the "means of production" are privately owned and the public or governmental role is at a minimum, then contemporary capitalist societies do not fit this definition. There is substantial governmental involvement in the economies of all capitalist societies. If communism is defined as an economic system centrally controlled and run by the government, then no communist countries fit this definition. All communist countries have preserved or reintroduced certain amounts of private enterprise.

Other economists and sociologists define capitalism and communism not primarily in terms of the role of the government but in terms of which social class controls the economy and government in a society. From this perspective capitalism is a system run by a relatively small class of owners who make profits from economic activity, whereas communism is a system in which both the economy and the government are run by workers, and private profits do not exist. With these definitions, all governments in the world are more capitalistic, regardless of what they call themselves, because workers as a class do not really hold power in any society today.

Other terms, such as socialist or "mixed" economies, are also used by some economists and sociologists. Socialism is usually defined as an economic system in which the main economic activities are owned and run by the government. "Mixed" economies are defined as those that are part capitalist and part socialist or communist, in the sense that there is a "mix" of government and private ownership.

It is difficult to separate sociological analysis of different economic systems from the intense ideological debates and arguments that frequently take place. It is perhaps easier to summarize the objections or criticisms that capitalists express against socialism or communism, and the objections that socialists and communists express against capitalism. The focus here is on social rather than strictly economic criticisms.

Capitalists believe that private enterprise is best suited to people's individual competitive nature. They feel that socialism or communism denies individuals the freedom to compete and get ahead and the motivation and incentive to try to accumulate wealth. Capitalists generally contend that communism concentrates power and decisionmaking in the hands of a small elite; thus making society undemocratic because the great majority of citizens must be workers who take orders from those who run the government. Finally, capitalists argue that allowing everyone to pursue his or her own self-interest is the best, if not the only way, to have a productive and free society.

Socialists and communists believe generally that capitalism is an undemocratic system in which workers must take orders from a small group of capitalist elite. The right of the capitalists to own property and accumulate wealth means that the majority of the population who are workers are, in reality, unable themselves to own property and accumulate wealth. Because the capitalists are primarily concerned with maximizing their profits and preserving their system of private ownership, they care less about the welfare of the workers or the welfare of the society as a whole. Unrestrained competition and selfishness can produce sharp conflicts and inequalities in capitalist societies.

The U.S. Economy and the World Economy

Karl Marx predicted that the system of competitive capitalism that existed in his day would soon evolve into a system in which there was much less competition and much more **monopoly** and **oligopoly.** Monopoly exists when one company controls a certain part of the economy, and oligopoly exists when a few companies control a certain part of the economy. Marx believed that intense competition between capitalists would destroy the weaker competitors. Periodic depressions would also eliminate many competitors, and the largest and strongest capitalists would take over or buy up many smaller businesses.

This process has pretty much taken place in all capitalist economies. In fact, the United States and other capitalist economies have been dominated by large corporations since the end of the nineteenth century. As a result, capitalism today is sometimes called corporate capitalism or even monopoly capitalism. The ascendancy of giant corporations is part of what Max Weber analyzed as the "bureaucratization" of modern societies. It has clearly transformed modern social life in many decisive ways.

About three-fourths of all working people in the United States are employed by the five hundred largest corporations, and a similar pattern prevails in other advanced capitalist societies. Most economic activity is controlled and directed by large corporations. Corporations are rarely controlled by one person or one family today. Corporate management is the collective responsibility of a group of people. Those at the top who run the corporations are the biggest owners of corporate stock and other economic assets. They possess a great deal of economic power and often can exert great influence over governmental politics as well.

National economies such as that of the United States are no longer sharply separated from each other. Today there is so much international economic ac-

Multinational corporations conduct business in many different countries.

tivity that many sociologists analyze economic institutions from the standpoint of a "world system." Most of the largest corporations have become **multinational corporations,** meaning that their activities are extensive in many different countries. The largest U.S.-based multinationals are oil giants such as Exxon and Texaco.

Multinational corporations are sometimes viewed favorably as progressive organizations that meet the economic needs of peoples throughout the world. They encourage interdependence among peoples, develop the economies of Third World countries, and provide millions of jobs throughout the world. On the other hand, the role of multinational corporations is criticized in many sociological theories.

The theory of **imperialism** is based upon an analysis of capitalist multinational corporations. This theory argues that when competitive capitalism gives way to monopoly and oligopoly, then large capitalist corporations expand beyond the borders of their own society looking for highly profitable economic opportunities. They often find the most profitable opportunities in Third World countries, because these countries contain valuable raw materials, because there are large populations of poor people who can be employed at very low wages, and because the often weak governments of these countries can be subdued and influenced by the large corporations and the governments of the multinationals' home countries.

Consequently, large corporations expand their investments in poor countries and extract great profits from them. Corporations from different countries compete with each other over these opportunities, each seeking to establish areas of economic and political domination. The great stakes involved eventually may lead to conflicts and wars between rival imperialist countries.

The Russian revolutionary leader Lenin set forth the classic Marxist view of imperialism in a short book written in 1916 during World War I. Lenin argued that imperialism is the highest, that is, the last, stage of capitalism, in which the leading capitalist countries have divided up the entire world economically and politically. After that point there would be world wars, in which capitalist countries would fight for redivision of the world among themselves. Meanwhile, both the people of the colonized Third World countries as well as the workers of the imperialist countries would become increasingly hostile to capitalism because of the suffering caused by these international conflicts. This would lead to communist revolutions in both imperialist and Third World countries and to the destruction of world capitalism.

Many Third World people believe that their countries have been oppressed by imperialism. Other people in the advanced capitalist countries believe that the theory of imperialism explains the immense inequalities between rich and poor countries and the many wars that have taken place throughout the twentieth century. Critics of U.S. foreign policy, such as some opponents of the Vietnam War and opponents of U.S. policies in Latin America or the Middle East, sometimes use the theory of imperialism to argue that the United States is pursuing harmful foreign policies that only serve the interests of U.S. multinational corporations.

The Nature of Work

To work is to occupy a role in the division of labor. Working is the source of most people's income. Relatively few people are able to live on inheritance or investments alone. Most of us will work, probably for someone else, for the money necessary to meet our needs and satisfy our desires. Likewise, being unemployed not only has severe economic consequences but also has consequences for emotional stability. In the following sections we explore employment, future work trends, unemployment, and the meaning of work.

Employment

The Bureau of Labor Statistics keeps a record of employment in eleven occupational categories: professionals, managers, sales workers, craft workers, opera-

Being unemployed not only has severe economic consequences but also has consequences for emotional stability.

tives, transport operatives, nonfarm laborers, private household workers, service workers, and farm workers. Of course, within each occupational category are many different types of jobs. For example, professionals include: accountants, clergy, engineers, foresters, lawyers, physicians, nurses, social workers, teachers, counselors, writers, and many other jobs. As you might imagine from the preceding list of jobs, there are wide differences in terms of who holds what jobs and the salaries that are earned.

Data are presented in Table 15.1 regarding the distribution of workers over nine occupational categories by race and sex. As illustrated in this table, males are about three times more likely to be managers than females. Conversely, females are about six times more likely to be clerical workers than males. In fact, females regardless of their race are most likely to be employed in some clerical capacity, as an operative, or as a service worker. White males are most likely to be employed as operatives, craftsmen, or managers. The distribution of work is more varied among minority males. Whereas black males are likely to be employed as operatives, laborers, and service workers, Hispanic males are likely to be employed as operatives, laborers, and craftsmen. Asian males are more likely to be employed as professionals than any other occupational category. The next most common occupations of Asian men are operatives, managers, or service workers. American Indian males are likely to be employed as operatives, craftsmen, and laborers.

Table 15.1 *Occupational Distribution in Private Industry by Race and Sex, 1981 (Percentages)*

Race/Ethnic Group/Sex	Total Employment	Officials and Managers	Professionals	Sales Workers	Office & Clerical Workers	Craft Workers	Operatives	Laborers	Service Workers
All Employees	100.0	11.7	9.7	9.0	16.3	12.1	19.1	7.5	9.1
Male	100.0	16.0	10.3	7.2	4.7	18.8	21.8	8.4	7.0
Female	100.0	5.8	8.9	11.6	32.5	2.7	15.2	6.1	11.9
White	100.0	13.3	10.7	9.7	16.4	12.7	17.6	6.2	7.5
Male	100.0	18.1	11.4	7.7	4.4	19.6	20.3	6.8	5.5
Female	100.0	6.4	9.8	12.6	33.7	2.6	13.8	5.2	10.4
Minority	100.0	4.9	5.2	6.1	15.9	9.6	25.3	12.9	15.6
Male	100.0	6.2	5.2	4.8	5.7	15.1	29.1	15.7	13.9
Female	100.0	3.3	5.3	7.7	28.1	2.9	20.8	9.5	17.6
Black	100.0	4.3	3.6	5.8	16.5	8.9	26.9	12.3	17.4
Male	100.0	5.4	3.2	4.4	5.7	14.6	32.5	15.6	15.0
Female	100.0	3.2	4.2	7.3	28.2	2.7	20.8	8.7	20.0
Hispanic	100.0	4.9	3.4	6.8	14.1	11.6	25.4	16.4	13.7
Male	100.0	6.1	3.6	5.2	5.0	16.9	27.3	18.6	13.4
Female	100.0	3.1	3.2	9.2	27.9	3.5	22.5	12.9	14.2
Asian/Pacific Islander	100.0	7.4	22.4	6.0	17.9	6.3	14.6	5.9	10.5
Male	100.0	10.6	25.9	5.7	8.3	9.4	13.4	6.0	10.2
Female	100.0	4.0	18.5	6.4	28.1	3.0	15.8	5.7	10.9
Amind/Alaskan Native	100.0	10.1	5.9	6.2	15.3	14.9	23.0	10.3	9.3
Male	100.0	12.6	6.2	5.0	7.2	21.8	24.9	11.1	6.3
Female	100.0	6.0	5.5	8.3	28.6	3.5	19.9	8.9	14.3

Source: Equal Employment Opportunity Report. (1981) *Job Patterns for Minorities and Women in Private Industry.* Washington, D.C.: U.S. Government Printing Office, 1.

If there is a common experience among working people in America, regardless of race and sex, it is within the occupational category of operative. Operatives share the experience of being employed in a factory or other manufacturing concern. Their work entails the operation of a machine in order to perform a routine task such as cutting, drilling, painting, or sewing. Perhaps the job that comes most readily to your mind is an automobile assembly line. There are, however, other jobs where workers operate machines in the performance of their work. These jobs include meat cutters, bottlers, canners, and pressers for dry cleaners. One of the authors of this text operated a hydraulic press for a steel fabrication plant before pursuing further education.

Despite these occupational commonalities, a closer examination of the detailed jobs within the category of operatives again reveals racial and sexual diversity. As indicated in Table 15.2, women are employed primarily in those jobs related to the textile and clothing industry. For example, 94.7 percent of the dressmakers and 96 percent of sewers and stitchers are women. Blacks and other minorities also operate machines to make or care for clothing. Almost 40 percent of clothing ironers and 28.4 percent of laundry and dry-cleaning operatives are either black or another minority. By contrast males and in particular white males are earth drillers, dry-wall installers, or miners. Roughly 95 percent of these operative jobs are held by white males. One of the major differences between the jobs that women and minorities perform and the jobs performed by white males is wages. The wage differential for occupational categories is shown in Table 15.3. As shown in tables 15.1, 15.2, and 15.3 women, blacks, Hispanics, and other minorities compete among themselves for the least prestigious, lowest-paying jobs. This pattern of women and minorities being concentrated in the least prestigious, lowest-paying jobs holds true in each of the occupational categories.

Blacks, Hispanics and other minorities hold the least prestigious lowest-paying jobs.

Table 15.2 *Employed Persons by Detailed Occupation, Sex, and Race, 1972–81*

	Percent of total	
Occupation	Females	Blacks and others
Operatives, except transport	39.8	16.2
Assemblers	52.4	17.1
Bottling and canning operatives	42.6	20.4
Checkers, examiners, and inspectors; manufacturing	53.8	13.8
Clothing ironers and pressers	80.5	39.8
Cutting operatives, n.e.c.	31.5	15.9
Dressmakers, except factory	97.4	15.4
Drillers, earth	—	3.3
Dry wall installers and lathers	—	4.9
Filers, polishers, sanders, and buffers	31.9	16.4
Furnace tenders, smelters, and pourers; metal	3.2	16.1
Garage workers and gas station attendants	5.7	10.9
Laundry and dry-cleaning operatives, n.e.c.	66.5	28.4
Meat cutters and butchers, except manufacturing	8.4	10.7
Meat cutters and butchers, manufacturing	29.6	18.4
Mine operatives, n.e.c	2.2	5.2
Mixing operatives	3.8	16.7
Packers and wrappers, excluding meat and produce	63.2	21.1
Painters, manufactured articles	16.9	13.9
Photographic process workers	50.6	9.2
Precision machine operatives	12.8	9.9
Drill press operatives	26.3	15.8
Grinding machine operatives	10.4	10.4
Lathe and milling-machine operatives	5.9	8.8
Punch and stamping-press operatives	31.8	10.3
Sawyers	9.7	16.1
Sewers and stitchers	96.0	21.6
Shoemaking-machine operatives	71.6	8.8
Furnace tenders and stokers, except metal	1.3	10.1
Textile operatives	61.0	28.7
Spinners, twisters, and winders	66.7	29.4
Welders and flame cutters	4.7	13.2
Winding operatives, n.e.c.	46.4	12.5
All other operatives, except transport	32.2	16.1

Source: Labor Force Statistics derived from the *Current Population Survey: A Databook, Vol. 1.* U.S. Government Printing Office (1981). Washington, D.C., 666.

Work Trends

The nature of work in America is changing. Although the operation of machines has traditionally provided the largest source of income for most workers in the twentieth century, opportunities to earn an income in this fashion are declining. The work force of tomorrow will be more technically skilled. Indeed, the greatest decline in job opportunities will be in those areas where only a modicum of training and formal education is necessary. According to the Bureau of Labor Statistics, the worst opportunities for employment in the future will include such jobs as farm laborer, private household worker, postal clerk, telephone operator, and stenographer. Ironically, the bureau includes on its endangered-species list the authors of introductory textbooks—college and university professors. Jobs of the future will require a greater degree of training. Although not all jobs will

Table 15.3
*Unemployment and Hourly Rate by Occupational Category**

Occupation	Unemployment Rate	Hourly Rate
White Collar	4.0	—
Professional	2.8	5.71
Managers	2.7	4.66
Sales	4.6	2.93
Clerical	5.7	3.72
Blue Collar	10.3	—
Craftsmen	7.5	6.40
Operatives	12.2	4.47
Transport	8.7	5.28
Laborers	14.7	4.07
Household	4.9	2.07
Service	9.2	2.93
Farm	10.6	2.91

*Note: Unemployment rates are derived from 1981 figures, whereas hourly rates are derived from 1978 figures.

Source: Labor Force Statistics derived from *Current Population Survey: A Databook, Vol. 1.* Bureau of Labor Statistics, Washington, D.C.: U.S. Government Printing Office, (1981). 546–50, 736.

require a college education in order to do them, most will require a college education to apply for them. Jobs in the field of computers, telecommunications, and energy management require a more educated work force.

Other significant trends in work projected for the future include an increase in the total number of employed persons, although the rate of growth of the labor force is expected to slow down towards the end of the decade. The largest share of jobs is expected to be in private industry. Growth of federal, state, and local government jobs is expected to be less rapid than the growth of jobs in private industry. Finally, the average number of hours that people work is expected to decline as work weeks become shorter. The sector of the population that is expected to benefit most from future employment trends is women.

Unemployment and the Meaning of Work

Just as the division of labor varies by race and sex, so too do rates of unemployment vary by race and sex. Unemployment rates also vary by occupation. Some occupations typically experience higher rates of unemployment than others. Blue-collar occupations that require more physical labor or involve unskilled factory labor experience higher rates of unemployment than white-collar occupations. Not only are the rates of unemployment higher for blue-collar occupations, but once unemployed blue-collar workers also tend to remain unemployed for longer periods of time. One reason for this is the shift in the productive emphasis from heavy industry to the provision of services. This shift displaces many workers. Because blacks, Hispanics, and women tend to be concentrated in blue-collar occupations, their rates of unemployment are often more than twice the rates among their white male counterparts. As shown in Table 15.3 the rate of unemployment for white-collar workers in 1981 was 4.0, whereas the unemployment rate for blue-collar workers during the same time period was more than twice as high as the rate for white-collar workers.

Recall from Table 15.1 that women are concentrated in clerical white-collar

The Nature of Work

jobs. The unemployment rate for clerical workers is the highest among white-collar positions. Women and minorities are also concentrated in the blue-collar occupational categories of operatives, laborers, and service workers. Notice that these occupational categories have the highest rates of unemployment among blue-collar positions.

Unemployment is only one of several problems that are associated with work. Underemployment, skidding (i.e., downward mobility), part-time employment, and job dissatisfaction are other work-related problems. The problems associated with working are significant because they often become the basis for other emotional and social problems. For example, Breed (1963:188) has written that "because in American society the work role is central for the man, work failure is not inadequacy in just one among many, but spreads through other roles and the self-image to threaten a general collapse of the life organization." In this same vein, some research has linked work-related problems to rates of suicide (Powell, 1958; Breed, 1963; Taylor, 1982). Breed (1963) found that more than half of the suicides in his study occurred among skidders—men experiencing downward mobility. Other research by Maris (1969) suggests that blue-collar workers have higher rates of suicide than white-collar workers, although suicide rates vary among the specific jobs within those statuses. Using official data from the city of Detroit, Taylor (1982) found that regardless of race or sex, suicide rates were higher among blue-collar workers than among white-collar workers.

Suicide is linked not only to work-related problems; it is also linked to occupation. According to Blauner (1974:236), "Work satisfaction varies greatly by occupation. The highest percentages of satisfied workers are usually found among professionals and businessmen." Blauner found that more than half of the professionals, salespersons, and managers in his sample would if given a

Computers have done to many white-collar office workers what robots have done to automobile workers.

choice continue in the same line of work. Less than half of the manual, service, and operative workers in his sample would continue in the same line of work. Again, although the actual amount of job satisfaction varies among the jobs within each occupational category, research has shown that job dissatisfaction tends to be high in those jobs that are easily automated (Kahn, 1973). Studies frequently point to the automobile assembly line as such an example. Job satisfaction increases as one can exercise initiative and creativity in affecting the work process.

More recently, a new form of automation has created job dissatisfaction among some white-collar workers. Computers have replaced many of the routine functions of secretaries and clerical workers. Computers have done to many white-collar office workers what robots have done to automobile workers. According to Zuboff (1980), computer-mediated work has created some job dissatisfaction because computers make work abstract, affect patterns of social interaction, and create new possibilities for supervision and control.

Despite the problems associated with working, including unemployment, skidding, suicide, and job dissatisfaction, some research has found that most workers express satisfaction with their work (Blauner, 1974). Working is a means by which people not only acquire money to purchase goods and services, it is also a means by which people express themselves. Working becomes a way of making a contribution to the society by contributing to the **Gross National Product** (GNP). The Gross National Product is the total value of goods and services produced in a country in one year. Finally, working becomes the way that most people acquire fame, social status, and social acceptance. Indeed, the research on suicide and work suggests that many people would not be caught dead without a job.

Workers were the focus of a great deal of ruthless business practices through much of our national history. Circumstances demanded some type of regulation that would provide protection for the worker. Government, mostly during the administration of Franklin Roosevelt, responded to this need by passing wage and hour laws establishing minimum wages, by facilitating union activities, by passing laws requiring protection of the work place from dangerous conditions, and by supporting retirement, disability, and unemployment benefits for workers. Such measures increase job security, reduce financial risks, and decrease occupational hazards for our work force.

Summary

In this chapter we examined the idea of the economy. The major function of the economy is the production and exchange of goods and services. We traced these processes through several historic periods and highlighted the shift from personal exchange to the open market.

Several theories explain the operation of a capitalist economy. Adam Smith's theory presented in the *Wealth of Nations* suggests that the economy operates best under the guiding influence of an invisible hand. Keynes's theory recommends government intervention in those instances where savings and investments have fallen off and the economy has become stagnated. Marx feels that the capitalist economy is only a stage in the evolution of society, and ultimately capitalism must be replaced by communism. Weber noted that the capitalist economy was most evident in societies where the Protestant Reformation had created a more tolerant ethic of business practices.

Capitalism and communism are the two main kinds of economic systems in the world today. Large multinational corporations dominate both the United States and the international economies. The theory of imperialism asserts that multinational corporations exploit Third World countries and cause many international conflicts.

The major source of income for most people is wages paid for their work. The distribution of work varies according to race and sex. Although the most common experience of working for all people is operating a machine to perform a routine task, a greater proportion of white and Asian males are located in professional and white-collar jobs than are blacks, Hispanics, and women. Higher salaries, less unemployment, and higher job satisfaction are also associated with white-collar positions. Despite the several problems associated with working, most people are satisfied with their work according to recent studies.

Key Concepts

bartering	**money**
economy	**monopoly**
Gross National Product	**multinational corporations**
imperialism	**oligopoly**
invisible hand	**primary sector**
laissez faire	**secondary sector**
marketplace	**tertiary sector**

References

Blauner, Robert. (1974) "Work Satisfaction and Industrial Trends in Modern Society." In Lionel S. Lewis and Joseph Lopreato (eds.), *Social Stratification.*

Bowden, V. Elbert. (1983) *Principles of Economics.* 4th ed. Cincinnati, Ohio: South-Western Publishing Co.

Breed, Warren. (1963) "Occupational Mobility and Suicide Among White Males." *American Sociological Review,* 28(April):179–88.

Heilbroner, L. Robert. (1972) *The Worldly Philosophers.* New York, N.Y.: Simon & Schuster, Inc.

Kahn, Robert L. (1973) "The Work Module: A Tonic for Lunch Pail Lassitude." *Psychology Today,* 9(February):35–39.

Lenin, Vladimir I. (1916) *Imperialism, The Highest Stage of Capitalism.* New York, N.Y.: International Publishers.

Levy, P. J. (1967) *The Economic Life of the Ancient World.* Chicago, Ill.: The University of Chicago Press.

Lipsey, G. Richard, Peter O. Steiner, and Douglas D. Purvis. (1984) *Economics.* 7th ed. New York, N.Y.: Harper & Row, Publishers.
Maris, Ronald. (1969) *Social Forces in Urban Suicide.* Homewood, Ill.: Dorsey Press.
Navarro, Peter. (1984) *The Policy Game: How Special Interests and Ideologies Are Stealing America.* New York, N.Y.: John Wiley & Sons, Inc.
Parsons, Talcott. (1958) in the Preface to Max Weber *The Protestant Ethic and the Spirit of Capitalism.* New York, N.Y.: Charles Scribner's Sons.
Powell, Edwin. (1958) "Occupations, Status and Suicide: Toward a Redefinition of Anomie." *American Sociological Review, 23*(April):131–39.
Smith, Adam. [1776] (1965) *An Inquiry into the Nature and Causes of the Wealth of Nations.* Reprint. New York: Modern Library.
Taylor, Maurice C. (1982) "Black Male-Female Suicide: A Case Study of Occupation and Rates of Suicide by Race and Sex." *The Western Journal of Black Studies, 3*(Fall):124–29.
Weber, Max. [1920, tr. 1930] (1958) *The Protestant Ethic and the Spirit of Capitalism.* translated by Talcott Parsons. New York, N.Y.: Charles Scribner's Sons.
Zuboff, Shoshana. (1980) New Worlds of Computer-mediated Work. In William Feigelman (ed.). *Sociology Full Circle.* New York, N.Y. Holt, Rinehart and Winston

16

Political Institutions

OBJECTIVES

By the end of this chapter the student should be able to:

1. Define power and assess its consequences for decision making in the political realm.

2. Identify three important types of polity.

3. Understand the importance of legitimacy of authority and identify the bases upon which it rests.

4. Characterize and contrast the elitist and pluralist models of the structure of power in the United States.

5. Identify factors that influence participation and partisanship in voting in the United States.

6. Identify some important trends in political behavior in the United States.

INTRODUCTION

Political institutions develop when the complexity of the society reaches the point at which kinship organization can no longer serve as an adequate mechanism for carrying out the political functions of the society. The following may be identified as political functions: (1) to protect the society from external threats, (2) to insure order in the society, (3) to resolve conflicts within the society, and (4) to allocate resources of the society.

In simple, homogeneous societies there seems to be widespread agreement on the values that underlie solutions to these social requirements. But complexity implies a measure of diversity of interests and values. Consensus cannot be taken for granted, for solutions that benefit one set of interests may have detrimental effects on another. Questions arise to challenge the assumption that there is a common interest and that universally satisfying solutions to problems can be devised: Whose interests need protection from external threats? Whose norms provide the basis for order? Whose interests are served in conflict resolution? Who gets what in resource allocation? Order at what price?

Because people at different positions in the social order tend to offer different answers to such questions, choices among alternatives are necessary.

It is obvious, then, that control of the apparatus through which these decisions are made and implemented is of crucial import. The essence of political process is the struggle between individuals and groups with different interests to gain the decision-making power. Power refers to the ability of an individual or group to have its will carried out even in the face of opposition to it (Weber, 1946). In terms of political functions it means being in a position to determine the answers to questions issuing from social complexity that concern whose interests and values are to be addressed.

Conflict and functional theorists differ in their conceptions of political power. Functionalists assert that only through some concentration of power can collective goals be achieved. They view the state apparatus as a mechanism for accomplishing these positive goals. Conflict theorists, on the other hand, view the state as serving the ruling economic class and see its function as maintaining the dominance of this class.

Power is not to be seen merely as an individual phenomenon. It is a social product. Bierstedt (1950) has identified three bases of power that indicate its social context: numbers, organization, and resources. The ability to mobilize the support of large numbers of people provides a strong power base. The old saying "the more the merrier" has profound import for generating power. However, even masses of people are ineffectual if they are directionless; organization is necessary. Sometimes a small, well-organized group can prevail over large, unorganized numbers of people. Control over resources is crucial to the ability to set the organization in motion. Resources may be widely varied, depending upon the context. Money, wealth, and property are major resources. Valuable resources would also include the energy, talent, knowledge, and skills the personnel have to offer. Such things as control over the mass media of communication, utilities, and transportation can be invaluable in certain circumstances. Individuals and groups that can bring all three of these factors to bear on any set of issues are in a very favorable position to have their will carried out even in the face of opposition. Those who are supported by large, well-organized groups with control over important resources have a great deal of power.

In this chapter we shall examine the way in which power to control the decision-making apparatus dealing with the political function is organized and distributed. First, we select three types of formal governments that have been of major significance either in the past or in today's world and consider their identifying characteristics. We focus on **proprietary states, democratic governments,** and **totalitarian regimes.** Each type of government attempts to gain legitimacy for itself, that is, to establish among the citizenry the acceptance of its right to control decision making. Weber identified three bases upon which such legitimacy may rest: traditional, charismatic, and rational-legal, each of which we examine in this chapter.

Turning our attention to the polity of the United States and its legitimizing bases, we then consider two models that attempt to describe the structure of power in this country: the **elitist model,** which emphasizes the dominance in public policy making of a unified ruling group with its major roots in big business, and the **pluralist model,** which posits the distribution of power among a number of interest groups and attributes real power to the electorate. In the context of the pluralist model, we discuss the nature of interest groups and identify some of the social factors that influence political participation and partisanship among the electorate in this country. We conclude with a brief overview of trends in political behavior.

Types of Government

Weber describes the **state** as the political organization that claims "binding authority and a legitimate monopoly of force within a territory" (Weber in Gerth and Mills, 1946:18). The modern nation-state, which emerged during the Middle Ages, has developed a set of institutions through which governance is achieved. The **government,** on the other hand, refers to the actual personnel who staff these institutions and constitute the ruling group. The government can change hands without disrupting the political institutions of the state. For example, the Italian government headed by Prime Minister Craxi fell when controversy arose over the release of one of the leaders of the hijackers of the ship the *Achille Lauro* in 1985. This did not, however, jeopardize the Italian state in any way. It merely formed a new government.

In the course of history human groups have developed innumerable types of **polities,** or formal organizations of governance, for ruling their societies. The special cultural and historical circumstances of each society transform even similar systems into unique structures. It would, of course, be impossible to discuss the entire range of such governmental organizations. We describe in the following sections a few types that have been of major importance historically or that are of special significance in the context of present world realities. We have selected three types: **proprietary states, democratic systems,** and **totalitarian regimes.**

Proprietary States

Historically, the form of government that has had the most far-reaching consequences has been based upon the notion of a proprietary state. In this type of polity the land is regarded as the private property of the ruler, often with only minimal restrictions upon what he may do with it. This is to say that no distinction is made between the private and political spheres of the ruler's jurisdiction, and the expectation is that personal advantage rather than social benefit will govern his decrees. Such license is legitimized through mythic and historical conceptions that elevate the ruling family to preeminence. Genealogical links to divine figures or legendary heroes establish the right of the designated member of the royal family to rule. The familial concept is closely intertwined with the kingship, and patterns of succession follow familial descent lines. For example, where primogeniture, inheritance by the firstborn, is the cultural pattern for inheritance, this rule generally applies to succession to the kingship. If a pattern of equal inheritance among male heirs is the norm, a ruler may divide his kingdom among his sons. A case in point was Charlemagne's attempt to divide the Holy Roman Empire among his three sons (Winston, 1960:373–74).

In the proprietary state, the ruler grants vast estates to those who have served him well. Although these tend to become hereditary, the claims of the crown are formally recognized by inheritors through ceremonies that renew fealty. The threat

In the proprietary state, the king was assumed to own all the land, and the granting of estates was a personal transaction.

of dispossession from the land as a result of the king's displeasure is ever present. The estate-holding families join with the ruling family in forming an elite governing class within the society. The peasants belong to the land; that is, they are a part of the estate. Therefore, the estate holders exercise both economic and political jurisdiction over them.

Developed to its most advanced stages in agrarian societies (Lenski and Lenski, 1982:198–201), this form of governing typified societies of ancient Asia, the Middle East, Africa, and medieval Europe. A recent example of this type is well described by John Beattie in his study *Bunyoro: An African Kingdom* (1960). Bunyoro is now part of the nation of Uganda. The ruler, called the Mukama, once exercised unchallenged power supported by myths and practices that set him apart as a descendant of gods, but he is now largely a symbolic figure. Such seems to have been the history of many proprietary rulers.

Democratic Governments

Democratic societies provide for a high degree of openness. The phrase commonly associated with democracy is "majority rule." If this were its only identifying characteristic, however, it would not necessarily provide safeguards for an open society. Alexis de Tocqueville, the astute observer of democracy in America (1969), cites as one of its inherent problems the **"tyranny of the majority."** By this he meant that where the majority rules, the rights of the minority may be disregarded. This problem confronts any society where decisions rest upon head counts. Modern democratic governments, however, attempt to provide safeguards against such abuses.

In general, modern democracies rest on constitutions that build checks and balances into the structure of government. Participation in the political process,

Widespread voter participation is one of the characteristics of a democratic state.

including access to public office, is broadly based. Provisions are made for periodic electoral competition. Democracies are typically representative governments. Officials are deemed to be accountable to those they govern; the sovereignty of the people is an underlying assumption.

Alternative centers of power have a chance to develop and act as a check upon the excesses of government. Responsible opposition is a part of the political process. Some criticism of government is tolerated, and electoral challenge is viable. Independent institutions flourish.

The realms of life subject to governmental action are limited. Civil liberties and individual rights are protected by constitutional guarantees. Although Thomas Jefferson's dictum that government is best that governs least has been largely replaced in contemporary life by a conception of government as having a more active role in the society, protection of the rights of individuals from governmental interference is a matter of concern. Freedom of speech, the press, religion, freedom to assemble, and freedom to petition are supports for democratic institutions.

Although modern democratic government emerged with the development of modern capitalism, it may be found in combination with other types of economic systems. For example, the United States combines democratic government with capitalism; Sweden combines democracy with a mixed economy.

Totalitarian Governments

Totalitarian governments, too, may develop in conjunction with a wide variety of economic systems (Washburn, 1982:352). Two major characteristics identify systems as totalitarian (adapted from Friedrich and Brzezinski, 1965): (1) One overarching ideology provides the rationale for the organization of the entire society. Dissent from this system of beliefs is not tolerated. The government promotes its official doctrine in the mass media, in schools and other agencies of socialization (such as youth clubs), and through symbolic occasions where the evocation of the ideology is expected to produce emotional response and recommitment. It controls and restricts access to ideas that might challenge the ideology. (2) The only center of power is in the intertwining power structures of the government and the single political party. No competing or opposing centers of power are permitted to exist. The government exerts total control over the economy and other social institutions. These two principles are enforced by terror and intimidation administered through the party and through the secret police, who control all the weapons in the society.

Cultural, economic, and social factors influence the development of totalitarianism. For example, a long tradition of authoritarian social relationships, weakness in potentially opposing institutions (such as family, religion, and education), or mounting economic crisis are all situations that foster the concentration of political power (Washburn, 1982).

Although these descriptions of proprietary, democratic, and totalitarian governments represent "pure" models, we may identify some societies that approach each type. The United States, France, Sweden and the Philippines under Aquino are examples of societies that follow the democratic model; whereas the Philippines under Marcos, Uganda, and the Soviet Union lean toward the totalitarian model. The old kingdoms of Europe, East Africa, and the Middle East exemplify the proprietary state. Most societies have developed systems that combine some of the features of two or more. Furthermore, as each society's polity develops out of its historical and cultural experience, each type is adapted to the particular circumstances of that society. We see this process at work today in the developing nations, where the desire for cultural continuity, the need for planning and discipline, and the wish for openness and the protection of individual rights combine to form unique, culturally specific polities.

Legitimation of Authority

Any type of government is faced with the problem of making itself acceptable to the people who are governed. This is the problem of **legitimacy,** which refers to the willingness of people to recognize the right of those who exercise power to do so. Because power is an element in the coordination of all large organizations, the issue of legitimacy is not unique to governmental structures.

Legitimacy converts power into **authority.** Authority gains compliance with orders and directives because the right of the person who issues them to do so is accepted by the people who must carry them out. Not all power is legitimate. For example, the crime syndicates may have power over small business operators in a given city, but the power is exercised by intimidation and force rather than through the businessman's acceptance of the syndicate's right to do so. By contrast, in your college, students accept the right of the instructor to establish course requirements and assign grades. This is legitimate power, or authority. It does not imply that one must agree with the number of papers required or approve of the grade received; but it means that students recognize the teacher's prerogative to make those decisions.

The same idea applies in political institutions. Although governments have force at their disposal (police, armies, and the like), most attempt to establish their legitimacy rather than depending upon naked force to have their mandates carried out. Acceptance of the right of individuals and groups to make decisions that affect the lives of people and to issue orders that people must follow grows out of the norms and values of the people, or at least some segment of the people. Authority, then, has a normative quality that other types of power do not have.

Various types of governments go about establishing their legitimacy in different ways. The three types discussed thus far illustrate such diversity. The ruling regime in the proprietary state justifies itself by genealogical links, real or imagined, to the past; by customary practices in the society; and/or by reference to what has gone before. By contrast, democratic societies are usually based on constitutional and legislative stipulations. Those who come to power through the legally designated procedures are recognized as having authority to perform the political functions. In totalitarian societies the founding regime is very often dominated by a revolutionary hero. His followers assume he has access to a higher truth, and their fervor demands that not only they but nonfollowers as well must abide by the mandates that embody it.

These situations illustrate Weber's three-pronged classification of the bases for the legitimation of authority: traditional, rational-legal, and charismatic. Each of these types represents a legitimate foundation upon which authority may rest (Weber, 1946).

Traditional Authority

When power has been achieved through patterns of accession that exist in the customs and traditions of a group, it is **traditional authority.** If in a particular society custom decrees that the oldest son of the king becomes the new king, then people in that society accept the right of the son to rule when the old king dies. This is implied by the ancient cry, "The king is dead; long live the king." People will obey the rule of the son because they accept the customary pattern through which he has acquired power. Tradition gives legitimacy to power, transforming it into authority. The authority of the father in a patriarchal family system or a hereditary chieftainship in a tribal society demonstrates the normative underpinnings of the traditional basis of legitimation.

Charismatic Authority

The term "charismatic" is often used today to refer to someone with a lively, appealing personality. Weber used it in a somewhat different sense. By **charismatic authority** he meant power legitimated through a group's attribution to an individual of such unusual and exalted personality or character that they are willing to do his or her bidding. Thought to have direct access to truth, the leader links the needs and aspirations of a group of people to some cosmic principle. The dynamic interplay between the yearnings of the group and the leader to whom they attribute powers beyond those of ordinary men and women is the basis for charismatic authority. The followers of the Reverend Jim Jones were willing to sell their property and turn the proceeds over to him, to follow him to South

Leaders of different political persuasions may acquire a following based partly on their charismatic personalities.

America, to give their daughters and wives for his sexual pleasure, and finally to give their children and themselves cyanide-laced Kool-Aid because they acknowledge his right to require those actions of them. Charismatic leaders include both the famous, like Martin Luther King, Jr., and Gandhi, and the infamous, like Hitler or Charles Manson.

Charisma is not a particularly stable basis for governance. Problems are sometimes created by the fact that the characteristics that attract followers to a social movement are not necessarily the qualities that are required for efficient day-by-day operations of governing. In addition, when charismatic leaders gain power, they are faced with the problem of translating their zealously advocated ideals into practical programs. This may lead to strong-armed tactics to achieve the goals. Furthermore, they are faced with everyday, nitty-gritty decisions that alienate some of the followers and take away some of the charismatic luster. Weber calls this tendency the **"routinization of charisma."** Another problem is that charisma is not transferable from one person to another. Unless the leader has used his authority to bring about the group's commitment to some institutional structures, his death will likely destabilize the group, because his successors will lack the personal authority to demand compliance.

Rational-Legal Authority

Authority that rests on compliance with a set of deliberately designed and broadly agreed upon procedures for gaining power is **rational-legal authority.** When a group draws up and accepts rules that specify how one reaches a position of leadership, the person who successfully follows those rules acquires legitimate authority. For example, the constitution of the United States, supplemented by various laws, contains a set of procedures for gaining the presidency. Because we are committed to these procedures, we accept the right of anyone who gains the office by following those rules to govern no matter how much we disagree with him or her. Watergate created a crisis of legitimacy because the committee to reelect President Nixon went beyond those rules, and the president conspired to cover up the "dirty tricks."

However, it is not merely the existence of regulations that gives legitimacy to authority gained under them. Legitimacy also requires commitment to the rules on the part of those who are governed. We find many coups d'etat occurring in countries that have constitutional governments. In such situations the desire for power or the dislike for the incumbent leaders of state outweigh commitment to the constitutional provisions for elevating one to such a position of power.

Rational-legal authority is limited by the rules. In the first place, the authority is vested in the office, not in the person. Secondly, the boundaries of the authority are circumscribed by the rules. For example, the First Amendment to the United States Constitution says that government has no jurisdiction over our religion or our speech.

Bureaucracies embody the principles of rational-legal authority. Governments resting on this basis for legitimacy are organized as bureaucratic structures. Government bureaus and agencies administer the major policies of government, and sometimes they take over the legislative functions, as when they develop regulations for interstate commerce or pollution standards. The problem of the accountability of the bureaucracy to the electorate is thought by many to be a serious one threatening the democratic principle of the sovereignty of the people.

In addition to constitutional governments, rational-legal forms of authority may also be found in other kinds of social organizations. As pointed out earlier, in our society we create many groups as we pursue our interests and goals. If such groups have any degree of formal organization, the specification of how positions of leadership are to be filled is most likely a part of their bylaws.

These types of authority may occur in combination. For example, Hitler was duly elected chancellor of Germany under the constitution of the Weimar republic. But this rational-legal authority was supplemented and eventually replaced by his charismatic authority. The Pope combines elements of all three types. Some leaders of nations emerging from the colonial experience, such as Jomo Kenyatta of Kenya, used their charismatic authority to further identification and acceptance by their followers of the rational-legal forms of the new national constitutions.

The alternatives to legitimacy in governing are the use of raw force to achieve compliance or continuing instability in political institutions. Unless normative supports for a given pattern of power are present, legitimacy will be withheld, and one or the other of the alternatives will probably result.

The Distribution of Power in the United States

The U.S. government is by design a democracy. It attempts to legitimize itself through democratic principles embodied in rational-legal forms. Constitutional and legislative provisions for a system of checks and balances among various interests, the protection offered to individuals to pursue their interests, and the ultimate sovereignty of the people are built into our political institutions. Debate arises, however, over whether these provisions for balance among diverse elements in the society are actually achieved or whether they are merely window dressing, a facade to mask the actual concentration of decision-making power in the hands of an economic elite that represents narrow interests and that is unaccountable to the electorate.

Models attempting to depict the major decision-making apparatus of the society have emerged in sociological studies. The **elite model** envisions power as concentrated in the hands of a small, unified group of men whose interests and backgrounds coincide. The **pluralist model** depicts a distribution of power among several interest groups whose diverse interests counterbalance each other.

The Elitist Model

Most of the elitist theories of power build upon the Marxian theme that the private owners of the means of production constitute the ruling class, that is, an economic elite. According to this analysis, the only reason for the existence of the state is to support the interests of this dominant group. So the linkage of economic and political institutions is a close one, with economic institutions being the determinative element. It should be noted that Marx predicted that if the private ownership of the means of production is eliminated through a proletarian revolution, the state will eventually wither away because its reason for being will have disappeared.

C. Wright Mills studied the power structure of the United States during the 1950s. He focused on the **"power elite,"** a group of men who headed up the major economic, governmental, and military institutions in the country. It consisted of heads of major corporations and financial institutions; top members of the government (those in key positions in the executive branch including the president, vice-president, cabinet officials, and heads of important agencies, as well as key members of both legislative bodies); and officers from the top echelons of the armed services.

Mills noted the cohesiveness of these groups and indicated that it rests on psychological, social, and structural bases (1956:19). In their respective groups, the elite share a similar background: they came from similar privileged positions; they attended the same schools and universities; they belong to the same clubs; they share a similar life-style. They know each other personally and interact with each other frequently both professionally and privately.

Elite members of the three structures coordinate their activities. Military leaders and corporate executives, especially those in defense industries, plan together for weaponry. According to Mills, military leaders have departed from their traditional role of implementing government policy and have entered the area of policy formulation. The tie between business and government is of a symbiotic nature: from business, large campaign contributions to sympathetic legislators and from government, repayment of the indebtedness through voting for the interests of the contributors. Furthermore, the key figures in the three elite groups move freely from positions of power in one structure to comparable positions in the others: corporate executives assume cabinet posts and retired military leaders become directors of major corporations (1956:202–3).

These interlocking structural relationships create a unity of interests, one of the most important of which is military spending. What benefits one benefits the others. Mills suggests that the major decisions affecting the entire society are strongly reflective of these interconnections: issues of war and peace, budgeting, international trade, and foreign policy. Mills's thesis, then, is that this three-pronged power elite are the real decision makers in our society.

Complementing Mills's argument concerning the power elite, William Domhoff (1967) attempted to show that it is rooted in the upper class. He stressed the degree to which key figures in the federal government and in the major corporations have been recruited from similar privileged positions in the society. There is, he insisted, an identifiable national upper class in this country that is "made up of rich businessmen and their descendants, who interact at private schools, exclusive social clubs, exclusive summer resorts, and similar institutions" (1967:140). From their ranks emerge the institutional leaders and decision makers of our society. The corporate rich finance federal office holders of both parties. They staff the most strategic positions in government. They control the channels for molding public opinion on vital policy issues. Their interests dominate the major decisions that are made. The evidence Domhoff amassed led him to conclude that the income, wealth, and institutional leadership of this business aristocracy warrant calling it a "governing class" (1967:156).

Domhoff has continued his research by examining: how the upper class formulates national policies (1970), and the culture of the upper class (1974). An extensive critique of the pluralist analysis (1978), and a recent restatement of his overall research (1983) has followed.

Representing a neo-Marxist perspective, Baran and Sweezy (1966) picked up on the theme that government exists to serve the interests of the ruling class. Our society, they said, is ruled by an oligarchy composed of leaders of giant corporations. They characterized our political system as "bourgeois democracy," a system in which the role of money is crucial. Votes are the nominal source of political power, and money is the real source: the system, in other words, is "democratic in form and plutocratic in content" (Baran and Sweezy, 1966:155). They pointed out that running political parties and campaigns requires a great deal of money; and because the big corporations are the source of big money, "they are also the main sources of political power." Government maintains a stable milieu in which monopoly capitalism can thrive, and the measures it undertakes promote the interests of the moneyed oligarchy. The corporate rich, then, exercise their dominance in decision making through federal officials, who constitute a subordinate segment of the ruling elite.

In summary, the elitist model of power portrays a unified elite group, dominated mostly by big business interests, who control decision making in the society. Political leaders are seen as either junior partners with the economic elite or under their control. The role of the electorate is negligible.

It should be noted that although some elitist theorists think that elite structures are necessary and desirable, those we have discussed here do not. Mills, Domhoff, Baran and Sweezy have been highly critical of the elite structures that they have identified in American society.

The Pluralist Model

The presumption of an identity of interests among the ruling elite is at the core of the elitist model. The pluralist model, however, rests on the assumption that power is distributed among various **interest groups,** each with its own elite, among whom interests are not only diverse but in many cases conflicting. An interest group is an organization of people who share a similar interest and who band together to attempt to influence public policy in a direction beneficial to that interest. The National Association for the Advancement of Colored People is an interest group promoting the interests of blacks. The National Association of Manufacturers promotes business interests. The AFL-CIO represents the interests of labor. Pluralists assume that interest groups struggle with one another for power to make or control the policy decisions that fall within the political realm. As indicated in our earlier discussion of associations, the tendency to organize to pursue certain interests is one of the manifestations of the rational orientation that characterizes modern societies.

Measures through which such interests are pursued focus on the electoral, legislative, and public opinion levels. One device is the Political Action Committee, or PAC, through which groups supporting a given interest contribute funds to assist candidates for election who are known to be favorably disposed toward that position. PACs also contribute to campaigns in hopes of winning future support from successful candidates. A group that has made a sizable contribution to someone's campaign expects that when its interests are at issue, the recipient will remember his or her indebtedness. Indeed, often PACs make contributions to both sides in contested elections to insure that whatever the outcome, their interests will receive favorable attention.

Other attempts to influence elections involve "get-out-the-vote" activities in support of candidates who are sympathetic to the interests of a particular group. Some groups pack political caucuses and attempt to get their members elected as delegates to nominating conventions. For example, much support for Walter Mondale in the Democratic National Convention of 1984 came from delegates representing the interests of the National Education Association, a teachers' organization.

Interest groups attempt to influence public policy at the legislative level, not only by electing sympathetic officials but also by lobbying actively in the halls of Congress. Professional lobbyists keep their eyes on policy developments affecting the interests of the groups they represent and use persuasive tactics to influence particular senators and representatives to vote favorably. Lobbyists also frequently make unofficial but significant input into the formulation of legislation.

Many interest groups maintain large staffs who engage in ongoing activities calculated to influence public opinion. Their spokespersons make effective use of the mass media to explain their positions and to create public support for them. For example, environmentalists hold news conferences, give interviews, or appear on television talk shows when issues affecting the environment are in the news. Public relations activities aim at creating a favorable attitude among the citizenry, who presumably influence legislators.

Given the extent to which many of these groups can effectively organize, mobilize large numbers of people, and draw upon considerable resources, it is obvious that many of them are powerful. Individuals who direct such groups control the use to which that power is put. As such, they constitute an elite within the structure. Robert Michels (1962), drawing from his classic study of the German Social Democratic party, concluded that the formation of such an elite, or oligarchy, is inevitable, no matter how democratic the principles upon which the group is based may be. His statement of the **"iron law of oligarchy"** holds that "who says organization, says oligarchy." A large group must organize to be effective in achieving its goals. The leaders chosen by the group may at first be merely the voice through which the group expresses itself. But as such leaders gain experience, knowledge, and skills beyond that of ordinary members, they increasingly make independent judgments, based on their own assessments of what is needed rather than just communicating the group's wishes. This tendency is abetted by the willingness of most group members to let someone else handle things. This sets the leaders apart from the rank and file. Eventually the leaders will move to solidify their position of leadership and will develop a cadre of trusted followers, who depend upon their patronage for their positions. This group plans for its own successors, insuring continuity of the oligarchy.

Although Michels is not customarily classified as a pluralist, his "iron law of oligarchy" is not incompatible with the views of pluralists. They do not deny the existence of power structures. As Rose (1967:484) suggested, power is the way any meaningful change can occur or be prevented from occurring in a complex, heterogeneous society such as ours. The major point of difference with the elitist theorists is that pluralists do not see such structures as culminating in a single, cohesive, monolithic group that dominates decision making in the society. Rather, they see multiple groups, each with its own power structure, each pursuing its own interests.

One leading pluralist theorist, David Riesman (1950:244–45), described the power structure of the United States as "amorphous." It consists, he said, of a number of "veto groups," which he identified as a "series of groups, each of which has struggled for and finally attained a power to stop things conceivably inimical to its interests and, within far narrower limits, to start things." He cited as examples farm groups, labor and professional groups, major ethnic groups, and the like. Although these groups are not powerful enough to accomplish their complete agenda, they are, nevertheless, able to neutralize those interests who might attack them. To illustrate Riesman's view, we may refer to the political strength gained by blacks in the South in recent years. Although they are not yet powerful enough to elect black governors or senators, they have succeeded in quieting those extremists, like Eugene Talmadge of Georgia or Cotton Ed Smith of South Carolina, who centered their campaigns for state offices around racist doctrines. Present-day candidates for office attempt to exploit this theme at their peril, for they confront at the polls the voting strength of blacks.

Another facet of the pluralist outlook is the idea that power must be viewed in terms of issues (Riesman, 1950; Dahl, 1961; Rose, 1967). As we have seen, the elitist theorists insist that a single, unified group makes the really significant decisions that our country faces. In contrast, the pluralists assert that a given issue will activate several interest groups or power structures whose interests relate to the issue. Other power groups will not be involved in the decisions. For example, an issue facing the second term of the Reagan administration concerns the continuation of farm price-support programs. That is, decisions must be made as to whether support for farm products such as milk or tobacco should be continued. The issue has mobilized powerful farm groups such as the Farm Bureau Federation and the Farmers' Alliance, but neither the National Association of Manufacturers nor the American Medical Association, both powerful groups, has shown any interest in the controversy. Arnold Rose sums up this idea when he says:

1. There are many power elites, each of which is somewhat specialized in the area in which it exercises its influence.

2. Power elites interlock only temporarily and on limited types of issues. (Rose, 1967:89)

While noting the power of the economic elite, Rose suggests that their power is brought to bear mainly on issues involving production and to a lesser degree the consumption and distribution of wealth. They do not involve themselves very much in other types of issues.

Even when such economic concerns are at issue, pluralists question whether business interests can be assumed to be unified. The competition and conflict among various business interests is sufficient, they say, to challenge the assumption that big business constitutes a cohesive group with one point of view. Policy that works to the advantage of one type of business may threaten the interests of other types of businesses. To illustrate this idea: A current controversy in Virginia concerns whether or not to build a coal slurry pipeline, connecting west to east, from the coal fields in western Virginia to the shipping terminals on the coast. According to the proposal, coal would be pulverized, mixed with water, and moved through the pipeline to port facilities, where it could be reclaimed and the water discharged. Major coal-mining companies, assessing the slurry as a more economical way to move coal than the present methods, vigorously support the project. The major electric and power utility company joins in strong advocacy for it. Vigorously opposed are powerful railroad interests, who stand to lose a major source of their income, the railway transporting of coal. These several members of the corporate elite are bitterly at odds over this issue. Pluralists see such opposition of interests among business groups as evidence of multiple and separate power structures rather than an interlocking business elite.

Basic to the pluralist viewpoint is the idea that a considerable amount of power resides in the electorate (Dahl, 1961). Whatever and wherever public policy decisions are made, they must be encoded and implemented through governmental channels. Public officials are responsible for this formal action, and as a

One of the disagreements between the elite model of power distribution and the pluralist model is whether the voters are real participants in decisionmaking.

result they exercise real power. Although other power centers may exert strong influence, in the long run, the decisions rest with them. Because public officials are accountable to the electorate, they must take the opinions and interests of their constituents into account in making their determinations. Lawmakers who are unresponsive to the needs of the citizenry face rejection at the polls when they present themselves for reelection. Armed with this ultimate sanction, the threat of removal from office, the people have real power over the actions of their representatives in public office. This is a counterargument to Baran and Sweezy's thesis that elected officials mainly serve the interests of the corporate elite.

To counterpose these two positions on the roles of the voter and the elected officials raises a number of questions about the efficacy of the electoral process. Does it make any difference that one candidate rather than another gets elected? Does anything substantial occur depending upon whether Republicans or Democrats are in office? Are we deluding ourselves when we talk about the importance of voting at election time?

To assume that voting is consequential appears to concede substance to pluralistic arguments of multiple interests. If we assume with the elitist theorists that the really important decisions are made in centers of power outside the political arena, then elections become merely a ratification device, a system of giving legitimacy to a process that operates behind the constitutional forms and essentially without reference to the electorate. On the assumption that who our officials are and which policies they represent does make a difference in the way the political functions of our society are carried out, we turn our attention to some of the social factors that influence political participation and partisanship.

Participation and Partisanship in the United States

Although the theory of democratic government assumes a broad, active, informed electorate, participation in the political process in this country is by no means universal. Levels of participation extend from total noninvolvement to full-time activism. Washburn (1982:147) has estimated that the category of inactives makes up about 22 percent of the American citizenry. The next most numerous category (21 percent) consists of those who vote regularly but who do not otherwise attempt to influence the actions of government. The remaining 57 percent represent more active participation at some level of community affairs and/or campaigning.

Studies of political behavior, particularly voting behavior, have shown that participation and political affiliation are not randomly distributed in the population. One of the points of view we have attempted to develop is the extent to which social structures influence individual behavior. The same type of explanations may be applied to differentials in voting behavior among various groups in the society.

Political Socialization

The institutions of our society perform a socializing function, meaning that they communicate attitudes, values, and norms, including politically relevant ones.

We learn political behavior from those with whom we interact. One of the most effective indicators of political choice is the nuclear family. The family group provides a context in which many of our subsequent political orientations develop. Some of these are specifically political and are communicated directly, such as voting habits, party preferences, and attitudes toward political issues. Other family influences are more subtle. For example, attitudes hinging on the development of confidence that one can manipulate one's environment develop in the family context and have an influence on political participation (Washburn, 1982:154). **Fatalism,** the belief that one is powerless to influence or control one's life circumstances, contributes to abstention from political activity. The family influence on political behavior is likely to be strongest in situations where the family is attractive to the child, where the emotional unity of the family is strong, and where the parents are interested in and in agreement on political matters (Washburn, 1982:155).

Other primary groups also influence political behavior. The peer group in the work place is a good predictor of voting preferences. One tends to take on the political norms of those with whom one works. A similar influence is exerted by intimate friendship groups. Some of this influence may be explained by the homogeneity of such group members;—they are likely to be "in the same boat." But some of it no doubt comes from going along with one's buddies—that is, evolving group norms.

The timing of political socialization seems to be relevant to voting behavior. The generation that became politically conscious during the lean years of the Great Depression of the 1930s is likely to have vastly different political orientations from those who became politically aware during the more affluent period of the 1960s. The political circumstances of a given period (for example, the Vietnamese War or Watergate) are bound to have repercussions in the attitudes of those whose political views are beginning to crystallize at that time.

Stratification

People in different class and status positions in the society tend to differ in their political orientations. Voting and other forms of political participation correlate positively with socioeconomic level. Individuals in higher economic levels tend to get involved more frequently in political affairs than those from low income levels. Low-income individuals vote less often and participate less often in other ways. The reasons for this are varied. Lack of knowledge about the issues is one factor. Limited education generally results in being less informed about political matters. Who the candidates are, what they stand for, and what the implications of their positions are may not be understood by those whose reading ability or access to reading material is limited. Similar factors also help to undermine a feeling of competence to deal with the actual registration and voting process. Transportation to polling places or registration sites can also be a problem for some.

Tweedledee and Tweedledum candidates for office may be perceived by voters as offering no real choice. If voters think that none of the candidates for office understands and addresses their concerns, they will probably consider it a waste of time to go to the polls. Because most political candidates are recruited from the middle class, this perception may be acute for low-income individuals.

Fatalism is also a deterrent to participation by low-income people. They are more likely than others to feel that they have no control over their own destinies. This attitude extends to the conclusion that one's vote does not count. Compounding this attitude, low-income individuals are more likely to belong to fundamentalist religious groups that deliberately eschew politics and advocate leaving everything in God's hands.

Middle- and upper-income people are better informed; they are more likely to feel that participation is important and they can influence the events that shape their lives; and they approach the process with greater confidence.

It has often been said that people tend to vote their pocketbooks; that is, they vote their economic self-interest as they see it. Traditionally this association is not as strong in the United States as it is in some countries with worker-based or ideologically explicit parties. Nevertheless, lower-income people have generally perceived their interests to be supported by the Democratic party, whereas higher classes have identified with the Republican party. Since 1968, class differences in voting preferences have diminished (Abrahamson, 1976), though the association remains.

Race and Ethnicity

Variations in political participation and partisanship are associated with differences in race and ethnicity. Whites tend to participate in political activities more frequently than blacks, Hispanics, and other minorities; although when socioeconomic factors are held constant, these differences may not stand up. For example, middle- and upper-income blacks participate in proportions equal to or exceeding their white counterparts (Blackwell, 1985).

Political participation of racial and ethnic minorities tends to be more frequent in situations where racial or ethnic issues or candidates are at stake and where members have a strong identification with the minority community (Olsen, 1970). An example of this would be the mobilization of Hispanics in the Southwest around the issue of bilingual education. The rallying of blacks to the campaign of Jesse Jackson for the Democratic presidential nomination in 1984 also illustrates the tendency.

One of the most striking developments in voter participation in recent years has been the growth of political strength among blacks and Hispanics. For blacks this has been a long struggle, and it is still going on. Although the Fifteenth Amendment to the Constitution barred racial criteria for voting, following Reconstruction southern states revised their constitutions to include measures that selectively disfranchised blacks without explicitly saying so. Grandfather clauses, poll taxes, and literacy tests were such devices. Southern Democrats claimed the right to exclude blacks from their primary (which was the effective election in the one-party South) on the basis that their party was a private organization and therefore not subject to the Fifteenth Amendment strictures. These formal practices were augmented by threats against and harassment of would-be voters.

One by one these measures were knocked down by the Supreme Court. The movement to secure the franchise culminated in the passage of the Voting Rights Act in 1965. Two provisions of the bill have been especially important in providing effective access to the ballot for blacks: (1) Federal registrars were sent into selected areas to insure that blacks would be able to register and vote, and (2) in states with a history of discrimination any action that would change the boundaries of political jurisdictions (such as annexation or redistricting) would have to be submitted for review by the Justice Department to insure that these measures were not being used to reduce the impact of black voting.

Congress extended the Voting Rights Act in 1975 and added provisions to protect the rights of Hispanic voters (Vander Zanden, 1983:249). One of the longrunning problems in voter participation among Hispanic citizens has been the language barrier, for large numbers of Hispanics do not speak English. The Voting Rights Act extension requires that bilingual ballots and other types of voting assistance be provided in areas where more than 5 percent of the residents do not speak English and where illiteracy is high and voter turnouts are low (Vander Zanden, 1983:249). Such measures have supported the increasing political clout resulting from the rapidly growing numbers of Hispanic citizens in this country.

Political partisanship varies among racial and ethnic minorities. Until the 1930s blacks had been staunch supporters of the party of Lincoln. They joined the Democratic New Deal coalition in the 1930s and have remained its most stalwart group. For example, in the presidential election of 1984, the Democratic candidate, Walter Mondale, received nearly 90 percent of the black vote.

Immigrant groups coming to this country in the early days of the twentieth century were wooed by the Democratic political machines in the cities where they settled. Catholic immigrant groups were wedded to the Democratic party in 1928 by the candidacy of Al Smith, the first Catholic candidate for president from a major party. In recent elections, this association has diminished. Hispanics of Puerto Rican and Mexican descent have also supported the Democratic party for the most part, one factor being its more generous social programs. Jewish voters were a part of the New Deal coalition and have continued to support Democratic candidates, though now perhaps not so overwhelmingly as at earlier times. Strategically located in the key states and major urban centers, they constitute a powerful political force in the United States.

In general, as minority groups assimilate, they tend to lose their political distinctiveness. As their interests become more diversified, they come to resemble more closely the general electorate in all its variegated dimensions.

Trends in Political Behavior

Throughout its history the United States has expanded the political base of its electorate. In the early days of our country only landowning white males were eligible to vote. The franchise has been steadily extended to other demographic categories. Landholding provisions were abolished. "Race, color or previous condition of servitude" as criteria for voting were made illegal by the Fifteenth Amendment. The Nineteenth Amendment gave women the right to vote and the Twenty-sixth Amendment lowered the voting age from twenty-one to eighteen.

Although the number of potential voters has increased, the actual percentage of voters has declined in recent years. Political analysts have attributed this drop to many factors: loss of trust in government, lack of viable candidates and political options, the increasingly technical complexity of public issues, and voter apathy and alienation. At least a portion of the decline must be seen in the light of the extension of the electoral base. Some demographic categories, for example eighteen- to twenty-one-year-olds, do not vote in proportions commensurate with the numbers they add to the base. But this merely pushes the question back one step. Why certain categories of people do not vote in proportion to their numbers is still to be explained.

The prominence of women and other minorities in the political process has increased dramatically in the past twenty-five years. This trend, which at first appeared to be mostly symbolic, is gaining in substantive import. There is no definitive evidence that the electorate in general enthusiastically endorses this development. Minority candidates still generate considerable opposition on the basis of their minority status. Still, there has been identifiable movement in the direction of greater inclusiveness in political affairs at all levels. The prominence of Geraldine Ferraro and Jesse Jackson in the presidential election of 1984 attests to this.

Another political trend of some importance is the diminishing partisanship of voters. The ranks of the independent voter have grown appreciably. The results of this may be seen in shifts in any given election from one party to the other depending upon the attractiveness of the candidate or the issues. Traditional alignments such as the old one-party Democratic South or rock-ribbed Republican New England have been largely shattered. Widespread ticket splitting is also a manifestation of the growth of the independent voter. This tendency has resulted in the past twenty years in local and state elections mostly favoring Democrats while Republicans were winning nationally (the Carter-Mondale victory in 1976 was an exception).

The extent to which television has changed the pattern of political campaigning in recent years has been marked. Candidates are "packaged" for media appeal, which tends to disqualify less "attractive persons" from major offices. The import of this trend is that serious discussion of issues becomes secondary to creating an attractive impression. In the process image supercedes substance in the evaluation many voters make of candidates. They key to success becomes more a matter of selecting a good public relations firm than of putting together a thoughtful, responsive political program.

Another trend that has helped to shape public affairs in recent years is one-issue politics. By this we mean the growth in the kinds of groups that support or oppose a candidate on the basis of the stand he or she takes on one particular issue. Some women's organizations make choices between candidates solely on the basis of their stands on women's rights. Pro-life groups may choose merely on the basis of the candidate's stand on abortion. Single-issue politics tend to undercut the balancing of interests that has characterized party politics in the past. Whether this trend portends a fragmenting of the two-party system remains to be seen.

Summary

We began our discussion of political institutions by identifying the functions that the formal structures of government carry out: protection from external threat, social order, conflict resolution, and resource allocation. Because complexity in the society creates diversity in the solutions to these problems that various groups find satisfactory, the struggle for power to control decision making has important consequences for the society.

Over time, human groups have developed many types of formal organizations of power for governance. Proprietary states have been historically important in most areas of the world. Democratic states have emerged on a large scale in more recent times. Totalitarian states are organized in terms of an overarching ideology and permit no centers of power to exist outside the linked structures of party and government.

Each government attempts to legitimize its power and convert it into authority. Bases upon which legitimation of authority rests were identified by Weber as traditional, charismatic, and rational-legal.

The polity of the United States is democratic. Its legitimacy is established through the constitution and enacted laws that embody this principle. Debate over whether decision making in public policy actually follows this principle has resulted in the development of two models of power distribution. The elitist model asserts that decision-making power rests in a small, unified group dominated by the corporate elite. The pluralist model depicts a distribution of power among many interest groups who counterbalance each other. Pluralists agree that one such locus of power is in the electorate.

The extent and direction of participation of the electorate in the political process vary among people with different socioeconomic characteristics and experiences. Primary groups influence the political orientations of their members. Socioeconomic factors such as class, race, or ethnic group membership influence not only the level of participation but political preferences as well.

The potential electorate of the United States has steadily grown more inclusive over the years. Women and minorities are assuming more prominent roles in political affairs. The development of television has changed the presentation of candidates for office. PACs have changed the methods of financing campaigns. The trends toward independent voting and one-issue politics raise questions about the future of the two-party system.

Key Concepts

authority
charismatic authority
democratic governments
elitist model
fatalism
government
interest group
iron law of oligarchy
legitimacy
pluralist model
polity
power elite
proprietary stages
rational-legal authority
routinization of charisma
state
totalitarian regimes
traditional authority
"tyranny of the majority"
veto groups

References

Abrahamson, Paul R. (1976) "Generational Change and the Decline of Party Identification in America," *American Political Science Review*, 70:469–78.
Baran, Paul, and Paul Sweezy. (1966) *Monopoly Capital*. New York, N.Y.: Monthly Review Press.
Beattie, John. (1960) *Bunyoro: An African Kingdom*. New York, N.Y.: Holt, Rinehart and Winston.
Bierstedt, Robert. (1950) "An Analysis of Social Power." *American Sociological Review*, 15:730–38.
Blackwell, James E. The Black Community: Diversity and Unity. 2nd edition, 1985. New York, N.Y.: Harper and Row, Publishers.
Dahl, Robert A. (1961) *Who Governs?* New Haven, Conn.: Yale University Press.
Domhoff, G. William. (1967) *Who Rules America?* Englewood Cliffs, N.J.: Prentice-Hall, Inc.
———. (1970) *The Higher Circles*. New York, N.Y.: Vintage Books/Random House, Inc.
———. (1974) *The Bohemian Grove and Other Retreats*. New York, N.Y.: Harper & Row, Publishers.
———. (1978) *Who Really Rules?* New Brunswick, N.J.: Transaction Books.
———. (1983) *Who Rules America Now? A View for the Eighties*. Englewood Cliffs, N.J.: Prentice-Hall, Inc.
Friedrich, Carl J., and Zbigniew K. Brzezinski. (1965) *Totalitarian Dictatorship and Autocracy*, 2d ed. New York, N.Y.: Praeger Publishers, Inc.
Lenski, Gerhard, and Jean Lenski. (1982) *Human Societies*. 3d ed. New York, N.Y.: McGraw-Hill Book Company.
Michels, Robert. (1962) *Political Parties*. New York, N.Y.: The Free Press.
Mills, C. Wright. (1956) *The Power Elite*. New York, N.Y.: Oxford University Press, Inc.
Olsen, Marvin. (1970) "The Social and Political Participation of Blacks." *American Sociological Review*, 35:682–97.
Orum, Anthony M. (1978) *Introduction to Political Sociology*. Englewood Cliffs, N.J.: Prentice-Hall, Inc.
Riesman, David. (1950) *The Lonely Crowd*. New Haven, Conn.: Yale University Press.
Rose, Arnold. (1967) *The Power Structure: Political Process in American Society*. New York, N.Y.: Oxford University Press, Inc.
Tocqueville, Alexis de. [2 vol., 1835; tr. 4 vol., 1835–40]. (1969) *Democracy in America*. Reprint New York, N.Y.: Anchor Books/Doubleday & Company, Inc.
Vander Zanden, James. (1983) *American Minority Relations*. 4th ed. New York, N.Y.: Alfred A. Knopf, Inc.
Washburn, Philo. (1982) *Political Sociology: Approaches, Concepts, Hypotheses*. Englewood Cliffs, N.J.: Prentice-Hall, Inc.
Weber, Max. (1946) *From Max Weber: Essays in Sociology*. Translated by H. H. Gerth and C. Wright Mills. New York, N.Y.: Oxford University Press, Inc.
———. (1964) *The Theory of Social and Economic Organization*. A. M. Henderson & Talcott Parsons. New York, N.Y.: The Free Press.
Winston, Richard. (1960) *Charlemagne: From the Hammer to the Cross*. New York, N.Y.: Vintage Books/Random House, Inc.

17

Education as a Social Institution

OBJECTIVES

Students who complete this chapter should be able to:

1. Discuss education as a social institution.
2. Analyze the impact of the social organization of schooling on the outcomes of the educational process.
3. Understand the expansion of educational institutions in modern society.
4. Explain and contrast functionalist and conflict theories of the relationship between education and society.
5. Analyze how social inequalities of class and race affect equality of educational opportunity.
6. Discuss the impact of busing and affirmative action programs on education.

INTRODUCTION

Education is usually a controversial subject because the most significant issues of the day often impact on the institution of education. For example, in the decade of the 1980s intense debate exists over whether busing for racial balance should be discontinued in order to permit a return to "neighborhood schools." There is heated debate over whether there should be organized prayer in the public schools. There is argument over whether the federal government should provide money to parents who want to send their children to private schools—the so-called voucher issue. Conservatives claim that American children are being wrongly taught to be disrespectful of authority and to be critical of American history and of great American heroes. On the other hand, liberals claim that American children are being indoctrinated into an unthinking patriotism, rigid conformity to authority, and neglect of the contributions of minorities and women.

Likewise, in the 1980s there is widespread concern that American education is a failure. The National Commission on Excellence in Education in its widely publicized 1983 report titled *A Nation at Risk* asserted:

> The educational foundations of our society are presently being eroded by a rising tide of mediocrity that threatens our very future as a nation and a people . . . If an unfriendly foreign power had attempted to impose on America the mediocre educational performance that exists today, we might well have viewed it as an act of war. As it stands, we have allowed this to happen to ourselves . . . We have, in effect, been committing an act of unthinking, unilateral educational disarmament (National Commission on Excellence in Education, 1983).

The sociological approach to the study of education cannot necessarily settle these arguments, but it can explain why education is such a controversial institution in society, and it can draw upon the findings of sociological research to shed some light on the issues that cause sharp political conflicts over education.

In this chapter we examine the relationship of educational institutions to the larger society by exploring the roles of education and the organization of schooling in America. A discussion of expanded educational opportunity is followed with a review of functionalist and conflict theories that attempt to explain education as a social institution. The chapter will conclude with a review of the controversies over differences in educational achievement and affirmative action programs.

Education as a Social Institution

As an institution, education plays several important roles in society. Education transmits the culture of a society to its members, mainly the young, and it is therefore an agent of socialization. In particular, education teaches those parts of a society's culture that are collectively agreed upon to be important and essential. Educational institutions are formal organizations that hire specially trained persons (teachers) and teach special subjects (courses, curricula) that have been planned in advance. This contrasts with the socialization that takes place in the family—socialization that just "happens" as we develop. The reason why cultural transmission generates much conflict over education is that there is much cultural diversity in society. There is controversy over the cultural values that should be taught in educational institutions, and that conflict over the values taught in school mirrors conflict over societal values.

Education is secondly a principal way of allocating status in society. That is, the educational system is used to place people into higher- and lower-ranking positions in the system of social stratification. In America education is supposed to provide everyone with an equal opportunity to achieve. Equality of opportunity means that the competition for higher-status positions is just and fair and based upon merit. Often, however, the equality of educational opportunity is mitigated by the ascribed statuses of sex, race, and family wealth. These ascribed statuses influence the schools students attend, the curriculum they pursue, and the opportunities available to them upon completion of their studies.

A third role of education in society is teaching necessary skills and knowledge. Although this aspect of education is relatively less controversial than trans-

Educational institutions transmit cultural values, teach skills and knowledge, and allocate status in society.

mitting values or allocating status, there is much disagreement over which skills and what knowledge are essential, to whom they should be taught, and what are the most effective ways to teach.

What Do Schools Teach?

The debate over what schools teach not only focuses on the roles of education as an institution but also on the information or messages that are transmitted through the educational process. Some analysts assert, for example, that schools teach students the cognitive skills that are appropriate for modern American society. Schools teach children not only basic skills but also a general scientific methodology, how to think, independence, tolerance of diversity, openmindedness, and adaptability to the challenges of a changing society.

Opponents in this debate assert that the American economic and political system needs citizens and workers who possess a very different set of skills and traits. Schools train students to follow instructions, accept authority, perform routine tasks, and assume a responsible position in society.

Others suggest that schools teach an ideological perspective, or an outlook on social events that occur in the students' environment. In a review of American history texts Fitzgerald (1979) concluded that American history is portrayed as "a triumphal story of increasing freedom and justice" and that the credit for this progress has been attributed to a small number of great white men. More recent texts have sought to establish some balance in the educational perspective by

Education as a Social Institution

pointing out faults as well as merits of various heroes and by paying attention to the contributions of women and members of minority groups.

The Social Organization of Schooling

In the 1960s and 1970s many educators and parents criticized schools for being organized in a rigid, authoritarian manner. In the 1980s schools are more frequently criticized for not exerting enough authority and control over students. The social organization of schools may either help or prevent the attainment of educational objectives.

Educational institutions may be analyzed as play organizations, as custodial organizations, and as work organizations. As play organizations, schools are places where young people explore social relationships, join and participate in extracurricular activities, compete for popularity, and engage in school sports. For many students this may be the most important aspect of educational institutions. As many researchers have noted, students develop a subculture that places particularly high value on popularity, sports, and social relationships. For example, the most popular students are frequently outstanding athletes, cheerleaders, or those with the most dates, rather than the students who are merely high academic achievers.

Schools as play organizations tend to perform certain **latent functions** for society. Latent functions are those that are not necessarily planned or intended. One latent function is the creation and transmission of patterns of age segregation in society. The youth subculture is one in which young people spend a great deal of time only with people their own age. Adults and even older and younger youth are viewed as outsiders and intruders who do not understand their world and their concerns. Because schooling is organized by age and because it brings together large numbers of young people, it strongly reinforces age segregation and fosters generational conflicts between youth and adults.

Schools may be analyzed in part as play organizations for youth.

One of the latent functions of schools is to serve as a marriage broker.

Another latent function of schools as play organizations is as a child-care institution that takes responsibility for children while parents work or engage in other activities. Parents who may be critical of schools for all sorts of reasons are nevertheless likely to appreciate the fact that schools relieve them from the caretaker responsibilities of their children for about six hours each school day.

A third latent function of educational institutions is that they often serve as a "marriage market" for young people. Not only do young people experiment with a variety of social relationships, they are also likely to select a permanent marriage partner, especially while they are in high school or in college, from among those relationships. Because high schools and colleges tend to sort people by social class and other social characteristics, this contributes to marriage patterns in which people tend to marry others who share many of the same social characteristics. Finally, a latent function is that, by prolonging play, educational institutions postpone the entry of youth into the labor force, and therefore unemployment rates are lower.

As custodial organizations, schools share certain characteristics with prisons and mental institutions. School attendance is compulsory, students may not arbitrarily leave school, they must be in assigned places doing assigned activities, and they are subject to the rules and authority of the institution.

As work organizations, educational institutions are much like factories or offices. Schools are places in which students are expected to work, even if they

Schools may also be analyzed as work organizations similar to factories or offices.

would rather not do so, under the supervision of persons in authority. As Hurn (1985) has pointed out, schools are likely to find it much harder than work organizations to get people to work. Schools face problems of motivation, authority, and control. Because schools cannot depend on motivating students with money, students must be motivated to work with grades, praise, and threats.

Schools also demand of students much behavior that runs counter to the natural inclinations of young people. Schools demand that students remain still, quiet, and attentive; that they not interact with fellow students; and that they perform many routine and often tedious assignments. It is often difficult to get adults to do these things, even when adults are being paid for their efforts, so it is understandably more difficult to require young people to cooperate in the performance of unpaid labor.

Play, custody, and work are different characteristics of educational institutions. Play often competes for student attention and energy. The custodial characteristics of schools allow the society to manage the daytime behavior of large numbers of youth. The worklike organization of schools often contradicts stated educational goals of encouraging students to think, explore, create, and gain independence.

Attempts to reemphasize education at the expense of play or other organizational characteristics of schools often generate much conflict and controversy. For example, the state of Texas, spurred by the efforts of H. Ross Perot, adopted a strict statewide rule prohibiting public school students from engaging in sports or any other extracurricular activities following the six weeks after a grading period if they failed a single class. When reports cards were sent out for the first time in the fall of 1985 under these new rules, thousands of football players, cheerleaders, band members, and others had to withdraw from their extracurricular activities, and many teams had to cancel the rest of their season schedule. Reactions ranged from angry condemnations of the new rule to enthusiastic praise for finally "getting tough."

Texas business man, H. Ross Perot spearheaded a successful effort in that state to restore the priority of academics over extracurricular activities with "no pass—no play" rules for students.

The Expansion of Formal Education in Society

During the twentieth century there has been a tremendous expansion of formal education. In 1900 most adult Americans had no more than a few years of elementary education. By 1940 some three-fourths of American youths attended high school, but only 15 percent went on to college. Today nearly one-half of American youth attend college. Minimum educational requirements for most jobs have risen along with this expansion of schooling. Occupations that previously had no educational requirements now demand a high school diploma. Occupations that previously required a high school diploma now require a college degree. Occupations that previously hired college graduates with a bachelor's degree now demand a master's degree or even a doctorate. Highly competitive professional positions that previously required a doctorate now routinely require several years of postdoctoral training. In sum, most people in the United States undergo from twelve to twenty years of formal schooling before entering the occupational world.

This educational expansion is clearly one of the most significant changes in the relationship between education and society. It is not at all clear, however, why such a vast expansion for formal schooling has taken place in the United States and, to a considerable degree, in most other countries throughout the world. To some observers the increased complexity of work and society has required an increasingly better trained and educated work force.

The extent to which minorities and women have participated in and benefited from educational expansion is subject to varying interpretations. In terms of years of schooling, both racial minorities and women have significantly narrowed the gap between themselves and whites and men. Women, for example, finish high school, attend college, and finish college at rates at least as high as men. Blacks on the average complete nearly as many years of schooling as whites. The percentage of black high school graduates who enter college is nearly equal to that of white high school graduates (Blackwell, 1985:182–84).

Nevertheless, great economic disparities persist for both women and blacks. If there is a direct linkage between education and occupation, increasingly equal educational attainments should produce increasingly equal economic attainments. In fact, the earnings for women and black workers remain only about 60 percent of the earnings of male and white workers. As a result, this "learning without earning" has meant that recent educational expansion has not significantly diminished the economic inequalities experienced by women and racial groups in American society.

Higher Education in the United States

Higher education has undergone rapid expansion and change in recent decades. The expansion of higher education has taken place mainly in public colleges and universities. The greatest growth in enrollments has taken place at public two-year community colleges and four-year state colleges and universities. Enrollment in more expensive private institutions has remained fairly steady or even declined.

Students from the upper classes predominate at the most expensive and prestigious colleges and universities, whereas students from lower socioeconomic groups are far more numerous at public two- and four-year institutions. Moreover, students who graduate from many private colleges are more likely to go on to graduate and professional schools, enter the highest-status occupations and professions, and receive the highest incomes. Students who attend the recently expanded public two- and four-year colleges are less likely to pursue graduate or professional education and are more likely to occupy the less prestigious and lower-paying white-collar and technical jobs.

Research has also shown that college students from lower-income families are much more likely than those from higher-income families to drop out before graduating because of financial or other difficulties. Consequently, students from the upper class benefit the most, and those from the lower classes benefit the least from opportunities for higher education. The **tracking,** or channeling, pattern in higher education resembles the tracking pattern that emerged early in the twentieth century in the then newly developed comprehensive public high schools.

Blacks and Higher Education

Desegregation of higher education has produced significant improvements in education for all Americans. The opening up of segregated colleges and universities to students of all racial and ethnic backgrounds came about only as the result of many forms of prolonged struggle in the courts, in the streets, and on campuses.

The efforts to open up higher educational opportunities for blacks in historically white institutions also led to expanded opportunities for lower- and middle-class white students, especially at institutions that adopted "open admissions" policies of accepting all high school graduates. Between 1960 and 1981, while the number of black students between the ages of eighteen and twenty-four enrolled in college increased from 134,000 to over 750,000, the number of white students in the same age group grew from just over 2 million to over 6.5 million (Blackwell, 1985:183).

In 1960 more than one-half of blacks attending colleges were enrolled at historically black institutions. By 1981 that percentage had declined to just 18 percent. Most of the blacks enrolled in traditionally white institutions, however, were at two-year community colleges or at four-year public colleges that were becoming or had already become predominantly black (Blackwell, 1985:1982).

Desegregation of higher education produced difficult problems for historically black institutions that had always struggled under great hardship to provide higher education for blacks when blacks had been barred from white institutions. Historically, black institutions, however, have continued to produce a high percentage of the most educationally and professionally successful blacks in the United States. Meanwhile, blacks in predominantly white institutions have achieved notable progress, but they have also encountered various problems.

College completion rates for young blacks have increased substantially, but they are only about one-half the rate for young whites. In 1981, for example, 11.5 percent of blacks aged twenty-five to twenty-nine and 21.3 percent of whites in that age group had completed college (Blackwell, 1985:184–86).

Blacks continue to be substantially underrepresented in graduate and professional schools in the United States. During the early 1980s blacks comprised about 6 percent of students in graduate school and medical school and about 4 percent of all law school students. Blacks also received about 4 percent of all doctoral degrees, but over half of these degrees were conferred in one discipline—education. In general, since the cry of "reverse discrimination" was raised during the middle of the 1970s, black progress in higher education has been slowed and perhaps even reversed (Blackwell, 1985:186–89).

Functionalist and Conflict Theories of Education

The functionalist theory of education and society begins with the idea that American society is basically a **meritocracy.** A meritocracy is a society in which status is determined by ability and effort. In our meritocratic society, functionalists argue, there are important positions that must be filled by highly trained and talented persons. In a fair and democratic society all persons have more-or-less equal opportunities to compete for these more important (and more highly rewarded) positions.

Educational institutions, assert the functionalists, play a central role in this meritocratic process. They provide equality of opportunity for all to compete for positions. They provide the necessary training for the various occupational positions in society. Finally, they provide a rational and basically fair selection and allocation process that places people into the appropriate positions in society.

Education thus performs the functionally necessary tasks of providing trained personnel to fill positions throughout the entire social system.

The functionalist explanation of educational expansion consists of three assertions about the relationship between education and modern society. First, since the modern economic system demands a labor force of educated people, workers must learn basic reading, writing, and mathematical skills. Their work environment requires a cognitive competence, because work is organized in an increasingly rational, technical, and efficient manner. Workers not only need to learn the particular skills to perform their job; they also need to learn rational ways of thinking and behaving in order to function effectively in the modern economic and social system.

Second, modern society requires that schools provide citizenship training and general moral education. Drawing upon the theories of Emile Durkheim, functionalists argue that schools must instill in people a set of common values and a sense of patriotism and membership in society. Because modern societies are made up of many different groups of people performing different work or functions, their unity or cohesion cannot be taken for granted. Educational institutions must consciously strive to create a "moral or cultural consensus" in society.

Third, the expansion of educational institutions is necessary to guarantee equality of opportunity to all citizens and to sort out and select the right people for the right positions in the society. Educational institutions discover and develop the most talented persons for the most demanding positions in an increasingly complex economic system. Educational expansion makes opportunities available to all youth, allowing them to compete for the most highly rewarded positions in their society. The expansion of the number of high schools and of colleges, which were available initially to white males and subsequently available to racial minorities and women, is viewed by functionalists as necessary to insure that society benefits from the contributions of all of its members.

Functionalists assert that schools instill common values and patriotism in a society's youth, while conflict theorists assert that schools impose the dominant group's values on young people.

The conflict theory of education and society begins with the assertion that society consists of conflicting groups who compete for control over educational institutions, as well as control over all other institutions in society. The group that establishes its dominance uses its position to control the educational system in its own interests, not in the interests of society as a whole. Although the dominant group may claim that the educational system and the society function in a meritocratic way, conflict theorists feel that in reality, the schools are run to maintain the dominance of privileged elites over subordinate groups.

Conflict theory thus asserts that those at the top of our society owe their position not only to talent or training but also to privilege and unfair advantages. "Those at the top essentially control the educational system and thus make sure that children of privileged groups have great advantages over children of disadvantaged groups" (Hurn, 1985:63). Social and economic inequalities thus undermine any real equality of opportunity that may be provided by education.

Conflict theorists believe that in addition to knowledge and skills, schools teach respect for authority, conformity, compliance, and acceptance of the social order. In other words, they socialize the children of the lower social classes to accept their subordinate position in the society. Additionally, if the schools can also convince people that all this has been done fairly, then people will accept their positions in society without challenging existing arrangements. For example, Bowles and Gintis (1976) interpreted three important periods of educational expansion—compulsory elementary schooling during the nineteenth century, secondary schooling or high schools during the early part of the twentieth century, and colleges and universities in recent decades—primarily in terms of capitalist efforts to discipline and control the working class. In their research they attempt to show that nineteenth-century factory owners promoted compulsory education for workers because they believed that this education would produce workers who worked hard, respected the bosses' authority, and avoided disorderly and rebellious behavior. Owners were more interested in this "moral" training than in the cognitive skills of their workers.

Later on, during the early years of the twentieth century, employers faced an increasingly militant working class that was fighting for unions and sometimes attracted to socialist political ideas. They also needed to train both industrial workers and the increasing numbers of white-collar workers. The solution to both these problems was the creation of the comprehensive high schools. Not only would the high schools indoctrinate all groups of workers into a greater sense of loyalty and identification with the capitalist order, the high schools would also produce skilled workers by providing an academic curriculum to train middle-class white-collar workers and a vocational curriculum to train working-class industrial workers.

Further, even though the comprehensive high school tracked, or channeled, working class youth into preparation for working-class occupations and middle-class youth into preparation for white-collar occupations, this was done in a way that appeared to be fair, scientific, and nondiscriminatory. Intelligence tests were developed and used to determine the track in which children should be placed. According to Bowles and Gintis, the tests were used to justify the channeling of working class and racial minority children into lower educational tracks.

More recently, the great expansion of higher education has again reflected the needs and interests of the capitalist order. The expansion of higher education has created a highly stratified system of colleges and universities, similar to the stratified tracking system that exists in high schools. Working-class youth who attend college mainly attend two-year community colleges and public four-year colleges, whereas elite institutions remain populated mainly by upper- and upper-middle-class students. Thus, Bowles and Gintis feel that education trains the various kinds of workers required by the capitalist economic system. While making it seem that everyone has an equal opportunity to get a higher education and a better job, the educational system actually continues to track people into unequal positions in the society.

A different kind of interpretation of educational expansion within the general framework of conflict theory comes particularly from the work of Collins (1979). In Collins's view, it is neither the general needs of society as a whole nor the interests of the capitalist elite that explain educational expansion. Rather, it is a process of status competition among groups in society that at least partly explains educational expansion. In the United States, especially, various racial and ethnic groups compete for the acquisition of educational credentials. Increasingly, the credentials, or the degrees, are more important than whatever knowledge, skills, and attitudes people may have learned. Intense competition for credentials causes an increasing number of people to seek and obtain an increasing number of credentials. Although the existing occupations, the needs of society, or the interests of the capitalist order do not require all this schooling, the competition for prized credentials and status does.

In summary, different theories of educational expansion are in a sense different views of the relationship between schooling and work. Functionalists believe that schooling provides people with the preparation they need to be effective

Students from high income families are more likely to attend prestigious and expensive private universities and colleges, while students from lower income families are more likely to attend two-year community colleges or four-year state colleges and universities.

"The Paper Chase!"—Schools encourage competition for prized credentials and status.

workers. Bowles and Gintis believe that schooling prepares workers to accept the authority and domination of capitalist employers. Whereas functionalists view education in a benign or positive light, Bowles and Gintis view it more critically or negatively. Collins sees much less of a "fit," or connection, between schooling and work. People are not necessarily well educated or well indoctrinated through schooling. By putting in a lot of time, however, they obtain valued credentials. Although the schooling itself may be unimportant and ineffective, the credentials are very important, or at least both employees and employers act as if they are.

Education and Equality of Opportunity

According to the functionalists, one of the most important objectives of educational institutions is to provide equality of opportunity for all members of society to compete for all positions in the system of social stratification. The view of American society as an open society rests in large part on the principle that regardless of social class or race, educational institutions provide opportunities for anyone to rise as high as his or her talents and efforts can take him or her.

In contrast to the functionalists, conflict sociologists assert that educational institutions maintain the inequality of opportunity. Conflict sociologists feel that the function of educational institutions is not to allow people to get ahead, but rather to keep people "in their place" and to reinforce social inequalities. Specifically, Bowles and Gintis (1976) argued that "equal opportunity" is merely rhetoric that conceals the process whereby schools reproduce and legitimate inequalities of social class in capitalist society.

Although much of the argument over whether there is equality of educational opportunity reflects strong ideological differences, research may contribute to our understanding of educational opportunity as well as any limits on that opportunity. For example, if the expansion of education has increased equality of opportunity, then children of disadvantaged groups in society should experience a general increase in upward social mobility in American society. Research on social mobility has shown that although a few outstanding representatives of disadvantaged youth, such as star athletes, may have experienced significant upward mobility, the vast majority of persons have remained relatively fixed in the economic position in the United States during the past century.

Another measure of equality of educational opportunity is reflected in meritocratic results. That is, the educational system will identify and select the most meritorious, or the best, students from all social backgrounds and channel them into the appropriate positions in the system of social stratification. If this is the case, then talented children from disadvantaged groups ought to be just as likely as talented children from privileged groups to achieve high-status positions. There is some evidence to support this expectation: greater numbers of children from disadvantaged backgrounds attend and complete college in comparison to earlier historical periods. On the other hand, research has shown that children from disadvantaged economic backgrounds whose standardized test scores and grades are high are much less likely to attend college and complete as many years of education as children from economically privileged backgrounds with the same test scores and grades. To put it another way, the economic status of one's family is often an important determinant of educational opportunities. For example, Coleman (1966) has argued in an influential government report that "school factors" are not as important as "family background" factors in determining educational achievement levels.

With regard to race and equality of opportunity, the integration of schools in the United States since the 1954 *Brown v. Board of Education* decision of the U.S. Supreme Court is often cited as evidence of the extension of equality of educational opportunity to blacks. Busing, Equal Employment Opportunity (EEO) programs, and other affirmative action efforts represent additional evidence of expanded educational opportunities for racial minorities.

Sociologists, however, have found many factors that limit or deny equality of opportunity to poor and minority students. First, there is a large network of expensive private schools that serve the children of the well-to-do. Not only do these schools have the resources to provide the highest-quality education; they also provide the contacts and the "networks" that perpetuate the privileges of the upper class.

An even larger group of private schools, although not as expensive as schools for the upper-class youth, are nonetheless racially exclusive. These are primarily "Christian" schools that in many cases were founded to escape court-ordered racial desegregation. Their enrollment has continued to increase rapidly during the 1970s and 1980s.

In addition to the inequalities between private and public schools, there are also inequalities among public schools. First, there are the inequalities between urban (inner-city) school systems and wealthier suburban school systems. The educational atmosphere is often much more favorable in the latter than in the former, even when there are not great differences in expenditures. Unequal opportunity may also be found within a single school system, because the schools that serve certain areas may provide better educational opportunities than others. Finally, a great deal of inequality of opportunity may be found within any individual school. The practice of "ability grouping," or tracking that is usually begun in the early grades and continued through high school, produces unequal educational experiences for children. Many analysts argue that "ability grouping" tends to increase inequality by accelerating the progress of some students and slowing down the progress of others.

There are additional factors that are obstacles to equality of educational opportunity for blacks and other racial minorities. These include significant resegregation that has taken place in many cities. The desegregated public school systems of many U.S. cities today, such as Atlanta, Baltimore, Chicago, Boston, St. Louis, Detroit, and Philadelphia, have enrollments that are between 60 and 90 percent black. "White flight" to nearby suburban school systems or to private schools has produced widespread racial resegregation. Finally, within desegregated public schools black students tend to have higher rates of suspensions and dropping out than whites. The authors of some studies in this area argue that many blacks are "forced out" by discriminatory administrative policies (Blackwell, 1985:160–61).

Busing and Affirmative Action

The U.S. Supreme Court in 1954 declared racially segregated schools unconstitutional and ordered that integration should take place "with all deliberate speed." From 1954 through the decade of the 1960s very little school desegregation took place; great majorities of both black and white children continued to attend racially segregated schools. Political and educational leaders employed a variety of techniques to preserve racial segregation. During the 1970s the courts ordered several school systems to make extensive use of busing to bring about an end to segregated school systems. Where busing programs had the support of local political leadership, there was only brief and limited opposition. In Boston and other cities, however, white politicians spearheaded violently racist opposition to court-ordered busing.

Even before busing programs had begun, "white flight" from the inner city to the surrounding suburbs was a well-established pattern, and many urban neighborhoods rapidly changed over from white to black. Busing programs that were

Busing has enabled children from segregated neighborhoods to attend integrated schools.

met with intense white hostility accelerated this white flight from both the city and the public school system. Under these circumstances, it was impossible for busing to be more than partially successful in integrating urban school systems. Many of the problems associated with busing, however, should be blamed not on busing itself, but on longstanding racial and social class inequalities, as well as often racially motivated white opposition to busing. Until and unless residential segregation by race is eliminated, busing will have only limited success in reducing school segregation or improving educational opportunities for minorities.

The principle of affirmative action involves the establishment of special procedures to encourage and consider minority applicants, as well as the setting of numerical goals or timetables for measuring actual progress. Affirmative action programs have been adopted in circumstances of education and employment where there was clear evidence of previous longstanding racial discrimination.

Affirmative action programs have been attacked as "reverse discrimination" by opponents who claim that such programs unfairly enable less-qualified minorities and women to be selected at the expense of better-qualified whites and males. Evidence provides little support, however, for those who make such claims. No affirmative action programs require that "unqualified" minorities be accepted, although racially discriminatory and irrelevant measures of "qualifications" have sometimes been eliminated as a result of affirmative action. Racial minorities are still substantially underrepresented both as students and faculty in colleges, graduate, and professional programs. Moreover, since the assault on affirmative action during the early 1970s, there has been little or no further progress for racial minorities in these areas. With black unemployment rates during the mid-1980s nearly two and one-half times as high as those for whites, it seems evident that what prevails is not reverse discrimination but continued discrimination toward blacks and other racial minorities. The widespread opposition to busing and affirmative action since the 1970s had hindered progress toward equality of educational opportunity in the United States.

Educational Achievement

If schools educated all students equally, the educational achievements of all students ought to entitle them to equal access to positions in the system of social stratification. In fact, however, educational achievement is very much related to both social class and race.

Coleman (1966) and Jencks (1972) have argued that inequalities in educational achievement are primarily due to differences in children and their family backgrounds. Coleman believed that his research showed that racial and social class differences in achievement could not be attributed to differences in the schools attended by black or poor students. Instead, cultural factors, particularly the home environment, were more decisive. In a reanalysis of Coleman's data, Jencks also concluded that lower achievement levels of black and poor students could not be blamed primarily on schools but on a combination of home, inherited ability, and "luck."

Critics of Coleman and Jencks argued that their research was both methodologically flawed and politically biased (Ryan, 1977). Coleman and Jencks failed to consider and measure the real educational inequalities encountered by black and poor students. By letting the schools off the hook for the inequalities in educational achievement of poor and minority students, they provided support to politicians looking for excuses to make drastic cutbacks in the funding of educational programs in general and educational programs for the disadvantaged in particular. The critics of this research countered further by asserting that the differential results in educational achievement as measured by test scores or grades are guaranteed by insuring that schools are geared to middle- and upper-class whites, that ability grouping and tracking places more black and poor children in "slower" tracks, and that standardized tests are subtly biased against black and poor students.

Intelligence and I.Q. Tests

When comprehensive high schools, with their different tracks for college preparatory and vocational students, were established early in the twentieth century, I.Q. tests became widely used as the means for deciding which children belonged in which track. The founders of I.Q. testing in the United States (Terman, Yerkes, Goddard, and others) asserted that the tests proved that white Anglo-Saxons and upper-class people inherited superior intelligence to other ethnic and racial groups and lower classes (Kamin, 1974; Chase, 1977).

Since World War I a debate has raged over the value of I.Q. and similar standard tests. Jensen (1969) has argued that efforts to improve the educational achievements of blacks were doomed to fail because blacks possessed fewer "intelligence genes" than whites. Herrnstein (1971; 1973) claimed that the lower classes of all races were sure to remain poor and unemployed because they lacked the intelligence to perform productive roles in society.

Critics (e.g., Kamin, 1974) have shown that claims that intelligence is inherited are derived from fraudulent studies and that I.Q. tests are biased in the aptitudes, values, and knowledge they measure. Explanations of unequal educational achievement that blame either the cultural or the genetic characteristics of racial minorities and the poor are ways of "blaming the victim" (Persell, 1977; Ryan, 1977). Bowles and Gintis (1976) further suggested that schooling necessarily produces unequal educational achievement because schools channel children from poor and minority group backgrounds into lower tracks and use the resulting unequal educational achievements as proof that those at the bottom have failed because they lack ability, intelligence, or motivation.

A more moderate view of testing suggests that despite the flaws in methodological design and cultural bias, tests do reflect a level of achievement. If schools teach knowledge and skills, tests can measure whether students possess that knowledge, and the tests can also measure the proficiency of the students' skills. These researchers argue that if the emphasis is placed on knowledge rather than intelligence or ability, tests are a very valuable tool. Problems with testing then are a result of the social and political interpretation of test results rather than inadequacies in the test design.

Summary

Educational institutions contribute to society by transmitting the society's culture, by sorting and allocating people into different positions in the structure of social stratification, and by discovering and teaching knowledge and skills. Functionalist theory asserts that these contributions meet the needs of the entire society and provide opportunity to all members of society. Conflict theory asserts that the dominant group in society controls educational institutions and uses them to reproduce and justify social inequality.

There is substantial disagreement among sociologists over what schools teach, how much they teach, and the consequences of what is taught. The characteristics of the social organization of schools include play, custody and work. These characteristics may interfere with the educational process, because the organizational framework and environment of schools often downplay the importance of learning and increase problems of discipline and motivation.

The expansion of higher education in the United States has created a stratified system of higher education. Although racial minorities have made some gains in learning, their educational accomplishments have not translated into comparable gains in earning potential.

The expansion of educational institutions can be viewed positively as a means of providing greater education and greater opportunities for all members of society, or it can be viewed more critically as a means of extending greater social control over all segments of the population while perpetuating social inequalities. Equality of educational opportunities is limited by the pervasive impact of the inequalities of social class and race in American society. Busing and affirmative action programs represent two attempts at improving educational opportunities for racial minorities.

Educational ability has traditionally been measured with I.Q. and standardized achievement tests. Unequal educational achievement is often explained by pointing to the alleged inferior characteristics of disadvantaged groups, but conflict theorists feel that differences in educational achievement are due to inherent contradictions in the organizational structure of educational institutions and the continued presence of racism in the schools.

Key Concepts

affirmative action
blaming the victim
desegregation

integration
meritocracy
tracking

References

Blackwell, James E. (1985) *The Black Community—Diversity and Unity.* 2d ed. New York, N.Y.: Harper & Row, Publishers.

Boudon, Raymond. (1974) *Education, Opportunity, and Social Inequality.* New York, N.Y.: John Wiley & Sons, Inc.

Bowles, Samuel, and Herbert Gintis. (1976) *Schooling in Capitalist America.* New York, N.Y.: Basic Books, Inc., Publishers.

Carnoy, Martin (ed.). (1975) *Schooling in a Corporate Society.* New York, N.Y.: David McKay Co., Inc.

Chase, Allan. (1977) *The Legacy of Malthus—The Social Costs of the New Scientific Racism.* New York, N.Y.: Alfred A. Knopf, Inc.

Coleman, James et al. (1966) *Equality of Educational Opportunity.* Washington, D.C.: U.S. Government Printing Office.

Collins, Randall. (1979) *The Credential Society.* New York, N.Y.: Academic Press, Inc.

Fitzgerald, Frances. (1979) *America Revisited: History Schoolbooks in the Twentieth Century.* Boston, Mass.: Little, Brown and Company.

Greer, Colin. (1973) *The Great School Legend.* New York, N.Y.: The Viking Press, Inc.

Herrnstein, Richard. (1971) "I.Q." *Atlantic Monthly.* (September):43–64.

———. (1973) *I.Q. in the Meritocracy.* Boston, Mass.: Little, Brown and Company.

Hurn, Christopher. (1985) *The Limits and Possibilities of Schooling: An Introduction to the Sociology of Education.* 2d ed. Boston, Mass.: Allyn & Bacon, Inc.

Jencks, Christopher. (1972) *Inequality.* New York, N.Y.: Basic Books, Inc., Publishers.

———. (1979) *Who Gets Ahead?.* New York, N.Y.: Basic Books, Inc., Publishers.

Jensen, Arthur. (1969) "How Much Can We Boost I.Q. and Scholastic Achievement?" *Harvard Educational Review, 39:*1–123. Jan.–Mar. (Quarterly).

Kamin, Leon. (1974) *The Science and Politics of I.Q..* Potomac, Md.,: Erlbaum Associates.

Katz, Michael. (1975) *Class, Bureaucracy, and Schools.* New York, N.Y.: Praeger Publishers, Inc.

Meyer, John W. (1977) "The Effects of Education as an Institution." *American Journal of Sociology, 83*(July):55–77.

National Commission on Excellence in Education. (1983) *A Nation at Risk.* Washington, D.C.: U.S. Government Publishing Office.

Persell, Caroline Hodges. (1977) *Education and Inequality.* New York, N.Y.: The Free Press.

Ryan, William. (1977) *Blaming the Victim.* 2d ed. New York: Vintage/Random House.

18

Sport as a Social Institution

OBJECTIVES

After completion of this chapter, the student should be able to:

1. Define sport and distinguish the different levels of sport.
2. Explain how sport is a microcosm of society.
3. Compare and contrast the functionalist and conflict views of the role of sport in society.
4. Discuss how sport promotes and reinforces the values of society.
5. Discuss the ways that sport promotes and impedes upward social mobility in society.
6. Describe the differences between black, Hispanic, and white involvement in sport.
7. Discuss the participation of women in sport.

INTRODUCTION

Sport is a social institution that affects the lives of almost everyone in the United States. The vast majority of American youth and adults participate in sports as athletes, spectators, consumers of sports clothing and equipment, gamblers on sporting events, or as members of a society whose culture puts great emphasis on competitive sports. It is thus not surprising that the sociology of sport has become an important area of study during recent decades. College courses, research, and writing on the sociology of sport have shown that the sociological approach can yield important and refreshing new insights into the study of sport.

Most of us have had a great deal of personal experience with sport, including some of the happiest and saddest moments of our lives. Because we tend to experience sport from a very early age and in a highly emotional and personal way, we usually do not get the opportunity to stop and think about sport in a more detached and scientific manner. This chapter begins by distinguishing between sport and recreation. We then discuss how the world of sport is a reflection of the larger society of which it is a part. Next, we examine how differences of social class, race, and gender affect the world of sport. Finally, we see that sport is both a source of opportunity and a source of social problems.

Definition of Sport

Everyone knows what **sport** is, but it is nevertheless not easy to define sport. Spreitzer and Snyder, two influential sports sociologists, assert that sport has three essential characteristics: Sport "is governed by established rules, competitive, and characterized by physical exertion." If one of these ingredients is missing, the activity is not sport. For example, such games as chess or bridge involve rules and competition, but, strictly speaking, they are not sports because they lack physical exertion. Dog racing involves no human physical activity and is not a sport, but horse racing and auto racing involve jockeys and drivers and hence are sports. Swimming or jogging for exercise or recreation is not sport, but when these activities are undertaken competitively with specific rules, then they are sports.

Sports may thus be distinguished from recreation, play, leisure, or games. You may occupy your leisure time with many activities other than sports. In fact, national surveys have shown that eating, watching television, listening to the radio, and reading books are the leisure activities engaged in by the most people in the United States (ABC News-Harris Survey, 1979). Play and games may lack the elements of physical activity, competition, and rules that are part of the definition of sport. Sport is only one kind of recreational activity, and recreational sports are often distinguished from more highly organized forms of sport activity.

Recreation also includes the so-called fitness craze of recent years. Millions of Americans today run or jog regularly, work out at health spas or other facilities, or participate in strenuous physical activity. The industry that provides the clothing and equipment for these activities has grown enormously. Many women have become involved in fitness-related activities, thus contributing to greater equality of women and men in sport as well.

Nevertheless, there remains good reason for concern over the lack of physical activity of the majority of citizens in the United States. Surveys have indicated that perhaps as many as four-fifths of all American adults do not engage in any regular physical activities (Persell, 1984). The President's Council on Physical Fitness (1979) reported finding a disturbing decline in physical exercise and fitness among both children and adults. Thus, the "fitness craze" may be mainly concentrated among certain sections of the population, particularly upper-middle-class young adults.

In addition to defining sport, it is also helpful to recognize the existence of different levels of sport. Eitzen and Sage (1982) identified these levels as **informal sport, organized sport,** and **corporate sport.**

Informal sport is sport engaged in primarily for the enjoyment of the participants. Backyard and playground games of touch football or basketball are examples of informal sport. The rules are mainly made up by the participants and not by a formal regulatory body.

Organized sport, as the name implies, involves formal organization, including established teams, leagues, and rules. Examples include most adult-organized

Corporate sport is more like work than play for the professional athlete.

youth sport programs, as well as community-based adult programs in such sports as softball and volleyball.

Corporate sport is sport that exists primarily for the purpose of making money. Teams are owned by business people, and the athletes are paid employees. Professional football, basketball, and baseball are the main examples of corporate sport, but big-time college sport also possesses many of the characteristics of corporate sport.

Sport sociologists have pointed out that the progression from informal sport through organized sport to corporate sport is also a progression from "play" to "work." The element of play or enjoyment is primary in informal sport, but the element of work—a job—tends to be primary in corporate sport. The progression from informal to corporate sport is also one of increasing bureaucratization.

Some sociologists have also identified a fourth category, called either **pseudosport** or **trash sports.** Examples include professional wrestling, roller derby, demolition derby, various televised "celebrity" competitions, and the like. These are "fixed" entertainment spectacles staged for the purpose of making money. They are not true competitive events and hence, not true sport.

Sport and its influence are found throughout modern societies. Sporting goods and clothing are a multibillion-dollar industry. Sport programming makes up nearly one-fifth of all television programming, and most of the all-time most popular television programs have been sporting events. For many the sports section is the most popular section of newspapers. Millions of children play informal and organized sports, and sport is often the most enjoyable and most memorable part of many children's lives. Businesses hire athletes to sell their products, and politicians try to use athletes to enhance their political causes. Our language is full of widely used sport cliches, such as "cheap shot," "ball-park figure," "out of bounds," and "game plan." Some sociologists have argued that sport has essentially taken over the weekend from religion and become the "civic religion" in the United States. A social activity that is as pervasive as sport should therefore certainly be studied in sociology.

Sport as a Microcosm

Sociologists have also pointed out that sport is a **microcosm** of society. That is, sport is a replica, a small-scale, "little-world" version of society as a whole. To the sociologist this means that you can gain important insights into the nature of a society by studying the nature of sport activity in that society. Also, you can better understand the nature of sport if you realize how it is shaped by the society in which it is located. These close relationships between society and sport are recognized and emphasized by both defenders and critics of the status quo in society and sport. Defenders emphasize how participation in sport teaches character traits valued by society and helps to maintain the existing society. Critics emphasize how sport reflects the problems that exist in the larger society and how sport diverts people's attention away from dealing with those problems.

The sportscaster Howard Cosell makes clear in the following passage why sport should be viewed as a microcosm of society:

> Once upon a time, the legend had it, there was a world that remained separate and apart from all others, a privileged sanctuary from real life. It was the wonderful world of sport, where every competition was endowed with an inherent purity, every athlete a shining example of noble young manhood, and every owner was motivated by his love of the game and his concern for the public interest. . . . The sports establishment—the commissioners, the owners, the leagues, the National Collegiate Athletic Association—would have us believe the legend. . . . The plain truth is that sport is a reflection of the society, that it is human life in microcosm, that it has within it the maladies of the society, that some athletes drink, that some athletes do take drugs, that there is racism in sport, that the sports establishment is quite capable of defying the public interest, and that in this contemporary civilization sport does invade sociology, economics, law, and politics. (Howard Cosell, "Sports and Good-bye to All That," *The New York Times,* April 5, 1971:33)

As Cosell points out, whatever problems are widespread in the larger society can also be found in sport, even if many people try to pretend otherwise. Drug abuse, racism, and conflict between opposing special-interest groups exist in sport, just as they do in the larger society.

Functionalist and Conflict Views of Sport

The two main theoretical perspectives in sociology—functionalist and conflict—have been applied to the study of sport. Jay Coakley (1984) has summarized and compared the functionalist and conflict views on sport and society.

The functionalist approach focuses on how sport contributes to meeting the basic needs of the social system. First, sport is a "backup" institution of socialization. It helps the family, school, and religion teach people the values of society. Sport teaches the importance of rules, hard work, competition, teamwork, efficiency, authority, and success. Sport also helps maintain the social system by providing an outlet for aggressive energies for both players and spectators.

Conflict theorists assert that the athlete's body may be harmed by overuse while the spectator's body is harmed by underuse.

Second, sport integrates, or brings people together, by promoting common identification with teams that represent a school, community, city, state, or even an entire society. Third, sport teaches members of society the goals they should strive for and the appropriate means for their attainment. In many sports the goal to be attained is actually called a "goal." Players try to reach or score a "goal" in football, in soccer and hockey. The rules of the game also prescribe the appropriate means for scoring a "goal."

Fourth, sport promotes adaptation and survival by encouraging physical well-being, fitness, and skills. In modern societies many people live and work in essentially unhealthful circumstances. Sport provides a means for adaptation to these conditions by engaging in wholesome physical activity. In sum, sport is functional for society because it contributes to socialization, to tension management, group integration, goal attainment, and adaptation to change.

The conflict approach sharply contrasts with the functionalist approach. The conflict perspective focuses on how sport is affected by the problems and inequalities of society. First, sport generates and intensifies alienation. That is, neither athletes nor spectators are in control of sporting activity. The athlete's physical and mental skills are used for business profit, and the spectator is also exploited and rendered passive and denied the benefits of active participation in sport. The athlete's body is often harmed by overuse, the spectator's by underuse.

Second, corporate and organized sport are increasingly set up like the bureaucratic, authoritarian capitalist work place. The athlete is essentially a worker who takes orders from owners, managers, and coaches. The world of sport thus trains people to accept the world of work.

Third, sport is an important source of commercial profit. Team owners, television networks, newspapers and magazines, the clothing and sporting good industries, beer advertisers, and other businesses all make large sums of money from sport. Though much attention is focused on the high salaries of a few athletic superstars, it is businesses that reap the greatest economic rewards from sport.

Fourth, sport promotes nationalistic, racist, and sexist prejudices. It arouses workers of different cities, countries, and nationalities against each other. In extreme cases it inflames violent militaristic conflicts between different groups.

Fifth, sport is an opiate—a drug—whereby extreme fan involvement with sport undermines awareness of political, social, and economic realities. Long hours of watching sport on television serve as an escape from the real world. At the same time, the belief that sport provides widespread opportunities for upward social mobility legitimates the existing social structure. Sport promotes the belief that success is the result of hard work and talent, and that failure and poverty are the result of inferiority and laziness. These beliefs encourage people to accept the inequalities of capitalism as just and appropriate.

Thus, whereas the functionalist view emphasizes how sport contributes to the maintenance of society, the conflict view emphasizes how sport contributes to social problems and injustices. The functionalist view may apply more to the informal and organized levels of sport and especially to youth sport, whereas the conflict view may apply more to adult corporate sport. Which view you think applies more to the United States probably depends more on your view of American society than on your view of sport.

Olympic organizers used the 1984 games to promote patriotism.

Sport and Societal Values

Because sport is a microcosm of society, it both reflects and promotes the basic values of society. Several writers have analyzed how sport mirrors the basic values of American society. Eitzen and Sage (1982) focused on the most dominant American values, such as success, competition, and the appropriate means for achieving success. Sport teaches the importance of winning or succeeding; it uses competition to motivate people to try their best; and it teaches people that hard work, continual striving, and deferred gratification are the appropriate means for achieving success.

Sports sociologist Harry Edwards (1973) has called the core values of American sport the American **sports creed.** This American sports creed consists of six essential parts: (1) sport builds good character; (2) sport develops discipline; (3) sport competition builds fortitude and prepares the athlete for life; (4) sport promotes physical fitness; (5) sport promotes mental fitness and educational achievement; and (6) sport promotes patriotism or nationalism and religiosity. After a careful and thoughtful analysis, Edwards concluded that these claims that are commonly made as part of the American sports creed rest on very little evidence. In other words, they are ideological beliefs rather than scientifically substantiated facts.

Functionalist and conflict sociologists agree that sport promotes and reinforces societal values, but they disagree over *which* values are promoted and reinforced by sport. Whereas functionalists assert that sport builds character, discipline, and competitiveness, conflict theories argue that sport often undermines character, substitutes repressive authority for discipline, and encourages excessive competitiveness. Too much emphasis on winning encourages illegal and unethical means of achieving success, dictatorial and dehumanizing coaching methods, and a sense of failure and inferiority among the great majority of athletes who are not the best.

Adults often make youth sport highly competitive.

Whereas functionalists assert that sport promotes physical and mental fitness, conflict theorists argue that sport sacrifices the physical well-being of the athlete to concern for winning or making money. Similarly, sport success often conflicts with academic success in high school or college. Many good high school athletes are unable to attend college because their academic record is too weak, and a majority of college athletes use up their varsity eligibility and never graduate from college.

Whereas functionalists assert that sport promotes patriotism and religiosity, conflict theorists argue that whipping up patriotic and religious fervor threatens international peace and diverts attention away from national problems.

Finally, whereas functionalists assert that sport teaches athletes the appropriate means for achieving goals, conflict theorists argue that the cheating, lying, win-at-all-costs behavior often found in sport reflects the dog-eat-dog struggle for supremacy found in the economics and politics of capitalism. In a sense then, functionalist and conflict theorists agree that people learn values from sports that they apply in life, but functionalists assert that people generally learn desirable values, and conflict theorists argue that people generally learn undesirable values.

Sport and Social Class

Social class differences affect all areas of American society. Because sport is a microcosm of society, we should expect to find that these differences also have a significant impact on the world of sport. Research has shown that there are significant social class differences in sports involvement. At least three important kinds of social class differences have been clearly identified. First, upper- and middle-class people are more likely to be involved in sports as active participants, whereas poor and working-class people are more likely to be passive viewers or spectators. Second, among active participants, middle- and upper-class people are more likely to be involved in individual sports, whereas poor and working-class people are more likely to be involved in team sports. Third, there are certain sports that are generally upper- and middle-class sports, such as polo, yacht racing, golf, and tennis, whereas there are other sports that are generally poor and working-class sports, such as basketball, football, baseball, softball, and ice hockey. To a certain extent, football, baseball, and basketball, as well as some other sports, are virtually national sports engaged in by members of all social classes.

Why do these social class differences in sports participation and preference exist? A number of reasons have been cited. Middle- and upper-class people are more likely than poor and working-class people to be active participants in sport because middle- and upper-class people have occupations that leave them with more leisure time and more energy to engage in physical activity. Upper- and middle-class people are also generally in better health than poor and working-class people. Working-class people may feel too worn out after a typical workday to do more than watch a football game on television.

Explanations for why members of different social classes engage in different sports activities take into account several factors. First, upper- and middle-class people are more likely to choose individual rather than team sports because participation in individual sports can be made to accommodate the highly changeable daily routine of business and professional people. Upper- and middle-class people can play golf, tennis, or racketball during any afternoon, during a long lunch break, or during any other time they may take a break from work. They need coordinate their sport activity with no more than one other person. Team sports, in contrast, usually require a rigid regular practice and playing schedule that must be adhered to by a large number of people. People playing an organized team sport must attend practice every Tuesday and Thursday afternoon or evening and play a game every Saturday or Sunday afternoon, for example. Many middle- and upper-class people prefer the flexibility of individual sports.

Working-class people, on the other hand, usually have fairly regular work hours and are accustomed to engaging in sports and recreational activities with larger numbers of other people at playgrounds, gyms, or bowling alleys. They can usually participate at the same time each week. They cannot take long lunch hours or take off afternoons, and they do not travel on business.

A second important reason for social class differences in sports preferences is obviously financial. The individual sports engaged in by many upper- and middle-class people are simply too expensive for most working-class people. Ownership of a boat for yachting or sailing, ownership of golf clubs and payment of greens fees, or keeping a horse for polo is clearly beyond the means of most working-class people. In addition, the facilities for yachting, sailing, golf, tennis, polo, and swimming are often available only at private country clubs. Membership in private country clubs is quite expensive, and many private clubs have traditionally restricted, formally or informally, their membership to wealthy white Protestants.

Children who grow up in a country club environment will certainly be more likely to participate in such sports as golf, swimming, and tennis and continue to enjoy these sports as adults. Children who grow up in a working-class environment in which they cannot afford to participate in these sports and are denied

Upper-class people are more likely to participate in individual sports that require expensive equipment or membership in exclusive clubs, while lowerclass people are more likely to participate in team sports using inexpensive equipment.

Pseudosports offer extreme versions of "good guys" and "bad guys" fighting it out.

access to sport facilities will instead play basketball, baseball, football, and the like on nearby streets and playgrounds.

The writer Thorstein Veblen, who frequently satirized efforts by the rich to portray themselves as superior to other classes of people, suggested another reason why upper-class people engage in particular sports. He argued that the rich engage in certain activities in order to show off their wealth and status. The rich use sport as a form of **conspicuous consumption** that demonstrates that they are rich enough to have both the money and the leisure time to do what the nonrich cannot do.

Sociologists have also used Veblen's concept of conspicuous consumption to explain why the upper classes support a certain version of the ideal of amateur sport. Only upper-class people can afford to devote great amounts of time to the Olympics or other forms of "amateur" sports without any kind of financial support.

Finally, a factor that seems to be involved in social class differences in sports preferences is physical contact. Upper-class people seem to be less likely to participate in those team sports that emphasize a great deal of physical contact, physical strength, and relatively high risk of personal injury, such as boxing, football, and ice hockey.

Although some analysts stress cultural differences between the upper and lower classes in explaining why working-class people are more likely to participate in physical contact sports, the primary reason probably has much to do with economics. Upper- and middle-class people have no need to subject themselves to the physical punishment and risks involved in such sports as boxing, football, and ice hockey. They have many easier and safer ways to make a good living and retain their middle- or upper-class status. On the other hand, many poor and working-class youth see these sports as offering them the best or the only opportunity to make money and get ahead. Other choices, such as dangerous blue-collar jobs or crime, pay less and involve at least the same risk of physical injury.

Thus, social class differences in sports participation are highly significant

Functionalist and Conflict Views of Sport

and have several important causes. Social class also significantly affects people's behavior as spectators or viewers of sports in a number of important ways. First, spectators for certain sports, such as golf or tennis, are mostly middle- and upper-class people, whereas spectators for automobile racing and pseudosports (particularly professional wrestling, roller derby, demolition derby) are mostly working-class people. Pseudosports try to appeal to working-class people by offering blatant violence or pseudoviolence, by encouraging intense emotional involvement of spectators, and by promoting extreme versions of "good guys" and "bad guys" fighting it out. Spectators are encouraged to hate the villains and cheer for the heroes.

The most popular spectator sports in the United States, however, owe their popularity to the fact that they more or less appeal to people of all social classes. Football, baseball, and basketball fans certainly come from all social classes. This does not mean, however, that social class does not have an important impact on how spectators enjoy these sports. Spectators who attend sports events are partially segregated by social class by means of ticket prices. Even the cheapest tickets for some sports events are too expensive for most working-class people. Newer sports stadiums have been built to include private suites, skyview boxes, and other luxurious accommodations for wealthy season-ticket holders. These suites and boxes cost hundreds of thousands of dollars a year and are frequently owned by corporations. The facilities include bar and restaurant service, and they are generally tax deductible for their business owners.

In sum, although involvement in sport as participant and as spectator sometimes brings together people of all social classes, there are also many ways in which people are separated by social class. Both as participants and as spectators, upper- and middle-class people have experiences in sport that are different from the experiences of poor and working-class people.

Sport and Social Mobility: The Glitter and the Reality

Perhaps nowhere is the American dream of rising from "rags to riches" through one's own talent and hard work more widely believed and pursued than in the world of sport. Millions of American boys have for decades spent the better part of their youth practicing their football, baseball, or basketball skills in hopes of becoming the next O. J. Simpson or Johnny Unitas, Magic Johnson or Larry Bird, Mickey Mantle or Hank Aaron or Roberto Clemente. In more recent years American girls have begun also to dream of becoming the next Chris Evert Lloyd, Mary Lou Retton, or Cheryl Miller.

These dreams are both realistic and unrealistic. It is necessary to look closely at both sides of the problem of sport and social mobility. On the one hand, sport does promote upward social mobility in a number of ways, and there are studies that document this upward mobility. On the other hand, many people who participate in sport do not achieve their dreams of upward mobility. They travel down a dead-end street and may even wind up worse off than if they had not become involved in sport.

At least eight ways that sport promotes upward social mobility have been identified and substantiated by sociological research. First, participation in sport may encourage or require a youth to obtain more education than he or she might otherwise obtain. A high school or college athlete must remain in school in order to play a sport. Acquiring more education in turn increases an athlete's opportunities for success outside of the world of sport.

Second, athletic participation generally requires that an athlete stay out of trouble and maintain a minimum grade point average. Schafer (1969) found that working-class athletes received higher grades and were less likely to be involved in delinquency than other working-class youth. As a result they were more likely to achieve upward social mobility.

Third, athletes generally have higher aspirations than nonathletes. They have better self-concepts, no doubt because of their athletic success and because of the recognition they receive from others. They are more likely as high school students to aspire to go to college. Their high status in high school enables them to associate with middle- and upper-class students in their high school. This association opens up new opportunities and contributes to higher aspirations.

Fourth, and more concretely, athletic participation earns college scholarships. Athletes from poor and working-class backgrounds who are good enough in their sport can receive scholarships that will pay for a college education that they otherwise could not afford and would not receive. A study of Notre Dame football players, for example, (Sack and Thiel, 1979) found that these scholarship athletes were more likely to be from more working-class backgrounds than regular Notre Dame students. A similar pattern prevails at many colleges and universities.

Fifth, studies have found that successful male athletes have more education and higher-status jobs than their fathers. Additional studies have also indicated that athletes who graduate from college obtain a higher economic position than nonathletes graduating from the same institution. Highly paid athletes who grew up in low-income families are tangible evidence of upward social mobility through achievement in sport.

Sixth, sport participation may lead to what is usually called sponsored mobility. An outstanding athlete may be offered a job in a business owned by a wealthy alumnus of the school or be hired by any business that might obtain a public relations benefit from the athlete's presence. Finally, an outstanding athlete might marry into a high-status family and obtain the usual benefits of such a marriage. These are all ways in which the upward social mobility of an athlete is sponsored by higher-status people.

Seventh, athletes may achieve upward social mobility because, through their participation in sport, they have acquired attitudes, skills, and experiences that are valued in the business world. The athlete may be regarded as a "well-rounded" person, or as someone who understands teamwork, leadership, or other traits considered desirable. These characteristics may give an athlete an edge in competition for positions that provide upward mobility.

Eighth, athletic participation may lead to a professional career in sports as a player, coach, manager, official, administrator, sports journalist, or in a sports-related business. There are professional football, baseball, and basketball players and professional boxers who came from very poor families who earn annual salaries of hundreds of thousands of dollars. These professionals represent the clearest examples of achievement of "the American dream."

Overall, studies of sport and social mobility have consistently pointed to one particularly important conclusion: Although the most dramatic and highly publicized examples of upward social mobility through sport are the examples of

Since 99 percent of all college athletes will never make a living as professional athletes, the most likely way they can achieve upward social mobility is by obtaining a college degree.

professional superstars, the most common way in which athletes achieve upward social mobility through sport is by using their athletic abilities to obtain a college degree. Athletes who are able to use their talents and efforts to get through college and graduate obtain the educational credentials they need for a lifelong career. Because few college athletes become professional athletes, their best opportunity for using sport for upward mobility lies in obtaining the educational qualifications needed for a good job. Their upward mobility is not as dramatic or highly publicized, but it occurs far more often and is more long-lasting.

This view of how sport promotes upward social mobility must be balanced against a view that focuses attention on the great majority of athletes whose dreams of success do not come true. Statistics show clearly and dramatically that over 95 percent of all high school football, basketball, and baseball players will not play for college teams and that over 98 percent of all college players will never have a major league career in these sports. Although there are several million boys and girls playing high school varsity sports, there is room for less than three thousand to make a living as professional football, basketball, and baseball players.

Several writers have pointed out ways in which sport is an obstacle to upward social mobility. Participation in sport is sometimes a barrier to educational attainment. Children who are still in elementary grades already neglect their school work to play ball and begin their quest for their dreams of becoming a superstar. By the time they get to high school, many fine athletes are years behind in their academic skills. Some coaches and school systems demand little educationally from athletes and allow them to slide through. One consequence is that there are hundreds of highly talented athletes who complete high school each year who are unable to get college scholarships because they do not meet the most minimal requirements for admission to college. Their athletic careers have ended at age eighteen, and they have few if any opportunities to earn a good living by any other means.

But what does the future hold for those athletes who do go to college? The College Football Association, consisting of those institutions with the nation's top Division I NCAA football programs, reported in 1985 that less than half of all football players who received scholarships at CFA institutions in 1979 graduated in five years. Only four of the sixty institutions that make up the CFA graduated over three-fourths of their scholarship football players in five years. Other studies have indicated that the majority of athletes who play football or basketball for top colleges and universities do not obtain their college degrees. Those athletes who become professionals often do not obtain a college degree, either. Approximately 80 percent of the players in the National Football League and the National Basketball Association do not have a college degree.

This pattern does not prevail at all kinds of colleges and universities. Athletes at Ivy League schools, at private liberal arts colleges, and at smaller Division II or Division III schools are generally expected to be students as well as athletes and have much higher graduation rates. This pattern, however, operates to reduce upward social mobility through sports, not to promote it. Most of the athletes at these kinds of schools come from middle- and upper-class backgrounds and participate in competitive sport for personal enjoyment. They complete their education and go on to higher status occupations, thereby retaining their middle- and upper-class status.

On the other hand, it is the athletes from poor and working-class backgrounds who are more likely to receive scholarships to participate in big-time money-making athletic programs that often force the athlete to sacrifice educational attainment to the goal of producing a winning team. Most of these athletes neither become professional athletes nor graduate from college. When they have used up their eligibility, they often leave school and eventually return to the ranks of the poor and the working class.

The consequence of this pattern is that the talents and aspirations of young athletes from working-class and poor backgrounds are exploited by the high school and college sports establishment, but the majority never experience the upward social mobility of which they dreamed. The college degree that would have provided them with a better opportunity to achieve upward mobility eludes them. It eludes them because they do not think they need it and therefore neglect academics, because they are often poorly prepared academically for college work, because coaches and administrators do not care about their athletes' education, or because coaches and administrators demand so much of scholarship athletes that the players literally do not have the time or energy left to get an education. The pattern just described occurs so frequently that it was highly newsworthy when basketball superstar Ralph Sampson chose to remain at the University of Virginia and graduate instead of accepting multimillion-dollar offers to enter the NBA's "hardship" (sic) draft.

Harry Edwards pointed out that the consequences for blacks of believing in exaggerated opportunities for upward social mobility through sport are very harmful. The outcome is that the majority of black youth who seek stardom "are foredoomed to be shuttled back into the black community . . . lacking any legitimate means of sustaining themselves." Jack Scott (1971) made the same point with respect to white working-class athletes:

> I make this statement as one who "escaped" an eastern Pennsylvania coal-mining town through the assistance of an athletic scholarship. . . . Yearly, close to two hundred athletes at my school would base their lives around varsity athletics, but at most three or four individuals would be rewarded with athletic scholarships. . . . For every Broadway Joe Namath there are hundreds of sad, disillusioned men standing on the street corners and sitting in the beer halls of Pennsylvania towns (Eitzen and Sage, 1982:287).

Because the world of sport is a microcosm of the larger society, social mobility through sport mirrors the patterns of social mobility that sociologists have studied in the larger society. As we have seen earlier in Chapter 8, "Social Class," only a few people actually rise from the bottom to the top. Most upward social mobility consists of relatively small steps. Moreover, great numbers of people experience little or no upward social mobility. Sport has certainly not been a means of upward mobility for the majority of the U.S. population that is female. The conflict sociologists seem to have a valid point in asserting that sport encourages acceptance of the existing social structure by greatly exaggerating actual opportunities for social mobility.

Race, Sex and Sport

Race and Sport

Until the 1950s sport in the United States at all levels—informal, organized, corporate, and youth and adult—was almost totally segregated by race. Since the 1950s all levels of sport have been desegregated, but sociologists have identified new forms of racial segregation and racial discrimination that exist in sport today. Black athletes today are largely concentrated in five major sports: basketball, football, baseball, boxing, and track and field. Relatively few black athletes are found in such other sports as ice hockey, tennis, golf, swimming, and soccer. Hispanic athletes are similarly found in greater numbers in such sports as baseball, boxing, and soccer, but in smaller numbers in most other sports in the U.S.

The virtual dominance by black athletes of certain sports is not the result of racial superiority and does not signify that racism no longer exists in those sports. Black dominance of basketball, football, and other sports may occur because racism continues to exist both in American society as a whole and in the sports world in particular. Because blacks are denied opportunities to achieve success in other ways, they are strongly encouraged to aspire to superstardom as athletes. While most sports remain white-dominated and discourage black participation, blacks are channeled into a few major sports.

In those sports dominated by outstanding black athletes, whites continue to occupy positions of authority and control. Blacks are extremely underrepresented as owners, managers, coaches, front-office personnel, officials, and journalists in basketball, football, and baseball. Blacks are mainly concentrated in the "worker" role in these sports, just as they are in the larger society.

Ninety-four percent of all college athletic scholarships are awarded to whites.

In addition, there is considerable evidence that segregation and discrimination continue to operate within those sports dominated by black athletes. The main evidence comes from studies of **stacking.** Stacking refers to the tendency for black athletes to be found mainly in certain positions in football, baseball, and basketball, whereas other positions are mainly filled by whites. Studies of college and professional football teams have found that black players dominate such positions as defensive backs, running backs, wide receivers, and defensive linemen, whereas whites dominate such positions as quarterback, kicker, punter, center, and linebacker.

Studies of major league baseball teams have found that black players are concentrated in outfield positions and underrepresented as catchers, pitchers, and infielders (especially shortstop and second base). Regarding college basketball, studies have found that blacks are overrepresented at forward and underrepresented at guard and center.

What all these patterns have in common is that whites dominate these positions that are most central and that are thought to require the greatest amount of thinking, leadership, and specialized skills. Blacks are concentrated in those positions that are most peripheral and that are thought to require mainly "natural" athletic ability and speed.

One of the authors of this textbook, who is a youth soccer coach, has also observed this pattern on some youth soccer teams. Blacks are often played at wing positions, which are noncentral and thought to require mainly natural speed and aggressiveness. Blacks are less often found at such central positions as center half, which involve more leadership, skill, and tactical awareness.

At least four explanations have been put forward for this pervasive pattern of stacking in those sports in which there are large numbers of black athletes. The first explanation asserts that the pattern simply reflects the different natural abilities of black and white athletes. We suggest along with Harry Edwards that there is no scientific evidence to support this explanation. The second explanation emphasizes that the adult athletes in these positions serve as role models for young blacks and whites and thus encourage youths to aspire to different positions. This may be a factor in perpetuating the pattern, but it does not explain the origin of the pattern. It also fails to account for the many blacks who are good quarterbacks but whose coaches insist on converting them into running backs. Moreover, since the central positions generally pay the highest salaries, this explanation does not account for why black athletes would voluntarily aspire mainly to relatively lower paying positions.

A third explanation emphasizes spatial location. Whites tend to occupy central positions, whereas blacks occupy peripheral positions. This maintains white dominance and black subordination. Edwards, however, argues that spatial location is not the really important factor. Rather, he offers a fourth explanation: It is the amount of control over the game and the amount of leadership associated with positions. Racial stereotyping leads to the relegation of most blacks to positions requiring mainly "natural abilities" and to white dominance of leadership positions. This is probably the most accurate explanation for stacking.

Recent studies have continued to find evidence of stacking in college and professional football and professional baseball. Because blacks numerically dominate all positions in college and professional basketball today, stacking appears no longer to exist in this area.

Stacking has financial consequences, because quarterbacks and pitchers tend to be more highly paid than defensive backs and outfielders. Players in central leadership positions tend to receive more media attention and more opportunities for commercial endorsements. Also, players in central positions in football suffer fewer serious injuries and have longer professional careers. Finally, since college and professional sports have such a great impact on tens of millions of fans and viewers, stacking reinforces racial stereotyping and prejudiced thinking among the population as a whole. It encourages the belief that blacks are only good at those things for which they have natural ability, but they cannot be taught to do as well as whites those things that require thinking and intelligence.

Other forms of racial discrimination in sport have also been identified in sociological research. There is, for example, "unequal opportunity for equal ability" (Eitzen and Sage 1982:313). In major league baseball, for example, black players must be better than whites to succeed. Black major leaguers have fairly consistently had batting averages about twenty points higher than whites. Black pitchers have averaged more wins per season than white pitchers. This suggests that there are higher "admissions requirements" to the major leagues for blacks than for whites.

Similarly, in professional football and basketball, research has found that blacks are more likely than whites to be starters. Blacks who are not good enough to be starters are not kept on teams, whereas whites are. Brower (1973) concluded that "mediocrity is a white luxury."

It is often argued that coaches and owners of sports teams are mainly interested in winning and therefore want the best athletes, regardless of race. This is certainly an important factor, and it helps to explain why professional and college football, basketball, and baseball have sought black athletes. To conclude, however, that racial discrimination has therefore been virtually eliminated from competitive sport would be incorrect. As the patterns of racial discrimination in American society have changed, but not disappeared, so have these patterns changed in the world of sport.

Sex and Sport

Historically, no group has suffered as much discrimination, stereotyping, and exclusion in sport as females. Until as recently as the 1970s it was widely argued that strenuous competitive sport was physically and emotionally harmful to females and contrary to feminine nature. It was also widely believed that females lacked both the ability and the desire to be good athletes. Females who nevertheless engaged in sport were channeled into such individual sports as golf, swimming, tennis, figure skating, or gymnastics, activities that emphasize grace and beauty rather than physical aggressiveness and competitiveness. Females who violated these repressive social patterns were labeled masculine or tomboys and subjected to many painful social sanctions.

It was also common practice for scholarships and other funds, facilities, and other privileges to be devoted almost entirely to male athletes. Females were expected to be short-skirted cheerleaders and majorettes for their male heroes not only in high school and college, but even for youth teams during their elementary years. While groups of boys played backyard and playground sports every day after school, girls were expected to stay indoors or jump rope. Boys might have gathered in large groups to play team sports, but girls were supposed to get together with only one or two friends at a time.

It was inevitable that the struggle for equal rights for females that developed during the 1960s would soon attack sexism in sport. The result has been an unprecedented transformation in female participation in sport. Although many

Since the early 1970s, there has been tremendous growth in girls' and women's participation in sports.

factors have contributed to these changes, perhaps the key has been what is known as *Title IX* of the Educational Amendments Act of 1972, which states:

> No person shall, on the basis of sex, be excluded from participation in, be denied the benefits of, be treated differently from another person or otherwise be discriminated against in any interscholastic, intercollegiate, club or intramural athletics offered by a recipient, and no recipient shall provide any such athletics separately on such basis. (*Federal Register,* 1975)

Considerable struggle followed over the interpretation and implementation of Title IX, but there were enormous increases in female participation in organized sports during the 1970s. At the high school level, about 300,000 females were participants in sport at the time when Title IX was adopted. That number had increased to over two million by the end of the 1970s. Similar increases took place on the college level. By the beginning of the 1980s females were over 30 percent of all college athletes and received about 20 percent of college athletic budgets. Over twelve thousand scholarships were awarded to female athletes, and national championships were held in seventeen different sports. Women have also benefitted from this increased participation in sport through improved physical fitness, self-confidence, and training in leadership, teamwork, and aggressiveness.

Despite this progress, however, serious problems remain. Female athletes and teams usually have to make do with less money, inferior facilities, equipment, and uniforms and less-qualified coaches. Women receive vastly less media coverage from television and newspapers. Male coaches, athletic directors, and athletic administrators run many female sports programs, often having replaced female personnel (Eitzen and Sage, 1982:344).

Progress for women's sports has also been threatened by the U.S. Supreme Court's 1984 reinterpretation of Title IX. The Supreme Court ruled that the term *recipient* referred not to an entire institution but only to a specific program receiving federal funds. Thus, a university receiving federal funds for its science labs could not discriminate in those labs and continue to receive the funds; but if its sports programs received no direct Federal funding, it could discriminate against female athletes without any penalty. This reinterpretation of Title IX has aroused widespread concern over the future direction of women's sports in the United States.

It is surely no accident that progress in women's sport greatly accelerated in the 1970s and may be under attack during the 1980s, for these developments mirror political and social trends in the larger society. The issue of sexism in sport clearly reveals once again that sport is a microcosm of society.

Summary

Sport may be defined as activity that is governed by rules, is competitive, and involves physical exertion. Three levels of sport are informal, organized, and corporate sport. Sport is a microcosm, that is a "small-world replica" of the larger society. It reflects both the values and the problems of the larger society of which it is a part.

The functionalist view of sport asserts that sport contributes to the maintenance of the social system by socializing people, managing tensions, bringing people together, encouraging the attainment of goals, and promoting adaptation to change. The conflict view of sport asserts that sport promotes alienation; trains people for the bureaucratic, authoritarian, capitalist system; generates profit; and arouses nationalistic, racist, and sexist prejudices.

Members of different social classes participate in different sports and also tend to enjoy different sports as spectators. Reasons for these class differences stem from both cultural and economic factors. Sport promotes upward social mobility by opening up educational opportunities, by bringing athletes into contact with upper-class people, by teaching certain vaues and skills, and by providing for some high-paying careers in sport. Sport impedes upward social mobility by interfering with educational achievement and distracting youth with unrealistic dreams of becoming a superstar.

Desegregation of sport has eliminated older forms of racism but given rise to new forms of discrimination and segregation. Blacks and whites tend to participate in different sports. Blacks predominate as athletes in a few sports, such as basketball, football, boxing, track and field, and baseball, but even in these sports they are segregated into certain positions and underrepresented as coaches, owners, officials, and administrators. They must often be better than their white counterparts in order to receive the same opportunities.

After being victims of a long history of exclusion from most sports, females have greatly increased their participation in organized sport during the 1970s and 1980s, thereby challenging many stereotypes. Despite this progress, however, problems and obstacles to equality in sport remain.

Key Concepts

conspicuous consumption **pseudosport**
corporate sport **sport**
informal sport **sports creed**
microcosm **stacking**
organized sport **Title IX**
trash sport

References

Brower, Jonathan J. (1973) "The Quota System." *Proceedings of the American Sociological Association.*, New York, American Sociological Association.

Coakley, Jay J. (1984) "Sport in Society: An Inspiration or an Opiate?" In D. Stanley Eitzen (ed.), *Sport in Contemporary Society.* New York, N.Y.: St. Martin's Press, Inc.

Cosell, Howard. (1984) "Sports and Good-bye to all That," New York Times April 5, 1971, p. 33.

Edwards, Harry. (1973) *Sociology of Sport.* Homewood, Ill.: Dorsey Press.
Eitzen, D. Stanley (ed.). (1984) *Sport in Contemporary Society.* 2d ed. New York, N.Y.: St. Martin's Press, Inc.
Eitzen, D. Stanley, and George H. Sage. (1982) *Sociology of American Sport.* 2d ed. Dubuque, Iowa: William C. Brown Company, Publishers.
Lapchick, Richard. (1984) *Broken Promises: Racism in American Sports.* New York, N.Y.: St. Martin's Press, Inc.
Michener, James A. (1976) *Sports in America.* New York, N.Y.: Random House, Inc.
Sack, Allen L., and Robert Thiel. (1979) "College Football and Social Mobility." *Sociology of Education 52* (January):60–66.
Schafer, Walter E. (1969) "Some Social Sources and Consequences of Interscholastic Athletics: The Case of Participation and Delinquency." In Gerald S. Kenyon (ed.), *Aspects of Contemporary Sport Sociology.* Chicago, Ill.: The Athletic Institute.
Scott, Jack. (1971) *The Athletic Revolution.* New York, N.Y.: The Free Press.
Sports Illustrated. (1984) (October 14) 45. "The College Football Association."
Spreitzer, Elmer, and Eldon E. Snyder. (1983) "Sport." In Robert Hagedorn. (ed.), *Sociology.* Dubuque, Iowa: William C. Brown Company, Publishers.

Crime and the Criminal Justice System

19

OBJECTIVES

After completing this chapter the student should be able to:

1. Explain the consensus and conflict definitions of crime and describe nine different kinds of crime.

2. Explain the different sociological theories of criminal behavior.

3. Describe the Uniform Crime Reports and the National Crime Surveys and summarize the major criticisms of their shortcomings.

4. Discuss research on police violence and corruption and compare theories of police behavior.

5. Discuss the bail process, preventive detention, plea bargaining, and the role of attorneys.

6. Explain four philosophies of sentencing, indicating which ones promise to reduce crime.

INTRODUCTION

Many Americans are critical of the criminal justice system for many different reasons. Some believe that the system is too harsh and punitive; others feel it is too easygoing and lenient. Many think that the law, the police, the courts, and the prisons are biased against the poor and members of minority groups and are riddled with widespread corruption. Still other people have a highly distorted or superficial view of the criminal justice system shaped by television programs and motion pictures.

A sociological approach to the study of the criminal justice system emphasizes how that system reflects the nature of the society in which it exists. Inequalities of class, race, and sex that influence the functioning of other institutions in our society also have their effect on criminal justice institutions.

We begin by defining and describing the many kinds of crime that occur in American society. The remainder of the chapter examines sociological theories of crime and the main sources of data about crime in the United States, the Uniform Crime Reports, and the National Crime Surveys. We conclude with an analysis of the police, the courts, and the prisons.

Crime in American Society

How is it that we come to label some behaviors as crimes? Sociologists have offered two different answers to this question. The consensus view, which is related to the functionalist perspective, asserts that members of society enact laws to express deeply and strongly held cultural values. **Crimes** are those acts that violate the laws a society has enacted. The law thus serves or functions to maintain the social system and the shared values of the people.

The conflict view asserts that the law is a product of conflict between different groups in society. These groups have different interests and different values. The strongest group enacts laws to protect its own interests and values. Crimes are thus mainly acts by weaker or oppressed groups that threaten the interests of the stronger group.

The consensus view tends to emphasize crimes that are **mala in se,** that is, acts that are inherently bad and more or less condemned by everyone, such as murder, rape, or robbery. The conflict view tends to emphasize crimes that are **mala prohibita,** that is, acts that are not necessarily inherently bad but are defined as crimes because laws have been passed against them. Examples of mala prohibita crimes are those relating to corporate regulations, drug abuse, sexual behavior, or labor-management conflicts.

Crime, then, is a special kind of deviance, and in order for crime to exist three specific conditions must be present. First, there must be an act. No matter how evil a person's thoughts, no crime exists until the person acts on those thoughts. Although conspiracy does not require the intended act to transpire, in order for it to be a crime the act of conspiring must occur. The act of conspiring may include phone calls, meetings, and sending and receiving coded messages. Often, conspiracy is a prominent feature of white-collar crime.

Second, the act must violate a law. In other words, "not all wrongs are crime" (Nettler, 1984:35). Sin, for example is not necessarily a crime. In some states there are no laws governing adultery or fornication, yet biblical passages repeatedly refer to both as sinful. Further, breaking hearts, transmitting sexual diseases, and standing people up on dates may be considered by some as grievous wrongs. However, none are crimes. Likewise, some crimes appear to harm no one; yet because the act violates the law, it is nonetheless a crime. For example, when laws exist prohibiting jaywalking, fornication, and profanity, commission of these acts constitutes crime. Crimes such as gambling, prostitution, and possession of drugs are transactions that occur with the consent of and often are initiated by the victim. These offenses, often referred to as victimless crimes, violate laws; and although there exists no apparent wrong to the victim, owning gambling establishments, solicitation, and possession of drugs are usually criminal activities.

Third, the act must not be justifiable by law. According to Nettler (1984:35), a defense or excuse "against the application of the criminal law consists of legally recognized justification for committing what otherwise would be called a crime."

Acceptable excuses for committing crimes include self-defense, being underage, and mental illness. Excuses for crime do not automatically mean that convicted criminals will completely escape responsibility for their behavior. In some instances, although the act has been excused as a crime, the perpetrators may be required to make restitution; be punished as a delinquent; or be confined to a hospital for periods even longer than if they were found guilty of a crime and subsequently sentenced.

Types of Crime

The subject of crime in the United States is frequently discussed as if there is only one kind of crime in our society—conventional, or "street," crime. In reality, there are many different kinds of crime in U.S. society, and it is necessary to include all of them in our discussion in order to get a balanced picture. Some people think that the poor and minority groups are responsible for most of the crime in our society, because they have in mind only the kinds of crime for which minority persons are more frequently arrested by police. Similarly, if we focused attention only on white-collar or corporate crime, we might conclude that wealthy white males are responsible for most of the crime in our society.

There have been many attempts to classify all the different kinds of crime in society. Criminologists Clinard and Quinney (1973) have identified nine major categories of criminal behavior, as described in the following listing:

1. Violent Personal Criminal Behavior. This category includes such crimes as murder, assault, forcible rape, and spouse abuse.
2. Occasional Property Criminal Behavior. This category includes petty property crimes such as shoplifting and vandalism and is largely the work of juveniles.
3. Public Order Criminal Behavior. This category includes alcohol- and drug-related crimes, prostitution, homosexuality, gambling, and the like. These are sometimes called "victimless crimes."
4. Conventional Criminal Behavior. This category includes the most common property crimes such as larceny, burglary, and robbery.
5. Political Criminal Behavior. This category includes both crimes committed against the government and by the government. Crimes against the government include draft evasion, treason, and the like. Crimes by government include police corruption and brutality, violations of citizens' rights by the FBI, CIA, and so forth, denial of equal rights (i.e., racism and sexism), violent repression, and unjust wars.
6. Occupational Criminal Behavior. These are crimes committed by the people "in the course of their occupational activity" (Clinard and Quinney, 1973:17). Malpractice by physicians or attorneys would be an example.
7. Corporate Criminal Behavior. These are crimes committed by corporations or by corporate leaders, and they include violations of workers' health and safety, pollution of the environment, manufacture of unsafe products, false advertising, price fixing, and violations of labor laws.
8. Organized Criminal Behavior. This category refers to organized systematic criminal behavior by syndicates that sometimes are referred to by such ethnic names as the "Mafia." Organized criminal activities include drug processing and distribution, loan sharking, racketeering, and the like.
9. Professional Criminal Behavior. This category refers to individuals who engage

in crime as a job or career. Counterfeiting, confidence games, pickpocketing, and forgery are examples of this category.

These nine categories make it clear that criminal behavior occurs among all sections of the population, rich and poor, white and black, youth and adult, men and women. It is important to keep this fact in mind as we examine various theories of criminal behavior, because some theories assume that criminal behavior is almost exclusively found among minorities, the poor, or the working class.

Theories of Crime

The theories of the founders of criminology are known as classical and positivist theories. Classical theory located the cause of crime within the individual who, of his or her own "free will," decided whether or not to commit a crime. Crime was thus essentially chosen by people who found crime more satisfying than conformity. Positivist theory, in contrast, did not view individuals as acting freely; rather, positivists felt that criminal behavior was determined by biological, psychological, or environmental factors. Crime was thus caused by a combination of heredity, mental illness, and poor environment. More modern versions of these classical and positivist theories exist today.

At least six different contemporary sociological theories of crime can be identified. These are class culture theories, anomie theory, opportunity theory, differential association theory, labeling theory, and conflict theory. Each of these theories is briefly described in the following paragraphs.

Class culture theories focus on the explanations of "lower-class" crime. Lower-class people commit crimes either in pursuit of such lower-class values as excitement and trouble (Miller, 1958), or in reaction against their failure to achieve middle-class values (Cohen, 1955). These theories may provide some insight into the cultural and environmental factors that lead to crime among lower-class youth and adults, but they have also been criticized for promoting negative stereotypes about the lower class. Another important criticism is that these theories do not account for middle- and upper-class crime.

Anomie theory (Merton, 1957) suggests that certain built-in structural strains in the society induce people to behave in unacceptable ways. Merton asserts that people who subscribe to society's goals of economic success but do not have the institutional means (i.e., education, occupation, and so on) to achieve them seek alternative ways to resolve this problem.

Crime is one of these alternative methods and occurs when people adopt illegal means to attain social goals or even a reorientation toward illegal goals. Merton's theory shows how social conditions and inequalities can produce crimes. Like class culture theory, however, anomie theory does not really explain the criminal behavior of middle- or upper-class people because they have acquired the institutional means to achieve societal success.

Opportunity theory is similar to the above theories in that it too concentrates on crimes committed by lower-class people in response to the absence or "blockage" of opportunity in society. Whereas anomie theory stresses blocked legal options, opportunity theory notes that not all would-be criminals have the same illegal opportunity. According to this theory, lower-class youth in particular turn to various types of crime such as violence and drugs because of the lack of opportunity to achieve economic goals legitimately or illegitimately.

Differential association theory is mainly a theory of how people learn criminal behavior. It asserts that criminal behavior is learned in the same way that any other behavior is learned. A person becomes a criminal by learning both the techniques for committing certain crimes and the values that justify criminal, as opposed to law-abiding, behavior. Someone who associated more consistently and more intimately with criminally oriented people than with law-abiding people will most likely adopt attitudes that favor criminal behavior. This theory points out that crime is learned through social processes and suggests that people in all social classes may adopt criminal patterns if their strongest associations are with criminally oriented people. A weakness of this theory, as Shafer has observed (1976), is that it only explains how the "second" criminal came into being, but it does not explain where the "first" criminal—the role model who taught the second criminal—came from.

Labeling theory focuses on the process by which people become labeled as criminal or deviant. According to labeling theory, no acts are inherently criminal. They are labeled criminal by those who have the power to do so. Persons who are labeled may then take on a new criminal or deviant identity. Labeling theory points out how society creates crime or deviance. It also introduces the elements of power; those who have power can label others and escape being labeled themselves. Labeled persons who either accept a criminal identity or have one forced upon them are not only treated as criminal by others, but they may also begin to act out this new identity.

Conflict theory refers to at least three somewhat different views of the causes of crime. First, the theory of cultural conflict notes that some groups in society may possess different cultural values. If one group is able to make laws reflecting its values, then other groups with different values are likely to come into conflict with the law. As we have seen in Chapter 6, a clash of cultures results in crime when conduct norms clash at cultural borders; one culture's norms are superimposed over another, as when one nation occupies the territory of another nation; or when one group immigrates or migrates to a group with varying conduct norms.

A more general type of conflict theory focuses not on values but interests. This approach adopts the general perspective of conflict sociology and views society as consisting of unequal groups with conflicting interests. The most powerful groups are able to shape and use the law to protect their own interests. For example, groups that favor legalization of marijuana or prostitution would be likely to come into conflict with laws passed by groups who have an interest in condemning marijuana and prostitution. Crimes are thus actions that harm or threaten the interests of the dominant group in society.

The third type of conflict theory locates the cause of crime in the system of capitalism. The economic conditions of capitalism—extremes of wealth and poverty—give rise both to crimes of survival among the poor and crimes of greed among the affluent. The cultural values of capitalism—competition, individualism, material success, and racist and sexist ideologies—also give rise to many kinds of criminal behavior. Although criminal behavior is widespread among all groups in the population, the capitalist upper class uses its power and wealth to escape punishment for its crimes. Instead, the attention of the criminal justice system is focused on the crimes of the working class, the poor, and racial minority groups.

Sources of Crime Data in the United States

The main source of information about crime in the United States is the *Uniform Crime Reports,* compiled annually by the Federal Bureau of Investigation (FBI) from arrest information submitted from local police departments throughout the country. A second source of information is the *National Crime Survey,* which gathers information from victims of crime and thus is called a **victimization survey.** These sources contain much useful information, but they have also been subject to important criticisms.

The *Uniform Crime Reports* (UCR) provide data on certain kinds of crimes that are reported to the police and on arrests made each year. Arrests are further broken down by race, sex, age, and geographical units. The reports divide crimes into two categories, referred to as Part I and Part II. Part I consists of what law enforcement agencies regard as the most important and most serious crimes. These are murder, forcible rape, robbery, aggravated assault, burglary, larceny, motor vehicle theft, and arson. These eight types of crime are collectively known as **"index" crimes,** and statistics about them receive the greatest amount of attention. Part II consists of more than twenty categories, including drug- and alcohol-related offenses, sex offenses, juvenile offenses, fraud, forgery, embezzlement, offenses against public order, and others.

In recent years upwards of thirteen million Part I index crimes have been reported annually to the police. Yet, according to the *National Crime Survey,* victims of crime report over forty million such crimes annually. Thus, only one-third to one-half of all index crimes seem to be reported to the police each year (*Report,* 1983:7). Some 90 percent of the Part I index crimes reported to the public annually are property or economic crimes (larceny, burglary, or motor vehicle

The great majority of arrests made by police each year are for property crimes and violations of the public order.

Only about one in fourteen burglaries is cleared by arrest.

theft); in fact, crimes in the larceny-theft category alone comprise over half of the reported annual index crime. Murder, forcible rape, aggravated assault, and robbery comprise only about 10 percent of the index crimes reported to the police each year.

Thus, the great majority of arrests for Part I index crimes are for property crimes, rather than crimes of violence. Although the FBI, the police, and the mass media often emphasize index crimes and violent crimes, police spend much more time arresting people for Part II crimes and property crimes. For example, more than one-third of all arrests annually are alcohol related: some 3.3 million arrests were made for the Part II offenses of driving under the influence, drunkenness, and liquor law violations.

The majority of crimes reported to the police, however, do not lead to an arrest. The percentage of crimes reported to the police for which an arrest is made is known as the **clearance rate.** The highest clearance rate is for reported murders (72 percent), and the lowest rates are for property crimes (17 percent). Given that no more than half of all burglaries are reported to the police in the first place, and only one out of seven burglaries that are reported to the police is cleared by an arrest, only about one in fourteen burglaries is cleared by an arrest!

The *Uniform Crime Reports* and the *National Crime Surveys* thus tell us that much crime is not reported to the police, that most crimes reported to the police

Sources of Crime Data in the United States

are property crimes, that most arrests are for nonindex and property offenses, and that no one is arrested for most crimes. The *Uniform Crime Reports* also tell us the race of people arrested by the police. For example, blacks comprise about one-fourth of those arrested by the police annually, one-third of those arrested for index crimes, and forty-six percent of those arrested for the four index crimes that are classified as violent crimes. A large majority of those arrested for most Part II offenses are white.

Evaluating Crime Statistics

The victim surveys point out the first important criticism of the *Uniform Crime Reports:* The UCR contain information only on those crimes known to the police. The majority of both Part I and Part II offenses are not reported to the police. The large volume of unreported crime makes it difficult to use UCR arrest data to make reliable statements about the actual amount of crime in the United States. At best, UCR data provide an estimate of the amount of crime.

Although the victim surveys reveal a larger amount of crime, their reliability has also been questioned. Repondents may not tell the truth, they may forget or exaggerate, or they may be unaware of having been victimized by certain crimes, especially white-collar, corporate, or political crimes. In addition, victim surveys tend to omit some rather serious crimes. "They (victim surveys) do not include kidnapping, and they omit being victimized by drunkenness, disturbances of the peace, impaired driving, drug abuse, sexual solicitation, and procuring" (Nettler, 1984:68). Consequently, neither the *Uniform Crime Reports* nor the *National Crime Surveys* allow us to determine with any real confidence how much crime there is in the United States.

A second important criticism of the UCR is that they do not describe criminal behavior but rather police behavior in the United States. That is, they tell us what crimes are most likely to attract the attention of law enforcement agencies. They do not tell us about criminal behavior as a whole because they do not include information about the great bulk of corporate crime, political crime, and occupational, or "white-collar" crime. Similarly, crimes directed mainly against women, such as forcible rape and spouse abuse, are extremely underreported in the *Uniform Crime Reports.*

A third criticism is that the *Uniform Crime Reports* promote and reinforce a class-biased and racist view of crime and criminals in the United States. The crimes that are regarded as most important and classified as Part I index offenses are those crimes that are more likely to be committed by poor people and members of racial minorities. The public is therefore encouraged to believe that the greatest criminal danger comes from racial minorities and the poor. This belief in turn justifies continued concentration by the police on arresting minorities and the poor (Reiman, 1979; Ryan, 1976).

Some critics have argued that corporate, political, occupational, and organized crime are more important and serious than index crimes, because the former inflict far greater physical and financial harm on more people in our society. Sutherland (1961), McCaghy (1976), Reiman (1979), Balkan and associates (1980), and Coleman (1985) have presented evidence that crimes committed by the rich and powerful are a greater threat to more people than Part I index crimes. For example, thousands of workers die each year in on-the-job accidents, and nearly two million workers are injured. More than 100,000 workers die from

Illegal dumping of toxic waste by corporations and organized crime syndicates threatens the health of millions of Americans.

occupationally related diseases annually, and hundreds of thousands more become ill. The economic costs of price-fixing, false advertising, and the like are far greater than losses due to robbery, burglary, and larceny. The Vietnam War, which many Americans came to regard as a political crime, took the lives of some two million Asians and sixty thousand Americans.

Neither the *Uniform Crime Reports* nor the victimization surveys provide much information about these kinds of crimes. The police almost never arrest people for such crimes, and the impact of the criminal justice system on the prosecution of corporate and political crime is limited because there tends to be a separate system of justice for upper-class offenders. The authors of one criminology text point out, "Corporate offenders are not even processed through the same criminal justice agencies as lower-class criminals.... Typically, business offenders are handled administratively before quasi-judicial boards of government regulatory and licensing agencies such as the Federal Trade Commission, the National Labor Relations Board, and the Food and Drug Administration" (Balkan et al., 1980:177).

In this separate upper-class system offenders may not be treated as "criminals." The punishments they receive often do not involve incarceration. The most common punishments for corporate and political wrongdoing are the issuance of administrative warnings or injunctions to "cease and desist." Sometimes, small fines are levied. Upper-class offenders are dealt with by their peers, because the administrators of these regulatory agencies and commissions are usually recruited from corporations and big business.

Criminal justice agencies and politicians sometimes justify this concentration on index crimes and neglect of upper-class crime by criminal justice agencies by pointing to a greater public concern about and a fear of index crime. Thus, the criminal justice system is doing what the public wants. This view is consistent with the functionalist/consensus theory that the behavior of the criminal justice system results from the shared values of the members of society. On the other hand, there are some research findings that cast some doubt on this view. The Bureau of Justice Statistics of the U.S. Department of Justice published the results of a 1977 "National Survey of Crime Severity," which measured how the public rates the severity of various kinds of crime. In this survey of sixty thousand people, such crimes as water pollution by a factory that injures or kills people, sale of dangerous products, and the taking of bribes by politicians or judges were rated as much more severe than many index crimes against property and against the person (*Bureau of Justice Statistics Bulletin,* 1984).

The criminal justice system's concentration on crimes of poor, minority, and working-class people and the relative neglect of corporate, political, occupational, and white-collar crime might thus be seen as a reflection of the powerlessness of the former and the power and influence of the latter in U.S. society. This interpretation that the criminal justice system is used by the dominant class to control the lower classes in society is more consistent with the conflict theory.

People in different social classes gamble in different ways.

This issue has important implications for interpreting the overrepresentation of poor racial minorities in arrest statistics. If the police concentrated equal attention on all kinds of crimes, there might be much less overrepresentation of these minorities among the ranks of those arrested. For example, because blacks and Hispanics are underrepresented in corporate, political, and professional leadership positions, they are involved in very little of the crime committed by people in those positions. Similarly, people in different positions in society certainly gamble in different ways. Some gamble in alleys; others gamble at private country clubs; still others gamble on the stock market or the international money market. If all forms of gambling were equally subject to arrest, minorities certainly would not comprise two-thirds of those arrested for this crime. It seems reasonable to suggest that if all serious crimes and criminals were dealt with equally, the overrepresentation of any racial group among those arrested in our society would be diminished.

The Criminal Justice Process

The criminal justice process has been described as a "filtering" system, because most people who enter the criminal justice system at the point of arrest are not processed all the way through the system to the end point of serving some kind of sentence. This process is called a filtering system because most arrestees are "filtered out" of the system at various stages in the criminal justice process. Reiman (1979) has called this a "weeding-out" process, because he believes that the criminal justice system "weeds out" the well-to-do and leaves behind only the poor and powerless. Shelden has labeled this a **"homogenization" process,** emphasizing that as defendants are processed through the stages of the criminal justice system, "the kinds of people involved become more and more homogeneous. For instance, they become more alike in terms of age (younger), sex (more are males), race (increasingly racial minorities), social class (increasing numbers of lower- and working-class people), offense (more and more 'index' offenses)" (Shelden, 1982:1–2).

Shelden concluded that "When we arrive at the last stage, the prison populations, we have the most homogeneous grouping in which the majority are poor, unskilled, uneducated" (Shelden, 1982:1–2).

The remainder of this chapter examines the stages of this criminal justice process. In it we analyze the police (the law enforcement institution), the courts (the judicial institution), and the prisons (the correctional institution). We note how the social class, race, and gender of the large society sometimes influence the various stages of the criminal justice process.

Law Enforcement: The Police

The police are the object of more attention today than any other part of the criminal justice system. There are local, state, and federal police bodies, and there are many kinds of specialized law enforcement agencies. The local municipal police, however, are by far the most numerous, and they are the focus of the following analysis. The size of the police grew considerably during the late 1960s and early 1970s in the United States, before shrinking somewhat because of budget cuts in subsequent years. There are today almost 500,000 local police officers in the United States. When state, federal, and private police personnel are added to this number, the total approaches one million.

American society has not always been so heavily policed. Although policing as a function of government has existed for thousands of years, the modern police institution has existed only about a century and a half. The first police departments were established in the United States in such cities as New York, Philadelphia, and Boston around the middle of the nineteenth century. Before the establishment of these police departments, there were two kinds of policing in the United States. First, there was a small voluntary night-watch or constable system in cities and towns. Second, there were repressive bodies that concentrated on racial minorities. These included the slave patrols in the South, armed forces and militias that fought native Americans, and agencies such as the Texas Rangers, formed in 1830s, that brutally oppressed Mexicans and Mexican Americans.

There is disagreement over the interpretation of why big city police departments were formed. Some writers argue that cities set up police departments to control a rapidly rising volume of crime brought on by population growth, economic inequality, and increasing ethnic diversity and conflict due to the immigration of new groups from Europe. Other writers argue that the development of capitalism brought about the creation of the police. Capitalist development created a rapidly growing urban working class and great economic inequality between the working class and the capitalist class. This class oppression was intensified by capitalist exploitation of ethnic immigrant groups and manipulation of ethnic conflict. Oppressed workers fought back with strikes, riots, and uprisings that threatened the property and position of the upper class. The upper class concluded that they needed a large armed body to try to control and prevent such working-class disorders.

Historians of the police generally agree that mass disorders were more important than "crime" in leading to the creation of police departments. A detailed study of one large city, Buffalo, New York, by Harring (1984), seems to provide evidence to support this point. The Buffalo police department was created during the second half of the nineteenth century. It was firmly under the control of business and industrial leaders of the city and regularly used to suppress worker protests, especially strikes. The size of the police force grew much faster than the amount of crime in the city, and police activities focused heavily on the city's immigrant Polish Catholic working-class community (Harring, 1984).

From the very beginning, police departments were beset with problems that remain central problems for the police today. Corruption, racial discrimination, brutality, and "politics" were widespread in early departments and continued to plague police work into the twentieth century. During the first two decades of the twentieth century, progressive reformers addressed these problems and sought to bring about changes in the police. Their agenda is still very much the agenda of police reform in the United States. Progressive reformers advocated centralization of administrative control over the police, better training and education to professionalize the police, and greater reliance on modern technology to improve the efficiency and effectiveness of the police. Except for a few departments, however, these reforms had relatively little impact (Walker, 1983).

During periods of widespread popular protest in the United States, there has been criticism of and opposition to the police. During the upsurge in labor struggles of the 1930s, many workers were killed or beaten by police, and fledgling labor unions viewed the police not as public servants but as servants of the business class. During the 1960s, many blacks, students, and others who protested against racism and the war in Vietnam came into direct conflict with the police. By the late 1960s the police had become the object of intense scrutiny. Investigative reports on the police were submitted by two national commissions, federal law enforcement agencies such as the U.S. attorney general's office and the FBI became far more involved in local law enforcement, law enforcement expenditures rose rapidly, and there was an upsurge in research on the role of police in the society.

The Police Function. Analysis of the role of the police in society today focuses on whether the main function of the police is law enforcement or **order maintenance.** The law enforcement image of the police emphasizes crime-fighting—solving crimes and catching criminals. It is the image conveyed in television shows about the police and the image held by many Americans. The order-maintenance role refers to such activities as controlling crowds, directing traffic, serving as an escort, and handling emergencies, family disputes, and the like, none of which usually involves crimes or arrests.

Studies of the police have found that much more police time is taken up with order maintenance than with law enforcement (e.g., Ryan, 1976). Similarly, only 10 to 20 percent of the calls that come into a police station are to report crimes. The majority of calls then represent requests for services, information, or reports of disorders. One important consequence of this is that much police work is routine and unexciting. It is a far cry from the glamour and excitement often portrayed on television in such shows as *Hill Street Blues, Police Woman,* and *Miami Vice.* Another important consequence is that the maintenance of the social order seems to be a more important actual function of the police than fighting crime. The ability of the police to reduce crime is limited by the fact that they must spend most of their time doing other things.

Sidewalk Justice. At the point of arrest police have wide discretionary powers (Davis, 1969). An alleged offender is not automatically arrested and processed through the criminal justice system. Depending upon such factors as race, sex, age, demeanor, and the wish of the complainant, police may choose to "come down hard" or "go easy" on an offender. These "low visibility decisions" (Goldstein, 1960) by the police contribute to the administration of a kind of sidewalk justice, as some offenders are arrested and processed but others who are presumed innocent or harmless by the police are not taken into custody. It is the administration of sidewalk justice that highlights problems that can occur when police abuse their authority.

The police are often charged with three kinds of abuses of their authority: brutality, the use of deadly force, and corruption. Police brutality refers to unjustified or excessive use of force by the police. It has been a widespread problem throughout the history of the police. As early as 1931 the Wickersham Commission, a national commission that investigated problems in the criminal justice system, published *Our Lawless Police,* which focused on the use of "the third degree" by the police. More recently, the police were often charged with brutality

Police killings of black men triggered major rebellions in Miami in 1980 and again in 1982.

during the suppression of the urban disorders and the campus protests of the 1960s. Blacks, Hispanics, and students most frequently charged police with brutality. In 1968 during the Democratic party convention, the police wildly assaulted demonstrators, newspersons, and bystanders in what was widely labeled a "police riot."

The use of "deadly force" refers to the killing of civilians by police. The number of people killed by the police has gradually risen from between 200 and 300 a year during the 1950s and 1960s to between 300 and 500 a year during the 1970s and early 1980s. Blacks and other racial minorities have consistently made up about half of those killed by the police each year, and such killings have frequently triggered major rebellions in various cities, both during the 1960s and more recently in the Liberty City and Overtown areas of Miami during the 1980s.

Defenders of the police explain the overrepresentation of blacks among those killed by the police as the result of greater black involvement in violent and dangerous crime. Young black male criminals are said to be more likely to be armed and dangerous. Critics, on the other hand, assert that this method of sidewalk justice is most likely to be administered to racial minorities. Studies during the 1970s indicated that about one-third of police killings occurred under questionable circumstances. A statistical study by Takagi (1974) found that even blacks between the ages of ten and fourteen were killed by police at a rate fifteen times higher than whites, and blacks over sixty-five were killed at a rate thirty-four times higher than whites. The implication is that all blacks, not just those young black men whom the police might regard as more dangerous, are more likely to be killed by the police (Takagi, 1974).

Police corruption is also an abuse of authority and has been a problem for as long as the police have existed. The most recent investigation of police corruption was that of the Knapp Commission in New York City during the 1970s. The Knapp Commission found widespread corruption, from which police officers received between several hundred and several thousand dollars monthly. Money came from payoffs from construction sites, bars, grocery stores, other businesses, prostitutes, and narcotics rings. The Knapp Commission rejected the traditional "bad apple" theory of police corruption. This theory suggests that corruption is caused by an occasional bad police officer. The commission found corruption to be too widespread to be explained in this fashion. As an alternative it put forth the "group support" theory, emphasizing that corruption was the rule, not the exception, and that it had the support of most members of the department.

Explaining Police Misbehavior. There are two popular explanations of the behavior of the police in our society (Shelden, 1982). The first explanation focuses on the values of the police occupational subculture and how police officers are socialized into that subculture. The second explanation emphasizes the class role of the police. The police subculture socializes its members into a distinct worldview, encouraging strong in-group loyalty, a sense of being isolated from the rest of the population, a common police language, an awareness of danger, and a highly cynical or negative view of human nature. This creates the "working personality" of the typical police officer, which in turn explains the general behavior of the police, including violent and corrupt behavior.

The second view asserts that the police are recruited from the working class, but that they are used by the upper class to control the working class from which they came. The class role of the police is the source or cause of the problems and contradictions in their behavior, because the upper class has to bring about a transfer of loyalty among the police from their class of origin to the class that controls them. This is accomplished by providing police higher pay and greater job security than other workers, by increasing their income and purchasing their loyalty with bribes and other forms of corruption, by intense ideological indoctrination into the value of capitalism, by imposing a military-bureaucratic system of discipline and organization, and by recruiting police from one ethnic or racial group to control other, usually more oppressed ethnic or racial groups.

The problems with these two explanations of police misbehavior is that both assume that police are completely resocialized to become predators rather than protectors of society. Even after administering sidewalk justice against minorities and other presumed undesirables and even with the widespread support for corruption that was identified by the Knapp Commission, it is still likely that police view themselves as public defenders. Thus, the question that needs to be asked about police misbehavior is, Why do people who are socialized to become public defenders commit acts that they know are illegal?

Several authors (Matza, 1964; Scott and Lyman, 1968; Sheley, 1980) have focused on techniques of neutralization to explain why people behave in ways contrary to their socialization. In other words, the excuses and justifications that police offer to explain their illegal behavior help them to neutralize the immorality of their crimes and at the same time allow them to continue to believe that they are still public defenders. Some common techniques of neutralization offered by police include the following: scapegoating—blaming other "good cops" or "bad cops" for their predicament; denying injury—claiming what they did (e.g., taking a payoff) did not hurt anybody; denying the victim—particularly in the administration of sidewalk justice the victim is seen as someone deserving punishment (racial minorities, junkies, drug dealers, and whores are easily viewed as people who deserve injury); and claiming that persons beyond the control of the police forced their hand or their actions, and that the brutality, the deadly force, or the corruption was an accident. This explanation of police misbehavior suggests that police believe themselves to be basically good people who perform necessary public defender services for the society but who occasionally behave in ways inconsistent with that belief. Then they find excuses and justifications that neutralize the moral constraints against their illegal behavior.

The 1984 Federal Omnibus Crime Control Act authorized the use of preventive detention by federal judges, and the number of federal pretrial detainees apparently increased substantially after the law went into effect. Conservative criminal justice leaders advocate the adoption of similar measures on the state and local levels.

Plea Bargaining. Many people think of trials as the most important events that take place in the judicial system, but, in reality, only a small percentage of cases come to trial. The overwhelming majority of cases are settled by means of **plea bargaining.** Plea bargaining occurs when alleged offenders admit their guilt to a lesser of several crimes with which they have been charged in exchange for a promise that the charge of the more serious crime(s) (and presumably a more serious sentence) will be dropped. Prosecuting attorneys represent the "state" or "the people," whereas defense attorneys represent the accused defendants. The original victim of the crime is, in a sense, not represented at all.

Prosecuting attorneys decide which cases to prosecute, and they may screen out or drop many cases. Defendants are legally entitled to a defense attorney. If they can afford one, they may have a privately retained attorney. If not, they either have a public defender or a court-appointed attorney. The majority of defendants have public defenders, who are full-time employees of the criminal courts.

Both prosecuting and defense attorneys try to settle the majority of cases by plea bargaining. There are several reasons for this. First, the court system is enormously overcrowded. Trials take up a great deal of time and are far more expensive than plea bargaining. If most cases went to trial, the entire judicial

Nearly ninety percent of all cases that reach the judicial system are settled by plea bargaining.

system would no doubt break down altogether. Second, most defendants who have come this far through the criminal justice system are guilty of at least some of the charges against them; thus, a guilty plea is a "correct" plea. Third, both prosecuting and defense attorneys are officers of the court. They depend on maintaining friendly relations both with the judges and with each other. They are not primarily adversaries, but negotiators attempting to reach an accommodation in most cases. Consequently, defense attorneys generally try to persuade most of their clients to plead guilty and accept a plea bargain.

This is especially true of public defenders. Public defenders are assigned extremely large case loads by the court and have little time for each client. They may spend no more than ten to fifteen minutes on a typical case, and they often devote this time primarily to convincing the client to accept the normal plea-bargaining terms.

What happens if a defendant refuses to plea bargain? Defendants who can prove their innocence to a judge or jury in a trial fare better, of course, than if they had agreed to a guilty plea. However, defendants who demand a trial and are found guilty are penalized for utilizing more of the court's time and resources. Research has shown that such defendants are convicted of more serious offenses and punished more harshly than if they had accepted plea bargaining. This harsher punishment is the threat that induces many defendants to plea bargain in the first place.

Plea bargaining has frequently been called assembly-line justice because it speeds up the system, and also because it treats each case in a routine "mass-production" way. Critics argue that plea bargaining fails to give individual attention to either the defendant or the victim. It keeps the system functioning, but it does not deliver justice either to criminals or to their victims. Critics also have emphasized that it is mainly poor, minority, or working-class defendants who are processed through the system in this fashion, because middle- and upper-class people generally obtain individualized attention for their cases in whatever courts they may appear. The National Advisory Commission on Criminal Justice Standards and Goals (1973) has urged that plea bargaining be eliminated from the criminal justice process.

The Judicial Process: The Courts

The judicial process begins after a police arrest and ends with the determination of guilt or innocence and, for those deemed guilty, the imposition of a sentence or punishment. Along the way, the weeding-out, or filtering, process continues, for the majority of those arrested are not punished.

Bail and Jail. Persons who have been arrested and charged with a crime are either released under some form of **bail** or detained in jail, pending resolution of their case. The principal constitutional purpose of bail is to insure the presence of the accused at trial. This may be accomplished either by the accused person posting a cash bond or a property bond, being released on his or her own "recognizance" (that is, without bail), or paying a bailbond person to put up bail. In the latter case, the arrested person usually pays 10 percent of the amount of bail to the bailbond person, who then puts up the full amount of bail.

An arrested person who cannot post bond remains in jail and becomes a

pretrial detainee. Pretrial detainees make up almost one-half of the daily population of the jails in the United States. The other half consists of persons serving sentences of less than one year for relatively minor crimes. In addition, there are a number of inmates convicted of more serious offenses who should be serving their time in a prison but who are "backed up" in local jails because of prison overcrowding.

There are many reasons why it is better to be out on bail before trial rather than incarcerated as a pretrial detainee. In the first place, most jails are very unpleasant places. There may be unhealthful and unsanitary conditions, untrained and uncaring jail staff, violent and dangerous inmates, no treatment, exercise, or medical facilities, and tight restrictions on visitors. Secondly, and perhaps most importantly, it is harder to prepare one's defense while in jail. Locating witnesses, gathering evidence, and working with one's attorney are made much more difficult by incarceration. Third, pretrial detainees often appear in court under guard and dressed in jail clothes, whereas those who have been out on bail appear in court without chains or guards and are usually dressed in their best clothes. The former "looks" like a criminal to the judge or jury, and the latter "looks" like a law-abiding citizen.

Consequently, research has shown that pretail detainees are more likely to be convicted than those released on bail (Shelden, 1982:198–99). Of those convicted, pretrial detainees receive harsher punishments than persons who were out on bail. Because being a pretrial detainee is a significant handicap, it is important to know whether the bail system operates in a fair and reasonable way. There are many reasons to think it does not.

First, the bail system tends to discriminate against the poor. Many arrestees cannot afford bail or even afford to pay a bailbond person. They remain in jail because they are poor, not because they are unlikely to appear for trial or because it would be dangerous to release them. Second, studies have shown that many more people could be safely released before trial. When the Manhattan Bail Project experimented in the 1960s with the concept of releasing more people without bail, it was found that almost all defendants still appeared in court at the appointed date.

Second, the bail system is often used to carry out the constitutionally questionable practice of **preventive detention.** Preventive detention refers to the practice of denying bail to those persons thought to be dangerous or likely to commit further crimes if they are released before trial. Supporters of preventive detention argue that such persons should not be allowed back on the streets. Critics of preventive detention argue that it amounts to punishing people for crimes they might commit in the future, and that predicting who will commit future crimes is highly uncertain. Critics also argue that preventive detention is sometimes used in a discriminatory way against poor or minority defendants.

Sentencing. Sentencing is the last stage of the judicial process. Most sentences do not involve incarceration in a jail or prison. The most commonly imposed sentences by far are fines and probation. Probation involves formal supervision in the community for a specified period of time. Restitution—paying back the victim or the community—is still another type of sentence.

Sentencing has long been controversial and inconsistent in our criminal justice system. Many studies have documented significant disparities in sentencing, that is, variations in the amount of punishment imposed. There is also much disagreement over what goals or philosophy should guide sentencing. The main sentencing philosophies are **retribution, deterrence, rehabilitation,** and **incapacitation.**

Retribution, or "just desserts," invokes the principle of revenge to "make the punishment fit the crime." It is morally right and necessary to punish criminals. Deterrence as a philosophy emphasizes the prevention or reduction of crime as the main goal of punishment. Rehabilitation emphasizes that treatment rather than punishment should be the goal of the criminal justice system. The criminal should receive the proper treatment needed to reform him/her into a law-abiding citizen. Incapacitation emphasizes the goal of incarcerating criminals so that they are not at liberty to commmit further crimes against society.

The philosophy of retribution suggests that we can deter or reduce crime only insofar as we can decide which criminals to incapacitate. Thus, selective incapacitation involves incarcerating those criminals who we believe would commit future crimes. Other criminals could be punished in other ways. The deterrence and rehabilitation philosophies claim to be able to reduce crime either by deterring future offenders or by reforming criminals.

Throughout most of the twentieth century the rehabilitation philosophy has dominated sentencing practices in the United States. Since the 1970s, however, the philosophy of retribution has gained ascendancy. It has brought with it the sentencing of more criminals to longer prison terms and has led to a substantial increase in the prison population in the United States and a revival of capital punishment.

Capital Punishment and Imprisonment

Capital Punishment: The Death Penalty. National surveys indicate that a large majority of Americans favor the death penalty. Some favor it for reasons of retribution, some for reasons of deterrence, and some invoke both philosophies. Opponents of the death penalty either invoke moral arguments, claim that it is not an effective deterrent, or argue that it is applied in a discriminatory manner.

Between 1930 and 1967 there were 3,860 persons executed in the United States. From 1967 to 1977 there were no executions, because the U.S. Supreme Court had declared unconstitutional existing death penalty statutes and instructed state legislatures to write new statutes that would not be discriminatory or arbitrary. By the mid-1980s some two-thirds of all states had adopted new capital punishment laws, nearly fifty people had been executed, and over 1,400 prisoners were on death row awaiting execution.

The issue of racial discrimination has been at the heart of the debate over the death penalty. Of those executed in the U.S. between 1930 and 1967, 55 percent were black. Nearly 90 percent of those executed for the crime of rape were black. Studies showed clearly that blacks convicted of raping or murdering whites were far more likely to receive the death penalty than whites whose victims were black or criminals whose victims were of the same race. Today, about 40 percent of all prisoners on death row are black. Some 6 percent are Hispanic. Class bias has also been an issue. Most of these executed have been poor. Today, only 41 percent of the prisoners on death row have completed high school (Bedau, 1982; Bowers, 1984).

If the death penalty is applied in a class and racially discriminatory way, this clearly undermines or weakens both its deterrent values as well as the moral justification of retribution. The death penalty cannot deter affluent whites who commit white-collar and organized crime and who also know that capital punishment is applied mainly to the poor and minorities. Similarly, if the death penalty is to be applied for the worst crimes committed by the worst criminals, it must be equally applicable to black and white, rich and poor.

The numerous studies that have investigated the deterrent value of the death penalty have generally failed to demonstrate that the death penalty effectively deters murder, the principal crime to which it applies. The debate is by no means resolved, however.

Prisons. There are both state and federal prison systems in the United States. The fifty state systems as a whole are much larger than the federal system, but both grew rapidly during the 1970s and 1980s. On June 30, 1984, the adult prison population had reached a record of 454,136—almost double the total ten years earlier. Only 34,168 inmates were in federal prisons.

As of June 1984 about 96 percent of this prison population consisted of males. Some 47 percent of inmates were black, and about 10 percent were Hispanic. Christianson (1981) has pointed out that the problems of black overrepresentation in prison is actually even greater than the above percentages indicate. Because 96 percent of all inmates are male, black males, who comprise less than 6 percent of the U.S. population, are more than 45 percent of all prison inmates. Other critics have stated that more black men enter prison each year than enter college. This is perhaps the most extreme example of the "homogenization" process in the criminal justice system.

Researchers debate whether the death penalty deters murder and whether it is applied in a racially discriminatory manner.

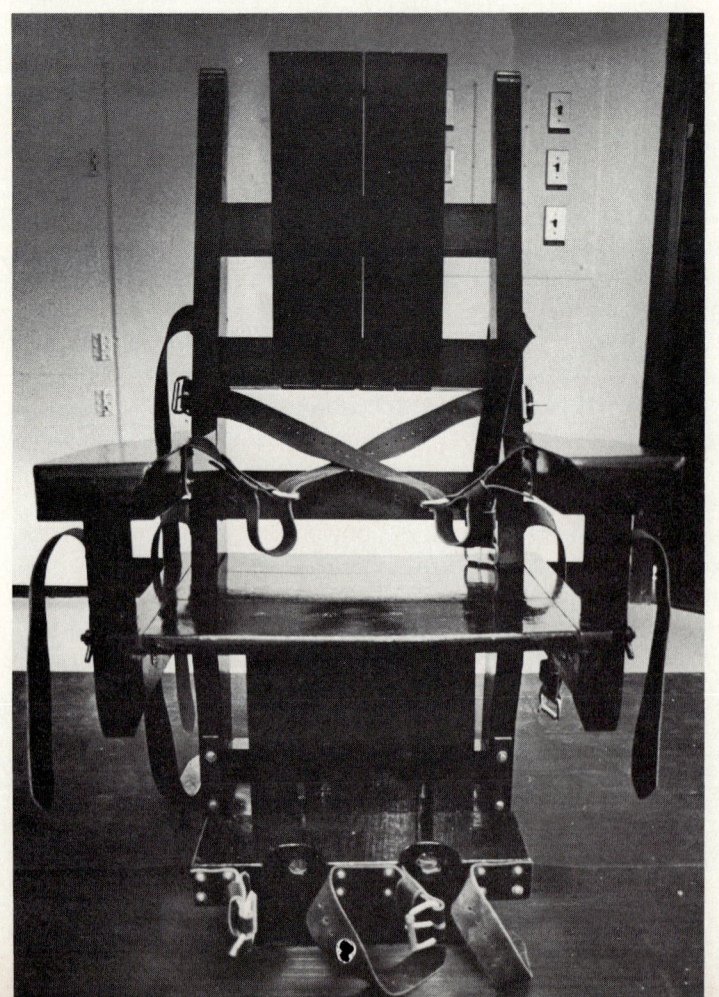

There are nearly six hundred federal and state prisons in the United States. The majority of all prison inmates are housed in maximum security prisons. As of 1983 the courts had declared unconstitutional the entire prison systems of eight states. One or more prison facilities were under a court order to institute reforms in twenty-one other states. Seven additional states were involved in on-going court actions. These facts provide some indication of the conditions that prevail in many prisons throughout the country.

Overcrowding is one of the greatest problems. In 1984 nearly ten thousand prisoners were being held in local jails because there was no room for them in already overcrowded prison facilities. Although states were spending hundreds of millions of dollars for construction of new prison facilities, the prison population was growing faster than new prison capacity (*Report to the Nation on Crime and Justice*, 1983).

This rapid growth in the U.S. prison population is related to the overall conservative movement in the United States since the 1970s. Conservatives emphasize the philosophies of retribution and incapacitation for cirminals. They have called for putting more people in prison for longer terms. Longer fixed sentences have replaced **indeterminate sentences,** which permitted the possibility of early parole.

Throughout most of the twentieth century the prevailing philosophy in the U.S. prison system was the philosophy of rehabilitation. The emphasis on rehabilitation grew out of the progressive movement of the early 1900s. Progressive reformers followed a medical model of crime and punishment. They believed that criminals were sick and in need of treatment. The experts who diagnosed their sickness would treat them until criminals were "rehabilitated" and could be released back into society. In recent years this **medical model of crime** has been widely criticized and rejected. Conservatives have argued that most criminals cannot be rehabilitated and that the emphasis should instead be on administering the proper punishment. Other critics have argued that the prison system never really put much emphasis on rehabilitation and that most of what was called "treatment" was actually punishment. These critics of rehabilitation also argue that the causes of crime lie primarily in the nature of society, not within sick individuals.

> More than 2.7 million adults were under correctional supervision in 1984.

The critics are largely correct that whatever the prison system did under the philosophy of rehabilitation was not very effective. Up until the 1930s the emphasis in prisons was on hard labor. The exploitation of prison labor to make a profit or at least to cover the costs of running the institution was a central concern of those in charge of the prison system in the United States. This emphasis on hard labor led Sellin (1976) to compare prison systems to slavery. Sellin argued that modern prison systems grew out of slavery and in many ways were a continuation of slavery.

Sellin noted (1976) that after the Civil War southern states developed first the convict-leasing systems, then chain gangs and plantation prisons to exploit the labor of black prisoners. These forms of punishment, Sellin argued, served as functional equivalents of slavery.

The exploitation of prison labor has declined significantly in the United States since the Great Depression of the 1930s. Before the 1930s there was a labor shortage in the United States, and employers sought to use all available labor power. Since the 1930s the United States has been plagued by chronic high unemployment rates. If there are no jobs for millions of workers in the free society, there are not likely to be any jobs for hundreds of thousands of prison inmates. Today the main labor performed by prison inmates consists of various forms of institutional maintenance that reduce the cost of running the prison. Most prisoners have a tremendous amount of simply idle time.

In American prisons today there are widespread problems of crime and violence. These include murders and assaults, homosexual rapes, widespread drug abuse, gang warfare among gangs usually organized along racial or ethnic lines, and an undergorund economy. These conditions give rise to large-scale prison riots or uprisings from time to time. Two of the most significant prison riots in recent decades were the 1980 New Mexico State Penitentiary riot and the 1971 Attica (New York) uprising. There were some significant contrasts between these two riots.

In the New Mexico riot thirty-three inmates were killed, all by fellow inmates. They were identified as "snitches," or informers for the prison authorities. Many were killed by the most savage and brutal methods. During the riot, drug-crazed inmates ran amok, and racial and ethnic tensions and conflict were widespread. In the Attica riot thirty-two inmates and eleven guards were killed, all by the state police who stormed the prison. The rioting inmates killed no one; they maintained order in the section of the prison under their control. Their chosen leaders presented a list of demands concerning conditions in the prison. There was a high level of interracial solidarity among the black, Hispanic, and white inmates. Consequently, there was a certain amount of pubic sympathy and support for the Attica rebels, whereas there was mainly a feeling of horror about the New Mexico riot.

The United States has one of the largest prison systems and the highest incarceration rates of any country in the world. Comparative statistics are unreliable, but probably only South Africa and the Soviet Union have higher incarceration rates than the United States. Locking up hundreds of thousands of criminals does not seem to make American society freer from crime and violence. In fact, Japan and certain Western European countries that have the smallest prison systems also have the lowest crime rates in the world. On the other hand, countries that have widespread poverty, oppression, and racism, such as the United States, South Africa, and the Soviet Union, have both large prison systems and high crime rates. Building a better society, instead of building a larger, more repressive prison system, would probably be more effective in reducing crime.

Summary

There are many different kinds of crime in American society that are committed by different groups. It is misleading to focus only on conventional crimes that are more often committed by poor and working-class people. At least six sociological theories of criminal behavior have been offered, including class culture, anomie, opportunity, differential association, labeling, and conflict theory.

The *Uniform Crime Reports* and the *National Crime Surveys* are the two main sources of official crime data. Both provide much useful information, but both have been subject to important criticisms. The police as a modern institution were formed during the middle of the nineteenth century, mainly to cope with rising urban disorders. They focus more today on order maintenance than on law enforcement. Today, as in the past, major problems associated with the police are violence and the use of "deadly force" and corruption. There are three main theories of police behavior. One theory focuses on the values of the police subculture and the ways that police are socialized into that subculture. Another focuses on the class role of the police in society. The third theory concentrates on ways police neutralize their socialization as public defenders.

The first stage of the judicial system involves bail or jail. Remaining in jail or getting released on bail is often affected by economic or political factors. The second stage of the judicial system involves trials or plea bargaining. Most cases are settled by plea bargaining. The final stage of the judicial system is sentencing, which may involve a fine or incarceration. Retribution, deterrence, rehabilitation, and incapacitation are the four main philosophies of sentencing.

Research on whether the death penalty is a deterrent is inconclusive; however, use of the death penalty has increased again during the 1980s. The United States has a large, growing, overcrowded prison system, containing disproportionate numbers of minority males.

Key Concepts

bail
clearance rate
crime
deterrence
differential association
fixed sentences
homogenization
incapacitation
indeterminate sentences
index crimes

mala in se
mala prohibita
medical model of crime
order maintenance
plea bargaining
pretrial detainee
preventive detention
rehabilitation
retribution
victimization survey

References

Attica: The Official Report of the New York State Special Commission on Attica. (1972) New York, N.Y.: Bantam Books.

Balkan, Sheila, Ronald J. Berger, and Janet Schmidt. (1980) *Crime and Deviance in America.* Belmont, Calif.: Wadsworth.

Becker, Howard S. (1963) *Outsiders: Studies in the Sociology of Deviance.* New York: Free Press.

Bedau, Hugo Adam (ed.). (1982) *The Death Penalty in America.* 3d ed. New York, N.Y.: Oxford University Press.

Bowers, William J. (1984) *Executions in America.* 2nd ed. Lexington, Mass.: D. C. Heath & Company.

Bowker, Lee H. (1982) *Corrections: The Science and the Art.* New York, N.Y.: Macmillan Publishing Co., Inc.

Brown, Edward J., Timothy J. Flanagan, and Maureen McLeod (eds.). (1984) *Sourcebook of Criminal Justice Statistics, 1983.* U.S. Department of Justice, Bureau of Justice Statistics, Washington, D.C.: U.S. Government Printing Office.

Christianson, Scott. (1981) "Our Black Prisons." *Crime and Delinquency, 27* (July–Sept.):364–375.

Clinard, Marshall B., and Richard Quinney. (1973) *Criminal Behavior Systems.* 2d ed. New York, N.Y.: Holt, Rinehart and Winston.

Clinard, Marshall B., and Peter C. Yeager. (1980) *Corporate Crime.* New York, N.Y.: The Free Press.

Cloward, Richard, and Lloyd Ohlin. (1960) *Delinquency and Opportunity.* Glencoe, Ill.: The Free Press.

Cohen, Albert. (1955) *Delinquent Boys: The Culture of the Gang.* Glencoe, Ill.: The Free Press.

Coleman, James W. (1985) *The Criminal Elite: The Sociology of White-Collar Crime.* New York, N.Y.: St. Martin's Press, Inc.

Davis, Kenneth C. (1969) *Discretionary Justice: A Preliminary Inquiry.* Baton Rouge, LA: Louisiana State University Press.

Federal Bureau of Investigation. *Uniform Crime Reports.* Washington, D.C.: U.S. Government Printing Office, published annually.

Galliher, John F. (1976) "Explanations of Police Behavior: A Critical Review and Analysis." In Arthur Niederhoffer and Abraham S. Blumberg (eds.), *The Ambivalent Force: Perspectives on the Police.* 2nd ed. Hinsdale, Ill.: The Dryden Press.

Georges-Abeyie, Daniel (ed.). (1984) *The Criminal Justice System and Blacks.* New York, N.Y.: Clark Boardman Company, Ltd.

Goldstein, Joseph. (1960) "Police Discretion Not to Invoke the Criminal Process." *Yale Law Journal, 69*(July):544.

Harring, Sidney. (1985) *Policing a Class Society.*, New Brunswick, N.J.: Rutgers University Press.

Institute for the Study of Labor and Economic Crisis. (1982) *The Iron Fist and the Velvet Glove: An Analysis of the U.S. Police.* 3d ed. San Francisco, Calif.: Synthesis Publications.

Knapp Commission Report on Police Corruption. (1972) New York, N.Y.: George Braziller.

McCaghy, Charles. (1976) *Deviant Behavior: Crime, Conflict and Interest Groups.* New York, N.Y.: Macmillan Publishing Co., Inc.

McNeely, R. L., and Carl E. Pope (eds.). (1981) *Race, Crime, and Criminal Justice.* Beverly Hills, Calif.: Sage Publications.

Matza, David. (1964) *Delinquency and Drift.* New York, N.Y.: John Wiley & Sons, Inc.

Merton, Robert. (1957) *Social Theory and Social Structure.* Glencoe, Ill.: The Free Press.

Miller, Walter B. (1958) "Lower Class Culture as Generating Milieu of Gang Delinquency." *Journal of Social Issues, 14:*(January)5–19.

National Advisory Commission on Criminal Justice Standards and Goals. (1973) *Task Force Report: Courts.* Washington, D.C.: U.S. Government Printing Office.

Nettler, Gwynn. (1984) *Explaining Crime.* 3rd ed. New York, N.Y.: McGraw-Hill Book Company.

Price, Barbara Raffel, and Natalie J. Sokoloff (eds.). (1982) *The Criminal Justice System and Women.* New York, N.Y.: Clark Boardman Company, Ltd.

Quinney, Richard. (1977) *Class, State and Crime.* New York, N.Y.: David McKay Co., Inc.

Reiman, Jeffrey H. (1979) *The Rich Get Richer and the Poor Get Prison.* New York, N.Y.: John Wiley & Sons, Inc.

Ryan, William. (1976) *Blaming the Victim.* Rev. ed. New York, N.Y.: Vintage Books/Random House, Inc.

Scott, Marvin B., and Stanford M. Lyman. (1968) "Accounts." *American Sociological Review, 33*(February):46–62.

Sellin, Thorsten. (1976) *Slavery and the Penal System.* New York, N.Y.: American Elsevier Publishing Co., Inc.

Shelden, Randall. (1982) *Criminal Justice in America: A Sociological Approach.* Boston, Mass.: Little, Brown and Company.

Sheley, Joseph F. (1980) "Is Neutralization Necessary for Criminal Behavior?" *Deviant Behavior, 2*(October–December):50.

Sutherland, Edwin. (1961) *White-Collar Crime.* New York, N.Y.: Holt, Rinehart and Winston.

Takagi, Paul. (1974) "A Garrison State in a Democratic Society." *Crime and Social Justice.* February, Vol. I, pp. 88–104.

Taylor, Ian, Paul Walton, and Jack Young. (1973) *The New Criminology.* New York, N.Y.: Harper & Row, Publishers.

U.S. Department of Justice. (1984) "The Severity of Crime." *Bureau of Justice Statistics Bulletin.* Washington, D.C.: U.S. Government Printing Office.

U.S. Department of Justice, Bureau of Justice Statistics. (Annual) *National Crime Survey.* Washington, D.C.: U.S. Government Printing Office.

U.S. Department of Justice, Bureau of Justice Statistics. (1983) *Report to the Nation on Crime and Justice.* Washington, D.C.: U.S. Government Printing Office.

Walker, Samuel. (1983) *The Police in America.* New York, N.Y.: McGraw-Hill Book Company.

Woodson, Robert L. (ed.). (1977) *Black Perspectives on Crime and the Criminal Justice System.* Boston, Mass.: G. K. Hall and Co.

20

Health Status and Medical Care

OBJECTIVES

After reading this chapter the student should be able to:

1. Define morbidity and mortality.

2. Identify synergistic forces that affect the incidence of morbidity and mortality in selected populations.

3. Outline the segments of the population that are at the greatest risk of contracting the most common notifiable diseases.

4. Discuss the impact of life-style on morbidity and mortality.

5. Note important social factors affecting a patient's access to medical personnel and health-care facilities.

INTRODUCTION

Sociologists are concerned with collective, or group, behavior. In each chapter we have seen how social forces such as socialization, deviance, religion, and education differentially affect categories of people. In other words, as one's membership in certain groups varies, so too do the social forces that impinge upon the behavior of that group. Researchers at the Centers for Disease Control (CDC) in Atlanta, Georgia, have labeled the social forces that affect the quality of one's health as "behavioral risk factors."

Behavioral risk factors that influence health status vary according to one's memberships in certain groups. As you move in and out of some groups and simultaneously remain a member of other groups, your health status will be influenced by the effects of combined risk factors upon the groups to which you belong. **Synergy** is the effects of a combination of factors on behavior. Thus, in this chapter we examine synergistic effects of factors that contribute to differences in the quality of health among various groups in the society.

Medical care in the United States is reflected largely in traditional practices recognized by such medical organizations as the American Medical Association (AMA) and the National League of Nursing (NLN). Although you may be familiar with a few home remedies for colds, hangovers, and minor cuts or scrapes, caring for serious health problems is likely to be reserved for professionally certified medical personnel. Likewise, where the ideas and values of some religious groups such as Jehovah's Witnesses regarding health care conflict with traditional medical practices, the weight of social and governmental support most often favors institutionalized medicine. Medical care then is one of several institutions, and like the other institutions that we have covered in this text, we can raise certain questions about its functioning in society. For example, to whom are medical services provided? Is medical care provided according to one's need or according to one's ability to pay for those services? Are the racial and sexual inequalities found in other social institutions also reflected in the provision of medical care?

The focus of this chapter is to review the health status and medical services available to people in the United States. Particular attention is given to segments of the U.S. population according to various age groups and racial and sexual categories. In this chapter we review leading causes of death, notifiable diseases, injuries, and access to medical facilities and health-care personnel. The effects of life-style are identified and examined for their influence on the health of segments of the population. Finally, where appropriate we seek to answer the questions associated with the functioning of medical care in society.

Social Forces and Morbidity

Medical doctors and sociologists are interested in the study of **morbidity.** Morbidity refers to the relative incidence of disease in a community. Doctors and sociologists, however, approach the study of morbidity in different ways. Whereas doctors concentrate on germs and viruses in order to develop cures for diseases, sociologists focus on social factors that are likely to place some populations at a greater risk of contracting disease than other populations. Social factors that help sociologists explain morbidity include income, race, sex, occupation, and life-style. This list of social factors, although not exhaustive, nonetheless helps us explain why certain groups are differentially affected by disease.

One way of examining the impact of social factors on morbidity is by reviewing their presence in association with selected **notifiable diseases.** Notifiable diseases are those diseases that by law require health-care personnel to report all known cases. The most frequently reported notifiable disease in America is venereal disease. Venereal disease is often referred to as a **sexually transmitted disease** (STD). Although gonorrhea and syphilis are the most well known of the STDs, there are many other diseases that are typically spread through sexual contact, including the following: acquired immune deficiency syndrome (AIDS), pelvic inflammatory disease (PID), chlamydia, herpes, trichomoniasis, nongonococcal urethritis, vaginitis, urinary tract infections, chancroid, lymphogranuloma venereum, genital warts, lice, and scabies.

Gonorrhea is by far the most frequently reported notifiable disease. The next most frequently reported notifiable disease is chicken pox. Salmonellosis, com-

Social factors, such as income, race, sex, occupation, and life-style, help us explain why certain groups are differentially affected by disease.

monly called food poisoning, is the next most frequently reported disease. Syphilis, the fourth most frequently reported disease, is the third most frequent communicable disease. Together, gonorrhea and syphilis annually account for almost a million cases of notifiable diseases. Although almost a million cases of gonorrhea and syphilis are reported to the CDC, public health officials generally concede that this number underestimates the total number of those infected each year. For example, the American Social Health Association (1983) estimates that 3,400,000 persons are affected by gonorrhea and syphilis alone each year. When other STDs are included, the number of persons affected is estimated to be between ten and thirty million people.

Age, Sex, and Disease

As you might expect, not everyone is at the same risk of catching gonorrhea and syphilis. Young people are more at risk than older persons. Specifically, young adults aged twenty to twenty-four are at greatest risk of contracting gonorrhea, whereas teenagers aged fifteen to nineteen are the second highest group at risk. According to the CDC (*MMWR*, 1983:33), "Teenagers accounted for 25% and young adults for 38% of all gonorrhea cases reported." Males and females differ in the age at which they are most at risk in contracting gonorrhea. Teenage females aged fifteen to nineteen are more at risk in contracting gonorrhea than their teenage male counterparts. Young adult males aged twenty to twenty-four are at greatest risk. Finally, males generally have a higher reported rate of gonorrhea than females. Presented in Table 20.1 are data regarding the rate of reported gonorrhea and syphilis per 100,000 persons in the population by age and sex.

One possible explanation for the differences in the age at which males and females are at risk in contracting gonorrhea is the cultural preference for older men to date younger women. Thus, young men aged twenty to twenty-four, who are at their greatest risk of contracting gonorrhea, are most likely to pass the

Table 20.1 *Reported Cases of Gonorrhea and Syphilis by Sex and Age, Per 100,000 Population, 1982*

Age in years	Gonorrhea		Syphilis	
	Males	Females	Males	Females
0–14	10.6	30.6	0.2	0.7
15–19	980.1	1424.9	24.5	21.6
20–24	2107.3	1356.2	65.4	25.3
25–29	1364.7	567.2	61.8	15.8
30–39	557.8	165.6	38.4	8.2
40–49	185.2	40.9	20.3	3.6
50+	29.6	5.6	3.4	0.5

Source: Adapted from (a) *Center for Disease Control Annual Summary, 1982: Reported Morbidity and Mortality in the United States* and (b) *Morbidity and Mortality Weekly Report,* 1983; *31*(54).

disease on to their younger female companions aged fifteen to nineteen. A similar pattern of age grading exists for rates of syphilis. Syphilis is primarily a young-adult and teenage problem. The highest rates of syphilis for females fall in those age groups just below the high-risk group for males (see Table 20.1).

Venereal disease is not just a problem for heterosexual couples. The CDC, for example, reports an increase in the proportion of men with syphilis who name other men as sexual partners. The CDC reported an increase from 23 percent of the men with syphilis in 1969 who reported other men as sexual partners to 44 percent in 1982. Perhaps the most fatal of the sexually transmittable infectious diseases for homosexuals is acquired immune deficiency syndrome (AIDS). To date, more than half of all AIDS patients have died. The groups most likely to contract AIDS are homosexual and bisexual males. Seventy-three percent of all known AIDS patients were either bisexual or homosexual males. Only 6 percent of reported AIDS cases have involved females (*MMWR,* 1983:104). Ninety percent of AIDS cases occur among persons between the ages of twenty and forty-nine. AIDS has been detected in whites, blacks, and Hispanics. Five percent of all AIDS

The segment of the population whose life-style and personal choices make them more likely to contract and transmit sexually transmittable diseases are young males.

cases reported to the CDC involve persons born in Haiti but living in the United States (*MMWR*, 1983:104).

Sexually transmittable diseases again highlight the influence of life-style and personal choices on the health status of a population. Although anyone can contract venereal disease, some people are more likely to contract a disease than others. For example, although there is no guarantee that remaining monogamous will prevent one from contracting a sexually transmittable disease, the choice to engage in sexual intercourse with a variety of partners greatly increases the chances of becoming infected and infecting others. The persons who are most likely to have a variety of sexual partners and therefore are at greatest risk are males and/or single persons between twenty and thirty years of age. Thus, the probability of contracting sexually transmittable diseases can be explained by such social factors as race, sex, and life-style. Race and income also help to explain the incidence of a particular disease among a given population. The following section highlights the influence of race, racism, income, and the lack of education on morbidity.

Bad Blood and Syphilis

In July 1982 the Associated Press revealed that the United States Public Health Service had been conducting an experiment for forty years on the effects of untreated syphilis on black men in Macon County, Alabama. According to Jones (1981), there were 600 men involved in the experiment, which lasted for forty years. Of those involved in the experiment, 201 men were controls, or persons free of syphilis. The other 399 men were purported to be in the tertiary, or final, stages of syphilis. This very controversial research on race and syphilis came to be known as the Tuskegee study. (The study was discussed briefly in Chapter 2.)

The Tuskegee study developed as an outgrowth of a demonstration project funded by the Julius Rosenwald Fund. The fund was set up in part by a Jewish immigrant who helped build the Sears and Roebuck Company. The fund was set up to finance benevolent projects for blacks. Most of the early money went to finance educational projects, including building schools. According to Jones (1981), by 1929 a medical division had been established and had as its goals increasing the number of trained black health-care professionals, particularly public health professionals, and improving black community health. The demonstration project began in 1930 and provided $50,000 for controlling venereal disease in the rural South. A second grant of $15,000 was provided by the fund in 1931, but the fund's executive board decided not to fund the demonstration project beyond 1931.

In 1932 officers of the United States Public Health Service who were administering the fund's grants decided that in the absence of funding from the Rosenwald Fund or from public health funds for control of syphilis among black males they would convert the treatment program into a nontherapeutic human experiment. Initially, the study was to last approximately six months, but again public health officials decided at the end of six months to expand the study indefinitely. Over the forty-year life of the study the officials who approved of and conducted the Tuskegee study included three surgeons general of the United States, four directors of the Division of Venereal Disease in the United States Public Health Service, a host of state and county health officials in Alabama, two public health nurses, two presidents of Tuskegee Institute, and two administrators of the John

A. Andrew Memorial Hospital on the campus of Tuskegee Institute. The study's design essentially involved the refusal by physicians, both public and private, to extend treatment of syphilis to black men in Macon County, Alabama, who had been identified by public health officials. Members of the control group who later developed syphilis were switched to the experimental group and also were refused treatment. The design of the experiment simply called for Public Health Service officials with the help of local medical personnel to monitor the development of syphilis over the men's lifetimes. When the men died, autopsies were performed to further document the effects of syphilis.

The men were never informed that they had syphilis. Rather, they were told that they had "bad blood." The men were led to believe by both the doctors and nurses that they were receiving treatment for their bad blood. In some cases they were given an assortment of tonics, pills, and rubs. But no effort was made by the doctors to cure the men's disease. The men did not give their informed consent to participate in the study. Thus, the men in this study were tricked into participating in an experiment that damaged their health and shortened their lives. Ironically, the medical value of the study was called into question long before any ethical issues regarding the morality of the experiment. Because most of the men had received some treatment for syphilis . . . there was never any true experimental or control groups. Thus, the poor research methodology meant that any findings were suspect. Because of the deficiency in design of the research, Dr. James B. Lucas, assistant chief of the Veneral Disease Branch, declared late in 1970 that the Tuskegee study was incongruous with the goals of the Public Health Service and "nothing learned will prevent, find, or cure a single case of infectious syphilis or bring us to our basic mission of controlling venereal disease in the United States" (Jones, 1981:202).

Several implications that help us explain differential morbidity among groups in society may be drawn from this review of the Tuskegee study. First, the relationship of black men to the medical institution, in the form of medical personnel conducting the syphilis research, was consistent with the relationship of black men to the other social intitutions of the period (e.g., economic, religious, educational). In short, the same racism found in other social institutions was found in the medical institution.

Second, as a result of the failure of medical personnel to treat black men the incidence of syphilis among black men and women in Alabama was higher than the incidence of the disease in a comparable group of whites. Finally, poor and uneducated men were most likely to be the victims of both the disease and the research. Likewise, it is the poor and uneducated who are more likely to experience higher morbidity than the well-to-do and educated of a community.

Social Forces and Mortality

The factors that contribute to **mortality,** the incidence of death within a given population, are both physical and social. Heart disease and cancer are examples of factors that may be considered physical or natural causes of death. Indeed, heart disease is the leading cause of death in the United States. The chances of dying from heart disease or cancer, however, are enhanced or minimized according to certain social factors. Social factors such as occupation, diet, exposure to environmental pollutants, exposure to violence, life-style including leisure-time activities, sexual activity, and drug use contribute to the probability of death from heart disease, cancer, or other natural causes. The Centers for Disease Control has noted in its *Annual Summary* (1983), for example, that three behavioral risk factors—hypertension, cigarette smoking, and elevated cholesterol level—are likely to increase the chances of developing heart disease (Rowland et al., 1983:16).

Note that these three factors—hypertension, cigarette smoking, and cholesterol level—are closely associated with one's life-style. In fact many of the morbidity and mortality problems of Americans can be traced to their life-style. In other words, the diseases that take our lives and the injuries that damage our health are for the most part a product of the choices we make throughout our lives. Relatively few of the life-threatening health problems for Americans are inherited. The surgeon general's report on health promotion and disease prevention claimed that the measures to enhance good health are within the practical grasp of most Americans. The surgeon general's report noted behavioral risk factors such as alcohol misuse, obesity, sedentary life-style, lack of seat belt use, uncontrolled hypertension, and cigarette smoking as the major influences on the health status of Americans (*MMWR*, 1983:v).

Social factors such as age, race, and sex also affect mortality. For example, hypertension increases with age and has a higher incidence among blacks than whites. Cholesterol level generally varies according to age and sex. Thus, although the leading cause of death for Americans may be heart disease, because some segments of the population are more likely to experience the synergistic effects of hypertension, cigarettes, and cholesterol than others, the death rate from heart disease or other natual causes will vary by race, sex, and age. The **death rate** refers to the proportion of a population to die from a particular cause. Table 20.2 contains data regarding death rate from heart disease.

Smoking and Health

Cigarette smoking is the largest preventable cause of illness and premature death in the United States. Smoking is a related factor in heart disease, circulatory problems, lung disease, and cancer. Cigarette smoking has been linked to cancers in the esophagus, urinary bladder, kidneys, pancreas, stomach, and cervix (*Report of the Surgeon General,* 1982). Cigarette smoking has also been cited as

Table 20.2 Leading Cause of Death by Race and Sex, Per 100,000 Population, 1980

Cause	White		Black	
	Male	Female	Male	Female
Diseases of the heart	277.5	134.6	327.3	201.1
Cerebrovascular diseases	41.9	35.2	77.5	61.7
Malignant neoplasms (cancer)	160.5	107.7	229.9	129.7
Pneumonia	16.2	9.4	28.0	12.7
Chronic liver disease	15.7	7.0	30.6	14.4
Diabetes	9.5	8.7	17.7	22.1
Accidents	62.3	21.4	82.0	25.1
Suicide	18.9	5.7	11.4	2.4
Homicide	10.9	3.2	79.5	13.7

Source: Adapted from National Center for Health Statistics. (1983) *Health, United States, 1983.* DHHS Pub. No. (PHS) 84–1232. Washington, D.C.: U.S. Government Printing Office, 105–6.

Cigarette smoking is the largest preventable cause of illness and premature death in the United States.

a factor in aggravating blood pressure levels, Burger's disease, and in aggravating the problems of diabetes by increasing blood sugar levels (Berkley, 1982:21–22). Overall, cigarette smokers have a 70 percent higher death rate than nonsmokers. Furthermore, cigarette smoking combines synergistically with other drugs such as alcohol and even oral contraceptives to increase the likelihood of cancer and heart disease. For pregnant women smoking increases the risk of spontaneous abortion, fetal or neonatal death, and retarded fetal growth.

The number of cigarette smokers (approximately fifty-three million) in the United States is not evenly distributed in the population. The percentage of current smokers and the percent of heavy smokers vary according to race and sex. Research (Rowland et al., 1983) utilizing data from the National Health and Nutrition Survey has shown that a higher percentage of males are current smokers. According to the survey, a current smoker is a person who has smoked at least 100 cigarettes and who now smokes, including occasional smokers. A higher percentage of males are heavy smokers, that is, smoke twenty-five cigarettes or more per day. Table 20.3 contains data regarding the rate of current smokers and heavy smokers for 1976 to 1980 according to race and sex. As illustrated in Table 20.3 black males constitute the largest percentage of current smokers, followed by white males, white females, and black females. White males, however, represent the largest percentage of heavy smokers, followed by black males, white females, and black females respectively. Males then are more likely to have their health status damaged from cigarette smoking.

Table 20.3 *Current and Heavy Smokers by Race and Sex Per 100,000 Population, 1976–80*

Race and Sex	Current Smoker[a]	Heavy Smoker[b]
White		
Males	37.6	17.5
Females	31.3	8.2
Black		
Males	46.5	9.6
Females	29.9	3.5

Source: Adapted from Michael Rowland, Robinson Fulwood, and Joel C. Kleinman, National Center for Health Statistics (1983). *Health United States, 1983.* DHHS Pub. No. (PHS) 84–1232. Washington, D.C.: U.S. Government Printing Office, 15.

[a]A current smoker is a person who has smoked at least 100 cigarettes and who now smokes; includes occasional smokers.
[b]A heavy smoker is a person who smokes 25 cigarettes or more per day.

Smoking by women did not become popular until the 1920s and 1930s. According to Diehl (1969), the greatest factor contributing to an increase in smoking among women was a tremendously skillful and intensive advertising campaign. The purpose of the advertisements was twofold: "to make smoking by women socially acceptable and associate smoking with characteristics that particularly appeal to women: romance, independence, glamour, and social success" (Diehl, 1969:13). The most successful campaign of this era was for Lucky Strike cigarettes. Their advertising slogan "reach for a Lucky instead of a sweet" offered smoking as an alternative to getting fat. "This was magic," according to Diehl (1969:13), "because most people, particularly women, have a fear of getting fat and know that candy is fattening." Within the year the sale of Lucky Strikes more than tripled.

In 1982 the report of the surgeon general on the health consequences of smoking estimated that in 1982, 197,000 women would die because of cancer. The report also concluded that 22 to 38 percent of the cancer deaths of women could be attributed to smoking. Because women began smoking approximately twenty to twenty-five years after males, it is necessary to subtract twenty-five years from the female cancer death rate in order to compare sex differences in lung cancer mortality and smoking habits. When this is done, morality trends "reveal no substantial difference in the risk of developing lung cancer between men and women" (1982:45).

Today, one-third of adults smoke. This is a decline from the 42 percent of adults who smoked in 1965. The surgeon general's report also noted that teenage smoking, particularly smoking among adolescent girls, is also declining. Despite this decline there are as many smokers today as there were twenty years ago. And since the 1950s lung cancer has been the leading cause of cancer death among males. Among females the lung cancer death rate is accelerating and is projected to surpass that of breast cancer in the 1980s (1982:145). Berkley (1982:22) concluded that "really good health is virtually impossible for those who smoke and inhale a pack or more a day."

Hypertension and Heart Disease

The leading cause of heart disease in blacks is **hypertension.** Hypertension is commonly referred to as high blood pressure. According to Berkley (1982:18), "high blood pressure is without question the number one killer of American blacks." Black women have a slightly higher probability of suffering from high blood pressure than black males. About 29 percent of black females and 28 percent of black males suffer from high blood pressure (Berkley, 1982:18).

The relationship between blacks, blood pressure, and heart disease clearly illustrates the synergistic effects of life-style and choice on a population's health. Blood pressure can be affected by a variety of factors such as stress, diet, and smoking. Stress is associated with work settings, discrimination, and living environment. Although all Americans experience some stress associated with work and living environments, some groups also experience racial, sexual, and/or ethnic discrimination. Black women experience the combined stress associated not only with working and living but also with racial and sexual discrimination.

Additionally, diets high in salt and fat contribute to hypertension; the fatter a population in America, the more likely they are to experience blood pressure problems. For example, Berkley (1982:25) notes that overweight individuals between twenty and thirty-nine years of age have twice the hypertension rate of those with normal weight and three times the amount of hypertension of those below normal weight. In America black women are more likely than whites or black males to be overweight. "Approximately 35 percent of all black women between the ages of 20 and 44 are overweight while less than 25 percent of white women of that age group fall into that category" (Berkley, 1982:26). Sixteen percent of white males and 10 percent of black males in the same category are overweight.

As we have seen earlier in this chapter, blacks are more likely to be current smokers, although they are not the heaviest smokers. Still, the synergistic effects that contribute to high blood pressure and heart disease and are common in the life-style of many blacks are stress, diet, and smoking. Although these synergistic effects combine to produce higher rates of hypertension in black females, in 1980, black males had a higher death rate from heart disease than black females.

Age and Cause of Death

As a leading cause of death, heart disease is primarily a health problem for adults thirty-five and older and/or males. By contrast, the leading cause of death for

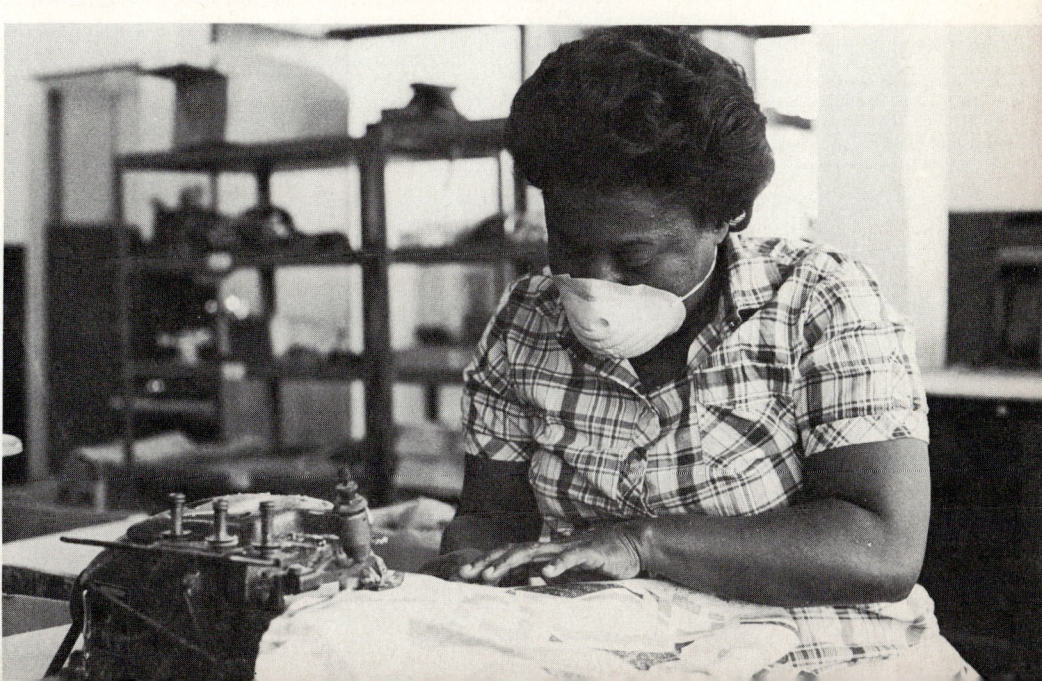

The combined stress associated with life-style, and with racial and sexual discrimination, often adversely affects the health of black women.

children aged 1 to 14, teenagers aged 15 to 19, and young adults aged 20 to 34 is accidents. The National Center for Health Statistics records data on several types of accidents, including motor vehicle, water transport, air transport, and rail transport accidents. Additionally, information is recorded on accidental fallings, drownings, poisoning, fires, firearms injuries, inhalation, and other accidents.

The two leading causes of fatal accidents for preschool children aged one to four years are fire and drowning. In 1979 "accidents accounted for 41 percent of all deaths of children 1–4 years of age" (DHHS, 1983:12). The Department of Health and Human Services (DHHS) notes that more school-age children die of accidents than of diseases (1983:12). The leading causes of accidental death in this age group are motor vehicle deaths and accidental deaths from fire and drowning. In the case of both preschool and school-age children the accident rate for males is higher than for females. This higher rate of accidental death is particularly evident in the cases of non–motor vehicle deaths. Differences in death rates decline for preschool and school-age males and females in the cases of motor vehicle deaths.

Among youth and young adults the leading cause of death is motor vehicle accidents. According to DHHS, motor vehicle deaths account for more than 40 percent of all deaths in young people fifteen to twenty-four years old. The death rate from motor vehicle accidents among this age group, however, is twice as high among whites than among blacks. The substantial difference in motor vehicle accidents between whites and blacks is probably not because of more careful driving habits by blacks. Rather, having access to and maintaining an automobile are expensive. Thus, it is probably more instructive to examine the differences in life-styles of those two groups to explain their accidental death rates.

Young adult whites are likely to have a higher standard of living as measured by parents' average income. A higher income means not only access to a motor vehicle but also more travel and travel of longer distances. More white youth between the ages of nineteen and twenty-four are in college and/or working than black youth of this age. Thus, travel to and from college, to and from work, as well as to and from places of leisure are likely to place white youth in automobiles more often than black youth. The Federal Bureau of Investigation's *Uniform Crime Reports* (UCR) note that the automobile theft is more common among white male youth than among black youth. Thus, the greater involvement of youthful whites with automobiles explains a great deal of the differences in accidental death by automobiles between white and black youth.

By contrast the leading cause of death for blacks aged fifteen to twenty-four is not accidents but homicide. Homicide is the leading cause of death for young black females as well as young black males. According to DHHS (1982:20), homicide accounts for a quarter of the deaths of all black females and 39 percent of the deaths of all black males between the ages of fifteen and twenty-four. Additionally, homicide is also the leading cause of death for black males aged twenty-five to thirty-four. In fact, the greatest threat to the health of minority youth is death or injury due to violence.

For all youth and young adults aged fifteen to twenty-four, regardless of race, the first three leading causes of death are either accidents, homicides, or suicide. This pattern of death from nonnatural causes among young people has led the DHHS to conclude that "natural causes account for only 1 in 5 deaths of young adults" (1982:22).

Medical Care

Thus far our discussion has centered upon factors that contribute to variations in the incidence of disease and death among segments of the American population. Obviously not all diseases are fatal. Some diseases only become fatal when they are neglected. Therefore, a major determinant of the quality of one's health is the nature of the medical care one receives upon becoming ill. Access to medical care implies several measures of medical service. For example, one measure of health care is how often one visits a physician. Another measure of health care is whether one has medical insurance to pay for visits to the doctor or for hospital emergencies. Still another measure of health care is whether the physician or hospital personnel were persons you felt comfortable with and therefore would visit again when you were ill. Note that the factors associated with these health-care issues involve the income, race, sex, and education of both the physician and the patient.

Recall the last time you visited a doctor or made a trip to the hospital. Whom did you see? Was it a family doctor, or was it a staff doctor? Had you been to this doctor before, or was the doctor a stranger to you? How did you pay the bill? Did you write a check? Did you use cash? Or did you show the medical personnel an insurance card and have them bill your insurance company? Your answers to these questions reflect, in part, your access to health care. Chances are that if your doctor was a stranger and you paid for your visit with either cash or check, your access to health care is limited.

Access to health care then implies visits to health-care personnel and some accepted method of payment for health-care benefits. Additionally, access to health care involves admission to hospitals or other emergency-care centers. In the following section, we examine health-care professionals, features of health insurance, and aspects of the hospital and patient interaction.

Health-care Personnel

Physicians provide the greatest amount of health-care services in the United States. According to Mugge (1983:49), "In 1980, 71 percent of the civilian noninstitutionalized population made ambulatory visits to physicians." Physicians include doctors of medicine and doctors of osteopathy. Other than physicians, the major health professionals responsible for providing care for humans include dentists, optometrists, pharmacists, podiatrists, and nurses. Thirty-five percent of the civilian population made visits to these and other health-care personnel including chiropractors and psychologists (Mugge, 1983).

Although the physician is the most conspicuous provider of health care in the United States, nurses are the most numerous. In 1980, for example, for every 100,000 people there were 202 physicians. But for the same number of people in the population there were 560 registered nurses. And evidence suggests that among active health-care professionals, nurses are experiencing the greatest increase (Kapantais, 1983:55). From 1965 to 1980 the number of registered nurses increased by 75.7 percent, whereas the increases in the number of physicians for the same time period was 39 percent (Kapantais, 1983).

In addition to the physician who provides the greatest amount of health care and the nurses who are the most numerous health-care personnel, there are other

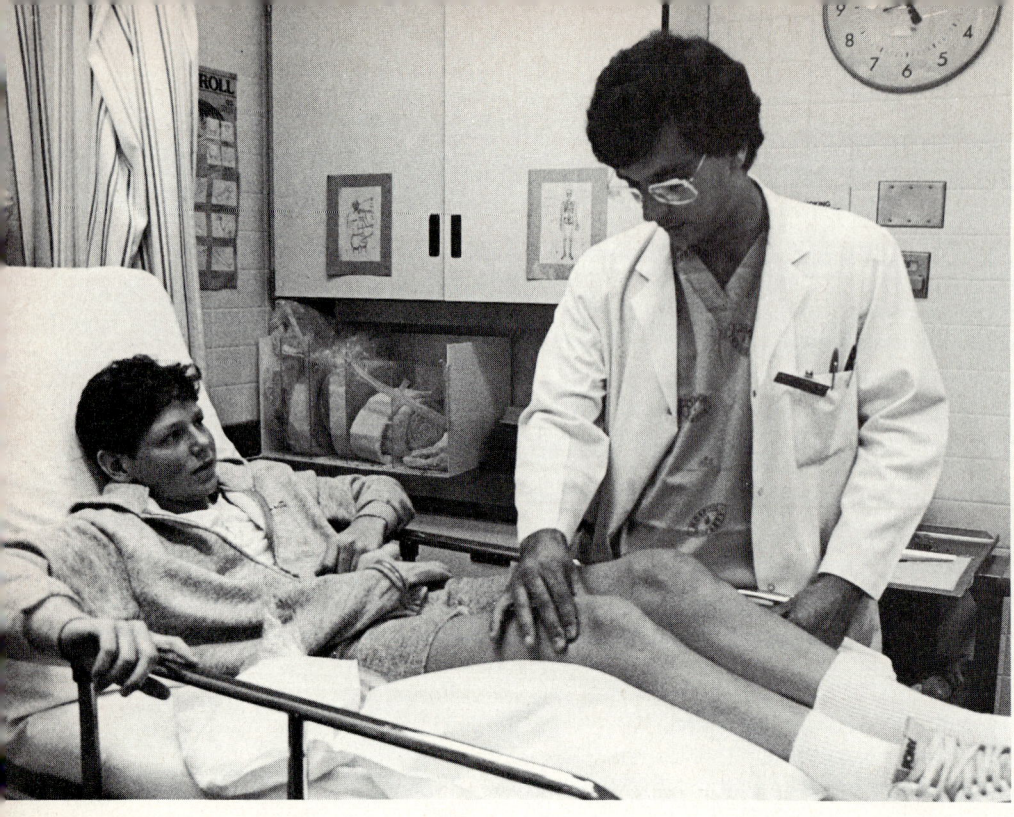

The physician is the most conspicuous provider of health care in the United States.

health-care personnel who assist either the physician or the nurse in the provision of health care. These health-care personnel include therapists, dieticians, administrators, technologists, practical nurses, aides, and orderlies. The technologist, who may be either clinical or radiological, provides information to doctors on the condition of the patient. Together, all of these health-care providers assist the doctor in making a medical diagnosis in the provision of health care.

Medical Diagnosis

The technologists' laboratory and X-ray information often helps the doctor to make the proper **diagnosis.** A diagnosis is the act of identifying a disease from the signs or symptoms. Simply put, a diagnosis is what the doctor thinks is wrong with the patient.

Diagnosis is perhaps the most significant act made by health-care personnel. According to Mumford (1983:68), the right to diagnose is central to the work, prestige, and power of medicine. For this reason, official diagnoses are generally restricted to physicians. Health-care professionals have gone to court over the right to diagnose. Psychologists have sued over the right to diagnose a person as mentally ill, "and the American Medical Association (AMA) wages lobbying campaigns to try to strike 'diagnose' from nurse practice acts that specify what nurses are legally approved to do" (Mumford, 1983:63).

If you consider closely the role of diagnosis in the medical and larger community, you will begin to understand the quest for power in the diagnosis. The diagnosis serves certain social as well as medical functions. One social function of a medical diagnosis is to absolve a person from social obligations. For example, your sociology professor may have required you to bring a note, that is, a diagnosis, from your doctor the last time you missed class. Excused absences for medical reasons are largely absolutions of personal responsibility granted by doctors through their diagnosis. Therefore, retaining a job, being able to take a make-up test, or being forced to avoid participation in some events have frequently been affected by a timely diagnosis from doctors.

Other than an absolution from social obligations the diagnosis also serves several functions for the medical community. First, diagnoses permit doctors to communicate with one another about the conditions of a patient (Mumford, 1983:65). Thus, a diagnosis becomes a cryptic message about the nature of the illness, its probable cause, and the preferred prescription. Second, diagnosis is a form of communication between the doctor and the patient. In this setting, the diagnosis may be used to disguise the doctor's ignorance of the problem; reassure the patient of the doctor's knowledge of the illness; and provide polite labels for "taboo topics" (Mumford, 1983:66). In this last instance, diagnostic terms such as halitosis and borborygums describe the common, distasteful conditions of bad breath and noise associated with gas.

Medical diagnosis then becomes not only the first step in the provision of health-care services to a patient but also a symbol of authority. Official diagnoses are the right of a few medical professionals. Not all health-care personnel are free to make diagnoses. Medical diagnoses have social as well as medical functions, serving as a means both to absolve responsibility and to communicate.

Sex and Health-care Personnel

Just as in other social institutions power and socioeconomic privilege are associated with males, the power and privilege assigned to medical care personnel varies by sex. For example, because the power and privilege of diagnosis are often restricted to physicians, one might expect that a majority of physicians are male. This is true. Although females constitute more than 90 percent of all licensed practical nurses (LPNs), registered nurses (RNs), and dieticians, they are 15 percent or less of the nation's physicians and only about 3 percent of all dentists.

Professions such as medicine and nursing become sex-typed and carry with them the expectations that the men and women in their respective organizations will conform to gender-appropriate behavior. Thus, in the profession of nursing, women are often expected to adhere first to the proper behavior for women and then to the requirements of her medical judgment. Mumford (1983:275) has referred to the adherence to gender roles in the interaction between nurses and doctors as "the rules of the game." The object of the doctor-nurse game, according to Stein (1967) is for the nurse to assume responsibility for patient care and make recommendations to the doctor without appearing to do so. The nurse must couch her recommendations about patient care in a manner and tone that make her recommendations appear to have been initiated by the doctor. Some of the gender-related behavior of nurses can be explained by the severe pressures that a Victorian society placed upon Florence Nightingale and a fledgling nursing profession to conform to the tenets of being a lady and providing "wifely support" (Mumford, 1983:290) to physicians. Much of any current gender behavior by nurses in the doctor-nurse game, however, must be attributed to social conditions that continue to support a view of nurses as auxiliary to doctors. Those conditions include nursing education, nursing pay, contradictions in authority, and continued resistance from the American Medical Association (AMA) towards having

Trends in the socialization of nurses point to an erosion of traditional sex-typing and sex-role behavior.

nurses assume greater responsibility for diagnosing patient illness. The discrepancy in pay between doctors and nurses serves to highlight the auxiliary roles of nurses. Likewise, those in the hospital setting who have the most contact with patients usually have the least authority to make medical decisions affecting the health of the patients. Often any decision that can be construed as having medical importance must await a doctor's release. The dispensation of aspirin as well as the dispensation of information about the patient's condition must usually await a doctor's sanction. These "contradictions in authority and responsibility" (Mumford, 1983:292) of nurses also maintain sex-typed behavior among nurses.

Recent trends in the socialization of nurses are pointing to an erosion of the traditional sex-typing and gender-related behavior. The trends include more active nursing associations, the development of the nurse practitioner, and an increase of male nurses.

The National League of Nurses grew out of a meeting of nurses at the Chicago World's Fair in 1893. From the beginnings of the NLN developed other nursing associations, including the Congress for Nursing Practice (CNP), the American Nurses Association (ANA), and the National Black Nurses Association (NBNA). Generally, these nursing associations have been responsible for developing a code of ethics, standards of practice, educational requirements, standards of licensure, nursing theory and research, and a forum for nurses to address issues important to their profession.

Nurse practitioners extend the role of nurses from one of being a medical caretaker to a health educator and health provider. Nurse practitioners today provide a variety of health-related services including outpatient care, preliminary diagnosis, primary medical care, and education of patients about preventive health care. The most frequent services performed by the nurse practitioners are midwifery and pediatrics. Nurse practitioners continue to face legal barriers and objections from physicians and other nurses, who often feel that the nurse practitioner oversteps the boundaries of good nursing practice.

Nonetheless, it is clear that the nurse practitioner will probably remain a permanent member of health-care personnel. Some research has shown that a majority of physician employers of nurse practitioners and their patients enthusiastically endorse the contributions of the nurse practitioner (Lewis et al., 1969; Mauksch, 1978; Sullivan et al., 1978). The extensions of primary medical care by nurses will affect the sex roles of nurses by eroding the sex-linked authority of the physician.

There has been a dramatic increase in the number of male nurses over the past decade. The immediate impact of the increase in male nurses on the nursing profession will be to blur the sex roles and gender-related behavior traditionally associated with nurses, because physicians will increasingly have to relate to nurses as professionals rather than as women. The increase in the number of male nurses is also expected to raise the overall pay scales for nurses. Male nurses hold a disproportionate number of the supervisory, administrative, and head nurse positions within hospital settings. These positions are marked by their greater prestige and pay. As the number of male nurses increases, large discrepancies in pay among various nursing positions may decrease.

Black Health-care Personnel

In 1982 blacks were 12 percent of the population and represented 12.7 percent of the total medical care personnel. At first glance, it would appear that there are sufficient black health-care personnel to care for black patients. A closer look at the distribution of black medical care personnel by occupation reveals that black medical care personnel are disproportionately represented in the least-skilled, lowest-paying, least-prestigious occupations.

Table 20.4 contains information on the number and percent of black and female health-care personnel by selected occupations. As shown in Table 20.4, blacks were overrepresented in the health services occupations and as dieticians. Twenty-two percent of the health services personnel, including practical nurses, trainees, aides, and orderlies, were black. Almost one quarter of dieticians are black. These occupations are similar in their lack of training, skill, and authority among those who hold them. This is not to claim that health service personnel and dieticians are not important in providing health care. Survey research by Ewell (1967) on patient respondents in a hospital setting revealed that a majority of the patients felt that nurses' aides provided the most frequent service followed by practical nurses. Likewise, it would be difficult to imagine hospital care without meals. Some patients require very special diets while they are under a doctor's care. The point is that these health-care occupations are virtually devoid of medical authority, with little say in the diagnosis of illness. Personnel in these occupations carry out the instructions of others and are minimally remunerated for their services.

Table 20.4 Employed Persons in Selected Health Occupations by Race and Sex, 1982

Occupation	Number (Thousands)	Percent Female	Percent Black
Total	5,513	74.9	12.7
Physicians et al.	869	14.9	2.4
Dentists	121	3.3	2.5
Pharmacists	168	23.8	3.6
Physicians	486	14.8	2.3
Registered Nurses	1,415	95.6	8.2
Therapists	252	70.6	7.9
Dieticians	70	90.0	24.3
Health administrators	228	50.9	3.5
Health technologists et al.	657	72.9	9.7
Clinical	266	76.7	9.8
Radiology	108	72.2	9.3
Health services	2,022	89.7	22.4
Health aides and trainees	333	86.2	15.9
Nurses aides and orderlies	1,136	87.1	29.0
Practical nurses	400	97.0	16.3

Source: U.S. Bureau of the Census. (1983) *Statistical Abstracts of the United States: 1984.* 104th ed. Washington, D.C.: U.S. Government Printing Office, 109.

By contrast, black health-care personnel are underrepresented in those occupations responsible for making diagnoses and prescribing treatments. In 1982 blacks were 3 percent or less of all physicians, of all dentists, and of all pharmacists. In all other health-related fields blacks were underrepresented, comprising less than 10 percent of each of these occupations.

This underrepresentation of black health-care personnel means that black patients are often treated by those who are unlike themselves in terms of race and socioeconomic status. Diagnosis can sometimes be affected by differences in the background of the doctor and the patient. Particularly in the area of mental health, where a great deal of the doctor's diagnosis may be open to several interpretations, cross-racial diagnoses produce measurable differences in the type of mental illness found among blacks and whites. For example, Gary (1981:65) has noted that "once admitted to mental health facilities, black and white men experience significant differences in terms of primary diagnosis at the time of admissions." Gary (1981:64–65) pointed out that with respect to diagnoses in state and community mental health facilities black men are three times more likely to be diagnosed as schizophrenic, eight times more likely to be diagnosed as having had childhood disorders, and about three times more likely to be classified as having organic brain syndrome than are white men. Similarly, Ruiz (1982:321) concluded that "black patients have a higher risk of being misdiagnosed than white." According to Ruiz, racial and cultural biases of the clinician contribute to the misdiagnoses.

In summary, black health-care personnel are concentrated in those occupations that have the least to do with curing black patients' illnesses. Instead, black patients' health status and medical diagnoses are likely to be in the hands of other than black physicians. This problem of medical diagnosis of black patients by other than black physicians is compounded in urban hospitals where an increased number of doctors, residents, and interns are foreign born. In these instances, cultural differences may exaggerate problems with medical diagnoses.

For example, some evidence suggests that differences in perceptions of pain by different ethnic and racial groups can affect medical diagnoses (Zola, 1973; Good, 1977; Adair and Deuschle, 1970). Adair and Deuschle (1970) have noted how Navajo women tend not to cry out in pain during childbirth. This culturally sanctioned tendency led at least one physician, who was assigned to the reservation hospital, to conclude that Navajo women feel less pain than Anglo women. The physician subsequently prescribed little medication for the Navajo women. Navajo women began avoiding the hospital for childbirth, reasoning that hospital births were as painful as births at home.

Finally, the prospects for increased numbers of black health-care personnel in the future are dim. A review of minority enrollment in selected health professions schools from 1977 to 1981 by the Health Resources Administration indicates that blacks are still underrepresented in all health professions except practical nursing and public health. According to Gloria Kapantis (1983) of the National Center for Health Statistics, when recent projections are examined, "the proportion of black and Hispanic people in the total supply of physicians and dentists will increase much less than their proportions in the population during the next two decades." In order to reach parity with their proportion in the population the number of black entrants into medical and dental school would have to double.

Other Health-care Personnel

Other than the selected health-care professionals identified thus far in this chapter there are other health-care personnel who contribute to the overall health status of the American population. These health-care personnel may be found in either of two professions: **public health** and **allied health.** In recent years, the American population has turned its attention to preventing disease rather than merely curing illness. A number of measures point to the focus on the prevention of disease. Cable television has had a proliferation of health programs. Independent television stations have programs that feature aerobic dancing. Hospitals often have fitness and wellness centers associated with them. And insurance companies advertise reduced rates for those who do not smoke.

Thus, as Americans have become more concerned with preserving good health, the public health profession has experienced a growth in numbers. Public health personnel attempt to prevent disease from occurring and to control existing diseases through community efforts. Public health personnel, then, are medical detectives of sorts. As such, they are concerned with identifying health hazards, educating the public about health hazards, and providing preventive health-care services. "Public health personnel contribute to environmental health-hazard detection and control, health education of the public, better nutrition, epidemiologic study of the causes and patterns of disease, management of health resources and services, and the provision of preventive and personal health services to high-risk groups, the needy and the disadvantaged" (Kapantais, 1983:57).

Public health personnel include physicians and nurses who have chosen to use their skills in public service rather than private practice. Typically, public health personnel are employed by local, state, or federal governments to provide health services to geographically remote areas or areas that may suffer from a lack of economic resources. Not all public health personnel are doctors or nurses, however. Public health personnel may include program planners, program administrators, scientists, technicians, sanitarians, teachers, researchers, and therapists. In fact, any persons, regardless of their occupational specialty, who use their occupational skills to contribute to a healthier environment may be considered public health personnel.

Finally, there is a set of health-related occupations that largely assist physicians in providing medical services. These occupations may be loosely termed allied health professions. Allied health personnel are a "cadre of professional and technical workers that complement as well as supplement the services provided by independent practitioners" (Kapantais, 1983:57). The supplemental service provided by allied health personnel is not merely unskilled assistance. Many community colleges offer associate degree programs in allied health occupations. These occupations include but are not limited to dental assistants, X-ray technologists, blood analysts, CAT scanner operators and respiratory machine operators.

Because allied health personnel require less training than traditional practitioners, allied health personnel are able to provide some health-care services more cheaply. Cleaning teeth, for example, does not require that a dentist do the job. A dental assistant, usually associated with a licensed dentist, can clean the teeth while the dentist is freed to perform more demanding medical services such as surgical reconstruction of a jaw. Even the actual construction of false teeth does not require a dentist's expertise. False teeth are as easily made by a technician as a dentist. Kapantais (1983) estimates more than 100 allied health occupations and specialties now exist.

Income and Health Status

One's health status is closely linked to one's income. Specifically, visits to physicians and the possession of health insurance to pay for those visits are largely controlled by income. As we saw in the chapter on stratification, one's income is also closely tied to one's race and sex, so health insurance coverage is also correlated with race and sex. Thus, poor people, in particular poor minorities and poor women, are least likely to possess health insurance.

A two-year survey of 132,000 persons under the age of sixty-five residing in fifty states by researchers at the National Center for Health Statistics found that about 12 percent of the U.S. population was uninsured for medical expenses (Trevino and Moss, 1983). The percentage of uninsured persons varied according to income, with low-income families being least likely to possess insurance. For example, regardless of race about one-fifth of all those with incomes under $10,000 have no medical insurance. Depending upon race, however, the percent of those with incomes under $10,000 who are uninsured ranged from a high of 46 percent for Mexican Americans to a low of 19.9 percent for whites. About a quarter of all blacks and Puerto Ricans with incomes over $10,000 lack medical insurance. Puerto Ricans with incomes over $10,000, however, are twice as likely as whites and slightly more likely than blacks who are in the same income category to be uninsured.

Regardless of income, Mexican Americans are least likely to possess health insurance. When all incomes are considered, the range for the percentage uninsured is lowest for whites and highest for Mexican Americans. Cuban Americans and Puerto Ricans are slightly more likely than blacks to lack medical insurance.

According to Trevino and Moss (1983:46), "inability to pay" was the most frequent reason reported by all ethnic and racial groups for not having health insurance. Inability to pay reflects not only the low income of some groups but also the fact that certain groups are more likely to be unemployed. Because much health insurance in America is group insurance provided by an employer as part of employee benefits, those who are unemployed are also likely to be uninsured. Thus, underemployment and unemployment are likely to place certain ethnic and racial groups at greater risk of having their health status jeopardized by an inability to afford medical insurance to pay for visits to a doctor when they become ill. Trevino and Moss (1983:46) found that Mexican Americans are the group with the highest percentage uninsured and are the most likely to report they could not afford insurance.

The lack of medical insurance reduces one's access to health care. Access to health insurance is closely linked to employment and family income. Research on income and visits to physicians reveals that a direct correlation exists between family income and visits to the doctor (Mugge, 1983; Trevino and Moss, 1983). Those who have higher family incomes visit the doctor more frequently than those with lower family incomes. For example, Mugge (1983) found that slightly over two-thirds of those with family incomes under $10,000 visited a physician in 1980. By contrast, almost three-fourths of those with family incomes over $35,000 visited a physician in 1980.

Other than income, race, sex, and education are also associated with visits to the doctor. According to data from the National Medical Care and Utilization of Expenditure Survey of 17,123 people, whites visited the doctor more frequently than did Hispanics or blacks (Mugge, 1983). Likewise, those with more education visited the doctor more often than those with less education. Approximately two-thirds of those with less than nine years of education visited a doctor in 1980, whereas three-fourths of those with sixteen years or more of education visited a doctor during the same time period. Other data support Mugge's research on visits to physicians and family income. Table 20.5 contains data on the percentage of visits to physicians by income and race. Regardless of race, those with higher incomes visit doctors in their offices more frequently than people with smaller incomes. Likewise, people with smaller family incomes are more likely to wait

Table 20.5 *Average Number of Visits to Physicians by Race and Family Income, 1981*

Annual Income (dollars)	Physician's Office		Emergency Room		Phone	
	White	Black	White	Black	White	Black
5,000 or less	65.1	51.2	15.5	34.1	10.8	3.4
5,000–9,999	68.6	54.6	13.2	32.3	12.8	5.2
10,000–14,999	69.1	59.2	13.1	24.1	12.9	5.0
15,000–24,999	70.2	62.1	9.6	25.2	14.4	6.4
25,000 or more	73.5	70.5	9.6	15.4	12.2	6.4

Source: U.S. Bureau of the Census (1983). *Statistical Abstracts of the United States: 1983* 104th ed. Washington, D.C.: U.S. Government Printing Office

for a medical emergency and visit a doctor at the hospital than those with higher incomes. Those with higher incomes are somewhat more inclined to phone their doctor than those with smaller incomes. Despite these similarities by race, whites are more likely than blacks to visit their doctors in the physician's office or phone them. Blacks are more likely to see a doctor in the emergency setting of a hospital.

Women visit the doctor on the average more frequently than men. According to the survey data, 76 percent of the women and 64.9 percent of the men reported visiting a physician in 1980. Regardless of sex, children (those under six years of age) and the elderly (those over sixty-five years of age) made more trips to the doctor than any other age cohort. Up to age sixteen there is little difference in the percentage of males and females visiting the doctor. At age seventeen, however, there is about a 20 percent increase in the number of women over the number of men who report visiting the doctor. This 20 percent difference remains through age forty-four, then drops to about a 10 percent difference until age sixty-four. By the age sixty-five the difference in doctor visits between males and females is only about 5 percent. A possible explanation for the differential rate of doctor visits between males and females is that ages seventeen through forty-four are childbearing years for women. Pregnant women are likely to visit the doctor for the prenatal care of their babies as well as for specific personal illnesses.

People who visit doctors are also more likely to visit other health-care practitioners such as nurses, optometrists, chiropractors, podiatrists, and psychologists. According to Mugge (1983:52), the more physician visits that people have, the more likely they are to have one or more visits to other health-care practitioners. There are many factors to account for this pattern of multiple practitioner visits. Some of the factors include: physician referral, perceived health needs by the patient, advertising campaigns, and word-of-mouth referrals. At the core of all of these factors, however, is the ability of the patient to pay for these health-care services. Thus, visits to other health-care practitioners follow the pattern of visits to physicians and family income. In other words, whites, specifically females, with more than a high school education and a family income above $10,000 are most likely to visit physicians and other health-care practitioners.

In conclusion, visiting doctors and other medical personnel is expensive. The usual method of paying for health-care services is medical insurance. We have seen that inability to pay for insurance is the most common reason given by the uninsured for their lack of medical protection. The ability to pay for insurance is tied most closely to family income. Those who are unemployed or underemployed are less likely to have discretionary income to pay for insurance. Because much of the medical insurance in America is provided as part of an employee's benefit package, those who are unemployed are least likely to possess medical insurance.

Patterns of family income vary according to race and education. Therefore, possession of medical insurance also varies according to race and education. Blacks and Hispanics are more likely to be unemployed or underemployed and to have smaller family incomes than whites. They are, therefore, less likely to be able to afford medical insurance. Lacking the ability to pay for visits to the doctor with cash or by insurance claims, blacks and Hispanics are also less likely to visit physicians or other health-care practitioners. Ironically, those who spend the most money and time visiting doctors and other health-care personnel tend to also be healthier and live longer.

Summary

The intent of this chapter was to examine the health status and medical care of diverse groups of Americans. In order to accomplish this, we reviewed the social factors associated with morbidity, mortality, and medical care.

Morbidity refers to the relative incidence or amount of disease in a population. The Centers for Disease Control (CDC) in Atlanta, Georgia, keeps records on morbidity. Some diseases that are contagious and/or communicable are required by law to be reported by health-care personnel to the CDC. These diseases are referred to as notifiable diseases. The morbidity data from the CDC indicate that the most frequently reported notifiable diseases are sexually transmitted. The most common social factors that affect morbidity are age, race, sex, and life-style.

Mortality refers to the incidence of death within a given community of people. Usually health researchers are interested in the incidence of death in a population that may be traced to a single factor. Thus, a given population's mortality is most commonly presented in terms of cause-of-death data. The leading cause of adult deaths in the United States is heart disease; among all youths it is accidents; and among minority youth it is homicide. The cause of death is very closely associated with one's life-style. The choices we make about the consumption of drugs, where we live, and what we do with our leisure time directly impinge upon our mortality. Thus, both disease and death are often the result of social rather than natural causes.

Access to medical care personnel is a factor in the overall health-care status of groups of Americans. Although physicians provide the most significant medical services, for some segments of the population access to physicians as well as other health-care personnel is affected by the underrepresentation of racial and ethnic minorities among medical professionals and a lack of medical insurance to pay for medical services. In conclusion, then, we can suggest that one's health is often a function of choice rather than chance, because the factors associated with morbidity and mortality are frequently the result of one's life-style.

Key Concepts

allied health
death rate
diagnosis
hypertension
morbidity
mortality
notifiable diseases
public health
sexually transmittable disease
synergy
venereal disease

References

Adair, J., and K. W. Deuschle. (1970) *The People's Health.* New York, N.Y.: Appleton-Century-Crofts.

Berkley, George. (1982) *On Being Black and Healthy: How Black Americans Can Lead Longer and Healthier Lives.* Englewood Cliffs, N.J.: Prentice-Hall, Inc.

Centers for Disease Control. (1983) "Annual Summary, 1983: Reported Morbidity and Mortality in the United States. *Morbidity and Mortality Weekly Report* (MMWR), *31*(54).

Department of Health and Human Services (DHHS). (1983) *Health, United States.* DHHS Pub. No. (PHS) 84–1232. National Center for Health Statistics. Public Health Service. Washington, D.C.: U.S. Government Printing Office, (Dec.):13–17.

Diehl, Harold S., M.D. (1969) *Tobacco and Your Health: The Smoking Controversy.* New York, N.Y.: McGraw-Hill Book Company.

Ewell, C. M. (1967) "What Patients Really Think About Their Nursing Care." *Modern Hospital, (109)* December:106–8.

Gary, Lawrence E. (1981) *Black Men.* Beverly Hills, Calif.: Sage Publications.

Good, B. (1977) *Culture, Medicine and Sociology.* Holland: Reidel.

Jones, James H. (1981) *Bad Blood.* New York, N.Y.: Macmillan Publishing Co., Inc.

Kapantais, Gloria. (1983) "Trends in Health Care Personnel." In National Center for Health Statistics, *Health, United States.* DHHS Pub. No. (PHS) 84–1232. Public Health Service. Washington, D.C.: U.S. Government Printing Office (Dec.):55–59.

Lewis, Charles E., Barbara A. Resnick, Glenda Schmidt, and David Waxman. (1969) "Activities Events and Outcomes in Ambulatory Patient Care." *The New England Journal of Medicine.* 280 (March): 645–649.

Mauksch, I. E. (1978) "The Nurse Practitioner Movement—Where Does It Go From Here?" *American Journal of Public Health, 68* (November):1074–75.

Mumford, Emily. (1983) *Medical Sociology.* New York, N.Y.: Random House, Inc.

Mugge, Robert H. (1983) "Visits to Physicians and Other Health Care Practitioners." In National Center for Health Statistics, *Health, United States,* DHHS Pub. No. (PHS) 84–1232. Public Health Service. Washington, D.C.: U.S. Government Printing Office (Dec.):49–53.

Rowland, Michael, Robinson Fulwood, and Joel C. Kleinman. (1983) "Changes in Heart Disease Risk Factors." In National Center for Health Statistics, *Health, United States,* DHHS Pub. No. (PHS) 84–1232. Public Health Service. Washington, D.C.: U.S. Government Printing Office (Dec.):13–17.

Ruiz, Dorothy S. (1982) "Epidemiology of Schizophrenia: Some Diagnostic and Sociocultural Considerations." *Phylon 4*(Winter):315–26.

Stein, Leonard I., M.D. (1967) "The Doctor-Nurse Game." *Archives of General Psychiatry.* Vol. 16, pp. 699–700.

Sullivan, J. A., C. Z. Dachelet, H. A. Sultz, and M. Henry. (1978) "The Rural Nurse Practitioner: A Challenge and a Response." *American Journal of Public Health.* 68:972–76.

Surgeon General of the United States. (1982) *The Health Consequences of Smoking.* U.S. Department of Health and Human Services, Public Health Service. Washington, D.C.: U.S. Government Printing Office.

Trevino, Fernando M., and Abigail J. Moss. (1983) "Health Insurance Coverage and Physician Visits Among Hispanic and Non-Hispanic People." In National Center for Health Statistics, *Health, United States,* DHHS Pub. No. (PHS) 84–1232. Public Health Service. Washington, D.C.: U.S. Government Printing Office, (Dec.):45–48.

U.S. Bureau of the Census. (1983) *Statistical Abstracts of the United States.* Washington, D.C.: U.S. Government Printing Office.

Zola, I. (1973) "Pathways to the Doctor: From Person to Patient." *Social Science and Medicine, 7:*677–89.

21
Collective Behavior, Social Movements and Social Change

OBJECTIVES

After reading this chapter the student should be able to:

1. Tell how collective behavior differs from institutional forms of social behavior.
2. Define and give several examples of collective behavior.
3. Identify characteristics of mass behavior.
4. Identify and discuss several theories of collective behavior and social movements.
5. Give examples of several social movements and describe stages in their natural history.
6. Discuss the relationship between social behavior and social change.

INTRODUCTION

It is very appropriate that we end this text with a discussion of collective behavior, social movements, and social change. We began the text by noting that sociology is the study of group or collective behavior. The chapters in the textbook have focused on various patterns of collective behavior. Culture, socialization, groups, patterns of stratification, and social institutions presuppose relatively stable and predictable forms of social behavior.

When we look around us, however, we see much evidence of social change. That change may be as innocuous as hairstyles or clothing fashions. Likewise, the change may be systemic, such as the changes that are taking place in South Africa, the Middle East, or Northern Ireland. The social changes occurring in these societies involve almost all aspects of social behavior. Yet, even social change is the result of collective behavior. One woman changing her "look" is not a fashion. Similarly, one person raising his voice in objection to patterns of inequality does not constitute social protest. Changes in fashion or forms of social protest are evidence only when groups of people adopt the "look" or assume the objection. Social movements may develop when a large number of people become organized to engineer or retard changes in patterns of behavior such as women's roles, racial inequality, religious intolerance, or even the consumption of alcohol.

Whereas the other twenty chapters in the text examined relatively stable patterns of social behavior, we begin this chapter by focusing on the crowd and the emergence of spontaneous forms of collective behavior. This chapter explores characteristics of crowd behavior; types of crowds; and theories of collective behavior. We distinguish between the crowd and social movements; identify characteristics of social movements; and integrate examples of various social movements to highlight our discussions. We conclude this chapter and the text with a discussion of social change.

Collective Behavior

A collection of people who happen to be in the same place at the same time are not necessarily an example of collective behavior. As we have seen in the chapter on groups, an aggregation does not behave in any collective sense. Rather, individuals in an aggregation pursue separate goals and lack a consciousness of one another. On the other hand, in order for spontaneous collective behavior to occur there must also be social interaction. The social interaction present in collective behavior is not as patterned and as predictable as that which we find in groups or social institutions. Indeed, the social interaction found in spontaneous forms of collective behavior may be based on something as elementary as a common impulse or a shared sentiment. Just as social interaction is the key element in other forms of relatively stable social behavior, it is also the fundamental characteristics of spontaneous forms of collective behavior.

The two sociologists who were among the first systematically to study unorganized and spontaneous collective behavior (Park and Burgess, 1921) noted that an aggregation of individuals exhibit collective behavior only when each individual acts under the influence of some shared mood or state of mind. Accordingly, they wrote that "Collective behavior, then, is the behavior of individuals under the influence of an impulse that is common and collective, an impulse, in other words, that is the result of social interaction" (Park and Burgess, 1972:364). The social interaction that is present in collective behavior is not yet institutionalized. Smelser (1962:8–9) has contended that collective behavior is not institutionalized; rather it emerges to meet undefined and unstructured situations. Thus, we can define collective behavior as the relatively spontaneous and unorganized social interaction that occurs among a collection of people responding to a shared sentiment.

Given this definition, there are many instances of social interaction that could qualify as collective behavior. Examples of collective behavior include crowds, riots, crazes, panic, revolts, revolution, mutiny, fads, fashions, mobs, and masses. Other authors (e.g., Evans, 1969) have also included disorder, protest, strike,

Collective behavior is the relatively spontaneous and unorganized social interaction which occurs among a collection of people responding to a shared sentiment.

disaster, rumor, audiences, publics, and cults as further examples of collective behavior. Although there are many different types of collective behavior, much of the focus in sociology to explain and identify characteristics of collective behavior has concentrated on the crowd.

The Crowd

According to Blumer (1969:71), "Much of the initial interest of sociologists in the field of collective behavior has centered on the study of the crowd." By carefully examining the crowd, sociologists have been able to outline the characteristics of collective behavior. One of the first efforts to describe features of the crowd was Gustave Le Bon's publication in 1895 of *Psychologie des Foules* (The Crowd). Le Bon (1977:24) suggested that the mere fact of a number of individuals finding themselves accidentally side by side does not constitute a crowd. A crowd develops from an aggregation only when "the sentiments and ideas of all the persons in the gathering take one and the same direction, and their conscious personality vanishes" (Le Bon, 1977:24). In other words, the crowd possesses a collective mind. Thus, individuals within a crowd often lose a sense of self and act in unison with other members of the crowd.

According to Le Bon, there are three causes of the development of a collective mind. First, an individual develops "a sentiment of invisible power" because of the anonymity and irresponsibility associated with large numbers of people.

The second cause is **contagion.** For Le Bon every sentiment or feeling as well as every act in a crowd is contagious. Contagious means that the sentiments and acts of some members in a crowd are likely to be duplicated or imitated by other members of the crowd. The third cause of the collective mind is suggestibility. Individuals in a crowd are more likely to adopt ideas presented to them than if the same ideas were presented to them individually. In summarizing the characteristics of the crowd Le Bon writes:

> We see, then, that the disappearance of the conscious personality, the predominance of the unconscious personality, the turning by means of suggestion and contagion of feelings and ideas in an identical direction, the tendency immediately to transform the suggested ideas into acts; these we see, are the principal characteristics of the individual forming part of a crowd (Le Bon, 1977:32).

Blumer (1969) has added to the characteristics of crowds by noting the existence of **circular reaction** and **social unrest** in spontaneous forms of collective behavior. Circular reaction refers to the interstimulation among individuals in a crowd that reinforces and enhances shared feelings, moods, and sentiments. An example of circular reaction is milling. "In milling, individuals move around amongst one another in an aimless and random fashion" (Blumer, 1969:68). The primary effect of milling is to make individuals more sensitive and responsive to one another. Collective excitement and social contagion are more intense forms of milling. When milling reaches this level of intensity, it can lead to crazes, manias, fads, mass hysteria, and panics.

For Blumer (1969:65–71) unrest, or disturbance in the routine norms and activities of group life, sets the conditions for the emergence of spontaneous forms of collective behavior such as crowds. Restlessness occurs when an individual's needs, desires, or feelings are not satisfactorily met. It is not merely the restlessness alone of individuals, however, that leads to the formation of crowds. Rather, it is social unrest, restlessness that involves circular reaction, or becomes contagious, that is likely to lead to a collective response. It is "the

According to Le Bon, the crowd possesses a collective mind, a sentiment of invisible power, and contagion.

Social unrest, one of the conditions favorable to the formation of collective behavior, occurs when individuals' needs, desires or feelings are not satisfactorily met.

socialization of restlessness" (Blumer, 1969:67), that is, social unrest, that is the cornerstone of collective behavior.

There are several characteristics of social unrest. Social unrest varies in scope and intensity. The unrest may be confined to a small community, or the unrest may transcend local boundaries. The unrest may be as mild as a letter-writing campaign to protest a new ordinance, or it may have the intensity of collective violence such as that exhibited by mobs, vigilantes, and riots. During periods of social unrest, the irritability and suggestibility among individuals become more pronounced. Ideas that might be discarded under more placid moments are more easily suggested and more readily adopted by members in a crowd. "Another significant mark of social unrest is excited feelings, usually in the form of vague apprehensions, alarm, fears, insecurity, eagerness, or aroused pugnacity" (Blumer, 1969:67). Given these characteristics of social unrest, rumors, gossip, and hearsay often play an important role in the quest for information.

Rumors

Rumors, which are unsubstantiated information on an issue or subject (Rosnow and Fine, 1976:131), are often an integral part of crowd behavior. Sometimes

Collective Behavior 465

rumors form the basis for collective response. For example, legislators recognized the power of a rumor to initiate panic buying and selling of stocks, bonds, and commodities when they wrote that it is against the law to make, circulate, or transmit any "rumor, written, printed, or by word of mouth, which is untrue in fact and is directly or by inference derogatory to the financial condition or affects the solvency or financial standing of the Federal Savings and Loan Insurance Corporation" (Rosnow and Fine, 1976:13).

In other instances rumors may serve to sustain or heighten sentiments already possessed by members of a crowd. Rumors are not simply the creation of pathological liars. Although it is true that some rumors are purposely begun by devious persons, many rumors emerge as a result of the conditions present in the formation of crowds. One of the conditions present in crowds that gives rise to rumors is a poverty of information. In *Improvised News,* Shibutani (1966:161) contended that rumors develop "as men caught together in an ambiguous situation attempt to construct a meaningful interpretation of it by pooling their intellectual resources." Rumors become a way of providing information to members of a crowd; therefore, they are likely to appear during periods of political turmoil, natural disasters, wars, racial and religious conflicts, or other periods of extended stress.

Knapp (1944) has identified three broad categories of rumors: pipe dreams, bogies, and wedge drivers. The pipe dream represents a hope or a wish. The bogie rumor reflects a fear or anxiety, whereas the wedge driver seeks to develop aggression and division among groups. During World War II, a pipe dream rumor surfaced among Americans that Japan was about to run out of fuel, thereby encouraging the hope that the war would be over soon. Some rather famous bogie rumors have been the cause of a variety of collective responses. One such rumor surfaced in 1938 following Orson Welles's radio broadcast about a supposed Martian invasion, and it initiated instances of mass hysteria and panic in American streets (Perry and Pugh, 1978).

A more recent bogie rumor involved the amount of gasoline available for American motorists during the "oil shortage" in the summer of 1979. Although there was evidence that imported gasoline supplies were being curtailed, the long lines of panic buying and topping off (buying gasoline to fill up a more-than-half-full tank) were generally the result of rumors that exaggerated the seriousness of the oil shortage. In another area, bogie rumors have arisen about the content of McDonald's hamburgers. One rumor had it that McDonald's was adding worms to its hamburgers. This rumor, which started in the summer of 1978 somewhere in the South, began to have an impact on 20 percent of McDonald's restaurants (Sheppard, 1984:636). Finally, wedge-driver rumors are often the spark behind race riots, vigilante, and mob actions. During periods of war and overt group conflict rumors often surface about the brutality and the lack of character among the enemy.

In summary, rumors may be a key characteristic of crowd behavior by enhancing the sentiments present during the milling process. Rumors also assist in the development of a collective mind by providing a common focus for individuals in a crowd. Rumors also help groups solve problems by providing direction in an otherwise ambiguous situation (Shibutani, 1966). Three conditions appear necessary for the emergence of rumors. First, sentiments, feelings, or moods are likely to be highly charged. Second, the need among members of a crowd for information is great. And finally, the flow of information from official authorities is limited. When these conditions are present, rumors are likely to surface to meet the needs of the crowd.

Mass Behavior

Another form of collective activity is **mass behavior.** Whereas crowd behavior requires face-to-face, or in the case of rumor, mouth-to-mouth, interaction, mass behavior is the result of people seeking to meet their separate needs. Mass behavior occurs when anonymous individuals attempt to satisfy their wants or needs by selecting from a variety of alternatives. According to Blumer, "The individuals' activities are primarily in the form of selections—such as the selection of a new dentifrice, a book, a play, a party platform, a new fashion, a philosophy, or a gospel—selections which are made in response to the vague impulses and feelings which are awakened by the object of mass interest" (Blumer, 1969:78). Because these choices or selections are made individually, there is little opportunity for milling or social contagion.

This is not to say that **masses** cannot be organized. Indeed, as the Coca-Cola Company discovered in 1985, organizations may develop from a mass in order to facilitate letter-writing or telephone campaigns. These organizations do not determine what the mass will do, however, as much as they facilitate selections or choices already made by individuals. A mass, then, may be defined as a collection of anonymous individuals from all walks of life, with little opportunity for interaction or exchange, who may be loosely organized and who participate in a large event (Blumer, 1969).

Fads are a kind of collective behavior adopted by people for a short period of time.

The large events in which masses participate are **trends, fashions,** and **fads.** Trends refer to gradual, long-term changes in behavior or sentiments. Trends in attitudes such as political conservatism are often recorded by pollsters, and trends in age, income, marital status, and education play an important role in advertising, marketing, and consumerism.

A fashion is the prevailing style of dress or manner of behaving during a given period of time. Fashions are not as lengthy in duration as are trends. For example, during the long-term trends toward smaller families and a longer life span, miniskirts, hot pants, and ankle-length skirts have all been in vogue, i.e, fashionable as women's clothing. Likewise, crew cuts, pampadours, long hair for white males, and "waves," afros, and close cuts for black men have all been fashionable hairstyles. Fashions do not necessarily refer to clothing or appearance. A certain philosophy or morality may also be in vogue during a period of time. Various attitudes about premarital sexual activity have been in vogue at different periods of time.

A fad is a behavior or interest adopted by a large number of people for a short period of time. Fads are often reflected in leisure-time activities. The hoolahoop, propeller beenies, Frisbees, and 3-D movies have all been a fad at one time. The relationship between trends, fashions, and fads is not merely spurious. Often trends in demographic patterns influence fashions and fads, and fashions and fads are most clearly reflected in the selection of consumers, or consumerism.

Cola Wars and Mass Appeal

Since 1886 when John Pemberton, a Georgia pharmacist, developed its original secret formula, Coca-Cola has been the most popular soft drink among Americans. In recent years, however, thanks to an aggressive marketing campaign by Pepsi-Cola, Coke was losing out to Pepsi in some markets. Pepsi spearheaded its campaign with a mass appeal to a younger constituency. The contrast between the image projected by the two companies could readily be observed in the choice of celebrities that Coke and Pepsi employed in their advertising. Coca-Cola used Bill Cosby, a favorite entertainer of the baby boomers who are now middle-aged consumers, to hawk Coke. In contrast, by featuring recording stars who are popular among children and teenagers such as Michael Jackson, the Jacksons, and Lionel Richie to peddle its product, Pepsi became the "choice of a new generation." *Newsweek* magazine noted the impact of demographic trends on this cola war when it wrote that "with aging baby boomers increasingly concerned about their weight and turning to non-sugar drinks, most growth in the sugar segment was expected to come from teen drinkers" (July 22, 1985:40). The combination of demographic trends and aggressive advertising was apparently successful, because according to *Fortune* magazine, Pepsi outsold Coke in the supermarkets during 1984 by nearly two percentage points—the equivalent of roughly $80 million in revenues (May 27, 1985:80).

But Coke did not become "It" just to lose its place as "the real thing" to Pepsi-Cola, and the Coca-Cola Company fought back. In October of 1984 Coke conducted taste tests of new Coke in over 30 cities involving 40,000 people. Fifty-five percent of those sampled selected new Coke over old Coke, and 52 percent selected new Coke over Pepsi (*Fortune,* May 22, 1985:80). With an eye on the future and not so coincidently an eye on Pepsi's younger generation Coca-Cola introduced new Coke.

Lionel Ritchie on the front lines of the Cola Wars.

Officials at Coca-Cola had perhaps underestimated the mass appeal brought about by the consumption of ninety-nine years (100 years in 1986) of old Coke. Old Coke loyalists fought back both through consumerism and active campaigns. Rather than switch to new Coke some consumers actually began buying Pepsi or other soft drinks. Other consumers began hoarding old Coke, and others threatened to import it from foreign countries. Some businesses, according to *Newsweek*, like Nick's Hamburger Shop in Brookings, South Dakota, stopped selling Coke altogether when the change was announced (July 22, 1985:42). In addition, old Coke loyalists began to form organizations to facilitate their expressions of dismay and protest. A Seattle man, Gay Mullins, formed Old Cola Drinkers of America and other Old Coke Clubs began to appear around the country. Through the efforts of these Coke clubs old Coke was portrayed as a national symbol. Some people claimed they relied on old Coke for medicinal purposes. Still others threatened lawsuits against the Coca-Cola Bottling Company for either the return of old Coke or the release of "7X," the code name for Coke's secret ingredients. *Newsweek* (July 22, 1985:40) reported that Coca-Cola received 1,500 angry calls a day and nastier mail than Joan Collins, the infamous star of a popular nighttime soap opera.

The pressure of the mass induced Coca-Cola to reintroduce old Coke, now called Coca-Cola Classic. According to vice-president Dyson, "We did not read the deep emotional ties that people had to the whole concept of Coca-Cola" (*Newsweek*, July 22, 1985:40). Of course some skeptics have claimed that Coke orchestrated the entire scenario as a coup in market advertising. Regardless of the perceived authenticity or historical significance of the Cola war of 1984, it illustrates very nicely the concept of the mass as a form of collective behavior. Individuals made largely anonymous selections of their choice of soft drink. Some

The pressure of mass appeal led the Coca-Cola bottling Company to remarket a familiar product.

of these choices were influenced by demographic trends and birth cohorts. Of course both Coke and Pepsi were aware of the demographic influences on consumer behavior of the masses and attempted to manipulate their choices or selections. When Coke pulled a product from supermarkets and soda fountains that appealed to large numbers of people, the consumers expressed their opposition by varying their individual selections and developing organizations to facilitate their protests. Finally, in response to the massive number of phone calls and letters the old product, albeit with a new name, was returned.

Theories of Collective Behavior

Thus far our focus has been on definitions, characteristics, and examples of collective behavior. Sociologists have not been content, however, with simply describing collective behavior. We are intrigued by the motives of individuals who participate in spontaneous forms of behavior. By developing theories of collective behavior sociologists have sought to explain why people participate in collective behavior and why they often lose a measure of self-control in these collective circumstances. Four theories, **contagion, convergence, emergent norm,** and **value-added theories** have traditionally been used to explain collective behavior.

Contagion Theory

Contagion theorists (e.g., Le Bon, 1977; Park and Burgess, 1921; Blumer, 1969) emphasize how the interactional processes of suggestion, imitation, and social contagion lead to the development of a collective mind. The collective mind can be seen in the similarity of behaviors and moods among members in a crowd. Le Bon specifically focused on the emotional and irrational aspects of the collective mind. He observed that among the special characteristics of crowds several were particularly noteworthy, including impulsiveness, irritability, incapacity to reason, the absence of judgment and the critical spirit, and the exaggeration of the sentiments (Le Bon, 1977:35). These special characteristics of the crowd tend to subject the otherwise important distinctions among people, such as education and class, to the controlling influence of crowd emotion. According to Le Bon (1977:42), "From the moment that they form part of a crowd the learned man and the ignoramus are equally incapable of observation." In summary, people are able to form a collective mind in a crowd situation because emotions are highly contagious.

Later modifications of Le Bon's contagion hypothesis focus on the circular reaction elements of crowd behavior (Blumer, 1969). Through the process of milling and under conditions of social unrest people who gather together are able to interpret each other's feelings, moods, and behaviors. Members of a crowd then react to one another's emotional state. In this way the feedback they receive from one another heightens and reinforces their own individual feelings. This interpretation of and reaction to feelings and moods moves back and forth among members of a crowd in a circular fashion to create a collective mind and a uniform response. Blumer (1969:70) feels that circular reaction in the form of milling, collective excitement, and social contagion serves to unite people on the most primitive level and thereby lays the foundation for more enduring and substantial forms of unification such as social movements and interest groups.

There are problems with contagion theory as an explanation of collective behavior. First, contagion theory takes a rather dim view of crowds and the individuals who participate in them. Le Bon (1977:18) claimed for example that "crowds are only powerful for destruction." He further contended that "crowds are too impulsive and too mobile to be moral" (1977:56). Blumer (1969) likened a crowd to a herd of cattle and suggested that the basis for their behavior is emotional and irrational. Contagion theorists also feel that individuals are powerless to resist the whims and sentiments of the majority. Given that much collective behavior happens rather spontaneously, contagion theorists claim that individuals have little time to assess and interpret their own or others' sentiments and behaviors in a more rational fashion.

Although many of the early studies of crowds focused on their destructive and often unflattering aspects, crowds are not inherently evil. Today crowds often emerge to celebrate an event. The Mardi Gras, state fairs, amusement parks, and championship teams often draw joyous crowds whose primary purpose for being is celebration. Likewise crowds that gather to protest are not necessarily destructive or disorderly. The March on Washington led by Dr. Martin Luther King, Jr., to underscore the quest for civil rights by blacks, the poor, and other minorities demonstrated that even massive crowds can be orderly. Since that march, others including farmers, veterans, the poor, and nuclear protestors have led orderly crowd demonstrations in Washington. Other theories including convergence, emergent norm and value added reject the dim-witted, irrational character of the crowd that is projected by contagion theorists.

Convergence Theory

Although psychologists (Freud, 1922; Allport, 1924) rather than sociologists have dominated the convergence approach, this theory provides an illuminating contrast to contagion theory. Freud (1922) was among the first to challenge the idea that contagion was the key element in crowd behavior. He also disagreed with the idea that an individual became a different person in a crowd. Rather, Freud pointed to the relationship between the leaders and members of crowds to explain collective behavior. Freud felt that because there are too many crowd members for each person to possess the leader individually, frustrated members can only identify with the leader's actions and suggestions. As the frustrated members identify with the leader, any rational or irrational behavior on the part of the leader will be adopted by individual members (Wright, 1978:18).

In contrast to Freud, Allport (1924) suggested that the leader in a crowd serves as a stimulus that is common to all members. A common stimulus is likely to elicit a common response, that is, uniform collective behavior. Further, uniform collective behavior is likely to occur because a crowd is likely to be made up of persons who already possess similar interests, sentiments, and tendencies and who have collected in or converged upon some area. Social contagion is not necessary because individual members of a crowd already possess whatever emotional fever they might catch from the crowd. Although Allport acknowledged that sentiments and behavior may be intensified by the crowd, he maintained that individual members nonetheless come together equipped with some fundamental similarities.

A popular version of this convergence hypothesis was used to explain riots in Watts, Detroit, and other urban areas during the civil rights movement of the 1960s. The central hypothesis was that riots occurred when "riffraff" converged in city streets determined to disrupt the social order. Riffraff were those poor, uneducated, mostly black but often Puerto Rican and Chicano persons who lived in the segregated ghettoes and barrios of America's major cities. Likewise, some explanations of the 1985 riots in South Africa against racial apartheid have focused on those who, although they may be genuinely opposed to apartheid, are nonetheless already predisposed to violence and who converge at convenient opportunities (e.g., funerals, marches, and other demonstrations) to disrupt the social order.

Despite the specific differences among convergence theories there are, according to Wright (1978), three important ways that they differ from contagion theory. First, convergence theories reject the idea of a unique group-level explanation of crowd behavior. Second, convergence theories do not accept the idea that individuals lose themselves in a crowd and become entirely different people. Third, all convergence theories hold the belief that there is a tendency for the crowd to be composed of individuals with like minds who collect in some area to express their interests. Convergence theory offers an explanation of spontaneous collective behavior that places more weight on the rational formation of crowds. Essentially then, convergence theory argues that crowds consist of people who share similar goals, beliefs, and sentiments and who come together precisely because they have these things in common.

A major difficulty with convergence theory is the assumption that the crowd is homogeneous in terms of the motives and characteristics of its members. Such an assumption, which is implicit for example in the riffraff theory, overlooks the participation in crowds of divergent groups. Evidence suggests that the composition of the crowds that rioted and took part in civil rights protests in America as well as in the crowds in South Africa that are protesting apartheid are composed of a variety of individuals including poor residents, community leaders, ministers, and other members of the community. Likewise, there is evidence that crowds historically have been composed of a heterogeneous mixture of individuals (Rude, 1964). Arrest records indicate that those who took part in the French Revolution of 1848 included building workers, carters, coal heavers, bronze workers, cabinet makers, and railwaymen (Rude, 1964:177).

Just as crowds may be composed of a variety of people, their reasons for participating in various forms of collective behavior may also differ. In a crowd that is protesting there may be along with the protestors, for example, those who have come merely to see, others who have come to be seen, and others who simply happened along. Although contagion theory suggests that individuals in a crowd are converted to a group mind, and convergence theory argues that the individuals come with a like mind, both erroneously assume that the crowd is homogeneous in terms of sentiment and behavior.

Emergent Norm

Emergent norm theory begins by assuming that the crowd is not necessarily homogeneous nor is it necessarily irrational. According to Turner and Killian (1972:22), "An emergent norm approach reflects the empirical observation that the crowd is characterized not by unanimity but by differential expression, with different individuals in the crowd feeling differently, participating because of diverse motives, and even acting differently." Individuals who participate in collective behavior nonetheless look to norms to regulate and guide their behavior. Given that there are many types of relatively spontaneous collective behavior, the norms could not exist prior to the formation of a particular crowd. Likewise, because crowds are often composed of a variety of people, they could not have converged with the same set of norms. Rather, the norms that regulate individuals in a crowd emerge even as the crowd is forming. Norms emerge within the crowd to regulate the nature and intensity of the sentiments and shape the behavior shared by crowd members.

Emergent norms are the result of collective interactions among the members and the interaction between the crowd and its leaders. Through these collective interactions definitions of the situation develop and are shared by the crowd. Thus, the sentiments and behaviors that appear are consistent with the shared definitions held by the crowd. One way in which shared meanings and definitions held by the crowd develop is through rumor. Rumors function in part as a way of giving members of a crowd the same experience. With such an experience individuals are able to share with others a similar sense of outrage, repulsion, relief, and so on and to develop appropriate conduct norms.

Emergent norm theory, then, contends that people in a crowd communicate with one another, often through rumors of other stories (hearsay, gossip, etc.), to create shared definitions and meanings of the situation. Norms emerge from the common definitions to regulate behavior. People behave in a uniform fashion not because they have caught an emotional fever or converged with a common cause, but because they have come to understand the appropriate behavior given this particular situation. "Such a shared understanding encourages behavior consistent with the norm, inhibits behavior contrary to it, and justifies restraining action against individuals who dissent" (Turner and Killian, 1972:22). The norms encourage some behaviors, such as trashing stores or stoning police, but discourage other behaviors, such as burglarizing churches or attacking community residents. Recent variations of this theory suggest that there is often more than one emergent norm shared by a crowd (Snow et al., 1981). Multiple emergent norms explains why there are different levels of participation in a crowd, because members do not necessarily share exactly the same definition of the situation.

A major problem with emergent norm theory is the failure of the theory to explain rapid changes in a crowd's sentiments and behavior (Wright, 1978:24). Because rumors or other stories take some time to filter through a crowd to create a common definition, how is it that crowds are able to panic—resort to flight in one moment and return to relative calm, organized behavior in another? Wright feels that spatial factors, gestures, and the proximity of crowd members are also important aspects of crowd interaction.

Value-added Theory

Value-added theory assumes that collective behavior is a response to structural conditions in the society that produce stress and strain for large numbers of people. According to Smelser (1962:71), "Collective behavior is a compressed way of attacking problems created by strain." Given the problems created by structural strain, Smelser's value-added theory attempts to explain how collective behavior develops and what direction or form it will take

Borrowing the idea from economics, Smelser suggests that like the monetary value that is added to raw materials as it passes through various stages of production, as from iron ore to steel to an automobile or to some appliance, value is also added in six stages to the underlying condition of structural strain in order to produce collective behavior. The six stages to which value is added to produce collective behavior include structural conduciveness, structural strain, spread of a generalized belief, precipitating factors, mobilization for action, and social control.

Structural conduciveness is a situation of social or political unrest that makes collective behavior possible. Structural strain occurs when there are problems such as racial apartheid in South Africa or religious animosity in Northern Ireland. Generalized beliefs serve to define the situation and suggest appropriate responses to the structural conduciveness and structural strain. Precipitating factors are any incidents that fan emotional fervor and "spark" people to action. Mobilization for action occurs as members of the crowd become organized in order to act. Members of a crowd may begin to collect debris, erect barricades, and generally prepare themselves for overt behavior. The final stage that arches over

all the others is social control, which consists of the various ways in which those in authority act to encourage or discourage a particular type of collective behavior (Smelser, 1981:443).

Using the riot in Watts that occurred during the civil rights protests of the 1960s, Smelser (1981) illustrated these six stages. The structural conduciveness in Watts was the tension between blacks and the police. The structural strain was the breakdown of trust between blacks and police. It was generally believed that the police were prejudiced and abusive. The precipitating factor was the forcible arrest of a community resident and the perception by community residents that the police were also about to arrest a pregnant woman. The crowd mobilized for action by stoning the police. Various displays of force by control agents (the police) served to infuriate members of the crowd and encourage them to respond in a violent and forceful manner.

Value-added theory is not without its weaknesses. One major problem with the theory is that it is vague. For example, the difference between structural conduciveness and structural strain is unclear and somewhat circular. It might be argued that structural conduciveness is structural strain. A second problem with value-added theory is that the six stages either do not necessarily occur at all in some forms of collective behavior, or they do not occur in the sequence that has been identified by Smelser. Spontaneous forms of unconventional behavior do not remain in the crowd phase for very long. Once crowds mobilize for action, the stage is also set for more enduring and more organized forms of

> Value-added theory assumes that collective behavior is a response to structural conditions in society which produce stress and strain for large numbers of people.

behavior. The regular appearance of crowds to protest structural strain often represents the beginning of a social movement that will attempt a measure of reform.

Social Movements

Somewhere between the spontaneous formation of the crowd and routine organizational behavior lie **social movements.** Although social movements are a form of collective behavior that are more organized and more stable than crowds or masses, they are nonetheless marked by changing membership and charismatic rather than bureaucratic leadership. Turner and Killian note that "as a collectivity a movement is a group with indefinite and shifting membership and with leadership whose position is determined more by the informal response of the members than by formal procedures for legitimizing authority" (Turner and Killian, 1972:246). Thus, social movements differ from crowds and other forms of spontaneous collective behavior in terms of longevity, membership, and leadership.

Social movements also involve a greater measure of planning in the development of strategies and the deployment of resources than do crowds. Finally, perhaps the most significant difference between other forms of collective behavior and social movements is that social movements are generally more committed to changing the larger society (Smelser, 1981:444) or resolving the social conflict

Social movements are a collection of individuals who share a similar set of attitudes and who act with some continuity to promote or resist change.

that arises from the structured arrangement of individuals and groups in a social system (Oberschall, 1973:33). Crowds, for example, may emerge merely to express some emotion, lynch a perceived undesirable, or praise a hero. None of these activities is designed to change social arrangements. The focus of any social movement, however, is change. The goal of the movement may be to resist impending change, encourage future change, or engender a return to the glorious past. Given these characteristics we may define a social movement as a collection of individuals who share a similar set of attitudes acting with some continuity to promote or resist change in the ideology and social arrangements in the society of which is it a part (Ash, 1972; Turner and Killian, 1972).

Types of Social Movements

Sociologists have attempted to classify social movements in a variety of ways. Blumer's (1951) description distinguished between social movements according to their degree of organization and style of behavior. Based upon these distinguishing features Blumer identified four types of social movements, including general and specific movements and expressive and revival movements.

General Social Movements. General social movements involve a collection of individuals groping in an uncoordinated fashion towards vague goals and objectives. An example of a general movement would be the youth movement during the 1960s and early 1970s. Students for a Democratic Society (SDS), the Weathermen, hippies, and college students were some of the principal actors in this movement. Their goals ranged from protesting the Vietnam war, trashing the establishment, and advocating free love to dismantling racial segregation. They embraced fashions of longer hair for men and unisex clothing for men and women. In summary, the youth movement included a variety of individuals representing divergent ideologies who participated in numerous uncoordinated activities designed to affect changing goals and objectives.

Specific Social Movements. By contrast, specific social movements are a collection of well-organized individuals with well-defined goals. Mauss (1975:45) said that specific social movements also have "generally acknowledged leaders, an overall organization broken down into a division of labor and roles, a guiding philosophy and set of rules, a body of traditions and expectations, and a kind of 'we-consciousness'." Examples of specific social movements include the Mohandas Gandhi–led movement for home rule in India and the civil rights and the Equal Rights Amendment (ERA) movements in America. Expressive movements consist of a collection of individuals who seek essentially collective adjustments to personal problems. Expressive movements do not necessarily seek to change existing social arrangements as much as they attempt to change the members who participate in the movements. Many expressive movements take the form of religious cults. The 913 members of the People's Temple who followed Jim Jones to Guyana, South America, and who subsequently committed "revolutionary suicide" on November 18, 1978, to protest social injustice were participating in an expressive movement. Finally, revival movements are composed of individuals who attempt to restore some past ideology or set of social arrangements. Many of the precepts and beliefs regarding abortion, birth control, and premarital sexual behavior held by members of the Moral Majority, a political-religious movement led by ministers such as the Reverend Jerry Falwell, reflect a revivalist approach to values that were purportedly held by a majority of Americans at some time in the past.

Norm-oriented Movements. Smelser (1962) differentiated between norm-oriented movements and value-oriented movements. Norm-oriented movements attempt to restore, protect, modify, or create norms in the name of a generalized belief (Smelser, 1962:270). Norm-oriented movements attempt to change the rules governing social behavior. The outcomes of such movements are likely to be new laws, new customs, or the creation of a new body of rule makers to effect normative change. The prohibition movement was a norm-oriented movement that resulted in the passage of the Eighteenth Amendment to the Constitution. This amendment, sometimes referred to as the Volstead Act, changed the way people consumed alcohol. It took another movement and another amendment to repeal the Volstead Act, which again changed patterns of alcohol consumption. Another example of a norm-oriented movement is the American labor movement, which resulted in new laws, new customs, and the creation of new rule makers to govern working in America. Specific normative changes affecting working conditions that were engendered by the labor movement include the establishment of unions, shorter working hours, higher wages, pension plans, and government bodies to oversee employee safety.

Value-oriented Movements. Whereas norm-oriented movements attempt to change rules and behavior, value-oriented movements "involve the restoration of past values, the perpetuation of present values, the creation of new values for the future, or any mixture of these" (Smelser, 1962:314). Value-oriented movements may be defined as a collective attempt to restore, protect, modify, or create values in the name of a generalized belief (1962:313). An example of a value-oriented movement is the Protestant Reformation. The Reformation sought to change theological beliefs in orthodox Christianity, and although some church ceremonies varied as a result of the Reformation, the most important and dramatic effect of this movement was changes in religious tenets. Generally, messianic, nativistic, and utopian movements qualify as value-oriented movements. Mauss (1975:46) suggested that probably all of the movements based on the great "isms," such as communism, fascism, millenarianism, and the like could be viewed as value-oriented movements.

Other Categorizations of Social Movements. Terms such as reform, revolutionary, conservative, and reactionary have also been used to describe social movements. These terms categorize a movement by examining its relationships to the existing social order. Reform movements, such as the suffragette movement, seek to alter some limited aspect—in this case, the right to vote for women—of existing social arrangements. Revolutionary movements like the American Revolution attempt radically to change the structure and social arrangements in the society. Because revolutionary movements threaten so many vested-interest groups at one time, radical change is often difficult without violent confrontations. Conservative movements, for example, antibusing or movements generally opposed to school desegregation, attempt to maintain current social arrangements by resisting proposed, perceived, or mandated changes. Reactionary movements, such as neo-Nazi and white supremacy movements, attempt to restore an ancient order of social arrangements. Reactionary movements envision a return to the "good old days."

There are several ways of identifying types of social movements. Sociologists do not have a preference for one classification or the other. The choice of typologies depends upon the sociologists' focus as they examine various movements. Regardless of the type, social movements have a life cycle and must contend with recruiting members and mobilizing resources.

The Natural History of Social Movements

Social movements have stages of growth and decline. As the movement increases in popularity, the size of its membership and the amount of available resources at its disposal are likely to grow. As the movement successfully realizes its goals or social control agents are successful in limiting its growth, a social movement will begin to decline. Oberschall (1973) has observed that social movements go through a period of mobilization in which conflict groups are formed and then through a period of disintegration where either the movement is successful in bringing about the desired change or authorities are successful in regulating the opposition to current social arrangements. These stages of growth have been identified as the "career" of the social movement or its "life cycle." Smelser (1962) and Mauss (1975) have referred to the process of growth and decline of a social movement as its natural history. According to Mauss (1975), social movements develop through five stages: incipiency, coalescence, institutionalization, fragmentation, and demise (see Figure 21.1). At each stage in its history a social movement may be terminated depending on "the changing mix of cooptation and repression applied by the society and the movement's response to that 'mix' " (Mauss, 1975:61). Identifying the stages of a social movement then is not to suggest that all social movements develop through these five stages. It is to say that ideally we can note five stages in a social movement that has progressed through its natural history.

The incipiency stage of a movement is characterized by people who have begun to feel that their collective interests are not being served by current social arrangements. There are no recognized leaders, no organizations, and no membership to speak of. Any protest is likely to be in the form of editorial articles, small, local meetings, and letters to various legislators. As the movement enters the coalescence stage, formal and informal organizations develop, and leaders of their respective organizations emerge. At this stage the movement has become

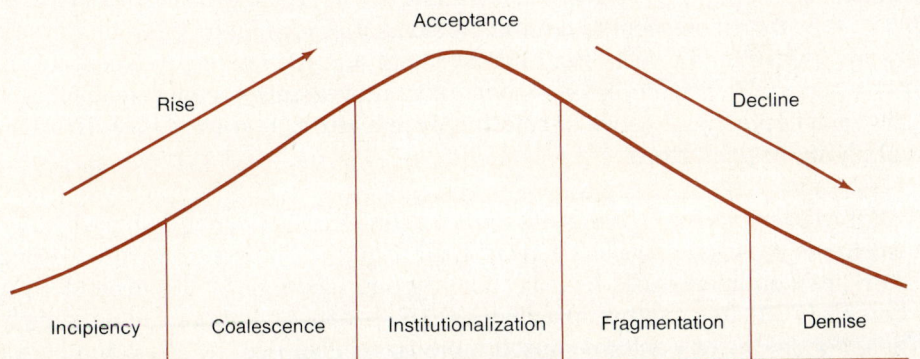

Figure 21.1

an influential force for change and cannot be stopped without severe sanctions or concessions by the larger society. The movement becomes institutionalized when other institutions, most notably governmental, religious, and economic institutions, acknowledge the legitimacy of the issues raised by the movement and begin to propose options to resolve those issues. A movement is at its peak of power and influence during the institutionalization stage.

Following the institutionalization of a social movement is a period of decline where the numbers of supporters begin to drift away until finally the movement is only recognized by a residue of changes. Thus, fragmentation occurs as a result of the success enjoyed by the movement in securing accommodations from the larger society. Once members feel that they have accomplished their goals, there is little reason for them to remain together because it was vested interests and not friendship that brought them together in the first place. In its final phase, the demise, "the co-optation process has appropriated the most critical elements of the movement's program, has 'bought off' many of its leaders and most effective members, and has choked off most of its outside support" (Mauss, 1975:65). It is an amusing irony that once the leaders and many of the members of a movement have exacted all possible concessions from the larger society, they often assume establishment, sometimes quite conservative positions in the society. Many of the leaders and members of the youth movement of the sixties and seventies are now entrepreneurs, managers, and legislators. Similarly, some leaders and members of the black power movement of the late sixties are now ministers, entrepreneurs, lecturers, writers, and legislators. If a movement is able to develop through each stage of its natural history, its decline is a signal of its success.

Theories of Social Movements

The explanations of spontaneous collective behavior have centered upon emotional contagion, the convergence of people who have similar interests, and the importance of emerging norms and values. The causes of social movements certainly contain elements of contagion, convergence, norms, and values. Social movements, however, persist longer than the actions of a single crowd; therefore, these theories do not adequately explain why people persist in collective interaction over a period of years to pursue a common cause. The question that theories of social movements attempt to answer is: Why do people come together and persist over a period of time, often in the face of very repressive governmental responses to their collectivity, in the pursuit of changes in existing social arrangements? For example, before unions became an acceptable feature of the work place, the labor movement in the United States met with bitter, often bloody and deadly opposition for years from management and the law enforcement agents of the period. To explain the cause of social movements sociologists have typically relied upon the theories of **relative deprivation, resource mobilization,** and **rising expectations.**

Relative Deprivation. When a group of people feel they are missing what they perceive as basic necessities or fundamental rights, a condition of want is created. Often this condition exists not because a group has none of the necessities or rights that it desires, but because they have less than other groups in the society. Thus, conditions of want are caused more by relative than by absolute deprivation. The perceived deprivation usually takes the form of economic and/or political discontent. The discontent felt by blacks in South Africa is not because they have absolutely no economic opportunity or political rights, but because they have less than the "coloreds" and the white Afrikaners in their country. When blacks compare their relative lack of opportunity and rights to others in South Africa, their discontent is enhanced. Similarly, the civil rights and women's liberation movements developed not because blacks and women had nothing, but because compared to whites and men, blacks and women had so much less. The basic assumption of the theory of relative deprivation is that a social movement begins and is sustained by people who are determined to bring about parity between haves and have-nots in the society. Thus, ideally a movement persists until the desired parity or some symbol (e.g., the Civil Rights Act of 1964) of the equality is reached.

Resource Mobilization. In contrast to those who see social movements as the result of a quest for parity in social arrangements others (Oberschall, 1973; Mauss, 1975) suggest that without resources a movement is doomed to failure. "Mobilization theory is concerned with how people with little individual power collectively resist or challenge established and organized groups that have a vested interest in maintaining the status quo" (Oberschall, 1973:102). The key factor then in a successful social movement is the ability to mobilize important resources. There are many resources upon which a collectivity may draw at various stages during the natural history of a social movement, including mass media, public sympathy, money, time, and political influence. The mobilization of these resources, however, is usually contingent upon the two most important resources a movement has at its disposal: effective leaders and a broad-based, loyal membership.

Leaders can be effective by drawing upon either their prestige or their authority. Their prestige is often the result of their having greater education, income, or social status than that possessed by the majority of those whom they lead. When Gandhi championed the movement for home rule and Indian independence from British colonialism, much of his effectiveness in mobilizing the support of his country's citizenry was the prestige he enjoyed as a result of his education in English schools as a lawyer. Weber (1957) noted that authority may be charismatic, rational, or traditional. Charismatic leadership is particularly important as a resource in the early stages of social movements, because charisma is useful in inspiring not only the zeal of a fledgling membership but also to marshall the support of the general public who are attempting to weigh the legitimacy of the issues raised by the movement. Finally, the recruitment and retention of members (Mauss, 1975) are likely to be based upon the leaders' ability to: (1) address collective issues relevant to a variety of social positions including but not limited to race, sex, caste, class, and religion and (2) articulate a satisfactory balance of risks and rewards in favor of participation.

Rising Expectations. Finally, there are those (Davies, 1962; Marx, 1955) who while acknowledging the discontent brought about by relative deprivation and the importance of mobilizing resources nonetheless feel that social movements occur when people begin to expect more from social arrangements than they actually receive. Tocqueville (1955) observed that the French Revolution occurred while the economic position of the French peasants was actually increasing.

Similarly, Marx and Engels (1955) felt that although English workers' financial lot was improving, a revolution was imminent because the workers' expectations would continue to rise, particularly when they compared themselves with the capitalists. Marx and Engels (1955:94) wrote that "while the enjoyment of the workers has risen, the social satisfaction that they have has fallen in comparison with the increased enjoyment of the capitalist."

According to Davies (1962), social movements and revolutions are likely when a group's position in the society that has been improving suddenly experiences a decline. The rising aspirations created by the improved social standing are not fulfilled because of the inability or refusal of the larger society to continue its support of the group's improved position. No matter what the actual position of a group is in the society, as long as the members receive close to what they expect from social arrangements, a social movement is unlikely. Thus, when a group's hopes for greater parity in social arrangements are met with a reduction in economic opportunity or political rights, a social movement can occur whose goal will be to assure that social arrangements meet the expectations of members of the movement. Both the farm workers movement, led by Ceasar Chavez, and the civil rights movement, led by the Reverend Martin Luther King, Jr., occurred during a time when the actual economic position of Chicanos and blacks had improved in comparison to their positions a decade earlier. Higher wages for agricultural workers and improvements in farming fueled rising expectations of a better life among the migrant, largely Chicano, farm workers. At the same time desegregation legislation in the military and schools fueled the hopes among blacks of greater social and economic opportunity. In the sixties and seventies when these two movements were enjoying their greatest popularity they addressed the fear shared by Chicanos and blacks that things had gotten no better and in some cases appeared to be worse. The theory of rising expectations suggests that a revolution or a social movement is the probable answer to the question posed by Langston Hughes when he asks, "What happens to a dream deferred?" in a poem by that title.

In summary, theories of social movements contend that people are likely to come together and persist in the pursuit of some goal when they experience discontent. That discontent may be caused by the relative position of one group in comparison to other groups in the society. Or the discontent may be caused by a perceived retreat of the larger society from supporting greater group gains. Regardless of the nature of the discontent, a successful movement must be able to mobilize its two major resources, effective leaders and zealous members. A major weakness is the inability of these theories to predict when a social movement will occur. We know that a social movement has occurred only because we are able to recognize in retrospect the relative deprivation, the resources, and the rising expectations shared by members of a movement.

Sociology and Social Change

We have reached the portion of this text where we must try to bring to a close our discussions, which took us through a myriad of topics. Each of the topics that we covered in our chapters have at least two things in common. Whether the specific topic happens to be culture, aspects of inequality, social institutions, or social movements, a common thread running through each is that human behavior, despite its many forms, is social behavior. To be human is to participate in the collective life of the community. Even deviance, or behavior that departs from the accepted collective norms, is social behavior in that it is learned, endorsed, carried out, and subsequently punished in the company of others. Regardless of whether it is relatively stable, patterned behavior such as that which occurs within the institutions of the economy, education, the family, criminal justice, and health care, or whether it is spontaneous, volatile, and often violent such as that which occurs in crowds, masses, and social movements, human behavior is collective behavior. In Chapter 4 we examined the rather serious problems that humans have in adjusting when their socialization is incomplete because of the failure of collective interaction.

A second common thread weaving through all of the topics in this text is the certainty of change. Change is an inevitable and predictable consequence of social interaction. As people interact within social institutions, groups, crowds, or social movements, they bring with them new ideas, new values, new aspirations, and new experiences that manifest themselves in special interests. As interest groups form and begin to mobilize their resources to protect and enhance their interests, they will conflict with other interest groups seeking to do the same. This conflict is an important feature of social change. In many instances change is improbable without conflict. Not all change requires conflict between interest groups. Some change comes about as a result of evolutionary processes, and some changes are welcomed and are the result of a consensus.

Thus, any useful explanation of social behavior must be able to account for both stability and change. In that sense we have come full circle in our journey through the topics covered in this text. We began Chapter 1 by examining theories that would help us explain the order and structure that we find in the society. The same theories that explain the presence of norms, roles, statuses, groups, and institutions are the same theories upon which we rely to explain how these very same structures change. Although there are many variations of these theories, we turn finally to functionalism and conflict to explain social change.

Functionalism and Social Change

The central idea in the functionalist approach to change is that societies try at all times to maintain a balance, an equilibrium among its many parts. For example, the institutions of family, religion, government, education, criminal justice, and health care, must coexist with one another. No one institution has complete dominance over the other, and in fact changes in one institution often produce pressures for change in another. The discovery of the birth control pill and the refinements in abortion techniques by health-care professionals have had a profound effect on all of the other social institutions. For example, the papal encyclical *In Human Vitae* denounced the pill as an immoral interference with potential life and virtually split the Catholic hierarchy from Catholic laity who have continued to use the pill to control family size. Similarly, while Protestant and Catholic ministers have preached of the sanctity of unborn life and the horror of abortion, rates of abortion nonetheless have continued to increase. Additionally, pressures have increased on legislators to make abortion legal, to make access to birth control generally available to anyone of childbearing age, and to make education about birth control the responsibility of schools. As family size has decreased in part due to the availability of birth control and economic pressures that made larger families a liability, one effect has been to reduce the number of children and young adults entering schools and universities. Thus functionalists see change as an attempt by the society to incorporate an invention occuring in one institution into a balance or equilibrium among the other institutions.

Change can be generated from any number of sources. Inventions, catastrophes, and cultural diffusion are common sources of change. Additionally change may be planned, as in the case of urban renewal projects or planned communities. Regardless of the specific source of change, functionalists view change as a series of adjustments by the institutions in the society to accommodate the change and reestablish a balance among them.

Conflict Theories of Social Change

Whereas the functionalists view change as a series of adjustments by the institution in the society to maintain or reestablish equilibrium, conflict theorists view change as a succession of skirmishes and occasionally large battles among various groups in the society. Individuals often converge to form crowds, groups, organizations, and social movements to change the social order. Even small-scale efforts at change, such as that occurring when special-interest groups lobby congressional representatives, involve conflict. Although conflict theorists acknowledge that change may include planning, inventions, natural disasters, or cultural diffusion, they suggest that the change will not come about without conflict between those groups who have a stake in the status quo and those who are seeking an alteration in the social arrangements.

Conflict theories feel that societies are always changing. The source of the change lies in the very organization of the society. As long as the organization of societies includes any form of inequality, those who are deprived will eventually rise up against those benefited by the current arrangements. In capitalist societies the two groups in constant conflict with one another are the bourgeoisie and the proletariat. The bourgeoisie are the capitalists, the owners of the factories, the mines, and the transportation systems. In short, the bourgeoisie owns the means of production in the society and profits most by the status quo. On the other hand, given the set of arrangements, the workers have only one way to profit, and that is to sell their labor to the bourgeoisie. The inequality in this arrangement is the source of conflict and provides the impetus for change. Structural change occurs as the proletariat acquires power at the expense of the bourgeoisie (Appelbaum, 1970:84).

Other conflict theorists (Dahrendorf, 1959) have modified the view of change based on class conflict to conflict among several groups based upon competing interests. Change comes about as various interest groups compete for positions of authority and advantage. Thus, the conflict among interest groups leads to changes in the nature of their relationships and changes therefore in the structure of social arrangements in the society.

In summary, we are able to note several important distinctions between functionalist and conflict explanations of change. Functionalists tend to view change as incidental to institutional stability. When change is introduced by any

Conflict theorists feel that change is often the result of conflict between groups who have a stake in the status quo and those seeking an alteration of social arrangements.

number of sources, the institutions in the society adjust to the change and to one another to achieve once again stability, balance, and equilibrium in the society. Finally, functionalists imply that change is orderly and "change is seldom conceived of as altering the fundamental structure of society" (Applebaum, 1970:81). Conflict theory, on the other hand, sees change as the primary factor in social arrangements. The source of all change is conflict among classes or special-interest groups. The conflict is a result of the organizational inequality that creates a constant source of tension between those who benefit by and those who suffer from social arrangements. Conflict theorists are more inclined to suggest that change can be revolutionary in that it occasionally alters the fundamental structure of society.

Summary

In this chapter we examined characteristics and explanations of relatively spontaneous forms of behavior. Included in this category of behavior are crowds, riots, crazes, panics, mutinies, and masses. Sociologists have labeled these types of behavior as collective behavior. Collective behavior is relatively spontaneous and unorganized social interaction that occurs among a collection of people responding to a shared sentiment. Rumors, any unsubstantiated information about some subject, are an important feature of collective behavior because they enhance the sentiments of the crowd and assist in the development of a group mind. Mass behavior is a form of collective behavior that occurs when anonymous individuals make similar choices from among several alternatives. Efforts by Coca-Cola drinkers to persuade the Coca-Cola Company to continue selling a ninety-nine-year-old product is an example of mass behavior. Fads and fashions are also forms of mass behavior that manifest themselves by the selection of consumers. Explanations of collective behavior have traditionally focused on emotional contagion, the convergence of similar interests, emerging norms, or values that are added at various stages of the crowd response.

Although social movements are perhaps a more stable form of behavior than crowds or masses, the behavior exhibited by movement participants is not yet institutionalized behavior. Social movements occur when people come together and persist over a period of time in an organized fashion to promote or resist change. The stages in the natural history of social movements include incipiency, coalescence, institutionalization, fragmentation, and demise. Explanations of social movements have concentrated on the relative deprivation, the mobilization of resources, and the rising expectations of movement members.

Finally, regardless of whether the behavior is spontaneous or routine, we can observe that human behavior is a product of collective interaction and is subject to change. Therefore any explanation of human behavior must be able to account for the stability we find in social interaction and the change that is likely to occur over a period of time. To do that we returned full circle to the theories we examined in Chapter 1, namely functionalism, conflict, and the various theories derived from them.

Key Concepts

circular reaction
collective behavior
contagion
convergence
crowd
emergent norm
fad
fashion
masses

mass behavior
relative deprivation
resource mobilization
rising expectations
rumors
social movements
social unrest
trends
value-added theory

References

Allport, Floyd H. (1924) *Social Psychology.* Boston, Mass.: Houghton Mifflin Company.
Appelbaum, Richard P. (1970) *Theories of Social Change.* Chicago, Ill.: Markham.
Ash, Roberta. (1972) *Social Movements in America.* Chicago, Ill.: Markham.
Blumer, Herbert. (1951) "Collective Behavior." In Alfred M. Lee (ed.), *New Outline of the Principles of Sociology.* 2d ed. New York, N.Y.: Barnes & Noble Books.
———. (1969) "Outline of Collective Behavior." In Robert R. Evans (ed.), *Readings in Collective Behavior.* Chicago, Ill.: Rand McNally & Company.
Dahrendorf, Ralf. (1959) *Class and Class Conflict in Industrial Society.* Stanford, Calif.: Stanford University Press.
Davies, James C. (1962) "Toward a Theory of Revolution." *American Sociological Review,* 27(February):5–19.
Evans, Robert R. (ed.). (1969) *Readings in Collective Behavior.* Chicago, Ill.: Rand McNally & Company.
Feuer, Lewis S. (ed.). (1959) *Marx and Engels, Basic Writings on Politics and Philosophy.* New York, N.Y.: Doubleday & Company, Inc.

Freud, Sigmund. (1922) *Group Psychology and the Analysis of the Ego.* London: Hogarth Press.
Fortune. (1985) "How Coke Decided a New Taste Was It." *11*(May 27):80.
Knapp, R. H. (1944) "A Psychology of Rumor." *Public Opinion Quarterly, 8*(Spring):22–37.
Le Bon, Gustave. (1977) *The Crowd: A Study of the Popular Mind.* New York, N.Y.: Penguin Books.
Marx, Karl, and Friedrich Engels. (1955) *Selected Works in Two Volumes.* Moscow: Foreign Languages Publishing House.
Mauss, Armand L. (1975) *Social Problems as Social Movements.* New York: J. B. Lippincott Company.
Newsweek. (1985) "Hey America Coke Are It!" (July 22):40–42.
Oberschall, Anthony. (1973) *Social Conflict and Social Movements.* Englewood Cliffs, N.J.: Prentice-Hall, Inc.
Park, Robert E., and Ernest W. Burgess. (1921) *Introduction to the Science of Sociology.* Chicago, Ill.: University of Chicago Press.
Perry, Joseph B., Jr., and Meredith Pugh (eds.). (1978) *Collective Behavior: Response to Social Stress.* St. Paul, Minn.: West.
Rosnow, Ralph L., and Gary Alan Fine. (1976) *Rumor and Gossip: The Social Psychology of Hearsay.* New York, N.Y.: American Elsevier Publishing Company.
Rude, George. (1964) *The Crowd in History, 1730–1848.* New York, N.Y.: John Wiley & Sons, Inc.
Sheppard, Jon M. (1984) *Sociology.* 2d ed. St. Paul, Minn.: West.
Shibutani, Tamotsu. (1966) *Improvised News: A Sociological Study of Rumor.* Indianapolis: Bobbs-Merril.
Smelser, Neil J. (1970) *Theory of Collective Behavior.* New York: The Free Press.
Snow, David A., Louis A. Zurcher, and Robert Peters. (1981) "Victory Celebrations as Theater." *Symbolic Interaction.* 1(May)21–42.
Tocqueville, Alexis de. (1955) *The Old Regime and the French Revolution.* New York: Doubleday/Anchor Books.
Turner, Ralph H., and Lewis M. Killian. (1972) *Collective Behavior.* 2d ed. Englewood Cliffs, N.J.: Prentice-Hall, Inc.
Weber, Max. (1957) *The Theory of Social and Economic Organization.* Glencoe, Ill.: The Free Press.
Wright, Sam. (1978) *Crowds, and Riots: A Study in Social Organization.* Beverly Hills, Calif: Sage Publications, Inc.

Bibliography

Abrahamson, Mark. (1983) *Social Research Methods.* Englewood Cliffs, N.J.: Prentice-Hall, Inc.

Abrahamson, Paul R. (1976) "Generational Change and the Decline of Party Identification in America," *American Political Science Review, 70* (June):469–78.

Adair, J. and K. W. Deuschle. (1970) *The People's Health.* New York, N.Y.: Appleton-Century-Crofts.

Adams, Jeremy du Quesnay. (1969) *Patterns of Medieval Society.* Englewood Cliffs, N.J.: Prentice-Hall, Inc.

Allport, Floyd H. (1924) *Social Psychology.* Boston, Mass.: Houghton Mifflin Company.

Almquist, Elizabeth M. (1984) "Race and Ethnicity in the Lives of Minority Women." In Jo Freeman (ed.), *Women: A Feminist Perspective.* 3d ed. Palo Alto, Calif.: Mayfield Publishing Company.

Almquist, Elizabeth M., and Juanita L. Wehrle-Einhorn. (1978) "The Doubly Disadvantaged: Minority Women in the Labor Force." In Ann H. Stromberg and Shirley Harkness (eds.), *Women Working.* Palo Alto, Calif.

Alperovitz, Gar. (1965) *Atomic Diplomacy: Hiroshima and Potsdam.* New York, N.Y.: Simon & Schuster, Inc.

Applebaum, Richard P. (1970) *Theories of Social Change.* Chicago, Ill.: Markham.

Ash, Roberta. (1972) *Social Movements in America.* Chicago, Ill.: Markham.

Astrein, Bruce, Adria Steinberg, and Joann Duhl. (1984) *Working with Abused Elders: Assessment, Advocacy and Intervention.* Boston, Mass.: University Center on Aging, University of Massachusetts Medical Center.

Atchley, Robert C. (1980) *The Social Forces in Later Life.* New York, N.Y.: Wadsworth Publishing Co., Inc.

Attica: The Official Report of the New York State Special Commission on Attica. (1972) New York, N.Y.: Bantam Books.

Babbie, Earl R. (1983) *The Practice of Social Research.* 3d ed. Belmont, Calif.: Wadsworth Publishing Co., Inc.

———. (1982) *Social Research for Consumers.* Belmont, Calif.: Wadsworth Publishing Co., Inc.

Bailey, Kenneth D. (1982) *Methods of Social Research.* 2d ed. New York, N.Y.: The Free Press.

Balkan, Sheila, Ronald J. Berger, and Janet Schmidt. (1980) *Crime and Deviance in America.* Belmont, Calif.: Wadsworth Publishing Co., Inc.

Baltzell, E. Digby. (1964) *The Protestant Establishment: Aristocracy and Caste in America.* New York, N.Y.: Random House, Inc.

Banfield, Edward C. (1970) *The Unheavenly City.* Boston, Mass.: Little, Brown and Company.

Baran, Paul, and Paul Sweezy. (1966) *Monopoly Capital.* New York, N.Y.: Monthly Review Press.

Bavak-Glantz, Israel, and C. Ronald Huff (eds.). (1981) *The Mad, the Bad and the Different: Essays in Honor of Simon Dinitz.* Lexington, Mass.: Lexington Books/D. C. Heath & Company.

Beattle, John. (1960) *Bunyoro: An African Kingdom.* New York, N.Y.: Holt, Rinehart and Winston.

Becker, Howard. (1963) *Outsiders: Studies in the Sociology of Deviance.* New York, N.Y.: The Free Press.

———. (1972) "Whose Side Are We On?" In William J. Filstead (ed.), *Qualitative Methodology.* Chicago, Ill.: Markham, 15–26.

Bedau, Hugo Adam (ed.). (1982) *The Death Penalty in America.* 3d ed. New York, N.Y.: Oxford University Press.

Bell, Daniel. (1973) *The Coming of Post-Industrial Society.* New York, N.Y.: Basic Books.

Bellah, Robert N. (1970) *Beyond Belief: Essays on Tradition in a Post-Traditional World.* New York, N.Y.: Harper & Row, Publishers.

Bennett, Lerone, Jr. (1970) "The Road Not Taken." *Ebony* (August):71–77.

Bequai, August. (1978) *Computer Crime.* Lexington, Mass.: D. C. Heath & Company.

Berger, Peter. (1969) *The Sacred Canopy: Elements of a Sociological Theory of Religion.* Garden City, N.Y.: Anchor Books/Doubleday & Company, Inc.

Bernard, Jessie. (1972) *The Future of Marriage.* New York, N.Y.: Bantam Books, Inc.

Bierstedt, Robert. (1950) "An Analysis of Social Power." *American Sociological Review, 15*(Dec.):730–38.

Bild, B. R., and Robert J. Havighurst. (1976) "Family and Social Support." *The Gerontologist, 16*(Feb.):63–69.

Birenbaum, Arnold. (1970) "On Managing a Courtesy Stigma." *Journal of Health and Behavior, 11*(September):196–206.

Black, Donald. (1970) "Production of Crime Rates." *American Sociological Review, 35*(Aug.):733–48.

Blackwell, James E. (1985)*The Black Community—Diversity and Unity.* 2d ed. New York, N.Y.: Harper & Row, Publishers.

Blau, Peter M., and Otis Dudley Duncan. (1967) *The American Occupational Structure.* New York, N.Y.: John C. Wiley & Sons, Inc.

Blauner, Robert. (1974) "Work Satisfaction and Industrial Trends in Modern Society." In Joseph Lopreato and Lionel S. Lewis (eds.), *Social Stratification.* New York, N.Y.: Harper and Row Publishing.

Bloch, Marc. (1962) *Feudal Society.* Chicago, Ill.: University of Chicago Press.

Block, Marilyn R., and Jan D. Sinnot (eds.). (1979) *The Battered Elderly Syndrome: An Exploratory Study.* College Park, Md.: Center on Aging, University of Maryland.

Block, N. J., and Gerald Dworkin. (1976) *The I.Q. Controversy.* New York, N.Y.: Pantheon Books, Inc.

Blumer, Herbert. (1969) *Symbolic Interactionism: Perspective and Method.* Englewood Cliffs, N.J.: Prentice-Hall, Inc.

———. (1969) "Outline of Collective Behavior." In Robert R. Evans (ed.), *Readings in Collective Behavior.* Chicago, Ill.: Rand McNally & Company.

———. (1951) "Collective Behavior." In Alfred M. Lee (ed.), *New Outline of the Principles of Sociology.* 2d ed. New York, N.Y.: Barnes & Noble Books.

Bostwinick, Jack. (1981) *We Are Aging.* New York: N.Y.: Springer Publishing Co., Inc.

Bottomore, T. B. (1966) *Classes in Modern Society.* New York, N.Y.: Vintage Books/Random House, Inc.

Boudon, Raymond. (1974) *Education, Opportunity, and Social Inequality.* New York, N.Y.: John Wiley & Sons, Inc.

Bowden, V. Elbert. (1983) *Principles of Economics.* 4th ed. Cincinnati, Ohio: South-Western Publishing Co.

Bowers, William J. (1984) *Executions in America.* 2d ed. Lexington, Mass.: D. C. Heath & Company.

Bowker, Lee H. (1982) *Corrections: The Science and the Art.* New York, N.Y.: Macmillan Publishing Co., Inc.

Bowles, Samuel, and Herbert Gintis. (1976) *Schooling in Capitalist America.* New York, N.Y.: Basic Books, Inc., Publishers.

Boyer, Richard O., and Herbert M. Morais. (1970) *Labor's Untold Story.* 3d ed. New York, N.Y.: United Electrical Workers of America (UE).

Breed, Warren. (1963) "Occupational Mobility and Suicide Among White Males." *American Sociological Review, 28*(April):179–88.

Brewer, Rose M. (1979) "Neglected Issues in *The Declining Significance of Race:* A Comment." *The Black Sociologist, 4*(Winter):69–72.

Brower, Jonathan J. (1973) "The Quota System." *Proceedings of the American Sociological Association.* Washington, D.C.: American Sociological Association.

Brown, Edward J., Timothy J. Flanagan, and Maureen McLeod (eds.). (1984) *Sourcebook of Criminal Justice Statistics, 1983.* U.S. Department of Justice, Bureau of Justice Statistics, Washington, D.C.: U.S. Government Printing Office.

Brown, Roger. (1983) *Aging: Continuity and Change.* New York, N.Y.: Wadsworth Publishing Co., Inc.

———. (1972) "Feral and Isolated Man." In V. P. Clark et al. (eds.), *Language Awareness.* New York, N.Y.: St. Martin's Press, Inc.

Burgess, Ernest W. (1925) "The Growth of the City: An Introduction of a Research Project." In Robert E. Park, Ernest W. Burgess, and R. D. McKenzie (eds.), *The City.* Chicago, Ill.: University of Chicago Press, 47–62.

Butler, Robert N. (1975) *Why Survive? Being Old in America.* New York, N.Y.: Harper & Row, Publishers.

Campbell, Donald T., and Julian C. Stanley. (1966) *Experimental and Quasi-Experimental Designs for Research.* Chicago, Ill.: Rand McNally & Company.

Carlson, Lewis H., and George A. Colborn (eds.). (1972) *In Their Place: White America Defines Her Minorities, 1850–1950.* New York, N.Y.: John Wiley & Sons, Inc.

Carmichael, Stokely, and Charles V. Hamilton (1967) *Black Power: The Politics of Liberation in America.* New York, N.Y.: Vintage Books, Random House.

Carnoy, Martin (ed.). (1975) *Schooling in a Corporate Society.* New York, N.Y.: David McKay Co., Inc.

Carsten, F. L. (1971) *The Rise of Fascism.* Berkeley, Calif.: University of California Press.

Centers for Disease Control. (1983) "Annual Summary, 1983: Reported Morbidity and Mortality in the United States." *Morbidity and Mortality Weekly Report* (MMWR), *31*(54).

Centers, Richard. (1949) *The Psychology of Social Classes.* Princeton, N.J.: Princeton University Press.

Chalmers, David M. (1965) *Hooded Americanism.* Garden City, N.Y.: Doubleday & Company, Inc.

Chase, Allan. (1977) *The Legacy of Malthus: The Social Costs of the New Scientific Racism.* New York, N.Y.: Alfred A. Knopf, Inc.

Cherny, Robert. (1977) "Economic Theories of Racism." In David M. Gordon (ed.), *Problems in Political Economy.* 2d ed. Lexington, Mass.: D. C. Heath & Company, 170–82.

Christianson, Scott. (1981) "Our Black Prisons." *Crime and Delinquency,* 27(July–Sept.):364–375.
Cicirelli, Victor G. (1981) *Helping Elderly Parents.* Boston, Mass.: Auburn House Publishing Company.
Clark, Colin. (1957) *The Conditions of Economic Progress.* 3rd. ed. London: Macmillan.
Clinard, Marshall B., and Richard Quinney. (1973) *Criminal Behavior Systems.* 2d ed. New York, N.Y.: Holt, Rinehart and Winston.
Clinard, Marshall B., and Peter C. Yeager (1980) *Corporate Crime.* New York, N.Y.: The Free Press.
Clinard, Marshall B., Peter C. Yeager, Jeanne Brissette, David Petrashek, and Elizabeth Harries. (1979) "Illegal Corporate Behavior." U.S. Department of Justice, Law Enforcement Assistance Administration. Washington, D.C.: U.S. Government Printing Office.
Cloward, Richard, and Lloyd Ohlin. (1960) *Delinquency and Opportunity.* Glencoe, Ill.: The Free Press.
Coakley, Jay J. (1984) "Sport in Society: An Inspiration or an Opiate?" In D. Stanley Eitzen (ed.), *Sport in Contemporary Society.* 2d ed. New York, N.Y.: St. Martin's Press, Inc.
Cohen, Albert. (1955) *Delinquent Boys: The Culture of the Gang.* Glencoe, Ill.: The Free Press.
Coleman, James W. (1985) *The Criminal Elite: The Sociology of White-Collar Crime.* New York, N.Y.: St. Martin's Press, Inc.
Coleman, James W., et al. (1966) *Equality of Educational Opportunity.* Washington, D.C.: U.S. Government Printing Office.
Coleridge, Samuel Taylor. (1983) "Youth and Age." In Virginia S. Reiser (ed.), *Best Loved Poems in Large Print.* Boston, Mass.: G. K. Hall and Company, 232–33.
Coles, Robert. (1967) *Children of Crisis.* New York, N.Y.: Dell Publishing Company, Inc.
———. (1971) *Migrants, Sharecroppers, Mountaineers.* Boston, Mass.: Little, Brown and Company.
Collier, Peter. (1980) "Better Red Than Dead." In Glen Gaviglio and David E. Raye (eds.), *Society As It Is.* New York, N.Y.: Macmillan Publishing Co., Inc.
Collins, Randall. (1979) *The Credential Society.* New York, N.Y.: Academic Press, Inc.
Cooley, Charles H. [1902] (1964) *Human Nature and the Social Order.* New York, N.Y.: Schocken Books, Inc.
———. [1909] (1962) *Social Organization.* New York, N.Y.: Schocken Books, Inc.
Cosby, Arthur. (1971) "Black-White Differences in Aspirations Among Deep South High School Students." *Journal of Negro Education,* (Winter):17–21.
Coser, Lewis A. (1967) *Continuities in the Study of Social Conflict.* New York, N.Y.: The Free Press.
Coser, Lewis A., Buford Rhea, Patricia A. Steffan, and Steven L. Nock. (1983) *Introduction to Sociology.* New York, N.Y.: Harcourt Brace Jovanovich.
Cowgill, Donald O. (1974) "Aging and Modernization: A Revision of the Theory." In Jaber Gubrium (ed.), *Late Life Communities and Environmental Policies.* Illinois: Charles C. Thomas.
Cox, Frances M., and Ndung'u Mberia. (1977) *Aging in Changing Society: A Kenyan Experience.* Washington, D.C.: International Education on Aging.
Cox, Oliver. (1970) *Caste, Class, and Race.* New York, N.Y.: Monthly Review Press.
Cox, William E. (1985) "Tufts Students Study Prejudice." *Black Issues in Higher Education, 2*(November):3.
Cumming, Elaine, Lois R. Dean, David S. Newell, and Isabel McCaffrey. (1960) "Disengagement: A Tentative Theory of Aging." *Sociometry, 23*(March):23–25.
Cumming, Elaine, and William E. Henry. (1961) *Growing Old: The Process of Disengagement.* New York, N.Y.: Basic Books, Inc. Publishers.
Dahl, Robert A. (1961) *Who Governs?* New Haven, Conn.: Yale University Press.

Dahrendorf, Ralf. (1959) *Class and Class Conflict in Industrial Society.* Stanford, Calif.: Stanford University Press.
Darling, Jon. (1981) "Late Marrying Bachelors." In Peter J. Stein (ed.), *Single Life.* New York, N.Y.: St. Martin's Press, Inc.
Davies, James C. (1962) "Toward a Theory of Revolution." *American Sociological Review,* 27(February):5–19.
Davis, Frank G. (1981) "Economics and Mobility; A Theoretical Rationale for Urban Black Family Well-Being." In Harriette P. McAdoo, *Black Families.* Beverly Hills, Calif.: Sage Publications.
Davis, Kenneth C. (1969) *Discretionary Justice: A Preliminary Inquiry.* Baton Rouge, La.: Louisiana State University Press.
Davis, Kingsley. (1949) *Human Society.* New York, N.Y.: Macmillan Publishing Co., Inc.
———. (1947) "Final Note on a Case of Extreme Isolation." *The American Journal of Sociology,* 3(March):432–37.
Davis, Kingsley, and Wilbert Moore. (1945) "Some Principles of Stratification." *American Sociological Review,* 10(April):242–49.
Dentler, Robert A., and Kai T. Erikson. (1959) "The Functions of Deviance in Groups." *Social Problems,* 7(Fall):98–107.
Department of Health and Human Services (DHHS). (1983) *Health, United States.* DHHS Pub. No. (PHS) 84-1232. National Center for Health Statistics. Public Health Service. Washington, D.C.: U.S. Government Printing Office, (Dec.):13–17.
Diehl, Harold S., M.D. (1969) *Tobacco and Your Health: The Smoking Controversy.* New York, N.Y.: McGraw-Hill Book Company.
Domhoff, G. William. (1983) *Who Rules American Now? A View for the Eighties.* Englewood Cliffs, N.J.: Prentice-Hall, Inc.
———. (1978) *Who Really Rules?* New Brunswick, N.J.: Transaction Books.
———. (1974) *The Bohemian Grove and Other Retreats.* New York, N.Y.: Harper & Row, Publishers.
———. (1971) *The Higher Circles.* New York, N.Y.: Vintage Books/Random House, Inc.
———. (1967) *Who Rules America?* Englewood Cliffs, N.J.: Prentice-Hall, Inc.
Douglas, Jack. (1985) *The Social Meaning of Suicide.* Princeton, N.J.: Princeton University Press.
Douglass, Richard L., Tom Hickey, and Catherine Noel. (1980) *A Study of Maltreatment of the Elderly and Other Vulnerable Adults.* Ann Arbor, Mich.: Institute of Gerontology, University of Michigan.
Durkheim, Emile. [1915] (1961) *The Elementary Forms of the Religious Life.* New York, N.Y.: Collier Books.
Duvall, Evelyn M., and Brent C. Miller. (1983) *Marriage and Family Development.* New York, N.Y.: Harper & Row, Publishers.
———. [1897] (1951) *Suicide: A Study in Sociology.* New York, N.Y.: The Free Press.
———. [1895] (1950) *Rules of the Sociological Method.* 8th ed. New York, N.Y.: The Free Press.
Earle, John R., Dean Knudsen, and Donald W. Shriver, Jr. (1976) *Spindles and Spires.* Atlanta, Ga.: John Knox Press.
Edwards, Harry. (1973) *Sociology of Sport.* Homewood, Ill.: Dorsey Press.
Eitzen, D. Stanley, and George H. Sage. (1982) *Sociology of American Sport.* Dubuque, Iowa: William C. Brown Company, Publishers.
Elderhertz, Herbert. (1970) "The Native Impact and Prosecution of White Collar Crime." U.S. Department of Justice, Law Enforcement Assistance Administration. Washington, D.C.: U.S. Government Printing Office.
Elkins, Stanley. (1963) *Slavery: A Problem in American Institutional and Intellectual Life.* New York, N.Y.: Grosset & Dunlap, Inc.
Erikson, Kai T. (1966) *Wayward Puritans.* New York, N.Y.: John Wiley & Sons.

Evans, Robert R. (ed.). (1969) *Readings in Collective Behavior.* Chicago, Ill.: Rand McNally & Company.

Ewell, Charles M. (1967) "What Patients Really Think About Their Nursing Care." *Modern Hospital, 109*(Dec.):106–8.

Feagin, Joe R. (1984) *Racial and Ethnic Relations.* 2d ed. Englewood Cliffs, N.J.: Prentice-Hall, Inc.

———. (1975) *Subordinating the Poor: Welfare and American Beliefs.* Englewood Cliffs, N.J.: Prentice-Hall, Inc.

Federal Bureau of Investigation. (Annual) *Uniform Crime Reports.* Washington, D.C.: U.S. Government Printing Office.

Feuer, Lewis S. (ed.). (1959) *Marx and Engels, Basic Writings on Politics and Philosophy.* New York, N.Y.: Doubleday & Company, Inc.

Filstead, William J. (1972) *Qualitative Methodology.* Chicago, Ill.: Markham.

Finch, Caleb E., and Leonard Hayglick (eds.). (1977) *Handbook of the Biology of Aging.* New York, N.Y.: Van Nostrand Reinhold Company.

Fitzgerald, Frances. (1979) *America Revisited: History Schoolbooks in the Twentieth Century.* Boston, Mass.: Little, Brown and Company.

Fitzpatrick, Joseph P. (1983) "Hispanics in New York: An Archdiocesan Survey." *America, 48*(March 12):185–88.

———. (1971) *Puerto Rican Americans.* Englewood Cliffs, N.J.: Prentice-Hall, Inc.

Fortune. (1985) "How Coke Decided New Taste Was It." *11*(May 27):80.

Foster, William Z. (1954) *The Negro People in American History.* New York, N.Y.: International Publishers.

Fox, Jacob H., Jordan L. Topal, and Michael T. Huckman. (1975) "Dementia in the Elderly—Search for Treatable Illnesses." *Journal of Gerontology, 30*(Sept.):557–64.

Frazier, E. Franklin. (1963) *The Negro Church in America.* New York, N.Y.: Schocken Books, Inc.

Freeman, Joseph T. (1979) *Aging: Its History and Literature.* New York, N.Y.: Human Science Press.

Freud, Sigmund. (1958) *Civilization and Its Discontents.* New York, N.Y.: Anchor Books/Doubleday & Company, Inc.

———. (1957) *The Future of an Illusion.* Garden City, N.Y.: Anchor Books/Doubleday & Company, Inc.

———. (1922) *Group Psychology and the Analysis of the Ego.* London: Hogarth Press.

Friedrich, Carl J., and Zbigniew K. Brzezinski. (1965) *Totalitarian Dictatorship and Autocracy.* 2d ed. New York, N.Y.: Praeger Publishers, Inc.

Furstenberg, Frank F., Jr., and Graham B. Spanier. (1984) *Recycling the Family: Remarriage After Divorce.* Beverly Hills, Calif.: Sage Publications.

Galliher, John F. (1976) "Explanations of Police Behavior: A Critical Review and Analysis." In Arthur Niederhoffer and Abraham S. Blumbert (eds.), *The Ambivalent Force: Perspectives on the Police.* Hinsdale, Ill.: The Dryden Press.

Gans, Herbert J. (1971) "The Uses of Poverty: The Poor Pay All." *Social Policy, 2*(July/August):20–24.

Garfinkel, Harold. (1956) "Successful Degradation Ceremonies." *American Journal of Sociology, 61*(March):420–24.

Gary, Lawrence E. (1981) *Black Men.* Beverly Hills, Calif.: Sage Publications.

Georges-Abeyie, Daniel (ed.). (1984) *The Criminal Justice System and Blacks.* New York, N.Y.: Clark Boardsman Company, Ltd.

Geschwender, James. (1978) *Racial Stratification in America.* Dubuque, Iowa: William C. Brown Company, Publishers.

Gibbs, Jack P. (1981) *Norms, Deviance and Social Control: Conceptual Matters.* New York, N.Y.: American Elsevier Publishing Co., Inc.

Giele, Janet. (1978) *Women and the Future.* New York, N.Y.: The Free Press.

Gilbert, Dennis, and Joseph Kahl. (1982) *The American Class Structure.* Homewood, Ill.: Dorsey Press.

Giles, Helen Foster. (1983) "Differential Life Expectancy Among White and Nonwhite Americans: Some Explanations During Youth and Middle Age." In Ron C. Manuel (ed.), *Minority Aging.* Westport, Conn.: Greenwood Press, Inc.

Glick, Paul. (1981) "Demographic Picture of Black Families." In Harriette Pipes McAdoo, (ed.) *Black Families.* Beverly Hills, Calif.: Sage Publications.

Goffman, Erving. (1963) *Stigma Notes on the Management of Spoiled Identity.* Englewood Cliffs, N.J.: Prentice-Hall, Inc.

———. (1961) *Asylums: Essays on the Social Situation of Mental Patients and Other Inmates.* New York, N.Y.: Doubleday & Company, Inc.

Gold, Raymond L. (1969) "Roles in Sociological Field Observations." In George J. McCall and J. L., Simmons (eds.), *Issues in Participant Observation.* Reading, Mass.: Addison-Wesley Publishing Co., Inc., 30–39.

Goldfarb, William. (1945) "Psychological Privation in Infancy and Subsequent Adjustment." *American Journal of Orthopsychiatry, 15*(April):247–55.

Goldstein, Joseph. (1960) "Police Discretion Not to Invoke the Criminal Process: How Visibiity Decisions in the Administration of Joseph." *Yale Law Journal, 69*(July):544.

Good, B. (1977) *Culture, Medicine and Sociology.* Holland: Reidel.

Gordon, Milton. (1964) *Assimilation in American Life.* New York, N.Y.: Oxford University Press, Inc.

Gove, Walter R. (ed.). (1975) *The Labelling of Deviance: Evaluating a Perspective.* New York, N.Y.: John Wiley & Sons, Inc.

Greer, Colin. (1973) *The Great School Legend.* New York, N.Y.: The Viking Press, Inc.

Griffin, John Howard. (1961) *Black Like Me.* New York, N.Y.: Signet.

Grimal, Pierre. (1973) *Larousse World Mythology.* New York, N.Y.: The Hamlyn Publishing Group, Ltd.

Gutek, Barbara, and Bruce Morash. (1982) "Sex Ratios, Sex Role Spillover, and Sexual Harassment of Women at Work." *Journal of Social Issues, 38*:55–74.

Hall, Edward T. (1959) *The Silent Language.* Greenwich, Conn.: Fawcett Publications, Inc.

Halsell, Grace. (1969) *Soul Sister.* Greenwich, Conn.: Fawcett Publications.

Harlow, Harry F. (1971) *Learning to Love.* New York, N.Y.: Ballantine.

Harring, Sidney. (1985) *Policing a Class Society.* New Brunswick, N.J.: Rutgers University Press.

Hauser, Robert M., and Featherman, David L. (1977) *The Process of Stratification.* New York, N.Y.: Academic Press, Inc.

Heilbroner, L. Robert. (1972) *The Worldly Philosophers.* New York, N.Y.: Simon & Schuster, Inc.

Heinz, Donald. (1983) "The Struggle to Define America" In Robert C. Liebman and Robert Wuthnow, (eds.), *The New Christian Right: Mobilization and Legitimation.* New York, N.Y.: Aldine Publishing Co.

Herberg, Will. (1955) *Protestant, Catholic, Jew.* Garden City, N.Y.: Doubleday & Company, Inc.

Herrnstein, Richard. (1973) *I.Q. in the Meritocracy.* Boston, Mass.: Little, Brown and Company.

———. (1971) "I.Q." *Atlantic Monthly, 228*(3)(September):43–64.

Higham, John. (1975) *Strangers in the Land: Patterns of American Nativism, 1860–1925.* New York, N.Y.: Atheneum Publishers.

Hill, Robert B. (1971) *The Strengths of Black Families.* New York, N.Y.: Emerson Hall Publishing, Inc.

Hindelang, Michael J. (1970) "Educational and Occupational Aspirations Among Working Class Negro, Mexican-American and White Elementary School Children." *Journal of Negro Education, 39*(Fall):351–53.

Hindelang, Michael J., Travis Hirschi, and Joseph G. Weis. (1981) *Measuring Delinquency.* Beverly Hills, Calif.: Sage Publications.

Hirschi, Travis. (1966) *Causes of Delinquency.* Berkeley, Calif.: University of California Press.

Hodge, Robert W., and Donald J. Treiman. (1968) "Class Identification in the United States." *American Journal of Sociology, 73*(March):535–47.

Hoebel, E. Adamson. (1960) *The Cheyennes: Indians of the Great Plains.* New York: Henry Holt and Company.

Hofstadter, Richard. (1971) *Social Darwinism in American Thought.* Boston, Mass.: Beacon Press.

Hollingshead, August B. (1949) *Elmtown's Youth.* New York, N.Y.: John C. Wiley & Sons, Inc.

Homans, George. (1950) *The Human Group.* New York, N.Y.: Harcourt Brace Jovanovich, Inc.

Hughes, Everett C. (1945) "Dilemmas and Contradictions of Status." *American Journal of Sociology, 50*(March):353–59.

Humphreys, Laud. (1970) *Tearoom Trade: Impersonal Sex in Public Places.* Chicago, Ill.: Aldine Publishing Company.

Hunter, Floyd. (1953) *Community Power Structure.* Chapel Hill, N.C.: University of North Carolina Press.

Hurn, Christopher. (1985) *The Limits and Possibilities of Schooling: An Introduction to the Sociology of Education.* 2d ed. Boston, Mass.: Allyn & Bacon, Inc.

Hyman, Herbert. (1954) *Intervening in Social Research.* Chicago, Ill.: University of Chicago Press.

Institute for the Study of Labor and Economic Crisis. (1982) *The Iron Fist and the Velvet Glove: An Analysis of the U.S. Police.* 3d ed. San Francisco, Calif.: Synthesis Publications.

Jackson, Jacquelyne J. (1980) *Minorities and Aging.* New York, N.Y.: Wadsworth Publishing Company, Inc.

Jackson, James S., Wayne R. McCullough, and Gerald Gurin. (1981) "Group Identity Development Within Black Families." In Harriette P. McAdoo, *Black Families.* Beverly Hills, Calif.: Sage Publications.

Jacobson, Solomon G. (1982) "Equity in the Use of Public Benefits by Minority Elderly." In Ron C. Manuel (ed.), *Minority Aging.* Westport, Conn.: Greenwood Press, Inc., 161–70.

Jaggar, Alison M., and Paula S. Rothenberg. (1984) *Feminist Frameworks: Alternative Theoretical Accounts of the Relations Between Women and Men.* New York, N.Y.: McGraw-Hill Book Company.

Jarvik, Lissy F. (1980) "Diagnosis of Dementia in the Elderly: A 1980 Perspective." In Carl Eisdorfer (ed.), *Annual Review of Gerontology and Geriatrics.* New York, N.Y.: Springer Publishing Company, Inc.

Jencks, Christopher. (1972) *Inequality.* New York, N.Y.: Basic Books, Inc., Publishers.

Jensen, Arthur. (1979) *Who Gets Ahead?* New York, N.Y.: Basic Books, Inc., Publishers.

Knapp Commission Report on Police Corruption. (1972) New York, N.Y.: George Braziller.

Knapp, R. H. (1944) "A Psychology of Rumor." *Public Opinion Quarterly, 8*(Spring):22–37.

Krauskopf, Joan M., and Mary Elise Burnett. (1985) "The Elderly Person: When Protection Becomes Abuse." In Harold Cox (ed.), *Aging.* Guilford, Conn.: Dushkin Publishing Group, Inc.

Ladner, Joyce A. (1973) *The Death of White Sociology.* New York, N.Y.: Random House, Inc.

Lapchick, Richard. (1984) *Broken Promises: Racism in American Sports.* New York, N.Y.: St. Martin's Press, Inc.
Lau, Elizabeth E., and Jordan I. Kosberg. (1979) "Abuse of the Elderly by Informal Care Providers." *Aging, 299*(September/October):10–15.
Le Bon, Gustave. (1977) *The Crowd: A Study of the Popular Mind.* New York, N.Y.: Penguin Books.
Lekachman, Robert. (1982) *Greed Is Not Enough: Reaganomics.* New York, N.Y.: Pantheon Books, Inc.
Lemert, Edwin M. (1951) *Social Pathology: A Systematic Approach to the Theory of Sociopathic Behavior.* New York, N.Y.: McGraw-Hill Book Company.
Lenin, Vladimir I. (1939) [1916] *Imperialism, The Highest Stage of Capitalism.* New York, N.Y.: International Publishers.
Lenski, Gerhard, and Jean Lenski. (1982) *Human Societies.* 3d ed. New York, N.Y.: McGraw-Hill Book Company.
Levy, P. J. (1967) *The Economic Life of the Ancient World.* Chicago, Ill.: The University of Chicago Press.
Lewis, Charles, Barbara Resnik, Glenda Schmidt, and David Watman. (1969) "Activities, Events and Outcomes in Ambulatory Patient Care." *The New England Journal of Medicine, 280*(Mar.):645–649.
Lewis, Oscar. (1965) *La Vida.* New York, N.Y.: Random House, Inc.
Liebow, Elliot. (1967) *Tally's Corner.* Boston, Mass.: Little, Brown and Company.
Lipset, Seymour Martin, and Reinhart Bendix. (1964) *Social Mobility in Industrial Society.* Berkeley, Calif.: University of California Press.
Lipsey, G. Richard, Peter O. Steiner, and Douglas D. Purvis. (1984) *Economics.* 7th ed. New York, N.Y.: Harper & Row, Publishers.
Lord, Walter. (1955) *A Night to Remember.* New York, N.Y.: Henry Holt.
Manuel, Ron C., and John Reid. (1983) "A Comparative Demographic Profile of the Minority and Nonminority Aged." In Ron C. Manuel (ed.), *Minority Aging.* Westport, Conn.: Greenwood Press, Inc.
Maris, Ronald. (1969) *Social Forces in Urban Suicide.* Homewood, Ill.: Dorsey Press.
Martin, Susan Ehrlich. (1984) "Sexual Harassment." In Jo Freeman (ed.), *Women: A Feminist Perspective.* Palo Alto, Calif.: Mayfield Publishing Company, 54–69.
Marx, Gary. (1967) *Protest and Prejudice.* New York, N.Y.: Harper & Row, Publishers.
———. (1967) *Critique of Hegel's Philosophy of Right.* Reproduced in L. Easton and K. Guddat (eds.), *Writings of the Young Marx on Philosophy and Society.* Garden City, N.Y.: Anchor Books/Doubleday & Company, Inc.
Marx, Karl, and Friedrich Engels. (1959) *Basic Writings on Politics and Philosophy.* Edited by Lewis Feuer. Garden City, N.Y.: Anchor Books/Doubleday & Company, Inc.
———. [1848] (1955) *The Communist Manifesto.* New York, N.Y.: Appleton-Century-Crofts.
———. (1955) *Selected Works in Two Volumes.* Moscow: Foreign Languages Publishing House.
Matza, David. (1969) *Becoming Deviant.* Englewood Cliffs, N.J.: Prentice-Hall, Inc.
———. (1964) *Delinquency and Drift.* New York, N.Y.: John Wiley & Sons, Inc.
Mauksch, I. E. (1978) "The Nurse Practitioner Movement—Where Does It Go From Here?" *American Journal of Public Health, 68(Nov.)*:1074–75.
Mauss, Armand L. (1975) *Social Problems as Social Movements.* New York, N.Y.: J. B. Lippincott Company.
McAdoo, Harriette Pipes. (1978) "Factors Related to Stability in Upwardly Mobile Black Families." *Journal of Marriage and the Family, 40*(November):761–768.
———. (1981) *Black Families.* Beverly Hills, Calif.: Sage Publications.
McCaghy, Charles H. (1985) *Deviant Behavior.* 2d ed. New York, N.Y.: Macmillan Publishing Co., Inc.
———. (1976) *Deviant Behavior: Crime, Conflict and Interest Groups.* New York, N.Y.: Macmillan Publishing Co., Inc.

McCandless, B. R. (1969) "Childhood Socialization." In D. A. Goslin (ed.), *Handbook of Socialization Theory and Research.* Chicago, Ill.: Rand McNally & Company.

McLuhan, M. H., and Q. Fiore. (1967) *The Medium Is the Message.* New York, N.Y.: Random House, Inc.

McNeely, R. L., and Carl E. Pope (eds.). (1981) *Race, Crime, and Criminal Justice.* Beverly Hills, Calif.: Sage Publications.

Mead, George H. (1934) *Mind, Self and Society.* Chicago, Ill.: University of Chicago Press.

Mead, Margaret. (1939) "Coming of Age in Samoa." In *From the South Seas: Studies of Adolescence and Sex in Primitive Societies.* New York, N.Y.: William Morrow & Co., Inc.

Melville, Keith. (1983) *Marriage and Family Today.* New York, N.Y.: Random House, Inc.

Merton, Robert K. (1949; rev. eds. 1957, 1968) *Social Theory and Social Structure.* New York, N.Y.: The Free Press.

———. (1938) "Social Structure and Anomie." *American Sociological Review,* 3(October):672–82.

Meyer, John W. (1977) "The Effects of Education as an Institution." *American Journal of Sociology, 83*(July):55–77.

Michels, Robert. (1962) *Political Parties.* New York, N.Y.: The Free Press.

Michener, James A. (1976) *Sports in America.* New York, N.Y.: Random House, Inc.

Milgram, Stanley. (1963) "Behavioral Study of Obedience." *Journal of Abnormal and Social Psychology, 67*(Oct.):371–78.

———. (1965) "Some Conditions of Obedience and Disobedience to Authority." *Human Relations, 18*(Feb.):57–76.

Miller, Daniel. (1979) *Marriage and Family Interaction.* 3d ed. New York, N.Y.: Dorsey Press.

Miller, Walter B. (1958) "Lower Class Structure as a Generating Milieu of Gang Delinquency." *Journal of Social Issues, 14*(Jan.):5–19.

Mills, C. Wright. (1959) *The Sociological Imagination.* New York, N.Y.: Oxford University Press.

———. (1959) *The Power Elite.* New York, N.Y.: Oxford University Press, Inc.

Moore, Joan W. (1976) *Mexican Americans.* 2d ed. Englewood Cliffs, N.J.: Prentice-Hall, Inc.

Morgan, Edmund S. (1958) *The Puritan Dilemma: The Story of John Winthrop.* Boston, Mass.: Little, Brown and Company.

Morris, Robert. (1979) *Social Policy of the American Welfare State.* New York, N.Y.: Harper & Row, Publishers.

Moynihan, Daniel P. (1967) "The Negro Family: The Case for National Action." In Lee Rainwater and William L. Yancey (eds.). *The Moynihan Report and the Politics of Controversy.* Cambridge, Mass.: The M.I.T. Press.

———. (1965) *The Negro Family: The Case for National Action.* Washington, D.C. Office of Policy Planning and Research, U.S. Department of Labor.

Myrdal, Gunnar. (1944) *An American Dilemma.* New York, N.Y.: Harper and Brothers.

Nachimas, David, and Chava Nachimas. (1981) *Research Methods in the Social Sciences.* 2d ed. New York, N.Y.: St. Martin's Press, Inc.

National Advisory Commission on Criminal Justice Standards and Goals. (1973) *Task Force Report: Courts.* Washington, D.C.: U.S. Government Printing Office.

National Center for Health Statistics. (1982) *Health, United States: 1982.* (PHS 83-1232) Washington, D.C.: U.S. Government Printing Office.

National Commission on Excellence in Education. (1983) *A Nation at Risk.* Washington, D.C.: U.S. Government Printing Office.

National Opinion Research Center. (1970–1979) *General Social Survey.* Chicago, Ill.: University of Chicago Press.

National Urban League. (1984) *The Status of Black America.* New York, N.Y., National Urban League Publishers.

Navarro, Peter. (1984) *The Policy Game: How Special Interests and Ideologies Are Stealing America.* New York, N.Y.: John Wiley & Sons, Inc.

Nettler, Gwynn. (1984) *Explaining Crime.* 3d ed. New York, N.Y.: McGraw-Hill Book Company.

Newsweek. (1985) "Up From the Underground." (September 2):33.

———. (1985) "The Nightmare at Hutton." (July 22):45.

———. (1985) "Hey America Coke Are It!" (July 22):40–42.

Oberschall, Anthony. (1973) *Social Conflict and Social Movements.* Englewood Cliffs, N.J.: Prentice-Hall, Inc.

Olsen, Marvin. (1970) "The Social and Political Participation of Blacks." *American Sociological Review, 35*(Aug.):682–97.

Olson, David H. (1983) *Families—What Makes Them Work.* Beverly Hills, Calif.: Sage Publications.

O'Malley, Helen, Howard Segars, Ruben Perez, Victoria Mitchella, and George Knuepful. (1979) *Elder Abuse in Massachusetts: A Survey of Professionals and Paraprofessionals.* Boston, Mass.: Legal Research and Services for the Elderly.

Omen, Gilbert S. (1974) "Behavior Genetics." In James Birren and K. Schaie (eds.), *Handbook of the Psychology of Aging.* New York, N.Y.: Van Nostrand Reinhold Company.

Oppenheimer, Valerie Kincade. (1970) *The Female Labor Force in the United States.* Berkeley, Calif.: University of California Press.

Orcutt, James D. (1983) *Analyzing Deviance.* Homewood, Ill.: The Dorsey Press.

Orum, Anthony M. (1978) *Introduction to Political Sociology.* Englewood Cliffs, N.J.: Prentice-Hall, Inc.

Park, Robert E., and Ernest W. Burgess. (1921) *Introduction to the Science of Sociology.* Chicago, Ill.: University of Chicago Press.

Parsons, Talcott (trans.). (1958) Preface to Max Weber, *The Protestant Ethic and the Spirit of Capitalism.* New York, N.Y.: Charles Scribner's Sons.

———. (1957) *Toward a General Theory of Action.* Cambridge, Mass.: Harvard University Press.

Parsons, Talcott, and Robert F. Bales. (1953) *Family, Socialization, and Interaction Process.* Glencoe, Ill.: The Free Press.

Perlo, Victor. (1975) *Economics of Racism.* New York, N.Y.: International Publishers.

Perry, Joseph B., Jr., and Meredith Pugh (eds.). (1978) *Collective Behavior: Response to Social Stress.* St. Paul, Minn.: West.

Persell, Caroline Hodges. (1977) *Education and Inequality.* New York, N.Y.: The Free Press.

Peter, Lawrence J., and Raymond Hull. (1970) *The Peter Principle.* New York, N.Y.: Bantam Books.

Pfuhl, Erdwin H. (1980) *The Deviance Process.* New York, N.Y.: D. Van Nostrand Company.

Pines, Mayor. (1981) "The Civilizing of Genie." *Psychology Today, 15*(September):28–34.

Pinkney, Alphonso. (1975) *Black Americans.* 2d ed. Englewood Cliffs, N.J.: Prentice-Hall, Inc.

Pope, Liston. (1942) *Millhands and Preachers: A Study of Gastonia.* New Haven, Conn.: Yale University Press.

Portes, Alejancho. (1984) "The Rise of Ethnicity." *American Sociological Review, 49*(June)383–397.

Powell, Edwin. (1958) "Occupations, Status and Suicide: Toward a Redefinition of Anomie." *American Sociological Review, 23*(April):131–39.

Price, Barbara Raffel, and Natalie J. Sokoloff (eds.). (1982) *The Criminal Justice System and Women.* New York, N.Y.: Clark Boardman Company, Ltd.

Quinney, Richard. (1977) *Class, State and Crime.* New York, N.Y.: David McKay Co., Inc.

Rains, Prue. (1982) "Deviant Careers." In M. Michael Rosenberg, Robert A. Stebbins, and Allan Turowetz (eds.), *The Sociology of Deviance.* New York, N.Y.: St. Martin's Press, Inc., 21–41.

Reich, Michael. (1981) *Racial Inequality.* Princeton, N.J.: Princeton University Press.

Reiman, Jeffrey H. (1979) *The Rich Get Richer and the Poor Get Prison.* New York, N.Y.: John Wiley & Sons, Inc.

Reiss, Albert J., Jr., and D. J. Black. (1967) "Interrogation and the Criminal Process." *American Academy of Political and Social Science Annals, 347*(November):47–57.

Rey, Antonio B. (1982) "Activity and Disengagement: Theoretical Orientations in Social Gerontology and Minority Aging." In Ron C. Manuel (ed.), *Minority Aging.* Westport, Conn.: Greenwood Press.

Riesman, David. (1950) *The Lonely Crowd.* New Haven, Conn.: Yale University Press.

Riley, Matilda White, and Anne Foner. (1968) *Aging and Society. Volume One: An Inventory of Research Findings.* New York, N.Y.: Russell Sage Foundation.

Rockstein, Morris, and Marvin Sussman. (1979) *Biology of Aging.* New York, N.Y.: Wadsworth Publishing Co., Inc.

Rose, Arnold. (1967) *The Power Structure: Political Process in American Society.* New York, N.Y.: Oxford University Press, Inc.

Rosenthal, Robert, and Lenore Jacobson. (1968) *Pygmalion in the Classroom.* New York, N.Y.: Holt, Rinehart and Winston.

Rosenthal, Robert, and Ralph L. Rosnow. (1984) *Essentials of Behavioral Research: Methods and Data Analysis.* New York, N.Y.: McGraw-Hill Book Company.

Rosnow, Ralph L., and Gary Alan Fine. (1976) *Rumor and Gossip: The Social Psychology of Hearsay.* New York, N.Y.: American Elsevier Publishing Company.

Rowland, Michael, Robinson Fulwood, and Joel C. Kleinman. (1983) "Changes in Heart Disease Risk Factors." In National Center for Health Statistics, *Health, United States,* DHHS Pub. No. (PHS) 84-1232. Public Health Service. Washington, D.C.: U.S. Government Printing Office, (Dec.):13–17.

Rubin, Zick. (1981) "Jokers Wild in the Lab." In Theodore C. Wagenaar (ed.), *Readings for Social Research.* Belmont, Calif.: Wadsworth Publishing Co., Inc.

Rubington, Earl. (1982) "Deviant Subcultures." In M. Michael Rosenberg, Robert A. Stebbins, and Allan Turowetz (eds.), *The Sociology of Deviance.* New York, N.Y.: St. Martin's Press, Inc., 42–70.

Rude, George. (1964) *The Crowd in History, 1730–1848.* New York, N.Y.: John Wiley & Sons, Inc.

Ruiz, Dorothy S. (1982) "Epidemiology of Schizophrenia: Some Diagnostic and Sociocultural Considerations." *Phylon, 4*(Winter):315–26.

Ryan, William. (1977) *Blaming the Victim.* rev. ed. New York, N.Y.: Vintage Books/Random House, Inc.

Sack, Allen L., and Robert Thiel. (1979) "College Football and Social Mobility." *Sociology of Education, 52*(January):60–66.

Sagarin, Edward. (1967) "Voluntary Associates Among Social Deviants." *Criminologica, 5*(May):8–22.

Savitz, Leonard D. (1978) "Official Police Statistics and Their Limitations." In Leonard D. Savitz and Norman Johnston (eds.), *Crime in Society.* New York, N.Y.: John Wiley & Sons, Inc., 69–81.

Schaefer, Richard T. (1979) *Racial and Ethnic Groups.* Boston, Mass.: Little, Brown and Company.

Schafer, Walter E. (1969) "Some Social Sources and Consequences of Interscholastic Athletics: The Case of Participation and Delinquency." In Gerald S. Kenyon (ed.), *Aspects of Contemporary Sport Sociology.* Chicago, Ill.: The Athletic Institute.

Schwartz, Howard, and Jerry Jacobs. (1979) *Qualitative Sociology: A Method to the Madness.* New York, N.Y.: The Free Press.
Scott, Jack. (1971) *The Athletic Revolution.* New York, N.Y.: The Free Press.
Scott, Marvin B., and Stanford M. Lyman. (1968) "Accounts." *American Sociological Review, 33*(February):46–62.
Sellin, Thorsten. (1976) *Slavery and the Penal System.* New York, N.Y.: American Elsevier Publishing Co., Inc.
———. (1938) *Culture Conflict and Crime.* New York, N.Y.: Social Science Research Council Bulletin 41.
Sells, Lucy. (1978) "Mathematics—A Critical Filter." *Science Teacher* (February):28–29.
Sena-Rivera, Jaime. (1979) "Extended Kinship in the U.S.: Competing Models and the Case of La Familia Chicana." *Journal of Marriage and the Family, 41*(Feb.):121–29.
Shanas, Ethel. (1961) *Family Relationships of Older People.* Chicago, Ill.: Health Information Foundation.
Shaw, Clifford R., and Henry D. McKay. (1942) *Juvenile Delinquency in Urban Areas.* Chicago, Ill.: University of Chicago Press.
Shelden, Randall. (1982) *Criminal Justice in America: A Sociological Approach.* Boston, Mass.: Little, Brown and Company.
Sheley, Joseph F. (1980) "Is Neutralization Necessary for Criminal Behavior?" *Deviant Behavior, 2*(October–December):50.
Sheppard, Jon M. (1984) *Sociology.* 2d ed. St. Paul, Minn.: West.
Sherman, Howard, Jr., and James L. Wood. (1979) *Sociology: Traditional and Radical Perspectives.* New York, N.Y.: Harper & Row, Publishers.
Shibutani, Tamotsu. (1966) *Improvised News: A Sociological Study of Rumor.* Indianapolis, Ind.: Bobbs-Merrill.
Shock, Nathan W. (1974) "Biological Theories of Aging." In Morris Rockstein (ed.), *Theoretical Aspects of Aging.* New York, N.Y.: Academic Press, Inc.
Shur, Edwin M. (1971) *Labeling Deviant Behavior.* New York, N.Y.: Harper & Row, Publishers.
Simpson, George E., and J. Milton Yinger. (1972) *Racial and Cultural Minorities.* 4th ed. New York, N.Y.: Harper & Row Publishers.
Slaughter, Oliver, and Mignon O. Batey. (1982) "Service Delivery and the Black Aged: Identifying Barriers to Utilization of Mental Health Services." In Ron C. Manuel (ed.), *Minority Aging.* Westport, Conn.: Greenwood Press, Inc.
Smelser, Neil J. (1962) *Theory of Collective Behavior.* New York, N.Y.: The Free Press.
Smith, Adam. [1776] (1937) *An Inquiry into the Nature and Causes of the Wealth of Nations.* Reprint. New York, N.Y.: Modern Library.
Snow, David A., Louis A. Zurcher, and Robert Peters. (1981) "Victory Celebrations as Theater." *Symbolic Interaction, 1*(May):21–42.
Social Security Administration. (1981) "The Income and Resources of the Elderly in 1978." *Social Security Bulletin, 44*(Dec.):3–11.
Sokoloff, Natalie J. (1981) *Between Money and Love.* New York, N.Y.: Praeger Publishers, Inc.
Spanier, Graham B., and Linda Thompson. (1984) *Parting: The Aftermath of Separation and Divorce.* Beverly Hills, Calif.: Sage Publications.
Spitz, Rene. (1964) "Hospitalism." In Rose Coser (ed.), *The Family: Its Structure and Functions.* New York, N.Y.: St. Martin's Press, Inc.
Sports Illustrated. (1984) "The College Football Association." 14(Oct.)4–5.
Spreitzer, Elmer, and Eldon E. Snyder. (1983) "Sport." In Robert Hagedorn (ed.), *Sociology.* Dubuque, Iowa: William C. Brown Company, Publishers.
Staples, Robert. (1981) *The World of Black Singles.* Westport, Conn.: Greenwood Press.
Stein, Leonard I., M.D. (1985) "The Doctor-Nurse Game." In Henslin, James M., *Down to Earth Sociology: Introductory Readings* (4th ed.) New York, N.Y.: The Free Press, 281–288.

Steinmetz, Suzanne K. (1983) "Dependent Elders, Family Stress." In Timothy H. Brubaker (ed.), *Family Relationships in Later Life.* Beverly Hills, Calif.: Sage Publications, Inc.

———. (1980) "Investigating Family Violence." *Journal of Home Economics,* ---(Summer):32–36.

———. (1978) "The Politics of Aging, Battered Parents." *Society, 15(5)* (July/August):54–55.

Straus, Murray A., Richard J. Gelles, and Suzanne K. Steinmetz. (1980) *Behind Closed Doors: Violence in the American Family.* New York, N.Y.: Anchor Press/Doubleday & Company, Inc.

Sullivan, J. A., C. Z. Dachelet, H. A. Sultz, and M. Henry. (1978) "The Rural Nurse Practitioner: A Challenge and a Response." *American Journal of Public Health,* 68(Nov.):1074–1075.

Summer, William G. (1906) *Folkways: A Study of the Sociological Importance of Usages, Manners, Customs, Mores, and Morals.* Boston, Mass.: Ginn and Company.

Surgeon General of the United States. (1982) *The Health Consequences of Smoking.* U.S. Department of Health and Human Services, Public Health Service. Washington, D.C.: U.S. Government Printing Office.

Sutherland, Edwin. (1961) *White-Collar Crime.* New York, N.Y.: Holt, Rinehart and Winston.

Sutherland, Edwin, and Donald Cressey. (1939) *Principles of Criminology.* 3d ed. Philadelphia, Penn.: Lippincott.

Sykes, Gresham M. (1978) *Criminology.* New York: N.Y.: Harcourt Brace Jovanovich, Inc.

———. (1957) "Techniques of Neutralization: A Theory of Delinquency." *American Sociological Review, 22*(December):644–70.

Szymanski, Albert. (1976) "Racial Discrimination and White Gain." *American Sociological Review, 41*(June):403–14.

Taft, Philip, and Philip Ross. (1969) "American Labor Violence: Its Causes, Character, and Outcome." In Hugh David Graham and Ted Robert Gurr (eds.), *The History of Violence in America.* New York, N.Y.: Praeger Publishers, Inc.

Takagi, Paul. (1974) "A Garrison State in a Democratic Society." *Crime and Social Justice, 1*(Feb.) 88–104.

Tannebaum, Frank. (1963) *Slave and Citizen: The Negro in the Americas.* New York, N.Y.: Vintage Books/Random House, Inc.

———. (1938) *Crime and the Community.* Boston, Mass.: Ginn and Company.

Taylor, Ian, Paul Walton, and Jack Young. (1973) *The New Criminology.* New York, N.Y.: Harper & Row, Publishers.

Taylor, Maurice C. (1982) "Black Male-Female Suicide: A Case Study of Occupation and Rates of Suicide by Race and Sex." *Western Journal of Black Studies,* 6(Fall):124–29.

Thornberry, Terrence P., and Joseph E. Jacoby. (1979) *The Criminally Insane: A Community Follow-up of Mentally Ill Offenders.* Chicago, Ill.: University of Chicago Press.

Time. (1985) "Placing the Blame at E. F. Hutton." (September 16):54.

Tocqueville, Alexis de. [2 vol., 1835; tr. 4 vol., 1835–40] (1955) *The Old Regime and the French Revolution.* New York, N.Y.: Anchor Books/Doubleday & Company, Inc.

Tönnies, Ferdinand. [1887] (1963) *Community and Society.* Edited and translated by Charles P. Loomis. New York, N.Y.: Harper and Row.

Trevino, Fernando M., and Abigail J. Moss. (1983) "Health Insurance Coverage and Physician Visits Among Hispanic and Non-Hispanic People." In National Center for Health Statistics, *Health, United States,* DHHS Pub. No. (PHS) 84-1232. Public Health Service. Washington, D.C.: U.S. Government Printing Office, (Dec.):45–48.

Trice, Harrison M., and Paul M. Roman. (1970) "Delabeling, Relabeling and Alcoholics Anonymous." *Social Problems, 17*(Spring):4.

Turk, Herman. (1965) "An Inquiry into the Undersocialized Conception of Man." *Social Forces, 43*(May):518–521.

Turner, Ralph H., and Lewis M. Killian. (1972) *Collective Behavior.* 2d ed. Englewood Cliffs, N.J.: Prentice-Hall, Inc.

U.S. Bureau of the Census. (1984) *Statistical Abstract of the United States.* Washington, D.C.: U.S. Government Printing Office.

———. (1983) *Statistical Abstract of the United States.* Washington, D.C.: U.S. Government Printing Office.

———. (1982) *Statistical Abstract of the United States.* Washington, D.C.: U.S. Government Printing Office.

———. (1980) *Current Population Reports,* Series P-60, No. 125. Washington, D.C.: U.S. Government Printing Office.

U.S. Department of Commerce, Bureau of the Census. (1983) *General Social and Economic Characteristics, United States Summary, Vol. I, 1980 Census of Population.* Washington, D.C.: U.S. Government Printing Office.

U.S. Department of Justice. (1984) "The Severity of Crime." *Bureau of Justice Statistics Bulletin.* Washington, D.C.: U.S. Government Printing Office.

U.S. Department of Justice, Bureau of Justice Statistics. (1983) *Report to the Nation on Crime and Justice.* Washington, D.C.: U.S. Government Printing Office.

———. (Annual) *National Crime Survey.* Washington, D.C.: U.S. Government Printing Office.

U.S. Department of Labor. (1977) *Dictionary of Occupational Titles.* Washington, D.C.: U.S. Government Printing Office.

U.S. Department of Labor, Bureau of Labor Statistics. (1983) *Employment and Earnings.* Washington, D.C.: U.S. Government Printing Office.

U.S. Senate Committee on Aging. (1983) *Aging America: Trends and Projections.* (PL 3377-584) Washington, D.C.: U.S. Government Printing Office.

Useem, Michael. (1978) "Inner Group of the American Capitalist Class." *Social Problems, 25*(February):225–40.

———. (1983) *The Inner Circle: Large Corporations and the Rise of Business Political Activity in the U.S. and U.K.* New York, N.Y.: Oxford University Press.

van den Berghe, Pierre. (1978) *Man in Society: A Biosocial View.* New York, N.Y.: American Elsevier Publishing Co., Inc.

Vander Zanden, James. (1983) *American Minority Relations.* 4th ed. New York, N.Y.: Alfred A. Knopf, Inc.

Veblen, Thorstein. [1899] (1973) *The Theory of the Leisure Class.* Boston, Mass.: Houghton Mifflin Company.

Vogt, Evon Z. (1970) *The Zinacantacos of Mexico: A Modern Way of Life.* New York, N.Y.: Holt, Rinehart and Winston.

Walker, Peter N. (1973) *Punishment: An Illustrative History.* New York, N.Y.: Arco Publishing Co.

Walker, Samuel. (1983) *The Police in America.* New York, N.Y.: McGraw-Hill Book Company.

Wallerstein, Immanuel. (1974) *The Modern World-System.* New York, N.Y.: Academic Press, Inc.

Wallerstein, James S., and Clement J. Wyle. (1947) "Our Law-Abiding Law-Breakers." *Probation, 25*(March/April):107–12.

Warner, W. Lloyd, and Paul S. Lunt. (1941) *The Social Life of a Modern Community.* New Haven, Conn.: Yale University Press.

Warren, Roland L. (1978) *The Community in America.* 3d ed. Chicago, Ill.: Rand McNally & Company.

Warwick, Donald P. (1981) "Social Scientists Ought to Stop Lying." In Theodore C.

Wagenaar (ed.), *Readings for Social Research.* Belmont, Calif.: Wadsworth Publishing Co., Inc.

Washburn, Philo. (1982) *Political Sociology: Approaches, Concepts, Hypotheses.* Englewood Cliffs, N.J.: Prentice-Hall, Inc.

Watson, Wilbur. (1982) *Aging and Social Behavior.* Beverly Hills, Calif.: Wadsworth Publishing Company, Inc.

Wax, Murray L. (1971) *Indian Americans.* Englewood Cliffs, N.J.: Prentice-Hall, Inc.

Weber, Max. (1946) *From Max Weber: Essays in Sociology.* Translated by H. H. Gerth and C. Wright Mills. New York, N.Y.: Oxford University Press, Inc.

———. (1925) (1964) *The Theory of Social and Economic Organization.* Translated by A. M. Henderson and Talcott Parsons. New York, N.Y.: The Free Press.

———. (1922) (1964) *The Sociology of Religion.* Translated by Ephraim Fischoff. Boston, Mass.: Beacon Press.

———. (1925) (1968) *Economy and Society.* edited by G. Roth and C. Willich. Totowa, N.J.: Bedminster.

———. [1920, tr. 1930] (1958) *The Protestant Ethic and the Spirit of Capitalism.* translated by Talcott Parsons. New York, N.Y.: Charles Scribner's Sons.

Weed, J. A. (1980) *National Estimates of Marriage Dissolution and Survivorship: United States.* Vital and Health Statistics: Series 3, Analytic Statistics, No. 19. Washington, D.C.: U.S. Government Printing Office.

Weeks, John R. (1984) *Aging: Concepts and Social Issues.* Beverly Hills, Calif.: Wadsworth Publishing Co., Inc.

———. (1981) *Population: An Introduction to Concepts and Issues.* 2d ed. Belmont, Calif.: Wadsworth Publishing Co., Inc.

Weitzman, Lenore J. (1984) "Sex-role Socialization: A Focus on Women." In Jo Freeman (ed.), *Women: A Feminist Perspective.* 3d ed. Palo Alto, Calif.: Mayfield Publishing Company.

White, L. A. (1973) *The Concept of Culture.* Minneapolis, Minn.: Burgess Publishing Company.

Willie, Charles V. (1981) *A New Look At Black Families.* New York, N.Y.: General Hall.

———. (1979) *Caste and Class Controversy.* New York, N.Y.: General Hall.

Wilson, Edward O. (1975) *Sociobiology: The New Synthesis.* Cambridge, Mass.: Harvard University Press.

Wilson, Everett K. (1972) "Conformity Revisited." In George Ritzer (ed.), *Issues, Debates, and Controversies: An Introduction to Sociology.* Boston, Mass.: Allyn & Bacon, Inc. 111–120.

Wilson, William J. (1978) *The Declining Significance of Race.* Chicago, Ill.: University of Chicago Press.

Winston, Richard. (1960) *Charlemagne: From the Hammer to the Cross.* New York, N.Y.: Vintage Books/Random House, Inc.

Wirth, Louis. (1945) "The Problem of Minority Groups." In Ralph Linton (ed.), *The Science of Man in the World Crisis.* New York, N.Y.: Columbia University Press.

Wiseman, Jacqueline P. (1970) *Stations of the Lost: Treatment of Skid Row Alcoholics.* San Diego, Calif.: University of California Press.

Woodruff, Diana S., and James E. Birren. (1983) *Aging: Scientific Perspective and Social Issues.* Monterey, Calif.: Brooks/Coles Publishing Company.

Woodson, Robert L. (ed.). (1977) *Black Perspectives on Crime and the Criminal Justice System.* Boston, Mass.: G. K. Hall and Co.

Woodward, C. Vann. (1955) *The Strange Career of Jim Crow.* New York, N.Y.: Oxford University Press.

Wright, Erik Olin, Cynthia Costello, David Hachen, and Joey Sprague. (1982) "The American Class Structure." *American Sociological Review,* 47 (Dec.) 709–726.

Wright, Erik Olin, and Luca Perrone. (1977) "Marxist Class Categories and Income Inequality." *American Sociological Review,* 42 (February):32–55.

Wright, Sam. (1978) *Crowds and Riots: A Study in Social Organization.* Beverly Hills, Calif.: Sage Publications, Inc.

Wrong, Dennis H. (1961) "The Oversocialized Conception of Man in Modern Sociology." *American Sociological Review,* 26(April):183–93.

Zborowski, Mark. (1952) "Cultural Components in Responses to Pain." *The Journal of Social Issues,* 18(4):16–30.

Zimbardo, Phillip. (1972) "Pathology of Imprisonment." *Society,* 9(April)4–8.

Zola, I. (1973) "Pathways to the Doctor: From Person to Patient." *Social Science and Medicine,* 7(Sept.):677–89.

Zuboff, Shoshana. (1980) "New Worlds of Computer-mediated Work." In William Feigelman (ed.), *Sociology Full Circle: Contemporary Readings on Society.* 4th ed. New York, N.Y.: Holt, Rinehart and Winston, 463–477.

Name Index

Abrahamson, Mark, 34
Abrahamson, Paul R., 368
Adams, Jeremy du Quesnay, 140
Ageton, Suzanne S., 79
Ali, Muhammad, 128
Almquist, Elizabeth M., 213
Alperowitz, Gar, 197
Amsden, 246
Astrein, Bruce, 246
Atchley, Robert C., 233, 240

Babbie, Earl R., 33, 35, 40, 42, 43
Bailey, Kenneth D., 28, 33, 36
Bales, Robert F., 223
Balkan, Sheila, 420, 421
Baran, Paul, 362, 366
Barnes, 42
Bavak-Glantz, Israel, 108
Beattie, John, 102, 355
Becarria, Cesare, 113
Becker, Howard S., 40, 108, 114, 116, 121, 122
Bedau, Hugo Adam, 431
Bell, Daniel, 332
Bellah, Robert N., 318–320
Bendix, Reinhart, 167
Bennett, Lerone, 192
Berger, Peter, 309, 310, 312
Berger, Ronald J., 420, 421
Bernard, Jesse, 215
Bierstedt, Robert, 353
Bild, Bernice R., 248
Birenbaum, Arnold, 111, 112
Birren, James E., 242, 248, 250

Blackwell, James E., 368, 380, 381, 387
Blau, Peter M., 167
Blauner, Robert, 348–349
Bloch, Marc, 140
Block, Marilyn R., 245, 247
Blumer, Herbert, 15
Bottomore, T. B., 141, 142
Bowers, William J., 431
Bowles, Samuel, 383–385, 389
Breed, Warren, 348
Brewer, Rose M., 170
Brower, Jonathan J., 408
Brown, Roger, 68
Brzezinski, Zbigniew K., 356
Bujak, Zbigniew, 125
Bureau of Justice Statistics Bulletin, 422
Burgess, Ernest W., 123
Burnett, Mary Elise, 247

Campbell, Donald T., 24, 35
Carlson, Lewis H., 197, 202, 203
Carmichael, Stokely, 185
Carter, Jimmy, 275
Centers, Richard, 157
Chase, Allan, 202, 203, 389
Chavez, Cesar, 119
Christianson, Scott, 432
Cicirelle, Victor G., 248
Cicourel, Aaron V., 38
Clark, Colin, 330–331
Clinard, Marshall B., 127, 415
Cloward, Richard A., 126

Coakley, Jay, 395
Cohen, Albert, 79, 416
Colborn, George A., 197, 202, 203
Coleman, James, 386, 388, 389, 420
Coles, Robert, 81–82
Collier, Peter, 83
Collins, Randall, 384, 385
Cooley, Charles Horton, 11, 12, 74, 75, 78, 94
Coolidge, Calvin, 202
Cosby, Arthur, 293–294
Cosell, Howard, 395
Coser, Lewis A., 129, 226
Cox, Frances M., 240, 241
Cox, Oliver C., 151
Cressey, Donald R., 124
Cumming, Elaine, 239

Dahl, Robert A., 364
Dahrendorf, Ralf, 90
Darling, Jon, 283
Darwin, Charles, 10
Davis, Kenneth C., 425
Davis, Kingsley, 68, 95, 137
Dentler, Robert A., 129
Domhoff, G. William, 82, 172, 216, 362
Douglas, Jack, 38, 39
Douglas, Richard L., 245
Drus, 109
DuBois, W. E. B., 2, 179, 193
Duncan, Otis Dudley, 167
Durkheim, Emile, 11, 108, 116, 117, 129, 130, 301, 305, 307

Duvall, Evelyn M., 274, 276, 278, 279, 287, 289, 296

Earle, John R., 314, 317
Edwards, Harry, 398, 405, 407
Eitzen, D. Stanley, 393, 398, 408, 410
Elkins, Stanley, 143
Elliot, Delbert S., 79
Erikson, Kai T., 129

Falwell, Reverend Jerry, 320, 325
Feagin, Joe R., 163
Featherman, David L., 167
Finch, Caleb E., 238
FitzGerald, Frances, 375
Fitzgerald, F. Scott, 142
Fitzpatrick, Joseph P., 318
Fox, Jacob H., 235
Frazier, E. Franklin, 12, 317
Freeman, Joseph T., 240, 241
Freud, Sigmund, 75, 324
Friedrich, Carl J., 356
Furstenburg, Frank F., Jr. 278, 287

Gans, Herbert J., 81, 165
Garfinkel, Harold, 109
Garvey, Marcus, 193
Gerth, H. H., 354
Gibbs, Jack P., 115, 116
Giele, Janet, 326
Gilbert, Dennis, 158
Giles, Helen Foster, 233
Gintis, Herbert, 383–385, 389
Glick, Paul, 291, 292, 294
Goffman, Erving, 110–112, 121
Goldfarb, William, 69
Goldstein, Joseph, 425
Gordon, Milton, 317
Gove, Walter R., 115
Griffin, John Howard, 30, 31
Grimal, Pierre, 304
Gutek, Barbara, 214

Hall, Edward, 57
Halsell, Grace, 30, 31
Hamilton, Charles V., 185
Harlow, Harry F., 66, 69, 79
Harring, Sidney, 424
Hauser, Robert M., 167
Havighurst, Robert J., 248
Hayflick, Leonard, 238
Heilbroner, L. Robert, 336–339
Heinz, Donald, 325
Hemingway, Ernest, 142
Henry, William E., 239
Herberg, Will, 318

Herrnstein, Richard, 194, 389
Hill, Robert B., 291–293
Hindelang, Michael J., 293–294
Hirschi, Travis, 126
Hofstadter, Richard, 11
Homans, George, 101
Huff, C. Ronald, 108
Hughes, Everett C., 39, 122
Humphreys, Laud, 29–31, 120
Hunter, Floyd, 158
Hurn, Christopher, 378, 383
Hutton, E. F., 127
Hyman, Herbert, 29

Jackson, Jacquelyne J., 235
Jackson, James S., 278
Jackson, Reverend Jesse, 88
Jacobs, Jerry, 39
Jacobson, Lenore, 83
Jacoby, Joseph E., 114
Jaruzelski, Wojciech, 125
Jarvik, Lissy F., 235
Jencks, Christopher, 388, 389
Jensen, Arthur, 164, 194, 389
Johnson, Lyndon B., 320

Kahl, Joseph, 158
Kahn, Robert L., 349
Kamin, Leon, 203, 389
Keller, Helen, 58
Kennedy, Robert E., Jr., 289
Kerbo, Harold R., 157
Keynes, John Maynard, 334, 336–338
Khomeini, Ayatollah, 316
King, Martin Luther, Jr., 120, 193, 316
Kingsley, David, 297
Kitsue, John, 38
Kosberg, Jordan I., 245, 246
Krauskopf, Joan M., 247

Ladner, Joyce, 42
Lau, Elizabeth E., 245, 246
Lemert, Edwin M., 114, 115
Lenin, V. I., 342
Lenski, Gerhart, 138–139, 143, 355
Lenski, Jean, 355
Levy, P. J., 333
Lewis, Oscar, 81
Liebow, Elliot, 31
Lincoln, Abraham, 192
Lipset, Seymour Martin, 167
Lipsey, G. Richard, 333, 336
Lunt, Paul S., 158
Lyman, Stanford M., 427

McAdoo, Harriette P., 20, 291, 292

McCaghy, Charles H., 42, 43, 120, 420
McCandless, B. R., 79, 80
McCarthy, Joseph, 129
McKay, Henry D., 123
McLuhan, Marshall, 53
Maris, Ronald, 117, 348
Martin, Susan Erlich, 214
Marx, Gary, 314
Marx, Karl, 11, 90, 144, 158, 171, 174, 312, 313, 334, 338, 341, 361
Matza, David, 122, 123, 124, 427
Mead, George Herbert, 12, 75
Mead, Margaret, 30, 31
Melville, Keith, 276, 278, 287, 290
Merton, Robert K., 90, 117, 120, 262, 416
Michels, Robert, 363
Milgram, Stanley, 34, 35, 40
Miller, Brent C., 274, 276, 278, 279, 287, 289, 296
Miller, Dorothy L., 279, 280
Miller, Walter B., 125, 416
Mills, C. Wright, 8, 9, 354, 361, 362
Moore, Charlotte Dickinson, 279, 280
Moore, Joan W., 79
Moore, Wilbert F., 137, 226
Morash, Bruce, 214
Morris, Robert, 42
Moynihan, Daniel P., 42, 164, 291
Myrdal, Gunnar, 59

Nachimas, Chava, 32
Nachimas, David, 32
National Advisory Commission on Criminal Justice Standards and Goals, 429
Navarro, Peter, 337
Nettler, Gwynn, 29, 38, 113, 114, 414, 420

Ohlin, Lloyd E., 126
Olsen, Marvin, 368
Olson, David H., 280
O'Malley, Helen, 245
Omen, Gilbert S., 235
Oppenheimer, Valerie, 214
Orcutt, James D., 115

Parks, Rosa, 120
Parsons, Talcott, 12, 137, 223
Perot, H. Ross, 378
Perrone, Luca, 158
Persell, Caroline Hodges, 389, 393
Pfuhl, Erdwin H., 111, 116
Pines, Mayor, 69
Polonko, Karen A., 279
Pope, Liston, 313, 314

Portes, Alejandro, 199
Powell, Edwin, 348
President's Council on Physical Fitness, 393

Quinney, Richard, 415

Rains, Prue, 121, 122
Reagan, Ronald, 221
Reiman, Jeffrey H., 420, 423
Reinhart, Bendix, 167
Report to the Nation on Crime and Justice, 433
Rey, Antonio B., 240
Riesman, David, 364
Rockstein, Morris, 238
Roman, Paul M., 109
Roper, Elmo, 157
Rose, Arnold, 364–365
Rosenthal, Robert, 27, 40, 83
Rosnow, Ralph L., 27, 40
Ross, Philip, 170, 200
Rubin, Zick, 41
Rubington, Earl, 122, 123
Ryan, William, 165, 166, 389, 420, 425

Sack, Allen L., 403
Sagarin, Edward, 121, 122
Sage, George H., 393, 398, 408, 410
Savitz, Leonard D., 38
Schaefer, Richard T., 185
Schafer, Walter E., 403
Schmidt, Janet, 420, 421
Schwartz, Howard, 39
Scott, Jack, 406
Scott, Marvin B., 427
Sellin, Thorsten, 125, 434
Sells, Lucy, 218
Sena-Rivera, Jaime, 297

Shafer, 417
Shanas, Ethel, 248
Shaw, Clifford R., 123
Shelden, Randall, 423, 427, 430
Sheley, Joseph F., 427
Sherman, Howard, Jr., 160
Shock, Nathan W., 238
Shockley, William, 194
Shur, Edwin M., 114
Simpson, George E., 187
Sinnot, Jan D., 245, 247
Smith, Adam, 334
Snyder, Eldon E., 393
Spanier, Graham B., 278 287, 288, 290
Spencer, Herbert, 10
Spitz, Rene, 69
Spreitzer, Elmer, 393
Stanley, Julian C., 24, 35
Staples, Robert, 289, 295
Steinmetz, Suzanne K., 245, 246
Straus, Murray A., 245
Sumner, William G., 10–11, 42, 51, 61
Sussman, Marvin, 238
Sutherland, Edwin H., 123, 124, 420
Sweezy, Paul, 362, 366
Sykes, Gresham M., 108, 124

Taft, Philip, 170, 200
Takagi, Paul, 426
Tannenbaum, Frank, 110, 142
Taylor, Maurice C., 117, 348
Teachman, Jay D., 279
Thiel, Robert, 403
Thompson, Linda, 287, 288, 290
Thornberry, Terrence P., 114
Tocqueville, Alexis de, 355
Tönnies, Ferdinand, 11, 266, 267
Trice, Harrison M., 109
Turk, Herman, 72, 73

Valenzuela, Fernando, 87

Vander Zanden, James, 369
Veblen, Thorstein, 82, 401
Vogt, Evon Z., 300

Walker, Peter N., 113
Walker, Samuel, 424
Wallerstein, Immanuel, 153
Wallerstein, James S., 108
Ward, Lester, 10–11
Warner, W. Lloyd, 158
Warren, Earl, 197
Warren, Roland L., 102
Warwick, Donald P., 41
Washburn, Philo, 356, 357, 366, 367
Washington, Booker T., 193
Watson, Wilbur, 239
Weber, Max, 11, 14, 40, 97, 137, 147, 166, 269, 315, 316, 334, 335, 339–341, 353, 354, 359
Weed, J. A., 287
Weeks, John R., 38, 235, 241
Weitzman, Lenore J., 217, 218
White, L. A., 58
Willie, Charles V., 292
Wilson, Everett K., 72, 73
Wilson, William J., 174, 169, 170
Winston, Richard, 354
Wirth, Louis, 181
Wiseman, Jacqueline P., 109
Wood, James L., 160
Woodruff, Diana S., 242, 248, 250
Wright, Erik Olin, 158
Wrong, Dennis H., 72
Wyle, Clement J., 108

Yinger, J. Milton, 187

Zborowski, Mark, 57
Zimbardo, Phillip, 34
Zuboff, Shoshana, 349

Subject Index

Aberrant behavior, 120
Abolitionism, 192
Absolute poverty, 162–163
Abstract rules, 99
Abuse of the aged, 245–247
Accidents, as cause of death, 448
Accommodation, 189
Achieved status, 87
   social mobility of females and minorities and, 168–169
Achievement orientation, of black youth, 293–294
Activity theory of aging, 239
Administration on Aging (AoA), 251
Affirmative action, 194–195
   in education, 388
Age. *See also* Aging
   cause of death and, 447–448
   sexually transmitted diseases and, 440–441
Age Discrimination and Employment Act, 250
Age grading, 235–236
Ageism, 241–242
Agency data, 34–38
Age-specific services, 250
Aggregate data, 37
Aging (the aged), 230–250
   abuse of, 245–247
   age-specific services for, 250–251
   biological, 233–234
   chronological, 232–233
   family and, 248
   health problems of, 242–243
   housing and, 244–245
   income of, 243–244
   legislation and, 249–252
   Marxist theory and, 151
   senility and, 234–235
   social roles and, 235
   support for, 247–252
   Weber's theory and, 152
Agricultural revolution, marriage and, 284–285
AIDS (acquired immune deficiency syndrome), 441–442
Alimony, 274
Allied health personnel, 455, 456
Altzheimer's disease, 235
American Indian movement (AIM), 129
American Indians. *See* Native Americans
American Medical Association (AMA), 450–452
Androgyny, 212
Animism, 304
Anomie, 116–120
Anomie theory of crime, 416
Anonymity, 40, 41
Anthropomorphism, 304
Anticipatory socialization, 77
Apartheid, 205
Ascribed status, 87
   social mobility of females and minorities and, 168–169
Asian Americans, 183–184, 196–197
Assimilation, 187–188
Assimilationist theory of racism, 185–186

Associations. *See* Bureaucracies
Authority
   charismatic, 358–359
   hierarchy of, 98
   legitimation of, 357–360
   rational–legal, 359–360
   traditional, 358

Bail, 429–430
Ban, 122
Bartering, 33, 333
Behavior. *See specific types of behavior*
Behavioral risk factors, 438
Beliefs, 59. *See also* Religion
   institutionalization of 302–304
Bigamy, 278
Bilateral descent, 287
Bilingualism, of Hispanic family members, 296–297
Biology (biological factors)
   and aging, 233–234, 238
   culture and, 53–54
   gender inequalities, and, 222–223, 226
Birth cohort, 233
Black Codes, 192
Blacks, 182–183, 192–196
   the church and, 314, 317
   current status of, 194–196
   equality of educational opportunity and, 386–387
   family of, 291–295
   as health-care personnel, 453–455

511

Blacks (*cont.*)
  higher education and, 380–381
  hypertension and heart disease in, 446–447
  marital status and, 294–295
  police killings of, 426
  political participation by, 368–369
  Reagan administration and, 195
  rebellions by, 194
  sexism and, 227–228
  social mobility of, 169–170
  sport and, 405–406
Blaming the victim, 389
  poverty and, 163–166
Bogie rumors, 466
Border norms, 125
Boundaries, 92
Bourgeoisie, 145
Brown v. *the Board of Education of Topeka, Kansas,* 42
Bureaucracies, 97–104
  formal organization of, 98–100
  growth of, 103–104
  impersonality of, 96–97, 102–103
  informal organization of, 100–101
  in a multicultural world, 102–103
  public reaction to, 101–102
  rational–legal authority of, 360
Bureau of Indian Affairs (BIA), 83, 191
Bureau of the Census, family as defined by, 277
Busing, 195
Busing for school desegregation, 387–388

Capitalism, 144–147, 149–151, 153, 337–343
  higher education and, 383–384
  Marx's view of, 338–339
  poverty and, 165
  spirit of, 339–340
Capital punishment, 431–432
Caste system, 139–140, 311–312
Centers for Disease Control (CDC), 34–35
Centralization of power, 104
Character stigma, 111
Chariots of Fire (film), 89
Charisma (charismatic authority), 358–359
  of prophets, 316
  routinization of, 359
Chicago, University of, sociology department at, 11–12
Children. *See also* Education
  feral, 67–68
  institutionalized, 69–70
  isolated, 68
  marriage and, 278–279

Chronological age, 232–233
Church and state, doctrine of separation of, 319–320
Cigarette smoking, 444–446
Circular reaction, 464
Civil religion, 318–320
Civil rights movement, 193–194
Class, 153
Class (class structure), 156–162. *See also* Stratification
  future changes in, 173–174
  in industrial societies, 172
  labels and, 157–158
  life chances and, 166
  Marxist view of, 144–147, 149–151, 153, 159–160, 162, 165
  objective approaches to, 159–160
  reputational approach to, 159
  socialization and, 81–83
  in the Soviet Union, 175–176
  sport and, 399–402
  subjective approaches to, 158–159
  tax structure and, 162
  in Third World societies, 172–173
  in the United States, 160–161
  Weber's view of, 147–148
Class bias, in death penalty, 431–432
Class conflict, 157, 170
Class consciousness, 171–172
Class culture theories of crime, 416
Classless society, 174–176
Class struggle, Marx's theory of, 338
Coca-Cola, 467–470
Cohort, birth, 233
Collective behavior, 461–476. *See also* Social movements
  cola wars and, 468–470
  the crowd, 463–465
  definition of, 462
  mass behavior, 467–468
  rumors, 465–467
  theories of, 470–476
    contagion theory, 471–472
    convergence theory, 472–473
    emergent norm theory, 473–474
    value-added theory, 474–476
Collective conscience, 305, 307
Collective deviance, 120–128
Collectivity, institutional religion and, 306
Colleges and universities, 380–384
Common-law marriages, 274
Communism, 146, 340
  fascism and, 204
Comparable worth, 226–227
Complete observer technique of field observation, 32
Complete participant technique of field observation, 29–30

Confederate, 35
Confidentiality, 40, 41
Conflict subculture, 126
Conflict theory, 14. *See also* Marx, Karl; Weber, Max; Marxism
  of crime, 417–418
  of education, 383
  law and, 62
  personality development and, 75–76
  of racism, 186, 192
  of religion, 312–314
  roles and, 90
  social change and, 484–485
  of social institutions, 261–262
  of sport, 396–397
  of stratification, 137
Conjugal succession, 278
Conservatives
  poverty as viewed by, 165
  prison system and, 433
Conspicuous consumption, 401
Contagion, 464
Contagion theory of collective behavior, 471–472
Content analysis, 39, 41
Continued subjugation, 188
Control groups, 23
Control theory of deviance, 126
Convergence theory of collective behavior, 472–473
Core nations, 153
Corporate deviance, 126–129
Corporations, multinational, 342
Correlation, 25
Corruption, police, 426–427
Courtesy stigma, 112
Courts, 429–431
Coverage error, 36
Crime, 109, 413–423
  anomie and, 119
  clearance rate for, 419
  corporate, 126–129
  definition of, 414–415
  index, 418–422
  sources of information about, 418–423
  theories of, 416–418
  types of, 415–416
Criminal justice system
  the courts in, 429–431
  death penalty and, 431–432
  homogenization process in, 423, 432
  index crimes as focus of, 421–423
  the police in, 423–429
    abuse of authority by the police, 425–428
    main function of the police, 425
    plea bargaining, 428–429

sidewalk justice, 425–427
prisons and, 432–435
Criminal subculture, 126
Cronyism, 101
Crowd, the, 463–465
Cuban Americans, 199
Cultural assimilation, 188
Cultural relativism, 53
Cultural variability, 52
Culture, 47–63
  beliefs and, 59
  biology and, 53–54
  definition of, 47
  dysfunctional patterns in, 51
  education's role of transmitting, 374
  environment and, 54
  ethnocentrism, 52–53
  extracultural contacts and, 54–55
  intracultural dynamics, 55–56
  learning and, 50
  material, 48–49
  nonmaterial, 49
  norms and, 59–63
  sexism and, 227
  sharing of, 50–51
  social transmission and, 50–51
  structure of dominance and, 56
  subcultures and, 56–57
  symbols and, 57–58
  technological development and, 55–56
  values and, 58–59
Culture of poverty theory, 164

Darwinism, 10–11
Data, 20
  aggregate, 37
Death penalty, 431–432
Deism, 302–303
Delinquency, 124, 126
Democratic governments, 355–356
Demography, 182
Denial, 124
Dependent variable, 23
Descent
  bilateral, 287
  patrilineal, 286, 287
Desegregation
  of higher education, 380–381
  of schools, 387–388
Determinism, moral, 309
Deterrence, 113–114
  as sentencing philosophy, 431
Deviance (deviants), 107–130
  anomie and, 116–120
  collective deviance, 120–128
  control theory of, 126
  corporate, 126–129

defintion of, 108–109
deterrence and, 113–114
deviant careers, 121–122
differential opportunity theory of collective, 126
explanations of, 114–120
labeling and, 115–116
responses to, 109–114
secondary deviance, 114–116
stigma and, 109–113
subcultures, 122–126
techniques of neutralization and, 124
Diagnosis, medical, 450–451
Dialectical materialism, 338–339
Differential association theory of crime, 417
Differential opportunity theory of collective deviance, 126
Discrimination. See Racism
Diseases. See also Health status
  heart, 446–447
  hypertension, 446–447
  notifiable, 439
  sexually transmitted, 439–443
Disengagement theory of aging, 239–240
Distribution of wealth, 162
Divergent norms, 81
Divorce, 278, 287–289
  blacks and, 295
  Hispanics and, 297
Dowry, 285
Dramatization of evil, 110
Dysfunction, 13–14
  cultural, 51

Economy, the (economic institutions), 329–349
  capitalist vs. communist systems, 340–341
  economic development theories, 334–340
    dialectical materialism, 338–339
    invisible hand, 335–336
    Keynes's theory (helping hand) 336–337, 335–336
    spirit of capitalism, 339–340
    exchange relationships, 333–334
    productive acitivty, types of, 330–332
    United States and world, 341–343
Education, 373–389. See also Schools
  conflict theory of, 383–384

equality of opportunity and, 385–387
expansion of, 379–384
functionalist theory of, 381–382, 384–385
higher, 380–384
roles of, 374–375
Educational achivement, 388–389
Egalitarian families, 291
Ego development, 75–76
Elder abuse, 245–247
Electorate, the, pluralist view of power and, 365–366
Elitist model of power, 353, 361–362
Emergent norm theory of collective behavior, 473–474
Employment, 343–345
Endogamy, 140, 142
Environment, culture and, 54
Equality of educational opportunity, 385–387
Error theory of aging, 238
Estate system, 140–141
Ethics of social research, 30, 40–44
Ethnic groups. See Ethnicity; Immigrants; Race; and specific groups
Ethnicity
  political participation and partisanship and, 368–369
  race vs., 181
  relations among, 187–189
  religion and, 317–318
  sexism and, 227–228
  Weber's theory and, 152
Ethnocentrism, 52–53
Ethnomethodology, 16–17
Eugenics, 201–202
European Americans. See White ethnics
Evil, dramatization of, 110
Exchange relationships, 333–334
Exchange theory, 14–15
Experiments, 34–36
Expressive functions, 223
Extended family, 276
Extended norms, 125
Extracultural contacts, 54–55
Extralinguistic behavior, 32

Fads, 468
Families. See also Marriage
  aging (the aged) and, 248
  of blacks, 291–295
  definition of, 274–277
  extended, 276
  functions of, 278–281
  group identity and, 279–280
  Hispanic, 295

Families (cont.)
  kin-assisted, 292
  matriarchal, 291
  native American, 279–280
  nuclear, 276
  of orientation, 277
  patriarchal, 291
  political behavior and, 367
  of procreation, 277
  socialization and, 279
  social policy issues and, 274–277
  as support system, 280–281
Fascism, 204–207
Fashions, 468
Fatalism, political behavior and, 367, 368
Federal Omnibus Crime Control Act, 428
Feminist theory of gender inequality, 224–225
Feminization of poverty, 163
Feral children, 67–68
Field observations, 27–34
  advantages and disadvantages of, 33–34
  ethical problems in, 30
Findings, 22
First Amendment to the Constitution, religion and, 319, 321, 322
Fitness craze, 393
Folkways, 60–62
Forced assimilation, 187–188
Functionalist theory (or perspective functionalism), 13–14
  of education, 381–382, 384–385
  of gender inequality, 223, 226
  law and, 62
  of racism, 185–186
  of religion, 306–312
  social change and, 483–484
  of social institutions, 261, 262
  of sport, 395–399
  of stratification, 137–138
Functions, 13

Garbology, 39, 41
Gemeinschaft, 266–267
Gender (gender roles). *See also* Sex; Sexism
  life expectancies and, 233
  sex vs., 211–212
  socialization and, 220, 224, 226–227
Generalization, 28
Generalized other (Mead), 75
Genocide, 188
Gerontocratic society, 240
Gerontology, 231

Gesellschaft, 267
Gods Must Be Crazy, The (film), 48–49
Gold, 31
Gonorrhea, 439–441
Goods, definition of, 329
Government. *See also* Bureaucracies; State, the
  definition of, 354
  democratic, 355–356
  as economy's "helping hands," 337
  legitimacy of, 357–360
  totalitarian, 356–357
Gross National Product (GNP), 349
Group cohesion, religion and, 307–308
Groups (group organization), 86–106
  associations, 96
  boundaries and, 92
  bureaucracies, 97–104
    in a multicultural world, 102–103
    formal organization of, 98–100
    informal organization of, 100–101
  classification of, 93–97
  the family and, 279–280
  nature of, 90–92
  norms and sanctions and, 93–94
  primary groups, 94–95
  role and, 88–90
  roles and, 92–93
  secondary groups, 95–96
  social mobility and, 170
  status and, 87–88
  statuses and, 92–93

Health-care personnel, 449–456
  black, 453–455
  public, 455–456
  sex and, 451–452
Health status, 438–448. *See also* Diseases
  age and cause of death, 447–448
  of the aged, 242–243
  income and, 456–458
  marriage and, 215
  morbidity, 439–443
  mortality, 443–444
  smoking and, 444–446
Hierarchy of authority, 98
Higher education, 380–384
Hispanics, 183, 197–199. *See also specific groups*
  families of, 295–297
  political participation by, 368, 369
  religion and, 318

Homicide, 448
Homogenization process, criminal justice as, 423, 432
Horizontal mobility, 167
Housing, for the aged, 244–245
Hypertension, 446–447
Hypothesis, 20

Id, 75–76
Ideal norms, 60
Ideology, 146
Illegal aliens, 198–199
Imitation, socialization and, 71–72
Immigrants, 201. *See also specific groups*
  political behavior of, 369
Immunological theories of aging, 238
Imperialism, 342
Impersonality, bureaucratic, 96–97, 102–103
Incapacitation, as sentencing philosophy, 431
Incarceration, 114. *See also* Prisons
Income
  of the aged, 243–244
  health status and, 456–458
Independent variable, 23
Indeterminate sentences, 433
Index crimes, 418–422
India, caste system of, 139–140, 311–312
Individual behavior, social behavior vs., 4–5
Industrial revolution, marriage and, 285–286
Industrial societies, 268
  social class in, 172
Inequality of educational opportunity, 385–387
Infrastructure, 146
Institutionalization of the criminally insane, 114
Institutionalized children, 69–70
Institutionalized racism, 185
Institutions, total, 77–78
Instrumental functions, 223
Intelligence tests, 383, 389
Interest groups, 362–363
Intergenerational mobility, 167
Interracial marriage, 201, 202
Interviews, 25–29
Intracultural dynamics, 55–56
Intrusion, 40–41
Invisible hand; concept of, 335–336
I.Q. tests, 203, 389
Irish Americans, 200
Iron law of oligarchy, 363–364
Iron law of wages, 145

Isolated children, 68
Issues, pluralist theory of power and, 364–365

Japanese Americans, 196–197
Job dissatisfaction, 348–349

Keynesian theory, 336–337
Knapp Commission, 426–427
Ku Klux Klan, 192–195, 201–205

Labeling (labeling theory), 115–116
Labeling theory of crime, 417
Labels, social class and, 157–158
Labor unions, 200
Laissez-faire, doctrine of, 336
Latent functions, 262
    of schools, 376–377
Laws, 62
Learning
    culture and, 50
    socialization and, 70–72
Legislation for the aged, 249–252
Legitimacy (legitimation)
    of authority, 357–360
    religion's function of, 309–312
Leisure activities, 393
Liberation theology, 323–324
Life chances, 147
    social class and, 166
Life expectancy, 232–233
Linguistic behavior, 32
Lobbyists, 363
Looking-glass self, 74
Lower class, 157, 158
Lynchings, 193

Macrosociology, 9–10
Mainstream deviance, 126–129
Manifest functions, 262
Manufacturing, 332
Marasmus, 69
Marital status, 281–290
    blacks and, 294–295
    divorced, 287–289
    Hispanics and, 297
    married, 284–287
    sex differences in, 281–282
    single, 282–284
    widowed, 289–290
Marketplace, 33
Marriage, 272–274. *See also* Divorce; Families; Marital status

blacks and, 294–295
children and, 278–279
common-law marriages, 274
conjugal succession, 278
definition of, 273–274
economics and, 284–286
functions of, 278–281
Hispanics and, 297
schools and, 377
sex and, 278
sex difference in health and, 215
types of, 278
Marxist theory, 14
    of gender inequality, 225
    racism and, 186–187
    of stratification, 144–147, 149–151, 153
    Weber's theory compared to, 149–152
Mass behavior, 467–468
Mass media
    research and, 39
    sexism and, 219
    socialization and, 80–81
Master status, 122
Material culture, 48–49
Matriarchy, 291
Matrilineal descent, 287
Matrilocal residence, 286
Medical care, 438–439, 449. *See also* Health-care personnel
Medical diagnosis, 450–451
Medical model of crime, 433
Medicare, 250
Mentally ill, the, 40–41
Merit criteria, 99
Meritocracy, 381
Mexican-Americans, 56–57, 83, 198–199. *See also* Hispanics
    health status of, 456–457
Microsociology, 9–10
Middle class, 157, 158
Minority groups, 181–182
Mobility. *See* Social mobility
Modernization theory of aging, 238–239
Monogamy, 278
Monopolies, 336
Monopoly, 341
Monotheism, 303
Moral determinism, 309
Morality, institutional religion and, 305–306
Moral majority, 320–321
Morbidity, 439–443
Mores, 60–62
Mortality, 443–444
Mortification ceremonies, 78
MTV (music television), 39
Multinational corporations, 342

NAACP (National Association for the Advancement of Colored People), 193
National Commission on Excellence in Education, 374
National Crime Survey, 418–420
Nationalism, 190
Native Americans, 190–192
    family and, 279–280
Nativism, 201–203
    I.Q. testing and, 203
Nazism, 204–207
Neolocal residence, 286
Neutralization, techniques of, 124
New Christian Right, 325
Nonconformist behavior, 120
Nonmaterial culture, 49
Nonverbal behavior, 32
Norms, 59–63
    for the aged, 237
    border, 125
    class differences and, 81–83
    enforcement of, 61–62
    extended, 125
    groups and, 93–94
    ideal, 60
    prescribed, 60
    proscribed, 60
    statistical, 60
    transposed, 125
Notifiable diseases, 439
Nuclear family, 276
Nurses, 449, 451–453

Objective approach to social class, 159–160
Observation, socialization and, 71–72
Observer-as-participant technique of field observation, 32
Occupational categories, 343–345
Older Americans Act (OAA), 251
Oligarchy, iron law of, 363–364
Oligopoly, 341
Opportunity theory of crime, 416–417
Order maintenance, as police function, 425
Oversocialization, 72–73

Pain response, 57
Palimony, 274
Palmer Raids, 202
Participant-as-observer technique of field observation, 31–32
Paternalistic system, 103
Patriarchy, 291
Patrilineal descent, 286

Patrilocal residence, 286
Peer groups, socialization and, 79
Periphery nations, 153
Personality development, 75–76
Peter principle, 101–102
Physical stigma, 111
Physicians, 449–451
Pink-collar jobs, 169
Pipe dreams, 466
Plea bargaining, 428–429
Plessy v. *Ferguson*, 11, 193
Pluralism, 188
Pluralist theory (or model)
   of power, 353, 361–363
   of racism, 185–186
Police, 423–429
   abuses of authority of, 425–427
Police departments, 424
Political Action Committees (PACs), 363
Political behavior, 366–369
   political socialization and, 366–367
   race and ethnicity and, 368–369
   stratification and, 367–368
   trends in, 369–370
Political institutions, 352–370. *See also* Government; State, the
   legitimation of authority and, 357–358
   religion and, 319–324
Political parties, Weber's view of, 148–149
Political partisanship, among racial and ethnic minorities, 369
Political power. *See* Power
Political socialization, 366–367
Polities, 354. *See also* State, the
Polyandry, 278
Polygamy, 278
Polygyny, 278
Polytheism, 303
Population transfer, 188
Posttest, 23
Poverty, 162–166
   absolute vs. relative, 162–163
   biological explanations of, 164–166
   blaming the victim, 163–166
   capitalism and, 165
   conservative vs. liberal view of, 165
   cultural explanations for, 164, 166
   feminization of, 163
   race and, 163
   social disorganization theory of, 164
   structural explanations for, 165
Power
   bases of, 353

definition of, 353
   elitist model of, 353, 361–362
   legitimate, 357–358
   pluralist model of, 353, 361–363
Power, centralization of, 104
Power elite, Mill's concept of, 361–362
Prayer in the schools, 321–322
Prescribed norms, 60
Prestest, 23
Pretrial detainees, 430
Preventive detention, 430
Priests, 309
   role of, 315–316
Primary groups, 94–95
   family, 78–79
Primary sector, 331, 333
Primary socialization, 76
Prisons, 432–435
Programmed theory of aging, 238
Proletariat, 145
Prophets, role of, 316
Proprietary states, 354–355
Proscribed norms, 60
Protestant Reformation, 339
Provincialism, 33
Pseudosport, 394
Psychoanalytic viewpoint, 75–76
Public defenders, 428, 429
Public health, 455–456
Public policy, research and, 41–44
Puerto Ricans, 197–198

Qualitative sociology, 39
Quantification of data, 33–34
Questionnaires, 25–29

Race (racial groups), 180–181
   ethnicity vs., 181
   life expectancies and, 233
   political participation and partisanship and, 368–369
   and poverty, 163
   relations among, 187–190
   sex differences in earnings and, 213
   social mobility and, 169–170
   social research and, 42–44
   sport and, 406–408
Racial discrimination, death penalty and, 431–432
Racism, 143, 179, 185, 204–207
   conflict theory of, 186, 192
   definition of, 185
   eugenics, 201–202
   functional theory of, 185–186
   institutionalized, 185
   I.Q. testing and, 203

Marxist theory of, 151, 186–187
   nativism and, 201–203
   responses to, 189–190
   reverse discrimination, 195
   sexism and, 220–221
   sociobiology and, 186
   in South Africa vs. the United States, 207
   Weber's theory and, 152
   white ethnics and, 199–204
Rationalism, religion and, 324
Rational–legal authority, 359–360
Rational orientation to social activity (rationalization), 269–270
Rebellion, 190
   anomie and, 119–120
   by blacks, 194
Reciprocity, 15
Reconstruction, 192–193
Recreation, 393
Reform, 190
Regimentation, 78
Rehabilitation, as sentencing philosophy, 431, 433
Relative deprivation theory of social movements, 480–481
Relative poverty, 162–163
Religion, 300–326
   black families and, 294
   civil, 318–320
   conflict perspective on, 312–314
   functionalist perspective on, 306–312
   in a multicultural society, 317–319
   institutionalization of, 302–306
      beliefs, 302–304
      collectivity, 305–306
      practices, 304–305
   institutionalization of morality, 305–306
   political institutions and, 319–324
   the sacred and, 301
   secularism and rationalism and, 324–325
   sexism and, 219
   social change and, 314–317
   television ministry and, 325–326
   women and, 326
Reputational approach to social class, 159
Research methods, 19–42, 40–44
   agency data, 34–38
   experiments, 34–36
   field observations, 27–34
   policy, race, and, 41–44
   research designs, 22–25
   survey methods, 25–29
   unobtrusive measures, 36–40
Resocialization, 77–78

Resource mobilization theory of social movements, 481
Restlessness, 464–465
Retreat, anomie and, 119
Retreatist subculture, 126
Retribution, as sentencing philosophy, 431
Reverse socialization, 77
Revolution, 190
Rising expectations theory of social movements, 481
Ritual(ism)
  anomie and, 119
  religious, 309
Role conflict, 69
Roles, 88–90, 92–93
Role set, 90
Role strain, 90
Ruling class, 157, 158
Rumors, 465–467

Sacred, the, 301
Sample, 22
Sanctions, 61–62
  groups and, 93–94
Scale, 26
Schools. *See also* Education
  as custodial organizations, 377
  debate over what is taught by, 375–376
  as play organizations, 376–377
  prayer in, 321–322
  private, 386
  socialization and, 80
  as work organizations, 377–378
Secondary deviance, 114–116
Secondary groups, 95–96
Secondary sector, 332
Secularism, 324–325
Self
  looking-glass, 74
  Mead's theory of, 75
Self-identity, 74–76
Semiperiphery nations, 153
Senescence, 234
Senility (senile dementia), 234–235
Sentencing, 430–431
Separatism, 190
Serial monogamy, 278
Services
  definition of, 329–330
  provision of, 332
Sex
  gender vs., 211–212
  health-care personnel and, 451–452
Sex differences
  Marxist theory and, 151
  Weber's theory and, 152

Sexism, 210
  biological theories of, 222, 226
  comparable worth and, 226–227
  culture and, 227
  definition of, 212
  feminist theories of, 224, 227
  functionalist theories of, 223, 226
  in the home, 214–215
  institutionalized, 216–220
  Marxist theories of, 225, 227
  mass media and, 219
  mathematical abilities and, 217–218
  minority women and, 227–228
  racism and, 220–221
  religion and, 219
  sport and, 219
  in the workplace, 212–214
Sex-role spillover, 214
Sexually transmitted diseases (STDs), 439–443
Sharing of culture, 50–51
Shaw, 123
Singles, 282–284
  black, 294
  Hispanic, 297
Slavery, 192
Smoking, 444–446
Social aggregate, 89
Social behavior, individual behavior vs., 4–5
Social category, 89–90
Social change, 482–485
  religion and, 314–317
Social class. *See* Class
Social Darwinism, 11
  poverty and, 164–166
Social disorganization theory of poverty, 164
Social institutions, 259–270
  conflict theory of, 261–262
  functional theory of, 261, 262
  Gemeinschaft and Gesellschaft, 266–267
  social functions and, 261–262
  social structure and, 262, 265
  specialization and rationalization and, 269–270
  urbanization and, 267–269
Socialism, 340
Socialization, 65–84
  agents of, 78–81
  animal studies of, 70
  anticipatory, 77
  class differences and, 81–83
  controversy over, 72–73
  definition of, 66–67
  failures of, 67–70
  the family and, 279–280
  family socialization and, 78–79

  gender-role, 217–220, 224, 226–227
  learning, 70–72
  mass media and, 80–81
  peer groups and, 79
  political, 366–367
  primary, 76
  resocialization, 77–78
  reverse, 77
  school and, 80
  self-identity and, 74–76
  types of, 76–78
Social mobility, 157, 166–170
  group, 170
  horizontal, 167
  intergenerational, 167
  race and, 169–170
  in the United States, 167–168
  vertical, 167
  women and, 168–169
Social movements, 476–482
  natural history of, 479–480
  theories of, 480–482
  types of, 477–479
Social policy, family and, 274–275
Social research, 19
  public policy and, 41–44
Social security, 250
Social structures, 262–265
  alternative, 264–265
Social transmission, 50–51
Social unrest, 464
Society
  classless, 174–176
  definition of, 4
  estate system, 140–141
  gerontocratic, 240
  infrastructure of, 146
  slave system, 142–143
  social class system, 141–142
Sociobiology, 53–54
  poverty and, 164
  racism and, 186
Sociological imagination, 8–10
Sociology
  contemporary theories of, 13–17
  definition of, 4
  development of, 10–13
  social change and, 482–485
Solidarity movement, 125
South Africa, 205–207
Soviet Union, social class in, 175–176
Space, cultural use of, 57
Spatial behavior, 32
Specialization, 270
  of task, 98
Sport, 392–410
  conflict theory of, 396–397
  corporate, 394

Sport (*cont.*)
  definition of, 393
  functionalist theory of, 395–399
  informal, 393
  as microcosm of society, 395
  organized, 393–394
  pseudo- or trash, 394
  race and, 406–408
  sex and, 409–410
  sexism and, 219
  social class and, 399–402
  social mobility and, 402–406
  values of society and, 398–399
Sports creed, 398
Stacking, 407–408
Stanley, 24
State, the. *See also* Government
  definition of, 354
  proprietary, 354–355
Statistical norms, 60
Status, 87–88, 92–93
  education and allocation of, 374
  master, 122
  Weber's view of, 148
Sterilization, involuntary, 201, 202
Stigma, 109–113
  character, 111
  courtesy, 112
  physical, 111
  tribal, 111
Stratification, 135–154, 137
  of caste system, 139–140
  conflict theory of, 137–138
  of estate system, 140–141
  functional theory of, 137–138
  Marxist theory of, 144–147, 149–151, 153
  nature of, 136
  political participation and, 367–368
  of slave system, 142–143
  social class system of, 141–142
  societal types and, 138–143
  Weber's view of, 147–153
  world-systems theory of, 153
Structural alternatives, 264–265
Structural assimilation, 188
Structural theory of poverty, 165, 166
Structure of dominance, 56
Subcultures, 56–57, 122–126
  conflict, 126
  criminal, 126
  opposition, 125–126
  recruiting, 123–125
  retreatist, 126
Subjective approaches to social class, 158–159
Subjects, 22

Suicide, occupational and work-related problems and, 348–349
Superego, 76
Superstructure, 146
Survey methods, 25–29
  advantages and disadvantages of, 27–29
Survival of the fittest, 10–11
Sykes, 108
Symbolic interactionism, 15–16
Symbols, 57–58
Synergy, health status and, 438
Syphilis, 43, 440–443

Tax structure, class and, 162
Technological development, 55–56
Technological revolution, marriage and, 286
Television
  evangelists on, 325–326
  political campaigning and, 370
Tertiary sector, 332
Theism, 303
Theology, liberation, 323–324
Theory, 22
Third World countries, 342–343
  social class in, 172–173
Tokenism, 188
Total institutions, 77–78
Totalitarian governments, 356–357
Tracking, 380, 383, 386–387
Traditional authority, 358
Traditional orientation to social activity (rationalization), 268–270
Transposed norms, 125
Trash sports, 394
Trend analysis, 37–38
Trends, 468
Tribal stigma, 111
Tunnel vision, 33
Turk, 73
Tyranny of treatment, 114

Underclass, 157, 158
Unemployment, 145, 347–348
Uniform Crime Reports (UCR), 418–421
United States, distribution of power in, 360–366
  elite model, 361–362
  pluralist model, 362–366
Unobtrusive research measures, 36–40
Upper class, 157, 158

Upper-middle class, 158
Urbanization, 267–269

Value-added theory of collective behavior, 474–476
Value-free research, 40
Values, 58–59
  class differences and, 81–83
  sport and, 398–399
Variables, 20
Venereal diseases, 439–443
Vertical mobility, 167
Victimization surveys, 418–421
Voluntary assimilation, 188
Voluntary associations, 96
Voting Rights Act (1965), 368–369

Wealth, distribution of, 162
Wear-and-tear theory of aging, 238
Wedge driver rumors, 466
White ethnics
  Irish, 200
  racism and, 199–204
  Southern and Eastern European, 200–202
White House Conference on Families, 275–276
Wickersham Commission, 425
Widowed persons, 289–290
  black, 295
Women. *See also* Sexism; Working women
  black, 291–295
  in the church, 326
  marriage and, 284–286
  single, 283
  social mobility of, 168–169
  sport and, 409–410
Women's liberation
  the church and, 326
  minority women and, 227–228
Work, 343–349
  future trends in, 346–347
  problems associated with, 348–349
Working class, United States, 157–158
Working women
  comparable worth and, 226–227
  in the home, 214–215
  in the workplace, 212–214
World-systems theory of stratification, 153
Written records, bureaucracy and, 99–100